Time of Troubles

Sponsored by the Hoover Institution on War, Revolution and Peace, Stanford University, Stanford, California.

TIME OF TROUBLES

The Diary of Iurii Vladimirovich Got'e

— MOSCOW —

July 8, 1917 to July 23, 1922

Translated, Edited, and Introduced by

Terence Emmons

❋

PRINCETON UNIVERSITY PRESS

PRINCETON, NEW JERSEY

Published by Princeton University Press, 41 William Street,
Princeton, New Jersey 08540

Library of Congress Cataloging in Publication Data will be
found on the last printed page of this book

ISBN 0-691-05520-3

This book has been composed in Linotron Granjon

Clothbound editions of Princeton University Press books
are printed on acid-free paper, and binding materials are
chosen for strength and durability. Paperbacks, although satisfactory
for personal collections, are not usually suitable for library rebinding

Printed in the United States of America by Princeton University Press,
Princeton, New Jersey

Designed by Laury A. Egan

The most trustworthy testimony is that of the eyewitness, especially when this witness is an honourable, attentive, and intelligent man, writing on the spot, at the moment, and under the dictation of the facts themselves. . . .

—H. TAINE

(from the preface to
The French Revolution)

Contents

✱

List of Illustrations

❊

(Following page 268)

Acknowledgments

❋

Among the many people who have contributed to the realization of this project, first mention belongs to Edward Kasinec, Director of the Slavonic Division, The New York Public Library, who first attributed the diary to Iu. V. Got'e while he was examining the Frank Golder archive in 1982 and turned to me for confirmation at a moment when I, quite coincidentally, was examining another Got'e autograph.

The resurrection of Iu. V. Got'e's deliberate and precise record of his thoughts and experiences over five turbulent years from an apparently indecipherable mass of faded scribblings was a process fascinating to behold and to participate in. Preparation of the finished typescript of the diary was above all the work of Mrs. Olga Dunlop and Mrs. Marina Tinkoff Utechin; they were helped in their long and scrupulous labors by Dr. Constantin Galskoy and Professor S. V. Utechin.

In preparing the notes to the text of the diary, I drew repeatedly on Professor Utechin's encyclopedic knowledge of Russian history, culture, and bibliography. Mrs. Utechin was similarly helpful, especially in regard to literary citations in the text. Professor Lazar Fleishman generously provided suggestions for the notes from his vast store of biographical and bibliographical lore on modern Russia.

Yet others have contributed to this project, in ways too numerous to mention. I should like merely to record here a note of thanks to Gordon Craig, Elena Danielson, Gene DeArmond, Delano DuGarm, Victoria Emmons, Peter Frank, Gregory Freiden, Hilde Hardeman, Nellie Hauke, Hilja Kukk, Marc Raeff, Jehanne von Stamwitz, Elena Stone, Lyman Van Slyke, and Wojciech Zalewski.

Generous support for this project was provided by several institutions, including Stanford University's Center for International Studies (the Hewlett Fund and the Center for Russian and East European Studies) and Division of Graduate Studies (the Pew Fund), and the International Research and Exchanges Board (IREX). The Hoover Institution and the Hoover Institution Archives supported this archival publication project in a variety of ways, but especially by releasing Mrs. Dunlop from other duties to work on the Got'e diary.

Finally, a note of thanks is due to Mr. Peter Kahn, who edited the entire English-language version of the diary and the notes; and to Mrs.

Gail Ullman, of Princeton University Press, whose enthusiasm for the project helped get it under way.

I have been sustained in this undertaking by the memory of my teacher, Professor Petr Andreevich Zaionchkovskii (1904–1983), who was a student of Iu. V. Got'e fifty years ago.

TERENCE EMMONS
Moscow, August 30, 1986

A Note to the Reader

This is a translation of the Russian-language diary kept by Iurii Vladimirovich Got'e between July 8, 1917, and July 23, 1922. That manuscript, in Got'e's own hand, is located in Box 16 of the Frank Golder Collection, Hoover Institution Archives, Stanford, California. An Appendix contains translations of the letters that Got'e attached to his diary and mentioned in the text. A number of other letters turned over by Got'e to Frank Golder together with his diary have not been included.

In presenting a translated text, there is no need to list the numerous rules that have been followed in transcribing the diary in its original language. Suffice it to say that the translation follows the original manuscript scrupulously: it is in no sense a paraphrase, and nothing has been omitted or embellished. Names of clearly identifiable people mentioned in the text are generally given in full, even if the author uses only their initials after first mention. A question mark in brackets [?] follows words whose proper reading is in doubt. Undecipherable words are represented by ellipses in brackets [...]. Omitted words are occasionally supplied, in brackets, as the sense of a phrase suggests. Omitted letters and obvious slips of the hand are corrected without special notice. An effort has been made to keep orthographic clutter to a minimum.

Place names have been translated if they are descriptive and unambiguous (Nikitskie Gates or Assumption Cathedral) but not otherwise (Bol'shoi Znamenskii Pereulok [the street on which Got'e lived]). Proper names have generally been left in their (transliterated) Russian form, except for names that are very well known in anglicized form (Nicholas and Alexandra and Witte; but Aleksandra Fedorovna is the form used when the empress is referred to with patronymic). This rule has been followed even in regard to names of foreign origin borne by Russian-speakers, including, with some hesitation, that of the diary's author.

Although he signed "Gautier" to his letters written in French or English, and to his articles written in French for the *Revue historique*, Got'e's principal publications are all in Russian, he is not well known outside the Russian context, and his name is entered in the National Union Catalog in its transliterated Russian form, "Got'e." Questions of consistency and bibliographic access aside, use of the French form of the name in the title and text of this publication would have misleadingly suggested that it is a foreigner's account of the Russian Revolution. By the same token, names of non-Russian origin from within the Empire are generally left in the Russian form used by Got'e if their bearers were principally known in the Russian-language milieu. (For any departures from his own rule owing to ignorance, the translator begs forgiveness.)

The same rule has been followed for geographical names, generally following cartographers' conventions (Moscow, but 'Perm'), albeit with a "Great Russian" bias for the names of towns in Russian territory, following Got'e (Kiev, Khar'kov).

English-language orthographic conventions are observed in the text, except for a few concessions to the style of the time or Got'e's idiosyncrasies ("bolshevik," "red army," etc.). Transliteration follows the simplified Library of Congress system (without diacritical marks) for the reformed Russian orthography (Got'e used the old orthography).

The notes to the diary are eclectic, including purely textual annotations, cross-references, biographical and historical information, and bibliographic references. The last are for the most part restricted to English-language publications. The notes are designed to be used in conjunction with the index: notes on individuals are provided at first mention in the text only; the location of the appropriate note can be found handily later on by looking up the name in the index. A Chronology of Principal Events has been included with similar intent.

Unless otherwise noted, all dates before February 1, 1918, in both text and notes, are given according to the Julian Calendar, which is thirteen days behind the Gregorian Calendar in the twentieth century. Thus, according to the calendar now in effect, Got'e and his family celebrated Christmas of 1917 on January 7, 1918, and greeted the New Year of 1918 at midnight on January 13, 1918.

List of Frequently Used Abbreviations

❊

Form used in text	Russian term in full	English translation
Cheka	Chrezvychainaia komissiia po bor'be s kontr-revoliutsiei, prestupleniiami po dolzhnosti i spekuliatsiei	Extraordinary Commission for Combatting Counterrevolution, Crimes of Office, and Speculation
Comintern	Kommunisticheskii internatsional'	Communist International
GPU	Gosudarstvennoe politicheskoe upravlenie	State Political Administration
KD, Kadet	Konstitutsionno-demokraticheskaia partiia	Constitutional-Democratic party
Narkompros	Narodnyi komissariat prosveshcheniia	People's Commissariat of Enlightenment
NEP	Novaia ekonomicheskaia politika	New Economic Policy
Rabfak	Rabochii fakul'tet	Workers' Faculty
RCP	Rossiiskaia Kommunisticheskaia partiia	Russian Communist party
RSFSR	Rossiiskaia sotsialisticheskaia federativnaia sovetskaia respublika	Russian Socialist Federal Soviet Republic
Sovdep, Sovdepiia	Sovet deputatov	[Government or Land of] Soviet Deputies
Sovnarkom	Sovet narodnykh komissarov	Council of People's Commissars
SD, Esdeki	Sotsial-demokraticheskaia partiia	Social-Democratic party
SR, Esery	Partiia sotsialistov-revoliutsionerov	Socialist-Revolutionary party

Tsekubu	Tsentral'naia komissiia po uluchsheniiu byta uchenykh	Central Commission for Improving the Living Conditions of Scholars
TsIK	Tsentral'nyi ispolnitel'nyi komitet	Central Executive Committee [of Soviets]

Chronology of Principal Events
Mentioned in the Diary of Iu. V. Got'e

❊

Note: Dates prior to February 1918 are given in the old style—thirteen days behind the current calendar.

1914

August 1   Beginning of the First World War.

1917

March 2   Abdication of Nicholas II; formation of the Provisional Government.

June 18   Beginning of Brusilov offensive.

July 3–5   July Crisis: unsuccessful uprising in Petrograd.

July 6   Austro-German counteroffensive begins.

July 8   Organization of the Kerenskii Cabinet.

August 12–15   State Conference in Moscow of all political groups except the Bolsheviks.

August 24–28   The Kornilov Affair.

September 1   Formation of the Directory headed by Kerenskii.

September 14–22   Democratic Conference in Petrograd.

October 25   October Revolution in Petrograd; organization of the Council of People's Commissars.

October 27–   Fighting in Moscow, ending in Bolshevik victory.
November 2

November 8   Arrest of Kadet leaders.

December 2   Brest-Litovsk armistice.

December 14   Nationalization of the banks.

1918

January 5   Opening of the Constituent Assembly.

January 6   Dispersal of the Constituent Assembly.

January 7   Murder of Kokoshkin and Shingarev.

March 3   Signing of the Peace of Brest-Litovsk.

March 12   Soviet government moves to Moscow.

April 11–12   Cheka raid on Moscow anarchist centers.

April 23   Nationalization of foreign trade.

May 26	Czechoslovak uprising; beginning of the Civil War.
June 28	Nationalization of large industries.
July 6	Assassination of Count Mirbach, German ambassador.
July 16	Murder of Nicholas II and his family.
July 30	Assassination of General Eichhorn, German commander in the Ukraine.
August 2	Allied occupation of Archangel.
August 30	Assassination attempt on Lenin; assassination of Uritskii.
September 10	Red Army takes Kazan'.
November 2	Extraordinary tax levy on the "bourgeoisie."
November 21	Nationalization of internal trade.

1919

January 6–13	Unsuccessful Spartacist uprising in Berlin.
March 2–7	First Congress of the Comintern.
March 21	Establishment of the Hungarian Soviet Republic.
August 1	Fall of the Hungarian Soviet Republic.
September 25	Anarchist bombing of Moscow CP headquarters.
October 11–14	Iudenich reaches Petrograd suburbs, Denikin takes Orel; highest point in the White advanced.
November 14	Red Army takes Omsk.
December 12	Red Army takes Khar'kov.
December 16	Red Army takes Kiev.
December 30	Red Army takes Ekaterinoslav.

1920

January 3–8	Red Army takes Tsaritsyn and Rostov/Don.
April 25	Poland begins hostilities against Soviet Ukraine.
May 6	Poland occupies Kiev.
June 12	Red Army retakes Kiev.
July 21–	
August 6	Second Congress of the Comintern.
August	Trial of the Tactical Center.
August 1	Red Army takes Brest-Litovsk.
August 16	Polish counteroffensive south of Warsaw.
October 12	Polish-Russian armistice.
November 14	Wrangel evacuates the Crimea; end of Civil War.
November 29	Nationalization of small industry.

1921

March 1–17	The Kronstadt Rebellion.
March 8–16	Tenth Communist Party Congress.

March 16	Decree on fixed tax in kind; advent of NEP.
July 21	Foundation of the Committee for Aid to the Starving (Prokukish).
August 21	Soviet agreement with American Relief Administration; beginning of ARA operations in Russia.
August 31	Dissolution of the aid committee; arrest of its organizers.

1922

February	Cheka replaced by GPU.
March 27–	
April 2	Eleventh Communist Party Congress.
April 10–	
May 19	The Genoa Conference.
April 16	The Treaty of Rapallo.
May 5	Indictment of the patriarch.
May 7	Eleven Moscow churchmen condemned to death.
June 8–	
August 7	Trial of the SRS.
July 5	Ten Petrograd churchmen condemned to death.
June 15–	
July 19	The Hague Conference.

Iurii Vladimirovich Got'e

TIME OF TROUBLES

Map 1. Russia in World War I—1914 to the Revolution of 1917. From Nicholas V. Riasanovsky, *A History of Russia*, 3d ed. 1977. Reproduced with permission of Oxford University Press.

Got'e and His Diary

❋

Russia in the summer of 1917 was in a state of crisis: a revolution in February, in the midst of the First World War, had overthrown the tsarist regime; a Provisional Government, committed to running the country until a constituent assembly could be called and determined to keep Russia in the war against the Central Powers, maintained a fragile hold on power. By mid-July 1917, the failure of the Russian offensive on the Galician front, which began in the third week of June and turned into a rout by the beginning of July, and the "July Days" demonstrations in Petrograd (July 3–5), which nearly ended in a Bolshevik-led *coup d'état,* had clearly revealed to contemporaries that the moderate Provisional Government would not be able to carry on the war against Germany and provide political stability at home. It was a sense of patriotic revulsion over impending national disaster[1] that led Iurii Vladimirovich Got'e, a forty-four-year old history professor at Moscow University and associate director of the Rumiantsev Museum, to begin keeping a diary on July 8, 1917, the day that Aleksandr Kerenskii replaced Prince L'vov at the head of the Provisional Government and two days after the beginning of the German counteroffensive on the eastern front. It was an occupation he had previously disdained:

> The army is an army no more. ... Russia has no future. ... The final fall of Russia as a great and unified power, as a result of internal, not external, causes, not directly due to enemies but to our own flaws and inadequacies, from complete atrophy of a sense of patriotism, motherland, common solidarity, and a sense of *union sacrée*— this is an episode with few analogies in world history. Living through all this, to my great sorrow, shame, and humiliation, I ... feel myself obliged to record my impressions and in this way to create a very imperfect, very subjective, but nevertheless historical source that may be of use to someone in the future. I do so contrary to all my former views on this account: I specifically did not want

[1] Got'e sets the tone at the outset with his "subtitle": "Lament on the Downfall of the Russian Land" ("Slovo o pogibeli russkoi zemli"), the title of a famous thirteenth-century literary fragment bewailing the Mongol conquest of Russia.

to write either reminiscences, or reflections, or a diary, for I have
always thought there was quite enough of that rubbish written
without me.

And he kept it up through five years of revolution, civil war, family tragedy, hunger, and progressively deteriorating living conditions—writing
on a stool in the doorway of the room in communal quarters where he
and his family took refuge after their own apartment had been seques-
tered in 1919, or on the sly at work in the museum, or in the country.
Toward the end, the entries become noticeably less frequent, mainly because by this time Got'e was afraid to keep the diary at home, but also
because of his exhaustion, which was no doubt mingled with awareness
that the new regime, having survived the Civil War, the Polish war, and
the internal rebellions of 1921, was there to stay: the great uncertainty
about the immediate future of the country that had sustained the chronicle for nearly five years had begun to fade.

As a matter of fact, we do not know for certain whether Got'e ceased
keeping a diary altogether on July 23, 1922. What we do know is that he
had decided by that time, as he was about to return to Moscow from his
summer refuge of Pestovo, that he would not be able to continue the
diary in town because of the danger of searches and the intolerable housing situation, and that shortly afterward he turned the diary through that
date over to Frank Golder for safekeeping abroad.

Frank Golder (1877–1929) was an American professor of history who
was in Soviet Russia collecting materials for the new Hoover Library at
Stanford (founded in 1919) and working at the same time as an agent of
Herbert Hoover's American Relief Administration (ARA). Golder was an
omnivorous and insatiable collector of books and manuscripts.[2] Got'e first
met Golder on October 23, 1921, and in his penultimate diary entry, on
July 16, 1922, Got'e wrote: "We visited Golder. . . . A proposal to ship off
my materials; I think I will accept it. This may yield a turning point in
my plans for the future [at this point Got'e was thinking seriously of
emigrating]; in any case, it will save the materials."

And so, soon after his return to Moscow, Got'e turned over the diary

---

[2] Golder's collecting activities are described in Allen Glen Wachhold, "Frank A.
Golder: An Adventure in Russian History" (Ph.D. diss., University of California, Santa
Barbara, 1984). See also Wojciech Zalewski, *Slavica Collections at Stanford University: A
History* (Stanford, 1985). After his 1921–1923 trip, Golder returned to Moscow in 1925
and 1927. He appears to have seen Got'e on both visits. Golder collected personal materials from others in both Moscow and Petrograd: in his papers there are two other diaries
from the revolutionary period, some family budgets evidently collected to make a case in
the United States for aid to Russian academics, and various other personal documents.

and its convoy of correspondence to Golder in order to preserve the record of his impressions for posterity. Golder shipped the diary off to the Hoover Library through channels that had been arranged between ARA and the Soviet government in the spring of 1922. The diary subsequently lay in the Frank Golder papers in the Hoover Library—unidentified except for the words "revolutionary diary of a Moscow revolutionary" [*sic*] written on its crumbling mailing envelope—until 1982, when it was correctly attributed to Got'e by Edward Kasinec, then curator of Slavic Materials at the University of California–Berkeley, who was searching the Golder archive for materials on the history of Soviet bibliography. The whereabouts, and perhaps even the existence, of the diary appeared to be unknown in the Soviet Union: Got'e's friends knew he was keeping a diary, as did members of his immediate family, but he may never have told anyone what he did with it in 1922, and it is unlikely he reminded anyone of its existence in later years, especially after his arrest in 1930 on charges of counterrevolutionary conspiracy.

The diary that Iurii Vladimirovich Got'e so painstakingly kept for five years and was able to preserve for "someone in the future" thanks to the fortunate meeting with Frank Golder (it would surely have perished had it remained in Got'e's possession) is an extraordinary document that plunges the late-twentieth-century reader directly into the first, critical years of the new Soviet order with a vividness surpassing that of any other source known to this writer.

To be sure, the picture is delimited by the author's geographical location, social milieu, and professional situation: we learn most about the Moscow of the middle-class academic intelligentsia, which was relatively isolated from both the mass movements below and the political regime above. Nevertheless, Got'e was a man who got around. His professional situation involved him with a variety of institutions and social groups, and brought him into fairly close proximity to the corridors of power: he sat on various commissions and convocations in the Kremlin (mostly connected with Narkompros, the Commissariat of Enlightenment); he knew personally quite a few politically significant figures in the new regime, such as Lunacharskii, Pokrovskii, Krupskaia, and Inessa Armand. He traveled extensively within "Sovdepiia": to Petrograd on numerous occasions, to Ivanovo-Voznesensk, Tver', Novgorod, Sergiev Posad and other towns, as well as to the countryside, where he and his family generally managed to spend most of their summers. He walked Moscow, in all directions, looking for food, visiting friends and relations, and going about his business. And to all that he saw, Got'e brought an unusually developed visual sense, a keen eye for detail. He also brought to his diary the terse and elegant style for which he was well known in his professional writing.[3]

At the most obvious, documentary, level, the contents of the diary for the most part belong to three categories: (1) description of major events and of living conditions in the city and in the countryside; (2) information on developments in the principal institutions with which Got'e was associated, the Rumiantsev Museum and Moscow University, and their relations with the new regime after October 1917; and (3) Got'e's assessment (and by extension that of his milieu, the professoriate, on which he regularly reports) of events and the general situation.

It is also, despite its author's intentions, a profoundly personal record. Beneath his stoic demeanor and matter-of-fact style, Got'e was a man of intense feelings, and these are constantly surfacing in the diary (he occasionally apologizes for lapses in his effort to avoid personal matters). In the end, we have the record, perhaps unique in depth and duration, of an individual consciousness living through the Russian Revolution.

Got'e was a man with a family and many friends, toward whom he maintained a touching solicitude and loyalty, even in the most trying times. He visited them regularly or kept in contact, sometimes with great delay, by mail. The Appendix, consisting mostly of letters to Got'e, documents these relations and the diaspora of middle-class Moscow in the Revolution.

The distinction between a diary, "a daily record, especially a personal record of events, experiences, and observations,"[4] on the one hand, and memoirs, reminiscences, or autobiography, on the other, must be insisted upon here. The former is a contemporary document and thus part of the historical record—subjective by nature, to be sure, but with its integrity undisturbed by the layers of interpretation and selectivity inevitably imposed by intervening events on even the best memory. The latter are *interpretations* of the historical record written well after the fact; despite their personal focus and the place assigned to memory in them (often prompted by reference to a diary or contemporary correspondence), they belong to the genre of historical narrative.

Got'e's manuscript is a nearly perfect example of the true diary: unlike many—perhaps most—personal journals that are eventually published, this one was never revised, censored, or embellished at a later time by its author. His entries are never separated from the events and experiences they describe by more than a few days; usually they were recorded the

[3] S. K. Bogoiavlenskii, "Akademik Iurii Vladimirovich Got'e," *Izvestiia Akademii Nauk SSSR. Seriia istorii i filosofii* 3 (1944): 109–16. V. I. Picheta, "Akademik Iurii Vladimirovich Got'e," *Istoricheskie zapiski* 15 (1945): 301–14.
[4] *The American Heritage Dictionary of the English Language*.

same day. By contrast, N. Sukhanov's famous personal record of the Revolution in Petrograd between February and October 1917 (which is often referred to as a "diary" or "journal" in the history books) is in fact a piece of historical reconstruction, although it evidently followed closely a diary or log kept by the author.[5] And Pitirim Sorokin's "diary" of his experiences in the early years of Soviet power, with pieces of a contemporary record inextricably mixed with ex post facto evaluations, represents a kind of bastard genre between the two.[6]

Like other great upheavals in modern times, the Russian Revolution has engendered a vast quantity of memoir literature, from full-scale personal histories to recollections about discrete events or individuals, with everything in between; their publication has been a minor industry both in the Soviet Union and in emigration.[7] True diaries are extremely rare. When Zinaida Gippius published the fragments of her Petersburg diary for 1919, she wrote in an afterword: "The diary in Sovdepiia—not memoir or reminiscences 'afterward,' but namely 'diary'—is an exceptional thing. I don't think many of them will be found after the liberation. Except perhaps those of commissars."[8]

Only a handful of diaries appear in fact to have been kept in Russia during the Revolution and Civil War, and the number kept inside Soviet Russia after October 1917 is even smaller, despite an epistolary tradition that was still very much alive. Few, at least, have found their way into print,[9] and the available archival guides do not indicate the existence of

[5] N. Sukhanov, *Zapiski o revoliutsii*, 7 vols. (Berlin, 1920). An abridged English translation appeared as *The Russian Revolution of 1917* (New York, 1955).

[6] Pitirim Sorokin, *Leaves from a Russian Diary* (New York, 1924).

[7] For the bibliographies: *Istoriia sovetskogo obshchestva v vospominaniiakh sovremennikov, 1917–1957. Annotirovannyi ukazatel' memuarnoi literatury* (Moscow, 1958; succeeding issues are under the same title); and Ludmilla Foster, *Bibliography of Russian Émigré Literature, 1918–1968*, 2 vols. (Boston, 1970). The final volumes of the exhaustive bibliography of memoirs and diaries on pre-Revolutionary Russia that are currently under way register materials that bridge the Revolution, but only those published in the Soviet Union: P. A. Zaionchkovskii, ed., *Istoriia dorevoliutsionnoi Rossii v dnevnikakh i vospominaniiakh. Annotyrovannyi ukazatel' knig i publikatsii v zhurnalakh*, 11 vols. to date (Moscow, 1976–).

[8] Zinaida Gippius, *Peterburgskie dnevniki (1914–1919)* (New York, 1982), p. 89 (these words were written in October 1920). And when Alexander Berkman in 1925 published his diary for 1920–1922, he wrote of it, "So far as I know it is the only journal kept in Russia during those momentous years." Alexander Berkman, *The Bolshevik Myth (Diary 1920–1922)* (New York, 1925), p. viii.

[9] The two most substantial true diaries kept by Russians inside Soviet Russia after October 1917 and subsequently published are probably Aleksandr Blok, *Dnevnik Al. Bloka. 1917–1921* (Leningrad, 1928), 250pp.; and the segments of Zinaida Gippius's diary mentioned above, which for the post-October period cover only November 1917 and the second half of 1919 (those parts originally published in *Tsarstvo Antikhrista* [Paris, 1921])

numerous unpublished diaries from that period either.[10] No published diaries approach even remotely the Got'e diary in richness of detail or number of entries, to mention only two objective characteristics.

The reasons are not far to seek. They are eloquently evoked in Got'e's diary: the extremely difficult living conditions, which, in Moscow at least,

---

and amount to less than one hundred printed pages. It is noteworthy that both are the work of poets, and typical that one was published in the Soviet Union in the 1920s and the other in emigration. Both are much more narrowly focused than Got'e's diary, although Gippius has a number of interesting observations about the political scene.

To them may be added the recently published fragments of the diary of another well-known writer, Vladimir Galaktionovich Korolenko (1853–1921): V. G. Korolenko, "Iz dnevnikov 1917–1921 gg.," Publikatsiia T. Tilia, in *Pamiat'. Istoricheskii sbornik*, vyp. 2 (Paris, 1979), pp. 374–421. Korolenko lived at the time in his native town of Poltava, which changed hands numerous times during the Civil War. The fragments, which are valuable especially for their revelations about Korolenko's attitude toward the Bolsheviks, break off at the end of August 1921; Korolenko died on Christmas Day 1921.

There are also several diary fragments published in Gessen's émigré journal *Arkhiv russkoi revoliutsii* in the 1920s, and such items of marginal interest as the juvenile diary of Nelli Ptashkina (Nelli L'vovna Ptashkina, *Dnevnik, 1918–1920* [Paris, 1922]; translated into English as *The Diary of Nelly Ptaschkina* [Boston, 1923]) and Irina Skariatina's "A Diary of the Russian Revolution" (March 1917–February 1918) (Irina Skariatina [Mrs. Victor F. Blakeslee], *A World Can End* [New York, 1931]).

It appears that more diaries of foreigners who happened to be in Soviet Russia in its first years may have been published than those of Russians. The most significant foreigners' journals include Pierre Pascal, *Mon Journal de Russie*, 4 vols. (Lausanne, 1975–1982); Capitaine Jacques Sadoul, *Notes sur la Révolution Bolchevique* (Paris, 1919); Claude Anet [Jean Schopfer], *La Révolution russe*, 4 vols. (Paris, 1919); and the Berkman diary already noted. Their bulk is somewhat deceptive: the first two volumes of Pascal's journal contain fragments of diary for the years 1916 to 1921 dispersed among other contemporary material and memoirs; Sadoul's journal consists of letters to Albert Thomas from October 1917 to September 1918; and Anet's work consists of daily columns written for the newspaper *Petit Parisien* between March 1917 and June 1918. Berkman's work is a highly embellished true diary. There are others, including two anonymous diaries of "an Englishwoman in the Russian Revolution"; most of them are from the year 1917 alone and were published within a few years of their composition.

[10] See, in particular, S. V. Zhitomirskaia, ed., *Vospominaniia i dnevniki XVIII–XX vv. Ukazatel' rukopisei* (Moscow, 1976); and *Lichnye arkhivnye fondy v gosudarstvennykh khranilishchakh SSSR. Ukazatel'*, vols. 1–3 (Moscow, 1962–1980). Among Got'e's circle of friends and colleagues, apparently only one, M. M. Bogoslovskii, kept a diary during the Revolution, and only for 1917. It is preserved in the Manuscript Division of the State Historical Museum in Moscow (GIM), fond 442, delo 4.

Special mention should be made of two as yet unpublished diaries. The first is that of Alexis Babine (1866–1930), sometime émigré to America, librarian at Indiana University, Stanford University, and the Library of Congress, who had returned to Russia in 1910 and found himself teaching English at Saratov University in 1917. His Saratov diary, which he kept in English from March 19, 1917, to November 18, 1922, is preserved in the Library of Congress. The second is that of an anonymous Petrograder, an archivist in the naval ministry who describes himself as an "average *intelligent*." It was kept from 1915 to 1922, when it, like Got'e's diary, was shipped off to the Hoover Library by Golder (Golder

more or less precluded spare time or privacy; and the political risk—since after mid-1918, searches of domicile became regular occurènces. (In this respect, Got'e's situation was unusual: as director of the Rumiantsev Museum's great library and archive, he had for a time relatively risk-free places to store his diary.) Few members of the writing public with the time and inclination to engage in the peculiar activity of diary keeping were favorably disposed toward the new Bolshevik regime in those early days of its existence; later on, prudence did not counsel preserving evidence of one's attitude toward the new regime in those early days.[11]

The motivations that lay behind Got'e's resolve to "create a historical source"—that is, to chronicle Russia's crisis for posterity—and to sustain it for so long in such trying circumstances are not entirely clear. By the time Got'e began to keep his diary, the genre had long since left its original moorings as a strictly private, usually confessional, enterprise; the second half of the nineteenth century, in Russia as elsewhere in Europe, saw a great florescence of diary writing by men and women who in one way or another were writing for the public. As a result, "it has become no longer possible to define clearly the motivations of diarists."[12]

Toward the end, as he intimates in the remarks about Golder quoted earlier, Got'e apparently entertained the idea that his diary was a kind of capital investment that would help him get started in a life of exile,[13] but that is an idea that could only have come to him after his resolve to emigrate had become strong and the diary had taken on substantial dimensions. For Got'e, his diary may have been above all a means of bringing order into the ongoing chaos of events, and thus of exercising a kind of control over them.[14] It has been remarked, in that respect, that diaries of the chronicle variety are usually the work of outsiders, people who feel themselves cut off by the course of events from power, from participation

---

papers, box 17). Like the Got'e diary, they are both true diaries and they are of comparable size: 259 and 418 typescript pages, respectively. Although the experiences and powers of observation reflected in these diaries are rather modest compared to the Got'e diary, they give comparable coverage, over the same period, to current local events and living conditions and the like, so that the three diaries taken together yield a geographically "triangulated" picture of life in Russia during the first years of Soviet rule. It is remarkable that all three of these diaries are in the United States—two of them in the Golder collection—and that all three authors were acquainted with Frank Golder.

[11] "I know a person who resorted to unheard of devices in order to keep a diary; it is impossible to recount them; and I am not even sure it has been preserved to this day," Gippius wrote in the afterword to her diary fragment cited above.

[12] Peter Boerner, "Place du journal dans la littérature moderne," in *Le journal intime et ses formes littéraires* (Geneva, 1978), p. 222.

[13] The notion of diary keeping as a kind of capital accumulation in a more general sense is suggested by Béatrice Didier, "Pour une sociologie du journal intime," ibid., pp. 246–49.

[14] Boerner, "Place du journal," p. 221.

in political and economic affairs in general.[15] In any case, Gippius was to be disappointed in her anticipation that the "commissars" would produce the diaries of the Russian Revolution: they were too busy making it, or trying to guide its course; Got'e was not.

Iurii Vladimirovich Got'e was born on June 18, 1873 (old style). His father was a bookseller, owner of a large bookstore on the fashionable street of Kuznetskii Most that specialized in fine editions and foreign literature, especially French. The business had been founded by Iurii Vladimirovich's great-grandfather, "Jean Dufayet dit Gautier,"[16] son of a French immigrant to Russia. Jean-Marie Dufayer Gautier, son of a magistrate of Saint-Quentin, had come to Russia as a young man in 1764 in response to Catherine the Great's 1763 ukaz inviting foreigners to settle in Russia with various privileges. This great-great-grandfather of Iurii Vladimirovich settled in Moscow in 1768, was inscribed, temporarily, in the Moscow merchantry, and took up the sale of musical instruments. His son, "Ivan Ivanovich," was in time inscribed as a regular member of the Moscow merchantry and established his bookselling enterprise in 1799, having married the daughter of his former employer, the bookseller François Courtener.[17]

Iurii Vladimirovich was the first eldest son of the Gautier/Got'e family not to take over the family business, choosing instead to go to university and pursue a scholarly career, and in 1895, the year before his father died, the business was accordingly sold to an employee, Félix Tastevin, who ran it until 1917. The business was thus in continuous existence for 118 years.

Though Iurii Vladimirovich was the first eldest son to leave the family business, members of the Got'e family had long since gone into other endeavors: one of his uncles, Eduard Vladimirovich, was a doctor and professor of medicine; another, Lev Vladimirovich, owned an iron works. Iurii Vladimirovich's younger brother, Vladimir Vladimirovich, was a lawyer and civil servant.

Iurii Vladimirovich Got'e attended Moscow University in the early 1890s (1891–1895), where he matriculated in the historico-philological faculty and took the courses on Russian history of the great Professor

[15] Béatrice Didier, *Le journal intime* (Paris, 1976), pp. 65–70.

[16] F. Tastevin, *Histoire de la colonie française de Moscou. Depuis les origines jusqu'à 1812* (Moscow-Paris, 1908), p. 70.

[17] N. G. Martynova-Poniatovskaia, "Materialy k istorii frantsuzskoi knizhnoi torgovli v Moskve," in Publichnaia Biblioteka SSSR imeni V. I. Lenina, *Sbornik* (1928), 1: 113–31; 2: 153–89. This history of the French book trade in Moscow is based in part on the Got'e family archive, which is preserved in the Manuscript Division of the Lenin Library, f. 83. Iurii Vladimirovich Got'e's personal archive is located in the Moscow Section of the Academy of Sciences Archive (MO arkhiva AN SSSR), f. 491.

V. O. Kliuchevskii and the young Privatdozent P. N. Miliukov, under whose direction he wrote his undergraduate thesis on the defense and colonization of the frontiers in Muscovy (it was completed just before Miliukov was exiled from Moscow for his political activities in January 1895). Got'e also studied ancient history and European history with P. G. Vinogradov (later Sir Paul Vinogradoff) and V. I. Ger'e (Guerrier). He and his later colleague and friend A. N. Savin graduated with highest marks among the historians.[18]

Following graduation, Got'e did his year of military service. Then, after the death of his father in 1896, he was obliged to go to work: he taught in Moscow high schools until 1902, when he began teaching in Professor Ger'e's Higher Women's Courses (the equivalent of university education for women); he continued teaching there until the Courses were merged with Moscow University in 1918, but at the same time, he took employment outside of teaching, first in the Archive of the Ministry of Justice (1897) and then in the library of the Rumiantsev Museum (1898), where he worked, first as academic secretary and then as associate director and head librarian, until his arrest and exile in 1930.

In 1900, Got'e passed the *Magister*'s examination and in 1903 he began teaching at Moscow University. In 1906 his Magister's dissertation, *The Moscow Region in the Seventeenth Century. A Study of the History of Economic Conditions in Muscovite Rus*, was defended and published.[19] In 1913 he defended and published his doctoral dissertation, the first volume of *The History of Local Administration in Russia from Peter I to Catherine II*.[20] He was elected professor by the Moscow University Academic Council on April 18, 1915. Got'e taught at the university until the mid-twenties, when most of the prominent historians left the university in connection with the creation of a special independent institute of historical studies (RANION). From 1907 to 1917, he was also professor at the Geodesic Institute, and from 1913 to 1918 at the municipal Shaniavskii University. (This kind of multiple appointment was standard practice among the Moscow professoriate.)

With the demise of the historico-philological faculty in 1919, Got'e began to teach a course on archaeology, a field of longstanding interest to him; he became a member of the new Academy of the History of Material Culture (the successor of the Imperial Archaeological Commission and the forerunner of the present-day Archaeological Institute of the

---

[18] Iu. V. Got'e, "Universitet (Iz zapisok akademika Iu. V. Got'e)," *Vestnik Moskovskogo universiteta, seriia 8, Istoriia*, 1982, no. 4, pp. 13–27.

[19] *Zamoskovnyi krai v XVII veke. Opyt issledovaniia po istorii ekonomicheskogo byta Moskovskoi Rusi* (Moscow, 1906), 603pp.

[20] *Istoriia oblastnogo upravleniia v Rossii ot Petra I do Ekateriny II. T. 1. Reforma 1727 goda. Oblastnoe delenie i oblastnye uchrezhdeniia 1727–1775* (Moscow, 1913), 472pp.

Academy of Sciences), and participated in numerous excavations in Europe an Russia. His lectures on the prehistory of Eastern Europe from the Stone Age to the Iron Age were published in 1925 and 1930.[21] In 1922, Got'e was elected a Corresponding Member of the Academy of Sciences.

Well before the Revolution, Got'e had established a reputation as one of the outstanding historians of his generation, a generation that produced more first-rate historical scholarship than any before or since. It was a unique moment in the development of Russian historiography: a generation of scholars, armed with positivist convictions about the scientifically objective character of knowledge based on documentary research and trained in source analysis in the research seminars of Kliuchevskii and Vinogradov in Moscow, and of K. N. Bestuzhev-Riumin, S. F. Platonov, and A. S. Lappo-Danilevskii in Petersburg, turned for the first time to the rich materials in state and church archives to write the social and economic history of Russia. Got'e was one of the leading and most productive scholars in this movement; he had a reputation as a particularly meticulous and exhaustive master of archival sources. His two dissertations were generally accepted as models of archive-based research works on the demographic, social, economic, and political-administrative structure of the provinces in the seventeenth and eighteenth centuries; both are still considered the standard works on their subjects.[22]

Got'e was particularly interested in land relations and the rise of the landed gentry; he wrote in 1915 what is to this day the only general history of landholding in Russia.[23] But his interests were unusually catholic and his capacity for work was prodigious: the bibliography of his works published in 1941 contains 161 entries.[24] He lectured and wrote on the history of the South Slavs, the Lithuanian-Russian State, and Poland; on Scandinavian and English sources for the study of Russian history; on historiography; on archaeology. Toward the end of his career, he turned his attention to the history of nineteenth-century Russia, one of the fruits of which was a book on Bismarck and Russia that has never been published. From 1910 to 1928, Got'e wrote surveys of current literature on Russian history for the French journal *Revue historique* and in 1929 he published there a survey of Ukrainian-language work on Ukrainian history for 1917–1928. His knowledge of languages was phenomenal, even for a

[21] *Ocherki po istorii material'noi kul'tury Vostochnoi Evropy do osnovaniia pervogo russkogo gosudarstva. 1. Kamennyi vek. Bronzovyi vek. Zheleznyi vek na iuge Rossii* (Leningrad, 1925), 275pp. *Zheleznyi vek v Vostochnoi Evrope* (Moscow-Leningrad, 1930), 230pp.

[22] L. V. Cherepnin, *Otechestvennye istoriki XVIII–XX. Sbornik statei, vystuplenii, vospominanii* (Moscow, 1984), pp. 315–20.

[23] *Ocherk istorii zemlevladeniia v Rossii* (Sergiev Posad, 1915), 207pp.

[24] N. M. Asafova, comp., *Iurii Vladimirovich Got'e* (Materialy k bibliografii trudov uchenykh SSSR. Seriia istorii, vyp. 1) (Moscow, 1941).

graduate of the historico-philological faculty of Moscow University, where Vinogradov required a knowledge of both classical languages and three modern languages of all undergraduate students in his seminar: in addition to French, which was still spoken on his father's side of the family and in the considerable French colony in Moscow in which the family circulated, Got'e knew at least Greek and Latin, Italian, German, English, Swedish, Polish, Ukrainian, and Serbo-Croatian.

❊

Got'e's views on politics, culture, and the nature of the contemporary crisis are developed in his diary with a clarity and fullness that require no lengthy elaboration here. Got'e was profoundly anti-Bolshevik. The Bolsheviks represented to him a mixture of the worst traits of the intelligentsia (fanaticism, indifference to legality, and devotion to the view that the end justifies any means) and of the *canaille*, the great unwashed, the "gorillas" (as he calls them). But Got'e was no apologist for the old regime, either: some of his most caustic comments are reserved for the imperial bureaucracy and for Nicholas II personally. Nor was he an uncritical admirer of the West: he feared the designs on Russia of the "imperialists," Germany in the first place, until the end of the war, but France and England, too.

Russia's collapse injured his national sensibilities. There stood revealed the thinness of Russia's civilized veneer, her despicable national character ("Russian swine" and "Russian carrion" are frequently used words in his lexicon), the weakness and fanaticism of her intelligentsia, and the perfidy of her nationalities (especially the Ukrainians, whom he could not forgive for dalliance with the Germans). He was fond of repeating the words spoken to him by Kliuchevskii on the eve of the Revolution of 1905: Russia would perish from the stupidity and avarice of the peasant and the betrayal of the nationalities.

Got'e was an elitist, but his elitism was not that of the aristocracy or of the revolutionary intelligentsia; it was the cultural elitism of a professional middle-class Russian of nonnoble background, Western oriented but deeply patriotic, and suspicious of the designs on Russia of the European powers and of international capital. Got'e's allegiance was to the country as a whole, whose cement was the supranational state, not to the nobility, or the merchantry, or the ethnic Russians, or "the people" (he is utterly hostile to any notions that smack of populist romanticism). If the supranational state were to disappear, so too would the basis of his national identity, for, despite his Westernism, Got'e was painfully aware that he was not a Westerner either (he had no family ties in France). He repeatedly bemoans the absence of "general-Russian patriotism" in the country, not only among the minority nationalities, but among the ethnic

Great Russians as well: "There are all kinds of patriotism in the Russian realm—Armenian, Georgian, Tatar, Ukrainian, Belorussian—their name is legion. Only general-Russian patriotism is lacking, and the Great Russians lack it as well."

In his despair over Russia's plight, Got'e spares no group or estate, and his remarks are not free of ethnic slurs—for the Russians in the first place, but also for Ukrainians, and for Jews. His greatest loathing is for the "gorillas" and for the Jewish Bolsheviks he encountered in great numbers in the organs of the Soviet government with which he had the most contact: the Commissariat of People's Enlightenment, with its train of would-be professors, and the Cheka, the political police. For him, these people embodied the traits—lack of patriotism, fanaticism, and opportunism—that he considered most destructive of the body politic, and there is no doubt that he tended to attribute these characteristics to an entire class—"the Jew in the new order."[25]

Got'e belonged to no political party during the time he kept his diary. He had been associated briefly in 1905–1906 with the main liberal-constitutionalist party, the Constitutional Democrats (Kadets), whose leader was his former teacher P. N. Miliukov. But he left the party in 1906, apparently out of disagreement with the party's endorsement of civil disobedience in the Vyborg Manifesto.[26] By 1917, in any case, he was convinced that the Kadets were fatally infected with the intelligentsia vices of partisanship and political ambition, just like the more extreme parties.

Got'e's political and social views were those of a fairly typical member of the academic intelligentsia. They echo themes expressed in the famous 1909 *Signposts* critique of the intelligentsia tradition, which Got'e cites in his diary, and in the 1918 "postrevolutionary" continuation of that discussion, *From the Depths*, which was confiscated before distribution and apparently remained unknown to him.[27] Colleagues of Got'e at the university contributed to both volumes.

[25] It is conventional wisdom that the highly visible role of Jews in the Bolshevik regime exacerbated negative attitudes about Jews in general in a country with a considerable tradition of anti-Semitic feeling. On April 3, 1919, two months after the Bolsheviks had retaken Poltava, Korolenko noted in his diary: "Hatred of communism and . . . judophobia are evident in the insurgent movement: 'We are now under Jewish rule.'" In the penultimate entry in his diary, as he is boarding ship in England to return to America (November 16, 1922), Babine writes: "The steerage and the second cabin of the Berengaria are full of Jews. Many of them are fleeing from Russia where life at present is impossible and where pogroms are expected of all the Jews [*sic*] for the sins of a few criminal anarchists who are Jews only in name, but who bring a curse on all Jewish race [*sic*]."

[26] Terence Emmons, *The Formation of Political Parties and the First National Elections in Russia* (Cambridge, Mass., 1983), pp. 364–65.

[27] *Vekhi. Sbornik statei o russkoi intelligentsii* (Moscow, 1909); *Iz glubiny. Sbornik statei o*

Got'e sympathized with the analysis of the Revolution as a crisis of spiritual and moral values, but the terms of discourse of most of the analysis in *From the Depths* were too abstract for Got'e's pragmatic historical turn of mind. However, the contribution of the editor, P. B. Struve, was in many respects close to Got'e's own analysis of the situation. Struve, whose essay was entitled "The Historical Meaning of the Russian Revolution and the National Tasks," began with the declaration "The Russian revolution has proved to be a national bankruptcy and a monumental disgrace" and placed the blame for the national catastrophe on the monarchy and the intelligentsia: on the monarchy for its jealous refusal to allow the cultured and educated elements of the population to participate in the affairs of state and for its failure to resolve the "peasant question" in the direction of transforming the peasantry into a class of small proprietors until it was too late; and on the intelligentsia for its "shortsighted struggle against the state." The task of the future was "the education of individuals and the masses in the national spirit."[28]

The analysis of the Revolution that appeared in a 1921 collection published in Prague, *Change of Signposts* (also for the most part the work of representatives of the Russian academic intelligentsia), elaborated on national and statist themes dear to Got'e's heart.[29] He read *Change of Signposts* soon after it appeared and comments on it at some length in his diary. For all his approval of what was written there about the state and the national interests, however, he could not accept the idea that the Bolshevik regime had taken up the national mission, and even less the underlying populist belief in the genius and "statism" (*gosudarstvennost'*) of the common people. He wrote that notion off to the "touching naiveté of the Russian intelligentsia." To have seen the Bolsheviks of 1921 as the bearers of the national tradition and *raison d'état* would indeed have required a leap of faith.

In the spectrum of academic intelligentsia thinking about the meaning of the Revolution, Got'e clearly belonged in the pragmatic middle, disinclined to think about it in terms either of metaphysical principles, at one extreme, or of romantic notions about the will of the people, at the other. Among well-known writers, it was probably Struve to whom he was closest in his assessment of the contemporary crisis.[30]

As Struve's biographer points out, Russian interpretations of the 1917

russkoi revoliutsii (Moscow, 1918 [1921]). *From the Depths* was set in type in 1918, but blocked by the censor. It was released in 1921—apparently in such small numbers that it never reached the bookstores—and was immediately confiscated. It became widely known only after its republication in Paris in 1967.

[28] *Iz glubiny* (Paris edition), p. 304.

[29] *Smena vekh. Sbornik statei* (Prague, 1921).

[30] See Richard Pipes, *Struve: Liberal on the Right. 1905–1944* (Cambridge, Mass., 1980).

revolution have drawn on two historical models, generally depending on whether one's political views were left of center or conservative. The model for the left was the French Revolution: Russia was experiencing the birth of democracy and the Bolsheviks were latter-day Jacobins whose rule would eventually yield to a synthetic regime, a strengthened and more democratic country. The model for the conservatives was the Russian Time of Troubles (1598–1613), a period of dynastic interregnum, anarchy, civil war, and foreign intervention—in short, unmitigated disaster.[31]

Like Struve, Got'e definitely preferred the native-Russian model: he even wrote a small book about the historical Time of Troubles in 1919.[32] Even though he claimed to have written it only for the money, his choice of subject was certainly not accidental, and in the diary he repeatedly refers to the present as "our Time of Troubles" and draws numerous parallels between events and personages in that epoch and the present. He certainly saw nothing good coming out of the Bolshevik Revolution at the time.

Nevertheless, the internal dynamics of the French Revolution were too compelling for Got'e to avoid: he repeatedly draws analogies between current events and personages and those of the French Revolution (especially as interpreted by Taine, one of his favorite authors). Perhaps these parallels were compelling because they provided a prospect of hope for the future. By the same token, in the introduction to his little book on the Time of Troubles, Got'e classifies that episode as a *revolution*, or a "whole series of revolutionary jolts and upheavals," and proceeds to define "revolution" in terms of an illness or fever. The organism is gravely endangered by the trial but emerges strengthened: "Living through the Time of Troubles, our motherland, however, found in herself a fund of new energy that allowed her to attain further successes on the historical path and to prepare for the highest elevation of her historical forces—the reforms of Peter the Great."[33]

We have no access to Got'e's thoughts about contemporary developments in the months and years after July 1922. It seems highly unlikely that he came to see in Stalin a new Peter the Great, but one can imagine that, as the country gradually emerged from anarchy, as the initial post-revolutionary attack against the national tradition yielded to a revived cultivation of the national past, and as the Bolsheviks began to demonstrate statist (some would even say Russian imperialist) proclivities, Got'e

[31] Ibid., pp. 298–99.

[32] *Smutnoe vremia. Ocherk istorii revoliutsionnykh dvizhenii nachala XVII stoletiia* (Moscow, 1921), 151pp. The book had been completed and turned over to the publisher in 1919.

[33] Ibid., p. 8.

must have come to see in the new regime some of the qualities necessary for the revival of "general-Russian patriotism" and made his peace, however grudgingly, with it. He had said on several occasions that, bad as they were, the Bolsheviks by late 1917 had constituted the only organizing force in the country.

Got'e tells us little about his religious views as such in his diary. He attended the Orthodox Church, especially during the main holidays. He buried his own and was married in the church. He knew his Bible, and he had a profound appreciation for the aesthetic and cultural-historical significance of the Orthodox Church in Russian life. He was interested in reports of miracles and omens, and he was not indifferent to the state of preservation of the relics of St. Sergius, which he was allowed to see in 1919. At the same time, he was quite critical of the contemporary moral state of the church and clergy. In any event, Got'e's intellectual frame of reference is not religious, but historical and cultural—that is, secular. If he found solace in religious faith during his trials in these years, which appears to be the case, he does not write much about it in his diary.

❄

During the years in which he kept his diary and for many years before, Got'e's professional life revolved around two institutions, the Moscow Public Library and Rumiantsev Museum, and Moscow University.

The Rumiantsev Museum had been established as a quasi-public institution in Petersburg in 1831 on the foundation of the Rumiantsev family collection of archaeology, art, and books and manuscripts. In 1861 the collections of the museum were moved to Moscow and incorporated with the just-created Moscow Public Library in the Pashkov House, a beautiful classical-style mansion built in the late eighteenth century near the Kremlin, which remains to this day a component of the Lenin Library. Although the Rumiantsev collections soon constituted only a small portion of the entire Moscow collection, and the library became the central part of the institution (it was designated a national repository library in 1862), the entire complex was habitually called The Rumiantsev Museum (compare The British Museum).

The Rumiantsev Museum had been administratively subordinate to the ministry of public enlightenment since 1867, and its senior staff (*shtatnye chiny*) were regular civil servants of the ministry.

The problems of physical space, budget, and staffing that preoccupied Got'e during the years he kept his diary had been plaguing the Rumiantsev library for years before 1917, as the size of its collection and the number of users grew steadily (the size of the library collection grew from about 500,000 volumes in 1900 to nearly 1,500,00 volumes in 1917).

The process of separating the library from the other divisions of the museum, which was the main response to the crisis of space, was completed on paper in 1921 with the rechristening of the library The All-Russian Public Library in Moscow, while the gradual physical removal of the other divisions (completed later in the 1920s) was begun even before the war. Upon Lenin's death in January 1924, it was renamed The Lenin Russian Public Library, and since February 6, 1925, it has been called The V. I. Lenin Public Library of the USSR, the national repository library.

A separate budgetary allotment for the acquisition of books—the first—was put through in 1912, and an expansion of the library staff from forty-five to sixty-two was put through in 1914.

Problems of space, staff, and budget were immensely magnified by the enormous influx of books—both confiscated and donated—that came with the Revolution. During the period that Got'e kept his diary, the library acquired over 400 institutional and private libraries of various sizes, amounting to almost 2 million books, of which 800,000 were not duplicates.

The main response of the Commissariat of Enlightenment to this crisis, despite its meager and uncertain budget, was to increase the size of the library staff: it was increased in 1919 to 305 persons. This undertaking, which is described in some detail in the diary, brought with it a whole revolution in the organization of the library that cannot be dwelt on here.[34]

Another serious problem faced by the library in these years was the interruption of foreign acquisitions, which began with the outbreak of the war and continued after the war's end because of the new regime's political and economic isolation from the rest of Europe. It was not until 1921, as we see from the diary, that some channels for acquiring current foreign imprints were revived, particularly through the Russian Peace Delegation in Riga.

The Rumiantsev Museum was not exempt from the crisis of authority that beset virtually all institutions from the outset of the Revolution. The staff of the museum before 1917 had consisted of three distinct groups: the ranking civil servants who made up the administration; the so-called "supplementary" workers (vol'notrudiashchiesia), who were in fact wage workers without benefits or pensions, people of some education who performed the basic library functions of cataloging, reference work, and the like; and the "lower personnel" who provided manual labor. Before 1917,

---

[34] See "X let bibliotechnogo stroitel'stva," in Publichnaia Biblioteka SSSR imeni V. I. Lenina, Sbornik (1928), 1: Istoriia gosudarstvennoi biblioteki SSSR imeni V. I. Lenina, 1862–1962 (Moscow, 1962), pp. 77–100.

none of these groups of museum employees were organized, though the civil servants constituted the Museum Council, the only consultative organ in the institution. The pay differential between them and the menial employees was enormous. The situation was ripe for a challenge from below, and it came immediately after the February revolution of 1917: two groups emerged—one for the intelligentsia "supplementary" staff, and another for the workers—each concerned with improving working conditions, salaries, and rights of participation. But when the workers announced a strike for higher wages at the beginning of October 1917, the majority of the "supplementary" staff sided with the administration against them. This was the setting for the staff relations that are frequently discussed in the diary.

These few facts should give some idea of the kind of upheavals that were occurring in the Rumiantsev Museum in the years the diary was being kept. Despite them, Got'e's position there seems to have remained secure until the appointment of a new director, A. K. Vinogradov, in March 1921. Relations between Vinogradov and Got'e went sour very quickly in spite of their previous association as museum employees.[35] Nevertheless, Got'e survived these vicissitudes—and Vinogradov, who was removed from the directorship in 1924 or 1925—and kept his position as chief librarian until his arrest in 1930.

The situation was worse in the university, which after the October revolution became a focal point of contention between the new Marxist regime and the overwhelmingly hostile, non-Marxist professoriate.

The history of relations between the professoriate and the state had been far from placid under the old regime. The general principle of university autonomy expressed in the right of the faculty to elect its own rector (president) had been recognized in the first university statute of 1804, removed in 1849, restored in 1863, removed again in 1884 (along with the right to elect faculty members), and restored once again in 1905. Although it was seriously violated at least once, in 1911, the liberal statute of August 27, 1905, remained in effect at Moscow University at the time of the October revolution: the authority to elect the university's administrative officers and to appoint faculty members belonged to the Academic Council.

For some time after October, the new regime did not interfere directly with the university's autonomy, despite the hostility toward it of the large majority of the faculty, and the lack of sympathy for the existing university on the part of the top men in Narkompros, A. V. Lunacharskii and M. N. Pokrovskii. By the spring of 1918, however, plans were elaborated in the commissariat for the "democratization" of student body, faculty,

[35] See the letters of Vinogradov in the Appendix to the diary.

and administration. A decree of August 2 abolished all entrance examinations and educational prerequisites and opened the university to all persons of both sexes (the prerevolutionary universities had been closed to women) of sixteen years of age or older. All entrance and tuition fees were abolished at the same time. A decree of October 1 abolished all academic degrees and announced that all professors who had been teaching for ten years in the same institution were to be deprived of tenure and their positions opened for reelection.

The first of these decrees led to the attachment to the university of the *rabfaki* or workers' faculties, special preparatory courses for workers (in fact for educationally deprived but politically precocious persons of various backgrounds). The first of these appeared in October 1919. In accordance with the second decree, elections for the "vacant" faculty positions were finally held in early 1919. The result might have been expected: the defiant faculty reelected all but one of the ninety professors who had lost tenure—the Communist professor of astronomy, P. K. Shternberg, who was head of the commissariat's division of higher education![36]

Still, the government did not move immediately against the institution of faculty autonomy, and until the autumn of 1920 the Academic Council retained considerable authority in the university. Then in November of that year the commissariat dispersed the Academic Council, set up an Interim Presidium of representatives of the students, faculty, nonteaching staff, and commissariat, and appointed a new rector ("president of the presidium"), the Communist lecturer in financial law, D. P. Bogolepov. From this time on, rectors were in effect appointed by the commissariat, and all professorial appointments were made by the commissariat. A new statute for the universities was promulgated in September 1921, which provided that executive authority in the university was to be vested in a directorate consisting of elected representatives of the professors, the students, the staff, and the commissariat; in December of 1921 the commissariat approved a new directorate of five and appointed as rector the Communist professor of history V. P. Volgin (who had been brought into the university in one of the compromises surrounding the formation of the faculty of social sciences). At this point the established professoriate lost effective control over the internal affairs of the university.

The prerevolutionary Russian university consisted of four faculties: medicine, physics-mathematics, law, and history-philology. Considering the ideological character of the new regime and Narkompros's techno-

[36] In 1918 the faculty had also elected two prominent anti-Bolsheviks, P. B. Struve and S. N. Prokopovich, to the law faculty. M. M. Novikov, "Moskovskii universitet v pervyi period bol'shevistskogo rezhima," in *Moskovskii universitet, 1775–1930* (Paris, 1930).

logical-utilitarian bias in regard to the university, the latter two faculties were the most vulnerable, and their day soon came. At the end of September 1918, the law faculty was abolished, the profession of law having been declared an irrelevancy in the new socialist polity. The following spring, the historico-philological faculty was also broken up, and a new faculty of social sciences was established to accommodate some of the social science departments of the defunct law faculty and the historical section of the humanities faculty. In 1921 the historico-philological faculty was formally abolished and a part of the philological section was then also absorbed into the faculty of social sciences. In 1922, a department of archaeology was added to that faculty (Got'e became one of the first professors to lecture in it).

In 1925 the faculty of social sciences was reorganized into a faculty of ethnography and a faculty of Soviet law. Got'e probably left the university because of this change and the removal from the university in 1926 of the historical institute that had been created there in 1921. This institute was the brainchild of Pokrovskii, who wanted to institutionalize historical research in research institutes separate from teaching.[37] It had been incorporated into a general association of social science institutes attached to the faculty of social sciences in 1924. When it was removed from the university altogether in 1926, it was put in the renamed Russian Association of Scientific Research Institutes of the Social Sciences (RANION). Although the first head of RANION was none other than Got'e's *bête noire*, Pokrovskii, Got'e and his "bourgeois" colleagues were taken into RANION. (It is not clear whether Got'e was there continuously from 1926; he may have entered it in 1927 when the Academy of the History of Material Culture was absorbed into RANION, or even as late as 1928, when he was appointed professor in the short-lived Institute of Eastern Peoples, which was a RANION adjunct.)

The 1930 handbook on the scholars of Moscow listed Got'e's affiliations as follows: "Corresponding Member of the Academy of Sciences of the USSR, Chief Librarian and Associate Director of the Lenin Public Library of the USSR, Active Member of the RANION Institute of History, Scholarly Associate of the State Academy of the Arts, Curator of the State Historical Museum."

Despite the obliteration of university autonomy and the institutional permutations in the academic study of history, a kind of coexistence between the "old" scholarship and the "new," Soviet Marxist, scholarship persisted until the late 1920s. Alongside the new Socialist Academy (1918) and the Institute of Red Professors (1921), the universities in Pet-

---

[37] See George M. Enteen, *The Soviet Scholar-Bureaucrat: M. N. Pokrovskii and the Society of Marxist Historians* (University Park, Penn., 1978).

rograd and Moscow, the Academy of Sciences, and even RANION were populated for the most part by prerevolutionary scholars who were allowed to go on with their "bourgeois-objectivist" studies.

The end to the period of coexistence came between 1928 and 1931, coinciding with the great upheaval of the first five-year plan and the collectivization of agriculture, and forming part of the great new offensive conducted by Stalin on all fronts. It began in the world of scholarship at the end of 1928 with the reform of the Academy of Sciences, which increased the number of academicians from forty-five to ninety. When the old guard in the academy blocked the election of Communist scholars to several of the new positions, the Party responded by purging the academy.

The arrests among historians began in October 1929 with Professor Rozhdestvenskii in Leningrad and continued into 1931: Academician Platonov was arrested in January 1930; Got'e's turn came in July. Arrested with Got'e and brought to Leningrad in July 1930 were his Moscow colleagues and close friends M. K. Liubavskii (who had just been elected to the academy), D. N. Egorov, S. V. Bakhrushin, A. I. Iakovlev, S. K. Bogoiavlenskii, and V. I. Picheta (from Minsk). In all, four full academicians (Platonov, Liubavskii, N. P. Likhachev, and E. V. Tarle) and more than 120 others (not all historians) had been arrested by November 1931 in what was popularly known as the "case of the four academicians," or the "Platonov affair." [38] Those arrested were accused of participating in a plot to restore the monarchy; the chief organizer of the plot was alleged to be Platonov, who was also to have been the prime minister of the new government. Got'e was accused of having been the head of the Moscow "section" of the secret organization.[39] Five of the alleged plotters were sentenced by an OGPU tribunal to be shot. Most of the historians among the accused were sentenced to various terms of exile, some in concentration camps. Got'e was sentenced to five years in the Ukhta-Pechora camps of the far north.[40]

---

[38] Konstantin F. Shteppa, *Russian Historians and the Soviet State* (New Brunswick, N.J., 1962), pp. 48–50. A. Rostov [pseudonym], "Delo Akademii Nauk," in *Vozrozhdenie. Literaturno-politicheskie tetradi* (1958) 81: 97–105; 82: 109–18; 83: 111–22; 84: 111–19. A. Rostov, "Delo chetyrekh akademikov," in *Pamiat'. Istoricheskii sbornik*, vyp. 4 (Paris, 1981), pp. 469–95.

[39] Rostov, "Delo chetyrekh akademikov," p. 478. It is easy to see why Got'e was given the "honor" of heading the Moscow "section" of the conspiracy: Got'e had traveled frequently to Petrograd/Leningrad and habitually stayed with the Platonovs while there. In those days the OGPU still sometimes took the trouble to build a plausible skein of evidence for its cases.

[40] Ibid. According to Rostov, who was apparently one of the Leningraders arrested in the "Platonov affair," the Ukhta-Pechora camps were reserved for those accused who had given false testimony and incriminated their fellows. According to him, Got'e "confessed"

But the story does not end there. The purge of the historians left over from before the Revolution had hardly ended before the purge of their successors, the first generation of Soviet Marxist historians began, and it was far bloodier. The physical liquidation of the representatives of the "Pokrovskii School" got into full swing after the murder of Kirov in December 1934 and was part and parcel of the general purge of those years.

The role of ideology in the fate of the Marxist historians of the 1920s is problematical, but there is no doubt that their sociological-schematic approach to history in general and their negative assessment of virtually everything in the Russian national past in particular (especially in the case of Pokrovskii, who died of cancer in 1932 before the blood purges got underway) ran afoul of Stalin's decision to cultivate Russian patriotism by rehabilitating the national past—great men, great battles, etc. The watershed year in this amazing reversal was 1934.[41]

In 1934 the history faculties in Moscow and Leningrad universities were restored, as were the history curriculums, including Russian history, in the schools; projects for the writing of Russian history textbooks at all levels were begun; and most of the "old" historians still alive in exile were brought back and put to work, often in the same positions as before their arrest. Only a few of them had in fact died in the meantime. Of the Moscow historians who were arrested with Got'e, Liubavskii and Egorov died in exile: Bakhrushin, Iakovlev, Bogoiavlenskii, and Got'e returned, as did their old university comrade Picheta.

Got'e himself did not return directly to the university but took up teaching at the Moscow Institute of Philosophy, Literature, and History (MIFLI), which had been founded in 1931. In 1937, his Magister's dissertation was republished, with an editor's preface that was more than respectful.[42] He began teaching again in the university in 1939 while continuing to teach at MIFLI until 1941, when he was evacuated to Tashkent, where he remained with much of the Moscow academic community for nearly two years. In 1939 he was also elected Full Member of the Academy of Sciences. In 1941, twenty years after its completion, the second

---

to having headed the Moscow "section" of the conspiracy and implicated S. K. Bogoiavlenskii. It is impossible to verify these assertions. In any case, the extortion of signatures on "novels," as stories fabricated by the secret police were called, was standard operating procedure going back to the first days of the Cheka, and it is doubtful that the act of signing such fabrications was taken seriously as proof of guilt by anyone involved. Got'e was certainly not shunned by his former colleagues in later years, least of all by Bogoiavlenskii, who made a point of stressing Got'e's excellent character in his obituary article.

[41] Shteppa, *Russian Historians and the Soviet State*, ch. 5, "The Subjection of Scholarship to the Party."

[42] *Zamoskovnyi krai v XVII veke. Opyt issledovaniia po istorii ekonomicheskogo byta Moskovskoi Rusi*, vtoroe, prosmotrennoe izdanie (Moscow, 1937).

volume of his large work on the eighteenth century was finally published.[43] A bibliography of his works, complete with a signed photograph, appeared the same year. From the time of his return from exile until his death, he contributed several articles to the *Great Soviet Encyclopedia*, wrote several chapters for the first Soviet college-level textbook on the history of the USSR,[44] and continued his writing and research on eighteenth- and nineteenth-century Russia.

❋

Iurii Vladimirovich Got'e died in Moscow on December 17, 1943, after a grave illness. He was seventy years old. He died in the midst of the second great war and German invasion of Russia in his lifetime, while two sons from the second family he had begun in 1921 were fighting at the front. One of them, his youngest son Mikhail, was killed a few weeks after his father's death. The fate of his first-born son, Volodia, remains unknown to this writer.

Despite the extreme vicissitudes of his life, Got'e left an astonishing legacy of work accomplished and of dedication to the best traditions of Russian historical scholarship. To the extent that those traditions have been preserved in contemporary Soviet scholarship, it is in large measure thanks to Got'e and a few others like him.

Got'e's old colleague, S. K. Bogoiavlenskii, wrote an obituary for one of the scholarly journals not long after Got'e's death. Bogoiavlenskii had known Got'e for at least forty years and had lived through it all, too. He ended his article with the following words:

> Even a short review of Iu. V.'s scholarly career is sufficient to evoke the lifelike image of a tireless intellectual toiler and a scholar actively engaged in the life of the community in the best sense of the word. Author of many works that demanded sustained and intensive labor, a master of detailed and meticulous research, Iu. V. Got'e was at the same time a fine human being who possessed the wonderful qualities of true benevolence, affability, and that inborn culture which is the possession of a select few.[45]

[43] *Istoriia oblastnogo upravleniia v Rossii ot Petra I do Ekateriny II. T. 2. Organy nadzora. Chrezvychainye i vremennye oblastnye uchrezhdeniia. Razvitie mysli o preobrazovanii oblastnogo upravleniia. Uprazdnenie uchrezhdenii 1727 g.* (Moscow-Leningrad, 1941), 303pp.

[44] V. I. Lebedev, B. D. Grekov, S. V. Bakhrushin, eds., *Istoriia SSSR, t. 1. S drevneishikh vremen do kontsa XVIII v.* (Moscow, 1939). For this textbook, Got'e wrote the introduction to sources, the chapters on the prehistory and early history of Eastern Europe before the founding of the Kievan state, and on medieval Georgia and Armenia, and most of the chapters on the eighteenth century. Bakhrushin, one of the editors, was Got'e's old friend and colleague who had been arrested and exiled with him a few years earlier for alleged involvement in a monarchist plot.

[45] Bogoiavlenskii, "Akademik Iurii Vladimirovich Got'e," p. 116. S. K. Bogoiavlenskii (1871–1947) was an historian of Old Russia and an archaeologist.

My Observations

Lament on the Downfall

of the Russian Land

Fututa est Russia,
nos fututi cum illa.

For since I spake, I cried out, I cried violence and spoil.[1]

Slavdom is not worth a pinch of tobacco.

The feast was ready, but the guests were unworthy of it.

—Prince D. M. Golitsyn[2]

1917

❋

JULY

8–16 July 1917. Finis Russiae. The army is an army no more. Russia has lost the capacity to defend herself. The fundamental cause, of course, is the century-long decomposition of the old regime. With its fall, it provoked the pendulum swing to the left and the rise to domination of forces that have developed in the underground and are fit only for destruction. The destruction of the army, undertaken in the name of underground slogans that were designed for the struggle against tsarism, has of course brought forth the fruit it was meant to yield: transformation of an army that had fought for two and a half years into a crowd of propagandized bandits.

I think Russia no longer counts for anything in the international arena. The Germans are being presented the opportunity they have been waiting for—to attain all their designated goals in the East. Reintroduction of the death penalty is a belated measure and is not likely to have any effect.[3] Russia is perishing, undermined by Nicholas II and finished off by her own revolution. It now (16 July) seems to me that the immediate future will take shape like this: destruction of the remains of the Russian armies will be completed within a month, and in the autumn pogroms[4] will spread across the country. Who will defend the innocent bystanders? Perhaps the Germans.

[1] Jeremiah 20:8. The corresponding passage from the Slavonic Bible, evocative of the celebrated image of laughter through tears in *Dead Souls*, is inscribed on the tomb of the great Russian writer Gogol.

[2] Prince Dmitrii Mikhailovich Golitsyn (1665–1737) was a member of the Supreme Privy Council that ruled Russia for several years following the death of Peter I (reigned 1689–1725) and was a leading figure in an attempt in 1730 to place "constitutional" limits on the authority of the tsar (in this case, tsaritsa: Anna Ioannovna); these words were supposedly uttered by him at the unsuccessful end of that drama. *Entsiklopedicheskii slovar'* (Brokgauz-Efron), vol. 9 (1893), p. 49.

[3] The death penalty in the army and navy had been abolished on March 12 by the Provisional Government. It was restored for the military by Kerenskii on July 12, although it was never implemented before the October revolution.

[4] Got'e uses the term "pogrom" for manifestations of popular violence—looting, burning, etc.—in general, not only in reference to violence directed against Jews.

The fate of Russia, an extinct dinosaur or mastodon, is to be transformed into a weak and poor country standing in economic dependence on other countries, most likely Germany. The bolsheviks are the true symbol of the Russian people—the people of Lenin, Miasoedov[5], and Sukhomlinov:[6] a mixture of stupidity, vulgarity, uncultured willfulness, lack of principle, hooliganism. And on the basis of the last two qualities—betrayal. The old regime, with its marvelously organized secret-police cadres and similar abominations created a first-rate network for the organization of all manner of evil forces—and they are now at work.

Heart and soul have been torn out, all ideals shattered. Russia has no future. We have no present and no future. The only reason left for living is in order to feed and preserve our families—there is nothing else. The final fall of Russia as a great and unified power, as a result of internal, not external, causes, not directly due to enemies but to our own flaws and inadequacies, from complete atrophy of a sense of patriotism, motherland, common solidarity, and a sense of *union sacrée*—this is an episode with few analogies in world history.

Living through all this, to my great sorrow, shame, and humiliation, I, an educated man who has had the misfortune to choose as his scholarly specialty the history of his native country, feel myself obliged to record my impressions and in this way to create a very imperfect, very subjective, but nevertheless historical source that may be of use to someone in the future. I do so contrary to all my former views on this account: I specifically did not want to write either reminiscences, or reflections, or a diary, for I have always thought there was quite enough of that rubbish written without me.

The peasants I talked with today in Zaprud'e and some from Pochep[7] are reacting feebly. [A people] has to possess greater awareness in order to play a role in the world. We are only fit to be manure for peoples of

[5] Colonel Sergei Nikolaevich Miasoedov (1865–1915) had been tried for treason in March 1915 by a court-martial and hanged.

[6] General Vladimir Aleksandrovich Sukhomlinov (1848–1926) was appointed war minister in 1909, removed in 1915 following major setbacks at the front, and arrested in 1916 on charges of gross misconduct and treason in connection with the conviction on spying charges of several close associates, including Miasoedov (see n. 5). These charges were never confirmed, but Sukhomlinov was found guilty of lesser charges by the Provisional Government and was sentenced to life at hard labor. He was amnestied by the Bolshevik government in 1918 and emigrated to Finland.

[7] Villages in Ves'egonsk district in the northeastern corner of Tver' province, immediately north of Moscow province. The Got'e family owned a small farm in this district, apparently a former gentry estate: "*usad'ba* Novoe Zagran'e." The farm, about two hundred miles due north of Moscow, was reached by traveling by rail as far as Krasnyi Kholm, and then by covering the remaining twenty-five miles or so by cart or wagon. Villages mentioned later in the diary are in that area, except when noted otherwise.

higher culture; and in our history only the negators have been right, beginning with Kurbskii and Khvorostinin and ending with Chaadaev, Pecherin, etc.[8] If anyone is feeling triumphant, it is only Empress Aleksandra Fedorovna.[9]

17 July. The newspapers are a little better. The hope has been kindled since July 15 that at the cost of yielding all of Galicia and complication of the already disgusting Ukrainian question (since, after all, the whole of the Ukraine lying beyond our borders is again in the power of the Germans), at the cost of hundreds of thousands of lives, the idiots will get smarter. Kerenskii's efforts to create a genuine coalition government, with the exception of the adventurist Chernov[10] and similar adventurists, ideologue-fools, and maybe charlatans, deserves every sympathy, but isn't it already too late? Haven't they been screaming and yelling and confusing the unfortunate Russian—stupid, ignorant, and unprepared for any kind of Rospublic (as Ivan Pavlov from Pochep says)[11]—for too long? The Germans play their game cleverly: treason on all sides. Why is it that in no other people drawn into the war is there so much treason as among the Russians? (1) From ignorance; (2) from the complete absence of a feeling of solidarity and fatherland; (3) from the fact that the leftist ideologues have been courting the minority nationalities for a good hundred years now; (4) from the benighted and anticultural deceitfulness that was remarked already by the foreigners' narratives of the seventeenth century.[12] The Germans have been able to take good advantage of this characteristic of the "Russian swine." Revolutionary Russia faces the task of either changing its ways or flying irreversibly into the abyss!

18 July. [My] mind turns always to the same [subject]. A quiet day without mail. A feeling of complete indifference on the one hand; [on the other] a feeling of regret that a people that could have made something of itself is committing suicide. What will we be—Muscovy, China, or

---

[8] A list of famous critics of the Russian order: Prince Andrei Mikhailovich Kurbskii (ca. 1528–1583); Prince Ivan Andreevich Khvorostinin (d. 1625); Petr Iakovlevich Chaadaev (1794–1856); and Vladimir Sergeevich Pecherin (1807–1885).

[9] The reference is to Empress Alexandra's German origins (she was a princess of Hesse-Darmstadt) and widely suspected pro-German sympathies. Of course, she was by the same token the daughter of the British princess Alice and was raised in Kensington Palace by her grandmother, Queen Victoria.

[10] Viktor Mikhailovich Chernov (1873–1952) was the leading theoretician of the Socialist Revolutionary (SR) party and held the portfolio of minister of agriculture in the Provisional Government coalitions between May and August 1917.

[11] *Rospublika* in Russian; cf. *respublika*: "republic." Ivan may have thought the word derived from the Russian verb *rospublikovat'*, "to promulgate, publish."

[12] Got'e was a specialist on these sources (see the Introduction).

Turkey? Will we have the energy to get on our feet? Although Kerenskii evoked the heavy hammer in the Soviet of Workers' Deputies, we may be only the glass that splinters.[13] In any case, of all the combatant peoples, we have turned out to be the weakest in nerve, and thus Hindenburg's thought is true—those with strong nerves will win. So everybody but us will win and logically should make peace at our expense: we will answer for all, and especially for our own stupidity, ignorance, and dishonesty. How often we all think: it's good to no longer be tied to mama's apron strings! In any case we are not a match for the Germans: they are unquestionably higher than we are in every respect, and most of all in personal endurance and courage; one can hate them, but it is impossible not to respect them.

19 July. Three years of war. A fine anniversary in all respects, except for the natural ruination, fatigue, and the like —not to mention defeat and the shame of desertion and treason. In Galicia today (according to the newspapers of the 16th) things are apparently (I have no illusions) a little bit better—the catastrophe is not yet final, perhaps. But the "Provisional Government" is already backtracking. Now it is no longer a matter of its reorganization, but only of some kind of partial adjustments. The damned leaders from among the "socialists" (I exclude here neither Kerenskii nor Tsereteli,[14] who are playing first violin right now, although they are undoubtedly better than the others) remain and will continue to remain dull-witted doctrinaires and will ruin any decent scheme in order to defend the arch-scoundrel Chernov. One catastrophe is obviously not enough to bring [them] to [their] senses—it will take more. It is impossible to make a revolution and fight a war at the same time; one of them has to be given up; and since the revolution is more important than Russia, that means we have to leave the war, ruin Russia, and save the revolution!

---

[13] An evocation of lines from Aleksandr Pushkin's poem, "Poltava":

No v iskushen'iakh dolgoi kary	Yet the ordeal of searching
Pereterpev sudeb udary	trials / Fortune's harsh
Okrepla Rus'.	blows and long denials, /
Tak tiazhkii mlat,	Steeled Rus. The heavy
Drobia steklo, kuet bulat.	hammer thus / Shapes iron
	while it shatters glass.

(English translation: *Alexander Pushkin. Collected Narrative and Lyric Poetry. Translated in Prosodic Forms of the Original by Walter Arndt* [Ann Arbor, 1984].)

[14] Irakli Georgevich Tsereteli (1881–1959) was a leading figure in the Menshevik fraction of the Russian Social-Democratic Labor party (SD); he was a member of the executive of the Petrograd Soviet in 1917 and held several ministerial portfolios in the coalition Provisional Governments.

20 [July]. The Moscow Conference?[15] What is it for and who needs it? The "minister-socialists" are going to say there that everything is bad beyond repair. Any sensible person knows without their help that our revolution has made Russia's situation worse in all respects, even by comparison with Nicholas II of cursed memory. Practically the only sensible thing they could tell us is that the war must be ended. But Kerenskii is hardly likely to say that, at least right now. Kerenskii is a sincere and strong individual, but I consider him to be Russia's greatest evil genius. In the February and March days, who organized the Soviet of Workers' Deputies and the other organs of disintegration? Who provoked the shift of the revolution in the direction of the "dictatorship of the proletariat"? Kerenskii, Chkheidze,[16] Skobelev,[17] and co.; that is, the extreme-left members of the duma. It is of no importance that Kerenskii entered the Provisional Government "at his own risk"—in doing so, astride two stools he had bound together by a slender thread, he held things together with one hand and with the other he broke them apart. Kerenskii is the most gifted of those evil geniuses, and he later came to his senses and began to think of himself as a man of the state and perhaps even a statesman. But all the same, in creating the Soviet of Workers' Deputies in the first days he did more for Russia's destruction than [he has done] for her fortification ever since. Therefore his responsibility is greater than anyone else's. Chkheidze can hardly be held responsible: he is not a Russian, and, by common tacit agreement, he is a "crystalline" fool—as suits a Georgian, by the way. Now all this so-called democracy is beginning to understand that it cannot remedy the situation: the slogans must be abandoned. But this they cannot do, just as they cannot give up power (which they seized as a long-awaited trophy). Therefore there is only one way out: endless negotiations and discussions and the downfall of Russia. Among those negotiations and discussions I include the Moscow Conference. The Russian people are a defeatist people. That is what makes possible such a fantastic phenomenon as the presence among purely Russian people of persons who passionately desire the final defeat of Russia. Defeat has always been more attractive to Russians than victory and triumph: the Russian is always feeling sorry for someone; therefore he

---

[15] The Moscow State Conference was convened by Kerenskii on August 12 as a forum of public opinion, or gallery of support for his Provisional Government. Its participants included former duma deputies and representatives of the soviets, unions, local government institutions, etc.; altogether, about 2,500 people participated in the conference.

[16] Nikolai Semenovich Chkheidze (1864–1926), a Georgian Menshevik, was a deputy of the last Imperial Duma and chairman of the first executive committee of the Petrograd Soviet in 1917.

[17] Matvei Ivanovich Skobelev (1885–1938) was another Menshevik deputy to the last duma and member of the Petrograd Soviet executive committee; he was minister of labor in the coalition Provisional Government.

prefers to feel sorry for himself and love his own misery rather than feel sorry for another whom he has harmed—egoism inside out. Our chronicles, *The Tale of the Host [of Igor]*, songs about Tsar Ivan [IV], [and] the tales about Kazan and the Time of Troubles mostly praise and recount defeats. The Battle of Kulikovo, the Stand on the Ugra, Borodino, Plevna: our greatest victories were in fact either half defeats or disguised defeats. For the most part our military glory speaks of defeats and failures: Narva, Borodino, Suvorov's Swiss campaign, and the like.[18] The doctrine of nonresistance to evil—formulated by Tolstoi—is the same pleasure in misery, humiliation, failure, and defeat. From the same source comes the contemporary doctrine of "defeatism," which is absolutely incomprehensible since the overthrow of the monarchy, but is nevertheless flourishing luxuriantly right now. And the situation cannot be explained by German spies alone: their seed, as in the matter of unalloyed treason, fell on fertile soil. This is our psychology—the complete opposite of the psychology of the German people with their doctrine of *Deutschland über Alles* and the cult of strength and exultation. *Ceteris paribus*, the Russians must be defeated in the conflict between these two peoples, and when everything else is unequal to boot? The answer is obvious.

Incidentally, on the subject of treason: the bolsheviks' mask has been torn off, but not yet the Ukrainians'. The more I think about it, the more I am convinced that there, too, German money is involved. Here I can testify [the following]: in the winter of 1916 the notorious Hrushevsky,[19]

[18] The references are to the most famous battles in Russian history:

The Battle of Kulikovo Field took place in 1380, and although the Russians under Prince Dmitrii Donskoi routed the Mongols in the end, their forces were decimated in a battle whose impact was hardly decisive. Nevertheless, it is traditionally celebrated as the beginning of the end of the "Tatar yoke."

The Stand on the Ugra River in 1480, during the reign of Tsar Ivan III (The Great), is traditionally recognized as the end of Muscovite dependency on the Tatar successors to the Horde; no battle occurred.

The Battle of Borodino in 1812, immortalized in *War and Peace*, was a classic example of the ambiguous victory: although the Russians withdrew at the end of the one-day battle, thus allowing Napoleon to occupy Moscow, the French probably suffered as many casualties as the Russians and were unable to hold Moscow.

The Russian storming of the Turkish fortress of Plevna in northern Bulgaria in 1877 during the Russo-Turkish War was unsuccessful and resulted in huge Russian and Rumanian losses; it was followed by a blockade that finally forced the capitulation of the fortress and the release of troops for the Balkan offensive.

The Russian siege of the Baltic fortress of Narva in the Gulf of Finland was routed by Charles XII of Sweden in 1700; this was the opening of the Great Northern War, which was ultimately won by Russia (the peace treaty was signed in 1721).

Field Marshal Suvorov's daring campaign against the French army in 1798–1799 ended in a retreat, the engineering of which is celebrated as a great military feat.

[19] Mykhailo Serhiiovych Hrushevsky (1866–1934) was a Ukrainian historian and leader of the Ukrainian nationalist movement; he was a member of the Ukrainian Central Rada

whose work in the Rumiantsev Museum I did everything I could to facilitate, as a matter of professional responsibility toward a persecuted individual, spoke with me (in the Rumiantsev Hall, near his desk), at the moment when the possibility of mobilizing men over fifty was being discussed, about how he might get himself assigned as a clerk somewhere in the [general] staff or chancery. A decent and honorable man would not be capable of such cynicism or carry on such a conversation with a perfect stranger. As many have been saying about him for a long time, this is an Austrian agent, as are also probably all his adepts; and the rest, as always and everywhere in Russia, are fools.

What more could I have done than to write these bitter lines, I, a professor, a specialist in Russian history? As much as I have thought about it, I have found no other answer than *nothing*. I am not a political activist; I don't have the temperament for it. In 1905, when I was in the Kadet party,[20] no one took advantage of my services, no one utilized me or involved me: in that "circle of good friends and acquaintances" they graciously offered me a place among the uninformed rank and file. The only thing I heard was the advice of P. N. Miliukov (my teacher)[21] to propagandize in the army (I was being mobilized into the Japanese war at the time), which, by my firm conviction, I would not have done and, of course, did not do. (I think that now Miliukov must think otherwise.) Neither Miliukov, nor Kizevetter,[22] nor any of my other acquaintances found anything for me to do in the Kadet party; at the same time I became disenchanted with it, and after the Vyborg manifesto[23] I left the

---

(council government) in 1917. The rada made a separate peace with the Germans in February 1918.

[20] The Constitutional-Democratic party (KD or Kadets) was founded in 1905 in anticipation of the first elections to the duma, the national legislature, held in the spring of 1906. Essentially a party of the professional middle class, the Kadets were able through skillful association with nationalist groups and peasant electors to emerge as the largest party in the first duma.

[21] Pavel Nikolaevich Miliukov (1859–1943) was the leading figure in the Kadet party throughout its existence. He was also one of the most influential historians of Russia before the 1917 revolution and had been a professor at Moscow University and Got'e's teacher for a short time in the early 1890s, before being expelled from the faculty for his political activities. Got'e's reminiscences about his teacher and his student years in general have been published: "Universitet (Iz zapisok Akademika Iu. V. Got'e)," *Vestnik Moskovskogo universiteta*. Seriia 8, Istoriia, 1982, no. 4, pp. 13–27. These reminiscences were apparently written in the mid-1920s.

[22] Aleksandr Aleksandrovich Kizevetter (1866–1933) was another prominent historian and Kadet leader; in 1917 he was a colleague of Got'e on the Moscow University faculty.

[23] The "Vyborg manifesto" was published on July 10, 1906, by a group of duma deputies immediately following the first duma's dissolution by imperial decree after only seventy-two days of existence. The manifesto protested the act (which was a constitutional prerogative of the monarch) and called on the population to engage in acts of passive resistance and civil disobedience as a means of compelling the government to reconvene the duma quickly. The issuing of the manifesto was an important milestone in the history

party of my own accord *before the governmental retribution* and became a "loner" for the rest of my life. As a loner I could make myself heard only in my own newspaper, like Ilovaiskii's *Kremlin,*[24] or at public meetings; but the former is out of the question, and at meetings they listen only to party orators, and again I am not fit for that. All that I could say is so at odds with the idiotic "slogans" of the ruling autocrats that in this respect, too, dissemination of my ideas would be difficult and useless at the present time. There remain private conversations and the classroom, where I have always tried to be objective and never to say what I did not think myself. Now, with the fall of the old regime, it may be a little easier and freer to breathe in the classroom, but maybe there will be no audience at all? It is likely that Russian youth will find it necessary to do anything at all next year except study, and will once again stop the advance of their civilization, such as it is, and the dissemination of knowledge, perhaps for a long time. If things turn out that way, the only thing left will be to write bitter lines.

21 July. We (Nina, L. Eg., and I)[25] worked hard at haying two days in a row in place of the workers. Physical work gives genuine satisfaction and calms one down (for a time, of course). I note this as another result of the times we are living through. Is it not this elementary satisfaction that causes lazy and flaccid Russians to "go native"; doesn't the secret of Tolstoianism, agricultural colonies of the intelligentsia and similar nonsense lie here, that is, in Russian sloth and superfluousness?

Always the persistent thought: Why has the flower of the Russian service-minded intelligentsia, for example the zemstvo activists and the animators of the zemstvo and town unions,[26] been swept away by events? They would have provided, of course, the best activists for the initial

---

of the Kadet party: the signers of the manifesto, including many of the party's leading figures, were put on trial and sentenced to short jail terms, as a result of which they could no longer stand for public office. Many party members—including Got'e evidently—disapproved of the radical tone and content of the manifesto and soon left the party.

[24] Dmitrii Ivanovich Ilovaiskii (1832–1920) was a conservative Russian historian and publicist, and the author of monographs, a general history of Russia, and many textbooks used in the schools. Between 1897 and 1913 he published his own Moscow newspaper, *Kremlin (Kreml').*

[25] Nina Nikolaevna née Dol'nik was Got'e's wife. "L. Eg.," who is mentioned several times in the diary, seems to have been a member of the Got'e household, but not of the immediate family.

[26] Reference is to the zemstvo institutions of limited rural self-government and the similar dumas, or councils, for the towns, which were established in reforms of the 1860s–1890s. Men from these institutions took the initiative in setting up the zemstvo and town unions (*zemgor*) during the war to help with supplying the army, providing medical aid, etc. Got'e has in mind the elected leadership of these institutions, mostly well-educated noblemen (in the zemstvos at least), not their hired technical employees, who were mostly of humble origin and politically on the left.

period of Russian liberty. I think that this is the result of the Razin- or Pugachev-like character that pervades every Russian political move-ment.[27] The destructive slogans with which the fanatics and provocateurs have been rallying the people against a criminal and stupid government for half a century could yield no other results when 100 million chained mad dogs were turned loose. Everybody who was higher culturally than the ignorant masses and the completely disoriented semiintelligentsia were declared enemies of the people—bourgeois—regardless of whether they had money or were just as hard-working as 99 percent of the Rus-sian people; they are regarded just like the noble masters were earlier. In some cases this led in the spring to the chasing off of health-service doc-tors and zemstvo employees, that is, the notorious third element (this occurred in the Volga region, where the spirit of Razin still lives).[28]

Why is it that in Russia they forgot about the war after the revolution and, under the fire of German cannons, began to rearrange everything both politically and socially—that is, have allowed something so mon-strous that it is hard to believe? In addition to all-Russian savagery, this is also to be explained by the fact that for a full hundred years, and maybe more, all the attention of 99 percent of Russians was focused on internal politics and the struggle with the regime (this is apparent from journal-ism, from analysis of Russian history, from a thousand indicators). When the fools were liberated from their chains, they began to scratch the backs on which they had always been beaten, not noticing that a sword had been raised over their heads that was more terrible than the old knout. One could have said *quem Jupiter perdere vult, dementat,*[29] if it weren't a matter of a people that has always been mindless. From the beginning of March I saw that reinforcement of the military forces was a necessary condition for Russian freedom to take root and for the happiness of Rus-sia, and predicted in the contrary case the downfall of the country, of freedom, and of all promises for a better future. It seems that the situation is now headed precisely in that direction.

I remember the words spoken to me by A. A. Kizevetter on the day of S. N. Trubetskoi's funeral (at the beginning of October 1905):[30] that the extreme right (progovernment) and the extreme left elements are touch-ing in their unanimity as regards bringing harm to Russia. This true

[27] A reference to the Cossack leaders of the great popular rebellions of the seventeenth and eighteenth centuries, Stepan Razin (who led the rebellion of 1670–1671) and Emel'ian Pugachev (who led that of 1773–1774).

[28] "Third element" was a term coined in the late 1890s for the hired technical employ-ees of the zemstvos to distinguish them from the mostly noble elected zemstvo men (the second element) and the regular bureaucracy (the first element).

[29] "Whom Jupiter wishes to destroy, he first drives mad."

[30] Prince Sergei Nikolaevich Trubetskoi (1862–1905) was a philosophy professor and the first elected rector of Moscow University (1905); he was a prominent figure in the constitutional-reform movement. He died suddenly in Petersburg in the autumn of 1905.

thought is becoming genuine reality today. Aleksandra Fedorovna and Lenin can serve as its symbols.

The absence of Russian patriotism in general and of Great-Russian patriotism in particular is an extraordinarily ugly phenomenon. There are all kinds of patriotism in the Russian realm—Armenian, Georgian, Tatar, Ukrainian, Belorussian—their name is legion. Only general-Russian patriotism[31] is lacking; and the Great Russians lack it as well. It is as though the Great Russians, having once founded the Russia that is now perishing, were completely exhausted, or else as though the notion of the general-Russian and the Great Russian was so completely identified with the political regime that has existed until just now in Russia that hatred toward the regime was transferred to everything general-Russian and provoked the atrophy of general-Russian patriotism. The partial, regional patriotism that was cultivated in bygone Russia is one of the most baleful types of particularism. It has ruined many Slavic states, and it will ruin us.

One of the results of the changes that are taking place will be the complete disappearance of Slavophilism in any form. Attempts, both cultural and political, to draw near to the Slavs were always *tirés par les cheveux*. But now Russia has failed to do the one thing that the Slavs have always expected and demanded: she has not defended them, and instead of saving them has herself fallen. Culturally, Austria was always closer for those same Slavs. But whereas tsarist Russia did not save the Slavs and was herself destroyed, free Russian democracy has proclaimed the slogan of internationalism, and in doing so has removed from its program any special relationship with Slavdom. To this it should be added that the Bulgarians, those longtime favorite children of ours, alas, have declared themselves to be non-Slavs. Good riddance to Slavophilism, Slavistics, Pan-Slavism, the little brothers, the kind and benevolent ideology, the blackmailings, the stupidities, and the many and varied speculations on incomparable Russian credulity.

22 July. A former holiday. Newspapers of the 18th, 19th, and 20th. On the front the situation is improving little and hopes are feeble. Inside the country, the same outrageous talk, speeches at mass meetings, arguments, and quarrels. One's attention is arrested by the telegram of the Moscow University Council (it would be interesting to know how many people were there, and how it went: probably there were no debates) and its intelligent concluding words: "Let it not be said that the revolution ru-

---

[31] "Obshche-rossiiskii patriotizm." Got'e uses a term here that is meant to convey the idea of loyalty to the state or the country as a whole, as distinct from the Russian or "Great Russian" ethno-linguistic group.

ined Russia." The message of the Moscow organization of trade and industry to the Provisional Government and several speeches of duma members in their private session[32] were also forceful and interesting. Voices are now being heard, after unheard-of defeat and humiliation, with which, as Uncle Eduard Vladimirovich says, "it is possible to agree." They were not heard earlier because they would have been considered counterrevolutionary. And indeed, the social hooligans of the Soviet of Workers' Deputies are already howling about counterrevolution. It's to be regretted once again that the state duma cut short its activity just to please someone. Was it really Miliukov who did that?[33]

But sober voices are still weak. Kerenskii (that surrogate nightingale) and co. have been in session in the Provisional Government a whole week dragging out discussions about a *national* government: long live slogans, let Russia perish! The Moscow Conference, if it takes place, will be a charade. The speeches of Lloyd George and Bonar Law, and several comments in the French press that have been printed in the newspapers, leave no doubt that Russia no longer counts for anything in international affairs.

23 July. The burden on the soul is worse than ever. Is it due to neurasthenia or a premonition of the next expected abominations? For we are a long way from having reached the limits of suffering. These days I have been reading Liubavskii's history of the Western Slavs.[34] Now it is our turn to perish in the international struggle for existence out of a lack of national self-awareness and a healthy instinct for self-preservation.

I would like to record my village impressions as well, although they are not cheerful either. More than ever, I am becoming convinced that the Russian village is the realm of anarchy. When it is calm, life is good; when it is brought to a kinetic state, it's every man for himself. Since

[32] The Fourth State Duma had been prorogued on February 27, 1917. A provisional committee or rump of the duma had created the first Provisional Government shortly afterward. The duma, though not convened in plenary session after February 27, was not dissolved until October 6, 1917, and in the meantime members continued to hold private meetings and to participate in state conferences.

[33] The reference is to Miliukov's apparently considerable role in detaching the first Provisional Government from the duma during political negotiations in Petrograd at the time of the February revolution. Miliukov held that a government responsible to the duma would be a liability in dealing with the Petrograd Soviet. See William G. Rosenberg, *Liberals in the Russian Revolution. The Constitutional-Democratic Party, 1917–1921* (Princeton, 1974), pp. 52–59.

[34] Matvei Kuz'mich Liubavskii (1860–1936) was an eminent historian of Russia and Got'e's senior colleague on the history faculty of Moscow University. A political conservative, he was elected rector of the university in 1911 following the resignation of A. A. Manuilov in a conflict with the ministry of education. He was replaced as rector by the liberal Professor M. A. Menzbir, elected after the February revolution.

almost all the peasants here are supplied with purchased lands, the general situation is calm, as I foresaw already in March, but there are individual hotbeds—for example, Mokei Gora.[35] That hotbed is sustained by muzhiks, stupid hooligans, confused and unbalanced people who consider themselves members of a party, sps or perhaps srs[36] (like Fedor Aleksandrov, they themselves don't know the difference), workers writing letters from Petrograd (Bochkov), and finally senseless, greedy, and stupid people like the Zamologins.

Relations got tense before sowing and haying time, when an assault was made on Zagran'e. At present the hotbed has cooled down (temporarily?). One of the reasons is probably the fact that the peasants of Zaprud'e and in part of Gora made a special assault on the Zamologins, who altogether have forty desiatinas,[37] and forced them to buy their way out with money. After that they calmed down—they defend their own [property] and don't lust after that of others. No other causes are clear to me. But of course, the hotbed can always ignite. So far there have not been any hostile manifestations toward us.

About two weeks ago, in connection with the census, I went to the township committee with Marietta[38] and had a talk with the chairman, the peasant Vasilii Semenovich Krasavtsev from Sushigoritsy. He is a bright, even rather diplomatic, half-intelligentsia peasant, apparently an sr, pretty well propagandized; they say he was in exile somewhere under the old regime. He creates rather a good impression, although it is clear that he relishes his position and authority—the future bureaucrat of the republic is already visible in him.

Marietta told about how she sat on the supply committee. The most interesting things were the role of the Sushigoritsy schoolteacher, an sr fanatic, who endlessly babbles the same old thing about the land, and how all these party activists and honorable Russian citizens occupied themselves first of all with the question of their salaries. It couldn't have been otherwise, of course.

24 [July]. Newspapers of the 21st and 22d. The Russian borderlands will have to pay for the lesson as well, of course. But perhaps even this will not be enough to bring them to their senses. Most recently, however, the internal decline has been even worse than the external. The Provisional

---

[35] A settlement in Ves'egonsk district, Tver province.

[36] That is, Social Democrats or Socialist Revolutionaries—the two main parties of the left whose members predominated in the Petrograd soviet.

[37] One desiatina = 2.7 acres.

[38] Marietta appears to have been a relative who lived permanently on the family's country property.

Government fell apart and by the 22d was no more.[39] The main fact was, of course, the resignations of Kerenskii and Chernov. The latter has been adequately unmasked, but what does the resignation of Kerenskii mean? Maybe he will again enter some kind of coalition? But maybe this means that the sincere and honest ideologue is becoming disenchanted with the bordello the Russian revolution has become. In any case, the latter is becoming more and more like a shameful comedy with every day that passes. The wish of that revolting sow bug I. I. Skvortsov-Stepanov[40] to transform the Moscow city duma into something like the Convention[41] is interesting: a proposal for roll-call voting with the public galleries packed with bolsheviks (for the question of reintroducing the death penalty).

Mr. Kerenskii's effort to create a special battalion or squadron of generals who have been relieved of their commands continues. The removal of Brusilov (see the interview with him in *The Russian Morning* for the 22d) leaves a strange impression. It is no less strange, it seems to me, to take Kornilov from the southwestern front at the moment when the situation there is critical.[42] One recalls Lermontov's verses:

> I want to say to the great people:
> You are a pitiful and empty folk![43]

What should be done immediately: curtail all liberties, all guarantees, all declarations and untimely reforms, and concentrate only on the army; for only the army can save Russia's life. But they won't do that and Russia will perish. Shame to the immoral and suicidal nation!

25 July. Today I thought all morning, both alone and together with Ninka, about the general and specific situations. Both are hopeless. There is no army, no money, no one wants to work, all the "democratic" strata

---

[39] Kerenskii had taken over as prime minister in the first coalition government following Prince G. E. L'vov's resignation on July 8. Kerenskii's own resignation on July 21, which appeared to Got'e at the time to signal the collapse of the Provisional Government, was in fact part of an elaborate maneuver by Kerenskii to preserve it by putting together a new coalition of socialist and "bourgeois" ministers; this was accomplished by July 24. Chernov returned to his post as minister of agriculture in that new coalition.

[40] Ivan Ivanovich Skvortsov-Stepanov (1870–1928) (real name, Skvortsov) was a longtime Bolshevik who at this point was editor of the newspaper of the Moscow Soviet.

[41] That is, the Convention in the French Revolution (1792–1795).

[42] General Aleksei Alekseevich Brusilov (1853–1926) was removed as commander in chief on July 18 and was replaced by General Lavr Georgievich Kornilov (1870–1918), commander of the southwestern front.

[43]
>   Mne khochetsia skazat' velikomu narodu:
>   Ty zhalkii i pustoi narod!

From Lermontov's 1841 poem, "Poslednee novosel'e" ("The Last New Abode"). The "great people" castigated by Lermontov was France, not Russia.

have been corrupted to the marrow of their bones, some by political intrigue, others by "a little land." Complete anarchy prevails in the towns and villages. The railroads are in ruins; the harvest is bad in a significant part of Russia. The foreign war has been lost; the internal war is intensifying. Life this winter is going to be a nightmare. Only a miracle can save us, and there are no miracles—St. Nicholas the Miracle Worker has retreated, too. The war is lost, and any future for what remains of Russia has been cut off at the root by the revolution! Thievery reigns. One can believe in Russia only in terms of specific individuals; in the mass—complete lack of responsibility.

What can the future international relations of "the remains of Russia" be like? They are spoiled with the allies; what do they care for the Russian carrion? Germany will butter us up, the better to eat us, and of course we will take the bait. Since the war will after all end in a compromise, there will be two systems: the Western powers, plus America plus Japan; and Austro-Germany. The first system will be sufficiently powerful to sacrifice Russia, which will become, economically and politically, the prey of Germany, the more so because the Western treasury will be closed to the latter.

The main causes of Russia's downfall:

1. The internal politics of the Holstein dynasty (egoism, despotism, cruelty, and shortsightedness).[44]

2. The inadequacy of the reforms of Alexander II: the peasant class that was called to life did not receive sufficient rights; the government could not come to terms with the new non-class social-political activists.

3. The impracticality, insensitivity, and narrowness, in terms of ideology and practical goals, of the revolutionaries from 1860 to 1917.

4. A lack of honesty, stealing from the treasury, which prevented the creation of organs of defense.

5. Backwardness, the result of the continuation of the same internal policies under Alexander III and Nicholas II; 3, 4, and 5 gave rise to the *treason* which flourished so brilliantly from 1914 to 1917.

6. Pan-Germanism.

7. Mistakes of the revolution—the product of items 1–5.

26 July. Yesterday evening Aleksandra Pavlovna, the deacon's wife,[45] paid us a visit with all her offspring. Had a conversation with Nikolai

---

[44] Got'e characteristically deprecates the former ruling dynasty by calling it "Holstein" rather than "Romanov." He is technically correct: Tsar Peter III (r. 1762) was the son of Charles Frederick, Duke of Holstein (and the grandson of Peter the Great). He was brought to Russia as a young man and married to a German princess of Anhalt-Zerbst, the future Catherine II (1762–1796). The remaining tsars of Russia were all descended from that union.

[45] The deacon's wife was from the district in Tver province where Got'e had a farm.

Pavlovich, a teacher in the factory upper-level primary school at the Gartman factory in Lugansk. Many interesting details about the bolsheviks; little that was new, but his stories about that small town confirm my thoughts. It is characteristic that all the former "passionate monarchists," all the good-for-nothings and charlatans, have turned into bolsheviks.

The newspapers from July 23. Kerenskii is taking power once again.[46] Things are no better at the front. General Kornilov expects many more failures on all fronts. The account of the meeting of statesmen in the Winter Palace produces a sorry impression. I was not left with the impression that Kerenskii will be able to cope with his task. The disintegration of all of Russia is undoubtedly going forward with gigantic steps, and the organic process of rebuilding some kind of remnants out of what used to be called Russia has yet to begin. At present, of course, we will go no further than words. Only the bolshevik leaders, who for various reasons—counterrevolution, treason, or self-aggrandizement—are leading to the definitive ruination of Russia, think and act logically. The revolutionaries and émigrés who were capable only of undermining Nicholas II are revealing their ability only to destroy the country; it will hardly help things that they are now "talking" about its salvation.

27 July. Yesterday I saw Oksa's carcass; when it was alive it had been a pig.[47] Now it is a carcass to be savored. Isn't that the symbol of Russia, which will be savored by the Germans as after the *Schweinschlacht?*[48] This morning I had a long discussion with Uncle Eduard,[49] all about the same cursed questions; almost complete accord in [our] thoughts and conclusions.

Once their main goal was achieved, the forces of destruction—the revolutionaries, the émigrés, the former terrorists—should have yielded their place to the elements that were trying to be constructive already under the old regime: the zemstvo and city unions, the military-industrial committees, etc. But having seized the pie of power, they will let go of it only when there remains neither pie, nor power, nor Russia. The right to vote for illiterates creates the following situation: universal suffrage is not secret, and a secret ballot cannot be universal. The possibilities for all kinds of falsifications are immeasurable.

Will Kerenskii be able to do anything?—an interesting question. There is much that indicates not, for the parties are unable to raise them-

[46] See n. 39.

[47] Got'e is apparently referring to a pig that had been known in the vicinity by a proper name.

[48] *Schweinschlacht*: the tariff conflict between Austria and Serbia (1905–1907) known as the "pig war" (pork being a major Serbian export to Austria).

[49] Eduard Vladimirovich Got'e (d. 1921), the brother of Iurii Vladimirovich's father, was a professor of medicine.

selves to consider the whole above the parts—Russia above the parties; and all questions are decided only by the parties; outside them there is nothing. Nineteen- seventeen resembles 1611. Will there be a Minin and a Pozharskii? Kerenskii is more like Liapunov.[50] So far I am still able to sleep, but loss of ability to work is complete. It is hard to experience the shattering of all one's illusions, however unfounded they may have been.

28 July. We saw off L. Eg. We admired the magnificent sunrise—a contrast with [our] frame of mind. Always the same thoughts and the same burden. We are incapable of bearing up under the transformation that is taking place—it is too burdensome, as it is burdensome for an infected organism to suffer two acute illnesses at once. A people gets the kind of regime and government it deserves. As much as you think, you can't find a solution or foresee anything. If only one had enough strength to become a genuine fatalist.

29 July. Yesterday I recalled my experiences after Tsushima in 1905.[51] First a sharp spiritual pain, then a feeling of dull indifference, and, finally, a certain relief and the hope that the war had become psychologically impossible and would soon come to an end one way or another. Yesterday I had exactly the same thoughts, although I recognized the enormous difference in the situation: then it was the navy that perished, sent to certain ruin by the Petersburg government and the court. Now, a free people, but one fundamentally corrupted by slavery and revolutionary propaganda, has itself brought about a defeat that could have exactly the same significance. Reading the newspapers today (from the 25th, 26th, and 27th) did not reinforce that feeling in me, but it didn't erase it either. Voices are heard from all sides about continuing the struggle; but they said the same thing then. Can we hold on? Lloyd George's veracious speech, with a good rebuke for Russia: "The defeat of Russia can provoke only deep regret"; but also "A people that departs from its true path is

---

[50] The references are to the last phase of the Time of Troubles (1598–1613), a period of Swedish and Polish intervention. In 1611 the Russians mounted two national efforts to drive the Poles from Moscow. The first, led by Prokopii Liapunov, a gentryman from Riazan, brought together a heterogeneous lot of armed gentry, peasants, and Cossacks. Liapunov gained the support of the Cossacks by promising various reforms, but these disparate elements soon fell out among themselves and Liapunov was murdered by Cossacks in July.

Kuz'ma Minin, a Nizhnii Novgorod merchant, and Prince Dmitrii Pozharskii, a seasoned military leader, then joined to lead the second effort in the autumn. They succeeded in driving the Poles from Moscow in November 1612. Minin and Pozharskii are preeminent heroes in the Russian patriotic tradition.

[51] Got'e refers to the annihilation of the Russian fleet by the Japanese navy in the Straits of Tsushima on May 27 (n.s.), 1905, during the Russo-Japanese War.

not a great people." We got the idea of astonishing and teaching Europe; but eggs don't teach the chicken, especially when they are soft-boiled, like we are. The frightening devaluation of the ruble is characteristic, but nothing to be surprised about. On the face of it the war news for these three days is rather better than before, but for how long? As for the new government, it gives no guarantee of stability or durability. Will Kerenskii find a way out? One would like to hope so, but in one's soul such hope is feeble. *Force* and *energy* alone can save dying Russia. If a sincere union were to be formed between Kerenskii and the supreme commander,[52] and if the army could be rebuilt and the internal disintegration at least arrested. But all this is dreams, and nothing else! The words of some bolshevik in the Moscow duma were characteristic: there is no need to worry about the motherland, since "they can't wreck it all." Simple and primitive. For an SR and democratic one, the duma all the same passed a decent resolution on the death penalty.

30 July. This morning they sent me a courier from the township committee with the demand to return the lists that had been entrusted to Marietta, and with an invitation to some kind of session which might or might not take place—such is probably the practice everywhere! Marietta read excerpts from her husband's letter yesterday; he writes that he is beginning to become disillusioned with the Russian people. It's about time! I recall his opinion on the road here, that "the socialists know where to lead Russia." Look where they have led us. . . . State of mind unchanged; the soul aches.

31 July. Newspapers from the 28th and 29th. The reports are relatively decent. Unfortunately, all is quiet once again on the Western front.[53] Here, I think, there is danger near Brody.[54] The next newspapers will show if that is so. The general mood is not improving, although it may be that the *leçon des choses* that has been received will not be without results for the town of Stupidity.[55] The question is after all interesting: will the revolution save itself or not? Its salvation lies in the reestablishment of the army, for the whole question is in the army, as it was from the first day after the fall of the monarchy. A long conversation yesterday with Nikolai Antip'ev from Gora: an astonishing mixture of inquisitive-

[52] That is, General Kornilov.

[53] That is, the Allied Western Front in France and Belgium.

[54] Brody was then located in Austrian Galicia, just across the border of Volynia province in the Ukraine; it straddled the southwestern front.

[55] A reference to M. Saltykov-Shchedrin's story "History of a Town" (1869–1870); the name of the town in the story was "Stupidity" or "Dumbsville" (*Glupov*).

ness, unusual and ardent patriotism, mistrust, revolutionary protest, and nonsense.

AUGUST

1 August. The state of mind remains the same. We went to Rozhkovo for butter, but didn't bring any back, because it was being sold yesterday for 2.50, but today they are asking 4. Nina and Marietta went to Shcherbovo and Sandovo after sugar. Will they bring something back? They brought back nothing new. The Germans were beaten back near Brody.

2 August. Newspapers from the 30th of July. Things are relatively decent in the war. For long? There are certain signs of sobering up to be seen— such as the publication of orders on the right to close congresses, meetings, and the like. But together with this there remains the same gibberish and stupidity in a thousand different forms and shapes. For example, the revolting Ukrainian question is heating up again due to the bloody conflict between Ukrainian soldiers and cuirassiers. Since the stirring up of that question is to the direct advantage of Germany and is entirely in conformity with German plans, we have here either outright treason or provocation by treasonous evil forces. What will the next catastrophe that awaits us be like? There is a letter of the SR B. Voronov[56] in *The Russian Gazette* for the 29th or 30th of July protesting his being forbidden to contribute to *The Russian Gazette* by the Moscow SR committee.[57] The order, printed alongside, was signed by Rudnev,[58] the new mayor of Moscow. O mindless imbecility!

3 August. I read Leonid Andreev's brochure *Ruin*.[59] There are many true ideas, similar to mine: ruin from hunger and from the disintegration of the army. But he, Leonid Andreev, will not curse his Mother Russia if everything perishes. I will curse her, though, since she is the union of all Russian men, who are ruining themselves and Russia by their dissension.

[56] Pseudonym of Boris Nikolaevich Lebedev (1883–1919).

[57] *Russkie vedomosti* (*The Russian Gazette*) (1863–1918) was a leading national newspaper published in Moscow; its political orientation was liberal-progressive, close to that of the Kadet party.

[58] Vadim Vasil'evich Rudnev (1879–1940) was a prominent Right SR who had been elected mayor of Moscow (*gorodskoi golova*) by the city duma in the spring of 1917.

[59] Leonid Andreev (1871–1919) was a prominent and rather controversial writer of stories and plays; he is probably best known outside of Russia for *Seven Who Were Hanged* (1908), a play that celebrates the heroism of revolutionary terrorists. "Ruin" ("Gibel") first appeared as an article in the Petrograd paper *Russian Liberty* (*Russkaia volia*) on April 30, 1917. Andreev was a member of the paper's editorial staff.

At best, we all face suffering through what is left of life, watching not only Russia as a state disappear, but also that light, thin, and fragile veneer of culture, those cultural values that have after all been created in Russia. The Pugachevshchina[60] of the present day extends not only to material, but also to spiritual values.

Several observations on local life. Zagran'e—reduction in the number of cattle, seizure of croplands by peasants, provoked not by the landowner's inability to cultivate a given area, but by a lust for seizures fed by propaganda. Boloto—the same: reduction of the herd from eighty to thirty head. The same on the Shvarts estate; in Iurev, selling off of cattle; in Kapustin, selling off of cattle. This means there will be no fertilizer in 1918 and the local clay-loam soil will revert to a primitive condition. That is the agricultural progress resulting from the policies of the sds and the srs. So matters stand in Ves'egonsk district, and how must they be in Russia's grain-producing regions?

4 August. What are the goals and what can the sense of the war be now? Why don't they move in the West? (1) Because they can't? (2) Because, having lost hope for Russia, they are waiting for America? In the first case, Germany's cause is won, and she will sacrifice only colonies and Mesopotamia, but will reward herself in Asia Minor and in Russia; and all the same *Mitteleuropa* will be established by swallowing up three-fourths of the Slavs, who have fully revealed their complete lack of brains and their antistatism. In the second case—the issue will be postponed for a year at least. Will we survive that year or not? Or will we live only to see the final disintegration and catastrophe? Or will we conclude a separate peace completely on German terms?

5 August. Newspapers and information from the 31st, the 1st, 2d, and 3d. Nothing particularly frightful at the front. Voices are continually heard saying that Russia must be saved. The only important and interesting fact is the removal of Nicholas II from Tsarskoe Selo[61] to somewhere else, maybe even to Tobol'sk. This was apparently decided already by the Provisional Government of June 5–22, the third. I think this is the result of a fear of counterrevolution. No other causes or reasons come to mind. S. A. Kotliarevskii[62] outlasted Prince L'vov in the governing circles and

[60] *Pugachevshchina* connotes the kind of mass rampage and anarchy associated with the Pugachev Rebellion (see n. 27).

[61] The summer palace south of Petrograd (now called Pushkin) where Nicholas and his family were being held under guard.

[62] Sergei Andreevich Kotliarevskii (1873–1941) was a gentry landowner (Saratov province), a veteran of the zemstvo movement and the Kadet party, a deputy to the first duma, and a publicist and professor of law at Moscow University.

remained to take charge of foreign confessions as the assistant to the Procurator of the Holy Synod,[63] while retaining his professorship. The gentle calf is suckling not with two, but with many more mothers.

6 August. The traditional pastoral visit yesterday evening. Gnawing boredom at Dubovikov's, the priest's; a more agreeable visit to Aleksandra Pavlovna—they are alive, at least. We went to the morning service today, and after that, reciprocal visits to Nikolai Antip'ev and Ivan Terent'ev. The same talk and impressions as before. Wonderful weather all day; autumn is in the air. You don't want to think about all that is going on. And one more impression: the Russian people are completely corrupted by slavery and the propaganda of the revolutionaries. These *extremités se sont touchées* always.

8 August. I didn't write anything yesterday, because I went to Zaluzh'e. The weather was gorgeous, as before. We returned by a beautiful road through Rastoropovo. A conversation with Shura Veselago—the same thoughts. He says that he is fed up with everything and tries to enjoy himself within the narrow limits afforded in Zaluzh'e. Much talk about the impending hunger, which will be felt in the country as well, but in different ways than in the cities. Shura is not submitting his candidacy for the township zemstvo.[64] Perhaps this is a mistake; perhaps the idea that they should sort things out for themselves is correct.

Newspapers from the 4th and 5th. Everything remains the same on the front: the Anglo-French have again gone over to the offensive. Here in Russia, Kerenskii and co. are trying to save face before the Soviet of Workers' Deputies, and the latter are trying to show that they have not yet gone down the drain. The speeches of "Blackman," as Lial'ka[65] calls Chernov,[66] are the speeches of a crude demagogue, perhaps a great vil-

[63] The Holy Synod was the state office in charge of the Orthodox Church, equivalent to a ministry; the Ober-Prokurator (or simply procurator) was its minister. The institution was created in 1721 upon abolition of the patriarchate. The patriarchate was restored in November 1917 by the first All-Russian Church Council (*Sobor*) to be convened since the seventeenth century; it convened on August 16, 1917.

[64] The township, or *volost'*, zemstvos were created by legislation of the Provisional Government published in May. Elections to them were taking place throughout the summer and fall around the country. In the original zemstvo structure, the lowest-level unit had been at the district or county (*uezd*) level. Creation of the township zemstvo was part of a general plan for democratic restructuring of local government.

[65] "Lial'ka," "Lialia": the unusual nickname of Vladimir Vladimirovich, Iurii Vladimirovich's younger brother, a lawyer and assistant procurator of the Novgorod District Court.

[66] A wordplay in Russian and English: Chernov's name suggests the Russian word for "black" (*chernyi*). "Blackman" is in English in the original.

lain. The attitudes at the trade-industry congress in Moscow are interesting for comparison (*The Russian Gazette*, 4 August).[67] The internal struggle is still ahead of us. We learned in Zaluzh'e about the constant ill-health of Talia Tomilovskaia. She is threatened with the lot of her mother. Lerin migrated to Moscow. I like that less.

9 August. Newspapers from the 6th. A growing impression of the insincerity of Kerenskii and co., and that a new wave of the Russian revolution is growing wider and higher. This is the wave against the arrangements set up after the fall of the monarchy. But the "comrades" go on repeating the same thing; as always, they are both stupid and intolerant. How will Kerenskii get out of this; who will he be in the end—an sr party man or a Russian statesman?

I have been reading these days in *The Russian Archive* (1888) the memoirs of K. N. Lebedev on the period of the Crimean War[68] and the memoirs of P. Kh. Grabbe on the Caucasian war and on the court of Nicholas [I] in the 1840s.[69] One constantly encounters ideas that bear on the present day. Apparently, Russia's successes over the last seventy years in matters of civilization, state administration, and social relations are illusory at best. The Moscow Conference[70] is beginning to take on interest. What will they dictate to the government there?

10 August. I have a growing feeling of apathy toward everything going on in the world—until the next powerful shock, of course. Perhaps it is the effect of the nearness of departure and the marvelous weather. Iul'ka Veselago arrived yesterday with her daughter. She tells how someone put forth the slogan of boycotting the landowners in the elections to the

---

[67] Congresses of representatives of trade and industry (the "big bourgeoisie" in Soviet parlance) dated back to the Revolution of 1905. An All-Russian Union of Trade and Industry was formed at a congress that met in Moscow in March 1917, and subsequent meetings were held in June and at the beginning of August.

[68] Got'e refers to the memoirs of Senator K. N. Lebedev (1812–1876), which appeared in installments over many years (1888–1911) in the pages of the popular historical journal *Russkii arkhiv* (*Russian Archive*).

[69] P. Kh. Grabbe (1789–1875) was an adjutant general and member of the State Council. His "Zapisnaia knizhka" (notebook) was published in *Russkii arkhiv*, 1888, supplement, nos. 4–11; 1889, nos. 3–6, 8–11.

[70] Got'e is apparently referring to the unofficial conference of public figures that had gotten under way on August 8 and would sit until the 10th. It was a convocation on the political situation attended by representatives of groups and organizations to the right of the socialists. Kerenskii, in his search for national unity, had ordered the convening of a huge state conference in Moscow, which met on August 12 through 15, with 2,400-odd representatives from across the political spectrum. Got'e later calls this the "big no. 2 conference."

township zemstvo;[71] accordingly, Shura and Koliubakin, who are members of the township committee, will not get into the Zaluzh'e zemstvo. The tone is being set by the teacher Mitrofanov, to whom Shura showed many kindnesses; he is the first candidate on the list. A truly Russian, customary, familiar picture!

11 August. They compiled the list of voters for Ramen'e commune yesterday (38 percent literate, 19 percent mobilized; in Krutetskoe the proportions were 28 percent and 15 percent; the literate percentage includes only persons over twenty years of age). A general list was compiled from the village lists. In the process it was discovered that (1) the chairman of the township committee, Mr. Krasavtsev, who compiled the list of voters for Zaprud'e, managed to triple the list of sixty voters; (2) there were similar foul-ups in the other village lists (it follows that the population is not even prepared to compile lists); (3) 4 kopecks are paid for each name in the lists (this is an unheard of price!!). Who received the money for us, more precisely for Marietta, whom Mr. Krasavtsev asked to take care of the compilation? I wouldn't be surprised if he took it himself.

The supply administration is establishing a price of 3 rubles 80 kopecks for a pud[72] of new rye; but it is imposing it only on the "manors," and the peasants are already speculating. Relying on the permission of the supply administration, they are making haste to buy up grain in Zagran'e at that price, not hesitating to say (Ivan Ivanovich from Andreitsevo, the brother of our Praskovia, for example) that they are buying for reserve, not out of need. There will probably be cases of resale for profit. The dishonesty and corruption of the people show up in this as well.

Ivan Terent'ev, Fedor Pavlov, and Marietta were appointed to the election committee by instruction of the township committee, that is, most likely, of the same Mr. Krasavtsev. The first two—kulak peasants, property owners, and acquisitors—so as not to have them elected deputies of the township zemstvo, where the people of the moment need types of the opposite character; and Marietta, so as to be able to say that the "landowners" were also involved in the common cause—Marietta is absolutely harmless for the current bosses.

12 August. Newspapers for the 8th, 9th, and 10th. The Germans are on the road to Riga. Nothing decisive yet. If things turn out the same as in Galicia, that might contribute to a further sobering-up; if they are able to turn back the offensive, that might contribute to the strengthening of some kind of authority. The Soviets of Workers' Deputies are starting to

---

[71] See n. 64.
[72] A pud equals thirty-six English pounds.

cook up something again, although the incident with the members of the Rumanian embassy was useful in undermining their authority.[73] The drunken ensign, a member of the executive committee of the Soviet of Workers' Deputies, assaulted them. Characteristic of Russian revolutionary democracy.

The first (minor, intelligentsia) Moscow Conference leads one to believe that they will have many good things to say to Kerenskii and co. at the big no. 2 conference. Some locomotive brigades have announced that if their demands are not satisfied by August 20, they will call a strike and will let through only military and medical trains. There you have the circumstances and persons on whom Russia's existence depends; that is how Russia's healing process goes in August 1917.

14 August. Newspapers for the 11th and 12th. The onslaught on Riga has not yet developed into the kind of catastrophe that occurred in Galicia. What will happen next? The situation is respectable in the other parts of the front, and also in Rumania. The bolsheviks are trying to wreck the Moscow Conference; the methods are the same—the threat of strikes. The revolutionary Moscow duma and the Soviet of Workers' Deputies are astride two stools: they condemn this bolshevik attempt and at the same time look askance at the Moscow Conference, considering it to be counterrevolutionary. The small Moscow Conference has already depicted itself as a loyal opposition on the right—no common language is to be heard, and it won't be found at the big state conference. The speech of I. A. Il'in[74] at the small conference was very characteristic; in an undoubtedly brilliant speech he castigated Kerenskii and especially Chernov for lack of patriotism and counterrevolutionary tendencies. But was it long ago, at the beginning of March 1917, that the same I. A. Il'in at the general meeting of university teachers made his vote for support of the government and for war to the end dependent on whether the "senior teachers," that is, the professors, would ostracize Statkevich, Veselovskii, and others from their midst?[75] The Ukrainians are making fools of them-

---

[73] On August 6, two Rumanian military attachés were assaulted and then arrested by a drunken soldier who was also a member of the executive committee of the Petrograd Soviet, "because they were speaking French in a streetcar." Rex A. Wade, *The Russian Search for Peace, February–October, 1917* (Stanford, 1969), p. 100. This incident is generally taken as a symptom of growing hostility in Russia toward the Allies, who in a variety of ways were showing their discontent with the Russians' inability to prosecute the war.

[74] Ivan Aleksandrovich Il'in (1883–1954) taught philosophy of law at Moscow University. In early 1918 he participated in the "Right" or "Moscow" Center, a group devoted to rallying anti-Bolshevik forces; he was exiled to Germany in November 1922.

[75] The names are of two faculty members: Pavel Grigor'evich Statkevich, professor of physiology, and the historian of medieval Russia, Stepan Borisovich Veselovskii (1876–1952), who taught in the law faculty.

selves and losing in municipal elections everywhere; perhaps the notorious Rada will fail in the end as well.[76] I wrote nothing yesterday. We
took a ride to see the future station of Toporovo. I began to think of a
future secure life—will we live to see it? A ride of only one and a quarter
hours! On the way back we saw Marietta in Pochep in the role of member of the election commission, verifying lists. In the evening there was a
meeting in Zagran'e to select a candidate representative from the two
Zagran'es and Dunaevskii khutor; they selected Marietta, who was apparently very pleased, but of course she will not be chosen as a representative, since six or eight have to be chosen out of twelve candidates selected; the buggers will choose their own people without doubt. The
price of 3 rubles 80 kopecks for the landlords' rye turns out to have been
established independently by the chairman of the supply committee and
his secretary, a female schoolteacher from Shcherbovo; that, too, is characteristic of Russian democracy! The lists for the villages of Ramen'e,
Andreitsevo, Zavrazh'e, and Pochep, which were compiled by a peasant
policeman, are beneath criticism.

17 August. I haven't written anything for two days. There were preparations the first day, and the journey the second. Arrival in Moscow today.
A distressing impression, both externally, vis-à-vis the regime, and on the
moral side. Disintegration, destruction, and deterioration in the museum:
the girls are being lazy, and the employee-comrades will be the source of
many difficulties in the future. A number of problems will have to be
resolved in order to keep the library going somehow. The mood of the
city is bad. Disillusionment, an elemental shift rightward, horrors on all
sides, an apparent hopeless disenchantment with the conference that extends to Kerenskii as well: it seems they are very dissatisfied with him;
the fact is, he is only an imposing and temperamental party activist, but
not a statesman—a surrogate nightingale.[77]

The response to the Moscow Conference was two breakthroughs near
Chernovitsy[78] and in Rumania, and the threat of a railway strike. Holy
Russia does not change. It is the realm of the comrades as before in Moscow. The same as at the railway stations. A mood of indifference, sadness,
and apathy.

[76] The Central Rada (council) was the self-constituted body established by moderate
Ukrainian nationalists and socialists shortly after the February revolution to govern the
Ukraine as an autonomous entity; its aim was federation, not total separation, until friction with the Bolsheviks led it to proclaim total independence in January 1918. Shortly
afterward, the Red Army took Kiev and the Rada disbanded. Its successor in the later
stages of the civil war was known as the Directory.

[77] "Na bezptich'i solovei."

[78] That is, Czernowitz, a front-line town in Bukhovina.

20 August. The Moscow hubbub doesn't allow for writing every day: I will have to sum up my impressions as I can. I am taking advantage of a trip to Pestovo[79] for that, while waiting for a settled life in my apartment to create normal conditions. The news from the front is not so bad as one might have expected two or three days ago. But no danger and no kind of horror has been or can be ruled out for the future, so long as 15 million mobilized but demoralized savages continue to constitute the Russian army. A powerful shift in public opinion compared to the month of May. I have in mind, of course, those circles with which I have contact. This is a shift to the right; recognition of the internal collapse of the Russian revolution is drawing near. In May, many who doubted the revolutionary capabilities of the Russian people still hoped and, in any case, were silent; now one hears unabashed and loud voices proclaiming the complete incompetence of so-called "revolutionary democracy." But the latter continues to do stupid things: among them, I include the protest against the death penalty in the Petrograd Soviet of Workers' Deputies, obviously arranged. Still, only good can come from the further loss of authority by the various soviets. For the first time one can make out counterrevolutionary voices, at least in regard to inveterate "revolutionary democracy." They will probably gather together near the army.

The situation of Kerenskii and co. is hopeless: they have no choice but to increase the fighting capacity of the army, since further German victories could lead even to a monarchical restoration; but a battle-ready army with an authoritative command staff is in itself a danger for any provisional governments and constituent assemblies.[80]

Destruction and disintegration in the Rumiantsev Museum: it is a microcosm in the macrocosm of Russia. Laziness has overcome everyone, beginning with my immediate assistants. The office and curatorial department are worse than they have ever been. A difficult and thankless job of raising work capacity lies ahead. Will it be possible to do anything?

A private dispatch appeared in *The Russian Word* in bold type about a "breakthrough" near Riga and the crossing of the Dvina by the Germans. Tomorrow we will probably know officially. There is nothing to be surprised at. The dying organism is no longer taking care of itself. In spite of familiarity, one still has the sensation of apathy and sorrow.

[79] Pestovo was a small resort on the Viaz' River about forty kilometers north of Moscow.

[80] This and the preceding paragraph testify to the anticipation of a military coup by this time, ten days before the attempt by General Kornilov, not only in the soviets and on the left, where it had been an obsession since the first days of the revolution, but among the educated public at large. Warnings of an impending military coup were being printed in all the newspapers by August 20.

21 [August]. Pestovo. The latest news will come only tomorrow; suffering and oppression. I remember a conversation with Picheta [81] in Moscow: he said that the Latvians have changed their sympathies so radically because the Russians devastated their land worse than the Germans; they have become Germanophiles out of fear of Russian barbarism. In other words, they have thrown themselves into the jaws of the tiger to save themselves from the claws of the bear. All this—alas!—very much resembles the truth. Rereading Maupassant's "Les dimanches d'un bourgeois de Paris," I found a passage that fits contemporary Russia well: "Vous avez une montre, n'est ce pas? Eh bien, cassez un ressort et allez la porter a ce citoyen Cornut, en le priant de la raccommoder. Il vous repondra, en jurant, qu'il n'est pas horloger. Mais, si quelque chose se trouve detraqué dans cette machine infiniment compliquée qui s'appelle la France, il se croit le plus capable des hommes pour la reparer séance tenante. Et quarante mille braillards de son éspece en pensent autant et le proclament sans cesse"[82]—and the further one goes the less the mind can conceive a way out of the present situation.

22 [August]. Everything about Riga was confirmed. A further step on the road to ruin, for one cannot count on their coming to their senses. On the surface the customary indifference reigns in Moscow. I sense that I am not alone in being overcome by lassitude. In the evening came the news of the arrest of Mikhail Aleksandrovich.[83] Kerenskii and co. are smiting the right-wing reaction. It is not the collapse of the revolution that is impending, but of *the entire nation*. The Russians have proven themselves incompetent before the entire world. At present Russia is a ship still afloat, but without a rudder.

23 [August]. Everything is developing according to program. Even if the Germans don't make it all the way to Petrograd, panic and talk of evacuation are proceeding at their own pace. How will Ninka get through; perhaps she will enter the wave of refugees. I had a conversation today with Uncle Eduard; then with Egorov,[84] Savin,[85] and Liubavskii. Always

---

[81] Vladimir Ivanovich Picheta (1878–1947) was a colleague of Got'e on the Moscow University history faculty and a specialist on the history of Russia's western borderlands.

[82] See Guy de Maupassant, *Contes et nouvelles*, vol. 1 (Paris, 1974), pp. 172–73.

[83] Grand Duke Mikhail Aleksandrovich (1878–1918) was the brother of Nicholas II in whose favor Nicholas had abdicated. On August 23, in response to rumors of a monarchist plot, he and his brother Pavel Aleksandrovich were placed under house arrest in the summer palace of Gatchina.

[84] Dmitrii Nikolaevich Egorov (1878–1931) was another colleague of Got'e on the history faculty, a specialist on Germano-Slavic relations in the middle ages.

[85] Aleksandr Nikolaevich Savin (1873–1923) was a historian colleague, a specialist on English (Tudor) socioeconomic history.

the same thoughts and opinions. Collapse and ruin! I took the fee for upkeep of the graves to the cemetery.

24 August. All morning revolting thoughts crept into my mind, as they have not done for a long time. We, that is, civilized people who consider ourselves Russians, are a small group of people lost in the world. Our fatherland has deserted us, no one stands behind us; "the people" will cast us aside, and no other society will accept us into its midst. All day long I heard only declarations that echoed my thoughts, mixed with mindless and boundless alarm. In the museum I urged the watchmen to arrange their work so that the reading room could be opened at 8 o'clock. I managed, with difficulty, to get a compromise agreement out of those shameless parasites. I am waiting for Ninka, so we will not be apart during this terrible time.

25 [August]. News of the same sort. In Petrograd, panic, that scourge of our time— *la grande peur.* The news that many workers are demanding severance pay is characteristic: it shows the cowardice of the comrade-bolsheviks. I talked with many people again today, and again everywhere the same feeling of dissatisfaction with Kerenskii and co. and a feeling that Russia's downfall has taken place. The long struggle between tsarism and the revolution for control of Russia is coming to an end before our eyes with the destruction and ruin of the aim and object of the struggle. The Russian slobs continue to search for fleas on themselves while the Germans are putting a noose around their neck. Pitiful wretches! My mood is such that I don't want to see anyone.

26 [August]. All day I think about how Ninka and Volodia[86] are traveling. I fear all kinds of unpleasant surprises in Bologoe.[87] Mood unchanged. In the museum today I spoke with many people about the impossible situation of library work: those with whom I spoke readily agreed. S. S. Podolinskii[88] came to see me in the museum in regard to the transfer of his uncle's papers to the museum. He was the vice-governor of Livland until the 27th of March. He said that in his opinion the fate of Riga was predetermined long ago. I asked his opinion of the murder of Stolypin, his relative of whom he remains an admirer: is one to think that he was killed by orders from the Court, not by terrorists? He replied

[86] Vladimir Iur'evich (Volodia), Got'e's son, was six years old in 1917. He was born on August 14, 1911.

[87] A rail junction where the line from Ves'egonsk joined the Petrograd-Moscow line.

[88] Sergei Sergeevich Podolinskii (b. 1879) served as vice-governor of Livland and Saratov and was a former member of the Tula zemstvo board.

that he thinks the same; that is, that the murder was planned by people at Court.

27 [August]. A respite all day Sunday owing to Ninka's arrival; I sat all day at Mertvyi Pereulok[89] and tried not to talk about all that was disturbing me. Ninka arrived in the direct third-class car from Kashin—the smartest and luckiest thing she could have done. Because of her fatigue, and mine, too, we went to bed at 9:30.

28 [August]. In the morning, while getting ready to go to Pestovo, I read the posted proclamation from the mayor about Kornilov's demand for the removal of Kerenskii.[90] One more page of the Russian revolution is being turned. By evening we were in Pestovo, where the rumors don't reach.

29 August. In the morning Shambi[91] called on the telephone, and even Gartung called.[92] This latter shows how great are the excitement and rumors in Moscow. It is hard to figure out what is going on so far, but it is evident that the affair is serious. A big struggle is shaping up. How will the Germans take advantage of it? Shambi arrived, but brought nothing new. We passed the evening peacefully, without additional news or rumors.

30 August. It is impossible to believe in the success of the Kornilov movement. Of course, numbed and brutalized former Russia will not now suddenly acquire good sense, and all will turn out in the worst possible way, and in the most helpful way for the Germans.

The appeal published yesterday in the newspapers by Iuzhin and Sobinov,[93] the commissars for the state theaters in Moscow, calling on citi-

---

[89] Part of the Got'e family lived on the side street called, in 1917, Mertvyi Pereulok, after the eighteenth-century owner of the main house, Mertvago. (Since 1937 it has been called Pereulok N. A. Ostrovskogo.) The street was located near the main radial, Prechistenka (now Kropotkinskaia ulitsa), a few blocks from Iu. V. Got'e's apartment on Bol'shoi Znamenskii Pereulok (since 1939, Ulitsa Gritsevets) just southwest of the Kremlin, in the area known as the Volkhonka. Got'e's apartment was less than two blocks from the Rumiantsev Museum.

[90] The principal documents of the Kornilov affair are available in English translation: Robert Paul Browder and Alexander F. Kerensky, eds., *The Russian Provisional Government, 1917*, vol. 3 (Stanford, 1961).

[91] The nickname of Sergei Konstantinovich Shambinago (1871–1948), a colleague of Got'e and a specialist in the history of Russian literature.

[92] Presumably Aleksandr L. Gartung (Hartung), an old acquaintance.

[93] Aleksandr Ivanovich Iuzhin (real name: Sumbatov; 1857–1927) was a prominent actor and playwright who had been associated with the Malyi Theater since 1882. In 1923

zens not to smoke in auditoriums, foyers, and other unspecified places, because a fire could result, was very typical. It symbolizes the cultural level of the Russian revolution.

Two world views have competed in Russian history: the messianic (the Third Rome, Slavophilism, "sound the roar of victory,"[94] and ... the desire to teach something to Western democracy); and the condemnatory (Kotoshikhin, Khvorostinin, the passion for things French and for Catholicism, Chaadaev, I. S. Turgenev through the mouth of Potugin).[95] Alas, it is now clear that the second is superior to the first in every respect!

31 August. Kornilov's attempt has unquestionably and irreversibly collapsed. Instead of waiting for Kerenskii and co. with all their minions to fall like a ripe fruit, the unintelligent but decisive generals—who are childlike in their lack of political experience and who earlier always disdained politics—have stepped forth as the leaders of an enterprise that has no ground under it. As a result, Kerenskii will grow stronger and a shift to the left will occur; and perhaps a terror from the left will also commence. I write this without adequate knowledge of the facts, solely according to my suppositions; it could be that everything will turn out otherwise. They are saying as fact that Kerenskii has gotten divorced and married some actress a few days ago; passers-by even assert that the marriage has taken place in the Winter Palace—*se non è vero.* How sad and sorrowful this all is—in the Russian manner! I had a conversation in the afternoon with Georgievskii, who has returned from Petersburg: the

---

he was appointed director of the theater. Leonid Vital'evich Sobinov (1872–1934) was a famous operatic tenor, who at this time was director of the Bolshoi Theater.

[94] "Grom pobedy raszdavaisia." Got'e is probably citing Pushkin here. See, *Pushkin. Polnoe sobranie sochinenii* (Academy edition), vol. 8, pt. 1, pp. 176, 206, and 218. The original source is a line from a patriotic ode by the eighteenth-century civic poet Derzhavin, "Khory, petye na prazdnestve po sluchaiu vziatiia Izmaila u ... kn. G. A. Potemkina-Tavricheskogo ... 1791 g., aprelia 28," which had been set to music in a polonaise by O. A. Kozlovskii.

[95] The references are to famous critics of the Russian order: Grigorii Karpovich Kotoshikhin (ca. 1630–1667) was a foreign-office official who fled to Sweden in 1664 and wrote there a scathing denunciation of Russian mores and institutions, *On Russia in the Reign of Aleksei Mikhailovich,* which remains a principal source on seventeenth-century Russia.

Prince Ivan Andreevich Khvorostinin (d. 1625), of the Iaroslavl' line, was a political figure of some note and a writer who is sometimes called "the first Russian Westernizer" because of his Latin learning and interest in Catholicism and other heresies. Kliuchevskii described him as "a remote spiritual ancestor of Chaadaev" (see below).

Petr Iakovlevich Chaadaev (1794–1856) was a Russian gentleman and man of letters whose first "philosophical letter" (published in 1836) set off the great debate between "Westernizers" and "Slavophiles" about the nature and prospects of Russian culture.

Potugin ("Sozont Ivanych") was the ultra-Westernizer and critic of Russian ways in Ivan Turgenev's novel *Smoke* (1867).

soldiers are munching sunflower seeds; the townspeople are in a panic over the Germans; in the state institutions the former bureaucrats write papers as before, but are overcome by the same paralysis as everywhere else, as in our museum. Conversation with the historians Iakovlev,[96] Bakhrushin,[97] and Bogoslovskii.[98] Their opinions entirely coincide: the collapse of the nation; the possibility of getting out of the situation only through unguided, elemental processes; the complete ruination of Russian agriculture; the impotence and lack of sense of the current leading figures—in a word, inevitable ruin. Their opinions about Kornilov's adventure also coincide with my own.

SEPTEMBER

1 September. It is becoming increasingly clear from the talk in town that behind Kornilov's venture lies a provocation, in which Kerenskii and Savinkov[99] were apparently involved. Russia is beginning to resemble Mexico. An interesting conversation with Iakovlev. He was in Mogilev and prepared an agrarian program for Kornilov, which consisted of allotting the soldiers land as property. He points to Zavoiko[100] and perhaps Alad'in[101] as the main authors of the affair. Kornilov impressed him as an attractive soldier, but not a politician—rather an infant in politics. He [Iakovlev] was not privy to the military and political part of the plot and left a day before the move began. In his opinion, V. N. L'vov played a dubious and stupid role here.[102]

[96] Aleksei Ivanovich Iakovlev (1871–1951) was a colleague of Got'e on the history faculty and a specialist on seventeenth-century Russia.

[97] Sergei Vladimirovich Bakhrushin (1882–1950) was another historian colleague, a specialist on the history of Siberia and the peasantry of Old Russia.

[98] Mikhail Mikhailovich Bogoslovskii (1867–1929) was still another colleague of Got'e, and, like Got'e, Iakovlev, and Bakhrushin, a student of Kliuchevskii. He had been a professor at Moscow University since 1911. Bogoslovskii was a specialist on the history of seventeenth- and eighteenth-century Russia, especially the reign of Peter the Great.

[99] Boris Viktorovich Savinkov (1879–1925), a former terrorist, was a writer and member of the SR party. Acting war minister under Kerenskii, he became a leading figure in the armed opposition to Bolshevik rule during the Civil War. He was expelled from the SR party in September 1917.

[100] Zavoiko was Kornilov's adjutant and speech writer.

[101] Aleksei Fedorovich Alad'in (b. 1873) was another adviser of Kornilov, a former populist duma deputy.

[102] Vladimir Nikolaevich L'vov (b. 1872) was for a time Procurator of the Holy Synod in the Provisonal Government. His role as go-between in the confused negotiations between Kerenskii and General Kornilov, though unclear, was undoubtedly considerable; Iakovlev's suspicions were well founded. L'vov emigrated after the October revolution, but returned to Soviet Russia in the early 1920s as one of the first repatriates of the "Change of Signposts" movement.

2 September. The political mess continues. Rumors of a provocation do not cease. Today I heard from Savin that Nekrasov[103] was one of the main provocateurs. It is clear that there are just as few honorable men among those who seized power as among the common people and educated society at large. The University Council [met]; everyone I happened to talk to was in a mood similar to mine. It appears that some of the students want to interrupt the academic year. Abstention from work remains the Russian's main activity; somehow it must be struggled against.

4 September. A *coup de théâtre* yesterday. Proclamation of a republic and of a directory consisting of Kerenskii, two military men with doubtful pasts—Verkhovskii[104] and Verderevskii,[105] the unprincipled Tereshchenko,[106] and the fool Nikitin.[107] This is something between an operetta and a fairy tale. The provocation is becoming progressively clearer; so too is the vengeance against the Kadets by Chernov. Is not Mr. Kerenskii playing into the hands of his friend Chernov by arranging the whole affair with a coalition ministry and then abruptly changing it into a dictatorship of five? Isn't the state conference, plus the fall of Kornilov, plus the crisis of the government on September 2–3, a conscious campaign of Kerenskii, based on provocation and leading to the dictatorship of the extreme leftists? Kerenskii and Azef[108] are closer than is customarily thought. A moral state beneath any criticism.

5 [September]. "The provisional government," or more correctly, OI PENTE TYRANNEYONTES,[109] have canceled classes in the higher educational insti-

---

[103] Nikolai Vissarionovich Nekrasov (1879–1940) was a prominent left Kadet who served as minister of transport and then as minister of finance and assistant premier in the Provisional Government. He was appointed governor general of Finland in September 1917. According to Rosenberg (*Liberals in the Russian Revolution*, p. 231n), Nekrasov was apparently the author of the declaration over Kerenskii's signature that branded General Kornilov a traitor.

[104] General Aleksandr Ivanovich Verkhovskii (1886–1938) was commander of the Moscow military district. He was appointed minister of war in the five-man directorate formed after the failure of the Kornilov coup.

[105] Admiral Dmitrii Nikolaevich Verderevskii (1873–1947) was commander of the Baltic fleet and naval minister in the Directorate.

[106] Mikhail Ivanovich Tereshchenko (1884–1956) was a Kiev industrialist who served as minister of finance in the first several Provisional Governments; in May 1917 he became minister of foreign affairs, a post he retained in the Directorate.

[107] Aleksei Maksimovich Nikitin (b. 1879), a lawyer and a Menshevik, was first chairman of the Moscow soviet, minister of post and telegraph in the Provisional Government, and minister of internal affairs in the Directorate.

[108] Evno Fishelevich Azef (1869–1918) was a notorious double agent (SR terrorist and tsarist secret police agent) whose exposure in 1908 nearly destroyed the SR party.

[109] "The five tyrants." Got'e so characterizes the Directorate of five set up by Kerenskii

tutions of both capitals, that is, in 75 percent of Russian higher educational institutions! Perhaps this is because the "student union" canceled these classes. In any case, the crudeness and stupidity of this order in regard to Moscow is beyond doubt. I heard from Kizevetter at the faculty meeting that Mr. Kerenskii is all the same thinking of creating a coalition ministry (he was repeating the words of Kishkin).[110] The ways of Mr. Kerenskii are unfathomable! Things are more decent at the front; but internal matters are worse than ever. There was a faculty meeting—we discussed the filling of the docentships; it seems there is hope that Shambi will make it.

6 September. A terrible mood all day, without any specific new cause. Today's newspapers don't report any astonishing villainies. The interview with Kerenskii was interesting, where in answer to Chernov's slanders he curses the latter: in a few days we will probably learn of a schism in the SR party—the Kerenskyites will rise up against the Chernovites. You hear only disgusting things on all sides—Mr. Kerenskii himself closed the higher educational institutions in accordance with the wishes of the student union; tomorrow the Moscow comrades are celebrating the victory over the counterrevolution; the comrades are growing stronger everywhere and in all respects. Perhaps all this creates the dejected frame of mind that I haven't been able to get rid of all day.

11/12 September. We spent almost four days in Pestovo; good weather, almost complete absence of newspapers, and daily mushroom gathering. If the soul didn't rest, it at least took a little break; but as soon as we got to the railway in Pushkino, one again sensed all the tragedy we are living through. Now the whole provocation staged by Kerenskii and co. is fully clear. But what was it all done for? The aim of the provocation is clear: the removal of the Romanovs to Tobol'sk so that they could not become a possible hindrance to the business at hand. The Moscow Conference was a general provocation, where everyone would reveal his cards. The provocation of Kornilov and Kaledin[111] as the most dangerous individu-

---

in the wake of the collapse of the second coalition government and the Kornilov crisis at the end of August. Kerenskii had persuaded the outgoing cabinet to vote him dictatorial powers at the beginning of the crisis.

[110] Nikolai Mikhailovich Kishkin (1864–1930), a Moscow physician and prominent Kadet, was commissar of Moscow from February to August 1917 and minister of welfare in September–October.

[111] Aleksei Maksimovich Kaledin (1861–1918) was a Don Cossack ataman and general who participated in the Moscow Conference as a strong advocate of restoring military discipline and an authoritarian government.

als, as revealed at the conference; the exploitation of Alekseev[112] in order to take care of Kornilov; and the ruination of Alekseev through the embarrassing situation in which he was placed—all this *ad maiorem gloriam* of the leftists. But in fact all this is to the detriment of Kerenskii and his closest friends; Kerenskii ruined himself as well. Didn't Chernov push him into this whole affair in order to ruin Kerenskii by ruining Kornilov and his ilk? In general, it is dancing on a volcano, and in the face of a German invasion. The army is obviously hopeless and one sees in the distance either German or general international intervention; in other words, a calling of the Varangians in a new form a thousand-plus years after the first one.

13 [September]. Everything remains the same; just as awful as yesterday, the day before, and so on. I was confirmed as a full professor. I went to see O. A. Talyzina to arrange a place for Liulia Veselago.[113] Conversations are all the same, and opinions coincide.

14 [September]. A dejected frame of mind all day, in spite of the beautiful weather; late in the evening of the 13th I received a report from Petrograd by Iur'eva about a new summons to Petrograd by Kerenskii of Kishkin and co.—all those who had already gone once as far as Liuban'.[114] This was confirmed by the morning newspapers. What kind of new trick is this?

In the evening we were at the Wilkens.[115] I feel very sorry for the poor old people; they are oppressed by both the general problems and a housing problem, since the surcharge of 100 percent compels them to cut back even further.

15 September. I got neither news nor impressions all day, except that the democratic conference opened with an SR hitting a bolshevik in the

---

[112] General Mikhail Vasil'evich Alekseev (1857–1918): chief of staff of the imperial army, then commander in chief following Nicholas's abdication; replaced by Brusilov in late May 1917. Alekseev was charged by Kerenskii to arrest Kornilov and his coconspirators.

[113] Ol'ga Anatol'evna Talyzina was the director of the Elizabeth Institute in Moscow, a finishing school for young ladies founded in 1825. Liulia Veselago was the daughter of an acquaintance; her parents were trying to get her enrolled in the Elizabeth Institute.

[114] Liuban' is a small town on the Moscow-Petrograd railroad, eighty-three kilometers from Petrograd; the reference is to an earlier unsuccessful attempt to set up a coalition government including the Moscow Kadets.

[115] The Wilkens ("Vil'ken," sometimes "Vil'kin") were old family acquaintances, Belgians living in Moscow. Emma Wilken, who figures repeatedly in the diary, lived on the Petrovka and was employed in a school for orphans.

mug.[116] There was a meeting of the editorial committee of the Moscow University teachers' press. N. S. Arsen'ev[117] and Prince N. S. Trubetskoi[118] did not give me the impression of being dispirited men. In the evening there was a meeting of residents for electing a building committee—I almost got elected chairman; thank God that lot passed me by, but it was impossible to refuse membership.[119]

16 [September]. The democratic conference is somewhere between failing and being insignificant. For two weeks now the library employees have been unable to divide among themselves a hundred rubles they were given for summer work—there you have the good judgment of the Russian people. In the evening the business meeting of the building committee took place without incident.

17 [September]. Six celebrants of name days that we hadn't seen for the most part since spring; everyday conversations of the usual type; no news.

19 [September]. The democratic conference is finally and irreversibly drowning in words. Things are getting worse and worse everywhere. Today I saw a marvelous depiction of Mr. Kerenskii in an emperor's crown—on a postcard, with the crown added by hand. A faculty meeting, the first with Privatdozents[120] attending; toward the end of the meeting we—that is, the senior members of the faculty—alone remained. A faculty meeting is obviously not a very gay thing. I received my full professorship and I was congratulated today in the customary way. I heard from the Kokoshkins the story, in F. F. Kokoshkin's eyewitness account, of how Kerenskii provoked the move of Kornilov's troops toward Pet-

---

[116] The All-Russian Democratic Conference, called in the wake of the Kornilov affair (September 14), was another attempt to rally support for Kerenskii's government; this time it was limited to the "democratic" (socialist) end of the political spectrum.

[117] Nikolai Sergeevich Arsen'ev (b. 1888) was a historian of Russian thought and literature at the university. See his memoirs, *Dary i vstrechi zhiznennogo puti* (Frankfurt/Main, 1974).

[118] Prince Nikolai Sergeevich Trubetskoi (1890–1938), son of S. N. Trubetskoi, was at this time Got'e's junior colleague at the university. The great linguist, founder of the Prague School, was also one of the founders of "Eurasianism," the doctrine that Russia was neither European nor Asian, but a separate cultural entity.

[119] The house or building committees (*domovye komitety*) were set up by order of the city government in mid-September to perform a variety of functions at the apartment-house level—especially to facilitate the implementation of the ration-card system. The committees were to be in charge of distributing the cards among the apartment dwellers and of collective purchasing of rationed foodstuffs for them as a means of cutting down on the size of food queues. Most Moscow apartment houses had committees in operation by early October.

[120] The Russian university equivalent of non–tenured assistant professors.

rograd and on the very next day disowned it. In this he showed himself in his true colors.

21 [September]. The democratic conference is getting completely lost. They are contradicting each other, changing resolutions—hindering everything and in addition hindering themselves. But still no way out is to be found. A letter of Gurko[121] to Nicholas II of March 4 has been published in *The Russian Morning* and *The Russian Word*: it prophesies the return of the monarchy. I began my seminar at the university today; afterwards I chatted with Schastnev.[122] The students' stories to the effect that he has become enamored of socialism are happily untrue. Pisarevskii[123] came to see me in the evening and carried on the same line of talk as we do.

22 [September]. Another railway strike has been proclaimed. How much German money has been spent on that? A story in the papers that a Russian monarchist newspaper is being founded in Switzerland with German money—*se non è vero, è ben trovato*. I began my lectures at Shaniavskii University.[124] The gorillas, male and female, took in my monologue about the Time of Troubles with lackluster interest. When I was in the streets and to some extent there, at Shaniavskii University, I was overcome several times by the feeling of a burning desire to cease being a Russian. In the evening we were at Mashkov pereulok:[125] we reminisced about the old days and drank a bottle of burgundy.

24 [September]. The strike has begun. What will come of it and how will it influence the Russian democraps?[126] I heard that expression yesterday, and I like it. In spite of the marvelous weather, I am sitting in my domestic retreat—the Moscow streets are physically repulsive to me, with their rude, unbridled, and idle crowd. We went to vote for the precinct duma (in my opinion one of the most useless stupidities of the revolu-

[121] General Vasilii Iosifovich Gurko (1864–1937) was Nicholas II's last chief of staff. The letter, predicting a restoration, had been written on March 4. (*Russkoe slovo*, September 21, 1917). His brother, Vladimir Iosifovich Gurko (1863–1927), was an official in the ministry of internal affairs at the beginning of the century who played an important part in the preparation of the so-called Stolypin land reform that commenced in 1906.

[122] Aleksandr Vsevolodovich Schastnev was one of Got'e's students.

[123] Pisarevskii apparently was a nonuniversity acquaintance of Got'e.

[124] Shaniavskii University was an unofficial institution with evening classes for people lacking the secondary education required for admission to the state universities. It was opened in 1908 and was administered by the Moscow city duma; it was dissolved in 1919–1920. It was common practice for Moscow University professors to give extra lecture courses in various institutions around town as a means of supplementing their incomes.

[125] Now known as ulitsa Chaplygina.

[126] In Russian, *der'mokraty*; a play on words using the word *der'mo*, "crap."

tion).[127] At 11 A.M. there was no crowd. The distributors of [party] ballots at the door were unkempt types with blank faces; there were two female college student-believers and a Caucasian-looking student representing the People's Freedom [party]. Inside, the scene was radically different from the earlier elections to the state duma: of all the people I saw there, only the chairman seated at the ballot box had a less than gorilla-like appearance—a well-fed, fat bourgeois. All the rest were female students or schoolmarms with the customary miserably intense and high-principled appearance, plus several comrades, one of whom was being chided by the schoolteacher sitting beside him about how he ought to be behaving. An impression of emptiness, boredom, and futility. The general impression is that the bolsheviks are trying harder than anyone else; if that is true of the first Tver precinct, what is going on in the outlying districts?

25 [September]. The railway [strike] is beginning to go into effect. Yesterday's elections gave a majority to the Kadets in the Arbat-Prechistenka precinct and half the votes in the Tver-downtown precinct. This is the first case of a Kadet victory. Elsewhere, the bolsheviks will probably win, for these are the only two competing tickets; the others, including the SRS, who won in the central duma in June, have apparently had no great success. The Kadets in the Arbat-Prechistenka and Tver dumas [will have to] show they are better than the others, or they, too, will be threatened with disaster. The other day a sailor and a civilian from the Baltic fleet showed up in the Rumiantsev Museum in search of various scholarly materials for a "sailors' university"; it appeared from their conversation that they are convinced they will hold onto Helsingfors.[128] Will they succeed?

27 [September]. The strike has been called off. Some say because they couldn't bring it off; but as a matter of fact the railway workers have gotten an enormous increase in pay, which will be paid for not by the impoverished state, but by us, for the rates will be doubled. The "democratic council," the devilish offspring of the notorious "democratic con-

---

[127] The precinct-level dumas (*raionnye dumy*), like the township zemstvos, were created as part of the Provisional Government's general plan to bring popular participation in governance to the grass roots. The elections for the seventeen Moscow precinct dumas gave a majority to the Bolsheviks (51 percent of the popular vote); the next largest vote went to the Kadets (26.2 percent); only small minorities went to the SRS (14 percent) and Mensheviks (4 percent). The elections to the city duma in June had yielded an SR majority (58 percent). These results illustrate the political polarization that was taking place during 1917, and in particular the growing popularity of the Bolsheviks after June.

[128] The official, Swedish, name for Helsinki before 1918.

ference," leaves a disgraceful impression: cursing, dissension, disintegration, and futility. Yesterday evening I examined Birukov's collection of incunabula,[129] and it seems the means to purchase it can be found; a small bright spot against life's dark background.

30 [September]. I have written nothing for three days, because I was very busy. The Germans have made a new move today: they have made a landing on the island of Ösel.[130] An interesting juxtaposition: at the moment they were preparing for this, the head of naval counterintelligence for the Baltic fleet was in Moscow selecting books for the "sailors' university" and claiming that the Baltic fleet was in full readiness for battle. Incidentally, this official was earlier one of the "staff members" of *New Time*.[131] Wasn't he a "staff member" of the "Okhranka"?[132] However that may be, a new step on the road to Petrograd has been taken, and the Russian nihilistic gorillas are again howling about raising the fighting capacity of the army, while Kerenskii is sending a "supreme" telegram to the Baltic fleet. All this would be funny if it weren't so sad. There are agrarian and urban pogroms everywhere—in Kozlov, Tambov, Riazan', Khar'kov, Odessa, Bendery, and so on. Demoralization is growing ever wider and deeper. I understand M. K. Liubavskii, who says that if he didn't have a family he would become a terrorist.

There was a University Council meeting today. The general outlook is panicky, fearful, and depressed. One feels that everyone shared the same thought: that we are approaching the final boundary, the limit of suffering. And yet we took care of our petty affairs. It was characteristic that Genzel proposed mortgaging the university to a loan company to help it find the means to provide heating. There is a deficit of over a million, and the government gives no money, but at the same time it is generously opening universities in Tomsk, Saratov, Irkutsk, and even Tashkent, where quite recently the Russians outdid the Turkmens themselves in savagery. What is this—stupidity or conscious deceit and grandstanding?

[129] Nikolai Nikolaevich Birukov, a Moscow lawyer, had one of the largest private collections of incunabula in Russia. Got'e hoped to buy it for the museum. *El'zeviry biblioteki N. N. Birukova v Moskve* (Moscow, 1917).

[130] The large island lying at the entrance to the Gulf of Riga.

[131] *Novoe vremia (New Time)* was a Petersburg daily, with a large circulation, published from 1868 until October 1917; its general orientation was moderate-conservative, progovernment.

[132] That is, the Special Department (Osobyi Otdel) of the department of police of the ministry of internal affairs—the secret police. For some reason this popular name for the secret police has passed into English as "Okhrana."

OCTOBER

2 [October]. Few impressions for two days. The Germans are successfully conquering Ösel, but I should think that further operations will go more slowly. We visited the cemetery yesterday;[133] it is beautiful there, but it took an hour and a half to get there, and the same to get back. The trolleys are jammed. Many of the comrades of all sorts were drunk; one of them cursed me for my bowler hat—*democratia triumphans!*

5 [October]. Ösel has been taken; the Germans are preparing to cross over to the mainland. The evacuation of Petrograd to Moscow is becoming ever more likely and imminent; there is more and more anarchy. In Moscow, there is a strike in the hospitals, and in the University Catherine Hospital, Professor Popov was carried out in a wheelbarrow.

Tables were ordered for the catalog in the museum. The cabinetmaker made a mistake and built them slightly narrower than they should be. In order to correct his mistake, he made the drawers for the cards a bit narrower as well, without paying any attention to the cards—a truly simian solution. In connection with the German communique about mine sweeping around Ösel, I recall that the "chief" of naval counterintelligence asserted that the Germans could not find our mines(!). My spirits are lower than they have been for a long time.

On Tuesday we went to the Art Theater to see *The Village of Stepanchikovo*.[134] A simian misrepresentation, and a simian audience, which watched Dostoevskii's heavy satire as if it were vaudeville. And on stage there was a madhouse that had little in common with Russia. Indescribable tedium. Obviously, the theaters, too, are going out of style for me; anyhow, it is unbecoming to go to theatrical productions at the present time.

6 [October]. In the sea battle in the Gulf of Riga and in Moonsund we of course retreated, gave up, and sank our old vessel *Glory*. That, too, is symbolic. The evacuation of Petrograd is approaching, with all its terrible effects. But this people—thief, traitor, coward, and anarchist—is not in the least concerned; indifference, hostility, hatred, and plundering. The dog deputies in Petrograd[135] proclaim that if the improvisional gov-

[133] Literally, "on Pokrov," that is, a church holiday (Intercession of the Holy Virgin) that falls on October 1.

[134] A dramatization of Dostoevskii's novel of the same title (1859).

[135] An ironic corruption using the adjectival form of "dog" (*sobach'ikh*) as a substitute for the Russian words for "soldier" and "worker"; hence, "Sovet sobach'ikh [soldatskikh i rabochikh] deputatov."

ernment[136] leaves for Moscow, they will set up their own government in Petrograd. Their stupidity exceeds even their shamelessness and criminality.

8 [October]. The Germans are coming up on the Gulf of Finland. In the preparliament[137] they quarreled on the very first day. The demobilized soldiers of the earliest call-ups are stirring up trouble everywhere. I heard from Shambi yesterday that comrade-soldiers in Trebizond have scribbled over and scratched up the frescoes that had been preserved under the Turkish stucco in the Byzantine churches and have befouled the shrines of those formerly Christian and later Moslem holy places. A strike of servants in all the institutions of the ministry of education is in the offing—on the grounds that the "Plekhanov" wage supplement of 100 rubles is long in coming.[138] When the "delegates" pointed this out to the minister of labor, Mr. Kuz'ma Gvozdev,[139] he replied: "Go on strike." Thus does the voice of the improvisional government encourage strikes in government institutions.

Yesterday there was a meeting on historical bibliography at my place; we talked of politics as well. There were few differences of opinion— evidently, a professional historical education leads to more or less sober views. How sad that there are so few historians. However, Picheta and Fokin[140] did lock horns—the former a passionate panslavist and member of Plekhanov's "Edinstvo,"[141] the latter calling himself a Junker and gentryman and admitting that he hates the peasant most of all.

11 [October]. The general situation hasn't changed for better or worse in the last few days. The Germans have had no great successes, but they have landed on the corner of Estland and have occupied the entire archipelago to the south of the Gulf of Finland, thus acquiring a base for

[136] More ironic punning: for "provisional government" (*vremennoe pravitel'stvo*), "improvisional government" (*bezvremennoe pravitel'stvo*; literally, "the untimely [or hapless] government").

[137] The preparliament (officially known as the Council of the Republic) superseded the Democratic Conference. A much smaller body (550 members), it was convened on October 7 to serve as an advisory body to Kerenskii's government; unlike the Democratic Conference, it included representatives of the "bourgeois" groups and parties.

[138] Wage supplements recommended by a committee chaired by G. V. Plekhanov, "the father of Russian Marxism," who returned to Russia in 1917 after thirty-eight years of exile.

[139] Kuz'ma Antonovich Gvozdev (b.1883) was a Menshevik member of the Petrograd soviet who served as minister of labor under Kerenskii in September-October 1917.

[140] Anatolii Mikhailovich Fokin was a member of the Moscow Historical Society.

[141] The Edinstvo group were SD followers of Plekhanov who advocated reunification of the party (*edinstvo* = "unity"). They supported continuation of the war to victory and, like the Mensheviks, held that the country was ready only for a "bourgeois" regime.

future moves against Petrograd. All this is being done, as Kerenskii correctly put it, "not because of their strength, but because of our weakness" (Kerenskii's speech in the preparliament). It appears that the evacuation of Petrograd will turn into the evacuation of Moscow. The idiots-in-charge want to evacuate the [cadet] corps and the institutes—once again the gang answers for everything. The strike of hospital workers, which involved the university clinics as well, has progressed; they are demanding the resignation of the provisional government and of the rector, Menzbir! On Monday the 9th there was an emergency meeting of the council, at which the university tried to preserve its autonomy. There will be a strike of city employees beginning on the 15th. Not enough object lessons yet.

13 [October]. Yesterday and today there was a meeting of men in public affairs, to which I was invited. I was at two of the four sessions, the general one and the military one; I was not at those where the question of the constituent assembly and economic problems were discussed. For me personally what was new at the first session of this meeting was the prevailing theme of love for the fatherland, for the homeland. In addition, it was proclaimed that the counterrevolutionaries are not we, but the bolsheviks. The third theme was a campaign against Kerenskii. The most interesting speeches the first day were those of Evdokimov,[142] a member of the cooperative movement from among the repentent SDS or SRS, who urged [us] not to condemn revolutionary democracy and recalled how he himself had sung *The Internationale* in a grove near Ivanovo-Voznesensk twenty-five years ago. Also interesting was the famous Fedor Botkin,[143] a former émigré and *intelligent*. The former I deduced from his statement that at the beginning of the war he fought in the ranks of the French army; the latter was apparent from his appearance and from his speech —he is also a born orator. He is undoubtedly a Caucasian—that is, a Russian with an admixture of Georgian or Armenian blood.

Prince Evgenii [Trubetskoi][144] also spoke articulately and forcefully. On the other hand, the speeches of Novgorodtsev[145] and Kizevetter were dry and scholastic: clear thinking, well-turned phrases, but no heart.

[142] Andrei Andreevich Evdokimov (b.1872) was a journalist and veteran of the revolutionary movement who wrote on the union and cooperative movements.

[143] This name could not be found in the reference works on the revolutionary movement.

[144] Prince Evgenii Nikolaevich Trubetskoi (1863–1920), brother of S. N. Trubetskoi, had been a member of the juridical faculty of Moscow University since 1906 and was also known as a religious philosopher and publicist.

[145] Pavel Ivanovich Novgorodtsev (1866–1924) was a historian of law and philosopher on the juridical faculty of Moscow University.

I retained a rather hopeful impression from the first session. Today it was the military question: three orators from the officers' union spoke sharply and to the point and shed appropriate light on the officer problem. The high points, of course, were the speeches of Brusilov[146] and Ruzskii;[147] the former spoke in a sharp tone, abruptly, and as drily and distinctly as the features of his face. Ruzskii speaks slowly, with pauses, but it is apparent that an intelligent man is speaking; he even wept when he spoke of the situation of the army. Brusilov, too, broke into tears. They both said that they had nothing especially new to say, and for me, indeed, they said nothing substantially new at all—it's clear that in order to re-establish the army, politics must be gotten rid of and discipline restored—not revolutionary discipline, but the one and only discipline that has always existed; and authority must be returned to the command staff. But it was interesting to see and hear these leading figures of the Russian army who have performed significant deeds and attained glory.

Will anything come of the conference? Who knows? There was talk of organizing a union of various unions in connection with the Moscow Conference. It could be that this will give real power to the public activists, and without real power all this is nothing but a mirage. In any case, I didn't carry away an impression of despair from the second day, either.

Moscow is full of rumors about a citywide strike and bolshevik manifestations—either on the 15th or the 20th. Is this the frightened fantasy of the terrorized townsman or is something really being prepared?

Another temporary remission in the war; only the French are consoling, having again won a partial but considerable victory.

15 [October]. Intensely depressed spirits again yesterday from all the conversations about strikes, disorders, etc. In the evening D. N. Egorov celebrated his *Geburtstag* (in a strictly German manner). A discussion of the subjects of concern: reasoning in terms of the welfare of the state were M. K. Liubavskii, M. M. Bogoslovskii, A. N. Savin, the host, and I; D. P. Konchalovskii[148] and one other Privatdozent, a jurist, were of a partly

---

[146] Brusilov (see n. 42) had been replaced as supreme commander by General Kornilov in July. He later served in the Red Army.

[147] General Nikolai Vladimirovich Ruzskii (1854–1918) was commander of the northern front at the time of the February revolution and continued there under the Provisional Government until April, when he retired because of ill-health. He later participated in the White movement and was taken hostage by the Red Army. On October 19, 1918, he was murdered by the Cheka in Piatigorsk.

[148] Dmitrii Petrovich Konchalovskii (1878–1952), Privatdozent, was a specialist on the history of Rome. After the closing of the history faculty in 1921, he taught German and Latin and did translations. He emigrated at the end of World War II and died in Paris in 1952. See his memoirs: D. P. Konchalovskii, *Vospominaniia i pis'ma (Ot gumanizma k*

socialistic inclination, but only partly. It is possible that Konchalovskii is laboring under the impression of what he saw and heard in the war; on several specific questions we were entirely of one mind.

The conference of men in public affairs has ended; I did not attend the last day. I don't know if all this will have any practical significance, but the principles proclaimed at the conference are correct: nonpartisan unification on a national-democratic platform—that is the only path to salvation. But can these few hundred individuals do anything in a sea of millions of gorillas? It is the question.[149]

The strike of city employees has been called off—probably because they themselves did not rise to it. Congresses of the Kadets and the Union of Towns are meeting, and fairly optimistic words are being spoken at both; as a result, the tone of the newspapers today is somehow encouraging. But something disgusting will surely happen tomorrow!

18 [October]. No need to write again. The 16th and 17th passed quite uneventfully. Today they have again suddenly begun to talk of a general strike in town, and have even ordered that the water be turned off at 2 P.M. It is now 6 P.M. and the water and streetcars are functioning. What is this, a provocation, *grande peur* of the townspeople, or is this crime in fact going to occur? The Germans have taken on the Italians and have beaten them mercilessly; if the Russians weren't scoundrels and betrayers, that would not have happened. Yesterday we had the visit of Gartung, who intends to become the assistant police chief of Tambov and, having left the Kadet party, is thinking of "signing on" with the Popular Socialists. What inconstancy, what an outstanding example of the Russian man. Another emergency session of the University Council is being called today because of the hospital strike. Ever more of the same thing, and no improvement in sight!

21 [October]. The matter of a city strike has ended with the city employees—Foma Fomich Opiskin,[150] too—mocking the townspeople—and the socialist duma and the insignificant mayor, Mr. Rudnev, above all—by again calling off their strike. It seems, however, that they have gotten all they wanted.[151] Some kind of "manifestation" of the bolsheviks, suppos-

---

Khristu) (Paris, 1971); and his reflections on the Russian Revolution: *Puti Rossii. Razmyshleniia o russkom narode, bol'shevizme i sovremennoi tsivilizatsii* (Paris, 1969).

[149] This sentence is in English in the original.

[150] The bullying villain of Dostoevskii's story *The Village of Stepanchikovo*.

[151] The newspaper *New Time* reported on the 12th that city employees were threatening to go on strike over demands for radical wage increases, improved working conditions, and the like. On the 20th, the same paper reported that a general strike plannned for the 20th had been called off and a compromise reached. An editorial in the same issue

edly throughout the country, was being predicted for the 20th. Of course, there was no manifestation on that day, nor could there have been, for those who want it will act only when the' others will least expect it. Things are getting bizarre. All the townspeople have begun to organize for self-defense; some apartment buildings were locked up last night as early as 10 o'clock. A strike of the lower employees of all the institutions of the ministry of education is coming to a head; it will probably be proclaimed tomorrow, since they cannot wait for the Plekhanov salary supplements. Those who have already received their money from local sources are striking out of solidarity. Some want the destruction of civil life; others, that is, the majority of gorillas, are indifferent—so goes Russian life.

Nothing new in the war; the rout of the Italians is not yet finished; and the Russian good-for-nothing is responsible for all this. Even if peace were to come soon, that would do no good, for the internal war will go on, as will the ruination that goes along with it, because the Russian gorilla will not stop the pogroms and atrocities until he is stopped by someone from outside. Our socialists, it seems, want to make the land committees[152] the main organs of local authority—a magnificent way to develop bribe-taking and malfeasance and, in the end, the oppression by the bosses of those very same peasant gorillas. Populism is fashioning new chains for the people with its own hands; truly, only Russian fools are capable of this.

22 [October]. The Italian defeat is taking on the character of a catastrophe. The same thing has happened to them as to us: discipline has been undermined by propaganda and part of the troops have fled without a fight, opening the way to the enemy. The Italians will leave the ranks in our footsteps; the only hope now rests with England, France, and America. The English made a false calculation in that they, proceeding with methodical slowness, figured that the Russian and Italian trash could go on fighting forever. *Fiat voluntas!* Russia has been ruined as never before.

25 [October]. Alarming new rumors were in circulation all day yesterday. The bolsheviks are undoubtedly preparing something in Petrograd. But what? A bluff, or really the seizure of power? It was reported in the

claimed the strike had been masterminded by the Bolsheviks as part of their effort to mobilize forces for the seizure of power in the city.

[152] Local land committees were set up by the first Provisional Government to collect information for agrarian reform and to settle minor land disputes. They consisted of both appointed and elected members, including representatives of local soviets. They very soon began to take on many more—and more radical—tasks, including imposition of rent controls.

papers today that Mr. Kerenskii has at last decided to make another speech in the preparliament. Will there be action behind the words? A new wave of strikes and pogroms is sweeping Russia. The strikes are being guided by the same hand—whose? At bottom, that of the Germans. Yesterday Georgievskii[153] told us about a spy trial: the spying was being done by Germans from the office of Wogau,[154] but the petty jobs were being done for them by Russians for two or three rubles a day. There you have the true symbol of Russo-German relations. There was also a session of the Archaeological Society yesterday: the old countess,[155] and two refugees, as it were, from Petrograd—Likhachev[156] and Turaev.[157] The meeting was on the Bersenevka;[158] it was just as if we were burying a close friend.

26 [October]. The bolshevik action has begun in Petrograd and Moscow with the proclaiming of the transfer of power to the Soviets of Workers' Deputies. One has the superficial impression that this action is somewhat different from all preceding ones—no one knows anything; no one is adequately informed; there is a schism within "revolutionary democracy," and in the armed forces, too. No one wants to be the first to start— both sides face each other and wait for something, perhaps to see who will win in Petrograd. There is no precise news from Petrograd, all kinds of rumors are circulating, but which of them correspond to the truth and which don't, you can't tell.

I gave a lecture at the Higher Women's Courses.[159] The students asked

[153] Probably Grigorii Petrovich Georgievskii (1866–1948): archaeographer and curator of the manuscript collection of the Rumiantsev Museum/Lenin Library from 1890 to 1937.

[154] Wogau & Co. was a German wholesale trade firm with offices in Petrograd.

[155] Countess Praskov'ia Sergeevna Uvarova (1840–1924) was an archaeologist and had been president of the Moscow Archaeological Society since 1884. She was the widow of Count A. S. Uvarov, the society's founder.

[156] Nikolai Petrovich Likhachev (1862–1936) was a prominent Petersburg historian and art historian, and a leading specialist on Old Russian sources.

[157] Boris Aleksandrovich Turaev (1868–1920), professor at Petersburg University, was an orientalist and a founder of Russian Egyptology.

[158] An area on the right bank of the Moscow River across from the Kremlin, near the Large Stone Bridge.

[159] The private Higher Women's Courses in Moscow were founded by Professor Vladimir Ivanovich Ger'e (Guerrier) (1837–1919) in 1872 to provide the equivalent of university education for women (Russian universities were closed to women until the very end of the old regime; women were first allowed to take the entrance examinations at Moscow University in 1912). Women's Courses, which existed in several large cities by the eve of the war, carried the right to teach in certain state schools. The courses in Moscow, as in other university towns, were closely linked to the university: Ger'e was a professor of Moscow University (European history). Most of the teaching was done by university professors; and the administration consisted of a council of university profes-

me during the second hour to say something about the current situation. I unloaded a lot of pessimistic thoughts on them. In the museum [the staff] paced about, because they weren't up to working.

27 [October]. All yesterday evening was passed on the telephone. Uncle Eduard came by, depressed and in a state of nervous exhaustion like all of us from everything that has happened. The news is contradictory: one version from the bolsheviks, another from other sources. It is impossible to get a clear picture of the situation, but it is clear that Petrograd is in their power to a significant degree. The general appearance of Moscow this morning was the same as yesterday; the streetcars are working. A one-day strike of employees of the ministry of education, including the museum, was called for today. It was wildly funny in the museum: only officials and volunteers were there—not all of them, to be sure; the lazy ones and the socialist-sympathizers (which is one and the same thing) were not there, of course. They opened and closed the shutters themselves, put on the samovar, and guarded the entrance, with Prince Golitsyn[160] at their head; the rest of the time they paced about. The news from Petrograd became more definite toward evening: the bolsheviks have taken over the city and are ruling in it. There is a quadrille of prisoners in the Peter-Paul Fortress: servitors of the tsar met with the servitors of Kerenskii; poor Tret'iakov[161] and Smirnov[162] have fallen into the soup for no good reason. I can imagine how Shcheglovitov, Maklakov[163] and the others are laughing.

Nothing is to be heard of any kind of Khlestakov-like attempts on the part of Kerenskii.[164] According to the comments of arrivals, there is more

---

sors headed by the university rector. The Women's Courses were assimilated into the university in 1918.

[160] Prince Vasilii Dmitrievich Golitsyn (d. 1927?) was director of the Rumiantsev Museum.

[161] Sergei Nikolaevich Tret'iakov was a leading representative of the Moscow "big bourgeoisie": head of the Moscow trade-industry organization, president of the Moscow stock exchange, and president of the economic council in Kerenskii's government beginning in July 1917.

[162] Sergei Aleksandrovich Smirnov (b. 1883) was another representative of the Moscow merchantry: chairman of the Moscow War Industries Committee; state comptroller in the Kerenskii government, September-October 1917. Both Smirnov and Tret'iakov were soon released and emigrated.

[163] Ivan Grigor'evich Shcheglovitov (1861–1918) and Nikolai Alekseevich Maklakov (1871–1918) were notorious reactionaries who had served in the post-1905 administration as ministers (justice and internal affairs, respectively). Both were removed from office in mid-1915 in a government attempt to conciliate the moderate opposition in the state duma.

[164] Khlestakov was the central character in Gogol's play *The Inspector-General.* The connotation here is of irresponsible, extravagant acts.

order in Petrograd than under the previous improvisional government; all the troops have turned out to be bolsheviks. Now we can anticipate a humiliating peace in the near future, if only the bolsheviks can hold out. And I think they will have no trouble holding out, for some time at least, and will be able to pay off their debt to the Germans. What fools are Kerenskii and his minions! Why, they are even more stupid than was Nicholas II and his hangers-on. And that is saying a lot.

28 [October]. The shooting began last night at midnight. The government forces consist of volunteers, junkers (there are several thousand of them in Moscow), and even university and Gymnasium students; the soldiers for the most part are on guard at the usual places and in the least critical locations—that is the extent of the activity of the soldiers who are loyal to the government. They took the Kremlin this morning. Right now they are fighting near the residence of the governor general and in places between Stoleshnikov, Petrovka, Okhotnyi, and Tverskaia,[165] and on the outskirts of town as well. If the affair is liquidated, it will take several days at least. The impressions are strongly reminiscent of December 1905.[166] We spent our time on the telephone; I think there were no less than fifty calls. I went out twice—once in the morning to buy newspapers and walk to Mertvyi Pereulok for milk; and then I accompanied Ninka to the orphanage. At that time occasional shots could be heard on Prechistenka and in the side streets; there was no feeling of fear, but rather an impulse to go and see something that looked like fighting. Tonight I will have two hours of standing guard at the entrance. At 6 P.M. the entire building was inspected by a patrol of two officers and three students; they claim that our Jew, Slavin, is a bolshevik.[167]

30 [October] (A.M.). Yesterday was a hard day. Involuntary inaction, contradictory rumors; small arms and artillery fire all around. We took a walk only in the courtyard. There are few government forces. They are expecting reinforcements, but from where? There are all kinds of contradictory rumors about that as well. The telephone is the only contact with the world. There was an inspection of the attics in our building. Among the officer-volunteers were Fedia and Andriusha Armand; Fedia is making amends for his bolshevik mama.[168] We treated them to lunch.

---

[165] All streets in the central district of Moscow, northwest of the Kremlin.

[166] At the end of the 1905 revolution, in mid-December, there was an armed uprising, complete with barricades, in the working-class district of Moscow known as Presnia (now Krasnaia Presnia). It was suppressed after a few days by government troops.

[167] Slavin was probably an employee of the building or of one of its tenants.

[168] Inessa Armand (née Stéphane) (1875–1920) was born in Paris and raised in Moscow by the family of her future husband, the Armands. She had five children. By 1917 she

Contact and acquaintance with all the tenants, as in 1905. Some are going out of their minds; others are taking it calmly. In the evening there was a group of four or even six standing guard, chatting away as if they had forgotten everything that is going on. I slept badly. There is less shooting this morning. The news information is relatively good; the bolsheviks, apparently, are asking for peace. In Petrograd the lengthy process of settling down is under way; will it last long? All the same, the rebellion, I am sure, will not be liquidated as it should be. The disintegration of society and the nation is ineluctable and will inevitably go on to the end. The endless hanging on the telephone is in the end irritating and tiring.

It is curious that the war has temporarily receded somewhere into the background; that is because there is no news at all in the papers. Have the Germans taken advantage of the new Russian crimes and stupidity? How will all that is going on reflect on the course of the world conflict, where the Russian carcass will become the object of general apportionment?

31 [October]. The situation is getting progressively worse. Regular firing on the center from the outskirts has begun; it turns out the bolsheviks have artillery and people who know how to shoot. They say that the rumored agreement between the two sides has not come off; in general no one has any information that is at all precise. We have been cast into an abyss; one can clearly foresee fires, lootings, and violence. A fire has already begun today at noon at Nikitskie Gates.[169] A depressed state of mind.

It is reported from Petrograd via the railway union that, supposedly, an agreement has been reached on a socialist government from the Popular Socialists to the bolsheviks. A strange and unstable combination! What will become of Moscow? I am afraid they are going to burn down the Rumiantsev Museum—what a frightful thing that would be! There was little shooting in the course of the day until 7 p.m.—approximately two or three times an hour. The fire at Nikitskie Gates has subsided. Tenants of the building have picked up shrapnel cannisters and bullets in the courtyard. A whole day without telephone service. Calls from private apartments should not have been taken from the beginning, but it is more oppressive without the telephone all the same. Tania ran over from Mert-

---

had long since abandoned family life for SD party work. Armand was on close terms with Lenin for many years, an association that gave rise to rumors of a love interest. Got'e had known her since childhood, and the Armand and Got'e families were close. Both had been in the Moscow French colony since its beginnings in the late eighteenth century.

[169] Nikitskie vorota: a square built on the site of one of the ancient gates to the city about a half-mile west of the Kremlin. The Bolshevik assault on the Kremlin began from there.

vyi Pereulok, having made her way through one or two patrols; we were glad of her arrival, as though it were the arrival of a person from another planet.

NOVEMBER

November 1. After a relatively quiet night and a good night's sleep, the first catastrophe has occurred: I never thought I would see Russian shrapnel and grenades in the courtyard of No. 4 Bol'shoi Znamenskii Pereulok,[170] but it's a fact; at 11:30 A.M. a grenade burst over the entrance of the courtyard wing, and all the windows were broken by the fragments and the concussion, except for some of the windows on the fifth floor. Just afterward, shrapnel flew in after it, which did not explode. A commotion was raised. Two people were wounded—the cook and a female tenant in Keneman's apartment, just under us; they have been sent to a field hospital. The proprietors left after them, abandoning the apartment. Together with two other occupants of the building I had to inspect the apartment and remove the valuables from the rooms with broken windows. The firing continued rather intensely until 3 o'clock; things seem to be calming down now. We decided to remain home for the time being, and have transferred to a bivouac in the rooms facing on the front. The general situation appears to be unchanged. For how long?

Evening of the same day. 10 o'clock: situation unchanged. Lialia left to do guard duty; we all intend to sleep in a bunch in the dining room.

2 November, A.M. The situation is unchanged as before, at least for those of us sitting in our apartments. According to rumors, a detachment of junkers has occupied the First Gymnasium; many anticipate intensified shelling as a result of that. The state of panic is increasing; it is being reinforced in our building by the servants gathered around Luker'ia, the doorman's wife, and by Luker'ia herself. Last night I stood guard at the entrance to the courtyard wing and drank tea with the old general and with Kasimov. We were all in the same numbed and vague state of mind; no signs of a way out. I think our present situation can be compared with that of the Parisians in the Commune; in the Russian revolution Petrograd itself has not gone through what we are enduring: Moscow under six days of shelling by Russian cannons! Il'ia ran over from Mertvyi Pereulok with provisions; apparently everyone there is in the same situation as we are. The day drags on, long and boring; it's a good thing we lay in bed until almost 10 o'clock.

[170] That is, Got'e's apartment building.

2 November, evening. Volodia Reiman[171] came over today; he was fed and got some sleep. His report is not much different from what had already reached us. In the evening I stood guard at the entrance. More rumors about reinforcements; it's hard to say what their real significance is. I read newspapers: one bolshevik and two sr; one gets the impression that all this terrible, fratricidal slaughter is a struggle between two Russian socialist sects. Is it worth spilling so much blood to save Kerenskii?

4 November, A.M. Volodia Reiman came by at 2 A.M. on the 3rd and said that peace has been concluded between the two warring sides; in essence this was not a peace, but the capitulation of the so-called "government forces," and with them of the entire sr Committee for Public Safety[172]—may God rest its soul! But what painful regret for all the young lives that were irretrievably and criminally destroyed. This time as well the affair was decided by armed force, by the same armed bands that wear soldiers' uniforms. Power rests with those who possess the force of arms. The Manilovs[173] of recent months could not understand that. I went to the museum yesterday afternoon; everything was in one piece there. Afterwards I went to Mertvyi Pereulok. Gloomy weather outside, to match my gloomy frame of mind. That is why, probably, the crowds of onlookers seem gloomy as well; lackluster faces, stupid and sometimes injurious—rarely regretful—remarks. The news from abroad is unclear, but very sad. The western front is collapsing; the Germans are in Åbo;[174] in Petrograd, they say, the state institutions are still not working. In the newspapers that were being sold on the street, one can find only sr wailing, covered with fig leaves, and the victorious invocations of the bolsheviks.[175] In terms of the number of horrors endured, last week exceeds by far all that have gone before. A reinforced guard on the building was organized in the evening. The night passed uneventfully.

[171] A relative. A Reiman and a Got'e had been in the book business in Moscow before Napoleon's invasion. F. Tastevin, *Histoire de la colonie française de Moscou. Depuis les origines jusqu'à 1812* (Moscow-Paris, 1908), p. 71.

[172] The Committee for Public Safety (Komitet obshchestvennoi bezopasnosti) was set up on October 25 at the initiative of the city duma for defense of the Provisional Government. Its members included Kadets and srs from the duma, the district zemstvo, the postal-telegraph and railway unions, and the Moscow military district staff. (The Mensheviks withdrew from the committee almost immediately.) The Committee for Public Safety was the nearest thing to an organized opposition to the Bolshevik offensive that existed in Moscow.

[173] Manilov was the "silly sentimentalist with pursed lips" in Gogol's *Dead Souls*. D. S. Mirsky, *A History of Russian Literature* (New York, 1955), p. 153.

[174] The Swedish name for the Finnish city of Turku, located on the coast about ninety miles west of Helsinki.

[175] The Bolsheviks closed down the "bourgeois" press between October 26 and November 6. Papers reappeared on November 7 or 8.

5 November. In the morning I went to the museum, and then to Kuznet-skii Most, moved by curiosity, which at the moment was stronger than any other feelings. Terrifying destruction—in that part of town the City Duma[176] and the Metropole Hotel were especially hard hit; but Nikitskie Gates, where we were in the evening, was still worse: the former Borghesti house and the Korobkov house are complete ruins. There, and on Arbat Square, there are trenches and barbed-wire barriers. The streetcar lines are lying on the ground; the clocks are smashed or stand helplessly stopped, leaning to one side. More terrible is the line of people in front of the university anatomy theater, waiting to identify corpses. When I was on my way home, the line extended, snakelike on the sidewalk, almost to the National Hotel.[177]

In the afternoon I was at Iakovlev's place, in Mertvyi Pereulok, and at Prince Golitsyn's for a meeting about the affairs of the museum. We decided to go on Monday to "put things in order," and to open it when calm is restored and there is something to heat the museum with. The discussions everywhere were mostly of an anticipatory character; the general impression is that the story is not yet over. At night I stood guard again for three hours, as did Lialia. It is characteristic that today one of the representatives of the democratic elements has already refused guard duty, and our security is rapidly falling apart.

The new regime is publishing decrees on the opening of all stores as of today—everything had been closed except food shops—and on replacement or covering over of all broken windows, also in one day. Obviously, in Russia any regime is capable of publishing orders that are impossible to carry out. There is no news from the outside world, and it is impossible to get any idea of what is happening in Russia, let alone in other countries.

6 November. Uncle Eduard came by this morning. He, too, has lost weight and become gaunt. We took a walk as far as his place and then on to Mokhovaia; the impressions are the same as the day before. I spent almost the entire day in Mertvyi Pereulok; there was a whist: "the elders" Vel'iaminov, Golenko, Lialia, and the whole family. The "bourgeois" who had taken refuge [there] had had a bit to drink to drown their sorrows. We returned home at 8:30 along completely dark streets. In the afternoon we also stopped by to see Egorov, and V. E. Kokoshkina came

[176] The City Duma Building, a large red-brick edifice, was situated on Voskresenskaia Square (now Revolution Square) just north of the Kremlin. It presently houses the Lenin Museum.

[177] About four long blocks, down Bol'shaia Nikitskaia Street (presently Herzen Street) and north along the Mokhovaia (Marx Prospect) to the corner of Tverskaia (Gor'kii Street).

by our place (her *beau-frère* has a very dark view of things).[178] Many conversations. Some exaggerate, others underestimate the situation; some think it will last a matter of months, others weeks. I do not share these optimistic outlooks, and I think we face a period of extremely heavy sufferings, before which the preceding three years pale. Apparently, the victors are not fulfilling the concluded agreement; they are routing the junkers and the cadets,[179] locking them up in prison to the accompaniment of various taunts on the part of the barbarized soldiers, who sense that strength is on their side. The situation in Moscow is reminiscent of the situation in Rome under Marius or Sulla.[180] As before, there is no news about the outside world. The new authorities deny the successes of the Germans, but can these denials be believed? Indeed, does all this have any meaning at all? The bolsheviks have dissolved the Moscow duma; the windbag SRs, led by Rudnev and grandpa Minor,[181] have gotten what they deserved.

7 November. Yesterday I was at the museum, and went around to see El. And., Uncle Emil', and Shambi. Crowds with the same morosely inquisitive look about them were in the streets. Rumors are proliferating, the more so in that there is no real news from anywhere: Minsk, Dvinsk, and Reval have been taken; Venice, too; Kornilov and Kaledin are surrounding Moscow. Where is the truth? It is probably worse than all the rumors taken together. It seems that we are approaching the final catastrophe. The banks are closed; that produces even greater alarm. In the afternoon I attended the memorial service for the students who have been killed; I even broke into sobs. The University Church was full of young people. Our theologian, Fr. Bogoliubskii, gave quite a forceful speech that provoked weeping. At the end he ordered everyone to sing "Eternal Memory"—it was powerful and moving. The University and Womens' Courses students nevertheless decided to continue with their studies. Poor scholarship, in what murderous conditions its dissemination in Russia is having to take place! Yet all the same it is necessary, business before all.[182] The entire chancel of the University Church has been riddled with

[178] Fedor Fedorovich Kokoshkin (1871–1918), an authority on constitutional law, a Privatdozent on the juridical faculty of Moscow University, and a leading figure in the Kadet party. He was state comptroller in the Provisional Government in July-August 1917. V. E. Kokoshkina was married to F.F.'s brother, Vladimir Fedorovich.

[179] The students of the military schools located in the Lefortovo district on the outskirts of town along the Iauza River, east of the Kremlin.

[180] Marius and Sulla were leaders of popular and aristocratic factions, respectively, in late Republican Rome, a time of Barbarian invasions and civil war.

[181] Osip Solomonovich Minor (1861–1932), an SR journalist, was chairman of the city duma.

[182] This last phrase is in English in the original text.

bullets, except for the altar; it would be good to leave this permanently for the shame of all our descendants. No news from outside the entire day, as before. Rumors of pogroms, panic; apparently everyone who can is quitting Moscow.

8 November. The newspapers that have been christened with the shameful name "bourgeois" appeared today. A few things have become clear from them. Former Russia has already been divided into the Caucasus, the Cossack lands, the Ukraine, an anarchist center, and, perhaps, Siberia. Finland has broken off. The Germans are proclaiming the separation of Lithuania and Courland. Russia is no longer on the edge of the abyss, but in its depths: we have passed the last barrier. The bolsheviks have taken over everywhere, relying on ignorant and dissipated soldiers; a touching marriage of Pugachevshchina and the most advanced ideas. This union can yield no benign results, but how much horror, suffering, and desolation will it take for the unhappy Russian people to stop killing themselves by systematic crimes and stupidities? I think that they will not come to their senses this time, either, and that the anarchy will go on getting worse, and that we can be rescued from it not by mythical Kaledins, but by the mutual extermination of our extreme doctrinaires, or by some as yet unknown Varangians.

A general observation: everyone you meet has lost weight; it is not easy to live through events. There is a strong urge to leave Moscow. With what joy would I quit this hateful city, if only there were the means and the possibility of cutting all ties and getting my family out. For me, not only the apartment, not only Moscow, but all Russia is becoming a suffocating cage. Few changes on the front for the time being, apparently; but the Germans are still moving forward in Italy. A mood of unrelenting gloom all day.

10 November. The "decrees" of the new regime are pouring forth as from a horn of plenty: demobilization of the army, nationalization of the banks, monopolization of newspaper advertising, etc., etc.[183] The Senate

[183] The Bolsheviks' assault on the "bourgeois" press began immediately after October 25 and was soon extended to the nonparty press as a whole. By the end of June 1918, the nonparty press in Moscow, and in most of the central territory of the country then under Bolshevik control, had been completely eliminated. Outright permanent closings were rare, however, until the breakup of the coalition government with the Left SRs in late March 1918; before then the assault was restricted to various forms of harassment, fines, temporary closing for antigovernment libel, etc. One of the earliest Bolshevik attempts to run the "bourgeois" press out of business without outright violation of freedom of the press was the scheme for instituting a state, or "soviet," monopoly on advertising, restricting advertising to the various *Izvestiia* of local soviets. On November 8, the government (Sovnarkom) published a decree on state monopoly of newspaper advertising; on Novem-

is not registering these decrees or publishing them. They will probably dissolve the Senate.[184] They are starting up peace talks directly, and are appointing a bolshevik ensign as commander in chief.[185] It will soon be the turn of the universities and scientific institutions, and very soon we may all be on the pavement. A passage in steerage looms ever closer. The funeral of fallen bolsheviks is today; excesses are expected. What kind, no one knows, but everyone is in a panic. More so than ever before, there is no energy for getting anything done.

11 November. Everything remains unchanged. No news from Petrograd. We opened the museum today; there were about twenty people at one time, but no more; cold, gloomy, not everyone showed up. The usual conversations. At the University Council the mood was more spirited than I expected; it was resolved to continue studies. I learned some amazing things: it appears that in Pieter[186] the remnants of the former government are holding sessions and carrying on current work, and that the Council of People's Commissars knows this and does not touch them—truly incomprehensible! So far there have been no assaults on the University.

12 November. The news is altogether depressing. "The struggle for peace" is being waged in such a way that we, *corps et biens*, are placing ourselves at the mercy of Germany: it will be hard to sleep! Few personal impressions for the day. I was at Shambi's this morning, where I saw Ivinskii[187]—how that old theoretical revolutionary has moved rightward! I did nothing all day. It is a shame to waste the time, but there is no energy for any kind of work.

13 November. Monday, a day without newspapers; that means little new depressing news—that will come tomorrow. I sat from 11:00 to 3:00 in the museum, trying to find something to do. At any one time there were

---

ber 18, an announcement was published that the law on monopoly would be put into effect on the 22d and measures to enforce it were to be begun on the 23d. However, neither the army of agents needed to enforce the decree nor the special offices for receiving advertising orders existed, and the "bourgeois" press continued to print advertising to the end.

[184] Like the state duma, the Ruling Senate, the old regime's highest court and organ of administrative oversight, did not disappear with the February revolution. Although some departments were soon closed, most remained without change and were abolished only by the Soviet decree of December 5, 1917.

[185] Nikolai Vasil'evich Krylenko (1885–1938).

[186] Pieter (*Piter*), from the Dutch, was a familiar name for St. Petersburg, dating back to the time of Peter I.

[187] A Populist from the generation of the 1870s?

twenty-five people in the reading room, not more. All evening I sat and wrote lectures, again in order to lose myself in work. Ahead is the revolting prospect of standing guard in the courtyard from 4:30 to 7:00; what have we come to—walking around in the roles of janitor and doorman in complete awareness of the dubious utility of it all? This morning I went to honor the memory of the fallen students for whom services were being performed at the Church of the Great Ascension; our new all-Russian patriarch himself, it seems, officiated. I was at the beginning of the ceremony, which lasted all day. Crowds of people, exclusively intelligentsia—or, rather, civilized—arrived every minute. They carried in the bodies with the singing of "Eternal Memory" while I was there. I confess I cried, for "Eternal Memory" was being sung not only for those unfortunate young people, who gave their lives for God knows what, but for all of unhappy, long-suffering Russia. What I saw was a counterdemonstration to the red funeral of the gorillas on the 10th: there there was the mob; here, civilized Russians. Right now, this evening, I don't know if the funeral went all right; if not, the battle was a battle of light against darkness, civilization against the barbarians. On Saturday, after the council meeting, the young people who were organizing the funeral said that some sort of local military-revolutionary committee refused to guarantee the safety of the procession to the communal cemetery, seemingly indicating not only that the procession would be attacked, but that the coffins would be thrown out; the idea then arose to bury them in the Novodevich'ii Monastery, but the nuns (oh, how characteristic this is!) did not want to give them any land. Then there was no choice, apparently, but to return to the idea of burying them in the communal cemetery. Tomorrow I will know how all that went.

14 November. The funeral went all right. There is relatively little bad news in the papers; tomorrow will probably make up for that. Something like work is going on in the museum. They have finally made Shambi a Dozent on the faculty; Speranskii's[188] presentation was well written. The English have taken Jerusalem; how shameful to read all this, knowing that the Russian forces are capable of taking only their own Moscow. They have replaced our windows, and today we will move back into our bedroom. For long? Won't we have to start renting out rooms?

16 [November]. Comrade Krylenko, the commander in chief of the bolsheviks, has started up negotiations with the Germans; three representatives have gone [to negotiate]—apparently all of them are Jews. Russia is

---

[188] Mikhail Nesterovich Speranskii (1863–1938) was a professor at Moscow University and a specialist on the history of Old Russian literature.

betraying and selling out, and the Russian people wreak havoc and raise hell and are absolutely indifferent to their international fate. It is an unprecedented event in world history when a numerous people, which considers itself a great people, a world power despite all kinds of qualifications, has in eight months dug itself a grave with its own hands. It follows that the very idea of a Russian power, a Russian nation, was a mirage, a bluff, that this only seemed to be so and was never a reality. That is so, but how shameful and grievous it is all the same. There is nothing to heat the Rumiantsev Museum with; there is nothing to pay raises to the employees with; and no one to turn to for explanations, since there is no administration—a unique state of affairs. And it is like that everywhere.

18 [November]. Things are going along their own way. We know nothing of what is happening beyond the Russian borders, probably because we are not being informed. In Russia, the bolsheviks are conquering staff headquarters, conducting peace negotiations, and freeing German war prisoners—in a word, they are preparing former Russia's fall into the embrace of Germany to the complete and sincere joy of the enormous majority of Russian gorillas, who are irresistibly attached to the dear and familiar knout of the master. All's well that ends well; the Russo-German war will end the same way the process would have without war: the Germans will conquer the Russians. Why then did they spill so much blood; why did they betray the French? It is curious to find great minds among the probolsheviks—or at least people who were so considered, such as Timiriazev.[189] N. V. Bogoiavlenskii spoke about that today in the library commission.[190] In the museum we discussed the question of how long we can hold out; we decided that we can hold out until Christmas so far as money and fuel are concerned—and then?

20 [November]. No particular facts for the last two days; everything is going along at its own pace. The allies spit on us, it seems. The salaries were paid again today. The university and the museum are not being touched for the time being. Does that mean that everything is all right? Even the mind is somehow more at peace; but it is the peace of death. The motherland has died; there is no more motherland. I went to vote

[189] Kliment Arkad'evich Timiriazev (1843–1920) was one of Russia's most prominent natural scientists, a plant physiologist. Timiriazev was sympathetic to the Bolsheviks and was elected to the Socialist Academy in 1918. In 1917 he held a chair at the university.

[190] Nikolai Vasil'evich Bogoiavlenskii (1870–1949 [?]) was a zoologist and professor on the medical faculty at Moscow University. He was also a member of the library commission.

for the all-national saloon;[191] I fulfilled my civic duty unhindered, and with that offered my last kiss to the late beloved Russia.

22 [November]. Dukhonin has been killed, and Kornilov, Denikin, and Markov have fled;[192] they will probably be caught. The separate peace is already a sure thing. The question now is, what is next—how will the coalition united under the name "bolshevik" and consisting of extremist fanatics, people working for German salaries, and black hundreds[193] fall apart? The death of Dukhonin is an instructive example for all the generals who are sitting between two stools; and judging by Savinkov's revelations (*The Russian Gazette*, 21 November), both Dukhonin and Cheremisov[194] and, apparently, many others took on a resemblance to the notorious *Vikzhel*[195] in the days of Kerenskii's fall—they all compromised and danced on the tightrope.

24 [November]. In the newspapers today: destruction of the law courts; rumors about the socialization of houses or, at least, putting houses under the control of building committees; the sending of sailors to guard Nicholas II; and the apparent lack of success of the peace negotiations. The

[191] *Vsenarodnyi kabak*: Got'e's derisive term for the Constituent Assembly, for which elections were finally being held on November 12.

[192] General Nikolai Nikolaevich Dukhonin (1876–1917) had been de facto commander in chief (the formal title was held by Kerenskii) following the arrest of General Kornilov. The Bolsheviks named Krylenko to replace him in November when he refused to begin negotiations with the German high command. He was lynched by a mob of soldiers and sailors in Mogilev, the Russian field headquarters, on the day Krylenko arrived (November 20). General Anton Ivanovich Denikin (1872–1947) and General Sergei Leonidovich Markov (1878–1918) had been under arrest for involvement in the Kornilov affair. Denikin, the future leader of the White Army in the south, was former commander of the southwestern front; Markov was his chief of staff. Generals Kornilov, Denikin, Markov, Romanovskii, and Lukomskii all escaped from Bykhov, near Mogilev, shortly before the arrival of Krylenko. General Markov died in the fighting between the Volunteer Army and the Bolsheviks on June 12, 1918.

[193] *Chernosotentsy*: a term dating from the revolution of 1905, signifying a right-wing mob.

[194] General Vladimir Andreevich Cheremisov (b. 1871) was commander of the northern front at the time of the October revolution. He refused Kerenskii's request for help in organizing a march on Petrograd immediately after the coup.

[195] That is, the railway union (literally, an acronym for the All-Russian Executive Committee of the Railway Union) founded in August 1917 at the first national congress of railway workers. In October, the Vikzhel pursued a policy of neutrality, plumped for an "all-socialist" government (as did the Left SRs), and negotiated with the new regime. On November 20, the Vikzhel passed a resolution agreeing to recognize the Soviet government on condition that it, the Vikzhel, be given control over the railroad system. In the end, these conditions were not accepted by the Bolsheviks, who were stalling for time: they successfully mobilized their own organization of railway workers and the Vikzhel was dissolved in January 1918.

first of these is shocking, although "they" had already talked of it earlier: poor Lial'ka, he will have a rough time of it for a while, and in general [the result will be] several tens of thousands of intelligentsia paupers. The second is perhaps not so terrible, but it will affect our dear, kind Mertvyi Pereulok; they are upset there, obviously. What can one say? The third sounds as if they are going to bump off Nicholas like Dukhonin, which will facilitate the resurrection of the monarchist persuasion. The fourth should have been expected. The question now is, will the comrades accept the German conditions in all their ignominy, or will they continue to play stubborn, pretending that they will go on fighting; or will peace really be postponed further? Technically, the process of Russia's sellout to the Germans is very interesting, if only it weren't so sad from the old-fashioned moral point of view.

25 [November]. The day passed without particular excitement; everything remains unchanged. There are many rumors and facts about the falsification of the elections to the all-national saloon, which by all indicators promises to be a zoo rather than a saloon. In the morning I had a conversation with Manuilov,[196] who said that in his opinion it would be possible to fight against the seizure of power by a band of men, but what can be done with a nation that has given them its votes in such quantity? He then asked me if I understand people like Pokrovskii.[197]

26 [November]. New rumors about the socialization of housing, reported in a ludicrous form in *The Russian Word.* If it is so, the bolsheviks have set themselves the goal of alienating all the intelligentsia, everyone who possesses anything at all. Perhaps the finale will come sooner as a result. Sasha Rar, Shura Grave,[198] and Shambi came to visit today. All have the same thing on their minds.

[196] Aleksandr Apollonovich Manuilov (1861–1929), an economist and agrarian expert, was a professor and former rector of Moscow University. A liberal-populist Kadet, he had been minister of education in the first two Provisional Governments. Manuilov emigrated shortly after the October revolution, but returned to Moscow in 1918.

[197] Mikhail Nikolaevich Pokrovskii (1868–1932) was a historian who, like Got'e, was a pupil of Kliuchevskii and Vinogradov. He had been associated with the Bolsheviks since 1905 and was the author of the first Marxist survey of Russian history (*Russian History from Earliest Times*, 5 vols., 1910–1913). Abroad from 1906 to 1917, he had just been named chairman of the Moscow Soviet, a post he held until March 1918. In that month he became assistant commissar of enlightenment, a post he retained to his death. Pokrovskii was to become the leading figure in the development of the Soviet system of higher education and in the ideological transformation of history and the social sciences. Although they were ideological enemies, Pokrovskii and Got'e were old acquaintances and were on familiar terms (na ty).

[198] Aleksandr Aleksandrovich Rar and Aleksandr Aleksandrovich Grave were relatives of Got'e by marriage. Grave was a medical doctor.

28 [November]. A savage appeal against Kaledin, Kornilov, Rodzianko,[199] and all those who have taken refuge on the Don has been pasted up in the streets. The lower university employees want to reorganize the administration of the university "on the principles of parity" between the representatives of intellectual labor and the representatives of physical labor. In Petrograd some sort of intelligentsia crowd is gathering near the Tauride Palace to defend . . . the abortive all-national saloon. A new mixture of the mindlessness, demagogic cruelty, stupidity, and that inexplicable Manilovshchina[200] of which only the Russians are capable. The Rumiantsev Museum has been closed for two days for lack of fuel, which had not been stored up thanks to the stupidity and mismanagement of our building manager. The University Council spent more than an hour discussing the individual words of a draft response to the opening of the all-national saloon, which failed to occur.[201]

29 [November]. Word from Marietta through Lena that the peasants are appropriating Soboliny, Boloto, and the Aleksandrovskii and Viazhinskii farms—in a word, the private farms around us. I would not be surprised if we were living our last days there, despite the arrival of Praskov'ia, who brought us edibles and is still here. Yesterday in Petersburg the rudiments of the all-national saloon met and elected Chernov as their chairman. How is he better than Lenin? Pitiful speeches about a pitiful gathering, and this sorry gathering is the last hope of former Russia. Once again we could not open the museum for lack of firewood and the incompetency of the building manager.

30 [November]. The decree on the arrest of the Kadet leaders,[202] the campaign against them, and the proscription of the Russian Girondists—somehow all this is more like Bulgaria under Stambulov than the French Revolution. Events are unfolding at a mad pace. Yesterday they did not even permit a private meeting in the Constituent Assembly; the dispersal

[199] Mikhail Vasil'evich Rodzianko (1859–1924) was a leading Octobrist and president of the fourth duma.

[200] See n. 173. The term can be roughly glossed as "dreamy ineffectiveness."

[201] Delegates to the Constituent Assembly began to arrive in Petrograd and to meet informally very soon after the elections. The first (and only) official session of the Constituent Assembly was repeatedly postponed, but finally took place on January 5, 1918.

[202] On November 28, a number of prominent Kadets who had been elected to the Constituent Assembly, including Countess Sof'ia Vladimirovna Panina, F. F. Kokoshkin, A. I. Shingarev, Prince P. D. Dolgorukov, V. D. Nabokov, F. I. Rodichev, and N. N. Kutler, were arrested in Petrograd. The arrests were preceded by a decree proclaiming all the Kadet leaders subject to arrest as "enemies of the people" who were allegedly planning a counterrevolutionary coup to coincide with the opening of the assembly. Though some Kadets foresaw civil war by this time, there is no evidence that the party was planning such an action.

of the all-national saloon is inevitable. There seems to be little reason to mourn it, however: being composed of pogromists, both sentimental and realistic, it would have been incapable of action all the same. The blow to the Kadets, in the opinion of A. I. Iakovlev, is an ingenious blow of the extreme rightists delivered by the hand of the bolsheviks. Is it so? *Qui vivra—verra*. They say the Germans have set impossible terms even for a separate peace. Logically speaking, they are playing a game they can't lose: either the bolsheviks must accept their terms or the Germans will occupy all of Russia in a victorious sweep in the spring, since the bolsheviks, mensheviks, srs, and the other Russian socialists have destroyed the organ of Russia's defense; by spring the last soldiers will have fled the front and it will turn out that the Russian people has destroyed its army itself. Woe to those who have prepared themselves an unheard of, unprecedented defeat and infamy.

DECEMBER

2 [December]. Yesterday there was again the rumor about the confiscation of money and a decree about not paying apartment rents to the landlords. Today there was the news about Nicholas II supposedly having fled Tobol'sk—that rumor, in my opinion, requires confirmation; I don't believe it and refuse to draw any conclusions. I spent the whole evening today reading the memoirs of E. A. Bogolepova about her husband; they were published in a few copies.[203] There is one-sidedness, but there is much of interest as well—for example, in the comments about Nicholas II, Pobedonostsev, and Witte. N. P. Bogolepov's opinions about the Russians are very interesting. In the 1870s, abroad, "he found the time to study the mores, customs and social organization of the Germans, and the comparison of the latter with Russian life and organization provoked a profound sadness in him. He was especially discouraged by the Russians' lack of will and character" (p. 36).

"The behavior of Dorobets, the unreliability of officials, the improprieties of certain university people, all deepened N. P.'s conviction that the majority of Russians, even educated ones, suffer from a lack of upbringing" (144). How applicable all that is to the present moment; how these opinions have been confirmed by life.

One more quote: "With their well-known lack of discipline and distaste for order, Russians frequently brand as a formalist someone who demands precision and order" (101).

[203] E. A. Bogolepova was the widow of Nikolai Pavlovich Bogolepov (1846–1901), professor of Roman law at Moscow University and minister of education from 1898 until his assassination by an sr terrorist in 1901. E. A. Bogolepova, *Nikolai Pavlovich Bogolepov: Zapiski* (Moscow, 1912).

5 [December]. New rumors and new decrees every day now: a rumor about the designation of commissars in the higher educational institutions; apparently, the designation of one such in the Archive of the Ministry of Foreign Affairs; we will probably have to face that heavy burden soon in the university and the museum as well. Today there was a sensational rumor to the effect that the Romanovs have been liberated. Can it be that the red is really yielding to the black? In the museum, the employees have again presented a paper with demands; the main one is to fire the head watchman. I am afraid to hope that the issue is more or less resolved. There was a faculty meeting today: Picheta's dissertation was accepted; if we still exist, the defense will be in January.

7 [December]. The most remarkable scene today was observing the conversations between the administration of the Archive of the Ministry of Foreign Affairs and the bolshevik commissar. Vasilii Kondrat'evich Evenko, a machinist from the Rostov/Don petty bourgeoisie, strode about in the main room of the archive in front of the assembled employees in an overcoat with a sheepskin collar, but bare-headed. The conversation was conducted in the sweet-and-sour tone so masterfully employed by S. A. Belokurov.[204] The commissar demanded signatures attesting to recognition of the authority of the Council of People's Commissars. He had already succeeded in seizing the keys on Tuesday, the 5th; the employees agreed to work on the condition that they not be forced to sign, that the keys be returned, and that there be no interference with their work.[205] How the affair ended, I don't yet know. Several instances were characteristic: the commissar asked how the archive could have sold something to the Rumiantsev Museum—the matter concerned several volumes of the *Complete Collection of Russian Chronicles*. To this Belokurov replied: "We sell books, and even print them—we work with our heads, you see." When the employees asked why there was such mistrust of them that he didn't want to give them back the keys, the commissar answered: "You see, it seems that certain documents were burned in the ministry of foreign affairs when it was being taken over by the new authority." Aren't they looking for secret treaties in the archive?

Later there was a meeting in the Rumiantsev Museum; what shall we do if we are awarded such a commissar? Opinions in general inclined toward adopting the platform of the archive. Elli Peterka [?] paid us a visit in the evening; we hadn't seen her in more than a year. She gave us

[204] Sergei Alekseevich Belokurov (1862–1918) was a historian and archaeographer. He had worked in the foreign ministry archive since 1886.

[205] According to a newspaper story of December 8, the employees' declaration also included the point that they recognized only the authority of the Constituent Assembly. Evenko, who had been named commissar of the archive, rejected the declaration and declared the employees fired. *Russkie vedomosti*, December 8, no. 271.

her personal impressions of the period of wartime agony, and by doing so she reinforced our thoughts and ideas.

8 [December]. The incident in the archive has been dragged out: the local Soviet of Dog Deputies claims that it is all a misunderstanding. Is it so? They have calmed down somewhat in the Rumiantsev Museum as well, especially because a rumor has reached there that commissars will not be appointed in institutions of culture and enlightenment. Is it so? In other respects the day passed without anything of interest happening.

9 [December]. Preliminary censorship of the newspapers, martial law, and revolutionary tribunals were introduced today in Moscow—the first and second until December 20. What is in store for the days ahead? The majority of people with whom I happened to talk today are of the opinion that this is either a symptom of the weakness of the existing authority, or a signal of an even greater acceleration of the last swing to the right. A third opinion is that this is directed against the unwanted so-called bourgeois newspapers, and for the liquidation of the strike of city employees.[206] If we live, we'll learn.

11 [December]. Yesterday passed without incident; no newspapers today. Things are going along at their own pace, it seems. The German peace is being prepared and the internal ruination of Russia continues. All persistently expect some kind of coup in the next few days; there are various views about what kind of coup it will be, but everyone thinks that the return of the monarchy is near. I would very much like to know what these rumors are based on. I met my university comrade I. N. Filatov on the street today. Under the old regime he had even spent some time in Siberia for his politics; now, it appears from my inquiries, he is a menshevik. Here is what he said to me on his own initiative: "We are about to lose everything. In a few days the Germans will take Petrograd from the front and rear and will restore the monarchy. This is a shame and a horror. Fifty percent of the bolsheviks are monarchists, 45 percent are scoundrels, and 5 percent are men of convictions." So these rumors are current on the non-bolshevik left as well.

14 [December]. I did not write for two days; there was no time. On Tuesday the 12th I talked with a pessimist and an optimist—Genzel' and

[206] The Central Strike Committee had announced that a strike of employees of charity hospitals, orphanages, and several other public institutions would begin on December 8 in protest of Bolshevik policies and in support of the Constituent Assembly.

Grushka.[207] The first says that the contemporary state of affairs will last until autumn, at least, and that the Allies will have to conclude an "indecent" peace as well; that the situation inside Russia can change only after the complete disintegration of the army and the total making over of the countryside on the ruins of private agriculture—then external forces can reestablish order. Grushka, on the contrary, affirmed that the bolsheviks' tactics as a whole are a toy pistol that is not to be feared; the noise it makes only demonstrates their powerlessness. The same day rumors began to circulate in gossip-ridden Moscow that a fight is under way in Petrograd, that a part of the armed forces has risen against Smol'nyi in favor of the all-national saloon; but all this is nonsense. A. K. Vinogradov[208] returned from Petrograd yesterday with Maksimov, an employee, and confirms that all is quiet there. Their trip was very interesting: Vinogradov cleverly extracted the Plekhanov and percentage raises from the bolshevik ministry, apparently without giving in to them and at the same time without senselessly tilting at windmills; he has shown, in my opinion, that he is a clever man. The comrades of the employee, on the other hand, were able to understand that without civilized people they can do nothing, that all is chaos and disorder with the bolsheviks and that it is not so easy to get something in Petrograd. Vinogradov's general impression is that the bolsheviks are entrenched and that no one gives a damn about the all-national saloon.

Yesterday evening there was a meeting of the Historical Society, where Picheta clearly and interestingly expounded his theme about the agrarian reform of Sigismund-August; it was more intelligent than the schemes of the Russian fools of the twentieth century.[209]

A conversation with L. M. Sukhotin.[210] He said that maybe he will leave for Siberia to make a life for himself; Prince G. E. L'vov has left for there already. What is it that draws our *ci-devants* to Siberia? That is interesting.

15 [December]. The standard news. Armed guards have been installed in the banks—yesterday in Petrograd, today in Moscow. What this will lead to remains to be seen, but one senses and feels the panic. The archive of

[207] Pavel Petrovich Genzel' (1878–1949) and Apollon Apollonovich Grushka (1870–1929) were colleagues of Got'e on the law faculty (finance) and the historico-philological faculty, respectively. Grushka was dean of faculty in 1917.

[208] Anatolii Kornelievich Vinogradov (1888–1946) was Got'e's younger colleague on the staff of the Rumiantsev Museum. Trained as a philologist, he was appointed director of the museum in March 1921, replacing Prince Golitsyn. He was removed from that position in 1924, and later became a well-known writer of historical novels.

[209] See n. 81. The reference is to Picheta's doctoral dissertation, which dealt with the agrarian reforms of the Polish king, Sigismund (August) (1548–1572) in the Lithuanian-Russian state (*Agrarnaia reforma Sigizmunda-Avgusta v Litovsko-russkom gosudarstve*).

[210] L. M. Sukhotin (1879–1948) was a literary scholar.

the ministry of foreign affairs has been purged and the proud and imperial S. A. Belokurov is being evicted from his apartment. Who could ever
have imagined that? I have again renewed my studies in the Archive of
the Ministry of Justice—as a narcotic. The German note on the peace
negotiations impressed me: it is almost a work of genius, considering that
"Russian" fools are sitting across from Kühlmann and Czernin.[211] I expect a trap, in which they will snare the comrades.

17 [December]. University Council yesterday; the mood was heavy, although so far there is nothing really catastrophic or hopeless. The financial crisis is very great, tuition will have to be raised; the "junior employees" give no peace and are putting forward all kinds of demands. The
clinics must be closed for lack of fuel, and the red guards have their sights
set on unheated buildings. There have been no conflicts with the bolsheviks yet, but one can expect them any minute. I left depressed and uncertain that the university will function in 1918. In the museum the ravenous
employees are dissatisfied with the Plekhanov supplements as well; they
wanted them continued to January 1, and not to November 1 as they
were issued. It took a lot of work to convince them that it is impossible
to do that. Then there was a new explosion provoked by the fact that our
truly Russian office staff issued these supplements to themselves and to
the nonsalaried workers, but let the wage workers wait until Monday. What insanity! The bank crisis has reached the point of nationalization of the banks and infraction of the inviolability of safe-deposit
boxes;[212] an act of blatant violence is taking place. Credit, industry, trade,
and private enterprise are being destroyed; we have broken through to a
new low with our numskulls!

19 [December]. Not much new for yesterday and today. There are persistent rumors from Petrograd about the gradual taking of the city by the
Germans; the Kadet matriarch E. V. Iur'eva[213] arrived today and con-

[211] That is, the German and Austrian foreign ministers, respectively.

[212] All banks were nationalized by a Soviet decree of December 14. In accordance with
another decree, inspection of safe-deposit boxes was begun in January and continued into
the summer of 1918; the numbers of the boxes to be examined in the presence of their
owners in a given week were regularly published in the newspapers. Precious metals in
all forms were subject to outright confiscation, as were stocks and bonds and the bulk of
currency found (a summary of the results of the procedure as of July 1, 1918, reported
10,127,976 rubles turned over to their owners out of a total of 64,649,091 rubles found).
In addition, taxes were levied on the contents of boxes containing over 5,000 rubles in
valuables and currency (*Izvestiia VTsIKS*, July 27, 1918, no. 158). According to the Soviet
press, the inspection revealed immediately that most of the jewelry and precious metals
had been removed from safe-deposit boxes by their owners well before October 1917
(*Izvestiia Moskovskogo Soveta Raboch'ikh i Soldatskikh Deputatov*, January 18, 1918). The
summary published in July confirmed this conclusion.

[213] One of Got'e's coworkers in the Rumiantsev Museum.

firmed this. The bank *coup d'état*, among other things, is being ascribed to the Germans, who want to destroy the last of our credit and interfere with the financing of the Don.[214] The famous Moscow policeman Stroev is working out of Smol'nyi.[215] The Kadet prisoners say that the bolsheviks need to isolate them, not to prosecute them. If that is so, it is equally the need of the Germans and of the black hundreds. In the Archive of the Ministry of Foreign Affairs things have taken a new turn: the mechanic has turned over the archive to the Soviet of Dog Deputies, the Soviet of Dog Deputies has given it to its cultural-enlightenment committee, and at the same time has recalled all the personnel. In this way, apparently, after the theater of the SDD there will appear the archive of the SDD. Well, the main thing is to preserve the creation of Müller, Bantysh et al.[216] Tomorrow we have to decide the question of the relation of the Rumiantsev Museum to the Commission for the Preservation of Monuments of the SDD; I will support a businesslike agreement, because cultural workers can enter a conflict only for very weighty reasons; I consider that there are none such. M. K. Liubavskii was at our place in the evening; we talked about general affairs, and were entirely of the same opinion about them. We discussed Picheta's book.

20 *[December]*. My salary from the museum was issued once again, and that is something. A meeting of the museum council. My point of view was successfully defended, although not without a fight. N. I. Romanov[217] wanted at any cost to take the bull by the horns and provoke a conflict with the dog deputies; I don't understand and cannot accept this typical outlook of the Russian *intelligent*—do it my way or a principle will be violated, and then let everything go to ruin. Nor do I see submission to the dog deputies in having a chairman appointed by them on the commission for the preservation of historical monuments. Who cares who is chairman—after all, at the present moment power is in the hands of those gentlemen. And if they call for help not in a political cause, but in a cultural cause, then we, for the sake of the cause as well as for the sake of our institution's welfare and its direct goals, should not aggravate the situation without weighty reasons or extreme need. An appointed chairman is even better, since in that case we bear less responsibility.

[214] That is, the formation of the Volunteer Army in the south whose primary purpose was to carry on with the war against Germany.

[215] Apparently a well-known member of the Moscow police force before the Revolution who now worked for the Bolsheviks.

[216] Gerhard Friedrich Müller (Miller) (1705–1783) and Nikolai Nikolaevich Bantysh-Kamenskii (1737–1814), the former a German and the latter a Ukrainian, were great archaeographers and collectors of documents on Russian history and foreign relations.

[217] Nikolai Il'ich Romanov (1867–1948) was a professor at Moscow University, a specialist on art.

The general draft of the German peace conditions was published today. They are depressing: it is now plainly clear what bait was used by the Germans to catch our *traitors* and fools, and what our traitors were after—the self-determination of the nationalities. It turns out that Lithuania, Courland, part of Livland (read: Riga and Ösel), and part of Estland (read: Dagö) have already opted for self-determination and have expressed a desire to separate from Russia. The bolsheviks pretend that they will not accept these conditions, but of course they will be accepted, because there is no other way out of the situation. Long live intelligence and may the fools and self-betrayers perish. I forgot: Commissar Malinovskii[218] came to the museum today—a repulsive, ugly little man who does not inspire trust. But he came with a request to accept the library of the Aleksandrovskoe School[219] and conducted himself (today, at least) very modestly—more modestly than V. V. Przheval'skii, who came in March as a delegate of commissar N. M. Kishkin of joyous and eternally worthy memory.[220]

22 [December]. We are accepting the library of the Aleksandrovskoe School at the risk of filling up all our free space. They had already begun to vandalize it. The school has been divided into six parts: six institutions and military units of the new regime are occupying it, including the red guard. This latter lounges about, gets drunk, curses its officers at the top of its lungs, deserts, and steals. Sometimes shooting and fighting between one group of gorillas and another occurs. In saving the library we are of course doing a service to the future school, but I fear that it will be with us for a long time. A characteristic detail: the truck driver tried to steal several books along the way! The conditions offered to us by Turkey are in today's papers; they testify eloquently to our decline: if it is woe to the defeated, then yet more woe to a people that has devastated and betrayed itself. But our peace will be concluded even on these conditions, because none of the gorillas care what it will be like and how the Germans will order us around.

23 [December]. The d. deputies have ordered an accounting of the currency in safe-deposit boxes. There are 25 rubles in mine, left by accident and belonging to Volodia.[221] On account of those 25 rubles, I stood two and a half hours today in a line on Skobelev Square, which should also be called the square of the dog deputies. The line consisted of bourgeois;

---

[218] Pavel Petrovich Malinovskii (1869–1943) was an architect who held the post of people's commissar for properties of the republic.

[219] The Aleksandrovskoe Military School was a large secondary school on Arbat Square that had been founded to prepare young noblemen for service as infantry officers.

[220] See n. 107.

[221] Got'e's son, Vladimir.

a thousand of them, perhaps, went before me. There were many Jews among them. The dominant reaction was irony, and not particularly bitter; people are firmly convinced that things cannot continue as they are for long and that everything will be as before. The attestations were taken by three outrageous wenches, one student of the Commercial Institute, and two worker-comrades, but a young man of intelligentsia appearance, a flyer, very handsome, was in charge. The whole procedure was extremely simplified and elementary; the job was terribly organized—a line, pushing and shoving, illiterate announcements and orders.

In the evening I dined in the English Club; there were quite a few generals in civilian dress (Zaionchkovskii,[222] Nilov[223]) and former people in general. There was a big, passionate game going on. The former people are reserved and well mannered, but in the club they try to distract themselves from woeful thoughts. The bolshevik peace is apparently experiencing some hitches; but I don't have too much confidence in the antibolshevik newspapers: they will all the same conclude a shameless peace and sell Russia to the Germans.

25 [December]. Yesterday and this morning we made the customary preparations for the holiday, but Nina and I thought: there has never been such a terrible Christmas as this one; our spirits plummeted again. We arrived from Mertvyi Pereulok in the evening and lit the small Christmas tree with its few presents; but Volodia had fun, as always. Never before, it seems, have I felt so acutely the revolt, incited by the demagogues and the German betrayers, of the mob of millions against the small nucleus of civilized people in Russia. It will certainly be easier for the Germans to lay their hands on the Russian people when it itself will have destroyed its leaders and again become a blind inert mass, ready for the German smelter.

26 [December]. Today is the second day without news. I was at the Kokoshkins and at M. I. Potulova's[224] in the afternoon; conversations of the

---

[222] General Andrei Medardovich Zaionchkovskii (1862–1926) was an infantry general and military historian who had retired from active service in May 1917. He served in the Red Army from 1919, and later became a professor in the Red Army Military Academy (1922–1926). While serving as a professor, Zaionchkovskii worked as an agent for the Soviet secret police at the same time he was head of the conspiratorial anti-Bolshevik Monarchist Union (The Trust).

[223] Admiral Konstantin Dmitrievich Nilov (1856–1918) was the former aide-de-camp to Nicholas II.

[224] Mariia Ivanovna Potulova taught German at the Usachevsko-Cherniaevskoe girl's school.

usual type. I met Professor Zykov,[225] who told me the following fact: in a psychiatric hospital in Saratov the patients, that is, insane or at least psychologically disturbed people, formed their own committee and union, and there were doctors who supported them. At the Kokoshkins the talk was about prisoners. The story was confirmed that the half-witted female student A. S. Shatskikh, an admirer of Shingarev[226] who had brought him a "little cake," made off with the minutes of the Kadet central committee and gave them to the bolsheviks. How can the party recruit agents among the insane? Or perhaps Shatskikh and the Saratov incident are a true reflection of Russia?

27 [December]. I sat home almost all day today; the triumph of the boorocracy[227] is too evident in the street, and so one's domestic refuge is the best solution on a day off. Tomorrow there will be newspapers after a four-day break; what disgusting news will they bring? Tania told how on the way home she saw a crowd of drunk comrades, led by a woman with an accordion, also drunk—a Muscovite Theroigne de Mericourt.[228] Today A. I. Iakovlev told several interesting things about a certain Logvinskii, a lawyer who had been called up as a lieutenant and had been Ruzskii's adjutant and at the same time an agent of the secret police. He apparently claimed that the affair of the first revolution had been prepared by Buchanan,[229] and that Ruszkii and Chernov had participated in it much more actively than is thought. As for the contemporary situation—it, supposedly, is the threshhold to a step backward. Where is the truth and where the falsehood here?

28 [December]. The newspapers bore us today the order of "supreme commander Krylenko"; he is summoning Russians into a voluntary "socialist guard" for war against the Russian, German, and Anglo-French bourgeoisie, that is, against the whole world. This order convinced me that at the head of what used to be Russia stand genuinely insane people

---

[225] Professor Vladimir Matveevich Zykov was a cancer specialist at the university clinic and a member of the medical faculty.

[226] Andrei Ivanovich Shingarev (1869–1918) was a member of the Kadet central committee who had served as minister of agriculture and then minister of finance in the Provisional Government. Along with F. F. Kokoshkin, Shingarev was hospitalized after his arrest in the November 28 roundup of Kadet leaders in Petrograd and was murdered by Bolshevik sailors in the Mariinskaia hospital on January 7, 1918.

[227] Another of Got'e's coinages: *khamokratiia* in Russian; cf. *kham*, "boor" or "lout."

[228] Theroigne de Mericourt (or de Marcourt) (1762–1817) participated in the taking of the Bastille in 1789 and other dramatic moments in the French Revolution through 1792; she led a band of women during the Terror. Shortly afterward she became insane and was incarcerated in a mental hospital from 1793 until her death.

[229] Sir George Buchanan, the British ambassador.

who belong in a psychiatric hospital. It is clear that nothing will come of this order. What was it published for? Either because its authors are insane, or so that its authors could later say: no one responded to our call, and therefore we must conclude peace with the Germans. Our forces are being removed from Persia, and as a result, former lovers of Christ are devastating Persia—all in the order of things. I frequently recall the words of my late father, that the arbitrariness and dishonesty of the Russians (*arbitraire et malhonnêteté*) undermine any faith in a Russian future; and also the words of M. A. Venevitinov,[230] who said to me in 1898–99 that Russia is heading for a catastrophe of unimaginable proportions. The one died in 1896, the other in 1900. I am distracting myself with the fourth volume of Gershenzon's *Russian Propylaea*, which has just appeared.[231] Under the title, "The Archive of Ogarev," the erudite and honest Jew has dredged up the whole drama of Ogarev, Herzen, and their common wife, Natalia Alekseevna.[232] Real-life drama is always interesting, and the drama of those striking individuals particularly so. I noticed a curious phrase in the diary of N. A. Ogareva: "the children must be protected from Russian life"; how that is true for our day!

29 [December]. Few impressions. The Germans have again put the squeeze on the Russo-yid traitors and fools and are putting them under the yoke. We have just come on foot from Lena R.'s at 11 P.M.—an impression of terror and complete lack of security. Some apparently drunk and overdressed women ran out of the door of the Aleksandrovskoe School, accompanied from within by the laughter of comrades.

30 [December]. A heavy weight on the soul all day, without particular reason. It didn't get lighter even in the theater, where we took Volodia to see *The Sleeping Beauty.* I am ashamed to admit that I even broke into tears from the music. Vava came by in the evening, and reported that all is well in Zagran'e. I read Chaadaev—truthful thoughts about the Russians.

---

[230] Mikhail Alekseevich Venevitinov (1844–1901) was an archaeologist and writer who had been director of the Rumiantsev Museum from 1896 to 1900.

[231] Mikhail Osipovich Gershenzon (1869–1925) was a literary historian and writer. *Russkie propilei* (*Russian Propylaea*) was a literary-cultural miscellany.

[232] The lives of these famous Russian exiles of the mid-nineteenth century are the subject of E. H. Carr's book *The Romantic Exiles* (New York, 1933).

1918

❋

JANUARY

1 January. Neither visits nor newspapers with their bureaucratic good tidings. Yesterday there were new rumors about the abolition of all state loans, inheritances, and so forth. Everyone is upset and yet everyone disbelieves it, or pretends not to believe it. In addition to the fact that it is possible to do anything under the present regime for a bribe, Russian dishonorableness is apparently manifesting itself intensely in the triumphant boorocracy.[1] We greeted the new year at Mertvyi Pereulok, where we also spent the night. I have just returned home; on the paper of one of the wall decrees on a fence I read the following inscription in a "democratic" hand:

> No hour passes without a soviet,
> No day without a decree,
> But there is no bread as yet[2]

Vox populi, vox Dei. But everything is going to ruin all the same, and all will be subjected to the ever more triumphant German: it is no accident that the Russian diplomats, Trotskii and co., "accepted the ultimatum" and continue in Brest to sell the rest of Russia wholesale and retail. And why shouldn't they sell? After all, there is no nation in Russia, nor is there a people. Where is there a single man produced by the revolution? Even those mediocrities of the old days have all disappeared. The SR Kerenskiada did not produce a single man; bolshevism—even less so. More than ever before, the "God-bearing people" is a panurgic herd rushing into the sea. There is no salvation for those who have destroyed themselves. Yesterday the Wilkens told about Georges's journey from Vladivostok to Moscow: there was order only in Manchuria, which is being guarded by the Chinese. They were searched nine times inside the Russian borders. In Perm' the train's passengers narrowly escaped being shot because some commissar who had requisitioned 2,800 rubles from the dining car wanted to shoot the passengers with the help of the militia

---

[1] A Got'e neologism: "khamokratiia." See note 227 for 1917.
[2] "Chto ni chas, to sovet. / Chto ni den', to dekret. / A khleba vse net."

and the red guard. Finally, their engine was stolen once by some soldiers for their "war" train. Where is the escape from this bedlam?

4 January. Rumors once again about abolition of the state loans, which will entail the ruination of persons who are unable to work or who have lost the habit, but who are for the most part civilized people. The "bourgeoisie" especially gave for the liberty loan;[3] now it must suffer as well for having had some money and for having had some germ of conscious patriotism. What will be the fate of all those who put their savings in so-called secure paper? One has to think that all this is a temporary phenomenon, but what crisis will pull us out of the abyss into which we are falling ever deeper; and what will remain of us when that crisis comes?

Along with this there are persistent rumors about the buying up of the Russian birthright: the English, the Americans, the Germans, are buying up land, factories, banks; and when Russia is delivered from the bolshevik nightmare, she will find herself in the power of foreigners. All these days I have been occupied with extracting things from the safe-deposit box. So far, I haven't succeeded, and I doubt that I will succeed in the future, but it did give me the opportunity to visit the bank. There is nothing more terrible than an empty, deserted bank in which former soldiers are holding sway. They gave out the rent allotments in the museum; that is simply amazing; we haven't been bothered at all so far. In Brest, the Germans have given our "delegates" hell for comrade Krylenko's appeal[4] and have used it to be even more merciless with Russia, but the comrade former soldiers are heading home en masse all the same. The stupidity of the Russian people, the most blatant and evident stupidity, which is being exploited by traitors and scoundrels—that is what in

[3] The "liberty loan of 1917," the last consolidated war loan, was issued on March 27, 1917. It was to have paid 5 percent, and to have run for fifty-five years, with redemption by forty-nine annual drawings beginning in 1922. P. N. Apostol, "Credit Operations," in *Russian Public Finance during the War* (New Haven, 1928).

[4] Reference is probably to Commander in Chief Krylenko's appeal of December 29 (January 10, 1918, n.s.) to workers and peasants to form a new people's army for a revolutionary "holy war" against the Russian bourgeoisie and the bourgeoisie of Germany, England, and France. ("Obrashchenie verkhovnogo glavnokomanduiushchego o sozdanii revoliutsionnoi narodno-sotsialisticheskoi armii," 29 dek. 1917 g., I. N. Liubimov, ed., *Revoliutsiia 1917 goda. Khronika sobytii. Tom VI. Oktiabr'-dekabr'* [Moscow, 1930], pp. 468–69.) The appeal was part of the initial Bolshevik response to the Germans' refusal from the outset of the Brest negotiations to give up the territories of the Russian empire they then occupied. On Brest-Litovsk, see J. W. Wheeler-Bennett, *The Forgotten Peace: Brest-Litovsk* (New York, 1939).

Nikolai Vasil'evich Krylenko (1885–1938), a longtime Bolshevik who had been active in the army, was the first Soviet commander in chief, from November 1917 until March 1918. He later became notorious as the chief prosecutor of political cases and as commissar of justice during the great purges. He fell victim to the purges in his turn and perished in 1938.

reality has appeared in the place of the legendary common sense of the Russian people. The newspapers failed to appear again today. The comrades have probably suppressed them because of tomorrow: in Moscow the order of the Soviet of Workers' Deputies forbidding demonstrations on the 5th in support of the all-national saloon and a proclamation calling everybody into the street on that day are hanging together on fences and walls. Shooting is expected. What will really happen? And if blood is spilled, what will it have been spilled for? For a chimera, for the abstract concept of the Constituent Assembly, for a utopia thought up by Russian doctrinaires.

5 [January]. Despite the demonstration, which did take place, the entire day failed to provide me with any new impressions. I sat home all day, worked a lot, and it was as if nothing was happening outside the house. They say that something could happen today in Petersburg. I don't particularly believe that, and I don't even know if it should be wished for, since the return of sr domination and the rule of the all-national saloon are not the way out of the situation.

6 [January]. The all-national saloon opened yesterday; the president is Chernov. The bolsheviks left the hall in the very first session, so a conflict is probably inevitable. They say the srs have decided not to leave the Tauride Palace and not to decide the issue of "authority," but to work at the promulgation of laws that will bring the love of the people, and then overthrow the bolsheviks—these are the "laws" "on peace," "on land," and the like. The struggle will begin, most likely, with the disbanding of the saloon and the proclaiming of the Congress of Soviets as a constituent assembly. They say that if they are victorious, the srs want to proclaim a presidium of the Russian republic consisting of Gots,[5] Minor, and Avksent'ev,[6] and to entrust the ministry to Rudnev. A sorry leadership!

So far I haven't succeeded in finding out anything definite about yesterday's happenings in Moscow. Apparently there was shooting, there were killed and wounded, but I don't know anything about the general mood or how many victims there were.

We had lunch at Savin's in the company of Bogoslovskii, Egorov, Kot-

---

[5] Abram Rafailovich Gots (1882–1940) was a prominent sr, member of the sr central committee, leader of the sr faction in the Petrograd soviet, and chairman of the first All-Russian Executive Committee of Soviets in 1917. He was an active opponent of the Bolsheviks during the October revolution.

[6] Nikolai Dmitrievich Avksent'ev (1878–1943) was an sr leader, a member of the executive committee of the Petrograd soviet, and chairman of the first All-Russian Executive Committee of Peasant Soviets. He was minister of internal affairs in the Provisional Government in June–July, and chairman of the preparliament in October. He emigrated in 1918.

liarevskii, N. V. Speranskii, and others. We talked a lot, all about the same thing. Apparently no one sees a way out. We talked of the university, whose economic situation is just as hopeless as the situation of Russia. What awaits us in the days to come; how will the latest outbursts and conflicts affect the university? It is clear that in the twilight of scanty Russian culture its propagators will not flourish.

7 *[January]*. The murder of Kokoshkin and Shingarev marked the entire day today.[7] They were killed while patients in hospital. It seems there is no reason to doubt this, and this at a time when they are giving freedom to the Beletskiis, Kurlovs, and their ilk.[8] What is going on here? Yesterday even more terrifying rumors were circulated about new murders and fighting in Petersburg, but they still require verification.

8 *[January]*. The murder of Kokoshkin and Shingarev has, alas, been confirmed; the other rumors about murders—no. The poor all-national saloon was dispersed after twenty-four hours of existence; and why should that saloon have existed, when all of Russia is a saloon, literally and figuratively. Sad news from Zagran'e. On the 28th of December the drunk citizens of Zaprud'e broke into our house and carried off two of my brother's guns. The first step has been taken; the rest will go along a beaten path. It is sad, although I expected it; it is sad that we won't be able to live in a Russian village, that we won't be able to raise Volodia in his native countryside.

Bolshevik manifestations are expected tomorrow; provisions are being stored up in anticipation of a new state of siege in Moscow. How tragically Kokoshkin died; he perished on the day of the existence of that very Constituent Assembly whose law he wrote; and that is a symbol of fallen Russia and of the failure of her revolution. The bank strike continues.[9] The city water system is beginning to fall apart—perhaps that is a result of the engineers' strike. The professors' deliberations at the council were saddening. It was decided to take contributions in the clinics from the

---

[7] See n. 226 for 1917. Kokoshkin and Shingarev were slain in their beds on January 7, 1918, by a band of men consisting mainly of Bolshevik sailors. The motivation and ultimate responsibility for their murders have never been established.

[8] Stepan Petrovich Beletskii (1873–1918), former director of the department of police (1912–1914), and assistant minister of internal affairs (1915–1916), had a reputation for activities on the far right, ties with Rasputin, and the like. He was shot by the Bolsheviks on September 5, 1918. Pavel Grigor'evich Kurlov (1860–1923) was assistant minister of internal affairs and director of the corps of gendarmes, 1909–1911. He was reappointed assistant minister by Protopopov on the eve of the revolution.

[9] Bank employees had gone on strike to protest the nationalization of all banks, which was decreed on December 14, 1917. "Dekret VTSiK o natsionalizatsii bankov," *Dekrety Sovetskoi vlasti, tom I. 25 oktiabria 1917 g.–16 marta 1918 g.* (Moscow, 1957), p. 230.

wounded or from someone standing behind them (the bolshevik city council?) for temporary support of the hospital. They have backed off from the Catherine Hospital altogether; they have decided to ignore the bolshevik government; i.e., not to correspond with it. That is perhaps the right thing to do, because if it gets entrenched it will ruin the universities all the same. Nevertheless, all the discussions about whether or not to write documents to Lunacharskii are nothing but a hollow threat.

9 *[January]*. It is now evening and, it seems, the demonstration of the bolsheviks came off more or less satisfactorily; however, there were episodes of shooting and one of them even had consequences for me: I was searched for the first time today. We went to V. E. Kokoshkina's in the morning; Vladimir Fedorovich had left for Petersburg; afterwards I was at the memorial service for the victims, and on leaving there I saw the march of the zamoskvoretskie[10] demonstrators. The sight of the red guard is terrifying: a crowd of workers of the usual type, sullen faces, are marching on order; they yelled hurrah to someone, also on order; red flags, as always, with slogans that were to be seen already in the spring; a great many adolescents, apparently completely corrupted—in a word, nothing special; it is just as everything should be in Russian social-hooliganism. An exchange of gunfire began as I was approaching home from there. It turned out the activity was on the Mokhovaia, opposite the building that is rented out by the museum. According to Nikitiuk,[11] whom I met an hour later, the first shot rang out from an unknown source, and the members of this crowd began to shoot at each other, with the result that, according to him, there were as many as one hundred killed and wounded. At 2 P.M. I accompanied Uncle Eduard from our place to the Vozdvizhenka,[12] and coming back along Vagan'kovskii[13] I was stopped by two red guard comrades and searched—in a polite way, incidentally. Going as far as the gates of the museum, I met Nikitiuk, who told me all that is written above. The heart aches again today from today's demonstration, yesterday's letters from Zagran'e, and the murder of Kokoshkin and Shingarev. One feels that everything is getting worse with every day that passes. The only way out in the future may be a German prince, installed with the help of the Germans, *um die russischen Schweine zu frischen*.[14]

Yesterday I again read Custine and truly I find that this derogatory

---

[10] That is, from the working-class district across the river to the south of the Kremlin.

[11] Vsevolod Stanislavovich Nikitiuk was bursar of the Rumiantsev Museum.

[12] Presently part of Kalinin Prospect, not far from the museum.

[13] Also known as Malyi Trekhgornyi Pereulok.

[14] Got'e apparently invests the German verb *frischen* with the meaning of the similar Russian verb *svezhevat'* "to skin or dress": "In order to skin the Russian pig."

foreigner's account contains much that is accurate; for example (IV, 72), La Russie, puissante chez elle, redoutable tant qu'elle ne luttera qu'avec des populations asiatiques, se brisera contre l'Europe. That is a veritable prophecy.[15]

10 [January]. Upon checking, it turned out that there were three killed on the Mokhovaia, and maybe three killed and wounded in all. It is characteristic that the demonstrators, panicking, broke out the plate-glass window in the Krasil'shchikov house opposite the Rumiantsev Museum and took cover there from the shooting. Few impressions or news for the day.

11 [January]. A new unpleasantness today: a proposition has appeared from the Union of Employees of State Institutions to receive salary for three months in advance and to go on strike with all the other institutions. A general strike is expected in a few days. I stand by the point of view that we (the Rumiantsev Museum) are an institution that must be preserved and must in no case take part in politics.

According to Nina, the memorial service in the Cathedral of the Savior for Shingarev and Kokoshkin was very majestic and crowded. In other respects, the day brought nothing new; still the same situation, without prospects or any hope ahead, amid universal disintegration and ruin. I am convinced that the bolsheviks will hold on for a very long time, because there is no one to take their place, with the sole exception of the foreigners, who must first make peace among themselves.

13 [January]. Yesterday was a sad and sorrowful St. Tat'iana's Day.[16] There has never been one like it before; I was in the university church with the feeling that it was perhaps for the last time. Afterwards I sat in the professors' meeting, where they talked with sadness and bitterness about the usual: about the new affronts of the clinic employees; about dealing with the bolsheviks; about the sad future of the poor university. One felt that we are all some kind of doomed men. In the museum, its own worries: on the one hand, the question of a strike was again discussed, although everyone generally accepts my point of view that we must not participate in the struggle of parties; on the other, we have to ask for money and protection from the bolsheviks, and in the first place we must shut the mouths of the boorish and bloodthirsty employees. It

---

[15] "Russia, powerful at home and formidable so long as she fights with Asian peoples, will shatter herself against Europe." See George F. Kennan, *The Marquis de Custine and His "Russia in 1839"* (Princeton, 1971).

[16] "Tat'ianin den'," January 12, was the anniversary of the founding of Moscow University.

became known today (from Prince Golitsyn's meeting with Mr. Malinov-skii) that the bolsheviks are preparing wage supplements for the louts, and perhaps for the auxiliary employees as well. But then our auxiliary ladies became agitated: could they accept raises from the bolsheviks? Things are going from bad to worse in the general situation—the civil war in the south and the Ukraine has led to the proclamation of the latter's independence and to a separate pact between the Ukraine and the Germans and, finally, to the open declaration of the Germans that they will not clear out of the Russian lands because the population of the ter-ritories they have occupied do not wish to experience the blessings of the Russian revolution. Thus the Russian tower of Babel leads to the reali-zation of all the German designs on the east.

14 [January]. The Russian revolution has one inherently characteristic feature—*stupidity*, carried to the extreme; everything in it has been stu-pid, from the formation of the first provisional government, hanging in the air, to the bolshevik peace negotiations. And a second feature is imi-tation of the stupidity of others: whatever and wherever it may turn up, nowadays any stupidity finds its imitators, and the wave of imitative stu-pidity is rolling toward complete and final absurdity.

15 [January]. A day without newspapers and with a small quantity of rumors; an extremely oppresive frame of mind, all the same. I saw V. F. Kokoshkin; that ebullient man is completely downtrodden and dispir-ited, and, in truth, he has cause to be. His impressions from Petrograd: there everyone is even more dispirited than here. The blacks, led by A. A. Vyrubova,[17] are playing some kind of role, but what kind is not clear to him. I have received information in the last few days from other sources as well that these forces are doing something. But to what degree are all these forces, those and others, organized? Isn't it simpler to think that everything is happening spontaneously, without plan and with a complete absence of any kind of organization, like everything in Russia?

17 [January]. The proclamation of Ukrainian independence is the apoth-eosis of the stupidity of the Russian tribe and of the Austro-German abil-ity to finish off in one way or another that stupid and unhappy nation; it is the furthest step of Russian dissolution. But if you take their point of view, they are perhaps right: for it is better to become the slave of the

---

[17] Anna Aleksandrovna Vyrubova (née Taneeva, b. 1884) was lady-in-waiting to the Empress Alexandra and her close confidante. Among other things, Vyrubova served as a contact between the imperial family and Rasputin. She emigrated to Finland in 1920. Her memoirs have been published in English translation: *Memories of the Russian Court* (New York, 1923).

civilized Germans than the slave of the benighted bolsheviks. The comrades have left for Brest in search of a shameful peace. Yesterday I was in a cinematographic studio for the first time and there forgot for a little while about all the dismay that is crushing and oppressing me.

18 [January]. Today I reached the firm conclusion that the bolsheviks are going to remain in power for a very long time. Evidence of this is the compromise of the bank employees, who are yielding to the bolsheviks and going back to work; the collapse of the strike of the finance-administration employees and of the city teachers; and the wavering of the cossacks. Today I heard the opinion from some former people that the war of bolshevism must sweep over all of Russia, and that something can grow again, perhaps, only on her ashes. I began to give lectures at the Higher Women's Courses; there were few auditors, but they were all the same ones as before; you ask yourself, what is it all for?

19 [January]. Today the bolshevik commissar of the "properties of the republic," the architect Malinovskii, discussed the budget of the Rumiantsev Museum for 1918 with us. The new boss was extremely polite; we had jacked up the budget to a sum of nearly a million, and he pared off much less, and that more politely, than the bygone imperial Petersburg bureaucrats. But I thought the while that he and we are like the Roman oracles, who must laugh when they are sincere. It is all a meaningless affair, and on our side, if we must participate in such talks, it is only for the active defense of our museum. The bolsheviks also sent the artist Oranovskii[18]—a complete fool and probably malicious as well; at the end of the meeting he raised the question of whether it wasn't possible to put all the temporary employees on the permanent staff and abolish the term "wage workers."

The Poles have annexed Mogilev province to Poland, but the bolsheviks say they have taken Kiev and that the Ukrainian regiments have gone over to their side. Things are getting worse by the hour. There is news of some kind of movements in Germany; of course, all this is blown up and can have no significance, but it would be good all the same if the Germans were to cut each other up a bit. I had the visit of the Franco-Italian Malfitano,[19] member of the Institut Pasteur and member of the Entendement Réciproque mission, which has been sojourning in former Russia since July. Their immediate aim is expansion of the French institute in Petrograd and establishment of a Russian institute in Paris. Oh, if only something were to come of this!

[18] E. V. Oranovskii was at this time assistant commissar for the properties of the republic.

[19] P. Malfitano was a scientist and permanent member of the Institut Pasteur in Paris.

21 [January]. There was no big news yesterday and today. Yesterday I arranged a discussion and meeting of historians with Malfitano. He is a reserved person, but much more sympathetic the second time. He turns out to be from Syracuse, and when I learned that, my trip to Sicily came to the surface; it seems he was touched by my enthusiasm, and I recalled old times and got an overpowering urge to visit Italy once more. The wave of bolshevism is rolling across all of Russia. I ascribe no significance to the German strike, but it is a fact that could have definite consequences. Oh, if only a general peace could be brought nearer! Perhaps it would hasten our pacification.

22 [January]. The paper *The Lantern* printed the documents that were published earlier in *Azov Territory*[20] concerning the German money that Lenin, Trotskii, and co. received from Germany for their "enterprise." Of course, all this was already known earlier, but a document always has a special power and weight. But did the Germans attain in Russia only what they wanted, or did matters take a somewhat different turn, not entirely desirable for them? We will know that in the next few months, depending on whether the Germans continue to support anarchy or try to establish order. Will they be able to do the latter? That will depend on the turn of affairs in the West. The centralizing efforts of the bolsheviks in Little Russia[21] and their position toward Rumania are not likely to suit the Germans either. And so Russia was sold, or perhaps more correctly bought, for less than thirty pieces of silver. What kind of nation is this that allows such experiments to be performed on itself? Is it worth talking about? One has to notice the intensification of the depressed mood among civilized people in the last few days: unconscious hopes for the rapid collapse of bolshevism have not been realized; the monetary situation is getting progressively worse—here is the source of the growing demoralization in society.

23 [January]. Today's newspapers brought less news than I thought they would. The effectiveness of the "decree" on the separation of church and state will depend on how it is carried out; I think, however, that only a certain amount of persecution can return our church and priests, who have grown fat and forgotten God, to a sense of their responsibilities, to the elevation of the church in general. Nevertheless, the procession of the cross in Petrograd apparently produced an impression on the bolsheviks.

[20] *Fonar'* (*The Lantern*) was a nonparty newspaper that appeared irregularly in Moscow in 1917 and 1918 (last issue: March 12, 1918). *Priazovskii krai* (*Azov Territory*) was a Rostov/Don daily newspaper, 1891–1918.

[21] "Malorossiia" was the traditional Russian name for the Ukraine. In Got'e's time, its use instead of "Ukraina" may have implied disparagement.

The movement in Germany remains unclear. I hear satisfaction on all sides over the dispersal of the Rada—and I share it to some extent myself; the question is, how do the Germans look at it. That should show up in connection with the bolsheviks' conclusion of a shameful peace—that is, in the next few days. One more basic feature of the Russian revolution is universal laziness and abstention from work; because of that we refused to fight and find ourselves without bread or transportation. The gorillas will go to work only when they have really "had their fill of hunger." Today the building committee invited the prosecutor of the Mogilev Court, Prince Iu. D. Urusov, to manage the house, with the consent of M. M. Petrovo-Solovovo.[22]

24 [January]. Today was a day without any particular news. Malfitano, Savin, and Iakovlev were here in the evening. We agreed that a small committee that could maintain permanent relations with the corresponding French organization should be set up in Moscow. Such was the practical side of the matter. What will come of it, I don't know, perhaps nothing; I am taking it up as a means of widening my weak ties with foreigners, with France in particular. I am doing this with the conscious thought that perhaps all this will be of use on the dark day when it becomes necessary to flee Russia. With business finished, we simply began to chat. He [Malfitano] proved to be a very agreeable partner in conversation, who recounted a lot about Mechnikov,[23] about his passion for the Russians, about his misadventures during the war. We tried to illuminate for him the situation in Russia from our point of view as historians. He seems to have listened attentively. N. P. Kiselev[24] had returned from Pieter and told us that the mood there was even more downtrodden than in Moscow and that no prospects are in sight there. And yet there are still optimists. What are they hoping for?

26 [January]. Little new for these two days. Everyone is saying that the goat of revolution will break its horns against the church wall. Is it so? Does the Orthodox Church have the strength to withstand persecution? I fear that it does not, and that autocracy, and Orthodoxy, and Russian

[22] The owner of Got'e's apartment house, Mariia Mikhailovna Petrovo-Solovovo (1858–1940), belonged to a well-placed noble family of Tambov province and was a maid of honor at the imperial court.

[23] Il'ia Il'ich Mechnikov (1845–1916), was one of the most famous of Russian scientists, a comparative pathologist and embryologist who received the Nobel Prize in 1909. Mechnikov was a product of the passionate scientism of the 1860s, a thoroughgoing positivist and materialist who chose a strictly scientific career. He emigrated from Russia in 1888 and spent the rest of his life as a member of the Institut Pasteur in Paris.

[24] Nikolai Petrovich Kiselev (1884–1965) was a historian of the book and editor on the staff of the Rumiantsev Museum.

nationality[25] are all a bluff, one like the other. Everything around remains in a decrepit state and in expectation of some kind of providential changes, which will probably never come, or will come when all hopes have long since disappeared.

27 [January]. Today they at last published the "decree" on the "annulment" of [state] loans; although all will of course change again, nevertheless it made a heavy impression on me—so many people thrown out on the street, and all of them people who lived as creditors of the state and did no harm to anyone. Was this really done *de bonne foi,* or intentionally in order to disenchant [people] with socialism? Really, if you look at it optimistically and with a sense of humor, it is possible that this is so—to wean socialistically inclined Russia from its fantasies. I am dismayed for my wife's parents: to work hard for so many years and then relax at last, less than a year ago, and now their entire situation is again in question. I do not believe today's news about an offensive by Alekseev; that would be too good, and everything good is too far from reality. The peace negotiations are being stretched out. The movement in Germany has stopped, but it seems the German subsidized press is beginning to vilify the bolsheviks.

28 [January]. There was a procession of the cross in Moscow today. Unfortunately, we didn't see it; they say there were many people; we don't know the details yet. I didn't go because my anthropophobia is progressing and because this morning I had "the ass's millstone" around my neck.[26] Afterward, we had a visit from A. A. Kizevetter, who told us an interesting thing: representatives from the delegation of Mirbach and Keyserlingk[27] have come to Moscow for talks with our captains of industry, in an attempt to obtain their sympathy for the cause of peace; they

[25] "Samoderzhavie, pravoslavie, i russkaia narodnost'" are the three elements of the conservative statist doctrine sometimes known as "official nationality," which was first expounded (without the adjective "Russian") by Nicholas I's minister of enlightenment, S. S. Uvarov, in 1833. See Nicholas V. Riasanovsky, *Nicholas I and Official Nationality in Russia, 1825–1855* (Berkeley, 1959).

[26] "... Na shee byl 'zhernov osel'skii'." That is, he was greatly burdened. In the Slavonic Bible, the upper, movable, millstone is called "the ass's millstone."

[27] Count Wilhelm von Mirbach was head of a German delegation to Petrograd in late December 1917; he was later appointed German ambassador in Moscow and was assassinated there on July 6, 1918, by a Left SR, Iakov Bliumkin, in an attempt to provoke resumption of hostilities between Russia and Germany. Walther Freiherr von Keyserlingk, a rear admiral, was chief of the operations group in the German admiralty. He was a member of the Mirbach delegation to Petrograd and head of its naval mission. Winfried Baumgart, *Deutsche Ostpolitik 1918. Von Brest-Litovsk bis zum Ende des Ersten Weltkrieges* (Vienna, 1966).

said they know the bolsheviks are only foam that will disappear, and that they would like to get talks under way with the substance of Russian society. Apparently peace with the bolsheviks does not appear reliable to them and does not satisfy them. That is interesting, but what will those devils do to remove the current lords of the Russian land? S. D. Kuchin arrived today from Kiev; he made his way through Sarny, Luninets, and Briansk. From his account, the situation in Kiev is similar to that of Moscow between October 28 and November 3; the bolsheviks are getting the upper hand because the hired red guards, who, it turns out, have been gotten drunk, are easily defeating the Ukrainian soldiers, who have disintegrated no less than ours, are quite unreliable, and seek only to "pack it in."[28] There you have the secret of the bolshevik victories.

30 [January]. My brother arrived—a liquidated person, but he looks at things optimistically. Yesterday we were in the Bolshoi Theater for one of the last performances in the loge that we had reserved for the season, but that it will be impossible to keep in any case. Triumphant louts from among the soldiers' deputies were sitting in the imperial loge—it was disgusting and revolting. Yesterday there was also the University Council. Our professors (I speak at least of the dominant group) are great ideologues: they persist in their nonrecognition of the bolshevik government and don't even want to answer the thus-far polite inquiries from the former ministry. The news arrived today that Trotskii and co. did not conclude peace in Brest, but proclaimed the war ended. This was done either by agreement with the Germans, in which case it is a fig leaf, or as an act of shameless bravado vis-à-vis the Germans. In either case, the Germans' hands are untied and they can do anything they please with former Russia. To end a war so shamefully constitutes an event without historical precedent.

31 [January]. I am taking a bromide to try to preserve my mental equilibrium. All the talk is about Mr. Trotskii's notorious "peace." In the majority of cases, judgments are identical to mine; the possibility of new, dizzying events is opening up, events that could produce the most unexpected results. I think this event constitutes some kind of turning point in the bolshevik yoke, but I still don't know what kind. The bolsheviks, in any case, continue to strangle the petty bourgeoisie—today there was a decree about a new, third levy of income tax, this time for the benefit of the dog deputies. Even with the best of intentions, there is nothing to pay it with. I am trying to convince myself and Nina that we should sell and liquidate everything, no matter how sad it is to part with the memory

[28] *Vtikati*: cf. Ukrainian *tikaty*, "to flee."

of an entire life past. There was another meeting with Malfitano; we worked out the text of an "appel" for mutual understanding.

FEBRUARY

1 OR *14*, I don't know; for the time being I will write both dates.[29] I am prepared to welcome this first sensible change to be introduced by the bolsheviks. Today we pawned our silver, which was lying in the loan agency for safekeeping; it seemed to us that it is better to get something for pawning it, because it is impossible to keep it at home, and if you leave it there without a loan you can expect it to be confiscated. It became apparent that the loan agency is currently the scene of action exclusively of bourgeois, who are pawning what little remains to them. The peace concluded by the Rada and not concluded by the bolsheviks is producing a big impression; all kinds of evil is spoken and foreseen about it, since the Germans will make Little Russia the object of their desires.

16 [February]. Today I heard from Manuilov that the comrade typesetters have announced that on the question of holidays they stand on the side of the church council; there the Russian shows himself in his true colors.[30] They say that Metropolitan Vladimir and General Ivanov have been killed in Kiev; it will be interesting to see if tomorrow's newspapers confirm this.[31] I began to give lectures at the university; to my surprise, the lecture took place, although with a very small number of auditors. There is general recognition that the bolsheviks are installed for a long time; they grow everywhere stronger.

17 [February]. Today Iakovlev invited S. P. Bartenev and his son V. S.[32] for *bliny*[33]; [the younger Bartenev] was kept on by us at the University for his good offices with the bolsheviks. The Bartenevs are collaborating and from this point of view represent an interesting phenomenon. We talked a lot about tactics for the present day. The opinion predominated

[29] On February 1, old style, the Bolshevik government adopted the Gregorian calendar for Russia, shifting the date ahead to February 14.

[30] That is, they were in favor of a great many holidays from work. On the church council, see John S. Curtiss, *The Russian Church and the Soviet State, 1917–1950* (Boston, 1953).

[31] Metropolitan Vladimir of Kiev was killed on January 25/February 7 in the Pecherskaia Lavra (Monastery) by a band of men. The rumor about the death of General Ivanov was false.

[32] Sergei Petrovich Bartenev (1863–1930) was a pianist and professor of music in the Moscow Nikolaevskii Institute.

[33] That is, Russian pancakes, shrovecakes.

that collaboration is the best solution. What was written today about Kiev exceeds all expectations and likelihood. The murder of Metropolitan Vladimir has exonerated his shady past; the suicide of Kaledin is a nightmare.[34]

18 [February]. The affair on the Don is ending; bolshevism is triumphing there, too, and perhaps the victory over the poor Russian generals and officers without soldiers will be more decisive and more solid than that over the crafty Ukrainians who, led by the cunning scoundrel Hrushevsky, have gone to the Germans for help.[35] A war also looms with the deceived and embittered Rumanians, to whom the Russians themselves have given the opportunity to take from Russia everything the Germans didn't allow them to take from Austria. In the museum they have set up a labor union of all employees and have elected Prince Golitsyn as its chairman. Its task: self-protection and getting raises for the boors. Pray God that we haven't miscalculated in this affair.

It was reported in the evening newspapers that the SRs celebrated the memory of Kaliaev on February 4.[36] Those gathered in the large auditorium of Shaniavskii University wept for "the poet-revolutionary who refused commutation for fear that the party would suffer morally." The old fool grandpa Minor "presented" to those present Kaliaev's brother, who "was so moved that he fainted." Poor Russia, you are still far from recuperating.

19 [February]. It has happened. The Germans have renewed the war; apparently they have already taken Dvinsk and will take Hapsal.[37] The Swedes, who are intervening for the Finland white guards—that is, for the civilized Swedes—are advancing on Torneo and have taken the Aaland Islands. The bolsheviks have ceased the demobilization and are

---

[34] General Aleksei Maksimovich Kaledin (1861–1918) was a cavalry general and Don Cossack ataman. He was commander of the Don Cossack troops that fought the Bolsheviks in the first phase of the Civil War. With the military and political collapse of the first anti-Bolshevik coalition, he shot himself (on January 30/February 12) rather than join the retreat from Novocherkassk to the Kuban. See Peter Kenez, *Civil War in South Russia, 1918* (Berkeley, 1971).

[35] The Red Army had taken Kiev on January 24/February 8, 1918. It remained in control of Kiev for about three weeks before it was driven out by the Rada with the help of the Central Powers.

[36] Ivan Platonovich Kaliaev (1877–1905) was a member of the terrorist Battle Organization of the SR party; he participated in the assassination of the minister of internal affairs, V. K. Pleve, in 1904 and of the Grand Duke Sergei Aleksandrovich (governor general of Moscow and Nicholas II's uncle) in 1905. He was apprehended and executed on October 5, 1905. February 4 was the anniversary of the grand duke's assassination.

[37] On the Baltic coast.

making summons to a holy war. It's late for that. As ye have sown, so shall ye reap. The just fruits of immorality. The people they have corrupted has perished, and nothing can arouse it to a love of motherland, which in the genuine sense it never had. A new page of the Russian time of troubles has been turned, and it is one of the most woeful; the God-bearing nation, alas, has sunken even deeper into the cesspool.

21 [February]. The bolsheviks are asking the Germans for peace, but the Germans are advancing and taking over the unhappy Russian land. Now they can do anything they want. But what do they want? To again wring from the bolsheviks favorable conditions, even more favorable than at Brest? Or do they want to get rid of them because they don't need them for the disintegration of Russia, which has reached the limit, and because a hotbed of Pugachevshchina extending over the entire territory of the former Russian Empire cannot be tolerated from the point of view of Western Europe? Such an infection cannot help but influence Europe as well. It is in the Germans' direct interest to restore an abbreviated Russia in the form of a monarchy and to hold sway in it, as before Alexander III.

If it is to be the first, that is, bartering with the bolsheviks, then we civilized people will have it even worse than it has been; and if it is the second, then that means we face new trials such as we have not seen before. The rule of the Germans, a possible German occupation: realistically that means the heel of the conqueror, insults, the contempt of the white for the colored, of the German for the Russian swine—but also, in all likelihood, restoration of the old mechanism, the integrity of savings, establishment of order. Morally that would be the collapse of everything; but I have already suffered over and mourned Russia, such as I imagined her and wished to see her. From my point of view, everything here is in the past, however lackluster that past may have been. Bolshevism, as an experiment in socialist Pugachevshchina, is so savage and oppressive that even the domination of the mailed German fist seems a lesser evil than the rampage of the Russian gorillas. It is terrible to admit this, even to oneself. But the fall of the Russian pogromists[38] is surely inevitable, so better it should come soon. But what of the national honor? Shame? Why, it is impossible to even associate those concepts with a people that has violated and sold itself, that hasn't even found it necessary to preserve its way of life.

22 [February]. Events are unfolding along the same course; the Germans have taken Minsk and, it seems, Polotsk. What will they undertake fur-

---

[38] That is, wreakers of havoc and pillage.

ther? The dull indifference of the Moscow public astonishes me: people are coming and going, amusing themselves; all the theaters are operating; nothing touches, nothing galvanizes these masses, in spite of the hysterical screams of the people's commissars that the "socialist fatherland is in danger." The term is a fantasy! Through the supreme command the idiots are issuing a summons to fight against the Germans behind their backs in partisan detachments. They are preparing to proclaim some kind of mobilization. Today I heard one young soldier, undoubtedly a bolshevik, say to another: "We'll see who carries out their orders." And a chambermaid or seamstress, reading the hysterical appeal, said: "Phew, how they have begun to shriek!" No, the murdered remains, or rather germs, of patriotism cannot be resurrected, especially by their murderers. I learned today of the unexpected, senseless death of my student A. Ia. Liutsh, an able, good young man who would have made an honest and conscientious academic worker. An ulcer in the stomach at the age of twenty-four. When I was told this I couldn't recover from the horror of it for a long time, despite the fact that nowadays it seems we have grown callous toward everything.

24 [February]. Poor Liutsh was buried yesterday; we escorted him to the cemetery, and I somehow couldn't believe that this modest, conscientious young man no longer exists. I haven't had very many students altogether, but Liutsh was entirely my student, and I hated to lose him just because this was my—genuinely my—student. I don't know what he would have made of himself, perhaps most likely something very modest. With all his abilities and undoubted giftedness, he was stubborn and a bit of an ideologue and fantasizer. He didn't want to concentrate on scholarly preparation, and in the space of two years he barely prepared two master's subjects. He was attracted by many subjects—recently, for example, by teaching in the Poltoratskie Courses.[39] There was much of the artist in him; he was attracted by music and by science. Judging by his conversations, he was able to take great pleasure in life, in spite of the more than modest living conditions in which he had been placed. But on the other hand, there was enormous conscientiousness in him, a fact explainable by his not entirely Russian blood. Whatever he undertook, he carried through; and he allowed himself to be epicurean after a fashion only in matters in which he owed responsibility to himself alone. He was an excellent worker in the museum, where he was valued and where he, almost alone in recent months, retained his ability to work. And here such a person dies from a stomach ulcer at twenty-four. We escorted him

[39] Vysshie zhenskie kursy uchrezhd. V. A. Poltoratskoi, one of the several higher women's courses in Moscow.

to the Piatnitskoe Cemetery, and after the burial went over to see the grave of Granovskii,[40] who rests in the Westernizers' corner together with N. Stankevich, Ketcher, Korsh, M. S. Shchepkin, and A. N. Afanas'ev, the great uncle of my Liutsh.[41]

The bolsheviks have accepted Germany's ultimatum; the terms are even harsher, but the bolsheviks will not be in a position to fulfill them: cessation of propaganda, removal of their troops from the Ukraine and demobilization not only of the white but of the red army as well. That means forswearing an intensification of the revolution, and they don't want that nor can they do it. There is much in their terms that the Germans will be able to play on, to play with the bolsheviks like a cat with a mouse. But having concluded peace, the bolsheviks will nevertheless hold on for some time; their calculation is based on that; let Russia perish, but long live the socialist republic. And they can be proud. They have ruined Russia, or completed its ruin, following in the footsteps of Nicholas II, L'vov, the Kadets, and Kerenskii. The shameful fools, may they all be cursed by the judgment of history. We were returning home just now and saw a drunk democrat, leaning against a lamp post and yelling: "Let Lenin and Trotskii shoot me, the accursed devils." And I am ready to repeat the same thing. A curse on those murderers of Russia; a curse on the Russian intelligentsia, which has brought the nation to the state it is in. And the reactionary bureaucracy has learned nothing: N. P. Muratov[42] dined today at Mertvyi Pereulok and talked such nonsense that I even protested; it is impermissible, after all, to blame the Decembrists for contemporary events.[43] Yesterday I learned from several sources, so there can be no doubts, that of a million and a half in contri-

---

[40] Timofei Nikolaevich Granovskii (1813–1855) was a leading figure among the Russian "Westernizers" of the 1840s. He was professor of world history at Moscow University (1839–1855), where he propounded a liberal Hegelian view of history. On Granovskii and the other Westernizers, see Andrzej Walicki, *A History of Russian Thought From the Enlightenment to Marxism* (Stanford, 1979).

[41] Nikolai Vladimirovich Stankevich (1813–1840) was a leading figure among the young Russian Hegelians of the 1830s. Nikolai Khristoforovich Ketcher (1809–1886) was a member of the Stankevich circle and the Russian translator of Shakespeare. See Edward J. Brown, *Stankevich and his Moscow Circle* (Stanford, 1966). Evgenii Fedorovich Korsh (1810–1897), a member of Herzen's circle, was a journalist, editor, and translator who also served as a librarian at the Rumiantsev Museum. Mikhail Semenovich Shchepkin (1788–1863) is generally considered to have been the greatest actor in the history of the Russian theater. Aleksandr Nikolaevich Afanas'ev (1826–1871), an archivist, writer, and editor, was famous as a student of Russian folklore.

[42] Nikolai Pavlovich Muratov (b. 1861) was a former governor of Tambov and Kursk provinces (1906–1915).

[43] The Decembrists were noble officers involved in the attempted *coup d'état* of December 1825. See Anatole G. Mazour, *The First Russian Revolution, 1825* (Stanford, 1961).

butions collected by the strike committee of city employees, one million has been stolen. One can go no further.

25 [February]. A bunch of scum consisting of Jew-internationalists, people without a fatherland, without honor, without law, crazed gorillas from the Russian workers and former soldiers, numbering 227, by a majority of 116 to 85 with 26 abstaining, have decided the fate of Russia and agreed to the German terms. The Germans have succeeded in taking Pskov, Reval, and Borisov. So go events in the Russian land. What will happen next—there is the fateful question you ask yourself every day, every minute. The game is not over; the bolsheviks have reason to show confusion and uncertainty about tomorrow. Malinovskii told Vinogradov that they don't know if they will still be commissars in a few days. I think they will be, and that they will hold on for some time yet.

27 [February]. Events are piling up. The Germans are headed for Petrograd without a doubt, and I think they will get there. As for Moscow—that is not clear. Lots of people are already reckoning on their arrival. They say, incidentally, that German agents are energetically buying up Russian bonds. Undoubtedly all of former Russia will be under the German heel; they are already casting lots for her clothing. One feels dismay, sadness, and shame for everyone and for the whole revoltingly savage nation. You catch yourself hating the bolsheviks more than Germanism.

28 [February]. Everything is continuing along the same path, although I think the fate of Petrograd will not be decided so soon—maybe in a week or even later. The question of Moscow will be drawn out. The worst would be if all the scum show up in Moscow and exhibit themselves in all their loveliness. It was saddening and painful today to lecture on the theory of the Slavophiles. What profound error; how mistaken were those fine men, dreaming of a brilliant future for a country that expired like the old alcoholic in one of Zola's novels—set fire to and burned up without a trace. Uncle Eduard and Malfitano were over in the evening. We had a good talk; Malfitano is a dreamer and soothes us in our grief.

MARCH

1 March. For some reason I have a terrible weight on my soul today. It will be awful if the Germans come, and awful if the bolsheviks remain. This is an insoluble dilemma, although intellectually one can imagine fairly clearly that only an external force can kick out the bolsheviks. The Germans have stopped temporarily after having penetrated quite far; what for?—in order to consolidate their position, or in order to seize Petersburg with their next leap?

There was a meeting of the building committee in the evening. I had not attended for a long time; but one should go—the dog deputies and their henchmen will soon make an assault on the bourgeoisie's apartments; a new tax is a possibility; so are attempts to squeeze in more tenants. They say, however, that one can buy off, and that the price is 500 rubles.

2 [March]. A kaleidoscope of news. This morning Lenin sent out a telegram that the talks have broken down; in the afternoon came the news that the unknown scoundrels sent to Brest decided to sign a peace that gave away Kars and Batum to the Turks, in addition to what had already been done. One can't even imagine what will come of this. If this peace is really ratified, it may happen that Pieter will not be listened to in Moscow and other towns, and the war will continue all the same. In any case, the Germans can continue to play with the bolsheviks like a cat with mice. But if they aspire to new seizures of territory from Russia, will they be able to present themselves as saviors? And that is precisely how it is, at least in Moscow. I was persuaded of this yet once again after visiting the English Club[44] today.

3 [March]. There is much that is unclear in the news. It is a fact that Pokrovskii and co. signed everything they were presented;[45] but it is not clear what effects will flow from this. Events are developing so fast even the imagination can't keep up with them. We celebrated our academic holiday today—V. I. Picheta's dissertation defense. Liubavskii and I were the opponents. As far as I am concerned, the defense was a success in terms of both the general mood and the character of the criticisms. Afterward there were refreshments at Picheta's house; tongues were loosened, it was cozy, but it was impossible to forget about the general horror. Much was said in the various speeches about what awaits us and what we are living through. Two tendencies emerged: there were pessimists, led by Liubavskii, and optimists, represented by Egorov. But all were agreed that we have never before witnessed such abominations; many

44 Moscow's oldest gentlemen's club (founded in 1772). Since 1924, the building of the English Club on Tverskaia (now Gor'kii Street) has been occupied by the Museum of the Revolution.

45 Pokrovskii was a member of the Bolshevik delegation to the Brest negotiations. In the early stages of the talks, he had sided with Bukharin and the other "left communists" who opposed making agreements with any of the imperialist powers.

talked of the need to cultivate national feeling—how tardily has Russian civilized society noticed that.

4 [March]. The peace treaty is not holding up; they have taken Narva; the authorities are moving to Moscow. In Moscow the anarchists are growing stronger; they are occupying houses, and today, they say, have seized the English Club. Something is in the air, like never before. I don't know what will happen—a pogrom, an invasion of the Germans, or something else, but something will happen. The rumor is circulating from bolshevik circles in the Kremlin that the German conditions include the right to remove such works of art from Russia as they see fit. Whether or not that is so, the gorillas don't need works of art, but such a condition shows that the Germans intend to treat the bolsheviks severely. The peace conditions were signed by M. N. Pokrovskii—there you have a truly perfidious name in Russian history and a disgrace to the school of Moscow Russian historians.

5 [March]. The newspapers did not appear, because, they say, certain newspaper idiots decided out of principle not to publish so long as the censorship exists; they are punishing all of us and their own pocket, thinking they will strike a blow against the bolsheviks, who could not care less about them. There are few rumors, but they say the Germans are demanding full restoration of order. On the one hand, this may be so, but then how can the Germans think that the bolsheviks will honorably fulfill this demand; on the other hand, the Germans cannot tolerate the bordello we have here. One's thoughts revolve ever around the Germans—Russia has perished if only the Germans can save us, and the Turks are driving us out of Trebizond. A disgrace; you feel yet again that it is possible to live only by one's personal interests—there is nothing else worth living for in former Russia, and there won't be for as long as we may live. A neurasthenic mood can come and go many times in a day, but reason leads you always to the same conclusion: Russia has ended, she has betrayed herself, the nation has dug its own grave; and what we have today is only the logical development of all we have seen over the last year. Today we presented to Liubavskii the only copy delivered to Moscow of a collection of articles undertaken four years ago. The collection is very good, and the presentation was warm; perhaps it will be the last collection of this kind.[46]

6 [March]. I heard today that the henceforth eternally famous M. N. Pokrovskii, who lived last autumn in A. N. Veselovskii's apartment, is dis-

---

[46] *Sbornik statei v chest' M.K. Liubavskogo* (Petrograd, 1917).

appearing somewhere and did not even come to Veselovskii's himself, but asked by telephone that his linen and personal effects be collected, saying that he would send for them. Most likely that loathsome creature feels guilty about even seeing people with whom he was acquainted in the old Moscow period of his life. It was also said that that same hero of the second Russian Time of Troubles is supposedly proclaiming that the bolsheviks' days are numbered. His speech in the Soviet of Workers' Deputies in Moscow is interesting: it is full of gloom—not a triumphant hymn, but a funeral dirge. The scoundrel and traitor who facilitated the betrayal of his fatherland to ruin and pillage by the Germans avowed with crocodile tears that they want to destroy us and, it seems, counseled against ratification of the peace. An accursed, self-infatuated Quasimodo, toward whom I have always felt a kind of disgust. Without making anything else of himself, he became the Herostratos,[47] or, more correctly, one of the Herostratoses, of Russia. So be it! The court of history will judge him. In Moscow the anarchists are proliferating and are seizing houses; it is still not clear whether they are the gravediggers of the bolsheviks or the next step in the Russian people's sinking into the cesspool.

8 [March]. The dog deputies, heeding comrade Lunacharskii, are closing all the institutions of learning in the city of Moscow, on the pretext of hunger, epidemics, and the evacuation of the "capital" to Moscow. This is the death of those fragile shoots of civilization that still survived in Moscow; or at least it signifies a long lethargy for them. The consciousness of universal ruin and destruction is increasingly overwhelming me; a consciousness of a general collapse of one's entire life and worldview. And they are transferring the notorious people's commissars to Moscow; the Bacchanalia of housing requisitions going on in Moscow makes all that has gone before pale by comparison. Arbitrariness and violence, and nothing more. The advance of the Germans is being covered up, but it is proceeding according to some kind of plan all the same. Like two nooses, bolshevism and Germanism are strangling poor, dying Russian life.

10 [March]. Yesterday we dined with Liubavskii in intimate company at Veselovskii's apartment; the occasion was the presentation of the book to him, but the real reason was to give the soul a rest, to forget about everything if only for one evening. The strictly nondrinking scholarly milieu betrayed its customs on this occasion and had a little to drink. Strained nerves gave rise to an exalted and animated mood. We talked much and easily, and the predominant theme was patriotism; this came from Liu-

---

[47] Herostratos was a Greek from Ephesus who in 356 B.C. burned the temple of Artemis in Ephesus (one of the seven wonders of the world) to make his name immortal.

bavksii who was, after all, the central figure, and from a shared feeling for the Mariuses who wept on the ruins of Carthage.

Another day without accomplishments today, because everything is falling apart. You involuntarily ask yourself: did you always do at least everything that was proper? Of course, it would have been better to volunteer for the front and put a timely end to one's existence there. But three things have prevented that: my congenital individualism, which has always caused me to try to live as I myself found necessary, rather than according to God's will; secondly, the fact that I have looked on my scholarly studies of Russian history as service to the motherland that I was obliged to continue all my life; and, finally, family. But now, happy is he who died in the war thinking that he was helping the welfare and salvation of Russia, and not knowing that the Russian people doesn't care whether it is free or enslaved. It is painful to think that all our scientific studies are also a luxury nobody needs, which the Russian gorillas have no use for now, as they will have none in the future; and our future rulers, the Germans, can use the material and written monuments of the self-destroyed nation themselves. A fantastic report today of a new Russian government of Prince L'vov and Putilov that has been formed somewhere in the land of the rising sun under the protection of Japanese bayonets. All this is utopian in and of itself, and if that flabby vegetarian is going to be in charge then certainly nothing will come of it. And even if it does have a future, we will all the same be suffocated before they get here. All the same, we will not escape ruin.

11 [March]. All day one has heard only about the "requisitions" of housing, that is simply the eviction of people from their apartments with twenty-four, forty-eight, or seventy-two hours' notice, seizure of mansions, and similar acts for the good of the people. They are taking away everything that was left; after money—they are robbing personal property. Soon the haves will become beggars, and the robbers will make off with the spoils, and "then will come Biron, Merzenshret, Gadenburg, and the great Sukenzon," as Prince Viazemskii wrote long ago.[48] I was at Malfitano's in the evening and made the acquaintance of his companion, Avenard, a very sympathetic type of Frenchman. It turns out that the whole Institut Français has relocated to Moscow. My student Kamernitskii read an excellent paper in the university seminar—a critical anal-

[48] The reference is to lines of the poet Prince Petr Andreevich Viazemskii (1792–1878), a contemporary and intimate friend of Pushkin. Ernst-Johann Biron (Biren) was the favorite of Empress Anna Ioannovna (1730–1940) and the most powerful and hated figure of her reign, legendary for his abuse of police powers. The other names are pseudo-German inventions based on the Russian words for "abomination," "vermin," and "son of a bitch."

ysis of Pokrovskii's history.[49] It was a good and healthy critique of Marxism.

12 [March]. I sat home all day from 2 P.M. and tried to work, on the whole relatively successfully; such moments should be used, they are becoming fewer and fewer. In the morning, despite the holiday celebrating the anniversary of the beginning of Russia's death and disgrace, I taught at the Higher Women's Courses in the presence of three auditors—good for them! There are few people on the street; here and there the red guard scum with rifles are waiting for something or searching for somebody. The impending horror of the rulers' migration from Petrograd is awful; the local population is even being threatened with the deportation of all unneeded mouths from Moscow—and no destination. And with what money? Obviously, they will create from this a new perfected means of eating the bourgeoisie and getting rid of persons they don't like.

13 [March]. The situation is not changing. The wave of requisitions continues in Moscow; people with the most astonishing physiognomies, which, if you were to meet them in a dark corner, would give you a fright, are riding about the streets in automobiles or "lout-shakers."[50] Meeting of the University Council; it was at last decided to enter into businesslike relations with the present authorities; it is about time, although I don't know if anything good will come of it. It was decided to defend university studies at all costs; and I don't know what will come of this, either. S. B. Veselovskii was elected extraordinary professor of the history of Russian law.[51] Will he ever teach in the university?

14 [March]. We cooked bliny at home—one time in Shrovetide. Shambi told us various soothing things, but I don't believe them. This morning I did a lot of walking about the streets, and saw various physiognomies of delegates who have appeared in Moscow. They could be recognized by the curiosity on their faces, their rude looks, and their walking in groups. I was seized by horror that this band of savages will decide the fate of our unhappy country; the refuse, dregs, led by demagogues, is stomping into the dirt "all that is great and sacred in the land," and there is not a single voice of a civilized person that would direct and caution them, to which they would pay attention. All this scum will do what their tsar,

---

[49] Presumably the five volumes of Pokrovskii's *Russian History from Ancient Times*, which appeared between 1910 and 1913.

[50] *Khamotriasy*: from *kham*, "lout," and *triasti*, "to shake." Cf. *lobotrias*: "idler."

[51] An "extraordinary" professorship was the approximate equivalent of an American associate professorship.

Ul'ianov, orders—and afterward? And afterward they will not be able to fulfill the peace terms.

15 [March]. I heard an expression that I liked a lot from the Frenchmen who are propagating Entendement Réciproque, because it is true. After the March coup, the Russians remembered only "leur peau et leur poche." Skin and pocket—that is what led to our ruin. It could not be otherwise; not only the people, but the intelligentsia as well thought itself free from all obligations contracted toward anyone at all; *ni foi, ni loi*; their own well-being, achieved by any means—that is what the goal became. But in fact the situation was no different earlier. If the intendants were, as they say, more modest than earlier, the military engineers and especially the doctors provided an example of bribe-taking and malfeasance of every sort. The Sukhomlinovs and Miasoedovs[52] sold Russia; now she is being sold by the bolsheviks. It was feared that Shtiurmer[53] would betray the Allies; what is so remarkable if now they have betrayed the Rumanians, and the Armenians, and the Georgians, and everyone else who could be sold out. Skin and pocket—there are the slogans by which the Russian nation perished, but it perished because these slogans were its only slogans earlier as well and because it is morally incapable of anything more—and not from ignorance alone, but from that deceptiveness and dishonesty which live still in the Russian *intelligent*.

Our meeting of *compréhension réciproque* met at 3 o'clock. There were about 100 people; warm words were spoken; one felt that the Russian *intelligent* is very much disposed toward the idea of such mutual intelligentsia contact, because such a notion is genuinely close and understandable to him. I am certain that if the social barometer stood at the level of last spring, our meeting would have had a great success; but at present the Russian *intelligent* has a guilty conscience about all he has done and is ashamed before his allies. I got the latter impression from quite a few discussions of the matter. One hears the answers—" now is not the time." "Is it really possible?"—and one senses the bitterness and shame behind them. However, our Frenchmen and Italians were very gracious and conducted themselves in the best possible way; and they continue to do so. All the same, I consider that the meeting was a success and that, perhaps, something will come of all this.

16 [March]. They have ratified the peace. After a session that lasted all day, and where the gorillas cursed each other and almost got into a fight,

[52] See nn. 5 and 6 for 1917.

[53] Boris Vasil'evich Shtiurmer (1848–1917) was an ineffectual prime minister between February and November 1916. Like the empress, Shtiurmer (Stuermer) was rumored to be pro-German because of his German background.

they confirmed the "obscene peace." Russia, bound and crippled, has been betrayed by them to their masters, the Germans. "Hēde hē hēméra toîs Héllēsi megálōn kakōn árxei."[54] I recall the words of Thucydides, although for Russia there have been so many days like that that one more or less makes no difference. One more page is being turned in the history of the Russian catastrophe, but it is not the last. I often remember the words of the late V. O. Kliuchevskii prior to the opening of the First State Duma. He said to me then: life will show what to do, life will show the way; *only the muzhik must be shown that he is a fool, and the borderlands must be appeased.* And now here the epigones of populism and the foxes—international, in part Jewish, traitors—have been crooning that there is no one better, higher, or more clever in the world than he;[55] and our borderlands have either fallen away from us themselves, fleeing the Pugachevshchina, or have been turned over by us to flood and pillage. How correctly Kliuchevskii pointed out our two gravest illnesses, and how deeply these illnesses have been felt in our time. Nation of idiots, who shall heal and guide you? Slavery to the Germans, slavery in shame—German *Viehzucht*, more precisely, *Russisch-Schweinzucht,*[56] that is the future of the self-betraying nation. History can repair everything except when a nation, out of stupidity and historically unprecedented thick-headedness and lack of awareness, has eliminated its own future by giving itself naked into the hands of the enemy, anticipating with stupid delight how that enemy will have its way with it.

In one of tsar Ul'ianov's speeches at the congress of gorillas there is a remark to the Left SR Kamkov (I don't remember his Jewish real name)[57] in answer to his questions: "One fool can ask more than ten intelligent people can answer." One can add to this only that those words could be addressed to Ul'ianov as well. Here we have not one fool, but tens of millions, perhaps hundreds of millions of idiots, among whom there is not to be found a single person with glimmerings of even national-social intellect, not to mention statesmanlike intellect (what is the state to them?). And this panurgic herd aspires to say something new to the world—idiots, fools, criminals toward their ancestors and descendants. Russia cannot change her ways. After 1861 the nobility perished, because it could not adapt itself to the new life; after 1917 the entire nation will perish, for it is incapable of sustaining either new ways or competition with Europe. And they still think they are God-bearers, if not on behalf of the old God, then on behalf of communism, anarchism, and suchlike

---

[54] "This day will be the beginning of great evils for the Hellenes." Thucydides, II.xii.3.

[55] The fable of the fox and the crow.

[56] "A German livestock operation, more precisely a Russian pig farm."

[57] Boris Davydovich Kats (1885–1938) was a militant Left SR and member of the Left SR central committee.

bugbears of Russian life, which in essence could go no further than Razin and Pugachev, nor will it be able to do so in the future.

18 [March]. Yesterday was a day without particular impressions; the malaise of the ruling group can be sensed in town. Rumors are flying about various retirements and shifts; so far everything is cloudy, but apparently yet another page in the Russian Time of Troubles is being turned. Classes were held without interference today in the university.

19 [March]. A burdened spiritual state; there are no direct causes, but this German peace weighs on me more and more. Worst of all are the territorial concessions to Turkey, which were once again extracted on the grounds of self-determination of nationalities—a principle that the Germans ingeniously used in order to pull the wool over the eyes of those fools of every sort and description who together with the traitors constitute Russian democracy. Oh, Russian stupidity, what can be compared to it? The Germans can write a second "In Praise of Folly," but only Russia's. Today I had a meeting and talk with Patouillet and his two assistants, Fichelle and Antonelli.[58] They expressed the hope, either sincerely or out of sympathy for us, that things will still get better in Russia; they said further that "la question russe devra être résolue au congrès," and that "il est impossible de laisser l'Allemagne libre de ses actions en Russie." There you have the Russian question, engendered by the suicidal nation. This question will be the subject of diplomatic negotiations, and the suicide will occupy the attention of Europe as that attention was earlier fixed on the sick man, Turkey. The Russian scum is certainly worthy of its fate.

20 [March]. Today is an unusually dismal day; there are no general changes or news, but there is some kind of fog all around, both outside and inside, in the soul, to the point that I cannot even work in the evening.

Today I was in the Kremlin for the first time; I attended a [meeting of the] Commission on the Preservation of Historical Monuments.[59]

---

[58] Jules Patouillet was the director of the Institut Français in Petrograd and head of the French Entendement Réciproque group. Fichelle was an *agrégé* in history assigned to the institute. Patouillet and his associates had been engaged in disseminating pro-Allied propaganda in Russia since the beginning of the war. See Pierre Pascal, *Mon journal de Russie, 1916–1918* (Lausanne, 1975). Madame Patouillet kept a diary during her sojourn in Russia with her husband. It is preserved in the Hoover Institution Archives.

[59] This commission, a quasi-public body attached to the Moscow soviet and under the supervision of the Commissariat of the Properties of the Republic, had been established in November 1917. It had four sections: archive-museum-library, plastic arts, architecture, and organizational-technical.

There was a crowd of people at the Trinity Gates, dressed in military uniforms, with shocks of hair sticking out from under their cocked caps and with stupid and boorish expressions—partly Russians, partly Latvians who spoke Russian poorly. These were all defenders of the rulers, rudely demanding passes. There was dirt, potholes, and puddles in the entranceway; automobiles are pushed through. And I saw one that was being pushed by some fools who were brandishing whips and yelling at it as if it were a horse. After that a pair of grown and still fairly stout horses strained to pull up there a relatively light cart of wood. On the square it was total chaos; some people were rushing about, who knows where and what for; aimless rushing about; an outward look of confusion—that is the general impression you get! After that I turned into Palace Street and in the building of the Commission I saw Oranovskii and co. eating on the palace china.

21 [March]. The general barometer has not moved; there are again rumors of impending action by the anarchists. At 3 o'clock the Tower of Babel commenced; some kind of naval ship's college and a commissariat of military-school instructors simultaneously presented demands for space in our house. We managed to assuage them with the Goncharovs' apartment, but there was much alarm—inspections, meetings in staircases, an emergency meeting of the building committee, disturbances, hopes, etc. We will know tomorrow which of the two competitors will win, but the requisition commission assures us that they will disturb us no more. We will see later if that is so. The result for us was that we are squeezing together and giving two rooms to the Timashevs. She was born a Trubetskoi; he may well be the descendant of one of Alexander II's ministers. Today I am writing for the last time in my study, where I have worked for five years.

22 [March]. The whole day was spent in a rush, moving things in the apartment. Toward evening we had things more or less cleaned up, now possessing three instead of five rooms, and began our new, semiproletarian life. The tenants moved in in the evening; so far it seems we will get along. The requisition battlefield was won by the sailors; today they were already demanding the entire Goncharov apartment and even threatened M. M. Petrovo-Solovovo. But the hope of keeping it is not yet lost. The senior sailor behaved with appropriate boorishness; he threatened General Gurko with a revolver and vowed to shoot the Timashevs' monkey.

There is little new on the general horizon. The bolsheviks are again vowing to form an army; probably even they see the manifest results of the most criminal of Russian stupidities—defeatism. The Russians can be pleased with the success of defeatism—it has genuinely achieved all possible results.

25 [March]. There is a German offensive on the Western Front; they are advertising it according to their custom. The Frenchmen with whom I met today and pondered mutual understanding are taking the offensive rather calmly—"ils ne feront pas plus qu'ils ne l'ont fait aux autres offensives."[60] God grant that it be so; the entire future of Europe depends on it. A state of suspense in Moscow: vague rumors, conversations, but the bolsheviks so far are not thinking of leaving. Studies in the higher schools are going along at their own pace; the decline is very gradual, and if they don't intervene to knock us off, we will somehow survive until Easter. The museum is still without heat, which is becoming positively unbearable—the girls are now showing up exclusively for tea, and on perfectly defensible grounds. Deterioration is increasing from the inaction, and it will be even harder to pick up the reins. Since the reshuffling in the apartment has ended, I have begun to work again since yesterday.

26 [March]. The Germans are having significant successes; although it is not a catastrophe for the Allies, the situation is alarming. For me it is my last hope for anything; if the Allies don't take care of the Germans there, universal German rule is inevitable—and all this because of the thick-headed and stupid depravity of the Russian people and its even more depraved intelligentsia, without conscience, without principles, and stupid. Today I had a visit from the Frenchmen Patouillet and Fichelle; they are taking the matter more calmly; maybe I have simply become a neurasthenic. In any case, I have not been in a mood like today for a long time. I tried to stifle the gloom by intensely writing a lecture about Kliuchevskii. They say the bolsheviks are going to give us money; I don't believe it all the same. But this is characteristic: comrade Malinovskii got terribly angry when he learned that our museum has been closed a week already because of a lack of firewood, and appeased his rage by berating our fool, the architect Sheviakov,[61] on the telephone for twenty minutes; Sheviakov (deputy from the laboring intelligentsia, *horribile dictu*) is his own comrade from the Institute of Civil Engineers. Thus do the drubbings of the old regime live on.

27 [March]. According to the evening reports, the German thrust appears to be weakening; one wants to believe it is so. Forty French officers are returning to Moscow to instruct the red army. Their reckoning is correct:

---

[60] "They will do no more than they have done in other offensives."
[61] Nikolai L'vovich Sheviakov was a civil engineer and the Museum Architect.

they say that so long as they can do something nasty to the Germans, they will stay here.[62] That is understandable: for them the Russians are now only material, at least potentially, for continuing the struggle. At present the Russians can count on nothing more under any circumstances. We are opening the museum; the pipes did not burst today, and there is a chance the institution can function once again. The shabbiness of the Russian intelligentsia can be seen from the following: on Monday, V. M. Khvostov,[63] with whom I walked to the university, began in my presence (we are not at all close) literally to curse Manuilov, with whom he had always been friends, whom he followed around like a puppy, and for whose sake he left the university in 1911. It turns out that Manuilov, while constantly saying that one should not pay the bolshevik municipal tax, himself paid it behind everybody's back. The reason given was that they would pay particular attention to a former member of the government and would punish him with special severity. On that score Khvostov said that in France there is a saying *noblesse oblige,* but that in Russia they act contrary to it; if prominent Kadets and members of the improvisional government behave that way, what can representatives of the simple Russian riffraff [be expected to] do? I am cutting out an excerpt from the latest edition of *The Kievan* that appeared in today's edition of *The Russian Gazette.*[64] I subscribe to it with both hands. Who, indeed, were the patriots in Rus'?[65]—part of the idealistic landed gentry, and the *métis* such as I and a great many like me. A part of the old nobility loved Russia and died for her in this war; and the métis loved her, too; as a matter of fact, love of the motherland in the middle strata, in the middling intelligentsia, was usually inversely proportional to the quantity of Russian blood. But after all, this handful of people was insufficient to

[62] These officers had been demanded by Trotskii in a letter to the French ambassador, Noulens. Pascal, *Mon journal de Russie,* p. 265.

[63] Veniamin Mikhailovich Khvostov (1868–1920) was a historian of Roman law and the author of works on historical theory and method.

[64] *Kievlianin* was a conservative Kiev newspaper (1864–1918). *Russkie vedomosti,* a leading national newspaper with close ties to the Kadet party, was published in Moscow between 1863 and March 27, 1918, when it was closed by order of Krylenko. It continued briefly (April 11–July 6) as *Svoboda Rossii,* with nothing changed except the title. The excerpt consisted of remarks by *The Kievan*'s editor, V. V. Shul'gin, about the socialists: "The socialists imagined that the so-called counterrevolution would come from the rachitic Russian capitalists or from the dreamy Russian landowners. . . . In the name of this nonexistent counterrevolution they shot and destroyed the small cultural class which in Russia was the only carrier of national pride and was prepared to submit to any experiments of 'socialism' if only their motherland's independence could be preserved. . . . Counterrevolution came in the form of the German officers and soldiers who have occupied Russia."

[65] The old, preimperial name for Russia, which was still in use as a familiar, sentimental term. Cf. "Rossiia."

save the country from the ruin desired by the full-blooded Russian intelligenty, who in the spring of 1917 were ashamed of the very word "victory" (for example, the blockhead Sheviakov), or from the plebeian gorillas who have never known anything except *la peau et la poche*.

28 *[March]*. The Germans continue to move. One grows fearful for
France, for the Western countries, for the last bastion against German
caesarism. If only they can survive—not for us, we are done for, but for
them; one can hope for nothing more. A characteristic case from the
museum chronicle: it was warm yesterday, the pipes had not burst, and
it had become possible to work after a two-week interruption. I proposed
this in a polite way to the ladies who had come to drink tea, but they all
left nevertheless, not wanting to start earlier than today. There you have
the Russian sense of responsibility; and the bolsheviks are going to pay
that lot 300 rubles a month each. All those salaries will be accepted, but
they will work as before. The justification will be that bolshevik salaries
carry no obligations.

Lialia has just returned and recounted, from the words of Lena Reiman, what is going on in Zagran'e. Everything is still standing, but the
situation is extremely tense; they anticipate, as everywhere else, that the
land will be divided up in the spring. The sailors and soldiers who have
come are trying to set the local gorillas on the socialist path and to
protect revolutionary order from the onslaught of anarchy. One can only
think that they will not withstand this onslaught, will conduct themselves
as they did in the war.

29 *[March]*. The news from the West appears to be a little better, but I
am still afraid to believe it. In the museum today 100 rubles were handed
out to each employee, alms from the bolsheviks drawn from the new
budget that was confirmed yesterday by comrade Malinovskii—thirty
pieces of silver. I tried to attend the Library Section of the Commission
on the Preservation of Historical Monuments, but I sat in vain until 4
o'clock, and then left before the session began, having only observed the
anteroom of this commission: again cups decorated with eagles, bureaucratic boorishness, overheated stoves, and the ironic attitude of several
persons who have taken up with the bolsheviks after a fashion.

30 *[March]*. The news from France is not better; the Germans are once
again gearing up; a feeling of numbness. In the afternoon there was a
session of the council of the Rumiantsev Museum, which has been renamed the learned collegium. The prince was reelected,[66] with expres-

[66] Prince Vasilii Dmitrievich Golitsyn, director of the museum.

sions of profound confidence; it was resolved to meet weekly in order to discuss business and to hear reports and communications from our envoy to the powers-that-be. In the library commission of the university the talk was about the new bolshevik job roster; it was decided to adopt a waiting posture until the matter is clarified in the faculties. This revolting farce is being carried over into the university, and it will have to be decided there what to do—save the university and risk our integrity, or safeguard the latter and risk the university. Today I made the acquaintance of General Zhilinskii,[67] one of the ex-Pompadours of the military variety: a cold and unpleasant gleam in the eyes; something very unpleasant about the whole expression of the face.

31 [March]. Few impressions. News from the West seems to be better once again.

APRIL

1 [April]. Today I saw A. E. Vorms,[68] who has been released by the bolsheviks following his arrest. He has the appearance of a man who has aged several years all at once. It turns out that the minutes of the Union of Landowners were seized in the affair of Countess Sollogub;[69] from them it was learned that the former minister Rittikh[70] and Vorms had spoken at the sessions in question, and they were arrested. Rittikh is still incarcerated, and Vorms has been released because the people's commissar of justice, comrade Stuchka,[71] decided that Professor Vorms's public image warrants his liberation. Incidentally, he sat for thirty hours in the basement of Sologub's house, where potatoes used to be stored, in the company of some speculators, a woman who was arrested for cause unknown, and some people who had been arrested for trafficking in alcohol, on which they had themselves gotten drunk. They were all threatened with shooting nearly every minute.

[67] General Iakov Grigor'evich Zhilinskii (1853–1918) had been commander of the northwestern front in 1914.

[68] Al'fons Ernestovich Vorms (b. 1868), a professor of law at Moscow University, was a specialist on peasant law and civil law.

[69] The reference is apparently to the seizure of the Sollogub mansion by the Cheka when it moved to Moscow in March.

[70] Aleksandr Aleksandrovich Rittikh (1868–1930) was a prominent official in the prerevolutionary land administration who played an important role in the implementation of the Stolypin reform. He was appointed minister of agriculture on January 12, 1917.

[71] Petr Ivanovich Stuchka (1865–1932) was a veteran SD, one of the founders of the Latvian Communist party, and commissar of justice from November 1917 to August 1918.

We got an awful piece of news today: Zarudnyi, whom Elli Peterka was planning to marry, was killed by a stray bullet in Rostov or Taganrog. How sad for her—what an unhappy existence. The general mood is depressed; everyone's expectations that the bolsheviks would fall have truly been deceived. But it was after all naive to hope for a quick deliverance. On the Western Front there is a lull in the burst of activity. That is better, but it is still a long way from good. Avenard and Malfitano were very sorrowful at our meeting today. I understand how the souls of the Frenchmen must be disturbed now; indeed, everyone must understand that the last stand against Germanism is being made in the West, and if fair France perishes because of the base Russo-Jewish nation, then the greater the shame on the foul Russian gorillas and the devils in human form like Leiba Bronshtein[72] and others of his tribe.

2 [April]. My brother's safe-deposit box was scrutinized today; he managed to get out the miniature of Napoleon's tomb, his enamel-inlaid watch, and the silver things; the snuff boxes are supposed to be given to the Rumiantsev Museum tomorrow. They were polite, but it was impossible to sneak out the bonds. At the faculty, the possibility of increasing salaries was discussed; it was decided that such an increase would be untimely; the Privatdozents came to the same conclusion. Resolutions of the faculty were probably drafted to that effect. I did not stay, because I had been summoned to the Commission on the Preservation of Historical Monuments to give my opinion on the affairs of the Historical Museum, against which it seems they want to mount a campaign of persecution; for the same reason I did not attend Golubtsov's[73] master's examination, although it very much interested me.

Things are without change in the West; it is hard to say what this will lead to further on. Here, whomever you talk to, everyone is in a numbed state of mind, and you really don't know what to expect in the future; and yet without an external force, the rebirth of Russia will take a very long time.

3 [April]. A young man from the Commissariat of People's Enlightenment appeared in the museum today on "important business" and asked for the director of the library. He proved to be a "chinovnik" of the new model—a philology student of Iur'ev University, Bogushevskii.[74] It turned out that "Vladimir Il'ich" would like to use some books, "foreign

[72] That is, Trotskii (pseudonym of Lev Davydovich Bronshtein).

[73] Probably Ivan Aleksandrovich Golubtsov (1887–1966), a historian of Russia and archaeographer. In the 1920s he worked in the state archives.

[74] A chinovnik is a government bureaucrat. Iur'ev University is now Tartu University (Estonia).

reference publications," from the museum library. I wanted to say that all this could be done by means of a decree, but they were seeking "legal" means, and I had to tell them that, in accordance with the unrevoked article of the unrevoked charter, all institutions, including the Council of People's Commissars in the person of its chairman, have the right to check out the books of the Rumiantsev Museum. The young man also went to the university on the same business; I was at that time in M. A. Menzbir's office and was able to forewarn him of the purpose of Mr. Bogushevskii's visit. I was very glad that Menzbir shared my point of view and understood that it was better to give Lenin his reference book voluntarily than to bring harm to the university for nothing. It was characteristic that the librarian, Kalishevskii, did not understand this at first and wanted, in talking with me, to defend the inviolability of reference books. In the evening Vinogradov and I composed a window-dressing constitution for the Rumiantsev Museum for the duration of bolshevik rule. I don't know how it will be received in the museum; all this is a matter of doing in Rome as the Romans do.

There were all kinds of rumors today; it is hard to figure them out, but it is characteristic that the bolsheviks are vowing that the war with Germany will soon be resumed. I very much fear one thing: the bolsheviks must rely on the Allies in reorganizing the army and resuming the war; the union of the Allies with the bolsheviks may estrange the so-called Russian bourgeoisie from them and thrust it into a German orientation, despite the fact that up to now it has been precisely the bourgeoisie that most of all supported the war against Germany. The situation is better in the West. Still, the outlook of the Allies toward Russia can be only one: to get at least a clump of wool from the mangy sheep.

4 [April]. I learned an interesting thing: Chicherin, who presently considers himself to be something like a minister of foreign affairs, is none other than the nephew of B. N. Chicherin: thus the pedigreed Russian nobility is in its turn taking part in the current final ruination of the motherland.[75] Andrei Belyi, or B. N. Bugaev, the poet, romantic, mystic, and follower of Steiner, turns out to be a Left SR.[76] [Is this] Genuine-Russian society,

[75] Georgii Vasil'evich Chicherin (1872–1936) was indeed a nobleman and the nephew of Boris Nikolaevich Chicherin (1828–1904). B. N. Chicherin was a celebrated philosopher, historian, and political commentator; with K. D. Kavelin and S. M. Solov'ev he founded the so-called "state" or "juridical" school of Russian historiography, which established modern historical scholarship in Russia. In April 1918, G.V. was as yet only assistant commissar for foreign affairs; he was appointed full commissar on May 30, 1918, and held that post until 1930.

[76] Andrei Belyi was the *nom de plume* of Boris Nikolaevich Bugaev (1880–1934), a major Symbolist poet and novelist. His father was professor of mathematics and dean of the physico-mathematical faculty of Moscow University. For several years before the First

idiotism, inconstancy, absence of social conscience and ethics, or simply the instability of the young Anacharsis of Scythia?[77] "Russia, Russia, Russia, the Messiah of the coming day"—that is his verse. This unhappy country with her self-appointed messiahs and unwanted, un-asked for messianism for four centuries now still remains the country of tomorrow. *Morgen, morgen, nur nicht heute*[78]—but for today it's pillage, act as if no one should interfere with my whims. A nation of idiots and criminals.

Ever more insistent rumors about officers entering the army. This may mark one of the possible ways out. Things are no worse in the West.

5 [April]. A lull in the West; perhaps before the storm! Today I attended the session of the Library Section of the bolshevik Commission on the Preservation of Historical Monuments. The session was of no interest, but it was interesting for me to see comrade Malinovskii in the guise of statesman and minister; there was, without a doubt, more importance and seriousness about him than any statesman of the old regime—and especially the appearance of being *affairé*.[79] The bolsheviks want to make us a gift of two houses at once: the Apraksin house, which had already been given to us, and the church house, which we ourselves have long wanted to acquire. All this is like a delirium.

7 [April]. Annunciation. But there are no good tidings; on the contrary. Yesterday there was the news of the landing of the Japanese in Vladivostok; the Germans have landed in Hangö and are sinking the remains of the Russian fleet; in the south they are taking Ekaterinoslav, and tomorrow will be the turn of Khar'kov; and here the war with the bourgeois continues. Finally, the news came today that the Germans have reached

---

World War, Belyi was a disciple of the German anthroposophist Rudolph Steiner. Like the great Symbolist poet Aleksandr Blok, Belyi developed messianic ideas about the Russian Revolution under the influence of the writer Ivanov-Razumnik (Razumnik Vasil'-evich Ivanov, 1878–1946); they formed a literary group in 1917 known as Skify (The Scythians). In 1917–1918 they published in the SR party press and were associated with the Left SRs during their coalition with the Bolsheviks in early 1918.

[77] Anacharsis was a Scythian who visited Athens at the time of Solon and became famous among the Greeks for his wisdom and inventiveness. According to legend, his attempt to Hellenize his people upon returning home cost him his life. The reference here is probably a literary one, to the book of Jean-Jacques Barthelemy, *Voyage du jeune Anacharsis en Grèce* (Paris, 1788), which was published in Moscow in a Russian translation during the reign of Alexander I (1801–1825).

[78] "Morgen, morgen, nur nicht heute! / Sagen alle faulen Leute" (Tomorrow, tomorrow, only not today, / all the lazy people say). This popular German saying is a paraphrase of the opening lines of a song, "Der Aufschub," by Christian Felix Weisse (1726–1804). The actual lines are: "Morgen, morgen! nur nicht heute / Sprechen immer träge Leute." Georg Buchmann, ed., *Geflügelte Worte* (Frankfurt, 1981), p. 82.

[79] Someone who is terribly busy.

Amiens. True, this was the "special correspondence" of the paper *Early Morning*[80] and it contains some geographical nonsense, but one has to get used to the fact that the worst possible does happen. You feel only one thing—that there must be some kind of end to all this. Yesterday and the day before there was news to the effect that the Germans are again trying to get talks going with elements of the Russian right and, allegedly, are now having more success. There is little doubt that the Russian Herostratoses will bring things to the point where those who fought against the Germans will become their friends in order to save at least the ruins of Russia.

9 [April]. In the West the fighting is proceeding apace, without success on either side. The rumors about the taking of Amiens turned out to be rubbish, thank God, as did the rumors about the taking of Rheims that succeeded them. The Germans ordered the Russian scum to disarm the vessels of the Baltic Fleet, and the Russian scum have made haste to carry out this order. The mutual relations of the German Empire and the Soviet republic are beginning to remind me of the relations of Rome with Carthage before the last Punic War, or with Egypt in the time of Pompey and Caesar. On the other hand, they have reached Khar'kov, and the Japanese have settled firmly in Vladivostok. The scum are screaming about the imperialists, who are preparing for war against Russia, and are expecting the legions of the red army to come out of the earth when Leiba Bronshtein stomps his foot.[81] Yesterday I had a visit from Malfitano and Avenard, and we painfully worked up a charter for the union of mutual understanding. I shared some of my woeful thoughts; Avenard said to me, "Vous etes indigné, nous le comprenons." That betrayed their attitude toward the Russian scum, concealed under delicate sensibility toward their hospitable host. Yes, one can understand everything down to the lowest foul deed and filth, but when the foul deed is performed only for purposes of suicide, without any hint of aggrandizement, you lose your reason in the face of the abyss of such stupidity; and yet this is how the notorious common sense of the Russian people has shown itself.

10 [April]. Tickets are being issued on the Kursk railroad only as far as Orel—any further, apparently, and you already have the Germans. The bolshevik Sablin is screeching about an internationalist army of war prisoners, some of whom, indeed, do not want to return home for fear of being sent to the front again. In Kiev they gathered to celebrate the anniversary of the revolution, but it was forbidden by the German com-

[80] *Rannee utro* was a Moscow daily newspaper, 1907–1918.
[81] This is an image from Russian folk tales.

mandant (oh, irony of fate!). In a word, the madhouse is burning as before and the madmen as before are jumping from the windows. In the West, perhaps, an equilibrium will soon be established again, but peace is not in sight. Yet how desirable it would be in the name of the salvation of European civilization; this is so clearly apparent now from our cesspool.

11 [April]. Today the curs ordered all land documents brought to them for destroying, and they intend to destroy all land acts in notarial offices, and comrade Lunacharskii has called the universities garbage heaps. In the council of the Rumiantsev Museum a voice is heard (of course, N. A. Ianchuk)[82] demanding the requisitioning of Count Sheremetev's house, which is occupied by the Hunters' Club, for housing the Ethnographic Museum—are not all these things manifestations, rich and diverse, of that all-Russian stupidity which, irresistibly rising to the surface, has demonstrated for all to see the uselessness and harmfulness of Russia's political existence. We will wait for the German ambassador, who will play the role of Prince Repnin in Warsaw in the 1760s.[83] More than ever before it is becoming clear to me that the landed nobility and dying industry will invite the Germans to help them against the socialists of all stripes. That is the only way out of the contemporary situation.

12 [April]. Today Ul'ianov demonstrated that he is smarter than Kerenskii: they have driven out and liquidated the anarchists; they have run them out of twenty-seven houses—what was destroyed and wrecked in the process is not known. At 4 P.M. automobiles were to have been sent out from the Kremlin, where I was at the time for the meeting of the Commission on the Preservation of Historical Monuments, to determine the damage and losses. In the evening they said that there will be a continuation of the same tonight, and that yet other forces are supposedly at work here.[84] I don't believe the latter. The news from the West is beginning to convince me that there, too, things will in the end die down; and then a partitioning of the demented zoo will be the natural outcome of the situation. The other day I learned—that is, I was told—that comrade

[82] Nikolai Andreevich Ianchuk (1859–1921), an ethnographer, was curator of the Moscow Ethnographic Museum. He had been an employee of the Rumiantsev Museum since 1892.

[83] Prince Nikolai Vasil'evich Repnin (1734–1801) was Russian ambassador to Prussia (1762–1763) and to Poland (1763–1768). In the latter post he was instrumental in the conclusion of the Warsaw Pact of 1768, which significantly increased Russian influence in Poland prior to the partitioning of Poland among Russia, Prussia, and Austria.

[84] On the raids against the anarchists on the night of April 11–12, see Paul Avrich, *The Russian Anarchists* (Princeton, 1967), ch. 7, "The Anarchists and the Bolshevik Regime," especially pp. 184–85.

Lunacharskii is a pederast with intimate friendly ties with certain well-known futurists; *se non è vero, è ben trovato.* It seems to me that this mixture of epicurean debauchery and social experiments, of fantastic futurism and khlestakovshchina,[85] whose models are comrade Lunacharskii's speeches about the Russian school, is extraordinarily characteristic.

14 [April]. I didn't write yesterday, because I wanted to finish the course of lectures on historiography that I am putting together this year;[86] in the autumn I did not expect that I would be able to give that course at all. Yesterday it was announced that the monuments of the tsars and the tsarist regime will be removed. They obviously have gotten in their reading of their guide to revolution to the destruction of the Vendôme Column.[87] In the West the Germans have again forced the English to retreat and have taken Armentières, but there has been no decisive success, nor will there be for either side. Yesterday we went to Petrovsko-Razumovskoe.[88] It was a fine spring day: the snow had not yet melted in the park, rivulets were flowing, there was slush in places. Nature was magnificent, and therefore the contrast between nature and people was even greater: cursing in the streetcar, the broken windows of the Leve house, the merchants' club, and the Pautinskii house (formerly Katuar); bestial mugs, little-boy hooligans, young college people with their manes swept forward (formerly they were worn back), disheveled and dirty; and above all the literature on the fences, from sexual stimulants to lectures on Esperanto and bolshevik decrees. I think that this would be a good subject for a social-psychological study—all this fence literature!

15 [April]. No changes in the West; the rumors about the Allies' flirtation with the bolsheviks continue; they say the Americans especially are flirting with them. I think this is the result of an absolute ignorance of Russia; it will only throw the Russian bourgeoisie sooner into the embrace of the Germans. More of Lunacharskii's futuristic babblings about the univer-

---

[85] From Khlestakov, the main character in Gogol's play, *The Inspector-General.* "In Khlestakov he symbolized the irresponsibility, the light-mindedness, the absence of measure that was such a salient trait in his own personality." D. S. Mirsky, *A History of Russian Literature* (New York, 1955), p. 154.

[86] A manuscript of this course survives among Got'e's papers in the Archive of the Academy of Sciences (Moskovskoe Otdelenie Arkhiva AN SSSR, f. 491).

[87] The Vendôme Column in Paris was constructed of captured bronze cannon between 1806 and 1810 in honor of Napoleon. On May 16, 1871, the column was destroyed by decree of the Paris Commune as a symbol of militarism, and Place Vendôme was renamed Place de l'Internationale. In 1875 the column was rebuilt and the name Place Vendôme was restored.

[88] The ancient estate of the princes Razumovskii on the northwestern outskirts of Moscow, the site of the Agricultural Academy.

sity slipped through today. They are after all probably going to undertake something against us; another tendency is that government employees should receive only one salary.

On Saturday the University Council produced a resolution to the effect that professors should be excluded from the request for salary increases, and that everyone else's should be submitted for decision by messrs. bolsheviks. I think that such a solution is the most honorable; it did not lower Moscow University. M. M. Bogoslovskii's speech was very good: it contained much force and feeling, and his great and honest soul came through; this speech, proposing to demand money for the university as an institution, but to ask it for those who have been aggrieved or receive nothing, and proudly to decline it for ourselves, put its seal on the whole discussion and in essence decided the issue.

16 [April]. Something like an equilibrium again in the West. In Moscow they await the arrival of Mirbach, proconsul of the German Empire in the devastated Russian tsardom. In the south the Germans are approaching Kursk and will, of course, take it. Today I had to sit in for the chairman in two museum sessions; in one—the administrative—I listened to the barbarities of the gorilla-employees, whereas in the session of the council I listened to the long diatribes of flabby Russian intelligenty. All this is useless, boring, and vulgar. Yesterday in "Tsik"[89] (Oh, poor Russian language) comrade Gukovskii, something like the minister of finance (they say he is not a bolshevik, but a speculator),[90] made an amazing report about the situation of Russian finances: the budget of expenditures is a matter of "astronomic" figures of several tens of billions, but revenues amount to only six million, and so on; as a result, he preaches economy and recommends immediate reestablishment of the banks. Reading all that, I understood that all our notorious bolshevik raises may turn into empty phrases in a month or two.

18 [April]. Yesterday the rulers celebrated the Lena massacre;[91] on account of that occasion we were deprived of newspapers today. The Turks have taken Batum, and the Mensheviks are warring against the bolshe-

---

[89] Tsentral'nyi Ispolnitel'nyi Komitet, the Central Executive Committee of Soviets—that is, the government.

[90] I. E. Gukovskii (1871–1921) was an Old Bolshevik who served as treasurer of the Bolshevik central committee in 1917. He was assistant commissar for finance in 1918.

[91] On April 4, 1912, workers at the Lena goldfields in Siberia who had gathered to present demands to management were fired upon unexpectedly by soldiers; about 250 workers were killed and as many more wounded. News of the massacre set off a wave of strikes and demonstrations in European Russia that served as the catalyst for the revival of the revolutionary labor movement, which had been in eclipse since the revolution of 1905.

viks in the rest of the Caucasus. The Germans have moved up to Kursk and are making their way in the direction of Voronezh. In the West an essentially aimless slaughter is going on. Apparently our rulers are gradually getting into a quarrel with the Germans. Yesterday, looking at the springtime, I recalled with painful clarity the lapping of the waves on the cliffs in the Crimea and the sale of flowers in the streets of Paris. *Nessun maggior dolore*. . . . We sent a letter to the Sovdep[92] in Zagran'e announcing that we are organizing a labor cooperative and that the land should be assigned to us. I don't know what will come of it.

20 [April]. Yesterday a short personage with a southern accent and a turned-up nose appeared in the museum—it turned out to be Madame Trotskii, who wished to receive *Kievan Thought* for 1915 and 1916 for her "spouse."[93] She was very polite. I indicated to her that certain formalities were required, to which she agreed. She appeared today, richly but tastelessly dressed, in an automobile with a soldier, who stood before her at attention, and received her *Kievan Thought* in exchange for a letter to "Citizen Librarian of the Rumiantsev Museum, Professor Iu. V. Got'e," in which, with all the bourgeois conventions, such as "I have the honor to request" and "I beg you to accept my assurance . . . ," Mr. L. Trotskii asked to be given the newspaper for no more than two weeks.

They continue to await the arrival of the German proconsul; in the West there is again nothing but partial successes of the French. My Frenchmen predict the development of activities by the Allies in the Far East; I answered them "que ce n'est que logique de dépecer le cadavre du mammouth,"[94] thinking to myself that a nation that has betrayed and killed itself is worthy of no other fate.

21 [April]. Intense fighting in the West; but the Germans are nevertheless incapable of overcoming the armies of nations that are strong and self-respecting. But when will this slaughter, this destruction and ruination of Europe, finally cease? Iakovlev told how he was received by comrade Lenin in the office of the prosecutor of the superior court in connection with the case of his father: [Lenin] was very polite and immediately sent a telegram to Simbirsk with orders not to touch old man Iakovlev;[95] not

---

[92] That is, the local soviet.

[93] *Kievskaia mysl'* was a liberal Kiev daily newspaper published from 1906 to 1918. Trotskii had been a correspondent for it for a number of years, including the war years, when he had written from Paris. He was apparently engaged in collecting or reviewing his own writings.

[94] "It is only logical to carve up the carcass of the mammoth."

[95] Iakovlev, a family acquaintance from Simbirsk, had been summoned to the Kremlin by Lenin on April 20 after having sent Lenin a letter about his father, "the well-known

a word was spoken about politics. The Dol'niks' tenant, Astaf'ev, former vice-governor of Khar'kov, is going to begin selling newspapers in the streets tomorrow; that's the Russian revolution for you. Today we had Picheta's second dissertation defense; in my opinion, this defense was also successful in the sense of a lively discussion of the book. It would be interesting to know if that is our last defense or not. Will this custom drown in the garbage heap or will Herostratos-futurist Lunacharskii not defile our sanctuary?

23 [April]. The battle of the nations in the West is experiencing a period of lull, before new storms, of course; here—the same old bolshevik sourness. Trotskii's project for creating a workers' army, based on compulsory training of all male and female workers and peasants in the use of arms, with cadres consisting of officers and generals, is interesting. This is nonsense, condemned to failure just like the project for a volunteer red army, whose collapse they have already admitted. One of two things: either there is an army, or there is not. If there is, it can only be with a command staff; and if there are officers, the officers will eventually devour the bolsheviks. They understand this in that milieu, and that is how I explain why Trotskii's project was not accepted by the Jews of the Central Executive Committee, but was turned over to some kind of commission.[96] The announcement of the French ambassador Noulens that the Allies may occupy Siberia can in its turn be explained in terms of the saying, "at least a clump of wool from the mangy sheep."

The *Instituto italiano* was opened yesterday in the hall of the Rumiantsev Museum; everything was done according to ritual, but there were perhaps too many salesmen from Daziaro and Cecato. A characteristic detail: Bal'mont was supposed to speak; they waited a long time for him, like a bishop; he arrived very late and the first thing he did was to have himself shown to the water closet; even the prominent Russian cannot help shitting all over himself.[97]

Chuvash enlightener" and inspector of the Chuvash teachers' seminary and the Women's Courses in Simbirsk, who was being threatened with expulsion from his positions by the Chuvash National Society. Lenin intervened with a telegram to the chairman of the Simbirsk soviet. Lenin received Iakovlev a second time near the end of April on the same account and had Bonch-Bruevich, chief of staff of Sovnarkom, send another telegram to Simbirsk. Ivan Iakovlevich Iakovlev (1848–1930) was a pioneer of Chuvash education who had been supported by Lenin's father, I. N. Ul'ianov, the provincial school inspector (and later director of schools). *Vladimir Il'ich Lenin. Biograficheskaia khronika*, vol. 5, pp. 392, 409–10.

[96] On this intensely debated issue, which was in fact resolved along the lines indicated by Trotskii—compulsory recruitment (beginning in mid-1918) and wholesale enlistment of officers from the old army—see Erich Wollenberg, *The Red Army* (London, 1938), or D. Fedotoff-White, *The Growth of the Red Army* (Princeton, 1944).

[97] Konstantin Dmitrievich Bal'mont (1867–1943) was one of the first modernist poets

There was a great alarm in our house, which lasted all night to 4 A.M. Slavin and Gurko got caught with their sugar operation. They had sold as much as seventy puds of sugar in the house, in the presence of enemies who are always ready to denounce. The denunciation came; I think that besides an envious and bolshevik-oriented servant, the former manager and an old woman, one Zograf, whom Slavin and Gurko had tried to evict from her apartment in order to expand their business operation, also took part here. Two comrades came to see us and take depositions; it is possible that earlier they had served in police investigation or the Okhranka (at least one of them). One was relatively civil, the other was very rude; it was revolting to see those mugs in our house—for the first but probably not the last time. A search was conducted only at Slavin's and at M. M. Petrovo-Solovovo's, where they were looking for some wine. The uproar lasted until 4 A.M., although I sat up only until 2. Today the alarmed bourgeois of the [building] committee gathered in an extraordinary session in order to establish a general line of conduct; afterward Slavin left for the Commission for the Struggle Against Counterrevolution, Sabotage, and Speculation,[98] and, it seems, has not yet returned.

Today I sat in the museum, working on statutes that no one needs and that will never be put into operation; how much time we waste—it is simply revolting! But it is especially revolting when you see that all the members of such an institution of enlightenment as the Rumiantsev Museum are, at best, Poshekhontsy who get lost in a forest of three pine trees,[99] or, in certain cases, simply fools who are out of their heads.

24 [April]. Yesterday, according to Bakhrushin, who is the neighbor of Count Mirbach, a crowd of rabble were gazing at the lit-up house where the Germans, led by the pronconsul of the Prussian caesar, were feasting. The boors are waiting for their master. Looking at the depth of social, political, ethical, moral, and all other sorts of debauchery, it occurs to me now that if this damned nation can in fact be cured of its insanity, it will only be by means of long-term enslavement to the Germans. This is the horse-cure: either it will kill the Russian nation (this possibility is not excluded), or it will cure it; no other remedy is in sight. There was a speech by Lenin today: hounding the small producer (that is the peasant proprietor), hoping for the envisioned West European revolution, and giving the finger to the Germans behind their back.[100] Today foreign

---

in Russia; his reputation had been made well before the revolution of 1905. He was well known for his immodesty.

[98] That is, the Cheka.

[99] The reference is to an episode in Saltykov-Shchedrin's *Poshekhonskie rasskazi (The Poshekhon'e Tales)* (1883–1884), a chronicle of provincial gentry life before the emancipation of the serfs.

[100] This is a reference to Lenin's speech in the Moscow soviet on April 23, which was

trade was "nationalized." The question occurs to me: can one buy a book at Tastevin's or Liedert's?[101] Our chairman, Slavin, passed the night somewhere in jail; he was home this afternoon, but I didn't see him. They say that this evening the Israelite was again "transported to heaven"— bolshevik heaven, of course.

25 [April]. There is an interview in the newspapers with the thick-headed German Jew Shternberg[102]—astronomer, bolshevik, and commissar for affairs of the higher schools. In April they intend to overhaul the historico-philological and law faculties, which from their point of view, of course, are to be considered nests of bourgeois scholarship. So, we'll wait and see what happens; we have to stay on and protect the university to the limits of the possible. Only it is revolting that some unknown, arbitrary people are disfiguring, without asking anybody, the little that was good in our universities. They are putting up a statue of Karl Marx in Penza; the mindless gorillas continue to play pranks.[103] The Germans have taken Simferopol. Soon Sebastopol will be taken by the Germans, by land, during a time of peace with Germany. I will say once again that the Russian nation deserves what it is getting, and that it is painful to live to the point of feeling hatred and contempt for one's native people.

26 [April]. Confused moods and impressions; a feeling of sinking deeper into the cesspool, although there are no particularly acute grounds. A new threat of requisitions is looming in the house; quarrels and squabbles over sugar in the building committee. In academic circles, discussions about the future fate of the university. I think that however much we may compromise, it is all the same: if the bolsheviks want to get rid of us, they will not be stopped either by our steps toward democratization of the university or by some kind of summer semesters. Young instructors of the type "ôte-toi de là que je m'y mette" can always be found. It remains to wait with philosophical calm on the will of Allah, who long

<hr/>

printed in *Izvestiia VTsIK* on April 24. In it, Lenin described the small proprietor as the main enemy of Soviet power, "stronger than all the Kornilovs, Dutovs, and Kaledins put together."

[101] Prominent Moscow booksellers. Tastevin had taken over the Got'e business in 1896 (see the Introduction).

[102] Pavel Karlovich Shternberg (1865–1920) was an astronomer who was professor of the physico-mathematical faculty of Moscow University and director of the Moscow Observatory. An Old Bolshevik, he was active in the revolution of 1917; in 1918, he was a member of the collegium of the Commissariat of Enlightenment in charge of the higher schools. He was later active in the party organs supervising the army.

[103] Sovnarkom passed a decree on April 12, 1918, "on the removal of monuments erected in honor of the tsars and their servitors, and the elaboration of plans for monuments to the Russian Socialist Revolution." *Dekrety Sovetskoi vlasti*, vol. 2, pp. 95–96.

ago abandoned the Russians. I was at the Wilkens yesterday and looked at the restaurant "Empire" from their window. There was a crowd of people and a performance on the stage that made it seem like not being in the socialist fatherland.

27 [April]. Meeting of the council of the [Higher Women's] Courses: the same uncertain situation as in the university; the future is all in a dark fog. Incidentally, we had to distribute the wages since Easter to the employees, 27,000 rubles, by check, and the check had to be witnessed in the Khamovniki precinct soviet of workers' deputies on the grounds that the Higher Women's Courses are a private institution. Kizevetter remarked to me after Chaplygin[104] had reported about this: "Write it in your diary, otherwise they won't believe it later." Such is the fate of higher education in the land of the gorillas. The cooperators—that is, the council of cooperative congresses, in other words the moderate-socialist simian panacea—got together to save monuments of art and antiquity (the cobbler should stick to his last . . .)[105] and formed an appropriate committee, to which I was invited, among others. The chairman is Grabar', the secretary Efros—the same "joint committee" that almost turned over all the museums into the hands of the bolsheviks.[106] The meeting of the committee was attended by cooperators of the SR and Popular-Socialist persuasions—all with gorilla mugs; stupidity and narrow-mindedness are written right on their faces. And here they have now decided to be pa-

[104] Sergei Alekseevich Chaplygin (1869–1942) was a prominent Russian scientist (theoretical mechanics), director of the Higher Women's Courses from 1905 to 1918, and a professor at Moscow University. He remained in Russia after the Revolution, took an active part in scientific and technical work, and became a "classic of Soviet science."

[105] Got'e quotes here the first words of Krylov's fable, "The Pike and the Cat": "Beda, kol' pirogi [nachnet pechi sapozhnik]" ("It spells trouble when the cobbler begins to bake pies").

[106] Igor' Emmanuilovich Grabar' (1871–1960) was a painter and art historian. At this time he was director of the Tret'iakov Gallery. Abram Markovich Efros (1888–1954) was a critic, essayist, and translator. In a letter to his brother, B. E. Grabar', dated April 26, 1918, Igor Grabar' wrote: "I think I will succeed in insisting on my idea of removing the Tret'iakovka from the city and transferring it to the new section of the Commissariat of Popular Enlightenment which is being organized there on the model of the French Sous-secrétariat des Beaux-Arts. Then all the museums will be there. . . . The Council of Cooperators' Congresses has elected me chairman of a new branch, which cooperation is setting up, a "Committee for the Preservation of the Cultural and Artistic Treasures of Russia." I have several assistant chairmen, some of them cooperative activists . . . , others activists in the artistic field—Romanov, Muratov. I think that at the present moment this is a most needed and important affair. . . ." *Igor' Grabar'. Pis'ma 1917–1941* (Moscow, 1977), p. 18. Grabar' was under pressure from opponents of his policies on the museum council to resign. On June 3, 1918, Narkompros published the decree nationalizing the Tret'iakov Gallery, and on June 17, Lunacharskii named Grabar' director of the nationalized museum.

trons of the arts. May God grant that something comes of this. In the West the Germans are trying to do something, but are getting nowhere; the scythe has struck a stone once again!

28 [April]. I went to the meager bolshevik Palm Sunday fair with Vovu-lia.[107] Maiden Field, or rather only one passage near the Cherniaevskoe School;[108] an absolutely democratic crowd, that is, exclusively gorillas; six or seven sorry booths, columns of dust from the pedestrians, and over it all there stands in splendor the balcony, draped in red cloth, of the local Sovdep, which is located in the confiscated mansion of Pospelov. Thus does the ancient Muscovite Palm Sunday fête die a miserable death.

In the evening I was at Patouillet's lecture, "L'armature spirituelle de la France." Russians should have heard that lecture, which was delivered in beautiful French; but by an irony of fate only Frenchmen, almost ex-clusively, were in attendance. He spoke of what the French can be proud of, and what the Russian scum lacked: not only *honneur et patrie*, but a feeling of general solidarity, a consciousness of the unity of the people, which is the cement of a nation and its internal strength and which cre-ates a *union sacrée* of a kind that is incompatible with Russian reality. The Frenchman could listen to all this with pride, and the few Russians with a feeling of shame and hurt.

30 [April]. I saw one of the new bosses today in the Vondrak store: in Lenin's words, a chambermaid, or something of the sort, who was buying herself a hundred-ruble hat.[109] "Other people came into the world, bring-ing with them other thoughts and aspirations."[110] Here is another case: a mangy type from the Commissariat of Foreign Affairs showed up at the Rumiantsev Museum and asked to be shown where treaties are pub-lished; he had been ordered to find some treaty with Austria. When Cherepnin[111] found him this treaty in the *Collection of Laws*, he almost wept when thanking him. That's what the strike of the functionaries has cost them! Preparations for the First of May were under way today; a banner is hanging from the Trinity Gates of the Kremlin: "Long live the universal republic." The question was raised in the Commission on the

[107] Diminutive of Vladimir—Got'e's son.

[108] Devich'e pole was an open area near the Novodevichii Monastery (whence its name); the Cherniaevskoe School was a girls' school located nearby.

[109] An ironic reference to Lenin's optimistic assertion, in *State and Revolution* and in other polemics of 1917, that the business of running the postbourgeois state would become a simple task for ordinary people with a knowledge of the four arithmetic functions and the ability to give out receipts.

[110] "Inye liudi v mir prishli, inye mysli i stremlen'ia oni s soboiu prinesli." I have been unable to locate the source of this quotation.

[111] An employee of the museum.

Preservation of Historical Monuments about turning Neskuchnyi Palace[112] into some kind of schools, and the lawn in front of the palace into vegetable gardens; and those people from the Commissariat of Enlightenment who spoke about this were unaware of their own impenetrable stupidity. Even comrade Malinovskii, even that one rose against them. (Mrs. comrade Malinovskii attended that same meeting; her outward appearance is quite decent.) Today they smashed Skobelev and removed the crown from Alexander III, and the eagles sitting on his pedestal.[113] There you have a bouquet of everyday news illustrating the fathomless stupidity of the Russian scum. The only sensible voice I heard from the crowd today was that of a ten-year-old boy who was looking at another banner on the Trinity tower, "Long live revolutionary labor discipline," and remarked: "What discipline?" Truly, from the mouths of babes!

MAY

2 [May]. They celebrated the first of May yesterday; we sat at home until 5 o'clock, and then went out and walked around the Cathedral of the Savior; clear, very cold weather, windy. Near [the statue of] Alexander III, covered with a black cloth and with a rope around the neck, were thirty or forty people; the words of professional orators sent by the Sovdep could be heard, answered by voices of protest; on the railings two youths, in former soldiers' dress, said: "We should write that down and send it to the Soviet of Workers' Deputies." They probably had in mind those who were speaking out of unison with today's celebration. The Kremlin is all in red flags; there is an enormous flag on the palace in place of the standard. These are all our direct impressions. By all appearances the holiday was not very animated; the stupid folk took a stance of passive protest, of which it is customarily capable; the streets (except for processions) were quiet and empty.

A miracle occurred today—the Nikol'skie Gates were draped in red, and so was the icon, which had been wrecked already in the October days. Suddenly today the red draping began to fall away and exposed the

[112] This imposing palace, built in the classical style in 1756, for some time after the Revolution housed a furniture museum; since 1935 it has been the home of the Presidium of the Soviet Academy of Sciences (Leninskii Prospekt 14–20).

[113] The statue of General Mikhail Dmitrievich Skobelev (1843–1882), hero of the Russo-Turkish War (1877–1878) and a main figure in the Russian expansion into Central Asia, had been raised in 1912 on Skobelev Square (formerly Tverskaia Square, presently Soviet Square). The bronze seated figure of Alexander III by Opekushin (1912) was located northeast of the Cathedral of Christ the Savior, not far from the museum (see Figure 15).

icon; the fabric unraveled along its fibers just as if some kind of acid had been poured on it. A crowd gathered, buzzing about the miracle; there was a public prayer, and then firing in the air to disperse the crowd.

I received a report about the negotiations with the Germans; if it does not correspond to the truth, it nevertheless foretells it for the future. For the time being, these negotiations are being conducted by three groups— Markov the Second[114] (the landowners), someone from the Moscow trade-industry group, and a certain Moscow public figure whose name is being concealed for the time being. The slogans on the Russian side are union with the Ukraine and noninterference in the war. They add that the negotiations are being conducted separately—genuinely in the Russian manner. I also heard from Iakovlev that the answer to the inquiry by the Baltic Germans about what they should do—leave or stay put— was "Man muss abwarten bis der Rittmeister nach Moskau kommt."[115] He who has a mind will understand. Walking along Denezhnyi Pereulok, I met two German civilians, two German soldiers, one French officer, and one French sailor—is that not a foreshadowing of the future fate of Russia under the protectorate of the Western nations once they have finally made peace among themselves?

3 [May]. The Germans have taken Sebastopol and Feodosiia. What a half-century ago required a year of superhuman efforts[116] has now been accomplished in one or two days and carried out on the first of May when official Russia, Soviet, federative, and the like, was celebrating their Mayday sabbath. Everything is going *planmässig* and *zweckmässig*,[117] only when and how will the villainous trap snap shut on the bolshevik sparrow, and Russian independence perish with it? We came to spend the holiday in Pestovo. A strange feeling. It is as if everything were as before, but the fact is that the gorillas can come and drive out the legal owners on "legal" grounds. We are settling down for five or six days; today was very cold; if we're lucky, we'll get warm again one day. A decree on the abolition of inheritances that was published today[118] does not concern me

[114] Nikolai Evgen'evich Markov (b. 1866) was a Russian noble landowner and a reactionary political figure. He was a leading member of the Union of the Russian People and one of the leaders of the Right faction in the third and fourth dumas. He was known as "Markov the Second" to distinguish him from a government official with the same surname.

[115] "One must wait until the riding master gets to Moscow." The implication was that the Germans would soon be taking over.

[116] In the Crimean War, the Allied siege of Sebastopol lasted eleven months, from October 1854 to September 1855.

[117] That is, according to schedule and plan.

[118] A decree on the abolition of inheritances, promulgated on April 27, was published in *Pravda* on May 3. See *Dekrety Sovetskoi vlasti*, vol. 2 (Moscow, 1959), pp. 187–90.

in the least, but if the bolshevik tsardom should unexpectedly last, there will be no other solution than emigration.

5 *[May]*. Easter. Cold; a north wind that hinders nature's work. We are passing our second day in Pestovo; complete restfulness, no one shows up, no one bothers us; a certain rest for the nerves is to be had here. We are living almost without servants, as one should in a socialist society; so as not to carry the dishes, we eat in the kitchen, which has become something like the kitchens on French farms—the dining room and the parlor are there as well. We ended the lenten fast yesterday at 10 o'clock, and were already asleep by 11. We decided against going to matins over two versts away because of the cold, and I also out of disinclination to see gorillas. I have no feeling of joy whatsoever from being in the country. All the time here, somehow, the feeling is even stronger than in Moscow that everything has disappeared, that everything has perished, that the Russian intelligent is left with the possibility of living only in the unhygienic and dusty cities; that the only thing that was good in Russia—the Russian village—is forbidden fruit for all nongorillas, since each of us can be driven from it at any moment.

I want to write down a thought that has come to mind many times recently. One of the peculiarities of the Russian Time of Troubles is the plenitude of newspapers, now appearing, now disappearing: everyone is seized by an urge to publish newspapers at any cost, not worrying about who will read them. The urge to publish a newspaper is greater the further left a given person or group is. The Russian sees his calling in the publishing of a newspaper and sees no further than that. This reminds me of an episode with the late priest in Pokrov-Barskii Konets, Mikhail Petrovich Tikhomirov. He was very well disposed toward me and frequently came to talk with me when I was in Zagran'e. When I had just finished, or perhaps was about to finish, the university (the winter of 1895 or 1896), in the winter, he arrived in a very highly excited state[119] (which happened to the poor fellow very often) and began to ask me in the course of our conversation what I was intending to do upon finishing the university. To my reply that I would like to devote myself to scholarly activity, he objected with disappointment in his voice: "But I thought you would publish a newspaper." The Russian intelligent of the middle and lower level has not budged in his development over the past twenty years.

6 *[May]*. The weather got better toward evening; we went out for a walk; out of the wind it was even warm. Newspapers were brought from Pushkino; the Germans are in fact dismissing the Rada—it serves the scum

---

[119] A polite way of saying the priest was quite drunk.

right. It is better for the unification of all Rus' in the future, too. I think that all sincere supporters of reunification are working to one end with the Germans against the Rada. But the Germans reveal here their basic shortcoming: the fact that they rely only on the power of the fist. In fact they are quarreling with their only friends. In the West everything is more or less all right. We broke up to go to bed at 10 o'clock and slept until 8—that is possible only in the state of nerves and with the sense of relaxation that I feel.

7 [May]. Emma Wilken and Shambi arrived from Moscow. There is no news of any kind. Shambi predicts rapid solutions, as usual. The newspapers will come out only on Thursday—O, heaven for the Russian loafers! The weather yesterday was quite decent and permitted a little enjoyment of nature. The population is polite; it would be quite possible to live if it weren't for that terrible feeling of fatality and hopelessness that never leaves me and is at times even stronger here than in Moscow—probably from the contrast between the peacefulness all around and the alarm inside oneself.

8 [May]. A big blizzard in the evening; today it is clear again, but cold as before. The priests paid us a visit today; the talk was about what is going on around. It turns out that all the shots are being called by the committee,[120] where in turn a few individuals run everything. Their aim is to get rich at the expense of everybody—that is, the landowners and the peasants—and then to beat it in good time and cover their tracks. There is no seed anywhere; there is nothing to plant potatoes with; but the committee is least of all concerned about how to relieve this genuine woe. Gnawing worry again today about what is going on in Moscow; haven't some unpleasant things been dumped on us? I have taken advantage of my stay here to draft a chapter of a French book that I have thought up; so far it has turned out better than I expected. It is a lot of work to be undertaking; if I finish it, it will be my political confession and my civic credo.[121]

9 [May]. Yesterday evening I borrowed for reading the weekly newspaper of the young Kadets.[122] The day before I had read two of the four issues that have appeared and was convinced that the young Kadets are all shouting the same thing in unison: motherland, fatherland, we must

[120] The reference is to the land committee or the local soviet.

[121] Got'e's "French book" was never published.

[122] Got'e refers to the weekly *On the Eve* (*Nakanune*), a few issues of which appeared in the spring of 1918. It was published by Iu. N. Potekhin, Iu. V. Kliuchnikov, and N. V. Ustrialov, all future contributors to the collection *Smena vekh* (1921) (see n. 93 for 1921). N. Ustrialov, *Pod znakom revoliutsii* (Kharbin, 1925), pp. 196–200.

be reborn; the Russian intelligentsia is responsible, it turned the people onto a false path, a healthy national feeling is needed, etc. Here and there Kadet venerables add their ripe baritones to these voices. But why didn't all of them say and write this earlier, from the beginning of the war, when it should have been written about, spoken, shouted? I have always been amazed by the paucity of Russian literature about the war and related to the war in comparison with what has come out in France, England, and Germany. Now it is clear why it was so: even civilized Russians needed a cruel object lesson in order to comprehend what should have been perfectly clear to everyone. In view of that, what is to be expected of the gorillas? One more thought gotten from the same source: in the second issue, there is an article by Kizevetter where he disparages socialism and argues its impracticality and inapplicability. Precisely five years ago the three of us were strolling in Simeiz, in Limeny,[123] Kizevetter, Bogoslovskii, and I, and I was listening to the argument of my companions: Bogoslovskii argued what Kizevetter is now writing, and Kizevetter defended the idea of socialism and argued for its practical possibility in the future (true, not in the near future, and not specially for the Russian people). But now he is saying not that Russia is unprepared for socialism, but that Russian experience proves the impracticability of socialism in general. Thus even a gifted and highly intelligent person, but one who has been infected by Russo-intelligentsia ideology, had to have an extremely cruel object lesson in order to recognize the truth.

We are continuing to enjoy the calm; it is cold but clear, and one can warm up in the sun by sitting on the porch facing south. One thinks more all the time about what is happening in the world. How good it would be if it were possible to escape from all that surrounds us.

10 [May]. The *coup d'état* in Kiev[124] can have enormous consequences for unhappy Great Russia, although there is little basis for predicting the details and planning for the short term, as they are apparently doing in Moscow. In any case, there is a certain animation in Moscow. I had a conversation in the train with two deputies of some sovdeps or other. A single impression: complete jumble in the head, complete stupefaction, which can be removed only by time or a very severe shock. Alarming news from Zagran'e. They are threatening to take away the plowland if we don't go there.

12 [May]. We stayed two more days in Pestovo; the weather got steadily better. Observation of the local population and conversations with it have

---

[123] A Crimean resort.

[124] At the end of April, the Germans had dispersed the Rada and replaced it in Kiev with the government of Hetman Skoropadskii (Skoropads'kyi).

convinced me that it will probably be possible to spend the summer there, although the peasants, while remaining rather amiable, have become quite familiar; in particular, the park is considered socialized, and in the last few days when it became warmer they began to appear in the park in large numbers. Since returning, I have seen few people, but judging from the tone of the newspapers the affairs of the rulers are not too good, although the process of their replacement, in my opinion, will not be short unless some kind of new factors, unknown to me, enter the scene. Some kind of turning point is in the air, however.

13 [May]. Rumors, rumors, rumors—like the malicious gossip in the aria from *The Barber of Seville*, they grow, are spread, and penetrate everywhere. Perhaps they will die down, in order to be resurrected on some new occasion; perhaps they really do presage the end of the bolsheviks. Their essence amounts to that, and to the appearance of a regime reminiscent of the current Little Russian one. On the other hand, something is in reality taking shape in the Far East; the day may not be far off when Asiatic Russia will be occupied by the Allies, and European Russia by the Germans, and they will cast lots for her, that is, Russia's, clothes. And what will the bankrupt nation do to prevent this?

15 [May]. Only rumors and more rumors for these two days, again of the most varied kind; there is some truth underlying them, but what is it? I consider the most valuable one to be that, according to Boris Sergeevich Petr..., who closely observes them, the bolsheviks' mood has changed sharply over Easter. The Germans have taken Yalta *and have liberated* (!) members of the imperial family who were sitting in confinement on their estates. The Germans are surrounding everything with their pincers, and the question is only when and how they will take us over altogether.

16 [May]. No new rumors; the old ones persist; there is a general conviction that the bolsheviks are done for, and a no less general one that German rule is inevitable. This conviction is much stronger than it was in February; it is perhaps on that account that everyone, myself included, is manifesting a certain indifference to whatever measures the bolsheviks may adopt.

17 [May]. Situation unchanged. Such are the rumors: certain commissariats have received instructions to wind up their affairs and be ready to move out in the direction of Nizhnii;[125] Garf reported that the Moscow-

[125] Nizhnii Novgorod, now Gor'kii, on the Volga about two hundred miles east of Moscow.

Kursk railway has received instructions to be prepared for evacuation; on the Moscow-Riazan'-Kazan' railway line orders have been given to build deadheads *beyond the Volga* for receiving rolling stock evacuated from here. Both pieces of information are more or less first hand, but what do they signify—the beginning of the end or prophylactic measures? There was a gathering at Liubavskii's in the evening; he and Countess Uvarova informed us of what they know concerning the German orientation. One gets the impression that some kind of negotations are in fact going on, but that Mirbach is being stubborn and difficult, and that both sides are biding their time and perhaps demanding too much. On the other hand, negotations with the Allies have been or are being conducted, but there they run into America's absolute refusal to agree to restoration of the monarchy. In general, the Allies understand us little, and the Americans haven't the faintest idea of how to deal with the Russian trash and what kind of horse-remedies are needed for our recovery.

18 [May]. Meeting of the University Council. Many stupidities were spoken about the branch division of the university in Irkutsk, on which the bolsheviks have already laid their hands. Afterward we had a visit from Malfitano, Avenard, [. . . . .], and uncle Eduard; we chatted about various issues broader than mutual understanding. Bolshevik troops seized the clinics today; it took a great effort to get them out of there, and it is still not even clear that they have left. The rumors are still the same, but there is little sense to them. The Germans cannot save the suicidal nation—what is it to them? I am reminded here of the long line of self-demobilizing soldiers who were making their way in the night along the Vozdvizhenka and the Arbat: they were leading us to German rule, and one got a feeling of dread in the soul from looking at them when one happened to run into them. Foodstuffs have risen sharply in price since Easter, and there are fewer of them. Hunger, real or artificial—I don't know—is beginning.

19 [May]. The rumors are still the same; they don't die down. There is much talk of the Far Eastern landings; they claim that the Japanese intend to go as far as the Urals by winter. Who is worse, the Germans or the Japanese?—for one must not think that the Japanese will be coming only out of love for us. They claim that Mirbach is demanding some kind of control over certain [rail]roads. The priest of St. Anthony's, they say, gave a sermon today in which Nicholas II was compared to Lazarus, "who will perhaps be resurrected." There was a general building meeting—boring, inert, ill-attended—which ended with the reelection of the old committee. Everything is like that in Rus'; however, I do not regret the decline of the building committees. They are preparing for new engagements in the West.

21 [May]. Yesterday I was invited to a meeting at the literary publishing department of the Commissariat of People's Enlightenment. I went there in order to look more closely at that insane asylum, and I don't regret it. The big hall of the lycee. In place of portraits of the tsars, red banners stuck up with red tacks. Under one of the portraits was a framed portrait of comrade Ul'ianova-Krupskaia—the same one that is in the book *The Bolsheviks*[126]—with a red ribbon in the corner. The marble plaques had been removed. I came an hour later than the appointed time; in the hall were Sakulin, Gershenzon, Grabar', Briusov, Veresaev, Chertkov, I. D. Sytin, and several comrades.[127] The "commissar," comrade Lebedev-Polianskii,[128] was a young man of about thirty, brunet, a smooth talker who interspersed his speech with pronouns—I, me, and the like: "I, as a revolutionary," and so forth. One sensed the conceit, the inflated exultation and self-infatuation, and, at the same time, the uncertainty about what to do next. The Jew Golosovker, who may or may not have been kept on at Kiev University, sat in as secretary. The presiding commissar gave a long speech, which contained a defense of the decree on the monopolization of the classics[129] and pointed out that all the rules and procedures for

[126] M. A. Tsiavlovskii, ed., *Bolsheviki. Dokumenty po istorii bol'shevizma s 1903 po 1916 god byvsh. Moskovskogo Okhrannogo Otdeleniia* (Moscow, 1918). The portrait (actually a mug-shot from police files) is opposite p. 113.

[127] Among those named, Pavel Nikitich Sakulin (1868–1930) was a historian of Russian thought and literature, of peasant origin, who taught at Moscow University. Although not a Marxist, Sakulin was sympathetic to the Soviet regime; he was elected to the Academy of Sciences a year before his death. Valerii Iakovlevich Briusov (1873–1924) was a poet and a pioneer of Russian Symbolism who became a Communist and an admirer of Lenin in 1917; he held a number of posts in the new government, including head of the censorship office, but was soon replaced because of his unorthodoxy. V. V. Veresaev (pseudonym of Vikentii Vikent'evich Smidovich, 1867–1945) was a well-known writer of fiction and memoirs in the realist tradition. Vladimir Grigor'evich Chertkov (1854–1936) was a dogmatic disciple of Lev Tolstoi and *eminence grise* of the Tolstoyan "community." Ivan Dmitrievich Sytin (1851–1934) was a leading figure in the Russian book trade and publisher of the large national newspaper, *The Russian Word*. After the Revolution, his enterprises were nationalized, but he stayed on to help establish the state publishing business.

[128] Pavel Ivanovich Lebedev-Polianskii (real name Lebedev, pseudonym Polianskii) (1881–1948) was an Old Bolshevik from the Geneva colony. At this time he was commissar of the literary publishing division of Narkompros. From 1918 to 1920 he was the head of Proletcult (Proletkul't), the proletarian culture association; and from 1921 to 1930 of Glavlit, the state censorship agency.

[129] The decree proclaiming a state monopoly on the classics of literature and calling for their dissemination in cheap editions was promulgated on December 29, 1917 (January 11, 1918). *Dekrety sovetskoi vlasti*, vol. 1, pp. 296–98.

publications, annotations, and editing have already been decided by someone in advance. In response, Gershenzon got up and replied with a very sharp rebuff. Its leitmotif was as follows: you invite us in the role of a charwoman, who is ordered to do one thing or another without reflection. Then Sakulin voiced a declaration signed by himself, Gershenzon, Veresaev, and me, in which it was stated that we support the idea of publishing the classics at state expense, in editions not intended to yield a profit, but that we are against monopolization and that we don't know what we are supposed to do in a case in which everything has been decided in advance. I asked comrade Lebedev what kind of commission there is in Petersburg and what the relation of the Moscow collegium is to it. The declaration of Chertkov was characteristic (I saw him for the first time—a remarkable patrician exterior, which was not concealed, but rather accentuated, by a ragged, unkempt suit). He said that he would also have signed our declaration if there had not been mention there of publishing at state expense, since he is against the state in general. There you have the stupidity of the repentant nobleman! Sytin remained silent the whole time, occasionally muttering his indignant comments to me (he sat next to me). It was strange to see him there: the bolsheviks have taken almost everything from him, and yet they invite him to this meeting. The reply of the comrade-commissar was long and smooth; he continued to speak in a show-off manner, listening to himself and smiling a saccharine and shameful smile. He was very offended by Gershenzon and declared that he was astonished that the citizen could say that someone was invited in the role of a charwoman; like the first time, he also tried to show his education and spoke of his philosophical principles, the "imperative category," and inserted French expressions, such as *au couran, au fond* instead of *à fond*, and so on in that way. But the arguments were to a considerable extent those of the mass meeting: he tried to demonstrate to us with sophisms that everything can be reexamined and redone, but that one thing is impossible—to change the decree on monopolization, whose aim is only to eliminate "literary piracy." How that will be done he could not explain. I, at least, got the impression that the bolsheviks, having committed stupidities, want sensible people to correct them and to shield their crime with their own authority, for their decree depriving authors and their heirs of their property can be considered nothing else than a crime. I got tired of sitting there and left, having announced that I could be a consultant of the commission (that term is in their program) within the limits of the declaration I had signed, but that I cannot be a member of a commission, collegium, or anything of that kind, insofar as I am not competent in matters of literary criticism and editing. I will try to find out what happened at the end of the meeting from Sakulin. Very characteristic was the composition of the Petersburg commission, which decided and planned everything in advance, but which, according to comrade Lebedev, can now die its own death in Petersburg, since it is to be replaced by a new—Moscow—commission that is being set up under the wing of the Commissariat of People's Enlightenment: its members are A. Blok,[130] Ivanov-Razumnik, who had declared himself the most left of the Left SRs, Benua,[131] who is at home everywhere and ready for anything, and two journalists, that's all. And now they have invited serious, balanced people to correct the actions of the insane decree and of the insane or ignorant people, or just scoundrels, who prearranged the procedure for putting the decree into effect. At this meeting we were shown one volume of Shchedrin,[132] one volume of Kol'tsov,[133] and the third volume of Kliuchevskii's course, all of which they have published. The commissar bragged that the printing had cost them very little, and Sytin whispered to me, "After all, they seized the print shops free of charge!" I left with the deep conviction that they will not succeed in attracting solid collaborators: the abyss of insolence, cynicism, and, at the same time, stupidity that opened before me convinced me once again of the true value of these latter-day organizers of Russia: scum, and nothing more.

22 [May]. Today there was an immense procession of the cross to Nikol'skie Gates, which have now become a place of devotion. I saw it—or rather a part of it and a crowd—on the Il'inka, on Nikol'skaia, and at the Iverskie Gates; it produced an extremely grand impression. This was no First of May, but something more inspiring. The masses are against the bolsheviks, of course, but that doesn't mean that they will be able to destroy them.

23 [May]. Nothing new; everything again in a state of suspension; whether that is because things are sooner said than done or because noth-

---

[130] Aleksandr Aleksandrovich Blok (1880–1921) was Russia's greatest Symbolist poet. Like Andrei Belyi, Blok had come to collaborate with the Bolsheviks through "Scythianism" and the Left SRs. At this time he had just written his most famous poem, the revolutionary-mystical "The Twelve".

[131] Aleksandr Nikolaevich Benua (Alexandre Benois, 1870–1960) was a prominent Russian artist and art critic, a leading figure in the Mir iskusstva (World of Art) movement. He emigrated to Paris in 1924.

[132] Mikhail Evgrafovich Saltykov (pseudonym N. Shchedrin, 1826–1889) was a civic-minded novelist and writer of satirical sketches who became very popular with the intelligentsia in the 1860s. His "fat journal" *Notes of the Fatherland (Otechestvennye zapiski)* was one of the most left-oriented of the legally published domestic journals.

[133] Aleksei Vasil'evich Kol'tsov (1809–1842) was a Russian poet of humble background who was celebrated for his lyrical verses imitating folk songs and who was known as "the Russian Burns."

ing can in fact come of it all, in any case one feels again the weight of a hundred puds on the soul, again the feeling of inconsolable disgrace and shame for everything Russian, and it seems as if nothing will ever change, and the destruction of our unhappy country will still continue. We are of use to no one, no one wants to put us in order, and at the same time the princes of this world are completing the destruction of the country. They are gearing up for new events in the West.

25 [May]. A situation without changes. The rumors either have died out or are the same as before: some say the rulers have grown bolder; others say that in Moscow they fear Mirbach, but are afraid to leave Moscow for the Volga, in view of the outbursts of disorder there. I might have gotten some news of the academic world, but I didn't get to the council meeting of the Higher Women's Courses because I was in the Donskoi Monastery for the anniversary of Kliuchevskii's death.[134] Incidentally, an article by L'vov about Kliuchevskii and the Russian revolution appeared in today's *Russian Gazette* (that is, in *Russia's Freedom*).[135] There was an interesting reference to his conversation with P. Struve (in Struve's collection *Patriotica*,[136] pp. 200–202) in which Kliuchevskii expressed doubt about whether the thin skein of state institutions could withstand the inevitable collision between the capricious reasoning of the awakened people and the government, which wants to protect the old regime at any cost. There are more and more indications of how much Kliuchevskii thought about the future revolution and how pessimistically he looked on Russia's future.

We roamed a good deal about the cemetery; how many persons there are here who are familiar from the history of the eighteenth and nineteenth centuries, from the chronicle of Moscow, and even from personal ties. We visited Venevitinov[137]—he also foretold the Russian Time of Troubles; we looked at the Muromtsev memorial: the bust, the wall behind, the naked stone barrenness in front—what a clear symbol for the Kadet party, that club surrounded by a void.[138] Today I had the pleasure

---

[134] Kliuchevskii died on May 25 (May 12, o.s.), 1911. He is buried in the Donskoi Monastery.

[135] The paper appeared under a new name after being closed by the Bolshevik authorities.

[136] P. B. Struve, *Patriotica: Politika, kul'tura, religiia, sotzializm* (St. Petersburg, 1911).

[137] See n. 230 for 1917.

[138] Sergei Andreevich Muromtsev (1850–1910), sometime professor of Roman law at Moscow University and veteran of the liberal movement, was one of the founders of the Kadet party and president of the first state duma in 1906. Got'e's remark about his monument in the Donskoi Monastery, which still stands, refers to the Kadets' failure to become a mass party. See Terence Emmons, *The Formation of Political Parties and the First National Elections in Russia* (Cambridge, Mass., 1983).

of making the acquaintance of one of the bolshevik leaders—Riazanov (I don't know his true name).[139] He appeared in the Rumiantsev Museum, evidently, to acquaint himself with institutions in connection with the enterprise he has undertaken—to set up a central administration of archives, museums, and libraries (the Rumiantsev Museum not to be included, by the way). He invited me again to some kind of meeting in the Commissariat of People's Enlightenment, for which thus far, however, I have not yet received an official invitation (but if I do, I will go to that bedlam, too). Afterward he honored me with a conversation that lasted more than an hour. This is a person of about fifty, very properly and cleanly dressed, with polite and correct manners; in the first minutes of conversation you are amazed to see such a bolshevik. It seems he, too, is a yid, but his exterior appearance does not give him away; it is only his speech that gives him away; his accent, although not especially strong, is rather repugnant, not purely Jewish but Jewish-Polish. He is infatuated and preoccupied with himself; he frequently referred to his scholarly work—apparently Marxism (I should remedy my ignorance and look at what he has written in general). He spoke of Russian professors with patronizing arrogance, and with the scholarly look of an expert talked about archival affairs, in which, in actuality, he went no further than good old Samokvasov.[140] He smiled superciliously when speaking of the too enthusiastic collaborators in our midst, those who especially willingly "take on protective colors"; here he apparently had in mind someone among the Petrograders. In general, for all the polite and correct manners, a strong urge to show off his scholarship, his superiority in everything, and, at the same time, his impartiality and his closeness to "my friend Lenin." An impression of an enormous, suffocating louse which tries to hide the stench it gives off with cheap perfume.

26 [May]. Everything remains unchanged. We strolled all morning around the Neskuchnyi [Park], where I hadn't been for at least twenty-eight years; the garden remains just as beautiful, just as cozy; in it you feel yourself somewhere in an oasis; the influx of democracy manifests itself only here and there in the beaten paths and trammeled grass, and also in the gorilla offspring that run in groups and feel themselves at

[139] "It proved to be Gol'dendakh." David Borisovich Gol'dendakh (pseudonym Riazanov) (1870–1938) was a Marxist scholar and SD veteran who joined the Bolshevik party only in 1917 (together with other members of the Mezhraiontsy group, including Trotskii and Pokrovskii). He was director of the Marx-Engels Institute in Moscow from 1921 until his expulsion from the party in 1931. He presumably perished in the purges in 1938.

[140] Dmitrii Iakovlevich Samokvasov (1843–1911) was an archaeologist and legal historian, sometime professor of Warsaw and Moscow universities and the author of a standard work on Russian archives (Arkhivnoe delo v Rossii, in 2 parts [Moscow, 1902]).

home. When we were leaving, hooligans with riding crops and topknots, costumed in military clothing (I can't describe it in any other way), began to appear. Nevertheless, the bourgeois element predominated until 2 P.M., the charm of the garden was in any case above all these defects, and we left in a good frame of mind.

28 [May]. I had a conversation with a Frenchman, the director of a factory in the Donets Basin; he said that all this catastrophe was inevitably bound to happen, and that when the first revolution occurred, the extent to which the workers' mood had long since been bolshevist became quite clear to them at the Donets mines. Today I received (alas!) an invitation to a conference from comrade Riazanov-Gol'dendakh; if it hasn't ended today, then tomorrow I will have to go once. What Iakovlev, Vinogradov, and Savin have told about this conference is rather dreary. I heard a story, issuing from Moscow German circles, that in Mirbach's opinion Chicherin is *ein reizender Kerl*,[141] who carries out all the bolsheviks' wishes, that so far no one fulfills German wishes better than the bolsheviks, and that no one except them would have undertaken to carry out the Brest treaty. This reinforces me in thinking that if the Germans do undertake something, it will only be when the Russians ask them for it. But so far this request—to dump the bolsheviks and to become dutiful servants of the Germans in exchange—has yet to be made. We shall have to have patience for a long time yet, and, who knows, we may perhaps have to save ourselves by fleeing to Kiev or Khar'kov, where Russian life will subsist precariously under the protection of the Germans. The calm in the West continues.

30 [May]. Another German offensive in the West and partial success once again, and all that due to the Russian scum. A government has been formed on the Don by General Krasnov, who had already gone to fight the bolsheviks near Gatchina;[142] this government is following the example of the Ukraine and has entered into contact with the Germans; thus the Germans will now fight against the bolsheviks within the boundaries of the Don region and Northern Caucasus. Region after region is being torn away; the war continues to deepen. Today the bolsheviks proclaimed martial law in Moscow. With what kind of new unpleasantness

[141] A charming fellow.

[142] General Petr Nikolaevich Krasnov (1869–1947), a Don Cossack, had been the leader of the only regular army troops to fight, briefly, against the Bolsheviks in the environs of Petrograd in October 1917. Captured by the Bolsheviks, he was soon released and made his way to the Don, where on May 16, 1918, he was elected Don Cossack Ataman and proceeded to organize a military campaign against the Bolsheviks with German help.

does that threaten us? My brother arrived yesterday from Zagran'e. The situation is such that we can and must go there.

31 [May]. Martial law has again led to the closing of all so-called bourgeois newspapers and to many arrests. Among others arrested yesterday were the Kadets who had gathered in the Kadet club, including Bochkareva and Iur'eva, employees of our Rumiantsev Museum. Iakovlev went to Lenin today for their release and, it seems, was successful.[143] The conversation between them, as Iakovlev conveyed it, was characteristic. Lenin: "We have arrested the people who will hang us." Iakovlev: "Not they, but others will hang you." Lenin: "Who, then?" Iakovlev: "I will tell you that when you are swinging." Their general tone and mood, according to Iakovlev, is confused and alarmed, but I nevertheless don't think that their end is near. I don't know against whom the blows of the bolsheviks are directed, but I know for sure that their end can come only with the cooperation of the Germans; and it is not clear that they want such a coup; there are no objective indicators of such a thing. The Don is all the same becoming a serious obstacle on the bolsheviks' path. The situation in the West is serious: the Germans are pressing on Reims and Soissons; that is, in a southerly direction toward Paris.

JUNE

1 [June]. No crisis is looming, nor will there be one this time, either. The stump has rotted, but there is no one to knock it over. The bolsheviks will hold on for some time yet. A. I. Iakovlev's initiative was successful, and Bochkareva has already been released; Iur'eva will be released today. Iakovlev's impression from visiting the court building is interesting: earlier it had been full of people and bolshevist life; now this life has subsided, and it is easier to get to the authorities sitting there than ever before. The same was confirmed to me today by Belokurov, who went to see Bonch-Bruevich[144] in an effort to free Ilovaiskii (they nevertheless

---

[143] The Lenin chronicle has no record of such a visit by Iakovlev, but it does note that at some time before June 10, 1918, Lenin directed Bonch-Bruevich to make inquiries in the Cheka about the cause of the arrest of Z. N. Bochkareva and E. V. Iur'eva, "for whom a Rumiantsev Museum group is vouching." Lenin, *Biokhronika*, vol. 5, p. 527.

[144] Vladimir Dmitrievich Bonch-Bruevich (1873–1955) was an important figure in the early Soviet government administration; at this time he was chief of staff of Sovnarkom. He was a trained historian with a special interest in the history of religion and popular culture.

detained the poor old man several days).[145] All the same, I see the inevitability of German suzerainty more clearly than ever before; it will come and engulf us totally and irreversibly. The letter we received by a chance opportunity today from our relatives in Iur'ev (now, alas, Dorpat once again) is characteristic: they *jubelnd* greeted the *ritterliche deutsche Krieger*, who brought them *herrliche Rettung*.[146] However bitter, however terrible it is for a Russian to read this, it is only the naked truth. For the Balts, the Germans are saviors, and the unbridled Russian scum, together with the thick-headed Latvian savages, have done everything to make the civilian population look forward to the German rescuers. The news from the Don is of a genuine white terror. In France, the situation of the Allies is difficult, as before. Lunacharskii has published a decree on the abolition of compulsory teaching of the Latin language—and the already wild Russian youth will in the near future be even wilder: it is not, of course, a matter of the Latin language as such, but of a modicum of discipline and assiduity in the schools.

2 *[June]*. A day without news. The whole story is so far only a bluff,[147] perhaps constructed by the interested parties themselves in order to emphasize their power and untie their hands. Today we opened our Franco-Italian mutual understanding at Patouillet's place in the building of the French Institute. Quite a few people came, and the customary speeches rang with sincerity; it could be, by the way, that the speeches of the non-gorilla Russians reflected a certain amount of shame in regard to France. In any case, the pursuit commenced two or three months ago is now near its goal; it only needs to be pushed further; who knows, perhaps we will after all do something, that is, achieve at least a more significant exchange between thinking and scholarly elements of both countries. If this succeeds in any measure, our efforts will not have been in vain. Much was said in the speeches of the bestial condition to which mankind has sunk, of the demons of war and revolution that, once unchained, cannot be reimprisoned. That is true, and the thought gradually comes to mind: will mankind be able to extricate itself from this awful condition, and will we know some measure of peace in our lifetime?

[145] This incident is described in the reminiscences of the poet Marina Tsvetaeva: "Dom u starego Pimena," Marina Tsvetaeva, *Izbrannaia proza v dvukh tomakh, 1917–1937*, vol. 2 (New York, 1979), pp. 215–46. According to Tsvetaeva, the detention lasted more than a week. (Ilovaiskii was the father of her father's first wife.)

[146] "They joyfully greeted the knightly German warriors, who brought them wonderful rescue."

[147] Reference is to the declaration of martial law and numerous arrests in Moscow. On the night of May 30, about one hundred people suspected of plotting against the regime were arrested in Moscow. The word "bluff" is in English in the manuscript.

3 [June]. I went to the Nikolaevskii and Iaroslavskii stations[148] to find out whether we have the right—having received a certificate giving us the right to enter Moscow—to *leave* Moscow with this certificate. On the same business, I went by the city railway office—and I received three different answers in three places: at Nikolaevskii station they answered that one cannot; at Iaroslavskii station that one can; at the city office that they sell tickets without [demanding] any papers at all. A truly Russian muddle and confusion. Rumors are circulating that the present burst of bolshevik repression has occurred on German initiative and that arrests are being made on the basis of German lists, because one of the aims of the discovered organization was resumption of the war with Germany. No news from the West; what is happening there is terrible.

4 [June]. So far we have not succeeded in liberating our museum lady, despite permission from important people. According to rumors, the arrests are continuing; if the authorities have decided to induce terror in that way, they are achieving it; the mood is depressed and frightened. They say that the war with the Czechoslovaks was also undertaken on German orders; there is something incomprehensible in general about the Czechoslovaks, at least for a completely uninformed person: where are they, how many of them are there?[149] Everything is seething, agitated; everything is shaking the throne of the bolsheviks, but the words going about Moscow are absolutely true: even if they are a corpse, there is no one to bury them, with the exception, of course, of those same Germans. They say that general military headquarters left for Murom today. Why? What does this mean?

5 [June]. "Very desirable, but untimely"—such is the answer that was given by the masters to their slaves who wanted to open a discussion. We will see what comes next. Moscow continues to be full of rumors, alarms, and disturbances; conversations about arrests and shootings; TsIK[150] is

[148] The train stations serving Petrograd and Iaroslavl', respectively.

[149] A corps of Czechoslovak soldiers formed from Austrian war prisoners and a brigade that had been attached to the Russian army before the Revolution was on its way eastward across Siberia to join the Allied armies on the Western Front in May 1918 when fighting broke out between the Czechs and the Bolsheviks along the railway. By early June, the Czechs had seized a number of towns along the railway, from Penza to Tomsk. An independent Siberian government was proclaimed in Tomsk on June 1, and another in Samara on June 8. The Tomsk government moved to Omsk on June 7. Both were led at first by SR supporters of the Constituent Assembly. The Czech rising is generally considered the starting point of full-scale civil war in Russia.

[150] The Central Executive Committee elected by the Fourth Congress of Soviets—its standing executive body. It was TsIK that nominally appointed the Bolshevik government, Sovnarkom.

proclaiming a crusade against the village rich; and Soviet Russia continues to shrink—it seems that the entire east has been cut off. However, the uninformed person cannot understand anything and must be lost in conjectures and suppositions.

7 [June]. No news from anywhere; all the same conversations, turning about the same sore subjects. A telegram came from Zagran'e summoning us there as soon as possible. Nina is determined to go on Sunday, the 9th. A completely black mood yesterday and today; one doesn't want to do anything; it seems that anything that can be done is pointless.

8 [June]. My mood is even worse; there are no prospects in sight; it seems that both the Germans and the Allies are simultaneously flirting with the present authorities. And both will change their attitude toward us after the end of the war. But when will it end? In the West, another stalemate that will again be followed by slaughter, and so without end.

9 [June]. Nina left for Zagran'e today. The testimony of my brother, who lived there for nearly two weeks, and information received from there in the last few days have once again convinced us that we must go there, that things are good there, and that we will be able to spend the summer there. Will our calculations prove correct? As with everything else, one can only guess about the answer to that. We managed to get them fairly good seats in the train—in the first-class car, even though the train was three-quarters heated freight cars. No general news of any kind. A standoff has taken shape again in the West; I fear that the periodic leaps of the Germans will nevertheless bring them closer to their cherished goal—Paris.

10 [June]. The Germans have attacked the French once again—so far, it seems, without great success. It is frightening once again. I was at the academic conference today;[151] this was the fourth session, I was at the opening. A strikingly sad picture. There are altogether 165–70 participants. Not more than 60–70 are attending, along with the ubiquitous female students. Drowsiness and boredom reign. And this when the academic world has been delivered a possibly fatal blow. What does it mean? Indifference? Cowardice? The wish to guarantee themselves a way out in order to accept the gift of the Greeks from the bolsheviks? When you see this, you involuntarily come once again to the conclusion that there is nothing to be done with such a people, and that nothing will come of it.

[151] An assembly held at Moscow University for discussion of university reform. It was convened on the initiative of Narkompros.

11 [June]. A new government has been proclaimed in Siberia; its real strength and significance are unknown. The regime has responded with something like a mobilization, which will lead to nothing. The fences are once again covered with horrific summonses. The third charge of the Germans in the West; it has only begun and it is impossible to foresee its outcome.

The last faculty meeting before summer was held; who knows, was it not the last in general? Golubtsov's master's examination; a superb response. Together with Novosel'skii,[152] who finished the examination on his main subject a week ago, these are the first representatives of those who have been summoned to replace us. We are already daddies in the scholarly world; God only spare both the daddies and the youth from together putting an end to their studies, and perhaps to their very existence.

12 [June]. Today L. Eg. saw V. Iu. Ge..., one of the most prominent Moscow Germans; he groaned in her presence like any Russian bourgeois. What does this mean?—perhaps that the Germans themselves don't know what they are preparing for us and what they will do with us. We inaugurated the activities of "Mutual Understanding"; there were few people—indifference, apathy, and weariness are taking their toll here, too. Noting all that with bittersweet words of comfort, we opened the activities. Will anything come of it? The mobilization of several districts has been announced (à la Kuropatkin);[153] it will be interesting to see the degree of its success. In the West, the news is better for the French today.

14 [June]. I went to Pestovo: good weather and on the surface everything is as before; but I could not shake the feeling that someone other than the legal owners can take charge of all this. I will probably have the same feeling in Zagran'e. Upon arriving [in Pestovo] I received word that Nina had arrived safely in Zagran'e. God grant that it will be possible to spend the summer. The day's rumors and news add nothing new to the long-familiar picture. Nothing decisively or essentially new in the West; nothing is being written about the so-called Czechoslovaks, about whom various rumors are circulating. I myself don't fully understand that action.

---

[152] Aleksei Andreevich Novosel'skii (1891–1967) was a specialist on seventeenth-century Muscovy. He was a student of A. I. Iakovlev.

[153] General Aleksei Nikolaevich Kuropatkin (1848–1925) was a former war minister and front commander, best known as commander in chief of the Far Eastern forces during the Russo-Japanese War (to March 3, 1905). During his tenure as war minister (1898–1904) Kuropatkin developed a plan for strategic readiness in key border districts (Poland, Turkestan, and the Amur districts).

Are they really departing for Vladivostok, or will they turn out to be the support of a semimythical Siberian government? But that government, if it has any real significance, will inevitably seek support in Japan, because the Czechoslovaks alone are not enough. Are those people who signed the telegram published by Lenin the same as the even more mythical government of Kolchak, or are these mutually hostile phenomena?[154] The mind seeks an answer, but finds none.

I think that one of the most interesting phenomena of our present day is the universal weight loss that is occurring, and not just from hunger alone. True, hunger is felt by many, but by no means all, and not as yet in a severe form; and yet everyone has lost weight—some 15 percent, others 20 percent of their weight, yet others even more. Undoubtedly nervous tension is of great significance here. Thoughts and anguish undermine and desiccate human organisms; the grief of people who in full awareness see the abyss into which we continue to slide is so strong and so deep that it cannot fail to be reflected in their physical nature, just as the fact that the well-fed inhabitant can at any moment be stripped naked and robbed cannot fail to affect him.

Recently I have been thinking often about why I did not become a revolutionary, when in the days of my youth, just as now, all Russia was divided into two camps—those in authority, and those who questioned authority. I never remained indifferent to this "fateful struggle" and never identified myself with the former, because I was unprivileged, not a nobleman, not a member of the ruling class, and always too independent to seek my fortune in that sector; but I always hated with all my power the blind moles who gnawed at the roots of their own country. I could never feel close to the Russian revolutionaries because I was alway sickened by their unprincipled lack of discipline, their barbarity, rudeness, and purely Pugachevian cruelty, combined with their impenetrable stupidity and thick-headedness. I think that in this matter my mother and father had a decisive influence on my thinking and development— an influence, by the way, almost unconscious, for it was never exercised directly but was assimilated unwittingly, automatically. My mother's ardent patriotism and her hatred of nihilism, together with her love for a great, flourishing, and united Russia, and by contrast my father's skepticism toward much in Russian life, a skepticism born of the common sense of the West European bourgeoisie that knew the meaning of real work

[154] Got'e refers to the Bolsheviks' June 10 declaration of war on the Siberian provisional government in Omsk, signed by Lenin and Trotskii. The text of the declaration incorporated the telegram sent from Omsk to Sovnarkom announcing the aims of the regional government. Got'e probably read it in *Svoboda Rossii* (no. 44, June 11, 1918, p. 1). For an English translation, see James Bunyan, *Intervention, Civil War, and Communism in Russia, April–December 1918* (Baltimore, 1936), pp. 325–28.

and was able to value it—those are the two forces which, probably, made of me for good a neutral person in the eternal Russian strife and inculcated in me a hatred toward both those who did everything they could to stop up the safety valves of Russian social life, and those who took every opportunity to arrange and prepare the blowing up of their native land.

15 [June]. The general news: arrests among the mensheviks and SRS, and the dissolution of TsIK —*la vermine continue à s'entre-manger.* A new breathing spell in the West. The scrutiny of my strong box occurred today. The bank was empty; unhappy bourgeois are sitting in line at the entrance to the vault; we enter the vault and fall into the hands of a comrade—rather polite and well disposed, it must be said. The scrutiny occurs quickly and without any particular feeling of irritation or bitterness. Irritation and conversations in raised voices can be heard all around.

In the evening I made the acquaintance of and conversed with Vl. I. Gurko; a very interesting and intelligent man.

The Germans are beginning to show a desire to talk with the Russians.

18 [June]. I didn't write for two days, because I went to visit my *belle-soeur,* Tat'iana, at Lake Senezh. This spot near Moscow has long attracted me, but I happened never to have been there; that was one of the stimuli for the trip, despite the fact that at first I was in no mood to go. I must admit that this is one of the most beautiful spots around Moscow: wooded slopes, valleys, and a very characteristic and beautiful view of the imposing heights that constitute part of the ridge separating the basin of the Oka from the basin of the upper Volga and stretching from Volokolamsk to the St. Sergius Monastery and, perhaps, farther to the east. Senezh itself, a half-artificial, half-natural lake, is very beautiful and attractive; I got great satisfaction from a walk along it. The estate where I was staying had been spared by the revolutionary tempest, and there was little in the area in general that reminded one of it; that is why my mood there was satisfactory. To make up for it, what a contrast when I got to the station—nothing but bagmen all around.[155] Well, they are relatively inoffensive—ordinary gorillas. Much worse were the soviet types who were at the station and around it—retired soldiers with topknots, young railway and postal-telegraph employees—*vikzheli, vikzheldory,* and *poteli*[156]—some in dirty shirts, others in turned-down collars with bared breasts, sticks, whips, riding-crops, and the smugly stupid faces of victors, unsuspecting that they are doomed fools and suicides.

During these three days the situation seems to have gotten even more

[155] *Meshochniki*: "bagmen," black marketeers.
[156] These are abbreviated names for the railway and postal unions.

muddled. The Czechoslovaks are turning into something serious, but for me so far essentially incomprehensible. Rumors are circulating about the murder of Nicholas II and the flight of Mikhail; for the time being I do not believe the one or the other, although the first is more likely than the second. They are saying that the Germans are entering into an agreement with the bolsheviks to combat the Czechoslovaks: if it is so, that will hinder a German orientation and will create the possibility of a struggle on some Volga front; and if Mikhail really did escape, it may turn out that the Siberian SRS and mensheviks will, led by Mikhail, fight against the monarchists of central Russia, who, perhaps, will adopt a German orientation. A situation without precedents in history. The absurdity of the Russian Time of Troubles is leading her to new and, this time, original developments.

20 [June]. The situation is getting more and more muddled; in truth, the time is not far off when we will assume the role of a slice of buttered bread, or rather of a filling, between the two enemies pressing on us. In Moscow, nervousness and, at the same time, apathy. One wants to leave as soon as possible, although I know that I am not headed for tranquillity. We had a meeting yesterday occasioned by an invitation from Mark.[157] We discussed in detail the tone and program of a possible colloquy, but I don't know if we arrived at a general united understanding of the aims and essence of the affair. L. is too primitively patriotic and lacking in subtlety; A.A.G. remained silent, seriously thought things over, but I don't know what he decided; S. wriggled like a grass snake and was a little shifty; D.N.E. was more interested in *how* everything will be rather than in *what* is happening, in the text of the welcome more than in the substance of the conversation. Ia. was the most sincere and consistent. I am dropping out in view of my departure and the fact that the colloquy was postponed until Saturday. Today I had a conversation with Ia. on the same subject. I advised him to go forward, without looking at possible hindrances, to go ahead as far as possible—that is, until the point of complete refusal by the other side to understand us and meet us halfway is reached. All the same, I think that we will have to live with them and sing to their tune, and that we should begin to take measures now. I will support Ia. as much as I can and insofar as this does not work at cross-

---

[157] A German resident in Moscow? This paragraph concerns discussions that were apparently being carried on at this time by Got'e and his colleagues with a view toward reaching some kind of agreement with the Germans in anticipation of a German occupation of Moscow. It was a risky business, as Got'e's rather transparent conspiratorial use of initials for his friends' names here indicates. Iakovlev ("Ia.") seems to have been the initiator of these discussions. "L." was probably Liubavskii; "A.A.G." Georgievskii; "S." Savin; and "D.N.E." Egorov.

purposes with my French ties and sympathies. An interesting question: what can come of this affair in practical terms?

24 June. Zagran'e. I am beginning my daily comments again where I began them in the first place—in Zagran'e. Once again we have had the chance to come here and live for a time; *I don't know* if it will be for long. The last day in Moscow was spent entirely on preparations for departure; from 4 to 6 P.M. there was a meeting of the administration of Compréhension Réciproque, which, unfortunately, was marked by an unpleasant incident. Malfitano *s'est embellé* against Khvostov, and Henri [Avenard?], for reasons that escape me, reproached them both for having retreated from the idea of union because they had offered to join in the work of, or more precisely enter into relations with, the academic commission for the study of Russia's natural resources. Malfi perceived in this some kind of *banquiers et industriels*, flared up, and left. That is most regrettable, because it is a bad omen for the activity of the society.

Five minutes before departure, Slavin suddenly appeared to announce that a cash fine had been assessed against everyone who had received sugar in March with the help of the house committee—that is, in the scheme that had been set up by that Jew and exposed by the doorman. What to make of it? I didn't inquire and left; I don't know what will happen next, but with my character, it will be a new source of worry and upset so long as the affair remains unresolved.

The journey to Zagran'e took twenty-eight hours. I traveled with my cousin, M. A. Kutorga; we bought third-class tickets, and they gave them to us only for as far as the Rodionovo station, since entry into Ves'egonsk district is supposedly forbidden owing to famine. That didn't prevent us from getting the needed tickets in Rodionovo for Krasnyi Kholm. In Moscow we had to crawl into the car through the window—that was the first time for me. I managed, with the help of one of my former students from the Polivanov courses (still wearing his military uniform and now a fireman in Raev; I just couldn't remember his name, and it was embarrassing to ask), to get a place for myself next to the window, and for Mania one of the sleeping platforms, so that the traveling was relatively decent as far as Rybinsk, and altogether satisfactory from Rybinsk to Sonkovo. Only on the way to Krasnyi Kholm did we have to stand on the platform, because all four passenger cars were crammed full of gorillas. I even managed to sleep a little at night, although two circumstances hindered sleep: the conversations of the gorillas about politics, and various noises, some accompanied by a foul odor and some not. It should be noted that the gorillas, being truly Russian people, are very fearful of drafts and therefore assiduously shut all the windows. One of the conversations stuck in my memory. The first participant was probolshevik:

a heavy [watch] chain, solid appearance, stupid remarks—he looked like a doorman who informs on the bourgeoisie. The second was a former soldier, sincere, and with an anguished voice—a typical SR. The third voice came from the depths, revealed the most common sense, and interrupted the conversation with ironic questions that put the first two on the spot. They talked loud and long; the bolshevik was the first to give up; but God, what horrors occur in the heads of the gorillas! What a mixture of memorized phrases, adopted or drummed-in "slogans," stupidity of a sort that knows neither bounds, restraint, nor criticism. The sickness has progressed far, and I don't know what kind of heroic remedies can cure it.

The journey by horsecart came at night; it would have been perfect, had there not been a fierce thunderstorm that pursued us an entire twenty versts. It had been a long time since I had seen such amazing lightning flashes. It was sad to cross the new railroad track. The rails had been removed, the ties lay there, and they say in many places the gorillas have considered them to be in the public domain as well and have taken them for firewood. The ruins of a railroad, there is the unanticipated result of the "Russian revolution." We arrived home at 2 A.M. I have been here a day and a half already; externally everything appears to be the same as before, but the gorillas know that they can now do anything, they let us know our dependence on them. Political corruption has progressed far since last year. However, external relations are polite; yesterday already I had a long visit from Nikolai Antip'ev from Mokei Gora; and I have talked with several others. It should be said that the latest tricks of Lenin and co. regarding the village poor and the "petty proprietors" have produced a definite reverberation here: the sovdep, led by the bolshevik P. Smirnov from the village of Besovo (according to Lena a typical bolshevik party member, a former ensign and commissar in Kronstadt, dense, stupid, and "principled"—and at the same time a rich peasant), was overthrown and replaced by the former township elder, who proved to be of a much more conservative orientation. A shift is taking place inside the village, provoked by the stupidity and thickheadedness of the bolsheviks themselves.[158]

Eat and sleep—that is what I want to do most of all. And for everything else—sorrow and apathy. This grudging, boring, northern climate is oppressive; one wants the south, and, as never before, one is overcome with longing for the Crimea.

---

[158] An acute supply crisis had been precipitated by the loss of the grain-producing regions in the civil war. In response, the Bolsheviks issued a decree on June 8 "on the organization and provisioning of the village poor" that called for the establishment of *kombedy*, "committees of the village poor," to extract grain surpluses from the "kulaks" or "village bourgeoisie."

25 *[June]*. All night "black thoughts, like flies, crawled forth one after the other."[159] Despite the summer day, the marvelous breezes, even in this poor north, a whole repertoire of garbage filed through my mind, both public and private—everything. How true is the thought about longing and the brave youth in the old song.[160] The only thing that affords me pleasure is sleep—I sleep sweetly and can't get enough. I talked with Aleksei [Ivanov] and Ivan Terent'ev—petty proprietors and bourgeois; they have experienced a big shift, and they are now feeling all the unpleasant effects of socialism. I had a look at the village of Zaprud'e—a new cabin has been assembled by every peasant. I noticed approximately the same in the other villages we went through—everything has been grabbed up and pillaged; the Russian people is taking advantage [of the situation] and is filling its pockets, and it seems to me that all the Shvarts estates will without fail be sold to the Germans and that German colonies or sawmills will appear here. What will this gorilla tsardom do then and where will it scratch itself? Today, perhaps, the conference is meeting that will decide the fate of the Russian higher schools and will introduce the statute I read at the last council meeting of the [Women's] courses: this is truly a monument to a completely unprecedented stupidity so great that it is almost unrealizable. I have gone four days now without news and somehow I don't want to receive any.

26 *[June]*. Aleksandra Pavlovna, the deacon's wife, was here; another change in worldview; she remembered everything I had said last year, and said that I have been proved correct. One could see from her stories that a turning point is being reached among the peasants; but it can only be slow, and by itself, undirected by a strong and independent force, will lead to nothing. The peasants say that the old government was better, but it was bad, too, after all, and no one will bring it back. They came over from the village of Zavrazh'e for the disk harrow, which "belongs to the people" now. It turned out that several screws had already been removed from it; there you have the result of turning over inventory to the people—it gets broken and no one will repair it, because only an owner can repair. In the evening we watched how the former battery commander and the wife of his colleague—Kutorga and Lena Reiman—hauled manure and piled it in heaps; if this constitutes the goal of the social revolution, then it has been accomplished. But the situation of unfortunate Grisha Shvarts is the worst of all here in Ves'egonsk district: a person whose education was a matter of great concern, but who has long since

[159] Lines from a Russian romance set to the music of Chaikovskii.

[160] In the folk song the brave youth begs his companions to throw him into the Volga to drown his sorrow from unrequited love. See A. I. Sobolevskii, *Velikorusskie narodnye pesni*, vol. 5 (St. Petersburg, 1899), nos. 105, 106.

taken the path of alcoholism instead of a brilliant career in the guards—
he lives in a hut in the village next to the central estate of his ancestors,
where he was not admitted, even "as a tenant." The descendant of
the district magnates has turned into a Job on the dungheap, and the
sovdep sits in the estate.

27 [June]. The citizen-proletarians of Zaprud'e are hauling anthills from
our wood for fertilizing the fields and knocking the fences down in the
process, as a result of which our crops are being trampled. The citizen-
bourgeois look at this negatively; the proletarians themselves are very
polite, but continue to do their business. Yesterday I learned an interesting thing: in Sandovo the shop of P. Kuz'min was looted by three villages
as early as last winter, and business was stopped; in Sandovo there is only
one cooperative shop, in which there is nothing. Yesterday the newspaper
that came was only Saturday's; the impression is the same as before:
something is developing, painfully and slowly, but what? I have as before
a feeling of melancholy, brought on by the local climate and by circumstances combined: Oh, how one yearns for the hot, bright south!

28 [June]. Only now do I understand the meaning of the old Russian
expression "Don't count on it"; looking about here, I feel precisely that I
"count on nothing" more here. The waterpipes are leaking, the house is
sagging in places, the kitchen porch has rotted, the forest is being cut
down, and I am completely indifferent to it all, as if it had never been
mine, as if I had never loved and never been concerned about Zagran'e.
The place, the whole region, these expanses and woods that I always used
to love so have become hateful to me. Nina said as much yesterday, and
I was unable to make any objection. The tsardom of the gorillas is felt
everywhere, a giant cage in which there is no refuge from the enraged
beasts.

29 [June]. A satanic syllogism: Russia needs a strong government, a
strong and intelligent monarchy; only Germany can give it—neither
France nor America can resurrect monarchy in Russia. They will try in
vain to establish a republican regime here; England doesn't care what
happens here. Therefore, the victory of the Allies will not yield the desired result for us, and therefore, oh horror, one should, thinking logically, wish for the victory of Germany. If anyone had told me even a year
ago that I would come to say such a terrible thing, I would not have
believed it myself.

I finished V. M. Khvostov's book *Sociology*; a useful book, although
there is no talent in it, as there is none anywhere in his works. In this
volume the main views on sociology and sociological processes are laid

out—how many profound thoughts have been expressed on the subject of the laws governing human interrelations, but how far we are from finding those laws. Thus far there are only clever suppositions, the groping discovery of a few objective norms, almost all of them mutually contradictory, and that's all. It would be good, if they did find such laws, to also find a means for reforming "evil and cunning men." Beautiful weather and a day without incidents; I cleaned up the garden.

The newspapers brought nothing new—all the same sickening muck; there is nothing in the West, either—neither good nor bad. Humanity is being dragged ever deeper into the abyss of self-destruction. A letter from Iakovlev; he reports that the meeting took place and that (in words, at least) they are ready there to come to terms with what we formulated in the discussion of June 19, if they can have serious guarantees. The whole question, of course, is in the latter. It is too bad that Iakovlev does not write about further possibilities in the matter of the broached relations.

30 [June]. Yesterday evening I was depressed and horrified by the sight of civilized people straining behind the plow; of course, one can put up with plowing, too, but it turns out that in order to acquire the right to live and work outside of town in this damned country, people who are capable of higher activities are obliged to stoop to the most elementary labors, useful as they may be. While we were plowing, a group of eight or so young people of socialist appearance passed by (female school teachers, comrade semiintellectuals, etc.); they were going to a play in Sushigoritsy! I was thinking all day that some steps should be taken for elucidating matters in regard to France before making a final choice of orientation; this should be undertaken with the help of Patouillet. In the final hour we, too, people of the study and the private life, must come forth. In any case, all this must be done before broaching the question of definitive emigration, a question that is on my mind ever more frequently and seriously and that must unavoidably be resolved if all this continues for long. The fact is that the same Russian animal that appeared in the Time of Troubles, under Razin and Pugachev, about whom Napoleon spoke when he said *gratter le russe*,[161] who was brilliantly foreseen by the German pan-Germanists already in the nineteenth century—he has grown great and swollen in the person of the *raznochinets*,[162] savage, uncivilized, but equipped with a bit of half-baked knowledge. Through

[161] That is, "Scratch a Russian and you'll find a Tatar."

[162] "Person of diverse status." This term was generally used in nineteenth-century Russia to identify a member of the intelligentsia of commoner background, most typically the son of a priest who had gone to the university after seminary instead of taking orders.

bazarovshchina,[163] nihilism, Marxism, and populism, this animal has taken over the country, has ruined and devastated his own house and land, and has swept away that porous and thin layer of gentry civilization that proved incapable even of adjusting to the reform of 1861.[164] All the same, this fragile stratum, reviled by the intelligentsia—along with people of foreign, European blood who nevertheless considered themselves Russians—were the only European-educated, the only conscious elements in Russia: they demonstrated this with their genuine patriotism and their understanding of the real state of affairs at a time when the Russian intelligenty were at first ashamed of victory, and then savored the idea of robbing the landowners, and, finally, took it into their heads to save the world with internationalism, and only began to feel the blow in their solid rear ends when their safes began to be dug into.

JULY

1 [July]. I turned forty-five today; I can see that so far in my life there has not been a year worse than the forty-fifth; I fear that the forty-sixth will outshine it. It seems the change in the calendar is causing everyone to forget about that date; I remembered it myself only because I sat down to write and put the date. Yesterday we went to Gora on a reciprocating visit to Nikolai Antip'ev. We saw many local gorillas, and the general impressions were the same as earlier from conversations with individuals: a complete confusion of ideas, a certain bewilderment from all that is happening, a certain contrast between expectations and what is really happening. The majority have no malicious feelings toward us—something, however, that can always change under the influence of the psychology of the masses. After that we went to the cemetery, where we found, by the way, a priest who was completely depressed and upset by all that is occurring; he asked me about our fate in the future, to which I could respond only with the same questions.

2 [July]. A day without incidents; heat. Saturday's newspapers brought nothing new besides the same old muck; a slow death—that is the only future for Great Russia I can imagine. Some kind of SR government flying

---

[163] From the name of the protagonist of Turgenev's *Fathers and Sons* (1862), Bazarov, the archetypical nihilist.

[164] Got'e refers to the economic decline of the landed gentry after the emancipation of the serfs. Very few gentry became technologically progressive large farmers after the reform; most rented out their land for cultivation by peasants, and by 1917 more than half the land fund left to the gentry in the emancipation settlement had been sold to nongentry proprietors (mostly peasants or peasant cooperatives).

the flag of the Constituent Assembly has been formed in Samara.[165] Forgive them, Lord, for they know not what they do, and deliver me from my pessimism, which torments me. In all my conversations with peasants, with one or two exceptions, I have never heard a word about Russia, about solidarity, about saving the country; prices of foodstuffs, land, easy gain—and nothing else. I note this not as something new, but as a constant and unchanging manifestation of the Russian popular mind.

3 [July]. Reading Presniakov's book, *The Formation of the Great-Russian State*,[166] and renewing in my memory the endless accounts of princely strife and internicine struggles, I am struck by the correspondence between the psychology manifested in them and the psychology of today's peasants: enmity, slander, fights, and suddenly, without any transition, something like friendship. You see such facts constantly among today's peasants, and you have the same thing, for example, between the Moscow and Tver princes in the fourteenth century: hatred, betrayal to the Horde, murders, treason, and then suddenly political and marriage alliances (I purposely take the example of the sharpest conflict between princes—Moscow-Tver). The heat is tremendous; in Moscow, no doubt, brains are melting. The Sunday newspaper gives the following impressions: in Austria, perhaps, something is in fact taking shape; the Allies, it seems, are in fact preparing to intervene from the east. On the Western Front, it seems, the situation is in fact taking a turn for the better for the Allies. That, of course, is the sum of impressions for several days.

4 [July]. The rumor that a railroad strike commenced on the 2d has reached even here; my brother did not arrive yesterday, probably for that reason. It remains terrifically hot; in Moscow it is probably quite unbearable. Compared with all those who are sitting in that prison this summer, I must consider myself in heaven. The mendacity of our Obraztsovs, who are in charge of us and our little corner, is confirmed every day (as was always the case, by the way); and these are after all good representatives of the Russian people. Our Volodia has gotten into the habit of going every day to his little cousin and announcing (of course, not only to her parents) that he will marry no one but her; a very promising character, in this as in many other, positive, respects.

[165] A committee of members of the dissolved Constituent Assembly formed a government in Samara following the city's occupation by the Czechs on June 8. Its slogan was "United Independent Free Russia! All power to the Constituent Assembly!"

[166] *Obrazovanie velikorusskogo gosudarstva. Ocherki po istorii xiii-xv stoletii* (Petrograd, 1918); translated into English by A. E. Moorhouse as *The Formation of the Great-Russian State* (Chicago, 1970).

5 *[July]*. My brother, Vladimir Vladimirovich, arrived; his stories were not extensive and added little. Apparently the English navy has disembarked at Murmansk;[167] one has to think that this is only the beginning of further actions. The hunger in Novgorod is very great. The notorious strike did not take place. He came for a short time only, mainly in order to stock up with provisions, and now the question arises of how to make it possible for him to remove provisions from here, in view of all the hindrances that are everywhere placed in the way of shipping out flour. It is too bad that he doesn't want to stay here—the affair would be resolved more simply.

The reading of Presniakov's book has led me to another element of analogy between the contemporary demos and the erstwhile social elite: is not the perfidy of the princes in the appanage and Muscovite centuries a symptom of the same dishonesty with which contemporary Russians are universally infected? I finished the book; it is the work of an intelligent and educated person who has specialized in microscopic analysis: there are many specific, minor observations, but frequently the whole is not seen behind the details.

6 *[July]*. We had the visit of Nikolai Antip'ev again yesterday: he came to find out from my just-arrived brother if there was not a rebellion against soviet authority. Dissappointment with the negative answer: "We are extremely fed up with them. The devil take them!" A remarkably inquisitive person, but you constantly sense the complete confusion of ideas in that agitated head. This morning I was supposed to have debuted on the disk harrow, but my Aleksei Ivanov failed to waken me, reasoning that he could sooner do it himself than teach us, and he in fact did it. This is either a resolve to keep me away from the work so as to say later that he does everything himself or a manifestation of the traditional mistrust of the inept master. I am waiting for news in the mail and the new abominations that we are fated to know of.

7 *[July]*. The newspapers have brought confirmation of the English landing at Murmansk; there is bolshevik confirmation that Mikhail Alek-

---

[167] It is not clear what event Got'e refers to here. There had been an Anglo-American presence in Murmansk since May. Major General Maynard, assigned to command the British expeditionary force at Murmansk, had arrived there on June 23 with six hundred men and a training mission. When Got'e wrote this note, the Bolshevik government's efforts to detach the Murmansk soviet from cooperation with the Allies had just collapsed, and Iur'ev, the chairman of the Murmansk soviet, had been declared an outlaw in a decree signed by Lenin and Trotskii and published in *Izvestiia* on July 1. The main Allied expedition, which the Bolsheviks were trying to forestall, did not disembark in the Russian north until September 4. See George F. Kennan, *The Decision to Intervene* (New York, 1967), chs. 11 and 16.

sandrovich has assumed leadership of something or other in Siberia;[168] news of new disorders in Austria and a new defeat of the Austrians in Italy; and there is the decree on the nationalization of all corporate enterprises.[169] It seems that once again some kind of page in the war is being turned, and the Allied cause is picking up again. We are busy preparing to send provisions with my brother, who is becoming altogether like a bagman. I have finished reading the few books we brought here and am sitting down to do the long-planned book in French.

8 [July]. An entire day yesterday without rumors or incidents. We were visited by the "squatters"[170] from Staroe Zagran'e. Afterward we went over there and sat for a long time on the old balcony facing the linden alley in melancholy contemplation of bygone Zagran'e, like the last Mohicans of a dying world. Today's communications bring no changes in the old impressions; confusion mounts, the fighting does not subside. The universities have been dealt a blow; the notorious charter has been published, and the council meeting called for today will not change it, of course. Poor Russian culture—*si elle a jamais existé.*

9 [July]. Under the influence of the recently decided fate of the university, somber thoughts have crept into my mind again, not because I was unprepared, but just like that, no doubt because the time had come. One of two fates awaits us: either we will be fired "for general cause," like the professors of the Nizhnyi Novgorod Polytechnic Institute, or we will be obliged to adapt to the new charter and put it into practice. I think that we should remain in the university and defend it as long as possible; our position should be preserved by holding it, not by evacuating from fear of being defeated at the time of battle. We have too often seen examples of the latter; but we may have to withdraw in this case as well, after all, since the position may prove to be untenable. And then the question will be, just as with being dismissed—where to go? What to do? Wouldn't it be better all together, as at least an impressive group of professors of Moscow University, to transfer our activity to the Ukraine, where circumstances will perhaps be more conducive to peaceful work and where it will be necessary to defend Russian culture and the Russian

[168] Prior to killing Grand Duke Mikhail Aleksandrovich on July 13, the Bolsheviks disseminated the story that he had fled his place of exile in Perm'. It appears that in fact he was simply taken from his hotel and shot on orders from Moscow.

[169] A decree of June 28, published in *Izvestiia* on June 30 and in *Pravda* on July 2, proclaimed the nationalization of a wide range of industrial corporations. *Dekrety Sovetskoi vlasti*, vol. 2, pp. 498–503.

[170] *Sidel'tsy*, literally "sitters"; in Muscovy the garrison of a besieged fortress. Got'e is referring to his relatives on the adjoining property.

language from Ukrainian particularism? I expressed all these thoughts in a letter to Matvei Kuz'mich Liubavskii, the more so in that he is occupied with the idea of organizing something like the Higher Women's Courses in Ekaterinoslav. I am asking him to share his thoughts with me.

We went to Sandovo yesterday, where we learned the astonishing news that the Czechoslovaks (who are omnipresent now) have apparently occupied Iaroslavl' and Rybinsk; one can take no stock in this rumor, of course. We stopped by to see Fedor Pavlovich Obraztsov, a rich peasant, property owner, former manager of Zagran'e and then the township elder in Shcherbovo; this is a typical little master, to use the words of the bishop. And now, like a practical man, he has not lost his head, but only retrenched. I finally got hold of the little archive of Zagran'e, whose very existence was even denied by earlier generations; it is more interesting than I thought it would be; I will have to select from it everything for the family archive.

10 [July]. We received no new papers today. Accidentally or not? Yesterday was all excitement. Shura Veselago and Talia Tomilovskaia with their offspring and households arrived; there were seven of them altogether, and we had a wake or, as Shura put it, a resurrection feast for the bourgeois all day. Both have remained in the same situations as earlier; the Tomilovskiis work [the farm] themselves, Shura works in a cooperative shop, but both feel the Damoclean sword of revolutionary democracy hanging over their heads. I quizzed them about all the local landowners. In general, there are few completely ruined or sacked estates: the Shvarts's "Pokrov," the Rodichevs' "Viatka." There are those that have been stripped, where the owners have been put on meager rations—for example, the Druris. The Izmailovs, or more exactly Arsenii Petrovich, an old man of seventy, still lives at home (it turns out his wife died in the winter, like Catherine II). The Kashtaevskiis are themselves working on a cooperative basis. Everyone holds onto the old ways; everything is hanging by a thread; we ourselves joked again yesterday that we are the last of the Mohicans here. In the evening we had supper, with something to drink, at our place—we should drink the wine that is here before the gorillas do. The nocturnal send-off of my brother took on truly Karamazov-like characteristics; I couldn't take it, and went to bed; poor Nina had to stay to the bitter end.

11 [July]. Aleksei Ivanov returned from taking my brother, who ordered him to wait for the return train from Sonkovo, since he thought he might come back on it. However, he did not come back on the return train. Only a few people came with that train; the Krasnyi Kholm red guards departed for Sonkovo, perhaps further; Aleksei Ivanov brought back a rumor that in Rybinsk houses are being burned and people killed. All this shows that something is happening. I think that the most likely thing is some kind of local rebellion. Yesterday I began to sort out the Zagran'e archive, which turns out to be more interesting than I thought.

12 [July]. A boring St. Peter's Day. A trip to church. I heard the astonishing news of a general strike, the alleged fall of the Soviet government, and, the main thing, the murder of Mirbach;[171] all this requires further checking and verification, for it all could have innumerable consequences. There are few facts for philosophizing or writing commentaries; therefore it is better to wait patiently. The day passed in the usual fashion: dinner in Staroe Zagran'e, the endless visits of the priests, the procession of drunks along the path next to the wood. All the same, judging from the rumors that vaguely reach us, something is happening in the world. How I would like to know precisely what it is.

14 [July]. I wrote nothing yesterday because we went to see Aleksandr Mikhailovich Veselago and spent twenty-four hours on the road. We stopped along the way for several minutes at the post office. There were no newspapers, except for the bolshevik *The Poor* for the 9th;[172] it reported that a revolt of the Left SRs in Moscow had been suppressed, but Mirbach was in fact killed! In Zaluzh'e we found the newspaper for the 7th, in which we found nothing new. There is nothing to say about our stay in Zaluzh'e: gradual continuation of the deterioration that was already noticeable long ago. They are hanging by a thread, like everyone else. The invalid with a head injury must work himself in order to defend his deteriorating home, and in order to defend himself from the bolsheviks from the sovdeps, he serves as chairman of the local cooperative, to which he was elected by the peasants because they unanimously consider him to be the only honest man in the entire district. It is interesting to note that M. A. Koliubakin, the son of the prominent Kadet and grandson of the longtime local *zemskii nachal'nik*,[173] and himself a Kadet, has been appointed a people's judge for Zaluzh'e township.

We reached home safely today. Here we found the newspaper for the 12th, in which I understood nothing. Apparently the bolsheviks have

---

[171] The German ambassador, Count Mirbach, was assassinated on July 6 by the Left SRs Bliumkin and Andreev in an attempt to provoke a renewal of hostilities with Germany. The assassination was allegedly accompanied by an attempt to provoke an uprising against the Bolsheviks, which failed.

[172] *Bednota* (1918–1920) was a Bolshevik party paper for peasants.

[173] The *zemskii nachal'nik*, or land captain, was an offical responsible for general supervision of peasant affairs at the local level. He was appointed by the government from among the local gentry.

won a victory over the Left SRs; but, also apparently, the whole story is not being told in the newspaper (*New Life*, St. Petersburg edition).[174] There is a report of the treason and death of the famous bolshevik leader Murav'ev[175] and a whole bouquet of mutually contradictory and internally inconsistent news. In addition, M. A. Kutorga passed on rumors, from Krasnyi Kholm and the railroad, of the fall of the Soviet government. I think this is an absurd rumor; but everything taken together creates a picture of confusion that there is no point in sorting out.

15 [July]. We went out to mow early in the morning; for the first time in my life I mowed the morning dew; physical fatigue, but an agreeable feeling of fatigue and of something accomplished, the more so in that it was a fine morning. The newspapers did not come at all; they brought no rumors at all from Sandovo, either, only two letters from Emma Wilken and from Iakovlev; from Emma's letter, as from the letter of Lena Reiman received in the last mail, it is apparent that living is not easy in Moscow and its environs, that the trains did not run for two days, even the commuter trains, and that there was panic. Iakovlev apparently concentrated his thoughts on the consequences of Mirbach's assassination. Apparently it was relatively calm in Moscow on Tuesday. There is nothing to do but wait, mow, and, so far as strength and time will allow, work at the writing desk.

16 [July]. We mowed again in the evening; this morning less, because the Obraztsovs went out late themselves and didn't wake us up—perhaps in order to say later that they did everything themselves. Nevertheless, when I woke up I went to the meadow and mowed for an hour and a half. In general, the work is going well; I think we can handle the mowing. Lena has just arrived; things are not going so well at their place and, what is worst of all, it is the workers; the best was the Pole, Franz, who returned home, and Khodzha, a Rumanian from among the Austrian war prisoners, but the Russians are good for nothing.

17 [July]. Intense work at haying, and in the intervals I work rather successfully at the writing desk. The absence of news does not get in the

[174] *Novaia zhizn'* was an independent SD newspaper, successor to *Svobodnaia zhizn'*, which appeared sporadically in June and July.

[175] Mikhail Artem'evich Murav'ev (1880–1918) was a lieutenant colonel in the imperial army who had taken up with the Left SRs and then the Bolsheviks in 1917. He was charged with the defense of Petrograd in October and then participated in campaigns against the Volunteer Army in the south. On June 13 he had been named commander of the eastern (Czech) front. In July he was involved in the Left SR attempt to revive hostilities with the Germans: he undertook to get the Czechs to agree to move on Moscow to support the anticipated uprising. He was killed while resisting arrest on July 11.

Map 2. Revolution and Civil War in European Russia, 1917–1922. From Nicholas V. Riasanovsky, *A History of Russia*, 3d ed. 1977. Reproduced with permission of Oxford University Press.

way, and maybe even facilitates the sorting out of the Zagran'e archive and practice with French stylistics. I look on the former as a final tribute to the home that was good to me; I look on the latter as a heavy obligation and, perhaps, a means to scrape together some money. Nina has just gone to the post office and in an hour or two I will receive my standard allotment of abomination. Nothing at the post office; the newspapers in Moscow are obviously shut down, but why didn't we get *New Life* for the 12th, which Mania brought me on Sunday? We got only a few copies of *The Poor* and Masha's letter, from which it is clear that there was shooting in Moscow, only not a lot, and on Friday the 12th, when the letter was written, all was quiet. What is going on; is anything at all going on?

19 [July]. I wrote nothing yesterday, because we worked all day; we had to mow about six hours in all; I note this as a not uninteresting phenomenon in the life of a respected professor who wishes to defend his home to the last. It is a strange thing: when you are mowing, you keep recollecting past journeys. If only some day one could look out on the wide world again, far from the realm of the gorillas! Today promises the usual excitement over the harvesting of the hay.

20 [July]. At the post office I read one of the bolshevik *Pravdas*—it seems that all is well in the West; if the Kadets are not adopting a German orientation, they are at least gravitating toward an understanding with them; the Czechoslovaks are squeezing the bolsheviks in various places. Everything else remains unchanged. A letter from Malfi—it seems they are leaving for France today. The good and gentle ideologue—but we will still do something. Work in the meadow all day; we all get dog-tired.

21 [July]. Against all possible odds, we arranged a "helping hand" today in order to mow our far meadow in Gorokhovo. It worked, but on the other hand we wore ourselves out, since this time, in contrast to previous years, we could not be the master, observing from on high, but had to be a participant in the work. They woke me up at 4:30; I had to march over two versts, work as hard as I could there with the scythe, and then take part in the reward; that is, amuse the gorillas with the gramophone, drink beer, and variously entertain them. This continued until 5 P.M.; twenty-four people were fed lunch, tea, and dinner, and eight buckets of beer were drunk. It must be said that the attitude of these people was quite normal, habitual, and during the "help" in no way reminded one that we are in a revolution—that is one of the contradictions of life.

In the evening I had a conversation with O. R. Volkov, a former land captain presently suspected of Kadetism; there were interesting details about several contemporary personages. In Krasnyi Kholm, the sovdep is filled with recidivist thieves and robbers, whom he named for me individually. In general, he lives, as we do, under a constant sword of Damocles. We went to bed from fatigue at 10 P.M.

22 [July]. We mowed clover beginning in the morning. There was nothing at all in the mail; that means the newspapers are shut down as before, but why are there no letters? Responses to the letters sent from here are hardly coming at all. Some respite today; there is no haying, and I can spend the day at my more habitual occupations. But toward evening we again worked for three hours drying the clover and stacking it.

23 [July]. Disgusting weather; a standstill in the work. I am taking advantage of the situation to work as much as possible. I feel that my nerves are in general stronger. I can coolly examine in my mind all the coming abominations that we will have to experience before we die or better times arrive; I have not got that oppressed feeling about surrounding nature, I even have less of that feeling of prison that I had upon arriving here. One has to think that this improvement in well-being will be helpful in the future as well. But these are only nerves, whereas one's judgment says the same thing as before, and perhaps with even greater clarity—everything has perished: country, people, and the future, both for us and in general.

25 [July]. The personal letters received from the post office have produced a pitiful impression. It seems the Moscow terror is intensifying: the telephones have been disconnected; the newspapers have all been suppressed, except for theirs, of course; people are in the dark; only rumors that as a rule make no sense creep out of the gloom. The only agreeable news was my father-in-law's report that he has been elected a member of the administration of the cinematographic enterprise "Neptune." God grant that this helps relieve their material situation and that the bolsheviks don't shut down the cinemas as well. I rushed to Sandovo in the rain for the sake of three registered letters, because one of them, it seemed, should have contained information on the procedures for recovering things from [safe-deposit] boxes; instead, I got the notice back. I just don't know what will come of this. Yesterday and this morning we again mowed. Why not live on an uninhabited island—sometimes it is better somehow without news. Work has been going well these days on the future French book and the Zagran'e chronicle.

26 [July]. I worked all morning in the meadow and, while raking hay, thought over the further scheme of my French book. Yesterday I read to

Nina what I had written; it is turning out better than I had hoped. Today I was seized by horror at the thought of our life next winter—at the thought of the completely unrelieved horror and hopelessness, for nothing is changing; everything remains thus far as before, and under such conditions further existence is impossible. I sometimes regret that I am writing down so little now, but in fact, thank God: it means fewer heavy thoughts in my head and stronger nerves.

27 [July]. No newspapers as before; nor letters, either; on the one hand you are outraged, on the other it is even better that you live as if on an uninhabited island. The weather is disgusting; I worked all day at the writing desk.

28 [July]. Volodia's nameday; they baked a tiny cake with white flour, and a large one of black-bread crusts. They went to church, but the priest, apparently tormented by his appetite, finished the mass at 8 o'clock, so that our people, that is Nina and Volodia, who left home at 8 o'clock, found the church locked. Volodia was overjoyed to be driving our nag. That was the whole of the celebration. Both Nina and I had a feeling of unrelieved melancholy all day from the present situation and from what lies still ahead; even here the situation is revolting, so far as people are concerned. It appears that our Obraztsovs stole cabbage from the Zaprud'e garden; on Saturday a "committee" unexpectedly appeared in Staroe Zagran'e and conducted an audit of the milking, and so on, but first heard the denunciation of the cook, which of course turned out to be false. There you have the existence of my cousins.

Perhaps the weather, which was awful until evening, is having an effect, aside from everything else, and also the absence of news. I tried to kill time with old letters and finished the Zagran'e chronicle; it turned out fairly interesting, although of course it would have been possible to collect even more. All the same, it is outrageous to think that it has been three weeks already since we learned anything about what is going on in the world.

29 [July]. A beautiful day; I worked in the field from 5 o'clock in the morning to 6 in the evening; that is good for the nerves. Nothing from the post office except a notice for a registered letter. The metal fixtures have been stolen from our bathhouse. There are burglaries everywhere; as a result, the peasants are removing the hay to their yards out of a very great fear that their brethren will rob them.

30 [July]. Work in the field all day. It makes you tired and dull-witted. A letter from my wife's mother, which left a sad impression. It is apparent that life in Moscow is harder than ever, and that my *belle-mère*'s mood is no better than my own. At times it is frightening to think that one has to return once again to that vale of tears, rage, and want. No, if this all continues for a long time, we won't be able to endure it and will have to flee as paupers somewhere abroad.

31 [July]. We traveled to the post office to find out what we could, and I found out that in Moscow all nonbolshevik newspapers have been closed until full consolidation of soviet power.[176] That means we are doomed to take nourishment from the soviet press for the foreseeable future. Japan is doing something after all, judging from the news that leaks through; it is apparent that in Siberia and in Samara things are settling down. The French are beating the Germans—that is the main thing. The Germans have sent Helfferich to Moscow—that means that great importance is attached to this post.[177] The stew thickens, and we are more and more turning into a *canneton à la rouennaise*, which is pressed to yield more juice.

AUGUST

1 [August]. A *coup de théâtre* last night. For the first time all summer, we went to take a walk beyond the Zaprud'e hill; we had gone about half a verst, when suddenly there were cries: "Return home, someone has come." "Who?" "We don't know!" At first I thought it was probably some local committee or something of that kind. We returned and on Zaprud'e hill at the windmill I met Ivan, the former doorman from Simeiz. At first I didn't even recognize him; Nina, on seeing him, imagined that one of her parents must have died. As it turned out, the notorious fine for sugar had been assessed to me and on Saturday, July 14, the comrades had appeared to collect 10,000 rubles from me or arrest me. According to Ivan, everyone in our house had hoped that the papers on that affair had perished in the revolt of 6/25–7/7 and were not at all worried. As I was not there, they asked my address. Somehow or other, someone

---

[176] A decree to that effect was published in *Izvestiia* on July 28. In fact, some non-Bolshevik SD papers were left in operation. The decree was directed specifically against the "bourgeois" press.

[177] Karl Helfferich (1872–1924), a former state treasurer and interior minister, had been appointed to succeed Mirbach as ambassador to Moscow. "On July 28, the new German ambassador, Karl Helfferich, one of the most prominent leaders in Berlin economic circles, arrived at Moscow. His appointment showed clearly the desire of the Germans to strengthen their economic relations with Soviet Russia." From Chicherin's report to the Seventh Congress of Soviets, November 6, 1919; cited in Bunyan, *Intervention, Civil War, and Communism in Russia*, pp. 127–28.

informed my wife's parents, and they entered negotiations for a settlement. This was on Sunday or Monday. They sent Ivan to warn us about all this and to say that the money had been found, that they are dickering, that there is a chance of reducing the figure, and that the matter has been taken care of. Since we bought for ourselves only seven pounds of the one pud and five pounds that we had the misfortune to acquire, the sugar is proving dear. Ivan also said that we should receive a telegram with a statement of how much all this is costing. Having eaten and taken what provisions could be sent, Ivan left during the night. It was a dream, but a nightmarish one. But the main thing is, when will the telegram finally ending the affair arrive? More than twenty-four hours have passed, and it has not yet appeared. And how will it be taken care of? How to pay back the borrowed money? Although I expected this affair, and it is better that it is being settled, one can only try to confront and deal with such horror and violence with equanimity and indifference, if not coolly. The general news conveyed by Ivan was for some reason optimistic; why, I don't understand myself. Everyone is waiting and hoping for something; the most interesting news he brought, however, was how to get abroad through the south. That is where we shall have to flee; the reality of that fact is becoming ever clearer to me. A very bad frame of mind all day and anguish, not from that episode, but from the new trials that are being prepared for us—cholera, chronic hunger, chronic mockery and humiliation, the possibility of war in the streets of Moscow, and so on. I took pleasure only in the fact that I had to work all day in the fields—we gathered the hay and clover rather successfully, so far as the weather was concerned.

2 [August]. A quiet day; we received no telegrams; in the evening they came over from the old estate to hear the Zagran'e chronicle, and while we were reading it, we were visited by the respected gorillas from Gora, Ivan Terent'ev and Ivan Iakovlev. A five o'clock was arranged, to which the Obraztsovs were invited; it was a touching communion with the people, which lasted about two hours. After that, the reading of the Zagran'e chronicle was continued.

3 [August]. No telegram; a feeling of dull anxiety, although reason dictates that if no one is bothering you that means the affair will somehow work out. I went to the post office: nothing, not even one letter. I got five issues of *Our Century*[178] from somebody, from which I learned that the Japanese are moving from Vladivostok, the English are moving into

---

[178] *Nash vek* (1906–1918) was a Petrograd newspaper of the independent left.

Tashkent, the Alekseevtsy[179] have occupied Stavropol' and Armavir, the Czechoslovaks Ekaterinburg, and the Allies Arkhangel'sk. A ring is being formed, and woe to all those who remain within it. I am thinking that Moscow will turn into a veritable flaming Gehenna. And that gang of fools is calling officers to active duty to occupy command positions.

4 [August]. We received a telegram: "So far, so good." We concluded from it that this story is not yet finished, but that there is a chance to get out of it not too expensively. Dinner and tea in the evening at Mania Kutorga's place; there were three engineers from the railroad and two Countesses Tolstoi, carried by the storm to the Popovs in Andreitsevo. These are typical *épaves de la révolution,* cousins of the Petersburg Counts D. I. and I. I. Tolstoi. Pensioners of the crown, they have lost everything; one works somewhere, the other is quite ill, but pleasant to talk with. All this was so strange and so sad, this feast in the house at Zagran'e, which is living out its last days.

5 [August]. Received a letter from Georgievskii; one senses that there is hunger in Moscow; he also writes that the bolsheviks are apparently intending to deprive us of our two-month vacation, but that is all the same to me—I have decided not to leave any earlier than the 15th. News in the papers: the assassination of Eichhorn in Kiev has further enraged the Moscow sovdeps against the bourgeoisie and the peasants.[180] That is fine; the more the German bigwigs suffer, the better. The Left SRs should be used for this; it is all they are good for.

6 [August]. I am trying to work as much as possible, first because the weather outside is terrible, such as I can't recall in a long time, and second because the time of my stay is limited, after all, and I want to do as much as possible here in relatively peaceful surroundings. Certainly in Moscow it will be possible to get only a little work done, and that will hardly be satisfactory. The more I think, the clearer it becomes that the time will come or is likely to come when flight will be necessary; we will have to make up our minds now, upon returning to Moscow, to prepare for an evacuation to the south—Khar'kov, for example. In any case we will have

[179] The reference is to the Volunteer Army, which was headed by General Denikin at this time. Its immediate predecessor had been known as the Alekseev Organization, after its founder, General M. V. Alekseev. During late spring and early summer of 1918, the Volunteer Army had a series of uninterrupted successes against the Bolsheviks in the south.

[180] Field Marshal Hermann von Eichhorn (1848–1918), commander in chief of the German occupation forces, was assassinated on July 30 by Boris Donskoi, a Left SR, in the same action that took the life of Mirbach in Moscow.

to rescue ourselves from Moscow, because Moscow is going to be the arena of unprecedented events of horror. What fortune that hunger has shown up here only in the last few days; otherwise I am sure that it would have been impossible to hold out. There is enough patience for two weeks; it is too close to the new harvest to expect excesses. But if one were to wait long, there would of course be excesses; it is enough to see these oppressed and strained faces seeking bread—for credit, so far. But will there be bread when the local bread is once again eaten up? They say that a part of the Ves'egonsk sovdep with a detachment of red guards is transferring to Sandovo. That is bad; it's a good thing, though, that we belong to another district according to them; that reduces the chances of being run off the "people's property" where we live.

I haven't mentioned here the death of Nicholas II,[181] but that is because I was able to assimilate that information only yesterday from reading *Our Century* for July 20. Nicholas II shared the fate of Louis XVI and Charles I, but in a modernized form, turned inside out *à la russe*, without the hypocritical solemnity of the English revolution or the unbridled, but still solemn, manner of the French. Nicholas was killed without a trial—that is especially characteristic of the Russians—far from the capitals, hurriedly, unnecessarily, by men who were afraid of their own shadows. He himself did everything possible to make this happen; but his disappearance constitutes the untying of one of the innumerable secondary knots of our Time of Troubles, and the monarchical principle can only gain from it.

7 [August]. Local rumors have it that the entire Ves'egonsk sovdep is moving to Sandovo; it seems that they have a foundation. This really can provoke our being run out of here; if only we can hold on for about three weeks. You also hear that here and there they are already reaping and milling, and that the milled wheat will supposedly be taken away and "put under the control of the committee"; the latter rumors are apparently making the local population nervous.

8 [August]. The newspapers for the 2d of August brought nothing new. The rumors about Sandovo fortunately turned out to be false. Toward evening there was a comical incident, *style moderne*. Two people approached our house: one was decked out in a double-breasted suit of sailcloth; behind him was a person in a soldier's uniform, with a saber and barefoot. I went out on the veranda. The first one says: "Representative of the militia of Ves'egonsk district." Scenes, one more awful and impossible than the next, leaped into my imagination. But the affair

[181] The murder of Nicholas II and his family in Tobol'sk had occurred on July 17.

ended in the most comical, and at the same time sad, way: a detachment of militia consisting of ten men had been sent to Sandovo; they had been there four days already, but they were given no rations and they were starving, and therefore they were begging outright—their request was to give them some bread. We invited them in and treated them to bread and milk, and gave them some bread to take with them, asking that this incident remain confidential, since we were giving them bread not from a surfeit, but from our own ration. From the conversation, it turned out that one of them was the former chief of the Ves'egonsk fire brigade, fired for no reason by the bolsheviks or, more precisely, by the individuals who are running things there under the bolshevik label; in the end they gave him compensation in the form of the job of secretary to the Sandovo militia detachment. The other turned out to be a former sausage-maker for Belov in Moscow, who entered the militia because he had nothing to eat and the sausage plant was not working! They offered to pay us for our hospitality. There you have a living picture from the Russian revolution—everything is mixed together here: hunger, bolshevism, charity, disorganization, and the poverty of people who have been pushed to the limit. As for the Sandovo rumors, they all turned out to be more or less nonsense; like everything here, by the way. The detachment of militia remains in Sandovo, but the detachment of the red "guards" or "army" (is it not all the same?) has been temporarily sent to Shcherbovo township to help the infamous poor.[182]

10 [August]. We paid a visit to the two Countesses Tolstoi, who have taken up domicile with the Popovs at Andreitsevo. We had a very pleasant chat with them; the sick one is not stupid; one feels very sorry for them, the unfortunates, the more so that it is not easy for them to live here either, because of the quarreling of the two Popov sisters. I have finally received answers to some of my letters. Iakovlev writes that new staff and thirty-five librarians are being brought into the library, but *qu'il s'en moque, j'en fais autant*, and if that happens I will try for only one thing—not to preside over that collegium. Bogoslovskii reports that university affairs are very bad and that beginning on September 15 "they" are going to put into effect their rules, which have now been worked out by some kind of new assembly, consisting of six professors, six commissars and sovdepshchiks, and six students, primarily of extremist leanings. Poor universities. But all the same, if the situation drags on, it will be necessary to relocate in other countries. One recalls the psychology of Pecherin—who renounced everything—as it is expressed in one of his

---

[182] The *kombedy*.

bad and sincere verses, where it is said that he is sailing on the sea, free in spirit.[183]

12 [August]. The former manager of Zagran'e, Marem'iana Gracheva, has become more than friendly with the former head of the sovdep, the bolshevik and Kronstadter[184] Smirnov from Besovo; whence, naturally, Marem'iana's desire to settle in Zagran'e, and Smirnov's desire to help her. The members of the current sovdep, or at least the director of the supply department, is on their side, the more so in that this latter fellow is himself from Parfen'evo, where Marem'iana lives. This explains all the unexpected audits in Zagran'e, all the reproaches to Lena as the manager and agent of Soviet authority. All this came to light yesterday at a "general meeting," to which my cousins were invited. It was proposed to remove them from the administration, with recourse to petty reproaches; but the evidence was in their favor and the general meeting itself did not go with the agitators, but supported them, which is very characteristic, a sign of the current times. A living picture of the activities of Soviet power in the village. I was at the Blagoveshchenskiis' place. My sister-in-law had just received a letter from her daughter in Lugansk: she invites everyone there, to revive from starving; those words may be prophetic for everyone. Young Blagoveshchenskii, Lesha, was indignant about the behavior in the Kashin normal school, where he finished the course a year ago: the pupils broke into the council meeting, smoked in classes, forced out unliked teachers. Along with this the narrator charitably added that if he were in the school now, he would probably be the leader of the troublemakers, but that he now understands how all that is terrible and unacceptable; a characteristic example of one of life's object lessons. The weather is the worst it has been here for a long time; I don't ever remember such a July.

13 [August]. Vague rumors of some kind of abominations in Petrograd; the newspaper *Our Century* has apparently been shut down; in Soviet Russia, that is, in the ressefeser,[185] there remains only the ressefeser press. I helped my cousins harvest clover all day.

[183] Vladimir Sergeevich Pecherin (1807–1885) was a young idealist of the 1830s, a classics professor at Petersburg University and Westernizer of the Chaadaev stamp, who emigrated in 1836 and took monastic vows in the Catholic church. He lived most of the remainder of his life in Ireland and died there.

[184] That is, a veteran of the Kronstadt garrison in the Gulf of Finland, which was a center of revolutionary activism and support for the Bolsheviks in 1917.

[185] From the initials for the full name of the republic, RSFSR. *Our Century* was closed on August 3.

14 [August]. Neither newspapers, nor money, nor letters from the post office—it's outrageous. We worked all day helping Lena and the Kutorgas take care of their clover; since they haven't got a handyman, their position is much worse and more helpless than ours. Today is Volod'ka's birthday—seven years old—already a big boy, a regular lad. Nina went with him to church; he drove, and there was complete satisfaction. We harvested clover again all day.

16 [August]. Two days of uninterrupted work in order to help Lena and Mania harvest the clover they had allotted to them. It was a fine school for learning the business—better than our haying, because we had the use only of our own bourgeois labor. A typical scene: we had not even finished harvesting the desiatina[186] lying near the village of Gora when one of the village inhabitants appeared with a basket and began to mow the stubble; if the desiatina hadn't already been raked, he would probably have taken the clover. In the evenings we had communal suppers: they took place in the old house, and the bourgeois rested at them. Yesterday's supper, however, was marked by a little domestic scandal between Mania and her husband, in which Kutorga manifested certain characteristic features of the Russian *intelligent*: already in the morning and then again at supper he talked about how to avoid offending the muzhik should circumstances change, but when his wife drank a little glass of liqueur, he shouted that he doesn't allow her to do that, made a scandal, and left the table, displaying despotism, instability, and poor upbringing.

It is difficult to live without news; one felt this especially today, when we have not been occupied with physical labor, perhaps because of the weather, which continues to be awful. I have not experienced such spells of bad weather here for a long time—a northern climate and nasty surroundings, that's all there is to it.

17 [August]. There have been no more newspapers, and there won't be any, that is obvious. From their newspapers it appears that we are in a "ring of fire." The information from A.S.[187] is interesting: the Germans have issued an ultimatum to the bolsheviks on manufacturing and on the liberation of former officers who are currently under arrest, and the bolsheviks have supposedly refused. There are a great many arrests in Moscow—among the officers and the "capitalists"—and yet those who write have the hope that something new is ahead. You don't know what to think; but Moscow is truly becoming a "flaming Gehenna," and there is no desire to return there.

[186] A standard Russian measure of land equal to 2.7 acres.
[187] Probably Got'e's colleague Aleksandr Savin.

18 [August]. Endlessly sad thoughts from the letters received yesterday. A genuine dictatorship of the proletariat has been introduced—mindless cruelty of the dark masses, stirred up by the demagogues, directed against the more educated elements. I am beginning to have a feeling of terror. Moscow will undoubtedly be the scene of the greatest horrors. What can be done to avoid them? This morning Nina admitted that she has now begun to share my urge to throw everything aside and leave for somewhere far, far away.

19 [August]. The Blagoveshchenskii family was here; they, too, confirmed the diverse rumors to the effect that various forces are moving from all points in the direction of Moscow. All this requires checking, of course, but one rumor confirms another and, in juxtaposing them, one can come to the conclusion that there is no smoke without fire. This, however, does not bode imminent happiness on any side—the bloodletting in Moscow will be the worst of all, either general excesses in the last days of rule of Soviet power, or some kind of siege of Moscow. Just so long as some kind of end comes as soon as possible. One is worried and thinks about all this especially when preparing to go to Moscow, and departure is not far off. In the evening we went to visit Countess A. G. Tolstaia, who has fallen completely into the hands of the half-witted and half-crazy Popov sisters. Nothing from the post office.

20 [August]. A terrible melancholy since morning, mainly owing to the fact that you absolutely don't know what to do—should the whole family go to Moscow to face hunger, or should we separate, with the risk of being cut off from each other? We should make up our minds to stay until Saturday, and then take some decision. In the afternoon Nikolai Antip'ev brought news confirming what A. S. had written: the demands of Helfferich, their rejection, and his departure.[188] Upon checking, it turned out that Lena had repeated my words about this to the Gora folk, and thus the story came back to me again. Nevertheless, it is stated in the issue of the newspaper that I received from Gora that the personnel of the embassy left for Petersburg; that confirms all the rest. In addition, the French are again giving the Germans a good beating.

21 [August]. Nothing from the post office. While in Sandovo, I looked through "their" newspapers—also little news of interest. Shenkursk has been occupied; that means that they are headed for Vologda; the aim of the Anglo-French is probably to seize the Zvanka-Perm' road, and we

[188] Helfferich's mission left Moscow on August 7 for Pskov, in German-occupied territory.

may all perish in the ring of fire into which we have fallen. And in these circumstances we have to go to accursed Moscow.

22 [August]. A telegram from Novgorod—my brother has been arrested for failure to observe the rules on registration of officers: "come quickly." A new accusation, perhaps a blow, perhaps a misfortune for him. I will have to be done with everything here early and go to Novgorod; to do what, I don't know myself. Oh, the insanity of the man who sees only what he wants to see, and doesn't face life. Another annoyance: a township committee of the village poor with unlimited authority is being formed. That doesn't concern us personally, as we are leaving here, but it is perhaps the end for our Zagran'e. I had such a feeling of melancholy all day that I took a bromide for it. In Staroe Zagran'e in the evening we saw Chudnovskii, who passed on the rumors—there are many of them, and they are quite diverse; according to them, changes will not be introduced by the Germans, but will come from the east. Whoever survives will see. I sent an inquiry to Novgorod before going there.

23 [August]. Worst of all is the knowledge that I have to go to Moscow; it is all the same to those who never left, but to return to flaming Gehenna is hard; it is also hard to leave the relative calm in which two months were passed, and also—to leave near ones, if only for two weeks.

24 [August]. Letters from Moscow that make clear (1) that life there is outrageously bad; (2) that hopes for changes for the better go on there unrestrained; (3) that the incident with the sugar, far from being liquidated, has only been postponed until my return. It is recommended that I not go to Moscow until some kind of changes have occurred; and how long will that be? All this obliges me to go straight to Moscow in order to clarify this whole business by myself and get rid of it. They have almost finished reaping and have done some seeding; yesterday Nina reaped two piles, and I—seven sheaves!! A record for the old professor.

25 [August]. A telegram came: "not yet released, come." That means I have to go to Novgorod, and then to Moscow to face a number of serious annoyances, the unknown. Now everything here is already receding into the background; it is too bad that I didn't have time to draft at least the sixth chapter of my future book. When will I now be able to return to it? The day today will have to be devoted to organizing my departure and preparations.

26 [August]. It has been finally established that I am going tonight; the family will stay on until the 1st of September or until word from me.

And so the summer of 1918 was spent in Zagran'e; and thanks be to fate for that. No news at all from the post office. I have to set forth into a world of darkness, horrors, and rumors. Yesterday the Blagoveshchenskiis said that a decree has been published according to which anyone, even an illiterate, can enter any institution of higher learning if he has reached sixteen years of age; moreover the poor peasants and the proletariat are given priority.[189] This is already *delirium tremens*.

SEPTEMBER

4 [September]. I wrote down nothing for a whole week; the cause was my movements, Moscow troubles, and living away from home. There are many impressions from those days, and they must be written down. The journey to Krasnyi Kholm was very unpleasant—the roads reminded me of the good old days when Nina and I traveled to Zagran'e on our *voyage de noce*. In Molokovo—the lamentations of Aleksandra Ivanovna and her spouse about contemporary events; the older generation has understood that it will get nothing from the new order. The road to Sonkovo was decent, but farther on was genuine pandemonium. At first I stood over the brake, where I was witness to an argument between a bolshevik officer, armed with a saber and a whip, and a worker of the Office for Preparation of State Papers, obviously a menshevik or sR; the argument was intensely passionate, with a threatening tone on the part of the "officer," who was probably from among the former accelerated-promotion ensigns. Afterward a lady traveling with four children gave me shelter in a second-class compartment, and I considered myself fortunate. From Bologoe to Chudovo I rode in another place, also at the feet of a lady, who was sleeping with a child. The train was late arriving in Volkhov, the steamer was missed, and I sat for eight hours at the Chudovo station, which had been transformed into the filthiest cloaca, and in order to receive the right to buy a ticket for Novgorod I had to pay a ruble tribute to the local sovdep. While I was in Chudovo, an echelon of the red army passed by—the horses and equipment in good order, the humans possessing the usual physiognomies, on which were written impudence, self-satisfaction, and everything else except military spirit. In each car, besides the soldiers, there was a girl, a miserable, cheap, Petersburg girl. If all the soldiers of the RSFSR are like that, there will be no victory. I arrived in Novgorod at 7 P.M. the 28th; I went on foot and, going as far

[189] On August 2 the Sovnarkom promulgated a decree on the rules of admission to institutions of higher education of the RSFSR (published in *Izvestiia* on August 6). It opened the universities to all comers, free of charge, with no educational prerequisites. *Dekrety Sovetskoi vlasti*, vol. 3, p. 141.

as Sophia and the Volkhov,[190] I was immediately struck by the beauty of the town. Going over to the Trade Embankment, I could no longer get along without a cabbie, and I found one for five rubles. There are more cabbies in Novgorod than in Moscow. I stayed in Novgorod from the evening of the 28th to 1 P.M. of the 31st.

My impressions are divided sharply in two—the business with my brother, and Novgorod itself. On arriving, I learned that my brother was in jail, having been arrested on the street, on the basis of a denunciation, for nonregistration, to which he was liable as an officer; moreover, in the "Extraordinary Commission,"[191] which exists in Novgorod, too, he quarreled with the Latvians there. I set myself the task of determining his situation, getting a visit with him, and facilitating his release. It turned out that he was in the custody of the Extraordinary Commission, which has to turn him over to the revolutionary tribunal. It was of course impossible to release him so long as he was in the hands of the Extraordinary Commission; with difficulty I got a visit with him. This is how it was. I show up at the Extraordinary Commission, which is filled with Latvian girls; I am sent into a room where one such personage is sitting. I lay out the request, she absents herself and then brings me the answer of an invisible deity: it is not allowed. I ask for a personal meeting with this deity, who is called "comrade Vitin," a thickset Latvian with a dull face and dirty fingernails, wearing a red necktie and a dirty jacket. I again lay out my request and show my documents: a paper issued to me for the right to return to Moscow by an institution called "Sovdep— evacuation commission" produces an impression on him, and he gives me permission for the visit. While they were writing a paper for me, he suddenly ran up to me again and asked, "And where did you learn my name?" with the intention of finding out something. "Why, it's on your door," I answered, pointing to the corresponding plaque. The malicious fool retreated with a crooked smile. Once I learned [my brother's] situation, I set about working for its earliest possible improvement following his transfer to the revolutionary tribunal. I had a discussion on that account with the military commissar of the province (who is also chairman of the tribunal), the former military investigator Makarov, with the chairman of the people's court, the former court investigator Vasil'ev, and with the investigator attached to the tribunal, Kupriianov (one of the intelligentsia type of military bureaucrat). All promised me help and were very polite; but in seeing these individuals from the former judiciary in the role of bolshevik judges, I marveled at the depth of corruption

[190] The Cathedral of St. Sophia (1052) and the Volkhov River, which traverses Novgorod.
[191] The Cheka.

into which the Russian people has fallen. I left after seeing my brother and getting a promise that they would summon me if the need arose; they promised to release my brother in a week or ten days. Now I fear that the wounding of Lenin will prolong the affair.[192]

I was able to use moments of the first day, half of the second, and the morning of the third for an inspection of Novgorod. If Novgorod were not in Russia, masses of tourists would visit it; it would be the object of pilgrimages. Here it is forgotten and run-down, although the latter characteristic gives it a special charm. Among the monuments, I inspected Sophia, Nereditsa,[193] St. George's and St. Anthony's monasteries,[194] and one or two churches. The impression was enormous; in addition, I walked around all the ramparts that surround Novgorod. The former life of Novgorod somehow could be felt especially vividly, particularly on the Sophia Embankment, where the streets have remained just as crooked and crisscrossed as in the old days, whereas on the Trade Embankment all the streets were replanned, probably after a fire. There was the same feeling at the view of the Volkhov and its embankment, where the timber stores and the merchants' row open, again as in the old days, right on the river. The view from the bridge in the direction of [Lake] Il'men, framed by Gorodishche[195] and St. George's Monastery, is magnificent—an extraordinary breadth and sweep of view. But the greatest impression is made by the solitary Nereditsa church on the bluff, with a few little houses nearby. Who built it, who painted those frescoes, and on whose initiative? The silence of the ages. Antiquity, overgrown with time and neglect, a vivid trace of bygone life, lost in the midst of the current chaos. My brother's apartment is on the edge of town and his windows look right out on Nereditsa. There is a wonderful view from the bluff: the plain in all directions, on which the monasteries can be seen as well as the town—St. Cyril's, Skovorodskii, Khutyn'—and individual churches from the same epoch as Nereditsa—Volotovo, Kovalevo, and others. Coming to Gorodishche, I sat for a long time on the slope, recalling how the princely vice-regents looked from here on the town they were forbidden to enter. I was able to cross over to the other bank of the Volkhov there to St. George's, the wealthiest of Novgorod monasteries

[192] Lenin had been shot on August 30, allegedly by Fania Kaplan (born Feiga Efimovna Roidman, 1890–1918), a woman who had been imprisoned for terrorism before the Revolution. Got'e later refers to her as "Roid-Kaplan," following the Bolshevik press.

[193] The frescoes in the Church of the Savior in Nereditsa, near Novgorod (1198) were among the most celebrated monuments of Old Russian religious art. They were virtually destroyed in the Second World War.

[194] Both were ancient monasteries (twelfth century) in the immediate environs of Novgorod.

[195] The "ancient settlement" just outside the city walls to the south.

until the bolshevik decrees. Fotii remodeled it magnificently with funds from Orlova, without particularly spoiling, by the way, the twelfth-century cathedral with its typical three cupolas and its shaftlike tower; but now the monks have almost all fled and I walked about the monastery as if in the castle of The Sleeping Beauty. Behind the monastery, under the ancient willows with their water-washed roots, there is a marvelous view of Il'men.

At St. Anthony's Monastery I was not able to get into the churches—everything was locked, and I didn't meet a single father. Sophia reminded me a great deal of the Kiev [Sophia]; it is, however, a little smaller. Its restoration of recent years is still too fresh, but the impression is nevertheless very strong; and when I looked at the Savior (unrestored) in the central cupola with his legendary right hand, I wanted the right hand to open and smite depraved and base mankind. The Kremlin, whose walls are all intact, is half-surrounded by the town park, whose trees frame the walls like the park of the Heidelberg Castle—this spot, too, is beautiful in its state of neglect. I returned by steamboat to the Volkhov station. The river in high water reminds one of the Neva; the banks are partly flat, partly hilly, and in places very pretty and picturesque. I was delighted and, as on the previous day during my walk at Nereditsa and Gorodishche, I was lost in reverie and forgot about the present. Traversing Kolmovo, historical memories of old Novgorod disappear and are replaced by the Arakcheevshchina:[196] its barracks and former military colonies—Krechevitsy, the Murav'ev and Selishche barracks—with the road connecting them planted with birches—majestic and solid structures. The recent excitement (reserve units were located here during the war) has now given way to emptiness and in part even ruin; they say that recently the soldiers, not wanting even to haul firewood, chopped up the floor and heated themselves with it. The Volkhov station woke me to the sorry life of the present: again standing over the brake, and then a night in a commuter car without the possibility of even leaning on something and with the tortuous inevitability of listening to the loud conversation of four gorillas about current events.

I arrived in Moscow on August 31, and the first thing I learned of from the fence literature was the attempt on Lenin's life. I don't know if it was necessary to do that; but it is apparent that the struggle between the bolsheviks and the srs is intensifying. This alone plunged me into the

[196] Aleksei Andreevich Arakcheev (1769–1834) was a general, high official, and sometime war minister during the reigns of Paul and Alexander I. His reputation as a ruthless martinet is legendary in Russian history. After the Napoleonic Wars, he instituted an experimental system of "military colonies," combining military service and agriculture for their state-peasant inhabitants. Got'e describes one of these settlements, which was established in 1825 on the Volkhov River.

nightmare of reality; panic, depression, terror, the death of any kind of normal life are felt much more strongly than two months ago. The urge to leave, to flee to the Ukraine, is everywhere; individuals who are either leaving or preparing to leave for the Ukraine are on all sides. This is only the beginning, and further on if nothing changes this great exodus will only grow, and the old centers of Russian life—Petersburg and Moscow—will decline and fall. How characteristic is the grass of neglect that is covering some Moscow side streets—it is a foreshadowing of the future. Bolshevik terror is growing, too—everything is stifled; arrests on all sides; people who have been arrested or are in hiding are everywhere. There are such among our relatives—for example, Sasha Rar. It is dark in the evenings; life comes to a halt early—and that is the beginning of great destruction. So far as I can make out, the situation is unclear and more confused than ever before. The Allies are pounding the Germans like never before; although I don't foresee a complete victory, the Germans are having a tough time and they are retreating and yielding. This compels them to make friends with the bolsheviks and even to protect them, not out of sympathy for them, but for their support against the Allies, who are marching against the bolsheviks and against the Germans. As a result, Great Russia will become the theater of an unheard-of civil war, where Russians will fight together with the Germans against other Russians marching together with the Allies. And the Russians will go against each other and will fight and slaughter themselves, providing an example of unheard-of meanness and stupidity. The supplementary agreement of the Germans with the bolsheviks—an addendum to the Brest peace—is fine: Sovdepiia is paying out six billion to the Germans for German capital investments, and a significant part of that sum in gold. It is impossible to go any further in the area of cynicism than the meaning the bolsheviks have given to the concept of "without annexations or indemnities." In Moscow I had, of course, to occupy myself with the liquidation of my sugar adventure. I went to see M. N. Pokrovskii in order to get a petition from the Commissariat of Popular Enlightenment to lift the 10,000 [ruble] fine; in need, in order to save myself from the bolsheviks, I had to pay obeisance to those same bolsheviks; I testify to this here, not wishing to look better than I am in reality. He received me as an old comrade, and the paper was signed. Yesterday I submitted my petition to the Extraordinary Commission,[197] and now I am waiting to see what will come of it, not sleeping at home or even looking in there—a stupid and vile situation. Everyone asks me about this affair and sympathizes. I have begun work only in the museum. The libraries and the museum remain the fetishes of the bolsheviks; they are always sitting,

---

[197] Got'e appended his draft of the petition to the diary. See Appendix, Letter 1.

conferring, fussing, and devising projects for increasing the staff, but how laughable it all is—nothing will come of it, and almost no work is being done inside the museum. And as soon as you look at it all, you want, uncontrollably, to throw everything aside and flee wherever your feet might take you. I absolutely have to think about this, and think seriously, because the time will come when material existence here will become completely impossible, and spiritual life will die out for good.

5 [September]. They would not give us our fur coats; another misfortune and another loss. They say that one should submit some kind of notice, and then a part [of them] will be given out. Lialia's table was sold, so there are 900 rubles for me. The term of the safe-deposit box has not expired yet, and that's good. There are no new rumors; the Allies continue to thrash the Germans.

6 [September]. There is a chance of getting two of my brother's trunks from the Kokorevka—this should be done immediately. Right now I am interested most of all in the psychology of the Germans in their new accord with the bolsheviks. The concessions that are being made to them—conditional, it is true, and capable of being taken back—are explained by some as the result of the fact that the Germans are in bad shape on the Western Front. I think the situation on the Western Front has an influence, but it is not a matter of that alone—the Germans are using the bolsheviks and the fact that the Russian East is in fact on the side of the Allies to rob Russia impudently and shamelessly. They also figure that they should make hay while the sun shines, until they have to make peace with their Western enemies, who have gained enormous successes again today.

In my private affairs, the day went calmly; there was a letter from Zagran'e: all is calm and so far there is no reason to fear the committee of poor peasants, one of whose members is Iasha Fishin[?] from Zaprud'e, who furnishes us with mushrooms. I will note the following as well: when V. I. Ger'e's house was searched, the poor old man who has done so much for Russia and his daughters were robbed of as much as 15,000 [rubles], and everything they had of value was carried off.

7 [September]. Mass executions in Moscow—Shcheglovitov, Khvostov, Beletskii, and the archpriest Vostorgov have perished.[198] They have all

---

[198] Ivan Grigor'evich Shcheglovitov (1861–1918) was a former minister of justice (1906–1915) and chairman of the State Council (1917) who was politically active on the extreme right. He was arrested after the February revolution and was shot by the Bolsheviks on September 5, 1918. Aleksei Nikolaevich Khvostov (1872–1918) was a former governor, interior minister (1915–1916) and representative of the far right in the state duma. He, too, was shot on September 5. Ioann Ioannovich Vostorgov (1866–1918) was a clergyman

done much, each in his own way, to bring Russia to her present state, but they hardly could have thought that they would perish because of the shot fired at Lenin by the Jewess sr, Roid-Kaplan. Alarming news about my brother—I fear he may become a victim of the same brutality; the only hope is that the news came from the least credible source. There is a complete break between the bolsheviks and the Anglo-French and the Americans, who continue to thrash the Germans like never before. Their successes, incidentally, make the situation inside Russia even more difficult. The atmosphere grows heavier in soviet Russia with every day that passes.

9 [September]. Yesterday I went to Pestovo, where summer life also passed satisfactorily; a novelty is that since it is impossible to use the telephone to make arrangements for one's arrival, one calls from the telephone at the Pushkino pharmacy and goes on foot to meet the carriage; I walked that way as far as Kurovo, that is, half the road. The return to Moscow today took five hours: the train was two hours late—such is the rule now on the Iaroslavl' line, which was always one of the best organized. There were no particular nuisances today in Moscow. It has become clear that the Razorenovs will probably be moved in with us.

10 [September]. I moved again within the remains of my apartment; the resolve to liquidate everything that can be liquidated grows stronger every day. I visited my old teacher, V. I. Ger'e; that old man has an amazing philosophical serenity, and there is much truth in the ideas he expounded yesterday, and which he has been expounding all his life— the ideas of a moderate liberal, against which so many rebelled. When we listened to his lectures on the history of the French Revolution, we did not think that we would live through the Russian one together. In the West, the retreat of the Germans continues; it is the only comforting thing. The bolsheviks have taken Kazan'.

12 [September]. New and constant successes of the French, English, and Americans; in places they are going farther than the line of 1917: *ex occidente lux*. My sugar affair is being dragged out; the Razorenovs have moved into the apartment; it is hard to say what kind of symbiosis we will have with them; our apartment once again resembles a furniture store that needs cleaning out.

13 [September]. A ruthless decree regulating evictions from apartments has appeared. It may not concern us or those near to us; however, that

who was also a well-known activist of the extreme right. (See n. 8 for information about Beletskii.)

decree is nothing other than theft provided with rules, of such a kind and scale as the world has not seen before.[199] One must try in every way possible to free oneself from everything superfluous: it is more necessary than ever. I went to visit Patouillet, and talked interestingly and at length with him. His views on the Russians are close to mine, but he blames his own people for many manifestations of tactlessness in relations with the bolsheviks. In his opinion, the future depends entirely on peace; and the matter of peace and war lies in the hands of Wilson, "qui dispose de l'argent et des armées." The Russian question will be decided then as well. He does not trust the Japanese. Characteristically, he has the same opinion of the French colony in Moscow as Paev, saying it consists of "parvenus riches." I am waiting for my family; today is the sad tenth anniversary of our wedding. How good those years were for us personally, and how terrible in general. It is interesting that Sasha Rar spent last night at the Dol'niks, and yesterday was his nameday; on leaving he said he doesn't know where or for how many nights he will be able to sleep in bivouac.

15 [September]. I got terribly upset yesterday because Nina has not yet arrived; the waiting began already on the 13th; Nina did not arrive in time for the anniversary—I waited four hours at the station in order to meet, at last, a late train half-filled with a band of sailors. Those bandits—the true descendants of the followers of Razin and Pugachev—produce a sinister impression. Yesterday again, through Mitia Kurdiumov, questions at the station. Finally at 2 o'clock a letter suddenly arrived; I attach it here.[200] In it Nina reports her wise decision to stay in Zagran'e until the 23d of September, mainly for Volodia's sake; it will, in truth, be better that way, although it is difficult without them. Fichelle, who came by the museum, reported a new victory of the French; the St. Mihiel salient has been cut off, Pagny-sur-Moselle has been taken, and the shelling of Metz has begun, with the taking of 13,000 prisoners.

[199] The housing situation in Moscow reached crisis proportions when the government offices and personnel were moved to Moscow in March 1918. In addition, the government sought as a matter of "class policy" to move workers from the slums on the outskirts of the city into the "bourgeois" houses in the center. The Moscow Soviet's "housing council" undertook a census of living space, and the process of "squeezing together" (*uplotnenie*) began. On July 30, *Izvestiia* reported that the systematic moving of workers and their families into the apartments of the "bourgeoisie" had begun and that "all apartments of the center of Moscow will be cleared of superfluous dark elements." Got'e reports here on a new decree that was published in *Izvestiia* on September 13, ordering a new offensive against bourgeois apartments. On the average, there were 2.5 people living in every room in Moscow in 1918. *Krasnaia Moskva, 1917–1920 gg.* (Moscow, 1920), p. 358.

[200] Letter of Nina Nikolaevna Got'e, dated August 26, 1918 (September 8, n.s.). See Appendix, Letter 2.

Thank God; even though we are dying here politically, we see the triumph of justice in the West, or, more correctly, the beginning of its triumph. There is a general recognition that the situation is not going to change in the foreseeable future. In truth, only a general peace can give an impetus to the resolution of the Russian crisis and the destruction of the putrid breeding ground of the infection that is spreading from our garbage heap, on which precious mushrooms have grown from time to time since olden days. I have an interesting collection of reports about the Czechoslovaks: (1) they are retreating; (2) they are doing this because they have gotten bored with defending the dead body of Russia, insofar as the Russians themselves are capable of nothing; (3) there is tremendous discord between the Russian groups standing behind the Czechoslovaks; 4) la garde blanche a fait une noce épouvantable à Kazan.[201] All this was reported by four different persons, but how like the truth it all is! A dead people and a dead society that must become material for exploitation by stronger peoples. I began to clean the apartment and took all the pictures over to the museum.

16 [September]. I got a letter from Novgorod, which I am attaching to the diary.[202] It will be indicative for future generations of how the powers-that-be are carrying out repressions—such behavior must provoke horror and revulsion. As a result I have to go to Novgorod to rescue my brother; that will take about five days. The general situation is unchanged—no new information or rumors; there are no reports from the Western Front. Yesterday was the wedding of my wife's cousin—Misha Dol'nik. I had a terribly strange feeling that something long-forgotten and blatantly antirevoluntary was happening.

18 [September]. Special permission is required in order to leave by the Nikolaevskaia railroad; it is granted in one of the premises of the former Noble Institute. I had to go up the staircase that led to the apartment of O. A. Talyzina. I had been there only a year ago—God, how terrible, what filth and abomination. The passes for business trips are given out on the fourth floor; the certificates were issued by a comrade-worker, whose rudeness was unmatched by anything I had heard or seen. And since our office had not seen fit to put a number on the certificate given to me, they didn't give me the pass at all, and I lost yet another day. The thrashing of the Germans continues on the Western Front.

---

[201] "The white guard went on a terrible bender in Kazan'." This is presumably a reference to the Red Army's capture of Kazan' on September 10.

[202] Letter of V. Bok to Got'e from Novgorod, dated September 12, 1918. See Appendix, Letter 3.

20 [September]. Yesterday I just didn't make it to the building where the passes are issued; there were horrendous lines, mixed-up and endless, at the door of the Talyzins' former entrance. Some sort of hooligans in semimilitary dress were simulating hacking with swords and beating with rifle butts, and were even pretended to be shooting. The motley, stupid crowd shied and knocked into each other, glancing fearfully at the hooligans, who were yelling that they had lost their patience and were going to clear everybody out. I stood for two hours and left without anything; I don't know what will happen today. I am appending Nina's letter with its sad notes about Zagran'e.[203] I think that the future there is simple and clear: thanks for letting us spend the summer; there is no point in dreaming about the future, especially since if nothing changes, we will in any case have to move away from here somewhere. There is little new in the West; the peace proposed by Austria risks being left hanging in the air, and the war will continue. Antisoviet forces have removed all the gold— 675 million—from Kazan'; according to my calculations that amounts to more than half of the total on hand, and if you add the 200 million given to the Germans, the soviets have no more than 300 million.

21 [September]. The Nativity of the Virgin, and we are working in the museum; that is the fruit of the new regime. The Jews have Saturday off today; such is the justice of the present day. The wave of horrors has swept as far as Zagran'e. On Tuesday the 17th Lena Reiman was arrested, having been declared a counterrevolutionary through the direct influence of the notorious Smirnov of Besovo, as military commissar; she was humiliated and sent off to Krasnyi Kholm, and is being threatened with execution while being forced to labor at digging potatoes. When this happened, Nina left immediately for Moscow, and, thank God, arrived safely yesterday and immediately busied herself with Lena's affairs. For that purpose, incidentally, I today visited my cousin, the bolshevik S. S. Krivtsov,[204] who politely agreed to intervene for both Lena and Lialia. He was self-important and full of a sense of his own worth, and he rebuked the professors of the university for not wanting to make peace with the "current authority." I am attaching Nina's last letter from Zagran'e as material for understanding the atmosphere there in our last days of living there.[205]

[203] Letter of August 28 (September 10, n. s.). See Appendix, Letter 4.

[204] Stepan Savvich Krivtsov (b. 1885) was a professor in the Institute of Red Professors in the early 1920s. A 1930 reference work identified him as a member of the Society of Marxist Historians and a specialist in historical materialism, dialectical materialism, and Leninism, head of the "methodological section" of the Lenin Institute, and a member of the Communist Academy.

[205] Letter dated August 31 (September 13, n. s.). See Appendix, Letter 5.

22–26 [September]. My second trip to Novgorod. How terrible it is to travel on the railroads. This was my odyssey: I left home at 6 P.M. on the 22d of September. At the Nikolaevskii station I sat on my suitcase a long time at the ticket window waiting for tickets to go on sale. I was not let on the express train that was leaving at 9 o'clock; that is the train of the privileged of the soviet republic, the train of the new bourgeois and patricians of democracy. I got a ticket on a rapid train leaving at 10 P.M. To get into a car, that is, even to get onto the platform, a line was formed; I took a place at the end that was near the entrance door. The line moved slowly; when I got to the second-class car, I was able to get a place in a compartment where ten people were already sitting; I was the eleventh. Later the corridor was also packed. In that state we traveled the whole distance; it was the same on the return trip. I cannot say that the public was nasty and unpleasant to each other; on the contrary, coming and going, all the people crammed into the compartment were mutually well disposed, meek and courteous. A hint of sad mockery in regard to the state of things prevailed; on the return trip only a few moaned because the toilet was jammed with people and consequently inaccessible. The lack of air also caused suffering; on the way there the window was opened at the stops; on the return trip the window was opened a crack until the Russian folk, who hate fresh air, protested. The rapid train got as far as Tver' in good time, but then a freight locomotive was attached, with which we arrived two hours late in Vishera. At one point I was even afraid that we would not make it to Chudovo by 2 o'clock. From Chudovo to Novgorod I rode in fourth class, completely empty, so I could catch up on my sleep after the sleepless night; in just the same way the return to Chudovo was excellent—I sailed on the Volkhov for a second time; the weather was entirely satisfactory and I once again admired the broad and full river and its interesting banks.

My task in Novgorod was to liberate my brother; I achieved that, moreover, quickly and without great effort. Apparently, the psychological moment had come. In the Extraordinary Commission I fairly quickly got to see its head, that is, the chairman, who received my petition and proposed that I get for him a memorandum on the "political reliability" of my brother. I turned to the commissar of the division to which he sent me, who in his turn directed me to the provincial commissar, Makarov, with whom I was already acquainted from my first visit. It was quite characteristic that the division commissar, a simple worker in a Russian blouse, said "my division"; although I am not an officer, I was hurt and offended when I heard him utter that. Makarov was just as polite as the first time and promised to talk with the chairman of the Cheka; that discussion decided the case. It was no less characteristic that it turned out that the former staff of the Novgorod Cheka—comrades Vasilit and Vitin—are being accused of robbing some treasury in Livland[206] during the evacuation of that region. My brother was released on Wednesday the 25th, with Makarov sending advice through me to leave Novgorod; we expect him tomorrow in Moscow. His life really was in danger and was saved only by luck, about which Bok wrote me. The circumstances of the execution were horrifying: my brother's fellow prisoners were taken out into a field and shot like grouses, and one who was not killed instantly was finished off point-blank. The murderers were boys from the red guard; and a former cavalry colonel, Niman or Neiman, gave the orders. Such are the mores of Sovdepiia.

In between business I again roamed about marvelous Novgorod; I was in several churches and in places that I hadn't gotten to earlier. I left with the same impression of enchantment as the first time.

28 [September]. Nothing has changed in the museum; I walked to the Commissariat of People's Enlightenment to ask for a security certificate for my apartment and for my library; for the first I was sent to Skatkin, Pokrovskii's secretary. Meeting [Pokrovskii] by chance, I told him the purpose of my visit; he answered me: "The more such certificates we give out, the less force they have." That is how those who consider themselves rulers talk. I was also at Fichelle's, who told me amazing things about the victories of the Allies in the Balkans, in Palestine, and in France. The Allies have at last found a weapon against the Germans. The poor Russians: the feast was ready, but the guests were unworthy of it.

29 [September]. The bolshevik newspapers did in fact put in print yesterday's French radio message, with the exception of Franchet d'Esperey's reply.[207] The situation has heated up for real; only what form will it take when it cools off? A meeting of the poor old museum committee which dates back to 1912. We had to decide what to do next, since the bolsheviks want to move the property of the museum into other buildings. The fate of the committee and of the museum itself is in the hands of Madame Trotskii, Grabar', and one impossible Iatmanov.[208] It was sad to look at the crowd of former generals and dignitaries who were members of the

---

[206] Part of Latvia or Estonia.

[207] Louis Félix Franchet d'Esperey (1856–1942) was Allied commander of the Macedonian front in 1918. At this time the Allied army had just completed the Balkan offensive that ended, on September 29, with Bulgarian capitulation; Franchet d'Esperey was about to sign an armistice with Hungary and Turkey as commander of the Allied forces in the Balkans.

[208] G. S. Iatmanov was head of the Commissariat of Enlightenment's (Narkompros's) Collegium on Museum Affairs and Preservation of Artistic and Historical Monuments, established in November 1917. (The commission attended by Got'e in the Kremlin was attached to this collegium.)

committee: Prince Odoevskii-Maslov, in a cheap jacket; Prince Shcher-batov, in a torn field jacket; the tattered generals Afanas'ev, Petrov, Ia-kovlev, Vorontsov-Vel'iaminov; A. A. Bakhrushin, in a poddevka and Russian blouse; and so on—former people and former business.[209]

30 [September]. Kizevetter was arrested last night; the search started at 10 P.M.; at 3 A.M. they took him, his wife, daughter, and stepdaughter away. His arrest should have been anticipated long ago. I was amazed at his equanimity. A faculty meeting: we deliberated about implementing the decree concerning the organization of knowledge-testing for ignora-muses. It was both funny and sad: how can you test the knowledge of ignorant people?[210] All the same, we must deliberate and conduct talks in the name of preserving the university personnel from blind and bar-baric destruction, without any hope of upholding anything reasonable. There are exaggerated discussions in town about the successes of the Al-lies; many think that the Germans have already been destroyed, but that is a profound delusion.

OCTOBER

1 [October]. Events in the West and in the Balkans are dizzying. On the French front, breakthrough after breakthrough; the clearing out of Bel-gium has now begun. There is some kind of confusion in Germany—the bolsheviks are already counting on a revolution there, but of course that is so far only a matter of imagination; nevertheless, the Germans' nerves are beginning to fail, and superiority might lie on the side of the Western nations. What wild self-confidence the Germans had when they set off the world conflagration in 1914. It is gratifying that although we have perished, the Germans, too, may end badly. The University Council unanimously decided to come to Kizevetter's aid; Iakovlev and Egorov went to the commissariat. It seems that Pokrovskii himself took steps for his release, but it is not so easy: Kizevetter is being charged with belong-ing to the central committee of the [Kadet] party and is threatened with

[209] Aleksei Aleksandrovich Bakhrushin (1865–1929), of a prominent Moscow merchant family, was a famous authority on the theater. He is included in this list of generals because he was awarded a general's rank (civil) and a patent of nobility for donating his theatrical museum to the Academy of Sciences in 1913. A poddevka was a light, tight-fitting coat. The other notables probably included General Nikolai Nikolaevich Odoev-skii-Maslov (1849–1919), Prince Nikolai Borisovich Shcherbatov (1849–1936), General Nikolai Ivanovich Petrov (b. 1841), and General Grigorii Mikhailovich Iakovlev (b. 1852).

[210] A second conference on reform of higher education that met in September approved amending the August decree's ruling on open admissions by requiring testing of students enrolling for laboratory work or other applied studies.

concentration camp. His family was arrested for "insulting" those who carried out the search. Perhaps all this is tied up with anticipated changes in the political situation and with the rumors that the Germans and Kadets, acting together in the Ukraine, intended to overthrow the bolsheviks. I don't believe this, but the fact of intensified persecution of the Kadets is obvious. Perhaps Bochkareva was arrested because of that. Lena Reiman has been released from the Krasnyi Kholm prison, but we don't have any details yet.

2 [October]. We are working on Kizevetter's behalf; his situation is serious. There was concern today about the library, for there is reason to fear that it will be looted. There was a meeting on setting up archival courses—a correct idea, in and of itself. It would be desirable to see it realized, but where to find enough mental resources to devote to realizing that task the way it should be? In the West and in the Near East the Allies are going from one success to another as before. In Belgium, Roulers and Menin have been taken; farther south Cambrai and St. Quentin; in Champagne, the French and Americans are moving northward. Something is cracking on the German side. In the Balkans, nearly a third of Serbia has been cleared; the liberators are approaching Üsküb; in Palestine fifty thousand Turks have been taken prisoner. I don't know what kind of potion the Allies have found against the Germans, but they have found something—whether technology, stronger nerves, or something else, it is a fact that in the fifth year, without Russia, superiority is shifting to their side. All this promises countless changes in the future, the most unexpected and fundamental departures, such as will completely contradict the expectations of people who consider themselves to be the most farsighted.

3 [October]. Further development of the same events in the West and in the Balkans. I have begun the fur-coat calvary; at Belkin's they are giving assurances that part of the fur coats are being given out.[211] A strange feeling overcomes me when I walk about the streets of Moscow—a feeling of death overall, of the termination, irrevocable and inevitable, of all life. I am free of that feeling only when I sit at home, or in the not yet completely looted apartment, or in the museum. Vava Varsonof'eva has returned from Zagran'e and finds that it is still possible to live there; my brother arrived from Novgorod and is intending to go to Zagran'e for an indefinite time.

4 [October]. A sudden alarm—we are being summoned today to a repeat audit and disemboweling of our safe at Iunker's. The building, by the

---

[211] Sergei Ivanovich Belkin had a fur shop with storage facilities on Kuznetskii Most.

way, has been requisitioned by the State Commission on the Retirement of Debts. It would be interesting to know what kind of debts they are retiring now, when they have all been annulled. That is the reason they are hurrying to clean out all storage facilities; and therefore one should expect a radical solution of the matter of the safe. Kizevetter's situation is not improving. It is characteristic that the individuals in authority to whom we turned decline to get involved in this affair, as it is in the hands of the highest and most powerful institution. In the West, the Germans have surrendered without a fight Armentières and Lens, which they so successfully and desperately defended over the course of two years. In Belgium the Anglo-Belgians are fanning out: if this movement continues, the Germans will have to clear out of Lille and Ostend.

6 [October]. Yesterday we took the whole day to eviscerate our safe-deposit box, and my brother's box as well. We waited three and a half hours. Afterward they took from us things weighing more than two hundred grams and recorded all bonds, which was transferred for safe-keeping to the People's Bank of the RSFSR. The comrades were polite, but just barely. I had a happy feeling when the whole ceremony was finished. That shoe-nail, that splinter that has been sitting there for ten months and causing pain, has been removed. We are no longer held back by the safe, which had ceased to be such; one anchor less in life—that has its charm. A new misfortune that same evening. We were informed, in a roundabout way, of course, that a telegram had been received in Moscow to the effect that someone wants me arrested. Today we learned one detail—[I am to be arrested] for counterrevolutionary propaganda at the dacha. One has to think that this affair is somehow connected with the affair of Lena Reiman and with the proclaiming of Zaprud'e and Gora counterrevolutionary. Someone found it necessary to mix us up in that affair. That is enough to poison one's existence for a whole two weeks, if not longer. We decided that I shouldn't spend the night at home. This is the second evening that I am being nomadic; it is both revolting and an unproductive waste of time, and, moreover, I have to start lectures tomorrow. Try to get out of that one! How long will I have to knock about like this?

The news from the West remains good; there is, moreover, news that Germany is agreeing to the conditions of the Allies; many are building exaggerated hopes on that, but I don't share them.

7 [October]. It was learned today that the notorious telegram was addressed to Trotskii himself; its author was probably Smirnov from Besovo. I can understand his line of thought: first he latched on to Lena, and then he extended his charge of counterrevolution wholesale to us, and in particular to me, as the head of the family. And being a military commissar, he informed the people's commissar for military affairs. When I learned of all this, I went to N. I. Trotskaia, presently the chairman of the Collegium on Museum Affairs, and told her about this affair. She was amiable with me and promised to give the necessary help. And so, a third unpleasant surprise has been more or less liquidated: the first was Lialia's arrest; the second was Lena's arrest and Nina's departure; and the third was the telegram. We shall wait and see what comes next. In any case, I will live at home. An attempt was made today to begin lectures at the university. At 10 A.M. S. A. Kotliarevskii and I. A. Pokrovskii, the mathematics Privatdozent Nekrasov, N. I. Novosadskii,[212] and I were there—no one's lecture was held. Later only Poznyshev[213] gave a lecture in the juridical faculty. No one else's lecture took place; a fine beginning of semester in the renovated university.

8 [October]. A day without any particular impressions. Successes again in the West: delivery of Reims from bombardment after four years of destruction. A mountain of rumors in Moscow, one more groundless than the other. I saw a man who had arrived from Kazan': on the 5th of August eight hundred men occupied the town, and several thousand red army men fled from them. They [the occupiers] organized a volunteer army numbering eight thousand; obligatory mobilization worked poorly—the draftees deserted. They carried off everything, and in the first place, gold; and when they saw that forces they could not match had been concentrated against them, they left. With them left all the bourgeoisie, but the bourgeois have returned for the most part from Laishev and Chistopol',[214] while the Czechoslovaks, the white guard, and the volunteer army went farther. The apartments of the returning bourgeois were confiscated. Such is the story of Kazan' in the telling of an eyewitness.[215]

10 [October]. The most outstanding event for these two days was the decree on reelection of all professors who have worked for more than ten years in one institution of higher learning or have fifteen years of accumulated pedagogical activity.[216] And so, we will be thrown out as of Jan-

---

[212] Iosif Alekseevich Pokrovskii (1868–1920) was professor of Roman and civil law at Moscow University. Nikolai Ivanovich Novosadskii (1859–1941) was a philologist and a specialist on epigraphy.

[213] S. V. Poznyshev (b. 1874) was a professor of law and a leading Russian representative of the sociological school of criminal law.

[214] Towns down the Volga from Kazan' on the Kama.

[215] Kazan' fell to the Bolsheviks on September 10.

[216] A Narkompros decree promulgated by Sovnarkom on October 1, 1918, abolished the traditional academic ranks and provided that all teachers with ten years' employment at the same university or fifteen years' accumulated teaching were to be deprived of their

uary 1, in the middle of the academic year; who will finish giving our courses, and how, remains unknown; who will reelect us in the form of an "all-Russian competition" is also unknown for the time being. The possibility of continued teaching is made dependent on some kind of unknown forces, albeit forces that are obviously hostile to us. Those comrades with whom I talked yesterday and today look on all this rather ironically—nearly nine-tenths of the entire university personnel will have to be reelected; many, in addition, think that things will change before January 1. I look on the matter dispassionately, with that sad and indifferent skepticism regarding the benign result of bolshevik undertakings that has stayed with me recently. Maybe this will facilitate our departure from Moscow; it will forcibly cut the knot that you will never voluntarily cut yourself. On the other hand, an interruption of salary in the middle of the year can put [us] in a hopeless material situation and make departure itself impossible. Well, we will be fatalists; it is probably better and calmer that way. In the West the Allies have again hit the Germans hard between St. Quentin and Cambrai. The idle Muscovites have already yesterday affirmed that a truce has been concluded and that everything will soon change. The old gossip Moscow remains true to herself, rumors are born and succeed each other: either they are signing a truce, or they are sending an international army of occupation to Russia for five years. But none of this is being confirmed, and, it seems to me, none of it will be confirmed for a long time. Today I began my lectures at the [Higher Women's] Courses; an attendance of twenty-five or thirty; more for the second hour; primarily the old auditors; an attentive attitude—they still have the naive faith that it is possible to get educated in Russia!

11 [October]. A new decree on the higher schools: (1) All curricular activities are to begin after 5 P.M. to make it possible for workers to study. How this is to be coordinated with laboratory and clinical work is truly incomprehensible. Everything is explained entirely and exclusively by pure demagoguery. Some react to the decrees with laughter, others with hopeless indifference. New successes in the West; Wilson's reply demands the withdrawal of German troops from the occupied territories before beginning peace discussions.

---

positions as of January 1, 1919, and would have to enter a nationwide competition for their former posts. The competition was to be held no later than November 1, 1918. *Dekrety Sovetskoi vlasti*, vol. 3, pp. 381–82. When the competition was finally held in early 1919, it produced no significant changes in the faculty: "As far as I remember, none of the professors was voted out except the Communist professor of astronomy, Shternberg." M. Novikov, "Moskovskii universitet v pervyi period bol'shevistskogo rezhima," in *Moskovskii universitet, 1755–1930. Iubileinyi sbornik* (Paris, 1930), pp. 156–92; quoted on p. 159.

12 [October]. I was visited today in the museum by the head of the investigatory section of the Cheka, comrade Romanov, who asked me to help them find instructions or regulations for the gendarmes,[217] so that these regulations, in altered form, can be applied to the current chaos, which is especially felt in the Extraordinary Commissions outside Moscow. It is impossible to go further than that. Avenard arrived, having spent two months in Kostroma province, and himself expressed the thought that French socialists of the type of Longuet[218] should come here and see for themselves what the socialist experiment leads to. In the West, the brilliant offensive of the Anglo-French goes on as before; you want to drink, or even get good and drunk, to Foch's health.

13 [October]. A letter from Aleksei: in Zagran'e everybody has been arrested; there is arson everywhere; the drying shed was burned down; it is forbidden to come to town to get any of us; he asks me to warn my brother to wait and not come, otherwise he will be arrested. He will have to be informed of all this so that he doesn't get involved in it. I won't have to save him myself. Aleksei Ivanov's letter fully exposes the circumstances in which the proposal about my arrest was sent to comrade Trotskii. A beautiful day; we went to the cemetery and were at the Kurdiumovs' housewarming near Iaroslavl' station.

15 [October]. A general feeling that peace is at hand; I don't think, however, that it will come very quickly; in any case, hopes for peace have given rise in many to other hopes. Of course, one of two things: either the entire world will become bolshevik, or we must live like everyone else. The victorious side will have its way with us, perhaps, together with the defeated. How strange to think that the Germans have been defeated, in the final analysis defeated, and how correct was Avenard when he said in the spring during the most difficult minutes of the final German offensive: "Attendez la réplique de Foch." *Réplique* turned into that genuine *revanche* about which the French have dreamed for a half-century. Further successes today—Douai and La Fère have been taken. The Germans continue to retreat. We discussed what to do about classes in two faculties—the university and the Higher Women's Courses. Lectures have been changed to thirty-minute [lectures], and all have been scheduled between 5 and 10 P.M. But it's all the same—nothing, one has to think, will come of the classes. Yesterday I was pleased that I was able to liberate the enameled snuffbox that had been requisitioned from the safe.

[217] That is, the Corps of Gendarmes, the political police instituted by Nicholas I.

[218] Edgar Longuet (1879–1950), the grandson of Karl Marx, was a longtime member of the French Socialist party.

16 [October]. The successes, both in the West and in the Balkans, continue; the Germans have been driven from Niš and Mitrovica; Laon and a huge area around that town have been evacuated. My bourgeois heart is warmed by the glory of the old nations of the West, which our God-bearers[219] considered degenerate. I read the draft legislation on the unified labor school: what a mixture of hypocrisy, stupidity, fantasy, and deliberate malice![220]

17 [October]. The fur coats have been released; Nina has been transferred to the third category from the fourth; I will probably go into the second—those are the three mundane joys I experienced today.[221] That is characteristic for the current time. Lena has again been arrested in Zagran'e. In accordance with the decree on reelection of professors, 9 out of 100 members of the council remain; 162 new members entered the council; 80 of them left in their turn—such is the renovation of the council. The same story will occur in the Higher Women's Courses. It is both sad and laughable. Little news today about the war; only a more detailed dispatch about the victory in Belgium, which gave the Allies Roulers, and also Wilson's reply to the German reply, which is severe and demands that the Germans cease committing outrages before peace can be concluded.

18 [October]. The successes in Belgium continue. Here they are expecting something from the south, but what, no one at all knows clearly, except, perhaps, the initiated. The fur coats were brought home.

---

[219] A reference to Slavophiles, Populists, and other extollers of Russia's moral superiority over the West in general.

[220] The First All-Russian Congress on Education introduced coeducational schooling at the primary and secondary levels at the end of August 1918. Children were to learn practical skills and to perform the basic chores around the school in order to learn the value of socially useful labor. There were many other progressivist, secularizing aspects to the reform, but these were main features identified in the title of the new school: "unified labor school." TsIK approved the project on September 30. *Dekrety Sovetskoi vlasti*, vol. 3, pp. 374–80.

[221] A bread-rationing system installed by the Bolsheviks in August 1918 recognized four "class" categories: those doing (1) heavy physical labor, (2) light physical labor, (3) intellectual labor, and (4) no work. The first two categories were soon conflated (bifurcation of the laboring population was recognized to have been a political mistake). In the autumn of 1918, the new first category received a ration of one pound of bread per day, the second a half a pound, and the third a quarter of a pound. However, as the author of a book on Moscow in the first year of Bolshevik rule notes, the norms, which were small to begin with, "were not always distributed in full, since despite all measures taken, bread reached Moscow irregularly." G. S. Ignat'ev, *Moskva v pervyi god proletarskoi diktatury* (Moscow, 1975), p. 256.

19 [October]. Today was the turn of Lille and Ostend; the thrust against the Germans is taking its course. Here alarm is growing stronger; I don't know what is threatening the authorities, but something is moving up from the south; if all this again ends in nothing, it will be more than stupid. The bolsheviks are appointing a commissar to the Higher Women's Courses—that was all that was lacking. This, incidentally, is to be rewarded by rechristening [the Courses] a university.

20 [October]. Bruges, Zeebrugge, Roubaix, and Douai have been swept; the perennial urge of Germany for the Pas de Calais, and in general for the sea around England, has vanished for many years, perhaps forever. The Allies are demanding a representative of a united Russia at the future congress; in the Ukraine there is a change in orientation from Germany to the Allies; a meeting of the former members of the State Duma in Kiev resolves that future Russia shall be a constitutional monarchy. I learned all this today from reading the *Izvestiia V.Ts.I.K.*[222] The affair is turning out to resemble the fifth act of *Macbeth*; soon, perhaps, Burnham Wood will rise up and move from its place. But there is no need to give oneself illusions—none of this will happen soon and we will have to suffer through much yet.

21 [October]. Vague conversations and vague hope; there is all the same a sufficiency of incurable optimists. The activities of the Compréhension Réciproque were renewed today. The mood was optimistic; we decided to work for the future. We began studies at the university in the evenings; a feeling of universal aimlessness; there are quite a lot of people milling about, but they all give the impression that they don't know what they want.

22 [October]. Courtrai and Tourcoing have been cleared; the push continues; it is obvious even from *Izvestiia* that Austria is collapsing, and that the Germans are entering into talks with Wilson despite the severe tone of his notes. A more satisfactory impression from classes in the university today, although the thought nevertheless remains that there are more professors than students.[223]

23 [October]. In the West the sweep continues, although to a lesser degree today; but the German reply to Wilson, in my opinion, makes further

[222] *Izvestiia*, October 20, 1918, p. 3, "Na Ukraine."

[223] Though the number of students registered in the 1918–1919 academic year nearly doubled over the previous year, to 36,000, actual attendance seems to have dropped off radically: only 178 students graduated from the university in Moscow in 1918–1919, as compared to 1,668 the year before! *Krasnaia Moskva*, p. 496.

talks possible. Lenin gave a strange speech in TsIK: on the one hand, he said, we are cracking, on the other we will win with the help of our German and Bulgarian comrades. What is this, conscious deceit or unconscious self-delusion? However, this speech was saturated with one thing: an unalterable German orientation. For Lenin, Germany remains the center, if not of the imperialist, then of the revolutionary world, and all the trash that blindly follows him believes unshakably that that very same Germany—this time a bolshevik [Germany]—will decide the fate of the world.[224]

24 [October]. My brother was arrested again today by the military commissariat. I think his wish to get a passport for travel abroad went too much against the order, just put up in the streets, calling on all, or almost all, officers under forty. Spells of upset and alarm again. I am thinking much about what has actually happened in Germany and how to explain her breakdown. Something in her collapsed inside. Perhaps there is an indirect influence of the Russian revolution here: Germany ignited it, and now that she has begun to feel the burdens of defeat on herself, that spirit which she planted in her neighbors has begun to elicit a response in herself. The Germans have suffered more than all the others from the pressures of the war, with the single exception of France, but the difference between France and Germany is that Germany, herself already worn out, has been deprived of all her allies, whereas powerful allied forces were constantly added to exhausted France. I forgot to mention that Zagran'e was liquidated several days ago now, unnoticed by us. The house has been sealed; some instructor said that we need not return there, since we have an apartment in Moscow. Frankly speaking, it did not touch me; I don't want a life in Zagran'e, but something else—departure for somewhere far away.

28 [October]. I did not keep my notes for three days because of another series of misunderstandings, problems, and complications. On Friday the 25th, my brother went to the military district commissariat to request a certificate attesting to the absence of obstacles to his going abroad, but

---

[224] Got'e refers to Lenin's speech on October 22 at a combined meeting of TsIK, the Moscow soviet, and other workers' organizations, which was published in *Izvestiia* on October 23 (p. 4). His remark about Lenin's obsession with Germany probably came from reading this passage, which has been changed in the version of the speech published in Lenin's *Collected Works*: "But coming to meet us, Comrades, is the German revolution. Knowing the power and organization of the German proletariat, we can say that the German revolution will break out with such force and organization that it will resolve hundreds of international questions. Only we must go in step with the German revolution, not running ahead of it, not spoiling it, but helping it. . . ."

he was held there, and was shown there the same telegram that Fedor Aleksandrov had sent from Mokei Gora. He was released after twenty-four hours, but he was refused a pass; he was interrogated about himself, and about me as well. Thus the question has been raised anew of the misfortunes that could befall me. It is clear that a telegram from the central commissariat has been sent to the district commissariat, and it remains there for the time being. After conferring with knowledgeable people, I went to talk about this affair with comrade Romanov, head of the investigative part of the provinces section of the Cheka. I found him in his residence in the National Hotel; everything looks the same as before in the hotel, but a comrade in an army uniform with a rifle is standing downstairs. Another comrade, speaking with a Jewish accent, gives orders from behind a special counter. Once past the control, there is freedom of movement. I found comrade R. in his room, living with his spouse. This is a very polite young man with a university education; they say he is a devoted communist, but we talked together like good old friends of a former day. Having heard me out, he advised me "to shrug it off and not get upset," but not to rush ahead, since otherwise I "might set [people] to gossiping about me," for "there is lots of slander about." His opinion was the same as that of N. I. Trotskaia—nothing in particular will come of this affair; it will probably die out somewhere, and if it doesn't die down and I am bothered by anyone other than him, comrade R., I should refer to him and other prominent "communists." In his opinion, if the affair doesn't die down, it will reach his hands, and, as far as he is concerned, he will order the affair extinguished. With this I have at present stopped and am awaiting events. In everything else, matters are the same as before. On the one hand, they are pushing their cause—they are nationalizing trade, and the trading streets of Moscow have come to resemble a cemetery;[225] everything is leading to universal socioeconomic death in the midst of proletcults,[226] cultural-enlightenment lectures, mass meetings, and other such attempts at cultural-Manilov undertakings.[227] The note of the Soviet government to Wilson with the question about the intentions of the Allies in regard to Sovdepiia was very fine: a re-

[225] A commission for the "municipalization" of trade had been set up in the Moscow soviet in July 1918, and the process began in earnest in the autumn: the liquor and dry-goods businesses, handicrafts sales, fur sales, and book publishing were municipalized in October alone.

[226] Proletcult (proletkul't) was the popular name of the organization Proletarskaia kul'tura (Proletarian Culture), which was founded in Petrograd in September 1917 as a voluntary organization to promote proletarian cultural activities. After the Revolution, it spread to many other cities. Its independence, "proletarian class-exclusiveness" (although it was founded and led by intellectuals), and radical rejection of traditional culture soon led to friction with the Bolshevik authorities. It was finally abolished in 1932.

[227] That is, sentimental and self-righteous. See n. 173 for 1917.

markable mixture of naiveté and insolence. The cause of peace is advancing slowly but surely, but it has a long way to go before getting to Russian affairs. Foch is smiting Hindenburg as before.

29 [October]. A day without particular personal impressions. Lesha Blagoveshchenskii arrived and reported that our house is being designated an agricultural school; Lena Reiman is being accused of speculation, having been denounced by Aksin'ia and the laborer Mikhail (the last [event] had already occurred in the summer). Fedor Aleksandrov appeared at our place, extracted forty rubles from Aleksei, and departed on our horse for Sandovo in order to send the telegram that has been mentioned here several times already. The deadly Spanish flu is spreading everywhere, epidemically.[228] I am completely philosophical about what is happening in Zagran'e; I don't care, because in the present conditions life there is impossible in any case.

NOVEMBER

1 [November]. Again I didn't write because there was a new alarm. My brother was arrested again and all kinds of maneuvers had to be concocted in order to free him. However, after a day and a half of sitting in confinement, in the Shamshin house on Znamenka, he was again released. There was another interrogation; he was again questioned not only about himself, but about me, about Sandovo, Sonkovo, our village connections, etc. Apparently, such is his impression, an inquiry is being conducted about an explosion on the Rybinsk-Bologoe railroad, which happened recently and was apparently very powerful. The notorious telegram of crazy Fedor Aleksandrov provoked the idea that we were possibly connected with that event. Truly, you don't know what affair blind fate will tangle you in in our day. If it weren't for the wear on the nerves, it would simply be funny. In my search for any means, I ran into F. A. Armand yesterday, who proposed that I turn to the famous comrade Inessa, his mother and my childhood friend. At first I didn't want to do this, but then, remembering that *Not kennt kein Gebot*,[229] I decided to; today I got from her a *billet d'introduction* to the commissar of the mili-

---

[228] The Spanish influenza or "Spanish disease" (*ispanskaia bolezn'*) reached epidemic proportions in the late autumn of 1918, when more than 150 cases a week were being reported in the newspapers. But it was a distant runner-up to typhus, of which over 1,000 cases a week were being reported at the same time. Fatalities from epidemic diseases in Moscow in 1918 were relatively modest: 2,445 deaths from typhus, cholera, and dysentery, or 20 percent of all deaths. Ignat'ev, *Moskva v pervyi god proletarskoi revoliutsii*, p. 290.

[229] "Need obeys no commandment."

tary district, Muralov, and a polite letter which I attach here, as a document.[230]

An interesting report again today in *Izvestiia* under the heading "Conspiracy of the imperialists against Soviet Russia," in which there is talk of a suspected agreement of virtually everyone against bolshevism. I would very much like to know whether this is a clever maneuver to frighten part of the readers, or whether a recognition of real danger is concealed under this communication? The English have reached Aleppo; all of Syria and Mesopotamia are in their hands; the French are in Herzegovina; the thrust continues, but seems less strong these days.

2 [November]. A day with few impressions. For that reason, perhaps, you dwell more on general thoughts. Austria is falling apart just like Russia; the bolsheviks are shouting that there is social revolution there. That is still far from obvious, but there can be no doubt that disintegration is occurring on a nationality basis. I am very glad that the loathsome clique of genuine imperialists, who long ago built their nest in central Europe (the Prussian Junkers, the Viennese Jewish bankers, the Austro-Hungarian aristocrats, etc.), and, finally, the war parties of both countries, Austria and Germany—in a word, all those who really did start the war, have been reduced to ashes and are being destroyed. It serves them right. Quem Jupiter perdere vult, dementat. The Germans committed three irreparable errors: (1) they started a war when they almost ruled the world already; (2) they dragged America into the war, although America did not want to fight at all; (3) they installed the bolsheviks in Russia. With all that, the ruling German circles demonstrated that behind their self-confidence was concealed the highest degree of genuinely German obtuseness, of a kind unmatched by any other people on earth, and the result was the destruction of everything for which the Germans and their satellites had worked for half a century, destruction of the monarchies at the hands of the chief European monarchists, and the destruction of imperialism at the hands of the supreme European imperialists.

3 [November]. I saw the celebration of the unveiling of the memorials: (1) to either Kaliaev or Danton, and (2) to Kol'tsov and Nikitin.[231] The first

---

[230] The letter could not be found in the manuscript collection. The note for Aleksandr Ivanovich Muralov (1886–1937) is there: "Respected Comrade! I beg of you to receive my acquaintance, Iurii Vladimirovich Got'e. I will be grateful to you. Inessa Armand."

[231] Got'e was showing indifference to the attribution of the first of these monuments. Since Lukin was speaking there, it was probably a statue of Danton. The latter two were dedicated to A. V. Kol'tsov (1809–1842) and Ivan Savvich Nikitin (1824–1861), respectively, "the people's poets." Both Kol'tsov and Nikitin were of humble parentage. Nikitin's "principal claim to attention lies in his realistic poems of the life of the poor" (Mirsky, *History of Russian Literature*, p. 226).

occurred, or was supposed to occur, in the Alexandrine Garden.[232] Near some bust, still draped, there strode the official historian of the present day, N. M. Lukin.[233] Later two orchestras came along, some sort of quasi-troops with red placards, and also 100-150 representatives of the public. The troops were led by a young man on horseback, in civilian clothes and a broad-brimmed hat; they said this was Smidovich.[234] Having looked at all this, I left. The two pitiful monuments to the people's poets had already been unveiled on Theater Square. There was no one near one of them; as many as 150 people were near the other, dolefully listening to the orators. The one I heard was mouthing memorized phrases about the sufferings of the hungry people celebrated by the poets, and about the crimes of the landowners who were fed at the people's expense. Such is the hypocrisy of life. Afterward I went to visit poor K. A. Wilken who is nearly dying, unable to endure the boons of our time. Such is the reality of life. Groups paraded in the afternoon with posters in honor of the revolution in Austria; it has been officially proclaimed so by the bolsheviks, but there is a complete chasm between their proclamations and the wire reports on which they are based.

4 [November]. They have arrested S. N. Vasilenko, a man less capable than anyone of political deeds or thoughts.[235] This is, of course, a misunderstanding, but what is it going to cost him! We are receiving a half-pound of candy each on the ration card on the occasion of the revolutionary festivities.

5 [November]. Moscow is preparing for the revolutionary anniversary—banners and decorations with bloodthirsty slogans. Having accumulated some sort of provisions, the rulers are giving out somewhat increased

[232] The Alexander Garden (Aleksandrovskii sad) is a large memorial park situated along the west wall of the Kremlin.

[233] Nikolai Mikhailovich Lukin (1885–1940) was a historian of Western Europe who was trained at Moscow University before the Revolution and taught there for a while beginning in 1915, by which time he was already involved with the Bolsheviks (a rarity among Moscow professors). He had recommenced teaching at Moscow University in October 1918. Later he held a number of important posts on the "historical front," including editorship of the journal *Istorik-Marksist* and directorship of the Academy of Sciences Institute of History. In 1938 he was arrested, while director of the Institute of History, and perished in the camps.

[234] Petr Germogenovich Smidovich (1874–1935) was a longtime Bolshevik and a high official of the government and soviets. Shortly before this time, he had been chairman of the Moscow soviet.

[235] Sergei Nikiforovich Vasilenko (1872–1956) was a well-known composer and conductor and a professor at the Moscow Conservatory. He survived to become a "classic" of Soviet music and Laureate of the Stalin Prize.

portions of sweets, meat, and butter, patently currying favor or wishing to show that we can pamper when we want to.

In the West, another blow against the Germans, and a very successful one: the Serbs, together with the Allies, have taken Belgrade; Serbia has been cleared in one month after three years of oppression. Honor and glory to them. Austria is apparently disintegrating, but is she disintegrating in the way the bolsheviks want? That is in no way apparent, and there is no way of knowing the true state of things, living in the dark. A letter came today from Aleksei, from which it is clear that Zagran'e has been liquidated. He reports that all the linen, even his own, has been taken away, "I don't know where"; that if we come in the summer we will have to live "in their apartment"; that he will feed us with bread; and that he has been deeply offended by us because we did not take care of him. The letter ends with the news that they have a "commune" and that things are bad in general. One has to think that this "I don't know where" signifies that the linen has been taken to Gora and that Messrs. Obraztsov, seeing that we were then being liquidated, notified the soviet and got into their hands everything they could. The dissatisfaction with us is very characteristic of a Russian gorilla, who stays on to live in our house, in our things, using our cow and our horse. On the whole, there has occurred what I foresaw from the spring of 1917: the Russian intelligentsia has been driven from the village, and our turn came in that process; we should remember with gratitude that after all, contrary to the experience of the majority of people with country residences, we were able to pass the summer of 1918 in Zagran'e. Lena Reiman, according to information that has reached us, is about to be released, but Petr Smirnov from Besovo, one of the main local activists, has demanded "that Reiman not set foot in the township." Mania, it seems, has resolved to remain in Zagran'e, in the small house, witnessing the destruction of all her worldly possessions and lacking the possibility at present to stop it. One thinks that she, too, will soon be thrown out; extra witnesses are not needed.

6 [November]. The latest event—the rupture of diplomatic relations between the Germans and the soviet government; an event pregnant with consequences, but I still can't grasp precisely what they will be or when they will be felt. Literally anything is possible; the authorities are concealing much, and the man in the street, as always, celebrates prematurely. In any case, some kind of events will ensue; I only fear that our fraternity is going to suffer not a little. It is impossible to imagine how the bolsheviks have decorated Moscow: the decorations betray an amazing mixture of progressive political and social ideas together with futurism, cubism, and the like. This evening was a sort of Easter night: fireworks were set off for about half an hour at the [cathedral of] Christ the

Savior; they probably burned some kind of effigies as well. We were disgusted and didn't go there, despite the proximity.

7 [November]. Moscow is celebrating. I was on Tverskaia only in the evening. The weather was fine; they say the crowds were big; the city was illuminated again in the evening; there were red lanterns even on Ivan the Great.[236] Il en a vu bien d'autre, ce brave vieux. The crowd on Tverskaia was democratic, unskilled laborers, factory hands, indeterminate—a genuine personification of that which has seized power. Like any Russian crowd, it was somber and dull; the side streets were dark and quiet, and there were even few flags. There are no newspapers, nor news bulletins, even cut and distorted; some are having a good time, others dissemble, yet others wait.

8 [November]. Universal tense expectation, expressed by the crowds reading the fence announcements or newspaper of "Rosta," that is, the Russian telegraph agency. The dearth of news only stimulates curiosity and disenchantment. I went to the nameday of my brother-in-law Mitia Kurdiumov near Iaroslavl' station and saw the decorations in the center of town. I think that every moment has its reflection in art. The decorations of Moscow in October 1918 exceed in level of deformity all the German art of the prewar period, epitomized by the Leipzig memorial.[237] The fullest expression of our art is the painting of the stalls in Okhotnyi Riad,[238] in which all the "isms" with which Russian life is filled are harmoniously mixed.

9 [November]. The Germans have broken with the soviet government.[239] Does this mean they will enterprise something right away? I think not. This was done, perhaps, in order the quicker and better to settle differences with the Anglo-Franco-Americans; perhaps it is a precondition for the talks that Erzberger and co. will conduct at the headquarters of Marshal Foch.[240] Between the break with Russia and the consequences flowing from it, there may be a fairly long period, unwanted by all, but in-

[236] The great bell tower in the Kremlin, dating from 1505–1508.

[237] The Volkerschlachtdenkmal in Leipzig, consecrated on October 18, 1913, was built to commemorate the Battle of Leipzig (The Battle of the Nations, October 16–19, 1813). It is a somber, foreboding granite pile, ninety-one meters high, constructed after the design of Bruno Schmitz.

[238] Apparently the butchers' stalls in Okhotnyi Riad had been decorated by some radical artists.

[239] The German government broke off relations with Soviet Russia and expelled its embassy from Berlin on November 5.

[240] Matthias Erzberger of the Center party led the German delegation that signed the armistice of November 11.

evitable. All frivolous Russian optimists should remember that. The holiday in Moscow is not yet over: the purely soviet institutions continued to celebrate today. The offensive in France still continues and if there is no truce the Allies will squeeze the Germans out of France altogether.

10 [November]. The main event of this day is the supplementary communiqué, published this afternoon, that power in Berlin has gone over to some kind of soviet, and that comrade Ioffe has been recalled to Berlin.[241] What the percent of truth is in this communique it is not given us to know; but the upheaval in Germany is in itself possible, because their retreat in the West has assumed a catastrophic character, which either indicates such an upheaval or foreshadows one. Any upheaval in Germany—at some level almost inevitable—can only be harmful to the remnants of the Russian bourgeoisie, to the Ukraine, and to all antibolshevik elements in Russia; therefore, the distant moment of rest and calm is made even more distant. But whatever happens, whatever comes of us, if anybody deserves a shaking-up and even possible destruction it is the German princes, Junkers, bankers, and industrialists, in a word, those who can justifiably be called world imperialists. The eviction from France and Belgium, the journey to pay homage to Foch, the severe conditions of the truce—all that is only the beginning, perhaps, of a great atonement for the greatest crime in world history, the war they started in 1914.

11 [November]. The general opinion is that what is happening in Germany is not quite what the Russian authorities are announcing. There is almost no fresh news: everything is in snatches and vague. Vasilenko has been released without any charges being made. I received a message from comrade M. K. Romanov that there is no need for me to be alarmed about the telegram of Fedor Aleksandrov.

12 [November]. Little reliable news; one will have to bide one's time for a while before saying anything about the present or predicting the future; right now I can make out nothing precise or likely. The more I reflect, the more I am amazed by the self-confidence and stupidity of the Ger-

---

[241] On November 9, the government of Prince Max von Baden resigned and Wilhelm II fled across the border to Holland. A struggle for power then ensued between the moderates, led by Friedrich Ebert of the sD party, who had been left in charge by the departing government, and the far left, led by the Spartacists (the German Communist party); the first phase of the German revolution ended with an abortive coup by the Spartacists in Berlin in January 1919. Adol'f Abramovich Ioffe (Joffe) (1883–1927) was the Soviet ambassador in Berlin who had been expelled on November 5. The communiqué Got'e read was wrong about both the nature of events in Berlin and the return of Ioffe.

mans, who in pursuing victory over the whole world have destroyed themselves and all of Europe—have done so with the same stupidity as Nicholas II destroyed Russia and the Russian nonrevolutionaries. For me the question is the following: will things in Germany reach the point of proclaiming war on the principle of property or not? If no, then the revolution will stop; if yes, it is bolshevism. The political order is essentially of no concern to us, and if the German rulers are kicked out, the world will lose nothing by it. How that will reflect on the victors is another question; but we have absolutely no real information about the state of mind in France and England and therefore cannot judge.

13 [November]. A situation without any particular changes: the truce has been concluded, but I still don't know its exact conditions; it seems they are severe; perhaps this is the influence of England, which is just as severe with Wilhelm as she was in her time with Napoleon. They say the princes of this world are not too pleased; that means they are not sure of the turn the German revolution might take. I spoke today with Avenard; he also fears that a movement might start in France as well. He considers severe conditions for a truce a mistake; it would be better to reconcile Germany with us than to set her against us—the French socialists, reinforced by all the discontented from the war, will, in his opinion, be against stringent conditions. In general, the present moment is unusually important and alarming: the future of all unhappy, old, berated, and plundered Europe has been wrapped in a fog that will not be lifted for a long time to come. And the Americans will, perhaps, come to Russia; they suffered very little, and they probably are impatient as well; and it is possible to do good *business*[242] in Russia.

14 [November]. Nothing new; the bolsheviks themselves admit, through their leaders, that they know very little about Germany; the information is vague and difficult to figure out. I am deeply sorry for the Germans; this is where blinding by nationalist pride leads. How stupid were all those German sovereigns, rushing headlong! If they had lived peaceably, they could have survived for several more centuries, but now they are like the old woman with a broken wash-trough.[243] The bolsheviks have joyfully destroyed the Brest treaty; what kind of consequences will flow from this?[244] Our apartment rent has been raised again: now we pay 600

[242] In English in the original.
[243] An image drawn from Pushkin's tale about the fisherman and the fish ("Skazka o rybake i rybke"), which has gone into the language to signify being no better off than before, or back where one started from.
[244] The Bolshevik government abrogated the Brest treaty on November 13.

rubles a month. I think we won't be for long in a position to live in this apartment.

15 [November]. The bolsheviks remain dissatisfied with the German revolution; this is the only objective indicator by which we can judge its course. The latest bombshell is the question of eviction from the apartment, which arises before us for the third time. Military control or counterintelligence, which has penetrated our house like a cancer tumor, wants to spread further and take over all our front wing. This time Nina and I think it is best to yield and move into the museum anthill. We will miss this apartment, which we picked for ourselves and loved, but now it is all the same, the old life is impossible, and therefore transfer to a bivouac of three rooms in all will be a step further on the path of relief from all attachment to things, to comfort, and the like. K. A. Wilken has died; among the people who were close to my parents, there remain in Moscow only Iu. E. Wilken and A. E. Armand, whose ages add up to 150 years, and in addition M. M. Cherkasskaia and L. N. Krasil'nikova in Khar'kov, who together have just as many [years].

16 [November]. Very interesting information has been printed in *Izvestiia* "from Kiev newspapers" about all the schemes of the Allies against the bolsheviks. I don't entirely understand why this was printed—there could be many explanations, but which is correct I don't know. The latest bombshell: an affair in the museum. Several fools of the Russian blockhead variety—the stubborn and stupid Belorussian ass, the supervisor Nikitin; the dolt with demagogic ways, the registrar Solodkov; the Quasimodo office clerk, Kozlov; and finally the anthroposophist of beautiful soul, Petrovskii—cooked up the idea of dumping Stratonitskii and even the prince, with the help of the employees.[245] The former will have to be sacrificed to save the situation. The question of eviction remains open and will be decided next week.

18 [November]. Yesterday and today I was hardly at home; there was the Wilken funeral, the procession to Mar'ina Roshcha to bid farewell to Lerik Veselago, and today a procession to Vvedenskie Gory.[246] It seems that it is even inconvenient to die nowadays: at the non-Orthodox cem-

[245] Aleksei Sergeevich Petrovskii (b. 1881), an employee of the Rumiantsev Museum and specialist on Russian literature, was a member of the Russian Anthroposophical Society and an acquaintance of Belyi, Blok, and other anthroposophists. Konkordii Andreevich Stratonitskii (b. 1865) was the academic secretary (*uchenyi sekretar'*) of the Rumiantsev Museum.

[246] Mar'ina Roshcha and Vvedenskie Gory were suburban sites of cemeteries. The "German" cemetery for Catholics and Lutherans was located in Vvedenskie Gory.

etery, which was always better organized than the rest, the gravediggers will not bury more than seven bodies a day and will not bury earlier than 1 P.M. When K. A. Wilken was buried, the grave had not been dug deep enough and the coffin had to be raised to the ground again; they lost the cross, which had been prepared beforehand, and they were rude and disgruntled—a typical manifestation of the Russian Revolution. The general situation is unclear; the rumors don't dry up, and the man in the street continues to live by them; there is no news from abroad; it seems that peasant disturbances are proliferating, suppressed in each individual case but flaring up anew in other places.

19 [November]. Silence in the newspapers; the rumors are all the same as before; you can't make out anything definite. In the narrow circle of affairs, a day without any particular impressions.

21 [November]. Almost no news; rumors are spread the more eagerly for that. They are talking about the approach of an Allied squadron to Petersburg; today they were saying that Petersburg has already been taken; I don't believe that, of course. Today I was in "town" and was horrified at the looks of Nikol'skaia and Il'inka[247]—everything is closed, there are hardly any people roaming about, it is as if there were a plague or a major holiday. Here and there they are tearing down signs that recall the dominance of the bourgeois in commerce and industry. The question of our eviction from the apartment seems to have gotten more acute yesterday, but there is no notice yet. We are trying to take all possible measures to stay on or, alternatively, to guarantee our moving into the museum properties. Worried about the collection of the ten-billion-ruble tax, the bolsheviks have decreed that everyone is obliged to show everything he has, down to and including cash kept at home. But a sheep can only be shorn when its wool has grown out, not when it is smoothly shorn like those Russians who formerly had means.

22 [November]. The matter of our eviction has not budged, with the exception only that I am making an effort to assure myself some kind of nook on the territory of the Rumiantsev Museum. It seems I have found it in an apartment used for storing manuscripts and archives. The general news is again vague; only the report of an exchange of fire between the Finnish fort Iniö and the "Russian" navy draws attention when juxtaposed with the reports of the appearance of an Allied squadron in the Gulf of Finland. More than ever before there is a feeling of universal

---

[247] The central shopping area of Moscow, where the GUM is now located; since 1935 the streets have been known as ulitsa Dvadsat' Piatogo Oktiabria and ulitsa Kuibysheva.

fatigue and, on the side of civilized Russian people, a universal passionate wish that the Time of Troubles pass. The longer it goes on, the more burdensome it becomes and the less patience there is.

24 [November]. The question of our eviction is apparently being postponed; our mangy building committee chairman told our tenants about this yesterday, but his words are like shifting sand. General news remains vague. Today is Sunday; I sat home and got very few impressions; it was pleasant to rest in one's shell.

25 [November]. Rumors, rumors, and rumors. In them it seems possible to grasp only one thing: that the Allied fleet has perhaps appeared in the Baltic Sea. In Moscow it is boring, dead, and ever hungrier; the day passed like all past and future [days].

26 [November]. One of the greatest injustices is that M. M. Petrovo-Solovovo, the landlady who has lived in this house for perhaps fifty years, is being evicted in two days and has nowhere to lay her head. For that matter, this kind of thing occurs in our day right and left. According to the latest reports, which Prince Urusov has just conveyed, they want to move M. M. Petrovo-Solovovo in with us, in exchange for the Razorenovs. There is the same opacity in the general situation as before.

27 [November]. The row at home is calming down and for the time being there will be no moving or changes for us. No definite news of any kind. The burden produced by the absence of news and by living the life of moles is becoming progressively heavier.

28 [November]. There are no changes; however, someone has taken Liski[248] from the Sovdepists. Voronezh has been declared in a state of siege and is being evacuated. I was in the office in charge of safe-deposits and saw there a prism in which a portrait of Trotskii had been inserted in place of the classic ukases of Peter; which of the bolsheviks were on the other two sides, I don't know. In the museum there is discontent again among the employees: now they want the staff that have apartments there to double up.

29 [November]. Something is being prepared, of where and how we know nothing; but there will be a struggle, and those who now rule Russia will put to use all the means at their command. Today I heard about one of the commissars of the Kremlin, the Estonian Veiman, who was on a

---

[248] A town in Voronezh province, presently called Gheorghiu-Dej.

secret mission to Germany for an entire six weeks in order to conduct communist propaganda there. That is what they are up to; those who supported them at one time are fools.

30 [November]. I heard from reliable sources that they are getting ready to either exchange or stamp money, and will exchange only up to the amount certified in the records provided by somebody. This is an excellent means of getting out of difficulties and liquidating an enormous amount of money in a single step. They are writing about the appearance of an Allied squadron in the Black Sea, but the date is not given; it probably happened a long time ago now.

DECEMBER

1 [December]. We traveled to Pushkino to bury my cousin and friend from childhood and youth, Volodia Reiman, who died at forty-seven from progressive paralysis. His life was full of mistakes; the last ten years he gradually went to ruin, and death was a deliverance for him and for all those near to him. He was buried in the Orthodox rite: the funeral service was in the Pushkino village church and he was interred in the Pushkino cemetery. His father attached himself to the Got'e family after the death of his wife; he [Volodia] also lived parasitically and parasitically attached himself to the Armand family, which he entered by his marriage, as his father had entered the Got'e family. At the funeral, which was in daylight, I saw some of the Armand family with whom my parents had once been friendly. The poor old folks, the last contemporaries and friends of my father—they are all looking into the grave, and Arkadii Evgen'evich Armand said today that all the old folks will surely pass away this winter. A contrast to this great sorrow was the fine winter day with new-fallen snow. Yesterday I happened to read the Kiev newspapers from last Sunday. They have an air of life about them, although in reading into them I couldn't help but be reinforced in my longtime conviction that we must not expect an end soon to our sufferings; and the uprising of the idiot Petliura is of course capable only of delaying the matter. The matter will come clear in 1919; may God grant that we will still be alive.

2 [December]. There have been no changes; but everybody wants them so, and unfailingly demands that they come soon, that there arise ever-newer rumors, which do not fall silent for a minute, not to mention a day, but cannot be taken seriously. The general situation is such that the victors will be obliged to police the world, and there is much evidence to suggest that the entire affair will end not with the triumph of the Russian bolsheviks, but with a return to order by the will of the cultured countries of the West; however, much time is needed for this. I received a letter from Lena Reiman; she writes that gradually everything is being stolen from us there. Kismet! The more so in that neither Nina nor I wants to return to Zagran'e.

S. A. Belokurov died. That is an irretrievable loss for the Archive of Foreign Affairs and the Society of History and Antiquities, where he was *everything*. He was an intelligent and important man in our petty world. His shortcomings were also great—enviousness, vengefulness, and ambition—but they were balanced by conscientiousness, devotion to his cause, and especially that flexible steadfastness he revealed in his last year, when he saved the Archive and all the employees without compromising his own dignity. This is the eighth death in one month. The Spanish disease, the general decline from which all suffer, poor diet, and the cold—all do their work. Moscow is not only scattering, it is dying off.

4 [December]. The holiday of the Presentation of the Blessed Virgin, but a working day; I had to work in the museum, but I canceled my seminar in the Higher Women's Courses; it was really very uncustomary and I very much did not want to work. Today I was for the last time in the "syphilitic" bank of the RSFSR; instead of my certificates I received only a receipt. Proletarization is going further and further. The rumors are all the same. There is no positive information of any kind.

5 [December]. The rumors do not quiet down; but there are only rumors; there was little new today. I am very much interested by the question of whether we professors will be allowed after the first of January to stay in our places until the reelections, or whether we will be forbidden to go within cannon shot of the university and the Higher Women's Courses: they are equally capable of the one or the other.

6 [December]. The situation remains unchanged, but the rumors persist, indeed grow constantly stronger; perhaps, however, it seems to me that way because, judging logically, either the entire world must become bolshevik, or we must live like the rest of the world; and as the latter is the more likely, it seems that deliverance will come soon.

I was invited to a meeting, session, or conference in the People's Commissariat of Enlightenment concerning the organization of cinematographic affairs in Russia, or, more precisely, in Sovdepiia. This is connected with the idea of creating a cinematographic picture, "The History of the Russian Liberation Movement," in regard to which I am something like an expert or consultant in the "Neptune" society. I first of all saw comrade Lunacharskii[249] at this meeting. A rather elegant gentleman with extravagant and foppish manners; a good dialectician, he conducted the session with talent, I must say, and strove for a clearly understood goal, despite the contrary actions of comrades of lower grade. Compared to the surrounding "comrades," Lunacharskii was undoubtedly much higher, a long habit of circulating among people who are inferior in all respects has not, perhaps, remained without influence on his highly developed conceit and self-delusion, which was undoubtedly bred into this born cubist-futurist and fop. Many deities of the local Olympus came to the meeting, beginning with comrade Pokrovskii, who reminds one more and more of Quasimodo; here there were scoundrels, repentant intellectuals, cinematography professionals, persons with an expression of narrow fanaticism on their faces, and the inevitable Jews, male and female, who essentially predominated here as they predominate everywhere. The whole was presided over by three goddesses: N. I. Trotskaia, a second-rate milliner; Kameneva, a Jew with the face of a parrot;[250] and M. F. Zheliabuzhskaia-Andreeva-Gor'kaia, etc., who, despite the "forty centuries" personified by her, has preserved some traces of her "antique" external qualities.[251] Here, too, participated "professor" Kogan, my old university comrade, now zealously publicizing Lenin in public lectures— *ad majorem "Dei" (Lenin's) gloriam.*[252] What was said at the session was of no interest: the customary Russo-Jewish twaddle, without substance and full of personal account settling.

7 [December]. A conversation with N. G. Semenov, my junker-school comrade.[253] He is a decorated officer who commanded a division; now, at the

[249] Anatolii Vasil'evich Lunacharskii (1875–1933) was the commissar of enlightenment from 1917 to 1929. Lunacharskii's background was bureaucratic-noble. Part of his education had been abroad (Zurich), and he had spent ten years in Western Europe between the 1905 and 1917 revolutions. He had been involved in Social Democratic politics for many years, but rejoined the Bolshevik party only in August 1917.

[250] The wife of Lev Borisovich Kamenev (1883–1936), head of the Moscow party organization and president of the Moscow soviet. She was also Trotskii's sister.

[251] Mariia Fedorovna Andreeva (1868–1953) was a well-known actress of the Moscow Art Theater and other companies who had been active in Bolshevik affairs since 1904. She was Maksim Gor'kii's common-law wife. After the Revolution, she held various government posts and continued acting for several years.

[252] Petr Semenovich Kogan (1872–1932) was a Marxist literary historian and critic who was appointed to the Moscow University staff after the October revolution. In 1921 he was appointed president of the State Academy of Fine Arts. He was "a popular lecturer and fervent propagandist of Soviet literature . . ." (*Bol'shaia Sovetskaia Entsiklopediia,* 3d ed., vol. 12, col. 1085).

[253] The junker schools were two-year officer-training schools for secondary-school graduates or the equivalent. After 1875, all army volunteers and recruits seeking officer

will of the bolsheviks, he is chief of staff of the Second Army, operating on the eastern front, but he took ill and fled from there. Here is his characterization of the Red Army: its worth is not great; there is no kind of internal link with the command staff of former officers, but among the commanders of the new formation, from among the red army men, there are those who command respect. They hobnob with the soldiers, but are able to inspire them with confidence as well on occasion. It would be hard to destroy this army, because its forces are dispersed, and when scattering they recruit former soldiers from the local citizenry, [so that] there have been cases when somewhat later they have regrouped in even greater numbers. They have a greater supply of ammunition than do their enemies, and that gives them the advantage. Their opponent is even weaker than they [are]. The core is the Czechoslovaks, who are joined by forces formed by the Siberian government; the soldiers there receive little, they have few supplies; the officers have learned nothing so far as relations with the soldiers and attitudes toward them are concerned. In addition, they are being demoralized by the bolsheviks' propaganda. A genuine armed force, well organized and outfitted technically, could easily gain the advantage. At present the military danger for the RSFSR is not on the eastern but on the southern front. The bolshevik newspapers report today that the Russian representation abroad has assumed the obligation of paying the debts and has recognized the former foreign representation of Russia;[254] also, the Germans have returned to the Allies the Russian gold they had taken, and supreme command over the Allied forces in the south will belong to Franchet d'Esperey.

8 [December]. Nothing is being reported today about the Russo-Jewish comrades' trip to Berlin, and there is mention of battle to the north of Liski. This means nothing is going the way they want. The rumors are all the same as before or just like them.

11 [December]. These days were all without changes; all the same tense expectation of something, and the same gloom surrounding us. Juxtaposing all the military news, I have now become convinced that the bolsheviks are lying viciously. They lie, conceal, and distort as no other govern-

---

status had to go to junker school. Got'e had apparently been sent to junker school during his year of military service after graduating from the university in 1895.

[254] This rather obscure statement refers to the conference of Provisional Government ambassadors in Europe, led by V. A. Maklakov, which at that time was in the process of convening a general Russian Political Conference of representatives of the Provisional Government and the centers of anti-Bolshevik forces in Russia. Its aim was to create a unified Russian representation for the peace conference. See John M. Thompson, *Russia, Bolshevism, and the Versailles Peace* (Princeton, 1966), chapter 3.

ment has done; in exactly the same way they lie in their reports from abroad. Neither in Germany nor in the rest of Europe are things going at all as they would like. Today I went to bid farewell to Patouillet, who is leaving in the hope, as he says, of returning to Russia toward spring. He questioned me a lot about my opinions concerning what ought to be done in Russia, raising the question, in particular, of whether the Allies were not making a mistake in befriending the counterrevolutionary elements outside Sovdepiia. I answered him that they have no other choice, that only the counterrevolutionaries had remained consistently faithful to them; one can only wish that the counterrevolution not manifest itself too strongly and not be too reactionary. He assured me that all this will be among the materials for his discussions with Poincaré and with several of the greats of this world in general. Masha the cook reported that a Latvian soldier had told her friend Gavrilych that they will definitely leave "for home" in two weeks. Bearing in mind the movement of the bolsheviks into the Baltic, I am beginning to allow for the possibility of a pull on the Latvians from within Sovdepiia to its periphery.

12 [December]. The day passed without changes and without particular impressions; it seems one has already grown accustomed to life in the manner of moles—blind and underground.

13 [December]. The rumors have worn out and seem to be dying down; the newspapers are empty as well. Now there is an alarm in the museum in the form of various funerals; they are assuring us that there will be searches and we will have to think again of moving relics of various kinds to other places.

14 [December]. The moment of calm—temporary, of course—continues. The rumors are not changing in content; however, the bolsheviks are signaling both a landing in the south and the possibility of the beginning of military actions in the north. As before, the most agreeable—indeed, only agreeable—passing of time is when you sleep or, having ended the workday and put on your felt boots, you lock yourself up in your shell.

16 [December]. A general lift in spirits again today: it is influenced by the little Menshevik newspapers that appear on Sundays and Mondays. We saw Avenard off today; we talked much of our coming arrival in France. God grant that it all occurs. In the last few days the conviction has grown in me that all this is going to change in the more-or-less near future, otherwise we will have to flee here forever. One hopes that poor Avenard will at last succeed in getting away from this horror to his *beau pays de France*.

18 [December]. I have seen the Petersburg historians Presniakov and Po-lievktov several times.[255] I was not aware of it earlier, but now with the intensification of life, the difference in the psychology of Petersburg and Moscow can clearly be felt. They adapt more easily to the RSFSR and look at the present more optimistically than we do. It is hard to explain this right off: the heritage of Petrine bureaucratism, a certain veneer of SR-ism that coexists with that same bureaucratic spirit of the former capital. The fact in any case remains that they get along better with comrade Gol'dendakh and all that goes with him. Something is going wrong in Kiev; it seems the autonomists Petliura and co. have again gotten the upper hand and have overthrown Skoropadskii. The bolsheviks report on this in muted fashion; whether everything is happening like that, or is really going somehow differently, we absolutely don't know.[256] That is the horror of our situation, that we are blind like moles—*c'est la bouteille d'encre*, as our friend Avenard, who left for good today, said. Will we ever see him again?

20 December. Yesterday we celebrated my father-in-law's traditional nameday; after workaday affairs in the museum, I spent the whole evening in warm and comfortable surroundings reminiscent of old Moscow, which none of us will ever see again; I even laughed, as if forgetting everything that has happened; we also drank a little vodka. This evening there was a colloquium of historians at Bogoslovskii's; we analyzed the causes of things and whose fault it all is. Voices differed, but a stranger listening to our discussion would have been struck by the cheerlessness and gloominess of the historians' opinions. Our Petersburg colleagues couldn't even stand it and, growing silent, very soon departed. As before, it is impossible to get any kind of understanding about what is going on around us. Contemplating the events in the Ukraine on the basis of scattered information, asking yourself with whose money Petliura is operating, and taking into account Foch's shouts at the Germans and threats to occupy Germany, you involuntarily think that Germany has still not laid down her weapons and, without resisting actively, all the same uses all available means to pour oil on the fire everywhere it smolders. We received news from uncle Emil', who had fled to the Ukraine. To them it seemed insufficiently calm in Poltava province. Whether from cowardice on their part, or from the real movements of Petliura and like trash, in any case he has left for Bendery. "The desert waves of Bendery" will now

---

[255] Mikhail Aleksandrovich Polievktov (1872–1942) was a specialist on the history of Russian foreign relations in the eighteenth and nineteenth centuries and author of a well-known book on the reign of Nicholas I.

[256] The army of the revived Ukrainian-nationalist Directorate, led by Petliura, occupied Kiev on December 14, ending the German-sponsored regime of Skoropadskii.

see our poor Muscovite ultrabourgeois uncle; we shall hope that he will find peace among the Rumanians. One other thought: it seems to me that the Poles of the end of the eighteenth century must have had the thought that a long rule by foreigners was the only way out of anarchy. Looking at the Ukraine, Sovdepiia, Siberia, and other scraps of unhappy, dead Russia that know no peace, seeing how troubles flare up there whence the Germans are retreating, I ask myself the question: do we not need a long, burdensome occupation by strangers, their ruthless rule, in order to recover from the gangrene from which Rus' has suffered for more than half a century?

21 [December]. A day without any impressions; a snowstorm is raging and one involuntarily thinks of the cold and frosts that await us in the next three months, without firewood and without provisions. I found out that the foreigners are continuing to leave; now it is the Belgians' turn. The process of turning Sovdepiia into a country deprived of any intercourse with the civilized world proceeds unswervingly; a country outside the law—that is what Russia is turning into.

22 [December]. The snowstorm raged all day, so that all sorts of transformations, forebodings, and the like involuntarily come to mind; it is just as if God himself has definitively withdrawn from us and is showing it to us clearly. At the meeting of the Society of History and Antiquities, Liubavskii read a eulogy for Belokurov. Some things in it were trite, but there was one fundamental idea: that the death of the main worker in the society calls attention to the fact that now it is the turn of the society as a whole, which will perish as all of Russian culture will perish. I spent the evening at Iakovlev's, at first with Presniakov and Nikolaev,[257] later alone with Iakovlev; among other things, we discussed the question of what will happen here if all goes on as it is going now. We unanimously decided that everything will gradually die off, the schools will close down, the towns will die of hunger and cold, the railroads will stand still, and gorilla-like troglodytes will live in the villages, somehow, after the fashion of prehistoric men of the Stone Age, working the field and living off it. Superficial Russian culture must perish, because the "people," in whose name the "intelligentsia" or, more correctly, the semiintelligentsia sacrificed everything that was superior in Russia, has need of nothing except the crudest satisfaction of its prehistoric instincts. We also talked about the Petersburgers; they seem to suffer from a kind of color blindness in regard to the bolsheviks; in their abandoned Petrograd they sin-

[257] Aleksandr Sergeevich Nikolaev was a Petrograd historian and professional archivist. He was still publishing documents as late as 1948.

cerely think that it is possible to talk about creative work with them, whereas we are convinced that such work is unthinkable under this regime.

23 [December]. The snowstorm has ended, but today the bourgeois are already being driven to clean off the snow, even from the railroads. I have truly never seen such snowdrifts. The talk is about the telegram supposedly received by the powers-that-be from comrade Zinov'ev to the effect that all naval bases on the Baltic Sea have been seized by the Allies, that there are no naval forces, and that the situation is grave. In the university, there are some kind of ominous rumors among the students about the assignment of communist monitors to replace the existing monitors. What is there to do? Let them, like the peasants, experience the charms of the regime. One student came to me today with the question whether he will be examined in my course for the entire course of the nineteenth century. I answered him that I don't know; then he said to me that there will soon be a meeting of socialist students—they will arrange everything, and will set up the administration of the university and set out all the requirements. At that I countered to him: then accommodate yourself to their requirements.

24 [December]. I heard the following story today: the bolsheviks themselves laugh at what they write in their newspapers; the news dispatches are complete lies; the radio reports, especially German radio reports, are invented in their entirety in Moscow. I gave my last lecture in the university as a professor before my transformation into a person without rights who may be allowed to teach. It will just have to be tolerated until warm weather comes.

26 [December]. Nothing new, all the same haze, the same impending final limit. Yesterday they destroyed all the law faculties as outdated and unneeded. Indeed, there is no need to know the law in a lawless country. This is a new milestone for that mindless, incredible stupidity and brainlessness which characterize the communist fortunes of poor Russia. Another snowstorm, as if it wants to cover up everything, as if it wants to destroy all life. There are no potatoes, nor will there be, as they have been spoiled, frozen, hidden, or stolen; and without potatoes the hunger in Moscow will grow more intense.

27 [December]. New rumors about the critical situation near Petrograd and about the equally critical situation in the south; we have heard so often about suchlike news that I let it all go in one ear and out the other. An "emergency revolutionary tax," expressed in astronomical figures, hangs over us at present. Everybody expects it, everybody talks about it, but no one worries about it, precisely because of its emergency status and its insupportable size: why get excited when it won't be paid anyway? The problem of Nina's diet worries me more and more; I am pondering all the possibilities about when and where to take her; but the fact is that wherever I might take her now would mean taking her to a certain death.[258]

28 [December]. I am worried about Nina's condition; our cook has fallen ill, apparently from the Spanish sickness, and Nina has to do everything for her, which aggravates her own sick condition even more. Lena Reiman was here in the evening; she invites us to Pestovo for the holidays; I am for taking advantage of the invitation while it is still possible; that will after all give us a bit of rest and some strength while the matter of our departure, away from the accursed Sovdepiia, is being finally prepared.

29 [December]. Yesterday I went by for B. V. Kliuchevskii,[259] who treated me to a magnificent hot loaf of white bread, and we went together to the funeral ceremony for S. F. Fortunatov.[260] For the first time in my life I was in the chapel for the deceased at the hospital; poor Stepochka lay there still without a coffin in the company of six other deceased, and the ceremony took place in a most difficult and miserable setting. I have the same funereal recollection of the meeting of professors and instructors of the historico-philological faculty on the issue of the notorious all-Russian competition: we tried to do something, but the university has already been devastated, and it won't even be in existence if the bolsheviks hold on for long. It all ended with a funereal tea, without food, in the rector's office, from which Menzbir is removing all his personal property, as he will no longer be rector in two days.[261]

In the evening I had to go to a meeting of the house tenants on the distribution of the revolutionary tax, for which I was assessed the amount of 2,000 rubles. The tax was undoubtedly distributed with complete contempt for justice, law, or any rules of ethics; it was obvious at the meeting that the committee wants only to push the matter through, without getting into any objections or making any amendments. The Jew Slavin, of course, managed to emerge unscathed from this unpleasantness; he assessed himself only 1,000 rubles. In the evening we had the visit of Marietta, formerly Kutorga who is to become Kuz'mina-Karavaeva, as she is

[258] Gote's wife suffered from diabetes.

[259] Boris Vasil'evich Kliuchevskii, son of the great historian.

[260] Stepan Filippovich Fortunatov, son of the great linguist, Filipp Fedorovich Fortunatov (1848–1914).

[261] Menzbir was replaced by M. M. Novikov as rector in the spring of 1919.

getting remarried to another. It appears, by the way, that Kutorga turned out to be a typical Russian intelligent-socialist: he fleeced her of all her money and is asking, and perhaps demanding, more from her for his support. Marietta reported about Zagran'e as well: they hauled off not only our linen, but our books; the executive committee of Iur'evo township plans to move into the house; and the Obraztsovs, the fools and impudent louts, have robbed us as best they could. They are working for the Sovdepists, turn up their noses, go about in our things, and shout that we did not pay their salaries. In the Russian land, the intelligent and the muzhik are equally good: Kutorga and Obraztsov can shake each other's hand.

30 [December]. I haven't had such melancholy as today for a long time; it has been a long time since I perceived so clearly the abyss into which the Russian people have fallen; lies, lack of principle, and lawlessness will not pull us out of this abyss, and we may be waiting in vain for the antici-pated radical change we are all expecting. The horror is that too many people have learned nothing and forgotten nothing and, flouting all the principles of ethics, continue to talk about republican sensibilities, liberty, and suchlike fantasies, although it would seem that the bolsheviks have in practice long ago weaned us from all that. I noticed today the extent to which I and everyone around us are irritable; in the museum I raised my voice from irritation in conversations with people who chose not to understand that there are established principles and demands of solidar-ity. The matter concerned only the establishing of the holiday duty ros-ters.

31 [December]. Liubavskii and Shambinago came by; we had an excellent chat, in spite of the fact that my pessimism and that of Liubavskii out-weighed Shambi's habitual optimism; we even gave ourselves over to dreams of some kind of better life. Today one lot was cast and measures were taken toward assuring our existence outside of Sovdepiia; true, these measures are meager, but if worse comes to worst, if we leave Sovdepiia, they will come in handy. Today is the end of the bolshevik year; although that is the only decree that should be left in force perma-nently, nevertheless, it would be something incompatible with one's feel-ing of propriety to celebrate today and greet the new year. Let the Lat-vians upstairs, who are already singing above my head, make merry. This is the second time I end the year in these notes, and now the situation is many times worse than a year ago. What will the coming year of 1919 bring? I hope that it will bring some kind of solution.

1919

❋

JANUARY

1 January. Although I am beginning the year according to the new style, and although I have always approved of the shift to the new style, I myself continue to feel the old style and will privately celebrate it in twelve days; perhaps this is a silent protest against the regime of the RSFSR. A day without impressions; I sat home and wrote lectures; there is pleasure only in studies.

2 [January]. I spent the evening at my wife's parents; I went there in a relatively good mood, perhaps because I had read all the beguiling news that the menshevik typographers printed today in their little newspaper;[1] but I left blacker than the night, after having keenly felt poverty in place of sufficiency, the loss of everything earned in a lifetime, and the shadow of hunger hanging over us. Sad news from Kiev, transmitted by Sobinov,[2] or more correctly by his officer-sons. It coincides with what is written today in the typographers' newspaper: a terror of the separatists is beginning there. I don't know which is better—that scum or the bolsheviks.

4 [January]. Pichon announced that they, the French, have smashed the bolsheviks near Perm'.[3] Today they were saying that Denikin's affairs are not bad and that order is being established in the supplying of munitions. Someone who came from Voronezh said that the Cossacks are within thirty kilometers, that the red army does not want to go to battle, and that the efforts of comrade Trotskii to compel them to go are mostly in vain; the opponent is at present, however, very weak; but it would only take a single effort to knock over the red army. Today an ukaz was

[1] *Gazeta pechatnikov* (*The Typographers' Newspaper*) was published by the Moscow Typographers' Union between December 1918 and March 10, 1919.

[2] Leonid Vital'evich Sobinov (1872–1934) was a prominent operatic tenor. At this time he was living in Kiev. Sobinov and Got'e were students together at Moscow University, although in different faculties (Sobinov graduated from the law faculty).

[3] Stephen Jean-Marie Pichon was the French foreign minister. Kolchak's Siberian Army had captured Perm' in late December 1918, without French participation.

issued to the effect that we are to continue teaching with retention of salary, but without responsibility and without the right to attend council and faculty meetings. One can only rejoice that they are taking away responsibility.

5 [January]. I felt fatigued all day from yesterday's outing to Maiden Field and Miusskaia Square.[4] These outings are also contemporary phenomena: they add their characteristic touch to the general picture of Russian life. My wife is being ordered to shovel snow tomorrow—that is yet another touch of contemporary life. We are surrounded by such "touches"; we can't escape from them. Odessa has been occupied by the Volunteer Army and the Allies. The tricolored flag has been raised there in the name of a united and indivisible Russia. At last! The menshevik newspaper *Evening Moscow* reports this; it of course does not approve of it.

6 [January]. This morning I hauled sauerkraut down the streets of Moscow in the company of A. I. Iakovlev, just as much a university professor as I, and O. M. Veselkina, the directress of the Aleksandrovskii Institute—more correctly the former institute[5]—and then I scraped snow from the street. Then I had the visit of Count P. S. Sheremetev concerning the rescue of the Mikhailovskoe Library, so that a touching unanimity of official and unofficial spheres on this matter has been revealed.[6] I have never been so pleased with the Christmas tree as this year and rejoice that we will light it upon returning from vespers.

8 [January]. Two quiet days, during which the bolsheviks have allowed us to rest; I tried to rest on those days, but hardly achieved any result; at least right now, on the evening of the second of those days, I feel just as exhausted as earlier. Today we took Volodia to the circus and watched how he enjoyed himself; but we could not enjoy ourselves. Nowhere, perhaps, is the ochlocracy that rules over us so obvious as at the circus: nothing but gorilla mugs. In the evening there was a long and hot argument with Nina about what we are going to have to do and what should be enterprised for our rescue. It is my impression that so far we still don't

---

[4] A square in the northwestern part of the city that was the location of a number of schools, including Shaniavskii University.

[5] The Aleksandrovskii Institute was a girls' school founded in 1891. It was closed shortly after the October revolution.

[6] Count P. S. Sheremetev (b. 1871) was a collector of literature and the owner of a great estate, Mikhailovskoe, in Podol'sk district, Moscow province. The Mikhailovskoe library, which dated to the eighteenth century, was one of the largest private libraries in Russia, with about 40,000 volumes, mainly foreign books and periodicals. It was acquired at this time by the Rumiantsev Museum. *Istoriia Gosudarstvennoi ordena Lenina biblioteki SSSR imeni V. I. Lenina za 100 let, 1862–1962* (Moscow, 1962), p. 61.

understand each other. That is very sad, the more so in that I myself vacillate every day, not knowing what best to do. But I am progressively coming to the conclusion that no kind of activity is possible in Sovdepiia and that, for Russia's sake and for my own sake, I should leave here.

9 [January]. The specter of hunger is looming ever nearer and tighter. I took a stroll around Moscow today and was somehow especially horror-struck by this dead and murdered city; one thought—to flee, and more than ever before I have the firm view that [we] should prepare for departure.

12 [January]. Life has fallen into its habitual pattern over these days. It is not the former holidays, but some kind of intermediate state—not without the ever-present upsets, and distinguished from ordinary workdays only by a smaller number of current obligatory tasks. Rumors to the effect that the bolsheviks are intending to destroy our faculty as well, by transforming it into part of a new general faculty of "social sciences," are becoming ever stronger. We even had a meeting on that account and decided that we will accept the probable invitation to participate in the meetings that are likely to be held on that subject, although all present, it seems, clearly understood that any discussions will be useless. Sakulin behaved in a very characteristic fashion: he is a good man, but a typical social traitor and collaborator, either a popular socialist or a menshevik, neither fish nor fowl; he curses the bolsheviks and at the same time is ready to enter into talks with them on some kind of conditions, although he himself should know that they will not observe any kind of conditions in any case. There are also rumors that they are not going to permit a competition at all, but will appoint those they wish to. It is all the same to me; the only thing is to hold out until summer and the opportunity to leave for somewhere, or to bide one's time until changes [occur]. I think this and say it everywhere. And there will be changes after all; the bolsheviks are changing their food-supply policy and allowing the free transport of almost everything; I don't think this could change the attitude toward them of the masses that are discontented with them, but if even 10 percent of the proclaimed favors are realized, we, the unfortunate bourgeois who produce no economic benefits, will be better off. On the other hand, there are rumors from everywhere about the collapse of the red army; and it cannot fail to collapse. There is a third, also persistent, rumor about new landings of men and technical equipment, mainly in the south. Finally, Finland has declared war on Estonia.[7] Col-

---

[7] Got'e's words echo the Bolshevik press. The reference is to the intervention of Finnish volunteers to fight with the Estonian Regular Army of the Päts government against the

lapse internally and an onslaught from without; all this is bound to occur in the course of 1919. So far I can say nothing about German events, because I can make no sense of them.

13 [January]. Today I heard that news has been received from Ent. and Pin. One says that relatives are coming, the other says that he will return in the spring. There is also a report that the monarchists and republicans are quarreling in the Denikin army, and that all the officers got drunk when the English officers arrived. How in the Russian manner that all is! If there are to be any changes, most likely some new people will surface after all from among those who have suffered through all this time and have studied Russian life in practice.

15 [January]. We greeted the "old" new year in the customary manner at my wife's parents—we rejoiced over two pies made with black flour and drank a sweet wine for lack of either vodka or champagne, with which we formerly toasted and saw in the year. Yesterday there were again remnants of the bourgeois life—dinner at E. A. Got'e's. Instead of the innumerable delicacies that were customarily there on that day, there was ham with potatoes, and we were all amazed at the splendor of the table. Such are the scenes of the hunger that grips us. But that hunger is gripping them as well: they talk insistently of evacuating the red army units from Moscow to avoid a hunger revolt; they themselves write about the catastrophic food-supply situation. One senses that some new, ineluctable events are in the offing. What will they bring us?

16 [January]. I unexpectedly received a letter yesterday from Princess M. M. Cherkasskaia from Khar'kov, dated September 19. Where it loitered remains a mystery. It is characteristic for illustrating the current time, and therefore I append it here:[8] such are the news about themselves given by inhabitants of two cities, between which two years ago communication was maintained by three pairs of courier trains that took fourteen hours. In today's *Izvestiia* there is an inimitable letter from the wife of "comrade Raskol'nikov,"[9] who has been taken prisoner by the English: the officers

---

Bolsheviks. They arrived in Tallinn on December 31, 1918. See Georg von Rauch, *The Baltic States: The Years of Independence. Estonia, Latvia, Lithuania, 1917–1940* (Berkeley, 1974), p. 53.

[8] See Appendix, Letter 6.

[9] Fedor Fedorovich Raskol'nikov (Il'in) (1892–1939) had been head of the Bolshevik organization at the Kronstadt naval base. In December 1918 he was captured in the Baltic by the British and jailed in London. In 1919–1920, after being released in exchange for British officers, he was commander, first of the Soviet Caspian fleet and then of the Baltic fleet. He later served as an ambassador and was editor of the important literary journal *Krasnaia nov'* (*Red Virgin Soil*). He died in Paris in September 1939, under mysterious

have openly gone over to the other side, and the sailors at the last moment began to salute them and address them as "Your 'Cellency,"[10] and turned over Raskol'nikov themselves. The Russian is always and everywhere true to himself: "We have long lacked moral fortitude."[11]

17 [January]. Nina's and Volodia's departure from Moscow is becoming more and more urgent, especially Nina's. Yesterday the thought entered my head that if Lelia moves to Vologda, Nina could go there temporarily, since the food situation is better there than here; on the other hand, although the matter is increasingly difficult, permission to leave Sovdepiia will have to be obtained. Thank God they have released A. A. Kizevetter; unfortunately, I have not yet seen him; he was here yesterday, but I wasn't at home, and today I missed him. Today there are neither big rumors nor interesting news, yet just today there is a kind of particular impatience and desire that everything be ended as soon as possible.

18 [January]. Liebknecht and Rosa Luxemburg have been killed.[12] Our rulers have raised a howl; this is a serious page in the German revolution. There was a time when I would have been sorry about his arrest, but now I want to say: a dog's death for a dog. Further, our [leaders] announce that the srs are seeking an agreement with them; today I discussed this turn of events with Iakovlev, and we came to the conclusion that such an exfoliation of *vermine* is probably a good thing; their peace will not be durable, and it will immediately alienate the communists' enemies from the sr scum. There was a meeting of the building tenants: we threw out the building chairman, who attempted to rape the daughter of the manager.

19 [January]. I was in the Cathedral of the Savior at the patriarch's service; it smelled of something old and good, but I think that was my love for Muscovite Rus', not recognition of the power of the Orthodox Church, which is weak and powerless despite the external beauty of the church service. A "protest demonstration" over the murder of Liebknecht was taking place at the same time; I didn't see it; they say it was

---

circumstances, after having been declared an enemy of the Soviet people. His wife was Larisa Mikhailovna Reisner (1895–1926), an intrepid young journalist of "bourgeois intelligentsia" background who became an enthusiastic supporter of the Bolsheviks after October 1917. She died of typhoid fever.

[10] *Vashe vskbrodie.*

[11] "Dushevnoi kreposti ne be v nas otdavna." A citation from the Slavonic Bible?

[12] Karl Liebknecht and Rosa Luxemburg were murdered on January 15 while under arrest following the failure of the Spartacist revolt in Berlin. The attempt by the German Communists to seize power was crushed by the regular army supporting the Provisional Government.

not particularly impressive. There is no encouraging news; I sat at home and worked. In the evening I was at the Society of History and Antiquities, where a chairman and secretary were elected to replace the late Glazov and Belokurov. Liubavskii and Bogoslovskii were elected; the latter announced after his election that his task is to observe religiously the charter and the sacred traditions of the society. I agree with him.

20 [January]. A vastness of rumors; one contradicts the other. In all, it seems, only one thing can be grasped: that something is apparently beginning in the north, and, perhaps, will be more effective than in the south. A new coup in the Ukraine: the Directory has been overthrown by some kind of military men; it is still too early to draw any conclusions, but the fall of Petliura and the rest of the scum can stimulate only the most pleasant feelings.[13] I began my lectures at the University: two-and-a-half degrees [above zero]; a few people were there all the same; I am amazed by these young people.

21 [January]. Narva has been cleared and the coup in Kiev has been confirmed. That is enough for everybody to celebrate, although perhaps without any basis; in other respects, the day passed, and thank God. We also thank him that Nina successfully begged in the Sovdep for an augmented diet of thirty eggs, three pounds of millet, and three pounds of rice; [she] literally begged and waited it out.

22 [January]. We are celebrating St. Gapon's Day and that of others of that ilk slain with him or without him, it's all the same.[14] Everything is closed in moribund Moscow, which makes no difference, since everything is closed on the other days as well. I walked to the Dorogomilovskaia suburb[15] for milk, to the retired carrier who is doing us the favor of providing a small quantity of milk for a high price. It was clear from

[13] A struggle between Soviet forces and the revived Directory ensued in the Ukraine after the removal of German forces and the fall of the Skoropadskii regime. On January 3, 1919, Bolshevik forces occupied Khar'kov; on January 16, the Directory declared war on the Soviet regime, and Symon Vasyl'ovych Petliura was made supreme commander of the Ukrainian forces; shortly afterward, a military dictatorship of Galician officers took over the Directory in Kiev. The Red Army reentered Kiev on February 6.

[14] On January 22 (January 9, o. s.), 1905, approximately 130 peaceful demonstrators and innocent bystanders were killed by government troops in Petersburg. Some of the demonstrators were attempting to deliver to the Winter Palace a petition with political and economic demands that had been drawn up by Father Gapon's Workingmen's Assembly. Gapon survived that confrontation, only to be murdered by a member of the SR Battle Organization on March 28, 1906. See Walter Sablinsky, *The Road to Bloody Sunday. The Role of Father Gapon and the Assembly in the Petersburg Massacre of 1905* (Princeton, 1976).

[15] A section of western Moscow on the right bank of the river, presently the location of the Kiev station and the Ukraine Hotel.

our conversation that the entire family is dissatisfied with the existing order of things; it is apparent that the lower classes are ready to tear their current rulers to pieces, but yet dare not, and will not dare to do so without outside help. There are many vague conversations and rumors, but one is afraid to lend them credence: it is very sad to be disappointed in everything.

23 [January]. Tense expectations of something or other continue; perhaps nothing will happen this time either, but life is getting harder and harder. In the morning I walked to Miasnitskie Gates[16] to the Samsonov store to get thirty eggs and three pounds of rice for Nina and Volodia. The very fact of such a long journey for so little is characteristic of our time, but the journey around Moscow during business hours in the morning once again produced a frightening impression on me—it is likely that the invasion of Genghis Khan affected the towns that were subjected to him in approximately the same way: all the windows have been boarded, everything has been killed, everything has stopped. It will take whoever will be summoned to do it a long time to fix everything and restore order. They are saying that Lenin was stopped while riding in an automobile in Sokol'niki,[17] that, moreover, the automobile was taken from him and he was threatened with a Browning—by whom it is not known. *Se non è vero*, then in any case it characterizes the disintegration of the current regime.

25 [January]. St. Tat'iana's Day. Mass in the big Ascension Church; beautiful singing; a middling number of professors and no students; perhaps, in fact, because this mass was known about only by word-of-mouth communication. Our archpriest Bogoliubskii gave a sermon on the theme that the ancient martyrs were not "ashamed" of Christ; he should have come to the natural conclusion that contemporaries are ashamed of him; that would be true, but he did not draw such a conclusion; perhaps he was himself ashamed, or, more precisely, afraid. The sermon could have been effective, but no effect was produced. At 1 p.m. there was a meeting of professors in the council hall—an unofficial meeting. There were about fifty professors, new and old, fired and retained; the meeting was

[16] A square, formerly one of the city gates, in the northeastern part of Moscow (presently known as Kirov Gates Square, Ploshchad' Kirovskikh vorot). Got'e walked clear across town.

[17] A region on the northeastern outskirts of town where Lenin's wife, Krupskaia, was convalescing for her goiter condition. Got'e's report of the incident, which apparently had occurred on Orthodox Christmas Eve (January 6), is confirmed by Krupskaia in her memoirs: N. K. Krupskaia, *Vospominaniia o Lenine* (Moscow, 1957), p. 399; in English, *Reminiscences of Lenin* (New York, 1960), pp. 494–95.

begun by Gulevich[18] with a very tactful and clever speech. In terms of content it was the usual opening speech for a meeting, but he very subtly touched on the present moment and no less subtly thanked Bogoliubskii for the opportunity to be in the cathedral today. At the end he proposed that Savin be elected chairman. Savin also handled well the task of guiding the discussions, about which one could say, in the words of Cicero, *cum tacent, clamant*. I don't know what those attending had on their minds, but the speeches were for the most part about how this is not our last St. Tat'iana's Day, and that we will celebrate it again in our cathedral, and that Moscow University will yet play a role in that resurrection of Russia that we all so passionately await. But I thought more than once today—isn't this the last St. Tat'iana's? Won't our university die of its own from cold and hunger, if the bolsheviks don't die first? I made bold to congratulate, on behalf of those gathered, Kizevetter and Novikov, who have recently emerged from prison or from the Butyrskaia sanatorium.[19] Several talked with sincere optimism, for example that same A. A. Kizevetter, who even astonished me by doing so. I am puzzled: is it firm conviction or manilovshchina? The speech of D. L. Cherniakhovskii, at one time my preceptor,[20] was characteristic: he spoke of the ideal autonomy of the university, including the participation of the students. His speech was not met with applause. We dispersed after sitting for about an hour and a half. Unfortunately, no gathering was arranged today to celebrate St. Tat'iana's; never have I wanted to celebrate it like I do today. Today the bolsheviks printed the appeal of the preliminary Peace Conference to all the Russian governments, inviting them to gather on February 15 on the Prinkipo Islands.[21] Of course, it is hard to say what the genuine character of this proposal or directive is; I interpret it as a challenge to the dictators of the world. Opinion in general is not pessimistic; the bolsheviks comment on it with sour grimaces, since they cannot take it sincerely. It may be that this is the last attempt to do something

[18] Vladimir Sergeevich Gulevich (1867–1933) was a member of the medical faculty and a prominent biochemist.

[19] That is, Butyrki (Butyrskaia tiur'ma), the large provincial prison through which generations of Russian revolutionaries had passed.

[20] Cherniakhovskii had apparently been ahead of Got'e at the university. It was traditional for St. Tat'iana's Day to be celebrated by professors and graduates together.

[21] This appeal was one of five attempts at the Paris Peace Conference to do something about the "Russian problem." Prinkipo, in the Sea of Marmara, was chosen because it would obviate the need of Soviet delegations to travel through any third country and because Clemenceau was adamantly opposed to receiving the Bolsheviks in Paris. The Bolshevik reply to the invitation was evasive and suspicious, and since the anti-Bolshevik forces refused to sit down at the same table with the Bolsheviks, the plan failed. See George F. Kennan, *Russia and the West Under Lenin and Stalin* (New York, 1961), pp. 121–25.

about Russia; perhaps it is the last attempt to unify the Russians or to scold them before active interference; well, we shall wait three weeks—we have already waited long enough. The elections to the German constituent Reichstag are very instructive and very comforting: not one Spartacist and twenty-three independents; the majority goes to the Scheidemannites, who are essentially no further left than our Kadets.[22] Europe remains Europe, and Russia has shown that she is nothing more than judified Asia. Yesterday I had to go on foot to lectures at Maiden Field, and from there on foot again to a lecture at Shaniavskii University; if this had to be done regularly, it would be impossible to give lectures.

26 *[January]*. I had the visit of N. A. Berdiaev, an unquestionably outstanding and agreeable person. Having lived off his literary work and, probably, capital, he has also been forced to the wall and talked with me about the possibility of getting a position in the museum and archive field. I of course gave him all necessary advice and instructions. In our discussion he expressed a thought that I entirely share, although it had not yet reached my consciousness: we have too many forces of destruction and too few constructive forces, or more precisely none at all; that is our greatest tragedy and danger. Earlier he was an optimist, but has now changed for the worse; nevertheless, his pessimism does not exceed mine. They say that yesterday's professors' discussion was attended by Artem'ev, "the assistant minister" from the bolsheviks.[23] How regrettable that no one showed me that fellow, who probably came in the role of a spy. Today they are writing sourly about yesterday's invitation to the Prinkipo Islands, and the mensheviks are altogether silent; that means something is wrong.

27 *[January]*. I attended the meeting of the library section; that is how they call some sort of new institution thought up in the Commissariat of People's Enlightenment for administration of the libraries in Sovdepiia. I entered the office of comrade Lunacharskii, where some kind of preliminary meeting was taking place (without him) and empty words were being bandied about; the unprincipled comrade Briusov was chairing. After about fifteen minutes, comrade Pokrovskii arrived and, after sarcastically excusing himself for some words spoken the day before, drove the meeting out of that office. They began to look for a place to go. It turned out that the former assembly hall is not being heated—it was plus five degrees in it. In the library? But there is an order that meetings

[22] The German elections of mid-January resulted in Philip Scheidemann, a Majority Socialist, becoming the first chancellor of the Weimar Republic.

[23] D. N. Artem'ev, a professor of mineralogy, was head of the "science division" of Narkompros.

should not be held in the library. What is this? Pokrovskii declared in Solonic fashion that the library session cannot meet in the library. We waited a long time among the stacks for someone to open the meeting. Looking on all this, I once again remembered the words of General D'A[. . .]de, uttered in Moscow: *Ah, le gâchis!*[24] Except for gâchis, the Russians are obviously good for nothing.

30 [January]. A meeting of the "library session," as are called some kind of periodic conferences that are supposed to rule the destinies of Russian libraries. They are attended in part by people of our ilk, such as the vice-director of the Public Library, Braudo, Vengerov, and Kalishevskii.[25] I must say that there are few Petersburgers; academicians Ol'denburg and D'iakonov[26] reported themselves sick and did not come. By contrast, the other camp is very fully represented, and even comrade Pokrovskii deigns to take part in the debates. Perhaps the most interesting case is S. D. Maslovskii (pseudonym: Mstislavskii), former librarian of the General Staff Academy, a Left SR, participant in the Brest negotiations, father of a family of ten, by appearance an alcoholic of whom they say that his actions always aroused perplexity at the very least.[27] He proposes to make all books in Russia public property, giving "the people" the right to destroy a book by using it when and where it pleases. Another type, A. P. Kudriavtsev,[28] is a clever rascal from among the émigrés who has for some reason set himself the task of protecting Russian antiquarians, perhaps out of personal interest in that. Who knows? I won't speak of the others: it is enough to look at the physiognomy of A. A. Pokrovskii, who for some reason enjoys popularity among the librarians in Moscow; comrade Chachina, who babbled something about extracurricular education, and others, to see that the last book will soon tumble out of the hands of

[24] "What a mess."

[25] Aleksandr Isaevich Braudo (1882–1940) was the librarian in charge of the "Rossica" collection of Petersburg Public Library. Semen Afanas'evich Vengerov (1855–1920) was a prominent literary historian and bibliographer. Anton Ieronimovich Kalishevskii (1863–1925) was a bibliographer and the director of the Moscow University library.

[26] Sergei Fedorovich Ol'denburg (1863–1934) was an orientalist who served as permanent secretary of the Academy of Sciences from 1904 to 1929. He had been minister of education in the Provisional Government for a time in 1917. Mikhail Aleksandrovich D'iakonov (1855–1919), a prominent legal historian, and a specialist on the history of Muscovy, had been a member of the Petersburg Academy of Sciences since 1912.

[27] Sergei Dmitrievich Maslovskii (1876–1943), who wrote under the pseudonym of Mstislavskii, had been an SR delegate to the Second Congress of Soviets. In the 1920s and 1930s he published a series of historical novels about the revolutionary movement.

[28] According to the Okhranka files, Aleksei Pavlovich Kudriavtsev (also known as Mashkovskii and Mirskii) was an SR living in Paris as of 1912.

these gorillas.[29] There were several pearls during the debates. Speaking about the antiquarians, M. N. Pokrovskii said that they are rogues and swindlers; Kudriavtsev, objecting, said that such a phenomenon can only be an exception, and that in general nothing based on theft can be solid—he missed the point. They talked of the possible drain of rare books abroad; Pokrovskii on that account declared that it is all the same, either the bolshevik island will swallow the sea or the sea will dry up, *as it apparently has a tendency to do*. Stupidity or doctrinaire naiveté? Incidentally, at this session we approved some kind of phantasmagorical library staff—of 250 people. Where will we put them? Will this horde be with us for long? Nothing definite on the general horizon; they say that Rakovskii[30] and Ioffe are going to the Prinkipo Islands, in order to make the Americans quarrel with the English and the French; that is also called missing the point. All the same, it is apparent that nothing will happen before spring and that in the end all Russia—hungry, weak, and ruined—will fall into the embrace of foreign capitalists and imperialists.

31 [January]. Today there were a few joys characteristic of the present moment: Masha arrived from the country and brought seven puds of potatoes, six pounds of butter, seven pounds of groats, and three enormous loaves of bread. I lectured at Shaniavskii; there were people there, and we got the money [for the term that began in] September. And, in the third place, there were no plenums or commission meetings. There are no general rumors at all; everything remains as it was yesterday; they say that they are not going to the Prinkipo Islands; that would be even better for us.

FEBRUARY

1 [February]. I heard from A. I. Braudo, who heard it from V. D. Bonch-Bruevich, that they will not go in response to an anonymous wireless

---

[29] Aleksei Alekseevich Pokrovskii (1875–1954) was a bibliographer and librarian, and archivist of the Synodal printing house. In the 1920s he became a senior archivist in the Central State Archive (Tsentrarkhiv). Ol'ga Ivanovna Chachina (d. 1919) was an old acquaintance of Lenin; according to the *Biokhronika*, Lenin attended a meeting of the Petersburg Union of Struggle for the Emancipation of Labor at her apartment on April 24, 1895.

[30] Christian Rakovskii (1873–1941) was a prominent figure in international social democracy before the Revolution and was head of the Soviet government in the Ukraine in 1918. He subsequently occupied a number of ambassadorial posts before being expelled from the party in 1927 as a member of the Left Opposition. He was reinstated in the party in 1934. In 1938 he was one of the accused in the show trial, along with Bukharin, and was sentenced to imprisonment.

message. From the same source: Lenin told Gor'kii, "We know that we will not succeed, but why should we leave when nobody is throwing us out?" Therefore they are driving full speed ahead without a worry, and will do so to their last moment. Yesterday I carried two loaves of bread in my hands from Iaroslavl' station to Mertvyi Pereulok—an original exercise. I had a conversation with P. S. Anti[pin?] about evacuations to the south; he thinks that at present it is out of the question to sneak off anywhere.

3 [February]. A sour report in *Izvestiia*, betraying discontent because they are not being invited to enough of the conferences. The other day they shot four grand dukes: Georgii and Nikolai Mikhailovich, Dmitrii Konstantinovich, and Pavel Aleksandrovich.[31] Riazanov called this "an odious execution." One has to think that there are two contradictory currents among them: (1) for rapprochement with Europe, and (2) against it.

4 [February]. The events of the day: comrade Chicherin's note to the Allied governments: concessions, amnesties, payment on loans are offered, with the condition that the internal social order of Soviet Russia remain untouched. Some consider this a capitulation, but I don't hold that opinion; the whole note is full of the customary bolshevik lie. They promise anything and then take the first opportunity to deceive and forswear all their promises.[32] For me the question is what the Allies will make of this or will wish to make of it: will they act as if they believed them and enter negotiations, or will this be the point of a complete break between them? I think that, at the worst, if they begin to negotiate, there will be a brief moment when relations with foreign countries will be possible; one should then take advantage of this and leave. My librarian's position in the museum is beginning to burden me heavily; endless troubles, growing ever greater, and no longer any kind of moral satisfaction.

[31] Georgii Mikhailovich (b. 1863) and Nikolai Mikhailovich (b. 1859) were the sons of the Grand Duke Mikhail Nikolaevich, a brother of Tsar Alexander II. Dmitrii Konstantinovich (b. 1860) was the third son of Grand Duke Konstantin Nikolaevich, another brother of Alexander II. Pavel Aleksandrovich (b. 1860) was the sixth son of Alexander II and the uncle of Nicholas II. They were all shot in the courtyard of the Peter-Paul Fortress on January 27, 1919. The official explanation of this act was that they had been hostages for Rosa Luxemburg and Karl Liebknecht.

[32] A diplomatic historian commented much later on Chicherin's note of February 4, 1919: "It goes without saying that inherent in this Soviet diplomacy of despair was the clear assumption that there was no nonsense about the sanctity of treaties; once power relations were changed, Soviet Russia would claim her own." Adam B. Ulam, *Expansion and Coexistence: The History of Soviet Foreign Policy, 1917–67* (New York, 1968), p. 97. See Jane Degras, ed., *Soviet Documents on Foreign Policy. Volume I: 1917–1924* (London, 1951), pp. 137–39 (translation of the text, edited).

5 [February]. The bolsheviks have taken Kiev and are retreating in the Pskov region; the eternal quadrille of *chemins croisés*; however, military actions continue everywhere, and that stands in complete contradiction with the conditions put forth by the Allies in their wireless message inviting the bolsheviks to the Prinkipo Islands. It is the more or less general opinion that the situation should become delineated—either war or peace, and, in any case, an end to the present indefinite state. Iakovlev, Bakhrushin, and I decided that if there is peace, of course temporary and probably short lived, we must immediately get ourselves out of Sovdepiia.

7 [February]. The latest rumors: someone among them is supposedly going to Paris, apparently Manuil'skii;[33] they are supposedly summoning him, but he is going on a Red Cross passport, which shows that the matter is not so simple. They were supposedly provoked into sending the Chicherin note by the fact that a large landing party was disembarked somewhere. In Finland there is supposedly a Russian organization headed by General Iudenich and Trepov.[34] A. E. Vorms has returned from the Finnish border; they would not let him pass with a bolshevik passport, while they are apparently letting people without them go through. Vorms sat for three days at the border, read Finnish, Swedish, and English newspapers, and carried away the impression that there will be no English intervention, because the internal difficulties of England are too great. I learned today that the most influential members of the building committee—Prince Urusov, Sokolov, and Krylov, have been arrested. They assure us that this is the calling card of the former chairman, Slavin. A gloomy mood all day today.

8 [February]. A depressed frame of mind; I feel that everything is falling from my hands and I don't want to do anything, since their bursts of creativity, which now threaten to wreck the universities and lock up the museum—that is, to spoil all my work—are even worse than their virtuosity at demolition. I had the visit in the museum of an officer of the

[33] Dmitrii Zakharovich Manuil'skii (1883–1959) was a veteran SD who had spent much time in France and had graduated from the Sorbonne (1911). At this time, he was a high official in the Bolshevik government in the Ukraine.

[34] General Nikolai Nikolaevich Iudenich (1862–1933), veteran commander of the Caucasian theater in the war, had emigrated to Finland in November 1918, where he began the organization of the Northwestern Army. This force helped to expel the Bolsheviks from the Baltic States in early 1919 and mounted a nearly successful offensive against Petrograd in the autumn of 1919. Aleksandr Fedorovich Trepov (1862–1928) was a former senator and one of the last chairmen of the Council of Ministers (November–December 1916). He was the head of a Russian Political Committee in Finland that gave its support to Iudenich and the Allied cause after the defeat of Germany. Iudenich maintained a "political conference" for handling these relations.

general staff, who was instructed by the "field staff" to figure out which regions of Soviet Russia can be given to whom on the basis of the Chicherin note. After a long discussion, it turned out that the Zamyslovskii atlas can serve as the basis of the work.[35]

10 [February]. Complete confusion in people's minds, but the rumors are apparently again picking up: they tell of some SR-type activist in the cooperative movement who arrived from England and whose words are on the whole confirmed by Vorms's words about the state of mind in England; there is talk of a volunteer army—non-Russian—which France and England are supposedly successfully raising and supporting. They are talking about the reconquest of Ufa; in the typographers' newspaper there is a letter of some revolutionary stalwart about how Kolchak has a fine army of 400,000. Where is the truth, and where the lie?

In the meantime, the bolsheviks are doing their job and demolishing the universities; now they have gotten the idea of putting us historians together with the jurists in a faculty of social sciences;[36] there will never be enough nonsense for them. They have also taken after the libraries, following the interest shown in them on the part of comrade Lenin— constant circulars, exactly as earlier when august personages took an interest in something.

11 [February]. I decided to spend the day at home, in order to take a respite from the museum and fortify my weakening nerves. This time I suceeded; I did give lectures, however, and was again amazed by our students who, although in small numbers, nevertheless stubbornly show up to listen to the course on prehistoric archaeology. The general situation is without change; the same rumors and the same morass.

12 [February]. One more day at home; I feel that I have less desire to be in contact with others than several days ago. I worked the whole day far from the newspapers and noise; apparently there is no particular news. In the evening I was at the Society of History and Antiquities, where M. M. Bogoslovskii read his reminiscences about V. O. Kliuchevskii (today is his nameday): in M.M.'s masterful rendition, there came alive

[35] *Uchebnyi atlas po russkoi istorii. Sost. i izd. pod red. E. Zamyslovskogo. Izd. 3-e* (St. Petersburg, 1887). This was a standard historical atlas used in the schools.

[36] A Narkompros resolution on closing the law faculty and organizing a new faculty of social sciences had been issued on December 28, 1918. Several of the law *kafedry* were then temporarily moved to the historical department of the historico-philological faculty. On March 3, 1919, the directorate of Narkompros approved the establishment of a faculty of social sciences that incorporated some of the kafedry of the defunct law faculty and the historical department of the historico-philological faculty. The history faculty was re-established at Moscow University in 1934.

memories of Moscow University in the 1880s and 1890s, when Moscow University was the center of Moscow's intellectual life. One felt something distant, good, and gone forever; I should write my reminiscences of university days, too.[37]

14 [February]. I met I. N. Borozdin,[38] who told me that "they" are intending to destroy the "secondary" unified labor school, which they themselves had invented, and want to replace it by having all the children work in the factories for four hours a day, the factory work to be accompanied by reading. There are no changes, except that we, it seems, are not to avoid fusion with the jurists, and that the notorious all-Russian competition, also announced by them, will be replaced by simple appointment. The general question—to be or not to be—remains unchanged.

15 [February]. Another big holiday spent like a workday; we sat after 3 o'clock in the scholarly publication committee of the archive administration and beat a dead horse, discussing the publication of documents that there will be no occasion to publish under either the present or the future circumstances of the Russian land. Those who came from Petersburg report that everything there is in order; however, comrade Chicherin burst forth today with a note to Finland concerning the concentration of troops on the Finno-Russian border.

18 [February]. Big and unpleasant events have occurred in these two days. The Military Control that had settled in our building has been renamed the Special Section of the Cheka and has begun to swell and spread out. They are evicting all the tenants of the old Solovovo house "due to strategic circumstances," and all ten vacated apartments are being moved into house no. 4—that is, ours. Along with this it is being said outright all around that the entire building will be gradually evacuated. We will have to think again about moving into the museum; discussions are going on about this, and we have already sent part of our furniture to the museum. Everything will have to be arranged and put in order, and there we will be able, perhaps, to do something with ourselves. Swells on the general horizon.

19 [February]. Nothing has changed; there aren't even any interesting rumors. For the matter of setting up the phantasmagorical staff of the Rumiantsev Museum, I was conducted to the Commissariat of People's

[37] See n. 21 for 1917. These reminiscences, only recently discovered and published by Got'e's son from his second marriage, apparently were written in the mid-1920s.
[38] Il'ia Nikolaevich Borozdin (1883–1959) was an archaeologist and historian of wide-ranging interests, and a literary historian.

Enlightenment to a meeting of the collegium of the commissariat. Comrade Pokrovskii chaired, and I never thought that he would conduct a meeting so laxly, poorly, and incompetently. N. K. Krupskaia-Ul'ianova-Lenina, the Russian empress-to-be, attended the meeting. I didn't expect her to look like she does: old and hideous, with the stupid face of a blind fanatic; her ugliness, moreover, is accentuated by clearly manifested goiter. The others attending were Pozner, Shapiro, Markus,[39] and other representatives of the ruling tribe, except for comrade Chachina, of the eternally embarrassed, blushing and blinking schoolteacher type, also with a fanatical look, who was to N. K. Krupskaia something like a mezzo-soprano is to the soprano in Italian operas. The first matter for which I was present concerned an unintelligible and confused note by Lenin, which essentially came down to the point that all Sovdepiia should be covered with a network of libraries, each of which should report on its successes, and all of them together should compete with each other.[40] Everyone treated the note exactly like the tsar's inscriptions on imperial reports were treated in the old days. The speech about this note by one of the participants, comrade Temkin, a Jew of course, was extraordinarily characteristic: he argued that the first thing to be done is to create librarians, because there are none of "our people" in the provinces, the cultured zemstvo has disappeared, and the intelligentsia has left. Ul'ianova and Pokrovskii were embarrassed when they saw how their comrade had missed the point. On the same account there was talk about some kind of institution that will be called Tsentrokniga,[41] attached to the TsIK, and will monopolize all the publishing houses in Russia. The Jews who drafted this proposal, it turns out, ate up the press of the Commissariat of People's Enlightenment, and one should have seen how the comrades who were present berated those who were absent and what discord there was between them. The words spoken by Pokrovskii dur-

[39] Viktor Markovich Pozner (1877–1957), a teacher, was head of the Narkompros department for the unified labor school. Lev Grigor'evich Shapiro (1887–1957) was head of the department of scientific institutions. V. A. Markus was Narkompros chief of staff at the time.

[40] This was evidently the note of seven lines written on January 30 and published in *Izvestiia* on February 7, which instructed the library section of Narkompros to monitor the growth of the library network and book-readership across the country. Lenin, *Polnoe sobranie sochinenii. 5-oe izdanie*, vol. 37 (Moscow, 1963), p. 470.

[41] Tsentrokniga was to be the "central authoritative organ for regulating book affairs," including coordination of publishing (but not nationalization of the big publishers) and distribution of printed matter. It was approved by Narkompros and Sovnarkom, but in the meantime a Party commission came up with a proposal to create a single state publishing enterprise for all official business, which would also coordinate publishing with cooperative and private publishers. The result was the creation of the State Publishing House, Gosizdat.

ing the discussion of that question were very characteristic: he talked about how part of the books have been hidden somewhere, "that in the provincial towns they have been hidden away by speculators who are still anticipating something, but will probably only have waited to find that the books have become scrap paper. The old books must be confronted by *our* books." This blind faith in the speculator, this fear of something that ought not to happen but will, and this juxtaposition of *ours and theirs* are remarkable. Then comrade Shapiro, a precocious fellow, insisted that some matter in which he had a personal interest be resolved; Pokrovskii disagreed. Another Jew, comrade Pozner, at first supported Shapiro, but then, deciding that Shapiro had done something without his knowledge, abruptly changed fronts and, addressing that one not as Lev Grigor'evich but as L. Shapiro, began to agree with Pokrovskii. Again a quarrel and bickering, undermining each other. Yet another issue was set aside by Pokrovskii on the grounds that the report on it had not been provided to the members of the collegium, but it turned out that the director of its affairs, comrade Markus, had already distributed it to everyone concerned six days before. Those present complained at length about the poor organization of their affairs. When the turn came to our staff, it turned out that I need not have come at all. I did not, however, regret that I had wasted time here; the picture of mediocrity and inability to do anything except drown in words was so clear that it left an indelible impression on me and convinced me once again that these creatures, who have only the form of human beings, cannot create anything.

21 [February]. The notorious order on moving in was received today, but tomorrow they will still be arranging whom to install and where. I was in the Archive of Foreign Affairs, where M. M. Bogoslovskii found me the Volynskii file, which I have long wanted to look at.[42] The work in the archives had a narcotic effect on me. In the museum I submitted a request for a business trip abroad; will it work out? A lull again on the general horizon; there are no new rumors.

22 [February]. I spent the whole day in meetings, one more useless than the other. In the museum we listened for three hours to the stories of Romanov and Borzov[43] about their Petersburg adventures at the "general

[42] Artemii Petrovich Volynskii was a protégé of Peter I who wrote several political tracts critical of the Russian government during the reign of Anna Ioannovna (1730–1740). Got'e published the results of his work on these materials in 1922: " 'Proekt o popravlenii gosudarstvennykh del' Artemiia Petrovicha Volynskogo," in *Dela i dni. Istoricheskii zhurnal*, 1922, kn. 3, pp. 1–31.

[43] Nikolai Il'ich Romanov (1867–1948) was an art historian and curator of fine arts at the Rumiantsev Museum; he later became director of the State Museum of Fine Arts.

museum conference," which was just as unnecessary as all the other undertakings of our day; afterward we engaged in some quiet sabotage in the Main Archive Administration, listening to some kind of rules for the printing of documents invented by A. N. Filippov;[44] and, finally, in the evening I sat in the building committee to defend us from doubling up and crowding in. A quite unexpected scene occurred there: the notorious Slavin does not wish to leave, and therefore the entire plan for jamming up our house ran aground. The matter remains open until Monday. Stupid, sickening, and funny.

23 [February]. I had a bourgeois rest, lying in bed until 12 o'clock, and went visiting all day with a vengeance. The resignation of Krasnov is being reported in the newspapers, as is the fact that the bolsheviks have come into conflict with the French somewhere not far from Odessa; perhaps this will set things in motion.[45] Today was the first anniversary of the founding of the red army; on the streets of the city where I was today, this holiday was manifested by nothing except a few ugly posters. D. E. [?] K[urdiumov?] told about the meeting he attended on unloading [the trains] on the Moscow railway hub: it turns out that there is no one to do the unloading, nor are there any mechanical means; on the Northern Railway the communists have themselves today given an example of unloading cars, but only 120 out of 2,000 employees showed up.

24 [February]. The question of doubling up is being clarified: today we spent the last day in our dining room; tomorrow we will give it up either to Babogin [?] with three children and a witch for a wife, or to Rubtsov, an engineer with a big family. Such are the vicissitudes of contemporary life. The thought is growing ever stronger that the complete liquidation of the apartment is inevitable. No news at all, unless one counts the fact that inspectors from among the Western socialists are coming here—

Aleksandr Aleksandrovich Borzov (1874–1939) was a geographer and assistant librarian at the museum; he later became head librarian of the Lenin Library.

[44] Aleksandr Nikitich Filippov (b. 1853) was Distinguished Professor of the History of Russian Law at Moscow University.

[45] General Petr Nikolaevich Krasnov (1869–1947) resigned his leadership of the Don army on February 14, 1919, after having submitted to Denikin's command, and emigrated to Germany. A French expeditionary force was in Odessa and the surrounding area between December 1918 and April 1919, in the most ambitious Allied effort at direct military intervention during the Civil War. The French fought principally against the forces of Ataman Nikolai Aleksandrovich Grigor'ev (1878–1919), a Ukrainian partisan who was collaborating with the Bolsheviks at that time and who occupied Odessa following the French evacuation of that city on April 6.

Kautsky, Adler, Hilferding, Henderson, Longuet, and the like.[46] What can they give us? Nothing, or something even worse than what we have.

25 *[February]*. The moving inside our apartment has been done; fatigue, disorder, dismay; all this is so barbaric and so unnecessary, and so contemporary. Nothing new from the outside, all as before. The fantastic staff roster of the Rumiantsev Museum has taken a new step toward its realization. The staff of the faculty of social sciences is also going through. In the evening I attended the trial lecture of A. A. Novosel'skii:[47] a very keen mind; an excellent lecture on the subject of "Noble Landowning After the Time of Troubles and After 1861." He is the first of the young generation of historians we are putting up as our replacements. I think he will be a good continuator of the school of Kliuchevskii.

27 *[February]*. Two days were spent in moving, and here we are now, crowded into two rooms that barely accommodate that part of our belongings we need for living. Try in such conditions to study and contribute to scholarship, that is, to fulfill the obligation from which the bolsheviks have not excused us. At first I was very sad to leave another third of the apartment and remain in the two back rooms; sad, because when we moved into this apartment, we thought it would be our apartment for life, because it suited us in all respects. But once having moved, I feel light and recall Pecherin's verses about the man sailing on the sea in a canoe; one more anchor cut away, one less hindrance. One should live in a bivouac until one dies, or leaves, or survives this terrible time. The fact remains that it is impossible to live in such crowded conditions and a way out will have to be sought by moving into the museum, which I have refused to do for an entire twenty years. Haze on the general horizon. I heard that they are offering jobs listening to private telephone conversations by right of military censorship; such an offer was made to my comrade, V.A.K. I am becoming ever more convinced that the coming of the socialist delegation bodes nothing good for us. By the way, the house of A. V.[?] Rerikh in Malyi Karetnyi Pereulok has been requisitioned for them; thus the luminaries of socialism will live in stolen property; that is stylish and fitting.

[46] Karl Kautsky (1854–1938), Friedrich Adler (1879–1960) and Rudolf Hilferding (1877–1941), Arthur Henderson (1863–1935), and Edgar Longuet (1879–1950) were leading figures in German, Austrian, British, and French social democracy, respectively—the Marxist equivalents of the church fathers.

[47] Aleksei Andreevich Novosel'skii (1891–1967) became a prominent Soviet historian, laureate of the Lenin Prize. He was a specialist on the history of seventeenth-century agrarian relations and foreign policy.

28 [February]. A day without big impressions; I managed to remember old-style Shrovetide and to eat bliny to my heart's content. I read no newspapers at all and therefore preserved a relatively good disposition. I heard no rumors.

MARCH

3 [March]. I kept no notes because we undertook a journey very characteristic for contemporary life: we went to Mashkov Pereulok to the Got'es to pass the night, and from there to Kurdiumovs near Iaroslavl' station; we rode there on a dray from the university to Sretenskie Gates for 10 rubles, and back with a cabby for 50 rubles. Everything else is unchanged; everything around is just as sickening as before.

4 [March]. Today we decided in principle to move into the building of the museum, into half of Menzbir's apartment. I had thought that we would move from our apartment on Bol'shoi Znamenskii only into the other world, but that shows what human expectations are worth; the bolsheviks came and wrecked them all. Moving into the museum, where for twenty years I not only did not try to move, but resisted doing so, threatens many complications and troubles. But at the present moment one should think that it will be calmer there, and if we must and are able to leave, our property will be safer there.

5 [March]. They say the fate of the history professors will be decided on Friday. The bolsheviks have set up some sort of commission of fifteen communists (including Storozhev)[48] and fifteen noncommunists, who are supposed to decide which of the professors of the law [faculty] and the history department of the historico-philological faculty are worthy of entering the faculty of social sciences. From among us, Bogoslovskii, Savin, Petrushevskii, and Vipper are obliged to go there. I am very sorry for them, especially the first two; they have gone there by special invitation. I consider myself a professor of the university by election of the University Council on April 18, 1915; I have made no claim on my relation to the princes of this world and I will continue to ignore them until I am either driven from the university or extract myself from Sovdepiia of my own accord.

[48] Vasilii Nikolaevich Storozhev (1866–1924) was a historian and archaeographer, and like Got'e a specialist on the seventeenth century.

6 [March]. The resolution of [our] fate will be on Monday, not Friday; our future depends on the flower of the socialist academy,[49] which, apparently unable to organize anything from its own midst, wishes to ensconce itself in Moscow University by force. That is the sense of the whole reform: embittered failures, nonentities filled with self-delusion, want to control the fortunes of Moscow University.

Lifelessness all around; hopes for liberation are rapidly fading, and the process of rotting through will take a long time. The bolsheviks have suddenly proclaimed tomorrow the holiday of the Third International. Somehow, to my shame, I don't understand what that means.

7 [March]. Taking advantage of the holiday of the Third International, I sat home all day and worked in the doorway of our bedroom; I have retained the impression that someone was going to the toilet all day behind me in the corridor. That impression [comes from] the excessive population growth in the apartment. In the evening the city was in darkness: I saw no external manifestations of joy over the Third International, but the Aleksandrovskoe School was all lit up: they must have been reveling there.

10 [March]. There is nothing clearly visible on the larger horizon; however, rumors have again revived recently, perhaps in connection with the uneasiness and dissatisfaction that they are apparently manifesting these days. They are talking again about some kind of offensives in the Baltic region, in Lithuania and in the direction of Minsk; I do not, however, attribute great significance to all this. On Saturday we arranged a feast at Kurdiumov's near Iaroslavl' station. I am recording this because this fact is characteristic of our time: twelve persons gathered for cooperative bliny, because everyone wanted to forget his troubles, drink some alcohol, and eat his fill of bliny; the feast began at 9 P.M. and continued until 4 A.M.; in truth, everything was forgotten, it was warm, bright, and cheery. On the same day before the feast, I was called into the Cheka, to its Special Section, which has installed itself in our courtyard. I was supposed to give testimony in the case of Prince Iu. D. Urusov, accused of "concealing state property," which turned out to be documents of historical significance. Urusov told me about them twice, and both times I advised him to turn them over to the state repository; he referred to those conversations, and that is why I was called for questioning. The first

[49] The Socialist Academy, renamed the Communist Academy in 1924, had been founded in 1918 for the study of problems of the theory, history, and practice of socialism, that is, as the center of "Marxist science." It was incorporated into the Academy of Sciences in 1936.

summons was on Thursday, the 6th; I received it after the time designated for the questioning. On Saturday they ordered me there by telephone and even threatened arrest if I didn't come soon. I set out for the mansion of M. M. Petrovo-Solovovo and found a filthy den filled with Latvian urchins and Latvian wenches. I was asked to wait in a room that had been stripped of all its furniture—only a few chairs remained; I could hear the Latvians frisking about next door, and read on the wall an announcement that the group of communists in the Special Section of the Cheka censures those comrades who permitted themselves to behave rudely toward the comrades of the female sex in the kitchen. Later, his boots squeaking, a golden-haired, blue-eyed man of about thirty, very polite and friendly, came in and said to me that he would be at my service in just a minute; after some time, I was called into the old bedroom of that house, with Corinthian columns and a marvelous mirror. Investigator Fel'dman,[50] with blond hair and faultless Russian, more like an old revolutionary populist than a contemporary Latvian-Jewish figure, questioned me politely and to the point and in conclusion informed me that the documents Urusov had had were the GHQ papers from February 25 to April 1, 1917, which he had received, most likely, as the then procurator of the Mogilev district court. I could not help saying that it was careless to keep such documents in one's possession.

As I learned this evening, the "elections" to the new faculty could not take place today, since the comrade-communists appointed to "sort out the riffraff" from among the so-called bourgeois professors did not show up. In that they showed themselves for what they are in all their beauty and slovenliness.

12 [March]. On Monday and today, Wednesday, the fate of the law faculty and the historians was decided and was not decided. Thirteen people of the academic group and three communists came on Monday; today— thirteen of the academic group and eighteen communists. On Monday they compiled their list; today another was compiled, longer and completely changed. In the first list there were Kizevetter, Bogoslovskii, Iakovlev, and Picheta from our group of historians; not included were Liubavskii, myself, and Bakhrushin. In regard to me, as it turned out, comrade Pokrovskii, who more or less runs everything, could not accept how it is possible, being the "director of an enormous library," to combine that with the university. Today that was cleared up and my candidacy passed, but the whole affair was ruined as a result of the fact that today, after a six-hour debate, the bolsheviks advanced the candidacy of

---

[50] This was probably Boris Mironovich Fel'dman (1890–1937), who later became a high official of the OGPU in Moscow and the Red Army before perishing in the purges.

Steklov-Nakhamkis, and the academic group would not accept that nomination. Then comrade Pokrovskii announced that this attempt at collaboration had failed, like every attempt at collaboration, and that therefore the new faculty will have to be filled by individual invitations. Both groups parted without saying goodbye. We discussed all this at Bogoslovskii's, who told us (Liubavskii, Iakovlev, and me) that he revived upon seeing us after having spent six hours looking at ugly, boorish Jewish mugs. We decided that it is our duty to perform our customary tasks and wait to see what happens; that, perhaps, all this happened for the better, for it relieves all of us of any individual responsibility. One more general impression confirmed by us: the bolshevik Jews are dying to work their way into Moscow University, and they are trying in every possible way to get there, while preserving some sort of fig leaves of regular procedure. I think it will be better if they appoint themselves there. A new flurry of rumors; there is insistent talk of an offensive of the Kolchak troops from the east having begun; perhaps this is only the latest self-comforting rumor.

13 [March]. A buoyant general mood from the various rumors, of unknown foundation, regarding what happened yesterday. The general view is that it is better that way.

14 [March]. It was decided in a private meeting of the defeated academic group to gather in council if an invitation from the bolsheviks comes. I am very glad that I am far from all this; let there come what may, because to remain in the university in the company that is getting in there is no longer to serve and to be a university professor. One could tolerate being appointed, but one shouldn't enter into an agreement or collaboration with them. The general news remains rather favorable.

15 [March]. Rumors continue to circulate about a movement from the east, about disturbances among the red army soldiers and workers; everyone is pleased. At the same time, hunger is unquestionably growing; bread has reached 30 rubles a pound, flour—1,100 rubles a pud. Our move to the museum was decided today; we are leaving the chandelier and the shelves for the wardrobe in the front hall as a deposit for our return.

16 [March]. The rumors are growing stronger; they are talking about rebellions in the red army, hunger riots; they themselves are not denying the strikes in Petrograd. There is unquestionably an impression that something is in the offing, but what and what form it will take—it is hard even to think about it. Today we actually begin the move; only now is all the unnecessary waste of time of this business being realized. The latest news on the academic question is that the historico-philological faculty will remain unchanged until the end of April, and that the economists will be transferred to our faculty before we, the historians, are transferred to the faculty of social sciences.

17 [March]. A letter has come from Patouillet; he writes that there is to be a meeting on issues of mutual understanding consisting of the *groupe promoteur* and persons who have been in Russia—himself, Avenard, and Malfitano. Malfi has returned from Italy, where he also tested the water of mutual understanding; how I would like to be at that meeting! He writes of life in Paris that only bread and sugar are rationed; "la boucherie abonde"; eggs cost 60 centimes, that is, according to the recollections of those who know the subject, four times more than before the war. I went to the Commissariat of Enlightenment to support and see through the staff of the Rumiantsev Library; we waited two hours with A. A. Borzov, after which they told us that all matters are being postponed; boors remain boors.

18 [March]. The holiday of the Paris Commune and the funeral of President Sverdlov;[51] I think that the Paris communards never imagined that the Russian barbarians would fete them a half-century after the charming events of 1871, and the president didn't imagine that the holiday, in whose arrangement he undoubtedly took part, would be clouded by his own funeral. From 10 to 1 o'clock today fifteen museum coworkers carried our things to our new living quarters in their hands and on sledges, and we also helped in all that. The remains of our apartment are peeling and empty; if one contemplates it all, one is seized by melancholy, but it is better not to consider it and to swim with the current; reason dictates living as light as possible. According to the rumors, they continue to be pushed from the east.

19 [March]. The gigantic staff of the museum has today taken another step toward its realization. I had once again to be in the "collegium of the Commissariat." Comrade Pokrovskii very graciously reported on the business of our museum. Pozner, Artem'ev, and a couple of worker-types, they say influential members of this organization, were at the meeting. I was very interested by Artem'ev. The look of a person from good society, a pale face, a bilious and unpleasant appearance; one senses either

    [51] Iakov Mikhailovich Sverdlov (1885–1919), the Soviet "president" (Chairman of the Central Executive Committee of the Soviets) and secretary of the Bolshevik central committee, died on March 16, 1919.

offended pride or unfulfilled ambition. A small detail during the discussions: the talk turned to extrabudgetary credits; Pokrovskii, laughing, announced that the commissariat had no funds for them, with the exception of those assigned to Perm' University, which has been occupied by the "Czechoslovaks." The rumors are all the same; attention is turning to the Volga region. We still aren't able to move to the museum apartment because there is no horse for moving the heavy things.

23 [March]. We have been moving all these days, and this is already the third evening we are living at 3 Mokhovaia, apartment 9, together with professor M. A. Menzbir. We are settling in quite well, in any case better than we were recently in the old apartment. The moving has been accomplished so far only by hand, since despite our best efforts we are unable to get a single cart, either through "cart transport" (as the bolshevik "central drayage" is called), or independently. That is also a phenomenon and sign of the times. The moving led to a sorting out of all the books; I did that with pleasure, and it awakened in me again the desire to collect books. I hope that tomorrow they will bring all the rest of the books here; my reference library, counting about three thousand volumes, will go in a modest corner that has been set aside for it. The situation is worst of all with the piano; we fear that it will be damaged in moving, as there are no experienced men and the inexperienced can't handle it. There you have one more consequence of bolshevism we have experienced: our lovingly built nest has been destroyed, and God knows where and when we will be able to build it again. We are living in a bivouac, as one should now. And yet it is sad. Thus far there have been no difficulties with living in the museum, except for the cold, which commenced here after our arrival because they have run out of firewood; they say there will be firewood, but there will probably be [other] difficulties with living here. Some hopes continue to flicker on the general horizon. Will they be realized this time?

24 [March]. We thought we would finish our moving today, but, alas, we were bilked on the cart and everything remains as before. In the evening I carried over the clock, wrapped up in a tablecloth, and, joining forces, we brought the kitchen equipment. The talk is all the same. The sixth or seventh wave of hopes has not yet subsided, the same with the movement from the east. In the south, however, the field belongs to the bolsheviks, who are even starting to move into the Crimea.

26 [March]. We were reelected to the university in an all-Russian competition; I received four votes for and two against, and thus for the second time it seems I have gotten into the university. What a stupid comedy it is. It must truthfully be said, however, that our young people conducted themselves with amazing tact and kindness and fully demonstrated their solidarity with us. It is characteristic that Sakulin received nine black balls, for his currying favor with the bolsheviks, of course. There is no news; the mood is the same; we are still waiting for a cart to move the rest of our things.

30 [March]. The interruption in the notes occurred as a result of the fact that we are continuing to settle in the new quarters; I had no corner [to write in] and no ink. No changes have occurred during these days; the war of the bolsheviks with the nonbolsheviks has again taken on the character of chess moves; the attitude of the Allies remains yet again just as unclear and indefinite as before. However, the bolsheviks are hoping for some sort of improvements. Yesterday I was received by comrade Pokrovskii regarding the matter of a trip abroad for the museum. He was gracious and even amiable; he declared that our undertaking is desirable and not so unrealizable as some think it is; it was added here that perhaps "our relations with the Entente will be normalized sooner than one might have hoped and that, perhaps, the embargo to which we are being subjected by initiative from Washington will be lifted from us." That is related to the rumors that have been circulating for several days now to the effect that negotiations between the Allies and the bolsheviks are under way. Perhaps they are, but it is unlikely they will lead to anything. I was satisfied with my meeting with Pokrovskii: he was sympathetic to the idea of an expedition abroad, and a lack of sympathy on his part could create many hindrances. Now the matter is entering the organization stage; it is not at all easy, but perhaps, God willing, it will lead to something positive.

The other day I was told that there exists a new, perfected trysting house on Saltykovskii Pereulok, which is visited expressly by members of the Cheka; the entrance fee is 500 rubles; orgies occur there every night. Such is the peculiar combination of debauchery and banditry with narrow-minded doctrinairism represented by Lenin, Pokrovskii, and their ilk. "Anarchy supported by terror," Pichon said of Sovdepiia the other day—and obtuse doctrine, I would have added. But the country is perishing and will perish further, because they [the bolsheviks] cannot retrieve her from the abyss alone, and it is profitable for the others to leave Russia in the hole. Flour has reached 1,500 rubles a pud; there you have the genuine, undisguised hunger that we are experiencing. All efforts are directed toward avoiding dying from hunger; thus far everyone is somehow managing, but it is getting harder every day.

APRIL

1 [April]. It is snowing; there is cold in the soul, and in the apartment, too. Several representatives of the academic world, including the two successive rectors of Moscow University for 1911–18,[52] were just here. Much of interest was said; someone is interested in the opinion of the Moscow academic world. In the afternoon there was a meeting of the reunited faculty—alas, apparently not for long. We welcomed our younger colleagues, and they welcomed us, but the whole idyll was overshadowed by the confirmation of the news that the historians are after all being transferred to the new faculty. They also showed a list of those who will be appointed there. Once again I am not on this list; however, all of theirs are there—Nakhamkis, Gol'dendakh, and *tutti quanti*. Several feelings are at war within me; I am sorry that my activity in the university will be cut short, but reason tells me that nothing could be better for me than that, having been elected by the council and now reelected in the bolshevik manner on the basis of an all-Russian competition, I not be appointed by the bolsheviks to their faculty-den of thieves, where one would have to sit with persons one wants nothing to do with. For the time being I remain a professor of the second university,[53] and we'll see what happens there. If nothing changes in the summer, there is still one alternative—to get out of here. Given the state of things that has developed, it is one anchor less; that is very good.

2 [April]. Today was the first day of thaw, but spring is advancing lazily. We bought a pud of flour for 1,300 rubles, as a result of which we are beginning to fall into debt. The bolsheviks have discovered, as they describe it, a new conspiracy, in which they are inculpating the srs and the sds.[54] *La vermine s'entremange.* The question of the faculty of social sci-

---

[52] Liubavskii and Menzbir.

[53] The Higher Women's Courses were transformed into a coeducational Second Moscow University (M.U. II) in 1918. It existed until 1930, when it was split up into three separate institutes (pedagogical, medical, and chemical-technical).

[54] The spring of 1919, with the crisis of the Civil War approaching, was a time of intensive and fluctuating Bolshevik activity vis-à-vis the Left srs, srs, and Mensheviks, the general aim of which was to consolidate support for the government in those quarters. A large number of Left srs had been arrested (or rearrested) on February 18 and the discovery of a Left sr plot announced; on March 1, *Izvestiia* proclaimed that Left srs and Mensheviks would be arrested and held as hostages in view of their disruptive activities in the army, industry, and transport. At about the same time, the Bolsheviks were negotiating for reconciliation with the sr party: the party was legalized on February 25 and for nine days at the end of March was allowed to publish its resurrected newspaper, *Delo naroda*. See Leonard Schapiro, *The Origins of the Communist Autocracy. Political Opposition in the Soviet State: First Phase, 1917–1922* (Cambridge, Mass., 1955).

ences remains open; they say they will make appointments directly to the departments. When our poor university becomes a den of thieves, there will be no satisfaction in being a professor in it. I have therefore decided to undertake nothing in order to be a member of the new faculty, which also has the character of a den of thieves.

3 [April]. Some kind of unrest reigns in Moscow; they are being strict about passes into the Kremlin; yesterday they wrote that some kind of conspiracy has been discovered, and they say arrests are once again taking place; they are saying that someone, somewhere, has stolen weapons; in a word, the usual wave of alarms. The military communiqués are very unfortunate for them. Starting today, all Moscow has begun swimming from the thaw.

4 [April]. A day without big impressions; every morning I find pleasure in the Archive of the Ministry of Foreign Affairs, studying the Volynskii case in order to elucidate everything possible about his general project; that is the best hour in the course of the day. The general situation remains the same—great unrest internally and thrusts from the east.

5 [April]. The offensive continues; they say that Sarapul has been taken; that means, then, that the arms factories of Izhevsk and Votkinsk are in danger.[55] The anxiety continues; however, according to the rumors that have reached me, the possibilities of revolts in Moscow have been either liquidated or set aside. Today A. N. Savin informed me that my noninclusion in the list of professors of the social science faculty is to be explained by the fact that comrade Pokrovskii supposes that my responsibilities in the museum are too complex (*sic!*). However, the new phase is that I am being offered the chair of archaeology. I continue to stand on my former point of view and leave it to them to do with me as they wish.

8 [April]. They have taken Odessa, probably because no one wanted to defend it. All the same, the policy of the Allies seems to me completely incomprehensible; now they start something, now they give it up. In regard to the Russian south, however, I do not see things as hopeless. Yesterday I had to undertake a journey to Iaroslavl' station and to Mashkov Pereulok, whence I brought home twenty-three pounds of bread, four and one-half pounds of salt, and eighteen and one-half pounds of rye; I had an Alpine sack on my back, and two other sacks in my hands; thus the professor strolls around Moscow. The university question is progres-

---

[55] Sarapul, Izhevsk, and Votkinsk were towns on the eastern front between Kazan' and Perm'. By the end of April, all these towns were under Kolchak's control.

sively turning into a big mush. The bolsheviks, that is, Pokrovskii and co., have eliminated both of our history departments and replaced them with some kind of fantastic ones; some kind of further meeting is being proposed, but it all comes down to the fact that whatever straightforward appointment they may think up is better than the fiction of cooperation that was offered earlier. Something completely unimaginable is occurring on the streets of Moscow—one great puddle, which is traversed only by those who absolutely must go out.

9 [April]. The onslaught from the east continues; on the other hand, Odessa has been taken. Judging from the stories of the few people who are penetrating here from the outside, bolshevism is a contagion for any soldier and any tired army; the foreign troops in the south of Russia are disintegrating under the influence of bolshevism, which is, moreover, reinforced by propaganda and bribery. That, perhaps, is the secret of the lack of success of the various interventions.

10 [April]. All is the same; there is unrest; several commissars, they say, are evacuating their families to the south. We gathered in the former premises of the seamstress Lamanova and, together with the jurists and the economists, discussed our fate under the chairmanship of the ex-member of the Provisional Government, S. N. Prokopovich, who today bore an amazing resemblance to an old woman begging from passers-by on the church porch. In general, this meeting was both pitiful and funny. I think that we should generally provide them everything possible and everything they want; all the same, under the present circumstances we can only be patient and bend our backs. My legs are completely refusing to obey as a result of the endless walking; I feel a terrible fatigue, magnified by Moscow's means of transportation, or rather by their complete absence. The memorandum on the business trip abroad was submitted today. Will anything come of that enterprise?

13 [April]. I have begun to write less conscientiously; the cause is the extraordinary accumulation of tasks—unnecessary, unimportant, but pouring forth in such a pile as I would never have dreamed of. Yesterday Nina and Volodia left for Troitsa;[56] I don't know if it will be for long or if this enterprise will be successful. I was supposed to go today, but I will have to stay until tomorrow because of museum affairs. The bolsheviks are sounding the alarm as they have not done for a long time—all against Kolchak! Such is the slogan; will they succeed in extricating themselves

[56] That is, the Trinity-St. Sergius Monastery, about seventy kilometers northeast of Moscow.

this time, too, or will a new page of our long-suffering history be turned? Yesterday I went again to the commissariat about the matter of the future business trip for buying books; a gracious reception, but they say there is no getting out of the RSFSR except with the help of the International Red Cross. We will seek that help. We have undertaken a new enterprise: a history publishing house together with the people from the Russian co-operative movement. On Friday the 11th we sat on that account in the National Bank, where, incidentally, I first saw the notorious Kuskova: a cantankerous but not stupid dame, accustomed to being taken seriously.[57] If external matters don't get in the way, this enterprise might work; I will have to write something myself in order to have daily bread. Yesterday evening I went to vespers at the Cathedral of the Savior; there was a pleasant feeling in that enormous edifice full of people undoubtedly hostile to bolshevism. There is no news on the university question. Whether or not the appointments to the faculty of social sciences have been made, I don't know.

16 [April]. Sergiev Posad.[58] The expedition here, planned nearly several months ago, has been realized. Nina and Volodia arrived on Saturday the 12th, and settled in a typical small house behind the monastery, on Staff Street in a relatively democratic section of the Posad.[59] In the old days such an enterprise would have been unlikely and unthinkable. We used to spend Easter in the Crimea; earlier I spent it in Petersburg, Kiev, the country, and the like; now, in order to get away a little from the horror of Moscow life, we have hidden in a wretched, although clean, little room of a former floor-mopper of the Posad and his wife and daughter-in-law, former embroideresses, and their son, a former painter and now a policeman. Thus here, too, everything is changing and falling into decay. In order to get here, I had to carry here myself a burden of nearly two puds, perhaps even more; I carried it from Mokhovaia to the station and here across the Posad at night, going up and down the local hills and ravines among the creeks and puddles. I was very satisfied that I was able to do all that relatively easily; it means we can get along without the gorillas in those matters as well. The train was not excessively crowded, but some kind of wreck occurred; we stopped five times for fifteen or

[57] Ekaterina Dmitrievna Kuskova (1869–1958) was a leading figure in the history of Russian Marxist "revisionism," a critic of SD policies, and a skillful polemicist. She was expelled from Soviet Russia in 1922 along with many other representatives of the intelligentsia who were deemed unfriendly toward the new order.

[58] The town adjacent to the Trinity-St. Sergius Monastery.

[59] Staff Street, located on the hill behind the monastery, was so called because civilian employees of the monastery lived on it. Got'e's landlords had all been on the monastery staff. The street is now called Academician Favorskii Street.

twenty minutes, the last time just before Sergiev itself, and in the end the train took four hours instead of two, so I had to waken both Nina and the landlords so they could let me in. Yesterday I went out on reconnaissance; a study of the locale revealed that there is more hunger here than in Moscow; however, it is possible to get a lot of milk products, although for exorbitant prices. There is no bread; with difficulty I bought a pud of potatoes; one way or another, provisions are assured. I only fear there won't be enough money; that is a constant nightmare now. We arrived here just after the exhuming of the relics of Saint Sergius; there are rumors here that they even want to remove the relics and close the monastery; but on the surface everything is calm here. The people are silent, although of course dissatisfaction, by all indications, exists; but it will manifest itself [only] if changes occur. Then these silent gorillas will disembowel and tie up bolsheviks of every type, shape, and origin. The weather is beautiful, to the extent it can be beautiful in the impoverished Russian climate; the sun warms and fatigues; despite the hard bed, I slept twelve hours and am prepared to sleep a great deal more and longer. I record one more Moscow impression: I stood for an hour and a half in the treasury to get the museum's advance of 25,000 rubles, in order to be the bursar of the library. I received only five; that is what everyone who should have gotten more than ten thousand received. The government doesn't even have its own currency; not the first hitch, they say, but a very big one at this point. Here Moscow affairs and interests have moved a bit to the rear of the stage; I think even less about the trip abroad, and about general news as well. However, this is only a temporary lull, which should be taken advantage of to gather all possible physical and moral strength.

17 [April]. Both days I devoured books—a strategic sketch of the war for July and August 1914, compiled by someone from among the current military liquidators, but intelligently and sensibly, and Wells's *Mister Britling*,[60] one of the most intelligent books about the war that I have had occasion to read. They aroused many thoughts in me: a recollection of the burning unrest and burning and bright hopes at the beginning of the war, when it seemed that, despite all the deficiencies and all the negative things, Russia had found herself. The sketch of the war gave me many explanations and confirmations of what I have always called the "cavalry-ism" in our conduct of the war: the cavalry leaders obliged the infantry to fight in a cavalry manner and exhausted it. The stupidity of the defeat of Samsonov and Rennenkampf in August–September 1914 is sim-

---

[60] H. G. Wells's, *Mr. Britling Sees It Through*, a novel about English experience during the First World War, was published in 1916.

ply astonishing; the author blames this mainly on Zhilinskii, but my conversation with Zhilinskii showed me that not he alone was at fault (see above);[61] isn't the author settling personal accounts with Zhilinskii? That would be "so in the Russian manner." And the Galician battle—our best victory in the war—was won with much more difficulty than it seemed at that time; so much stupidity and improvidence make it quite understandable why we ran out of steam so soon. On the other hand, the reading of Wells's book explains much about the slowness and lack of preparation of the Allies, about how they dragged out the war and in so doing allowed us to become exhausted earlier than was desirable. The psychology of the English is also interesting: they, too, are inclined to curse themselves and all their ilk and to castigate themselves for their deficiencies. Very interesting, finally, are the thoughts about how the retribution for all kinds of speculation during the war will be revolution. God forbid that it occur anywhere else: for if revolution in fact settles accounts with speculation, it elevates to the place of the overthrown speculators others who construct their own speculative calculations and fish in troubled waters even more successfully than their predecessors; the experience of our country demonstrates this best of all.

I was in the Trinity Cathedral for mass and took a close look at the uncovered skeleton of Saint Sergius; they have left it as it was upon exhumation; as I learned today, that is being done deliberately and, in my opinion, correctly; they say that the examining doctors confirmed that the skeleton has lain there for five hundred years, and that the yellow hair that was discovered was gray, but yellowed by time. Thus our priests, using their wits and leaving the relics uncovered, correctly wish to show: look, we do not conceal what was and what is—and in doing so, of course, they only strengthen religious feeling. After church we sat for a long time on the steps of the monastery bell tower, but there is neither religious nor historical feeling in me; the one and the other have been destroyed in me by what is going on. Opposite the monastery, the shops full of requisitioned goods were burning; they say the fire started in the shop where there were shoes designated for distribution to the population. The comrades probably plundered them and set the fire—an illustration of the thought about speculation that was introduced above. The public looked indifferently at the fire and did nothing to put it out; one heard many conversations on the theme of how before when there was a fire it was immediately extinguished because it was one's own, but now it belongs to no one and is for no one. We completed our outing with bliny, paying thirty rubles for ten bliny (excellent, it is true); that is

[61] See the entry for March 30, 1918.

characteristic for an economic evaluation of the present moment. The reading of the twelve gospels was held in the Academic Church, which as a result of the arbitrariness of the comrades has migrated to the refectory. The public there was more refined than in the Trinity Cathedral; an excellent reading, but murderously cold; we met the young generation of the professoriate of the [theological] academy (which has migrated to Moscow), Kapterev and Golubtsov.[62]

18 [April]. I continue to catch up on my sleep—again twelve hours in a row. In the monastery from 5 P.M.; a beautiful day and just as beautiful an evening. From the balcony of the refectory there is a marvelous view in the direction of Vifaniia[63] with warm spring tones; it stimulates and encourages a certain vague hope, which you immediately suppress in yourself. A curious detail heard there: the local bolsheviks are not having kulich and paskha,[64] but are observing the holiday with pies with jam in order to distinguish themselves from ordinary people. I like the observance of Holy Week here, especially yesterday—the carrying of the shroud of Christ from one church to another. Despite the humiliation of the church and the academy, it all preserves its grand and ancient beauty. I catch myself comparing this Easter with last year's equally bolshevik one, which we observed in Pestovo. Then I had no hopes at all until Thursday, when I learned of the coup in the Ukraine and the proclamation of the hetman; I thought then that this was Russia's chance for salvation. But I was very much deceived; a year of the most impossible trials, sufferings, and destruction followed. And yet, despite the fact that the situation is even worse now than a year ago, I still have some kind of hope that all this can change because of the internal crisis that is beginning to show up just now as a result not only of the bolsheviks' crimes, but also of their stupidity. They have lost the people, and its stupid and dense sympathy for them will not return. That is what this year has yielded, it seems to me. On this ground a national dawning from the east is possible, without the Germans and even without the Allies; if it comes, it will be the stronger and brighter. But will it come?—that I don't know and cannot say.

[62] Pavel Nikolaevich Kapterev (b. 1889) was a philosopher and historian of philosophy; in the 1920s he worked in the Academy of Fine Arts. Ivan Aleksandrovich Golubtsov was Got'e's student.

[63] A monastery dependency of the Trinity-St. Sergius Monastery, about five kilometers to the southeast.

[64] In Russian Orthodox tradition, these two confections, extremely rich and laden with eggs, are blessed by the priest and form the centerpieces of the Easter table.

19 [April]. A day spent at services: the liturgy of Holy Saturday in the Trinity Cathedral with its captivating antiquity. Bortnianskii's[65] "Rise, O Lord" reminded me of old times when my mother and I regularly, year after year, stood through these services at the Cathedral of the Savior. I met Kapterev, who informed me that Trotskii's train passed through Sergiev for the Viatka front; according to rumors, there is confusion and fleeing at Viatka. The weather is gray and not too warm; we are sitting at home after noon, working a little, resting, and occupying ourselves with the rationing out of our meager fare.

20 [April]. Matins in the monastery; I have had occasion to observe Easter in many places, but the atmosphere of the monastery has its special charm, despite the humiliation to which the monastery and the academy are currently subjected. We stood through almost the entire matins and, splashing through the mud, returned home and broke our fast with modest kulich and paskha, which have never seemed to me so tasty as this time, although in recent years I have often ironically called the paskha putty, and although this year's kulich resembles those one could formerly get in bakeries ready-made for 80 kopecks—with a small amount of butter. Today after a late and abundant lunch (I underline this element because it expresses the essence of the time we are living through), we went visiting to the Kapterevs and Golubtsovs and had a very good time until 9 P.M. The residents were walking in groups about the Posad; there was a holiday mood, which accorded little with our feelings (at least mine). Little was learned of the general news; there is increased movement back and forth on the railroad; there are rumors about the evacuation of Kostroma, based on what I don't know. We saw a train headed for Moscow with automobiles—presumably evacuation from the north—and another headed north with machine guns—figure it out. Probably the kind of mix-up without which neither they nor those who preceded them can get along. At the Kapterevs I became acquainted with P. A. Florenskii;[66] he seems to be an interesting person. With the younger generation of the Posad, that is, with I. A. Golubtsov, my student, and the Kapterevs, the time passed very quickly in an animated and pleasant discussion. I learned much about the present situation of the monastery and its prin-

---

[65] Dmitrii Stepanovich Bortnianskii (1751–1825) was a Russian-Ukrainian composer, best known for his religious choral music.

[66] Pavel Aleksandrovich Florenskii (1882–1943), the great Russian polymath, was a scientist and religious philosopher, a graduate of Moscow University (mathematics) and of the Moscow Theological Academy who took religious orders in 1911. He had been a professor at the Theological Academy. In the 1920s and 1930s, until his arrest in 1933, Florenskii was a professor in a technical institute, editor of a technical encyclopedia, and an inventor.

cipal relic, which is apparently threatened with further complications owing to the activity of a group of Jews who are twisting the Russian fools
around their little fingers in those "elective courses" which have gripped
the academy. The lack of concern of the higher monastery administration
and the Moscow patriarchal administration is very curious: on the question of relics they resemble ostriches hiding in their own feathers. It appears that most of the energy is being provided by that secular university
youth of the monastery with whose representatives we passed the time
yesterday.

21 [April]. The whole day at home, not going out in the air; it is fairly
warm here, but outside there is a north wind, cold, rain, and snow toward
the end of the day. Isolation works wonderfully on the nerves; absolutely
no news or information; reading and concern with food—dinner and
supper—and whether the bread, which Nina is baking herself, will come
out all right. Such are the occupations of the professor's family, which is
spending Easter at Troitsa in 1919.

22 [April]. Preparations for the railroad; I am determined to go this afternoon, because it is very unpleasant to go for the morning train in the
slush. In Moscow the sum of news received is in general satisfactory. The
movement from the east remains unchanged; that is the most intelligent
and powerful of the movements directed against Sovdepiia, but it cannot
of course yield quick results; nowhere do I feel contempt for the Russian
people so sharply as when traveling on the railroad: vile physiognomies,
filth, conversations about rations, the charms or the liabilities of the present regime—that is all you hear.

23 [April]. I have plunged into Moscow life; it just hit me in the nose with
its abomination. To begin with, I remain completely without money; the
advance, from which I, incidentally, was also to have received payment
for myself (that is, more precisely, for Nina) I did not receive; I paid all
the money I had on me for provisions obtained at the archival administration, and now I have to find the money to live through the coming
week. Secondly, I dove into the abyss of contradictory rumors about the
movement from the east. There is a chasm between the pessimists and
the optimists: some have no hopes, others are prepared to expect rescue
tomorrow; all this creates such confusion that you feel your wits dim-
ming and you don't know what to believe or what to expect. In the evening, together with A. A. Borzov, I wasted four hours in the "Little
Sovnarkom,"[67] where we were to have reviewed the personnel list of the

---

[67] Malyi sovet narodnykh komissarov, or the Little Sovnarkom, was the inner admin-

library of the Rumiantsev Museum. It is located in the former office of the assistant procurators of the court; next door, in a room opening on the stairway, there is a kind of reception room furnished with several chairs and armchairs dragged in from all the rooms of the court office-building, which seemed to me today so poor, unhappy, and abandoned. The physiognomies that passed into the room of the small council and crowded into the reception room were striking—they exude a lack of culture. The thought of *who* is ruling us fills one with horror. We, however, did not succeed in "getting admitted" to the most august meeting. They spent three hours examining the question of some kind of agricultural census, after which we were informed that "the small council has not had supper," and that comrade Pokrovskii himself would try to put through our business over supper. Our long wait was interrupted by a discussion on two occasions with the dictator of Russian enlightenment, who was quite "graciously" inclined toward us. Most characteristic were his words, spoken with laughter, about how the university in Khar'kov had fallen under the unlimited authority of seven students—a "student dictatorship." What is this—sadism, or something else? The sole result of the visit to the Kremlin was a horseshoe, big and in excellent condition, which I picked up on Senate Square, which is, incidentally, permeated with a stench and surrounded by a fence from the gates of the Arsenal up to the middle of the square and to Nikol'skie Gates; from under the fence you can see fragments of Vasnetsov's cross on the spot of the murder of Sergei Aleksandrovich.[68]

25 [April]. Two days of desperate running about Moscow on petty business and in search of money. The most interesting was my visit to the foreign section of the Red Cross, located in the Hermitage;[69] how strange to be in this temple of Moscow gluttons, and in general how revolting to see a building designed for one purpose suddenly and hurriedly rearranged for another. Neglect, dirt, a sense of something abandoned, forgotten, discarded, and broken. A conversation with the director of the foreign section, our Privatdozent, Korovin.[70] The trip, perhaps, is not out

---

istrative group of four members that handled day-to-day affairs and did the preliminary work for the full Council of People's Commissars, the Sovnarkom.

[68] The Grand Duke Sergei Aleksandrovich, the Governor General of Moscow, was murdered there by Kaliaev on February 4, 1905. A cross to mark the spot of his assassination had been commissioned from Viktor Mikhailovich Vasnetsov (1848–1926), a famous painter and decorative artist who cultivated historical and patriotic themes.

[69] The Hermitage was a famous prerevolutionary Moscow restaurant on Petrovskii Boulevard near Neglinnaia. Moscow University students and professors traditionally celebrated St. Tat'iana's Day there.

[70] Evgenii Aleksandrovich Korovin (1892–1964) graduated from the law faculty in

of the question, but the question of it is difficult and complex and depends, in the end, on the Finnish senate, to which a request for admittance into non-Sovdepiia must be addressed through the offices of the Danes and the Norwegians. There is little new in academic affairs; on Friday there was to have been an organizational meeting of the "faculty of social sciences," but it was postponed because, in Pokrovskii's words, "our people" have not yet arranged things and have not compiled their list, and the negotiations of the commissariat with them have been dragged out. On the evening of the 24th there was a meeting at Bakhrushin's, where there was the entire complement of Russian historians, and also Savin and Egorov. I like Bakhrushin more and more: this is a very subtle, intelligent, and talented person with a great future, if on the whole the Russians have any future. On the general horizon, all is the same: for impatient people everything seems lost because the offensive is not going fast enough; for the pessimists its very slowness provokes doubts; but the geographical map should disperse any doubts: in the very best of conditions the affair can move only very slowly. In the west, the Poles have taken Vil'na. They will probably try not to return it.[71]

26 *[April]*. Again a day in Troitsa; the first storm, charming spring weather in the intervals between rains. There is a question of setting up here for the whole summer, or at least until such time as it will be possible to undertake something new and definite. A day of rest without news or information. They say that the local commissars are either fleeing or being replaced.

27 *[April]*. They are reporting a success over Kolchak; this success is not too great, in fact quite insignificant; however, the most pessimistic thoughts about the future are nevertheless aroused. Perhaps this last hope will collapse, and then there are before us years of ruination, troubles, and anarchy, from which there will be no way out. We have provisionally resolved the summer question and have rented two rooms from A. A. Tikhomirov[72] (did I ever think that I would live under one roof with that

---

1915. A specialist in international law, he was a member of several Soviet delegations to international conferences, a professor, and a judge.

[71] Poland occupied most of Belorussia and part of the Ukraine between April and August 1919, when the Red Army was still preoccupied with the White armies. Vil'na (Wilno, Vilnius) was taken on April 19. The city and its district were in fact retained by Poland at the conclusion of the 1920 Soviet-Polish War.

[72] Aleksandr Andreevich Tikhomirov (1850–1931) was a prominent zoologist who had been a professor and rector of Moscow University (1899–1904) and a high official in the education ministry. As rector, Tikhomirov was notorious as a strict disciplinarian and enemy of the student movement and "progressive" professors. He was an outspoken anti-Darwinist.

repulsive "marquis"?) in the Kapterevs' house. The arrangement of the house and garden is very good. This will be something like living in Voskresensk;[73] there are woods and fields nearby in the direction of Vifaniia and Chernigovka. It seems to me that under existing conditions this is one of the best solutions of the problem.

28 [April]. Return to Moscow. The information is rather satisfactory: today there was the first meeting of the faculty of social sciences; according to Egorov, it was a complete saloon; they refused to give lecture courses, and showed themselves to be complete ignoramuses in the business of university teaching. I regret that I was not at that vile, but apparently entertaining, spectacle.

29 [April]. I stood for four hours in a line at the State Bank in order to receive a twenty-thousand advance for museum acquisitions. The bank was bespattered and dirty; the line for the commissar—a boy of about twenty-five—consisted of about seventy persons in front of me and about forty behind me. I heard all kinds of expressions of resentment vis-à-vis the bolsheviks; the discontent has mounted, it is ready. Bad news from the east; the comrades are boasting of a victory over Kolchak near Orenburg. It would be interesting to know the relation between the appearance and what really happened.

MAY

1 [May]. Yesterday I went to the Danish Red Cross—the only offical foreign institution existing in Sovdepiia. The reception was very amiable, there was willingness to help the realization of the expedition for books. In regard to the present moment, there was an indication that "les relations sont tres tendues" between the RSFSR and Finland, "mais peut-être que sa s'arrangera." There was the impression that the matter is not hopeless, but a lot of time and effort will be expended before it is realized. Not another word about victories in the east. One gets the impression that this was some kind of inflated report intended for the first of May. The usual rumors of some kind of complications with Finland, and in general with the northwest, which is supposed to be more dangerous for Sovdepiia than all the rest. Going on foot from the Danes on Pimenovskii Pereulok to Iaroslavl' station in order to go to Troitsa, I saw a crowd of unfortunates being sent from the Cheka to Butyrki; a sad and onerous

---

[73] Present-day Istra, about fifty kilometers northwest of Moscow.

spectacle. In the train there was a crowd of people, part of which probably wants to spend the first of May outside Moscow.

2 [May]. Moscow. The news, in general, is satisfactory. The first of May seems to have gone rather laxly; there was no boasting of victories. On the railroad one again heard cursing and only cursing. I was again in the State Bank, in order to queue once again for my advance; after another three hours I at last received the money. The entire function of the State Bank now seems to amount to distributing an infinite quantity of *kerenki*[74] and 250-ruble notes; everything else has come to a halt. They say that the entire supply organization of the bolsheviks on the eastern front is especially fouled up: they thought they would be fed by the bread of the Transvolga, but instead they got the finger.

5 [May]. Two days in Troitsa; an excellent walk in the woods and fields on Sunday, the 21st; fifteen bourgeois and bourgeoises who had escaped from horrible and revolting Moscow, forgetting for several hours the woe and sufferings they were experiencing, and enjoying the meager Russian nature. I was very sorry for these poor bourgeois and bourgeoises when at night they had to go to the train so as not to be late for their soviet jobs. The Russian intellectual bourgeois is amazingly meek and submissive to fate; in this company there were very rich men and very rich women, and all of them have accepted their fate with amazing simplicity; I don't know whether to praise them for their philosophical worldview or to despise them for their lack of character. Life goes on getting entangled; the complications in the west and northwest are undoubtedly increasing, and their victories in the east turn out to be a bluff.

6 [May]. The situation remains unchanged. I was in the Danish Red Cross; there was again no rejection. The person in charge, Dr. Martini, is undoubtedly a great and skillful diplomat; personal permissions will have to be sent for to Finland and beyond. They posed this question to me: what if they give you a secretary who will conduct soviet propaganda? I answered that in that case I will not go at all. I have resumed lectures in the university.

8 [May]. The situation remains unchanged. Again despondency everywhere: the accursed and stupid Russian intelligentsia once again contemplates in despair its weakness and collapse. Today I heard that the cause of the bolsheviks' successes near Samara is the Magyar prisoners of war;

---

[74] Kerenki were the paper rubles that were printed in great quantities—as many as fifty million a day—by the Provisional Government.

that is possible, although Magyars are usually stuck everywhere, so this is suspicious. Churchill's speech, fragments of which the bolsheviks published yesterday in *Izvestiia*, seemed to me very interesting. From it one can conclude that Sovdepiia will after all not be ignored, especially if the peace is indeed signed.[75]

11 [May]. Two days [spent] in the usual Moscow bustle; the main fuss was over the Rumiantsev Museum, as a result of the fact that the phantasmagorical staff roster was passed and confirmed. Besides that, more teaching has been added in the institutions of higher learning. It is now very difficult to bear this work; there is no kind of *entrain* at all; the audience is drifting away for good, but it is still not clear when the lessons will stop by themselves. We are moving to another apartment today in Troitsa. The general news is again becoming more interesting. You have to have patience, just when you feel that it is at an end. My projected business trip will also be for the university. The papers have been prepared and have to be taken to the Danish mission.

12 [May]. The peace terms for Germany were published in yesterday's newspapers; the comrades are exaggerating their onerousness and unacceptability to Germany. They are indeed very burdensome, but there must be such hatred and ill-will toward Germany in the West that this burden is understandable; all of Bismarck's work has come to naught through Wilhelm's stupidity. There is a curious reference to Russia, probably distorted by the comrades: the treaty of Brest is revoked, and Russia (somehow new and different) has the right to seek damages from Germany. My conversation with the Serb D. I. Ilić, who comes here with his semicompatriot Kriukova for provisions, was very interesting: he told me as a fact that Franz Ferdinand was indeed killed by a Serbian organization that was grouped around the Serbian general staff, that Austria was correct in this point of her claims; but that Franz Ferdinand was indeed killed for cause, as he was the biggest enemy of Slavdom. We have definitively settled in the Kapterevs' house, in the apartment of Aleksander Andreevich Tikhomirov, former rector and administrator, and are using part of S. M. Solov'ev's furniture.[76] I had never imagined such a coincidence!

[75] The May 7 *Izvestiia* article "Churchill on Russia" picked up the text of a Churchill speech in the House of Commons of March 25 from a Berlin Russian-language newspaper, *Golos Rossii*. The speech was a *tour d'horizon* "about the actual operations on the different fronts where fighting is in progress on the vast frontiers of Russia," with special reference to British involvement.

[76] Sergei Mikhailovich Solov'ev (1820–1879) was Got'e's great predecessor at Moscow University and the teacher of Kliuchevskii. He was a professor of history (and sometime

13 [May]. The news is vague and indefinite; a quadrille in the east and in the south. The bolsheviks can't beat the enemies, and the enemies can't beat the bolsheviks. Iakovlev brought the news that in the Volga region the regime is just as worn out as it is here, and that if the occasion arises, there will be very savage reprisals there as well. I was in the Danish mission today and submitted my papers; they said to come by and check in a month; they say that there is a chance for me to be allowed into Europe. That still doesn't mean that I will be released from here or that the money question will be satisfactorily resolved. The latest rumor: in the south the atamans Grigor'ev and Makhno have pronounced themselves some kind of separatists, have made use of a billion and a half in money taken from the bolsheviks, and have proclaimed themselves enemies of soviet authority.[77] Poor Russia! They can't stop torturing even her corpse. Today I saw the clearly perceptible signs of the absence of fuel in Moscow: the fences of the Cherniaevskoe School and the magnificent Nemchinov garden in Maiden Field are being dismantled for firewood. This is only the beginning. I was at a meeting of the history department of the faculty of social sciences. The tone is being set by comrades Volgin and Udal'tsov,[78] who have taken leave of their own kind but have not taken up with those alien to them: they know nothing, understand absolutely nothing at all in academic affairs, but do not want to hear us. The result is an unimaginable saloon, hopeless and irreparable; we ourselves cease to understand anything, so that to the questions of the students, who just like us don't understand anything, we must answer that we are completely uninformed and understand nothing. Impenetrable Russian stupidity, superficiality, and ignorance are being applied to the destruction of the higher school.

14 [May]. Only now, thinking about what we are going through, I have understood why three hundred years ago Russia so easily became the prey

---

dean and rector) from 1847 until his death. Solov'ev's monumental *History of Russia from Earliest Times* in twenty-nine volumes is the classic work of its kind.

[77] On May 7, Grigor'ev rebelled against the Bolsheviks and took over a considerable part of the southern Ukraine. In July he joined up with Makhno, who had him killed on July 27. Nestor Ivanovych Makhno (1889–1934) was the extraordinary leader of an anarchist band, based at Guliai-Pole in the southern Ukrainian steppe, which fought against every authority to appear in the Ukraine in the course of the Civil War, including the Bolsheviks. He also entered into agreements with the Bolsheviks three times and broke them all. He fled to Rumania in August 1921.

[78] Aleksandr Dmitrievich Udal'tsov (1883–1958) was one of the Bolshevik-sponsored new members of the history department appointed in the spring of 1919 (although he did not become a Party member until 1928; his brother, Ivan Dmitrievich, was a well-known Old Bolshevik). He later became a high official in the academic bureaucracy. He wrote on the history of early medieval Europe.

of pretenders: gullibility, benightedness, and the fragility of Russia's whole social structure made possible then, as they do now, such unacceptable and, it would seem, unthinkable metamorphoses. I visited M. N. Pokrovskii to thank him for the personnel increase of the Rumiantsev library. The reception was again amiable, and I heard the following regarding the question of buying foreign books, which interests him as before: "The Entente again wishes to make peace with us; a month ago nothing came of it; now, perhaps, something will. They have shipped to Stockholm 900,000 puds of all kinds of things—stewed fruit and jam for children—and are promising to deliver all this if we will stop military actions against Kolchak and Denikin. Amazingly strange people: as soon as things get bad for Kolchak, they begin to offer us peace."

16 [May]. They continue to be horrified by the peace terms presented to Germany; but in my opinion the terms are altogether normal if one considers what Germany has done during the last five years. Of course, the Germans will be resurrected in the end, but they face hard years ahead. Everything in its turn; after the triumph of Germany comes the revanche of old France. Here everything is rotting as before.

18 [May]. There is some kind of new pressure in the west, near Petersburg; I, however, can't grasp the sense of this pressure, insofar as it comes from inadequate forces and not all at once from all sides; poor Russia is truly turning into some kind of "living relic," which lies motionless and is being taken apart by everyone. A terrible bustle over the expansion of the museum staff; there is only one refuge from the bustle—Sergievo.

20 [May]. I spent two days in Sergievo sorting out letters of Herzen, Granovskii, Granovskii's wife, and several ladies connected with the Westernizers' circle; the letters were preserved in the Korsh family and are presently being offered for acquisition by the Rumiantsev Museum. I love the people of all the Moscow circles of the 1840s; I love that small nucleus of cultured people who shone with their light on all of simian Russia, despite their gossip and their eternal *Grübelei*, to which Herzen devoted space in *My Past and Thoughts*,[79] and about which Granovskii's wife talks repeatedly in her letters. Among the sorted letters, I found the most interesting to be one of Granovskii to M. F. Korsh, where he speaks of the constant attacks of melancholy that overcome him and from which he finds solace in wine and cards. This talented man, too, was a Russian man, despite his belonging to the Westernizers, and he paid homage to

[79] *Byloe i dumy*, Herzen's autobiography, on which he worked from the early 1850s until the end of his life (d. 1870), is one of the great works of nineteenth-century Russian literature.

1. Archibald Cary Coolidge (1866–1928)

"I visited Coolidge for the last time: he is leaving for America. That is too bad. He is an interesting, symphathetic, highly cultured, and sincere American." February 13. 1922.

2. M. M. Bogoslovskii (1867–1929)

"M. M. Bogoslovskii's speech was very good; it contained much force and feeling, and his great and honest soul came through." April 15, 1918.

3. M. K. Liubavskii (1860–1936)

"I understand M. K. Liubavskii, who says that if he didn't have a family he would become a terrorist." September 30, 1917.

4. S. F. Platonov (1860–1933)

"A meeting with S. F. Platonov. His appearance is not bad; a great deal of energy, as always—it just flows from him." March 12, 1920.

5. A. K. Vinogradov (1887–1946)

"It is becoming difficult to work with A. K. Vinogradov in the museum: with all his major positive qualities as a worker and defender of the museum's interests, he is an operator, a careerist, and a lout." November 23, 1921.

6. The Supreme Council of the People's Commissariat of Enlightenment (*left to right*) M. A. Reisner (1868–1928), A. V. Lunacharskii (1875–1933), M. N. Pokrovskii (1868–1932), P. K. Shternberg (1865–1920)

"For the first time I saw close up comrade Lunacharskii-Lunaparkskii-Lupanarskii. A vigorous man of about forty-five, of a very healthy and well-fed appearance. His self-satisfaction is apparent in his every movement, every word. It is unlikely, however, that he has much authority among his comrades." March 6, 1920.

"[Pokrovskii is] an accursed, self-infatuated Quasimodo, toward whom I have always felt a kind of disgust." March 6, 1918.

"There is an interview in the newspapers with the thick-headed German Jew Shternberg—astronomer, bolshevik, and commissar for affairs of the higher schools." April 25, 1918.

7. "Wednesday—a new excursion: I went to participate in the unloading of a barge of firewood for the museum . . . the guarantee of warmth and life in the museum was in that barge. And so, all the employees are taking part in this work, carrying wood from the barge and depositing it on the ground." August 9, 1920.

8. "On Arbat Square there are trenches and barbed-wire barriers." November 5, 1917.

9. Unprocessed acquisitions in the Rumiantsev Museum (1922)

"Then I had the visit of Count P. S. Sheremetev concerning the rescue of the Mikhailovskoe Library, so that a touching unanimity of official and unofficial spheres on this matter has been revealed." January 6, 1919.

10. "My wife is being ordered to shovel snow tomorrow—that is yet another touch of contemporary life." January 5, 1919.

11. Patriarch Tikhon (right) and Metropolitan Veniamin (1922?)

"There was no getting through to the Trinity Cathedral; the patriarch was officiating there. Yesterday he rode past us—incidentally, the Russian pope rode in a simple one-horse cart. He has a sympathetic and intelligent face." June 8, 1919.

12. Inessa Armand and her children (1914)

"Among the officer-volunteers were Fedia and Andriusha Armand; Fedia is making amends for his bolshevik mama." October 30, 1917.

13. The Metropole Hotel in November 1917

"Terrifying destruction—in that part of town the City Duma and the Metropole Hotel were especially hard hit." November 5, 1917.

14. The Rumiantsev Museum (1922)

"Today we decided in principle to move into the building of the museum, into half of Menzbir's apartment. I had thought that we would move from our apartment on Bol'shoi Znamenskii only into the other world, but that shows what human expectations are worth." March 4, 1919.

15. Frank A. Golder
(1877–1929)

"We visited Golder. He is no less interesting than Coolidge, even livelier than he is. A proposal to ship off my materials; I think I will accept it." July 16, 1922.

16. "Today they . . . removed the crown from Alexander III, and the eagles sitting on his pedestal." April 30, 1918.

17. Map of Central Moscow from Baedeker's *Russia* (1914)

Got'e's life was centered in the area shown on the lower left of the map, due west of the Kremlin. His apartment was across the street from the Alexander Military Academy.

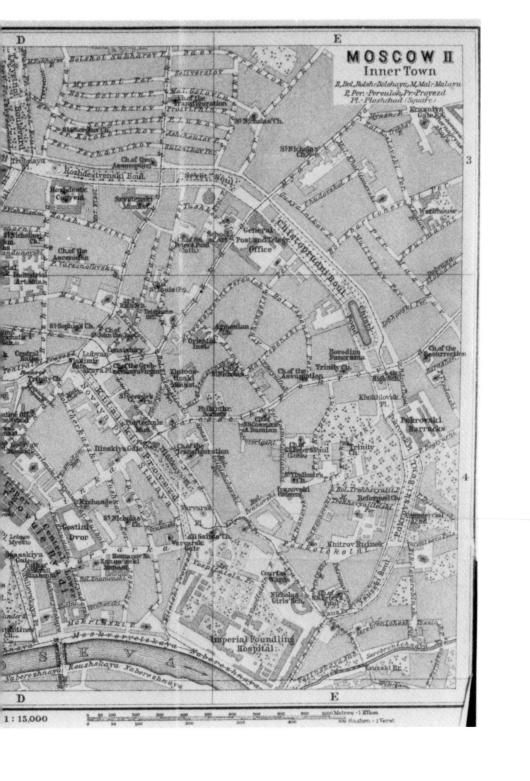

MOSCOW II
Inner Town

B. Bol. Bolsh. = Bolshaya, M. Mal. = Malaya
P. Per. = Pereulok, Pr. = Proyezd
Pl. = Ploshchad (Square)

1 : 15,000

18. Townspeople dismantling a wooden house for firewood (1919).

19. "The hospital ship *The People's Will* is lying on its side in the Neva. That is symbolic: the People's Will in the water." May 17, 1921.

all the charms of Russian life. There is for me some kind of special charm in reading the letters of long-departed people; it is the same feeling as in archival studies, but something more alive and intimate. We had a house-warming; there were the Kapterevs, Tania, and the Serb Ilić. The conversation revolved around the sick man, that is, Russia (Turkey has practically died, and Russia is close to it). Ilić said that in his opinion Clemenceau and Lloyd George should have set up special missions of all those wishing to acquaint Europe more widely with bolshevik Russia: that would have facilitated a quicker and more successful sobering up from socialism. Today A. A. Tikhomirov paid a visit to me and had a long conversation with me, more precisely a monologue, because even if I had wanted to participate in the discussion, I would not have been able to do so, because he would not have allowed me to. An astonishingly strange person: one sees, even through his immeasurable conceit, over-flowing sense of his own genius, and constant striving to see Jew-Kadets and Masons everywhere, a man of intelligence. [He holds] very accurate opinions of Manuilov and Chuprov[80]—those artificial notables created by the stupidity of the Russian intelligentsia. No less interesting was his opinion of Kasso,[81] whom he at first considered to be an intelligent and decent man but later became convinced he was a petty cheat and adventurer. He spoke of Nicholas II as a very strange man, but not stupid (with the latter I, of course, cannot agree), but he accurately evaluated Aleksandra Fedorovna as one of the most revolting of women. Of Nicholas he correctly says that he seemed intentionally to have appointed as ministers the worst and most insignificant men, as if fearing that they would diminish his authority. Our conversation ended with his usual attacks against Darwinism. To be fair, he bears his difficult situation with dignity, when he is even half-starving. The end of the day was devoted to work in the garden; thanks to the kindness of the Kapterevs, we have a small garden, and our appetites are whetted: we even want to plant potatoes; such are the dreams of bourgeois in Russia in 1919. Masha the cook left for somewhere near Rostov to exchange the parlor curtains for potato flour. This, too, is something contemporary.

21 [May]. Two days in Moscow and again running about and a most senseless waste of time. The news, however, is fairly cheery; something

[80] Aleksandr Ivanovich Chuprov (1842–1908) was one of the founders of Russian statistics and a professor in the law faculty (department of economics and statistics) of Moscow University. He was a leading figure, like Manuilov, of the liberal-populist school of Russian economic thought.

[81] Lev Aristidovich Kasso (1865–1914), a Bessarabian nobleman, was minister of enlightenment from 1911 to 1914. The mass resignations at Moscow University in 1911 were made in protest against his violation of university autonomy.

is in fact beginning to threaten Petersburg; the peace is also growing near, and that, in the final analysis, may be to our advantage. All evening today they sorted out the "wage rates" for the museum employees and made a row because the rates commission (to such nonsense do things go now in the state institutions) has insulted our employees. One more curious observation: Pokrovskii was present today at the saloon-faculty of social sciences; I was amazed by his wish—and it seems a sincere one—to somehow draw near again to his old comrades. This could be felt in all his words and actions. I think that he would be quite amazed if he could read the absence of such reciprocal feelings in the hearts of those present.

22 [May]. There is much discussion of Trotskii's telegram about how Petrograd, the birthplace of world revolution, is being menaced. What is this—a tactical maneuver or the real situation? We will see in a short while.

23 [May]. Discussions are buzzing over the possible taking of Petersburg. I am not aware of the degree of seriousness of that undertaking. One will have to wait. Is this a constituent part of a general movement or something disconnected? The likely outcome of this affair and of the entire fate of Russia depends on which of these it is. Today I carried a half-pud of bread from Novinskii to Mertvyi on my back; a nice scene for my professor's status. In the evening there was a meeting of Russian historians at my place: we talked of teaching plans for next year, without believing for a minute in their realization.

25 [May]. Sergievo. The first day of summer. Volodia and I climbed up the monastery bell tower and admired the wonderful view: a fine summer day does after all have a stimulating effect; it takes your thoughts away from all that is going on and makes you think less about the charms of world revolution. The news is satisfactory; almost everywhere in the quadrille there is the command *reculez*, but nothing is written about the main danger spots, and about Petrograd and Riga—silence. Today I was able to do some reading and further prepare the work about the Time of Troubles for the cooperativists.

26 [May]. Sergievo. The whole day [was spent] in complete calm and without any news; wonderful weather; on such days living is after all easier; I am working quite a lot. The latest chat with A. A. Tikhomirov, who says as a matter of speculation that Nicholas II in his day was not uninvolved in Masonry and participated in black masses; in this connection he cited persons who had been close to the Court by the back door. Who knows, perhaps there is a grain of truth in this.

28 [May]. The Moscow bustle again, and whole days of construction in the Rumiantsev Museum, without hope of seeing any good results from that construction. The general news is becoming ever more interesting; someone is taking something, but when will there be an end to this terrible fratricidal war? The more you think about it, the clearer it becomes that the society that gave birth to a Nicholas II with his Rasputins, Miasoedovs and Sukhomlinovs, and the Artsybashevs and Kuzmins in literature, should have ended as it has ended.[82] Interesting things are happening in the university question: today comrade Volgin, the latter-day professor of bolshevism, is talking about the need to work out a plan of compulsory classes for the students, and a paper comes from the commissariat with a proposal to monitor how the students attend lectures. How good it would be if the commissariat would come to the idea of resurrecting the inspections and informants.

29 [May]. Ascension, left by some miracle in the list of holidays. I did not go to Sergievo, because that is really too tiring. But I was bored. I was at the cemetery and marched on foot across all of Moscow, and once more was convinced of the horrible abomination that Moscow now is—stench, dirt, and the complete absence of intellectual physiognomies. Brutalization is felt at every step. I slept a whole two hours from fatigue. The news is satisfactory, but once again affirmative of the fact that the matter of our rebirth is a rather long matter. I received a letter from Sasha Gartung, which I append here as a "human document" depicting the Russian intelligent.[83]

30 [May]. The general situation is without change. I gave a lecture at a meeting of lawyers about authority and law in Russian history in which I introduced the idea that an independent Russian court has been wrecked three times by fault of the government and society. Filat'ev, Liadov, Kossovskii, and several other personages from the world of the former legal profession were present. It seems that in general the talk corresponded to the set purpose; at least the audience stayed put and there were rather lively discussions. It is characteristic that Filat'ev, and Liadov to some extent, who are in general men of Kerenskii's time, nevertheless revealed themselves to be unreconstructed populists. The

---

[82] Mikhail Petrovich Artsybashev (1878–1927) and Mikhail Alekseevich Kuzmin (1875–1935) were the outstanding representatives of decadence in post-1905 Russian literature. In their work they celebrated sexual freedom—homosexual love in the case of Kuzmin.

[83] See Appendix, Letter 7, from Aleksandr Gartung to Got'e, no date, but ca. May 6, 1919.

Russian is so pigheaded that he remains after all an intelligent with all that high-sounding nonsense that is characteristic of him alone.

JUNE

1 [June]. Sergievo; excellent weather; again some recovery and you take advantage of two days of freedom. Apropos, a very curious discovery: when giving the lecture to the lawyers, I learned from Kossovskii that Martini's assistant, Skart [?] is as much a Dane as I am, and just like the rest of us sinners was trying to get out of Sovdepiia and has recently at last made off. There is a rumor about abolishing all faculties of social sciences except one; that doesn't surprise me, because such an idea flows logically from the existing situation, and the teaching personnel of the university, the Higher Women's Courses, and the Shaniavskii University almost coincide.

3 [June]. In Moscow it is again possible to witness a curious but customary phenomenon: dispiritedness among the ex-bourgeois because matters are not moving as quickly as wished. As for personal matters—overwork as before at the museum; I don't know when I will get out of the kettle in which I am boiling owing to the expansion of the library staff. As for general news—they are saying as a fact that the Siberian government has been recognized; whether that is so or not, today all consulates left in Moscow have been seized, or more precisely consular personnel, since all those remaining here were sojourning here as private persons; the poor Wilkens, who have never been involved in any politics, are under house arrest. The former Norwegian consul Halmby is under arrest in exactly the same way, together with E. A. Got'e, the mistress of the house in which he lives. The persecution of foreigners was reflected today in the newspapers by public notice of the abolition of all the immunities granted them (it appears that all such immunities were actually violated long ago, at least in all those individual cases where they [the Bolsheviks] found it expedient to do so). So far it is not clear just what the real reason for this amazing action is. The decree allowing travel on the railroad only with a permit has already been reflected in bread prices—they have again leaped to 1,200 rubles a pud.

5 [June]. The roundup of consuls and foreigners is turning out to be far wider than one could have thought at the beginning: all nations have been subjected to one and the same fate; evidently something far bigger than we know is happening. In the evening I worked with pleasure in the Archive of Foreign Affairs; it was quiet and cool, and there was nobody there; I spent two and a half hours with complete satisfaction.

6 [June]. Here is Dima Wilken's story: at 1 A.M. on Wednesday they came to them from the Cheka with an order for a search of their apartment, along with the neighboring apartment of the Nazes. They rummaged through everything and dug around until 7 A.M., after which they took Georges Wilken to Liubianka 14. Incidentally, they took away 16,000 in currency belonging to various people and announced they were leaving them 200 rubles; later they reconsidered and left them 1,000 rubles. In the morning an old Jewish woman and her secretary appeared for questioning and interrogated them for a long time about all their connections and acquaintances; on leaving, she announced that their testimonies were such that they would be released immediately; release came toward evening of the day after. Apparently the same thing has happened to other foreigners; they detained five other Belgians at Wilkens' place; they also grabbed some Swiss and other members of minor nationalities and states. The newspapers today are howling about the movement on Viatka, and Nakhamkis is talking about the landing in Archangel.[84] Moscow's inhabitants have again picked up in spirits a bit. I arrived in Sergievo in the evening; a spring evening with a thunder storm—warm, light, and cozy.

7 [June]. While traveling on the railroad recently, I saw the following scene: two youths in their twenties replied to a remark made to them that the car was for nonsmokers that they "do not celebrate antiquity," that now everything is new and they don't give a hang about the old. However, under the unanimous assault of some suddenly emboldened intelligenty the base and stupid gorillas quickly yielded and threw their cigarettes out the window. Going to Vifaniia this morning we met a crowd of urchins with saws and axes. My friend Shambinago addressed them sharply, in his usual manner: "Well, are you going to plunder someone else's woods? According to a new decree?" They answered him rudely: "Of course according to a new one, and not an old one. What is the old to us? Everything is new now." The psychology of both is the same: the faith of primitive men that everything has changed, that all that was before has disappeared and been entirely replaced by something new. This is the sense that the people have of the revolution, or that part of

[84] Got'e refers to the arrival of a British relief contingent that was ostensibly sent to cover the withdrawal of the entire force in Archangel, although it did undertake an offensive in midsummer. The decision to withdraw had apparently been taken by the British in March; in June the Americans were already departing. See Kennan, *Russia and the West*, p. 88.

the people that shares such a faith; the sense will remain unchanged until an authoritative command is given, whereupon the gorilla herd will freeze in the pose of the old woman at the broken trough. For in negation of the old law, there is rooted negation of any law, and faith in the new consists of the conviction of being free from any formal or moral obligations and of the rule of one's own individual arbitrary will, whose beastliness surpasses "Kit Kitych" many times over.[85] The mistake of the ideologues of bolshevism consists in the fact that they do not understand this psychology, and to some extent don't want to understand it. Where the "worker-peasant masses" is not a tool of demagogy, it is an idol on a pedestal: both corrupt the people. At present there is no education, not to mention training, of the people, as there was none under the tsars; once more the saying is proven correct: "*les extremités se touchent.*" An excellent stroll in Vifaniia; a tropical day with a thunderstorm; swimming in the Vifaniia ponds. The newspapers are like yesterday's.

8 *[June]*. Trinity at Trinity. A stroll in the monastery to mass; a great crowd of people; the usual fete on church holidays, but on a larger scale. There was no getting through to the Trinity Cathedral; the patriarch was officiating there. Yesterday he rode past us—incidentally, the Russian pope rode in a simple one-horse cart. He has a sympathetic and intelligent face. An excellent stroll in the evening to Chernigovka. I recalled two more incidents from the life of the museum that depict the Russian man. Our "inspector" Nikitiuk, a stupid and stubborn churl from Podlasie,[86] has now received the title "director of the maintenance division" and has imagined himself to be all-powerful. On that basis, without asking anyone, he began to break through the fireproof wall into the adjacent archive, which provoked a conflict with the neighboring institution; in addition, he wrote a most insolent document in his own name. The next day, learning that Prince Golitsyn had ordered his wife's grave edged with sod, he revoked that order, announcing that [only] he (he is a former gardener and estate manager of the same Prince Golitsyn) has the right to give orders having to do with maintenance. There you have the type of uncivilized Russian for whom the wine of power has gone to the head. According to the newspapers, they are retreating everywhere, but they are feigning courage and boasting. I read the Austrian peace conditions; I would have pruned her in exactly the same way.

[85] Kit Kitych was the merchant in Ostrovskii's comedy *Your Drink—My Hangover (V chuzhom piru pokhmel'e)*, "the essence of the *samodur*—the willful domestic tyrant . . ." (Mirsky, *A History of Russian Literature*, p. 238).

[86] A region of eastern Poland.

9 [June]. A day without happenings or news from outside; magnificent weather and a good rest; the holiday was not too obtrusive; there were even few people around the house.

12 [June]. In all three days spent in Moscow, I wasn't able to write a word: too much work, it is all too piled up, there is hardly time to deal with urgent everyday matters. In Moscow my mood changed greatly. There everyone is certain of the opposite of what the bolsheviks write in *Izvestiia.* This conviction is founded on a multitude of rumors that come along unnoticed, stemming in significant measure from the most frightened, embittered, and quarrelsome bolsheviks. Reports are persistently coming from various quarters that news, even in boring summaries, will be more and more suppressed. It is forbidden to report defeats. From all the data that can be collected, it is apparent that the offensive against the RSFSR is indeed continuing and that the front-line territory is all enveloped in uprisings; an echo of this is the declaration of martial law for the entire Ukraine and all of Tambov province. I cite two facts: D.A.K. writes from Orel: "I am coming, and L. and S. are following." Sh. G. received a letter from K. G., from which it is evident that in the west near M[insk?] there were battles, as a result of which M[insk?] has been taken by someone or is about to be taken. Moscow, too, has begun to be agitated. The cause of this is the nondistribution of bread; there is no bread, and there is nowhere to get it. The transporting of it is unthinkable, and, what is more, the most hungry time before the new harvest is just ahead. There is agitation among the workers and the rabble in Moscow: there were demonstrations already last Sunday, repeated on Monday and Tuesday; they say they will occur again today. The demands are—bread, down with the civil war, free trade. Of course, this will provoke repressions, which will elevate the Cheka even more over the Council of People's Commissars. They are also saying that a desperate struggle is going on between Trotskii and the head of the special section of the Cheka, Kedrov,[87] who wants to take Trotskii's place. There are rumors coming from the Cheka that Trotskii has gone mad; but he is still fighting back, although he is indeed ill and suffers from neurasthenia. On Friday I was at the faculty of social sciences and was a witness to how the communist students—the Jew Genin and the Armenian Ruturian—demanded that they be admitted "with deciding vote," on the basis

---

[87] Mikhail Sergeevich Kedrov (1878–1941) was a longtime Bolshevik who was made head of the Special Section of the Cheka in 1919; before that he had served as a high-ranking military commissar and commander. In 1941 he was brought out of retirement to be imprisoned and shot by order of Beria, whom he had tried to expose for wrongdoings as early as 1921.

of the just-published decree on admitting student-communists to the faculty. They were asked to show their mandates; for lack of such the matter was postponed until the next time, as were the elections to the "presidium" of the faculty. Their boorishness was amazing; I must say that this incident did not bother me at all—I sincerely found it funny. But many, for old time's sake, still felt obliged to get offended and angry. Only one thing is clear: it is impossible for a man who wants to preserve his integrity to be a dean at the present time. A long talk today with A. A. Tikhomirov; he cursed Pobedonostsev and reported to me that the half-wit metropolitan of Moscow, Leontii, used to call Pobedonostsev "dog mummy." That is characteristic for the metropolitan, and extraordinarily apt for Pobedonostsev himself. Coming from swimming, I thought a lot about the essence of my historical research work: what kind of idea unites it? And I came to the conclusion that I am, essentially, a historian of gentry civilization in Russia. The Moscow region is one link, local administration another; a book about the fall of the empire [would be] the last; the planned essays on the history of the sixteenth century the first. The social-estate policies of Peter, and Pushkin as the summit of gentry culture, are questions that interest me. If all this were developed, it would make a series, internally united and whole. Today's news summary is rather decent: Tsarev and Novyi Oskol[88] lost, and regression in the west.

14 [June]. A magnificent bicycle jaunt with S. N. Kapterev. It is impossible to even imagine how charming are the environs of the Posad; if this weren't Russia, people would journey here, they would come on foot, there would be restaurants here—*schöne Ansicht*, and so forth. And what is happening today in Paris! We would give dearly, all the unfortunate civilized Russian people who remain true to the precepts of the past, to get just a glimpse at that universal triumph. Alas, "not for us has the spring come"!

15 [June]. Another day without news. We get it only in the evening. Today I dreamed of Zagran'e in my sleep for the first time. I think that is because they are mowing hay everywhere, and that reminds me of last year's harvest work, which, despite all the fatigue, had its charms. What is going on there? Who is mowing our hay? In the morning Nina and I went to the monastery; when you go through the central part of the Posad and see the sovdep gorilla mugs, you have the sensation of a kind of rotten belch, just as if you had eaten something spoiled. On Sunday the bolsheviks wrote that in Khar'kov N. I. Astrov is supposedly forming

---

[88] Towns on the southeastern front.

some kind of new government with the SRs and the Popular Socialists.[89] If that is so, it means that poor Russia has still not learned anything; it means that one should flee at the first opportunity, because this foolishness will not save us.

16 [June]. The news gleaned from *Izvestiia* again leaves a vague impression; continual movement to the east—now toward Zlatoust and Ekaterinburg. What does it signify—only the collapse of Kolchak's armies or also something else? Marking time in the south. What is the percent of lies and what the percent of truth in all they write? After spending three or four days far from rumors and conversations, you always pose yourself these eternal, burning questions. One must think about how to survive the winter somehow. Those are the routine and most burdensome tasks of the immediate future; to survive, emancipate oneself from everything superfluous, and, at the first convenient opportunity, to get out of this stinking toilet. Those are the desires you restrict yourself to at the present time.

18 [June]. Despondency in Moscow; they have taken Ekaterinburg and Ekaterinoslav. On the other hand, though, there is complete confidence that reality does not correspond to what is written in *Izvestiia*. I have even been told that *Izvestiia* is forbidden at the "fronts," and that another newspaper is published there, in which corresponding lies are printed about Moscow. *Se non è vero.* . . . From this it is clear (1) that no movement *from without*, taken alone, can take care of the RSFSR, although the latter is collapsing, and (2) that we must prepare for hibernation. And this latter is the most difficult matter. *Wir müssen durch!* For the rest—disgusting, boring, nasty, and hopeless!

19 [June]. Unexpectedly for myself, as a result of the necessity of substituting for V. D. Golitsyn next week, I came to Sergievo on Friday instead of Saturday. It is amazing: a stay in Moscow is morally invigorating owing to the multitude of the most varied rumors—you choose which you want to believe. You come here, therefore, invigorated, but here you learn only from the newspapers and therefore toward the end of your stay in Sergievo your spirits fall. I paid tribute on the streetcars—they stole my wallet with forty rubles and my gold cuff links; at least my watch is intact. Worries about winter occupy me more than anything else; whatever firewood there is is all requisitioned by institutions that

[89] The Khar'kov city duma reassembled after the Whites took Khar'kov and elected a council of five Kadets and one Popular Socialist (June 24, 1919), which had aspirations to rule the entire province of Khar'kov.

have authority but from neglect or incompetence have not bothered about laying in firewood; among them, alas, are the railroads!

20 [June]. Last evening Nina suddenly said that she would have nothing against leaving for somewhere in the Russian south. I immediately began to consider some kind of plan in this direction. It seems to me that if the whole situation remains unchanged, I should get myself a business trip to the south for buying books in Kiev, Khar'kov, and Odessa, and at the same time settle the family, and myself, somewhere in a warmer place. There was no news received today; thanks to that, the tense concern with events relaxed a little. For long? Until the next news. It should be noted that yesterday's official communiqué was rather satisfactory.

21 [June]. Nina left for Moscow. I stayed with Volodia in Sergievo. In the morning I worked as usual; afterward I listened to the memoirs of A. A. Tikhomirov. He read to me for the period from 1898 through 1902, that is, for the time, roughly, of his rectorship and the Bogolepov and Vannovskii ministries.[90] I must say that I listened to them with great pleasure. A great deal in them complemented what I knew earlier; much seems to me quite different from what it seemed at that distant time. I always cursed him as a rector, but now I must admit that he was more direct and honest than the others and that in some things he was right, for example in his judging the student disturbances to be a purely political phenomenon. I also completely agree with him that Germany even then encouraged our disorganization and disorders out of her notorious *Wille zur Macht.* Only nearsighted Russians can say that the Germans are better than the Allies. The Germans could have had everything from us, but that seemed little to them and they decided to enslave us; when that didn't work, they destroyed us.

22 [June]. A magnificent bicycle jaunt to the monastery's country property, Tarbeevo[?]—confiscated, as is the custom now—and swimming in the lake. Along the way I pondered what to do for winter. I thought up a new version—stay here, store up a lot of supplies from autumn, and sit it out. Or else go south for sure. It will be possible to live in Moscow only if fuel, food, and light are guaranteed.

[90] Nikolai Pavlovich Bogolepov (1847–1901), a professor of Roman law at Moscow University, sometime rector and head of the Moscow education district, was appointed minister of enlightenment in 1898. He was assassinated in 1901. Petr Semenovich Vannovskii (1822–1904) was a general and served as minister of war for seventeen years (1881–1898). Appointed minister of enlightenment to replace Bogolepov in 1901, he was dismissed a little more than a year later.

23 [June]. A thunderstorm with hail, a downpour, and heat before and after that. Gloom in the soul, intensified by worry about Nina's health. Will the peace be signed?—that is the most important question for us, the unfortunate civilized Russians.

24 [June]. Damp weather after the storms; wind; gloomy outside and gloomy in the soul. I am transporting the Stessel' archive, which I acquired for the Rumiantsev Museum;[91] I am reading over some of it, and that makes my mental state even worse. In Port Arthur they kept two generals for one role—isn't that in the Russian manner; could two Russian generals not quarrel? When you remember and relive everything that happened fifteen years ago, Russian public stupidity, to which there is no equal on earth, stands up to its full height. They took it into their heads to build Russian imperialism with their bare hands under the nose of the Japanese; they went too far, received a terrible lesson, yet went on and continued to handle matters in such a way that they fell into an even deeper and more fetid abyss. All this is so painful and shameful! And when you look ahead, into that *grand au delà des bolcheviki*, for which we are all hoping so, is it not clear that the present lesson, too, is insufficient and that Russian stupidity will continue to grow and develop? Because of this the future seems even gloomier.

27 [June]. The mood in Moscow is mixed. Some are expectant, others expect nothing. The peace, thank God, will be signed. This is possibly a step forward toward the pacification of the world, but one must not give oneself illusions: it will all continue for a very long time. I work in the archive every day; that is the best way to spend time that I can imagine at present. In Moscow arrests and searches are continuing on an extremely large scale: on the one hand, you are terrified; on the other, you see how untenable and futile it all is. There is talk about discontent on the railroads. I think that this, too, is a symptom, but it will take a long time before it develops into something concrete.

29 [June]. The thought is growing ever firmer that the immediate future will be far harder than anything we have experienced thus far; this flows not only from intuition but from logic. On the way out they will "slam the door," but many will have headaches from the slamming. Sasha Rar's

[91] Anatolii Mikhailovich Stessel' (Stoessel, 1848–1915), a veteran of the Russo-Turkish War, was commander of the military region that included Port Arthur at the tip of the Liaotung Peninsula, the site of the Japanese attack that began the Russo-Japanese War in February 1904. His archive contains both memoirs and a diary covering events in Port Arthur (Otdel rukopisei Biblioteki im. V. I. Lenina, f. 289, 1.10/1,2).

head, for example, has begun to ache again; he was arrested yesterday on a warrant that, it seems, was not even in his name; many more will have headaches before the rulers either fall or calm down. The "leaving" of Khar'kov has been announced. It would be very interesting to know what kind of excesses were permitted there and how firmly Denikin will rule Khar'kov; much depends on that. I didn't very much like what was written today about the peace. In Germany, apparently, there are some kind of waverings; they even tell me that a monarchist counterrevolution is being prepared. But peace is necessary, otherwise the struggle against bolshevism will be difficult. Yesterday I saw in Moscow a thoroughly contemporary sight, and one that may become even more widespread: a wooden house razed for firewood, in which people were scurrying about like worms or flies in carrion. The housing problem in Moscow threatens to become very, very serious in the near future.

30 [June]. The peace was signed on Saturday at 4 P.M. August 1, 1914– June 29, 1919 = four years and eleven months—such was the length of one of the most terrible epochs in the history of unfortunate mankind. I don't know whom the judge of history will finally find guilty in this horror, but it seems to me that the basic perpetrators were not elemental circumstances, but specific people: the German military, the German industrialists, the German and Austrian diplomats, the Viennese Jews and adventurers. All these people expected to get rich quickly by means of the millions of well-trained and well-equipped Germans, fanaticized by the idea of *Deutschland über alles*; instead, they have ruined Germany, Austria-Hungary, and Russia, have destroyed twenty monarchies by which they themselves were supported, and have undermined the well-being of all the rest of Europe, wrecking her finances and, in part, her industry. Of course, this peace is such that it will not be a lasting peace. There was the idea of French revanche; now the idea of German revanche will grow, and someday the cannons, bayonets, gases, and suchlike contrivances of destructive technology will sound again. The struggle for the banks of the Rhine, which has continued for twenty centuries, will not end in 1919. What is beginning now in the West will also have an influence on our situation: if it proves to be the growth of imperialism, it must destroy bolshevism; if it proves to be the growth of the labor movement, bolshevism will thereby receive indirect support. In any case, a hard and difficult fall and winter await us, if only we don't perish from political upheavals and coups. The movement from the south is growing, but so far I don't have a sense of its strength or its long-term future. The supply problem gets more dragged out and difficult every day.

JULY

1 [July]. Today I am forty-six years old; five of these years ought to be crossed off my life. I always said and am now more convinced than ever that it is far better to live in times of quiet and stagnation than in such "interesting" times as we are living through. I am peacefully enjoying myself in Sergievo; I have just now come from a swimming hole, which I found at half an hour's walk, in Torgosh creek. Today nature is fragrant and radiant; even this vile northern climate has its own beauty. The bolsheviks have set the clocks back by half an hour; they even play with meteorology! There are persistent rumors about Kursk; I don't know what they are founded on.

5 [July]. I have recorded nothing all these days, and all for the same reason: I am afraid to write at home, in view of the uneasiness of the situation and the possibility of a search any minute. (I am writing this in order not to suspect myself later of fantastic exaggeration.) In the museum I have to grab a free minute in order calmly to record my thoughts, and in existing conditions it is not easy to find one. These days the attention of the people who are agonizingly waiting for rescue has been fixed as before on the south, where the advance of Denikin's armies has continued as far as Belgorod, Borisoglebsk, and Balashov;[92] "their" alarm is great. They are trying to draw everyone they can to the defense of their socialist state; little is coming of it, but I fear all the same that it will be enough to roll back the avalanche. I fear it, because earlier ones were rolled back and because we absolutely don't know anything about the advancing army and what kind of help it can get from the phenomenon of the day—the so-called green army; that is, the enormous collections of deserters that are accumulating in all corners of Sovdepiia. There is much talk of an impending offensive from the west; but so far it is impossible to get a hold on it. In Moscow they have stopped distributing bread and console [us by saying] it is not known when it will be distributed; thus there may be a real, genuine famine in Moscow. Its origin is clear—there can be no transport from the south now insofar as all remnants of transport are being used for military freight. But that situation in the making may also be rich in consequences.

6 [July]. Sergievo. After three sweltering and uneasy days in Moscow, the peace and abundance of this place again. Upon arriving, after the sweltering train car and the even more horrible Moscow swelter, I even went

---

[92] Towns in Kursk, Tambov, and Saratov provinces, respectively.

swimming in the evening; and late in the evening Nina and I took a little stroll, basking in the descending cool of the night. Yesterday they admitted their loss of Balashov and Bogodukhov; in addition, something has flared up between Iaroslavl' and Vologda—a bridge blown up and tracks dismantled; the Cheka has been sent there.

7 [July]. Thinking the whole day about what to do in the material sense. Prices are rising unbelievably. Here in Sergievo today butter costs 170 rubles a pound, milk 75 rubles a quarter,[93] horsemeat 30 rubles, farmer's cheese 32 rubles, eggs 120 rubles: I record this for the memory of future generations. It is possible to wait another month or two; after that we will have to leave for somewhere; but how to decide all this? Where? How? In the winter we are doomed to both hunger and cold; a cord of wood costs up to 1,000 rubles here now. What will it be in Moscow? We will likely have to flee to some grain-producing region; but again, what to choose and where to find it? The weather is charming and there has not been such a summer for a long time.

One more remark: Inessa [Armand] has refused to vouch for Georges Wilken; such is her memory for hospitality extended to her in her youth. I admit that I didn't expect that even from her.

9 [July]. An extra day in Sergievo; sometimes you forget the whole surrounding nightmare. Prices are leaping upward so fast the mind can't keep up with them. Milk has reached 75–80 rubles in the course of two weeks; there is not enough money for anything. Despite all the optimistic rumors and all the nonsense that is circulating, I remain a pessimist and have little faith that Denikin will reach Moscow. And there can be victory over bolshevism only if Moscow is taken and "red" Moscow—that is, the whole nest of the "international" that has been built in stupid old Moscow—destroyed. So long as the seedbed of the infection is not destroyed there can be no victory over bolshevism. Aside from that, I am presently worried about the matter of winter fuel. What will happen if matters go on as they have been going up to now? The best solution would be to live together around some hearth, like the Eskimos or Chukchi,[94] in the one heated room in the whole house. Those are the winter prospects as I sketch them to myself.

27 [July]. A big gap again, explainable by the Moscow jostle. The latest new sensational rumor for these days: the entry of the Germans into the struggle with the bolsheviks. They even say they have declared war, but

[93] *Chetvert'*: approximately three liters.
[94] Aborigines of northeastern Siberia.

wars are not declared nowadays, they simply certify the state of military operations. This is possible, since the rumors come from many bolshevik and military circles. If it is confirmed, then of course it is a new indication that the bolsheviks have all the civilized world against them. An indirect confirmation of the rumors about Germany is the animation of military operations in the Dvinsk–Pskov region. The news of Denikin is also better than it seemed a week or two ago. Ekaterinoslav turns out not to have been taken: the grip of the bolsheviks on the Elets-Valuiski line is apparently being broken by the fist of Denikin, who has gathered considerable forces precisely on that line. In the east the retreat is not happening in the way the bolsheviks write. Here is a detail concerning the railroad situation: all personnel are being evacuated and the signals are being taken down, but the big equipment is not being destroyed. I heard this from N. K. G-n. My firm conviction that all their war communiqués are full of lies was reinforced by the stories of P. N. Kapterev, who has just returned from Voronezh province. The red army is fleeing from Cossack patrols, and it is clearer than ever before that they cannot withstand any kind of even minimally organized and firm force. Another rumor P.N.K. told me was that in the Moscow sovdep they told him this: this is how we live—run for your life. If all that I have written here is taken together, one would think that I am in a radiant mood. In fact it is not like that at all: I am just as skeptical as ever; I have been deceived many times. That the rumors reaching us are not always false is demonstrated by the story of G.N.N., the Simeiz astronomer who came to reestablish his laboratory's tie with Pulkovo.[95] He confirmed almost everything that, one way or another, reached us from there, and reported much that was interesting for me about all the Crimean misfortunes of 1918 and 1919. Saddest of all was the story about Sebastopol: it has been much harder hit than in 1855; there is absolutely nothing left there—not one usable vessel, not one military structure. Thus do the Russian gorillas treat their native land. These days I was a witness to how Muscovites get firewood for themselves: from Preobrazhenskoe, Cherkizovo, Lefortovo, even from around Sukharevka, people are going to Moose Island with axes and even knives, and they are carrying back slender trees.[96] They extend in a string like ants, carrying the slender trunks, exhausting themselves from the burden, and frightfully damaging the forest. There is a scandal in the museum: for the third time the jug-headed Kozlov[97] has been ar-

[95] Pulkovo was the site of Russia's principal observatory, near Petrograd, constructed between 1837 and 1839. Moscow University maintained a small observatory in Simeiz in the Crimea near Yalta.

[96] Losinyi ostrov (Moose Island) was a park northeast of Moscow. Now within the city limits, it had originally been a hunting preserve of Tsar Ivan IV.

[97] Kozlov was the bursar of the Rumiantsev Museum.

rested as an SR; but he is in addition an SOB, for his arrest brought in its train the seizure of 327,000 rubles that were lying in his cash drawer. Now we have to get that money out of the Cheka. The Commissariat of Enlightenment has sent a paper to the saloon faculty [telling them] to wait with the election of the dean and his sidekicks in view of the anticipated reorganization of the administration of the university and faculties. They say they are very dissatisfied with the action of the communist students three weeks ago and don't know how to get out of the situation they got themselves into.

28 [July]. A gray day; I am reading over the essay on the Time of Troubles that I have written. Yesterday's newspaper reports were fairly satisfactory, but it will take a great deal of patience yet. We are celebrating Volodia's nameday. The presents offered him are very characteristic: a wooden pail for twenty rubles, a small bread roll, and a penknife.

AUGUST

1 [August]. Three days again in Moscow without a chance to record anything. I am afraid to keep even a single sheet of paper at home (that is also characteristic of the moment), and in the museum there is simply no time. The basic fact of Moscow life for the past few days: universal searches, or at least searches on an unprecedented scale. The question can be posed: don't they want in fact to search every apartment in Moscow? These searches, however, differ from searches based on a definite suspicion of one person or another. They are a little different: they are looking for weapons, deserters; along the way they remove silver and gold things and sometimes currency, if there are more than 10,000 rubles on hand. That gives full range for arbitariness; they do not, however, make arrests. So far, the searches have been in several areas of town; now everyone expects them and the attitude toward them, of many at least, has become one of indifference. On the general horizon there is new animation and new hopes in connection with the continuing onslaught from the south and the revived onslaught from the west. Kamyshin and Poltava have been taken. Someone's paws are stretching toward Kiev from Poltava and from Kovel; the news from Minsk is such that it will be someone's property tomorrow, if not today. But who are they? They say it is the Germans, the Poles, the English who are on the move; just now they have begun to talk about how the campaign against the RSFSR is nothing less than the campaign of the League of Nations against bolshevism. The latter seems to me the most likely; although such a collective enterprise has to be arranged, which in turn will take a lot of time. Of course, there can be no peace with people who set themselves the task of corrupting the whole world with propaganda, who lie and cheat on principle, and never keep their word or obligations.

The treasurer of the Rumiantsev Museum, who was arrested a week ago, was released after three days, along with the money. Bread and flour are getting cheaper in Moscow; they say that is occurring because the workers, who are allowed to buy bread, are transporting it in such quantities that they are speculating with it, selling it to those who are not allowed to buy bread.

2 [August]. St. Elijah's Day. Glorious weather after rain. Yesterday's newspaper was very insignificant in content; no news from Moscow. Thus, impressions equal zero. This morning we dreamed for a long time about someday getting to Western Europe and returning to the lap of civilization, for you sense more strongly every day how we and all that surrounds us are sinking into an abyss of barbarism.

4 [August]. The comrades yesterday reported with embarrassment the demise of Soviet Hungary.[98] "The wire is not yet clear," but the fact is communicated nevertheless. This is a big step toward the liquidation of bolshevism; despite its small size, Hungary is a disturbing country in Europe, and her pacification, even though somewhat forced, will not harm the peace of Europe and will compel focusing attention on the sole hotbed of worldwide upheaval—the RSFSR. The news summary was rather satisfying. A magnificent stroll yesterday about the environs of the Posad, which impress me more all the time with their beauty. We wandered for seven hours and covered nearly eighteen versts. That is the best distraction from painful reality.

5 [August]. One more calm day; excellent weather, a stroll with Nina, which showed that she has gotten some strength. Today an inspection of the monastery: we walked about the walls and crawled up into the attic and the choir loft of Assumption Cathedral under the guidance of P. N. Kapterev. Every opportunity to examine as much as possible should be taken advantage of; every such excursion is in essence a small journey; lacking the possibility of going far away, one should study what is near that there will be no time to see later on. No news came from Moscow.

6 [August]. The news summaries are of no consequence; one gets the impression that they want to paint over and stop talking about some-

---

[98] The Hungarian Soviet Republic was proclaimed on March 21, 1919, and existed for 133 days. The Communists were forced out of the government on August 1.

thing, and therefore are shouting loudly, trying to demonstrate something that never was. In the evening Lialia and Tania arrived unexpectedly; they reported that in Moscow all the talk is about the fall of Soviet Hungary. I agree that this is an event of great importance; it is characteristic that, as the bolsheviks themselves report, their Hungarian brethren will be judged for political and criminal offenses and for the most part the latter.

10 [August]. A break again owing to a trip to Moscow. The general impression is that the bolsheviks have been shaken by developments in Hungary. For ourselves, we can for the time being draw the conclusion that, having finished with Hungary, they will someday give [us] favorable attention; we only fail to realize that a great deal of time is needed for this. The Muscovite, fantasizing as always, goes further; the taking of Petersburg, Saratov, and Minsk are being chalked up, and as always it is impossible to tell where the fantasizing begins and where the lies and concealment of the bolsheviks end. Nevertheless, the conviction that all this must end sometime is apparently growing stronger. Predictions and plans based on "afterward" continue. I finished my essay on the Time of Troubles, which was written for the cooperative press with which we made a contract a few days ago. S. V. Bakhrushin is now looking at it to decide if it is suitable for the broad reading public. I took on that work only out of a desire to make the money that is needed to support myself and my family; if I had been able to choose, I would have worked exclusively on specialized works from which those who wish to could take the material they need. Meanwhile, it is necessary to earn kerenki. For that purpose I sold one hundred copies of my doctoral dissertation for 1,500 rubles to the so-called book center—that is, to the bolsheviks, who can at least paper rooms with it. Prices (I mention for reference purposes those at which we bought various supplies): a pud of flour, 1,600 rubles; cabbage, 20 rubles a pound; eggs, 150 rubles for ten; meat, 70 rubles. On Friday I was in the hospital church of Novoekaterininskaia Hospital for the requiem for Misha Ostrovskii. The church is in the garden inside the hospital property. I was struck by the phenomenal filth and antihygienic conditions of the hospital environs. The hand of the times is visible here, too—no one wants to do anything. Here as everywhere the Russian understands freedom in his own way—as freedom from any exertion or obligation. The same Friday, in chasing after money in order to buy a little stove for the winter, and to get to the aforementioned mass, I had to go on foot to (1) Maroseika,[99] (2) Maiden Field, (3) Donskaia, and (4)

[99] One of the oldest streets in Moscow, northwest of the Kremlin, now known as Bogdan Khmel'nitskii Street.

Strastnoi Boulevard. Such is the fate of the Muscovite who has no automobile at his disposal. The little stove[100] *was bought for 250 rubles* for the
purpose of heating in the winter. I am writing down these petty details
because they will probably be of some interest one day.

12 August. Strolls in the woods for mushrooms two days in a row; one
lasted four hours, the other seven. I was once again impressed by how
beautiful the environs of the Posad are; such an expanse, such a wealth
of forest, such space for human activity, such considerable vestiges of the
primeval forest in which Sergius once took refuge. Nothing is so invigorating as nature; you go off into the forest and you forget about the bolsheviks. Today's news summary was very lamentable for the bolsheviks.
Of course, the reality is perhaps even worse, but the summary is the minimum—it can't be better than that for them. That is why I attribute
significance to it, if only in a relative way. Minsk and many important
points in the south have been taken.

13 [August]. Rain all day. I went to see off Lena Reiman and saw a long-
distance train at the station—it was packed tight with "them." In the
evening I listened to Tikhomirov's memoirs, which were interesting as
usual; the rest of the time I sat and worked. A conversation with A. A.
Tikhomirov, who told me why he *hated Kliuchevskii* and considered him
a *scoundrel (sic!)*. In January 1904, when Tikhomirov was rector, Inspector Fominskii (a great fool—that is my opinion) informed him that there
was going to be a gathering at Kliuchevskii's lecture where the Japano-
philes were to have a fight with the Japanophobes. Tikhomirov wrote
Kliuchevskii a letter, asking him not to lecture that Saturday and to reply
to his letter. Kliuchevskii did not reply. On Saturday, Tikhomirov asked
V. O. to come see him before the lecture. Kliuchevskii arrived [at the
university] and sent word to Tikhomirov, asking whether he *ordered* him
to appear at his apartment, or ordered him to wait for him in the rector's
office. When Tikhomirov arrived at the rector's office and explained to
Kliuchevskii what was going on, and reproached him for not replying,
Kliuchevskii said that he could not reply to him because he was busy, and
that he *would not lecture* only by order of the rector. Tikhomirov refused
to give such an order, but to spite Kliuchevskii he sent the inspector to
accompany him to the lecture hall. The behavior of both here is characteristic and very typical of the one and of the other.

[100] *Pechurka*, a little brazier about the size of a shoebox in which wood and paper scraps
could be burned for heat and cooking, was a basic necessity in Moscow during the Civil
War.

17 [August]. Running about in Moscow, I am not even going to try to record my impressions for Thursday through Saturday, but am postponing that duty until Sunday. In the course of those days the pressure on the bolsheviks has broadened and intensified. According to the latest news—from their newspapers, that is—according to the minimum that is to be used as a point of departure, Sumy has been taken and Borisov has probably been taken; the red army has retreated beyond Mozyr', that is, almost to Gomel'; in the south they indicated battles at Oboian' and again admit the loss of Borisoglebsk. Their articles and appeals are either malignant or monotonous. They tell of some new delegation that has supposedly appeared and is meeting in the Kremlin, and also of some supposedly new ultimatum submitted to the bolsheviks. I have little faith in these stories. If it is a German delegation, it is at best a traveling-salesman affair, as was the first one that was here in the spring; I can't imagine there being another one here except a German one. Whatever ultimatums they may put to the bolsheviks, they cannot leave because they have nowhere to go. It remains therefore to await the results of the assault. There has been a gay mood among the Muscovites these days, despite anticipation of a winter without firewood, and despite the constant requisitions of apartments, now become even more frequent because everybody from everywhere is being evacuated to Moscow. The searches have stopped; they are saying that in the last days of the epidemic of searches, warrants for them were being sold for 150 rubles on Sukharevka—that resembles the truth. Things are calm for the time being in university circles; they are waiting for an appeal from the professors (in the name of equality!) and the merging of the universities into one, as was done today in Petersburg, where everything has been divided among a medical academy, an academy of mechanical or applied sciences, and, finally, the university with two faculties—social sciences and physico-mathematical. It would be interesting to know what has become of the faculty of eastern languages.[101] What barbarous stupidity to hack everything up according to completely new and arbitrary principles. But why talk of their stupidity? Their ways are inscrutable. Today I ran around the market all morning, where I spent 800 rubles without noticing it; you are struck by the enormous number of Muscovites you meet there. The most unexpected meetings; everyone is trying to get to Troitskii bazaar, which in the last few Sundays has assumed enormous proportions. I have just chatted with V. S. Miroliubov, the publisher of the

---

[101] The faculty of eastern languages, which was moved to Petersburg University from Kazan' in 1854, was the only such faculty in the Russian university system. After undergoing several organizational permutations in the 1920s, the faculty was restored in 1944 and exists to this day. In Moscow, eastern languages were taught in a separate institution, the Lazarev Institute (founded in 1872).

Magazine for Everyone.[102] He met Lenin and co. living abroad in 1908–1913, and he told me of Lenin's persistence and lack of principle and of how few honest men there were among them. To tell the truth, there was little honesty under the old regime, which was entirely immersed in dishonesty; but this order, which is itself built on lies and deceit, is even more suitable for all sorts of villains and scoundrels. Everything that was false and dishonest under the tsars has now flourished, and everything honorable has been rejected, abased, and trampled by them.

18 [August]. I have heard several not uninteresting stories. The bolsheviks are admitting three of their "difficulties": (1) somewhere beyond the Dnepr, at Ekaterinoslav or further, where an entire army of theirs has been surrounded; (2) at Vorozhba,[103] where something similar has happened; and (3) near Borisoglebsk. At the same time, they were preparing to go over to the offensive themselves on the 15th. Thus, their cards are mixed.

19 [August]. This year the bolsheviks have for some reason decided to celebrate the Transfiguration, whereas last year they considered it a workday. Yesterday evening there was a big five-hour outing for mushrooms, and a great many were brought home; that works wonders for the nerves and makes you forget about reality. As this is Monday, we sit without news.

20 [August]. It may be that we are now experiencing a critical moment of the bolshevik regime. The pressure is mounting—they are moving on Gomel', Orsha, Dno, Kiev, and Kursk.[104] Oboian' and Gadiach have been taken in the south, but there has been a breakthrough in the direction of Tambov and Kozlov (that is, officially). But the bolsheviks had themselves been preparing to take the offensive everywhere; they say this is their all-or-nothing gamble. Today they write that they are advancing on Novyi Oskol, on Biriuch, and along the Voronezh-Rostov line. Now the question is, whose offensive will prevail and whose will be the stronger? The future depends on that.

V. I. Ger'e has died; I learned that from a student who has arrived from Moscow. He passed away, it seems, on Sunday. That was to be expected, because his moral and physical strength had been declining

[102] *Zhurnal dlia vsekh* (1896–1906) was an unusually successful magazine featuring articles on popular science and stories and attracting many of the leading writers of the day, generally those of "progressive" reputation. It was closed by the government for printing articles about the strike movement in the autumn of 1906.

[103] An important railway junction on the northwestern border of Khar'kov province.

[104] Got'e refers to movements of the White armies.

since spring. With him a great pillar of Moscow University has disappeared; the life of the historico-philological faculty has been closely connected with him for the entire second half of the nineteenth century. The university, women's education (including the Higher Women's Courses—founded twice by him), and the city of Moscow owe a great deal to him. He was the last epigone of the Westernizer circle, and he liked to emphasize that. But future generations will repay his services and appreciate him better than his contemporaries. His abruptness, his coldness, and an appearance like the blade of a knife (*lame de couteau*, as my late father called him) repelled people and caused them to fear him. In addition, he lacked tact, which frequently caused him unnecessary unpleasantness and conflicts. For us, students of the 1890s, he was still a terror, although less of one than for our predecessors; myself, I feared him for a long time after university, although he always treated me with great kindness. The evolution of his political views is interesting: he had the reputation in the '80s and '90s of being a liberal; later on he became a convinced Octobrist. For that he was censured by the Russian intelligenty from the Kadets leftward, and for the ignorant youth after 1905 he became almost a black reactionary. However, precisely that evolution was the only normal one; he remained a moderate liberal, but in the process of Russian society's mad leap into the abyss that swallowed it, those who did not participate in this *course à la mort* appeared to be backward. Perhaps his sobriety reflected his non-Russian origin. In recent years, it seems, he disdained contemporary Russians of prominence. At least I retain such an impression from chats with him last winter. And that, perhaps, reflected his genuine Westernism: he was a liberal of the Western type, which did not take hold in Russia and is incomprehensible to the Russians, with their reckless urge for the absolute. That feature, together with certain angularities of character, prevented him from occupying that place in Russian society, poor in people, to which he was fully entitled. May you rest in peace, one of my last teachers, and thanks for what you taught me!

24 [August]. Ger'e was buried on the day I went to Moscow. According to friends who were there—Iakovlev, Egorov, Bakhrushin—and later according to V. I.'s daughters, the funeral was very heartwarming; there was even a prayer service in front of the university. Yet the official side, which in normal conditions would undoubtedly have been very noticeable, was almost absent. On Friday I visited his daughters, and that night there was a search at their place, and poor E. V. was taken for the second time to Cheka headquarters; incidentally, they took V. I.'s correspondence for 1896 and 1897, two group photographs of the '80s, and a guide to the Crimea. It is hard to understand what the purpose of the idiots who searched the house was; but it is a characteristic phenomenon of the present moment. Ger'e was buried in Piatnitskoe Cemetery, in the necropolis of the Westernizers, where he lay down as their last epigone.

The general situation has taken shape as follows over these last few days: the centripetal movement on Kiev has developed unhindered; the danger, however, consists in the fact that three [forces] are aiming for Kiev at the same time, the Poles, Petliura, and Denikin. I very much fear that their coming together will lead not to a coalition, but to mutual conflict. The offensive in the west is not going badly, either; the bolsheviks are announcing that the Poles are approaching Bobruisk and are shelling Borisov. A very complex game is being conducted in the south; the breakthrough to Tambov was successful; Kursk, apparently, is almost under fire; but the bolsheviks have mounted a counterattack to the south of Voronezh and in the direction of Kamyshin. Rumors were circulating in Moscow yesterday about the taking of Kamyshin and Valuiki by the bolsheviks. Thus mutual pressure is being exerted in the south and the question is who will overcome whom. They say the bolsheviks regard their movement as an all-or-nothing gamble. There is a great deal of talk about some sort of delegation that is supposedly in Moscow either for negotiations or under arrest. There is no end to discussions about the surrender of power, about the departure of the bolsheviks, about someone's extradition—but for all that, it is impossible to figure out what reality is concealed behind these rumors. In academic circles—the usual abomination: the merger of all faculties and universities into one institution. Only idiots could do such a thing, but again there is no reason to be surprised at anything here. For that matter, everyone looks on all this with indifference, since there prevails a general certitude that it will all end soon. They are even setting dates. I am not setting any, but something will change sooner or later—I am more convinced of that than ever. The bolsheviks are presently at war with the whole world, and inside [the country] everything creeps along as before.

25 [August]. They are boasting that they have taken Kamyshin and Valuiki. Private information, quite reliable by the way, reports that in Tambov everything has been burned that could be set on fire, that in Kozlov the same thing is happening, and that the Cossacks are fanning out in three directions—Morshansk, Dankov, and Elets—to destroy or cut in two the railroads that serve as the base for the bolshevik southern front, thus dooming their southern offensive to failure. They are silent about the rest today. Whether because some kind of critical point is approaching, or for some other reason, I have been gloomy all day. The weather

is revolting: a genuine Moscow August. How I would like to go south, to the sun and warmth. To leave Moscow—that, it seems, is the most passionate dream of my life. To leave, so as to see no more these horrible gorillas—savage, self-satisfied, and stupid.

26 [August]. Monday. There is no news. There is a private rumor that a wire has been received here, in the Posad, about an ultimatum (which in number?), and to forestall the spreading of this rumor the radio-telegraphers have been arrested. I. A. Golubtsov, who arrived from Alatyr',[105] reports that there are several tens of thousands of *barefooted* red army men begging alms and pillaging in the vicinity. An outing for mushrooms to take one's mind off gloomy thoughts; we walked for seven and a half hours. I brought back a fair amount of fungus food.

28 [August]. The situation, in my opinion, is getting more and more complex. The battles in Kursk province continue; they are on the march at Kursk, but on the other hand the reds are boasting that they have taken Volchansk at eighty versts from Khar'kov. They say that the commander in that place is General V. I. Selivachev,[106] who was released from prison on the condition that he command an army. I met him in the winter when he was in charge of the Lefortovo archive, and he seemed to me to be an honorable man. Is utter selfishness so great among the Russian generals that they really will fight honorably for the bolsheviks? By the way, all reports concur that Mamontov is working miracles in the Kozlov-Riazhsk-Dankov corridor, and is extending from there toward Riazan', Morshansk, and Penza on the one side, Tula on the other, and Elets on yet another. If they wreck and cut all the lines, they say that the southern offensive might end in disaster.[107] Kiev has undoubtedly been taken; somebody is sneaking up on Polotsk, but in return the reds have again taken Pskov; they say that the Russian white guard generals—Rodzianko, Liven, and Balakhovich—have quarreled among themselves

[105] A town in northwestern Simbirsk province.

[106] Lieutenant General Vladimir Ivanovich Selivachev (1868–1919), a graduate of the General Staff Academy who fought in the World War, came over to the Red Army in December 1918. In August and September 1919, he was commander of the southern front. He died of typhus on September 17.

[107] Lieutenant General Konstantin Konstantinovich Mamontov (1869–1920) was a Cossack veteran of the World War. In August and September 1919, he led a celebrated forty-day cavalry raid behind Red Army lines on the southern front, destroying rail lines and bridges and seizing supply depots. Mamontov's forces were finally repelled by the Red Army, which had formed a special "internal front," and the Red Army's offensive was resumed in mid-August. Mamontov died of typhus in February 1920.

there.[108] I know those spirited steeds![109] There are rumors that Finland is playing very dirty tricks on us, and even wanted to expel within twenty-four hours all Russians located there. According to the same rumors, Iudenich is a poor diplomat. All this is very disturbing because one senses that we are on the verge of a possible turning point, which, however, might not come this time. Another source of upset is Nina's health; a new recurrence of the disease. Those are the reasons why I have been in a very gloomy mood for two days. I feel that liberation must come before the cold weather sets in, otherwise we will not survive the new winter in conditions even more terrible than last winter. The establishment of an apartment here in the Posad is not working out, and yet it is necessary to keep a refuge here; here, after all, it will be easier to keep oneself warm and fed.

31 [August]. Without any doubt, the situation is becoming more tense daily. The bolsheviks, through the mouths of Nakhamkis and others, would have us believe that an offensive of all the imperialists in the world will begin in a few days; this is already not twelve, but fourteen tribes.[110] They are not writing the truth about matters on the southern front. However, they did talk yesterday about how they have avoided the danger of being surrounded at Valuiki and Kupiansk, and about the raid of Mamontov, who is conducting a sweeping operation. Trains to the south go no farther than Riazan' and Tula, and therefore the transport of foodstuffs to Moscow has completely stopped. Prices are rising madly; there is almost no distribution of bread; bread has reached 80 rubles at the Sukharevka market, and flour is on sale for 2,800 rubles. Very numerous arrests occurred last night: Kotliarevskii, Alferov, D. D. Pletnev, our Iureva, Kishkin; they wanted to arrest I. A. Il'in, but he hid out; and, they say, Samarin, probably D. N. Shipov, S. A. Pervushin, D. K. Budinov, and

[108] General Aleksandr Pavlovich Rodzianko (b. 1879) was a former guards officer and brigade commander on the northwestern front. He was one of Iudenich's commanders in the Northwestern Army. Prince Anatolii Pavlovich Liven (Lieven, 1872–1937), a native of Riga, had been a cavalry guards officer before the Revolution who took up arms against the Bolsheviks in Latvia after October 1917. He later joined forces with Iudenich's Northwestern Army, in which he was a division commander (the 5th Liven Division). Major General Stanislav Nikodimovich Bulak-Balakhovich (Bei-Bulak-Balakhovich) (1883–1940) was another of Iudenich's commanders, a defector from the Red Army. Following Iudenich's defeat, he eventually joined the Polish army and fought against the Bolsheviks in the Soviet-Polish War in 1920.

[109] "Uznaiu konei retivykh!" The source is probably Pushkin again; namely, his 1835 translation of a fragment of the Greek poet Anacreon, which begins "Uznaiu konei retivykh / Po ikh vyzhzhennym tavram" ("You can tell spirited horses by their brands"). *Pushkin. Polnoe sobranie sochinenii* (Academy edition), vol. 3, pt. 1, p. 373.

[110] The "twelve tribes" (*dvanadesiat' iazykov*) was a standard Russian literary allusion to Napoleon's multinational army that invaded Russia in 1812.

even Iu. I. Bazanov. The searchers were polite everywhere. If you compare these names, it is clear that this is an affair of the Kadets, "prominent" persons, and former rich people. But why was D. K. Budinov included, why did they arrest such female Kadets as the Kareevs, mother and daughter, or Natalia Andreevna Vinkel'man?[111] They look on all this as the taking of hostages; but it must be recognized that even from this point of view their enterprises can't stand up to criticism. Their tense situation does not prevent them from continuing their notorious reforms; the affair of the merging of all the faculties into one pile is apparently acquiring the character of some kind of general garbage heap, in which all higher education in Moscow will be destroyed. The one hope is that all this is [happening] before the end.

SEPTEMBER

1 [September]. Last fall we historians guessed that the bolsheviks would hold out until Assumption; but here it has passed, and they are still sitting there, although their thrones are apparently shaking. Yesterday's news summary indicates fighting on the Oskol line, that is, forty-five to fifty versts farther east than the day before. Thus the breakthrough to Khar'kov is apparently not succeeding. The arrests carried out on Friday surpass all plausibility: they picked up [people] in all circles. Apparently the arrested number in the hundreds: they took Kadets, other party people, they snagged the Religious-Philosophical Society, theosophists, lawyers—you can't tell what guided those who were doing the arresting, that is the Cheka. The general impression remains that they are taking hostages. I have been and still am thinking about myself— since it is impossible to discern the motives, it would be very easy to find oneself among the victims. Having conferred with Nina, I have decided

---

[111] The Kotliarevskii in question was S. A. Kotliarevskii. Aleksandr Danilovich Alferov was a former Moscow duma member and Kadet, and a teacher in a girls' school. Dmitrii Dmitrievich Pletnev (1872–1953) was a prominent doctor (the same Dr. Pletnev who was one of the three physicians indicted in the great purge trial of 1938; he was sentenced to twenty-five years and died in a Vorkuta camp). "Our Iureva" was E. V. Iur'eva, and "Kishkin" was N. M. Kishkin. Aleksandr Dmitrievich Samarin (1868–1932) was a former Moscow marshal of nobility, member of the State Council, and head of the Russian Red Cross during the war. He had been Procurator of the Holy Synod for a few months in 1915. Sergei Aleksandrovich Pervushin (b. 1888) was an economist and professor at Moscow University. Dmitrii Timofeevich Budinov (b. 1875) was a radiologist. "Bazanov" was Iu. I. Bazanov. "The Kareevs" were the wife and daughter of the historian and sociologist Nikolai Ivanovich Kareev (1850–1931), who had been a Kadet deputy to the first duma. Natalia Andreevna Vinkel'man was headmistress of the Sixth City Needlework School.

to be careful and on my next trip to Moscow try not to spend the night at home—at least I will be gaining some time. I very much want to avoid getting arrested for two reasons: it is quite possible that their convulsions are at hand, that is one thing; another is that they will be very vicious and one could perish for nothing.

I am reading *Vie et correspondance de Taine*. Here is what he writes about the struggle of parties after December 2, 1851: "Entre les coquins d'en haut et les coquins d'en bas, les gens honnêtes qui pensent vont se trouver écrasés."[112] That was written on December 11, 1851; how applicable that is to bolshevisia![113] Wonderful autumn weather. A long walk in the woods in the company of P. N. Kapterev and A. I. Ognev.[114] Nina is better, thank God.

2 [September]. A day without news. We spent it walking to the hamlet of Sharapovo, about ten versts away. We were received by local peasant-"craftsmen,"[115] who formerly worked in the silk factory in Sergievo; now all that awaits a better future. They regaled us (we were nine people) with a dozen eggs, tea, cream, three or four pounds of bread, and a gallon of milk; by contemporary pricing that amounts to nearly 500 rubles, and they took nothing for all this. That permits two conclusions: (1) the visit of the "masters" is still an object of vanity for the peasants, and (2) they are far richer than we are. The walk was charming. I think that if I have to emigrate I will miss most of all the fine summer and autumn days in the Russian countryside, from which Russian intelligentsia propaganda has expelled civilized people! Looking at the sea of forest spreading out from the local foothills, I thought: there is the country that is perishing from lack of fuel! A walk like this and communion with nature is an exercise in moral hygiene. Thanks to it, you forget about Sovdepiia, if only for a few hours.

7 [September]. I spent four days in Moscow, where the main subject of conversation and concern continues to be the arrests numbering in the hundreds and thousands. To the extent it is possible to understand their causes, they are to be explained as follows. According to rumors originating with Riazanov and D. I. Ul'ianov,[116] the bolsheviks stumbled onto

[112] "Honest thinking people are going to find themselves crushed between the crooks on high and the crooks below" ("Taine à Prévost-Paradol, Nevers, 11 Decembre 1851"). H. Taine. *Sa vie et sa correspondance. Correspondance de jeunesse, 1847–1853*, 4th ed. (Paris, 1905), p. 170.

[113] *Bol'sheviziia.*

[114] Apparently the son of I. F. Ognev, a professor at the Theological Academy.

[115] *Masterki*, a diminutive or familiar form of *master*, "craftsman."

[116] Lenin's brother, Dmitrii Il'ich Ul'ianov (1874–1943), who was at this time head of a party organization in the Crimea.

the threads of some kind of conspiracy, or onto lines of communication with nonsovdep Russia. A variant of the rumors has it that somewhere in Moscow they found a list of a Kadet government to be formed in the event of Mamontov's coming; its members were to be Avinov, Leont'ev, Kotliarevskii, and (supposedly) Chaplygin. They said this list was found either at N. N. Shchepkin's or in the possession of yet other Kadets as well.[117] If this isn't simple provocation, is it possible to imagine a greater stupidity? How in the Kadet manner it all is—in the first place, all [the posts] go to them, who have let everything slip; secondly, everything is naively put down in writing. Ex ungue leonem? I know those spirited steeds. Thanks to that, the bolsheviks decided to make a large catch with a big net, and, following the Kadet lists, they are catching in that net [people associated with] the party from nearly the beginning of its existence. The net is also catching the popular-socialist fools, the renegade spawn of the Kadets. One can see how the arrests and ambushes took place from the fact that Kizevetter and his wife went a week ago to Petrushevskii's, and just after their arrival (at 6 P.M.—they were probably followed) the Cheka suddenly appeared there and arrested both guests and host. That evening Petrushevskii was to have had [other] guests. S. B. Veselovskii came, with sheet music to play on the piano and with foreign currency in his pocket—and they grabbed him as well. Later came R. P. Bogoslovskaia, who also fell into the trap; and finally, at 2 A.M., M. M. Bogoslovskii appeared to find out what had happened to his wife, and was caught in the ambush. Ambushes like these were set up in the houses of very many of those who were arrested. Bogoslovskii and Petrushevskii, who did not participate in politics (and M.M. is not even a Kadet), will be released in a few days. But more important personages, especially Kadets, will have a great deal more trouble extricating themselves. The situation is such that no one is exempt from the possibility of sitting in Butyrki or in one of the innumerable houses of detention in Moscow

[117] Got'e is describing the National Center, a clandestine organization of anti-German, anti-Bolshevik liberals, mostly Kadets, that was set up in Moscow in the spring of 1918. It had branches in a number of other cities on both sides of the Civil War front. The Moscow organization was liquidated by arrests and numerous executions during August and September 1919.

Nikolai Nikolaevich Avinov (d. 1937) was a former member of the Moscow City Administration (Gorodskaia uprava) and assistant minister of internal affairs in the first Provisional Government. He taught finance at the Moscow Commercial Institute and was head of a fuel cooperative after the October revolution. He was shot by the NKVD in November 1937. S. M. Leont'ev was a founding member of the Moscow group and a Kadet from Rostov. Of the others mentioned, Nikolai Nikolaevich Shchepkin (1854–1919) was a prominent Moscow Kadet and former duma deputy who served as chairman of the National Center. He was one of those executed by order of the Cheka following his arrest.

(monasteries, detached houses, police stations, and so on). And I admit that I have never felt the Damoclean sword of the bolshevik jail so close over me, despite my perennial estrangement from politics. Whatever happens later, I am more than ever convinced and understand how profoundly right I was in staying out of Russian political life, where besides intrigues and cliquishness there was—and, alas, will be—nothing. All the parties are only masks for ambitious men and traps for fools; and ruling parties are in addition an instrument for scoundrels.

The situation at the fronts for the week has taken shape favorably for the antibolsheviks; one senses the possibility of liberation near at hand; but, as Veniamin Mikhailovich Khvostov said to me yesterday, "There may still be hitches." Aside from that, the fanatical bolsheviks like the Ul'ianovs will hold on to the last minute and make the two-fingered sign of the cross even as the house they are in bursts into flames on all sides. In their psychology there is much in common with the psychology of the schismatic self-incendiaries.[118]

Yesterday there was a meeting of all the packed-together humanities faculties; it was stupid and sad. They have successfully committed hara-kiri, which will be completed today in a meeting in the commissariat.

Today is the day of soviet propaganda: the comrades promise to ring all the bells in Moscow and make all the noise they can. One of the numbers in the divertissement is "the burial of the old, bourgeois, obsolete Marseillaise." For that reason, probably, the newspapers are completely empty today.

8 [September]. A traditional family day of celebration. A bicycle jaunt with S. N. Kapterev. Wonderful spots, unknown to anyone; vacation houses, vacation settlements could arise here if this were a land of people and not the land of gorillas. The situation at home is this: Nina needs a sanatorium; there are no sanitoriums, for they have all been seized or their diet is unsuitable for diabetes. But she needs constant and attentive treatment. That is how matters stand in simian Bolshevisia.

9 [September]. The news summary is indifferent. Gomel' is in a state of siege. Some stupid wires of some sort of Estonians who want to enter peace negotiations with the bolsheviks. Either that is a false rumor or, in the worst case, a sign that dissensions on the white northwestern front continue and are getting worse. On the other hand, some news—from the article of Nakhamkis about the deals in Riga—on how to act against

[118] Got'e draws a parallel between the Bolsheviks and the Old Believers, the schismatics who renounced the official church following its adoption of various reforms in the seventeenth century. Persecuted by the state, many groups of Old Believers committed mass suicide rather than fall into the hands of the "Antichrist."

the bolsheviks. In Moscow it is forbidden to go out after 11 P.M. I am sitting at home all day and nothing cheers me up.

10 [September]. In anticipation of news. The newspaper is not adequate. There is too much deliberate and shameless lying in it. The rumors, which do in part turn out to be true, serve as a corrective to the verbal torrent of the triumphant Russian nihilists. I am becoming ever more convinced that if we live to see a better time, I should immediately take my family away and sell everything except the bare necessities, for the replacement of the bolsheviks will only be a new page in the sad history of the so-called Russian revolution. I should not repeat mistakes and remain here when it will be possible to leave. Anarchy, upheaval, and coups await us in the future, and probably not in small quantity.

12 [September]. I am distracting myself by reading *Vie et correspondance de Taine*. Yesterday I read about 1870 and 1871. I am extracting several separate sentences here; they are easily applicable to our present situation and to my thoughts before the war, during the war, and in the revolution. "On souhaite la paix, le commerce, le travail, le bien-être pour soi et pour le moment, et l'on résiste de plus en plus énergiquement aux raisonnements qui, dans la tête d'un souverain, feraient tuer cent milles hommes pour le bénéfice des générations futures et pour le maintien d'une prééminence" (II, 336). "Le 12 (juillet 1870) j'ai écrit à une personne influente (? Princesse Mathilde), pour lui dire que nous allions avoir contre nous les passions de 1813, que la *guerre était imprudente*; presque tous les hommes cultivés pensaient comme moi" (III, 16). "Pour moi le sentiment des maux publics est si vif que je ne sens plus véritablement le beau" (III, 27). "Il est bien probable qu'à mon retour, je ferai à Paris des articles politiques de fond, malgré ma répugnance et mon insuffisance; il faut maintenant que tout le monde mette la main a l'oeuvre; mais la parole est si peu de choses contre les institutions et le caractère national! Enfin je ferai ce que je pourrai, malheureusement avec peu d'espoir; tu sais ce que je pense de notre pays et cela depuis des années" (III, 480; 7 fevrier 1871). "(21 mars:) La bêtise inouie de la garde nationale et la trahison de l'armée nous mettent aux mains des gens du ruisseau" (III, 68–69).

"Mon chagrin est si profond et mes prévisions sont si tristes que j'aime mieux ne pas en parler" (26 mars, III, 74). "D'après mes entretiens avec plusieurs personnes bien informées et dont l'une revient de Londres, les menées et l'argent bonapartistes sont pour beaucoup là-dedans" (28 mars, III, 76–77). "L'argent va manquer à la Commune; on parlait hier de menaces contre la Banque; il y aura des violences contre les grands établissements de crédit, contre les financiers, les riches; la Commune les forcera à signer des traités, on emmenera plusieurs comme otages; elle va se trouver acculée à des crimes" (30 mars, III, 81). Comme banquier, magistrat etc., ils sont menacés; on parle de quinze cents personnes arrêtées à Paris comme suspectes" (1 avril, III, 85). "Conversation aujourd'hui avec un professeur de science et un vieux peintre. Ils sont tous les deux favorables ou presque favorables aux insurgés. Cela me confond toujours; on ne comprend pas qu'un homme intelligent ait une si faible notion du droit et de la justice" (8 avril, III, 99). "Il y aura une terrible bataille dans Paris; les insurgés ont des chefs très résolus" (17 avril, III, 102). "Paris—c'est un pandémonium; la mère d'une dame qui est ici (Tours), sortant de chez elle ces jours-ci en robe très simple, a été apostrophée dans la rue par une mégère: 'A bas les aristocrates en toilette; on vous mettra bientôt à bas'" (30 avril, III, 104). "Je mange et dors bien, mais ma barbe a grisonné" (5 mai, III, 107). "Deux principes inconnus en France, admis universellement et appliqués fidèlement dans tous les pays libres: (1)quand la majorité a prononcé, se soumettre franchement, sérieusement, ne pas garder l'arriere-pensée de la violenter par un coup d'Etat; (2) permettre à la minorité de dire et imprimer tout ce qui lui convient" (21 mai, III, 121). "J'apprends à l'instant les horreurs de Paris ... les misérables! Ce sont des loups enragés" (25 mai, III, 128).[119]

[119] "One desires peace, commerce, work, and well-being for oneself and for the moment, and one resists ever more energetically the reasoning that, in the head of a sovereign, would have a hundred thousand men killed for the benefit of future generations and for maintaining a preeminent position. ... On the 12th (of July 1870) I had written to an influential person (Princess Mathilde?), to tell her that we are going to have the passions of 1813 ranged against us, that *the war was imprudent*; almost all cultivated men think as I do. ... For me the feeling of public ills is so acute that I no longer genuinely sense the beautiful. ... It is quite possible that upon my return I will write some genuinely political articles, despite my repugnance and inadequacy; everyone must contribute to the task now; but the word is so little against institutions and the national character! Anyhow, I will do what I can, unfortunately with little hope; you know what I think of our country, and have for years. ... (21 March:) The deplorable stupidity of the national guard and the betrayal of the army put us in the hands of men of the gutter.

My chagrin is so profound and my expectations are so somber that I would prefer not to speak of them. According to my discussions with numerous well-informed persons, one of whom is returned from London, the schemes and money of the Bonapartists have a lot to do with it. The Commune is going to lack money; there was talk yesterday of threats against the Bank; there will be violence against the big credit establishments, the financiers, and the rich; the Commune will force them to sign agreements, many will be taken as hostages; it is going to find itself forced into crimes. ... As banker, magistrate, etc., they are being threatened; one speaks of the fifteen hundred persons arrested in Paris as suspects. ... A conversation today with a professor of science and an old painter. Both are sympathetic or almost sympathetic to the insurgents. That always amazes me: one can't understand how an intelligent man can have so feeble a notion of law and justice. There will be a terrible battle in Paris; the insurgents have very resolute leaders. ... Paris is a pandemonium; the mother of a lady who is here (Tours), who set forth from her place the other day in a very simple dress, was cursed in the street by a shrew: 'Down with the dressed-up aristocrats; you will soon be brought down.' ... I eat and sleep well,

This is an analysis in dicta of the Russian so-called revolution, and repetition of my own thoughts.

I went with Volodia to Pushkino[120] for a pud of flour that the Reimans exchanged for our revolver, which had been lying for a year in the hollow of a tree. Incidentally, we stopped by to see the Armand old folks. God, what horror in Pushkino! In the garden they are cutting down the trees for firewood and calves are grazing in the flower beds. The old folks are immobilized in anticipation of death, which has already overtaken half of them. The lanes are uncared for, the gate in the park stands wide open. I left with a heavy feeling. The general news, official and unofficial, differs as never before: they write about a forward movement near Konotop and Bakhmach. Rumors coming from reliable sources speak of a defeat near Oskoly and Kastornoe, near Tsaritsyn, and near Gomel'. The negotiations with the Estonian mensheviks have turned out to be a worthless scrap of paper, as should have been expected.

13 [September]. Several more dicta from Taine: "le suffrage universel, dans un pays apathique tend toujours à mettre le pouvoir aux mains des bavards déclassés (III, 172). L'éssentiel est que les classes éclairées et riches conduisent les ignorants et ceux que vivent au jour le jour (III, 173)."[121]

While taking a walk I saw some Russian intelligenty sawing wood; at the risk of making a vulgar joke, I will say that an intelligentsia that has by its own efforts brought things to the point where it has to saw wood itself fully deserves it; it is good for nothing else. Many conversations about the movement of the Germans toward Bologoe, which is being proclaimed in the bolshevik newspapers: for me this is still unclear.[122] I learned that Bogoslovskii, Petrushevskii, and Bakhrushin have been released. The commissariat, that is, comrade Pokrovskii, has cut our lectures by a third, because their credits have been cut by a third; a fine method for appraising scholarly teaching in the higher school.

---

but my beard has turned gray. . . . Two principles unknown in France, but universally recognized and applied in all other free countries: (1) when the majority has spoken, submit honestly, seriously, without entertaining the thought of doing violence to it by a *coup d'état*; (2) allow the minority to speak and print everything it pleases. . . . I have just learned of the horrors of Paris . . . the poor wretches! They are mad wolves. . . ." Cited from Volumes 2 and 3 of Taine's correspondence (see n. 112 above). The parenthetical remarks and italicizations are Got'e's.

[120] A town thirty-six kilometers northeast of Moscow on the Iaroslavl' line.

[121] "Universal suffrage in an apathetic country tends always to put power in the hands of déclassé babblers. . . . The essential thing is that the enlightened and rich classes lead the ignorant and those who live from day to day. . . ."

[122] On September 12, *Izvestiia* carried a brief report "from Finnish newspapers" to the effect that the troops of General von der Holz in Latvia were planning an offensive into the interior of Russia aimed at the Bologoe station (the junction of the Pskov and Petrograd lines). Von der Holz and his troops were described as a band of renegades who had cut their ties with Germany.

14 [September]. The newspaper: the comrades admit that they have been beaten back from Tsaritsyn; they also admit the taking of Elets and Staryi and Novyi Oskol, which indicates that the entire Elets-Valuiki line is in the hands of Denikin. This can have very great consequences. They are arresting notary publics, including Uncle Kostia. All morning today I lugged various things: two puds of cabbage. There was a big exchange: for various old possessions we received a sack of potatoes, a measure of horseradish, some mushrooms, milk, and the like. An excellently spent *dimanche d'un bourgeois.*

15 [September]. A day without news, as usual. However, on Sunday, yesterday, the comrades reported that they have been knocked out of Bakhmach. It turns out that a month after the offensive began on August 15, the successes of the comrades amount only to the taking of Kamyshin. A visit to the monastery library located over the refectory; also located there is the old archive, in which there is a great wealth of unused material on the monastery economy and landholding for the sixteenth and seventeenth centuries. The entire archive is in complete order, thanks to the work of the completely unknown monk-librarian, Father Aleksei. That is where I could work if only there was the possibility of pursuing my plans for a study of the sixteenth century. Tomorrow it's off to cursed Moscow again! I don't want to go!

I am copying out several more dicta from Taine, which fully correspond to my thoughts:

"Vous savez si j'aime la Révolution; pour qui la voit de près, c'est l'insurrection des mulets et des chevaux contre les hommes sous la conduite des 'singes qui ont des larynx des perroquets'; mais l'ancien régime n'est pas beau non plus . . ." (III, 266).

"Ma seule thèse intime est contre le pouvoir arbitraire et absolu, soit de la foule, soit d'un individu. Un être humain ou une collection d'êtres humains, qui est despote et ne subit pas le contrepoids d'autres pouvoirs, devient toujours malfaisant et fou"(III, 272–73).

"Le suffrage universel qui est un chancre toujours coulant" (IV, 45, 24 mars 1878).

"Je vous assure que les Girondins de la législative ne sont pas jolis à voir de près; l'orgueil doctrinaire et juvenile est le fond, et ils se permettent jusqu'au 10 août tout ce qu'on fera contre eux après le 10 août" (IV, 93; 28 Juin 1879).[123]

Isn't that our Kadets?

[123] "You know how I love the Revolution: for one who sees it up close, it is the insurrection of mules and horses against the humans under the direction of monkeys with the larynxes of parrots'; but the old regime is not beautiful, either. . . ."

"My only essential thesis is against arbitrary and absolute power, whether of the crowd or of an individual. A human being or a collection of human beings that is despotic and

15 [September]. Sitting in Sergiev Posad, I have thought up a general plan of my studies for the rest of my life. The plan is greater than the time that I have left to work. I want to write it down just in case.

1) Introduction to Russian history—a scholarly elaboration of the archaeological material for Eastern Europe before 862 (taking that date provisionally, of course). This has not been done.

2) Mutual relations between the Russians and the Balkan Peninsula and the Slavs before the conquest of the Balkans by the Turks and the formation of the Muscovite state. This is *terra incognita*.

3) An experiment in the comparative study of Slavic law—*Russkaia Pravda*, the Pskov charter, the law codes, the Wislica statute, the law code of Stefan Dušan, the *Vinodol Law*, the Poljica statute, etc. The Nieszawa statutes, etc.[124]

The third flows in part out of the second.

4) Here begins the main part of the projects: formation of the Muscovite state—in the form of essays on the history of the fifteenth and sixteenth centuries: *Ivan the Terrible; Formation of the nobility; The architectonics of the Muscovite state of the sixteenth century: conscious efforts of the Muscovite sovereigns in the creation of their state.* "The ideology of the sixteenth century: Josephites, ties with South Slavdom; theory of power, heresies." The Muscovite state in the accounts of foreigners; relations with Lithuania, Poland, and other states; the cultural contributions of the Italians. Moscow and the Crimea in the fifteenth and sixteenth centuries. The economic state of Muscovy, especially before the crisis of the 1560s (the archive of the Trinity Monastery). The main thing is to emphasize that the tsars created the nobility as an instrument obedient to them.

5) My essay on the Time of Troubles and my other works about the Troubles formulate my thoughts about this epoch.

6) The Moscow region—in essence it is the history of the nobility in the seventeenth century in its main features.

---

is not subject to the counterweight of other powers always becomes malevolent and mad. . . ."

"Universal suffrage is a constantly running sore. . . ."

"I assure you that the Girondins of the legislature are not pretty to look at up close; doctrinaire and juvenile pride lie underneath, and they permit themselves to do until August 10 all that will be done against them after August 10. . . ."

[124] *Russkaia Pravda* is the oldest known East Slavic (Russian) law code, dating from the eleventh century. The Pskov charter (*Pskovskaia sudnaia gramota*) is a collection of fourteenth- and fifteenth-century laws from the medieval Republic of Pskov, which partly incorporated the norms of the *Russkaia Pravda*. The Wislica statute was a major law code issued in 1347 by the Polish king Casimir the Great. The law code of the Serbian tsar Stefan Dušan was issued in 1349. The Vinodol law was issued in 1288; Vinodol was the historic name of a region on the Croatian coast of the Adriatic. The Poljica statute was a Dalmatian law code of the late fifteenth century. The Nieszawa statutes were privileges granted to the Polish nobility (*szlachta*) by Casimir IV in 1454.

7) The social-estate policy of Peter the Great. Begin with the idea of the 1680s; the nobility at the end of the seventeenth century, awakening to the political desires of the eighteenth century. Peter and the nobility: this is something completely unknown.

8) The history of regional administration, which took on enormous proportions—this is nothing other than the *everyday* history of the nobility from Peter to Catherine II, when they definitely conquered everything.

9) Pushkin, as the quintessence of noble culture. The best that it produced before the arrival of the moment when it began to doubt itself.

10) The fall of the Russian Empire, which I have already begun.

$$
\begin{array}{ll}
1 & / \\
2\text{-}3 & / \quad 3 \text{ cycles} \\
4\text{-}10 & /
\end{array}
$$

Of the biggest part, 5,6, and 8 are done and 10 has been sketched out.

It would take two lives to do all the rest; but all of it together would constitute a series of monographs in which all my views on the entirety of Russian history would be developed. In particular, the result would be an integrated cycle on the history of noble Russia, which arose in the fifteenth and sixteenth centuries and fell in the twentieth.[125]

20 [September]. Sergiev Posad after four days in Moscow. The frightened Moscow bourgeois and "bourgeois-oids"[126] are extraordinary fools. They still think that everything should change in the winking of an eye, and therefore they cry and weep if something in the bolshevik newspaper seems disagreeable. For example, on Wednesday of this week they wrote that the Estonians want to make peace with the bolsheviks, and in Moscow there was despair. As if something could change because some Balt

---

[125] Got'e uses the term *dvorianstvo, dvorianskoe* throughout this plan to signify Russia's version of the first estate. It is translated in the text consistently as "nobility," "noble," although the character of the "first estate" changed considerably over time—from a group of military servitors supported by land grants to a quasi-independent corporation or estate of privileged landowners (and, until 1861, serfowners). That change, and the overall process of Russian social and political evolution of which it was a crucial part, was in fact the subject of Got'e's inquiry. As he notes, he had already essentially completed items 5, 6, and 8. He later realized item 1 with his works on the history of material culture in Eastern Europe (*Ocherki po istorii material'noi kul'tury Vostochnoi Evropy do osnovaniia pervogo russkogo gosudarstva*, 1925) and the Iron Age in Eastern Europe (*Zheleznyi vek v Vostochnoi Evropy*, 1930). He made substantial contributions to several of the remaining items (a collection of English travel accounts about sixteenth-century Muscovy in his translation; a study of the political crisis following the assassination of Alexander II in 1881, etc.). A list of Got'e's published works was published in 1941: N. M. Asafova, comp., *Iu. V. Got'e* (*Materialy k bibliografii trudov uchenykh SSSR, Seriia istorii, v. 1*) (Moscow, 1941).

[126] *Burzhuidy.*

social-traitors—mensheviks, laborites[127] and suchlike trash—thought of kissing up to the soviet government. On Thursday the military communiqué was rather interesting; the main thing was that they have retreated everywhere; among other things, fighting is going on near the town of Tim—almost due east of Kursk. And so spirits are suddenly lifted, with just as little foundation as they had fallen the day before. On Friday we sat in session with comrade Volgin in a meeting of the history department and talked about the canceled courses. The new Magnitskii or Runich[128]—comrade Pokrovskii—did all the crossing-off either single-handedly or together with his famulus or Wagner, the same Volgin. One had to see with what self-satisfaction that scoundrel reported that such and such course had been canceled by mistake, that Pokrovskii's personal opinion need not be considered, and suchlike deliberate lies. I returned here by the night train; what a horror is the darkness on the railroads! The locomotive runs with one lit lantern, instead of three; at each station there is one light for the whole territory of the station; there is absolute darkness in the cars, so that someone could kill a man and you wouldn't notice. The bolsheviks want to clamp down on Sukharevka on the usual pretext of combating speculation, but then a Sukharevka would spring up on every corner and crossing. With the doctor's prescription I got five pounds of cheese for Nina—that is noteworthy! On Friday I went to Sergievo; in the course of September I am going to go on the sly, skipping days in the museum. I must take care of my family and protect my health—that is all that remains. Arriving here today, I dug potatoes and split firewood.

22 [September]. Denikin has unquestionably gone over to a general offensive along the entire front. This shows that he has withstood the bolsheviks' offensive, which began on August 15 and yielded no results except the taking of Kamyshin, and that he has now found sufficient forces to respond with an offensive. My conjectures that big things were happening in the south are being justified. Now we have to await the results of the action that has been undertaken; they could be very great, but they could fall through. If Denikin achieves an advance toward Moscow, even as far as Briansk, Orel, and Elets, then the danger for Moscow will be sketched out more clearly. But for the moment I still can't perceive the

---

[127] Trudoviki, the group formed in the first duma by deputies of the independent left to recruit adherents among the nonparty peasant deputies. It became the second largest "party" in the duma after the Kadets.

[128] Mikhail Leont'evich Magnitskii (1778–1855) and Dmitrii Pavlovich Runich (1778–1860) were the two most notorious agents of the anti-Enlightenment campaign mounted in the education ministry toward the end of Alexander I's reign (ca. 1819–1826). Their names became symbols of obscurantism.

beginning of a Moscow operation; I think that it would be very difficult to do it all in one blow. However, the first result has already made itself felt: everyone has cheered up; even telephone conversations from Moscow revealed the cheerful mood of the inhabitants. It is possible that they possess some kind of supplementary information, but it is also possible that the newspaper stories were sufficient to put the Muscovites in a joyful mood: a new sign of the Muscovite's extraordinary frivolity and flabbiness.

I jotted down several words for a characterization of old Ger'e in order to read them at the meeting in his memory that will certainly be held in the Historical Society. I think that "Calvinist pastor" was created in order to "demand things" from people and therefore, despite his enormous contributions, he was never popular. Glorious September weather; I went with Nina to the monastery and basked in the sun as if it were springtime; it is strange to think that it has already been six months since we settled in the Posad. I am absent from the museum today on the sly.

24 [September]. Yesterday was nightmarish in terms of the number of impressions received. Alferov, Astrov, N. N. Shchepkin, and A. A. Volkov have been shot as spies of Denikin.[129] The impression is that a like fate could befall each of us any day. "They" have become completely enraged, perhaps under the influence of the failures in the south, where Kursk and L'gov have been surrendered [and the whites] have crossed the Seim and are moving up on Voronezh. But today the newspaper is empty. The impression has to be weakened, of course. I am going to the conference of academic libraries—God, what boredom.

25 [September]. The advance continues. Today, however, the newspapers are unusually empty. Obviously there is nothing to boast about. I saw V. N. Shchepkin, who is the sole intercessor for the affairs of his brother's family; it turns out that in addition to [N. N. Shchepkin] his two sons-in-law were shot. According to [V. N.], comrade Pokrovskii felt uncomfortable receiving him on business and at first told him he didn't recognize him. To this, V. N. Shchepkin replied that he had, of course, aged

[129] Members of the National Center. Aleksandr Danilovich Alferov was executed together with his wife, Aleksandra Samsonovna Alferova, who was the director of a girls' school. Aleksandr Ivanovich Astrov (1871–1919) was a Kadet and a professor at the Petrovskaia Agricultural Academy. Killed at the same time was his brother, Vladimir Ivanovich Astrov (1872–1919), who was a Moscow duma deputy and a justice of the peace. Aleksandr Aleksandrovich Volkov was a former zemstvo man, a Privatdozent in mathematics at Moscow University, and professor in several other Moscow higher schools. A list of sixty-seven persons shot by order of the Cheka was published in *Izvestiia* on September 23, 1919. It included the brothers Astrov, the Alferovs, and Volkov from among those whose arrests were remarked by Got'e in his diary.

a great deal. The general impression is that the executions have provoked not terror but animosity. It is not clear to me what the foundation for such an opinion is, because I have no concrete data on that account. But what an enormous accumulation of rage.

26 [September]. A bomb was thrown into the building of the Russian Communist party, otherwise known as Countess Uvarova's house, and several second-level functionaries were killed. The heart shudders in advance at the thought of the repressions that will follow on this event. Of course, this is the doing of the Left SRs, who wanted to make mischief with this act simultaneously *on the right* and *on the left*, but innocent people will pay for it. At the front their affairs are bad. Today the station Zolotukhino was mentioned, almost in the vicinity of Orel. They say that there is already an order for the evacuation of Smolensk; that in the south near Orel they are left with only 4,000 bayonets; and that they are throwing in there unformed, unclad, and barefoot divisons from the vicinity of Alatyr' and Ardatovo, about which I heard a month ago that the soldiers were begging for alms. I am continuing to go to the library conference, where today we had to save the conservatory library from the advances of one of the "narkompros" departments and defend the libraries of institutions they want to crowd together.

27 [September]. The trip to Sergievo with the evening train, in complete darkness. Gorilla conversations on all sides, generally hostile toward the bolsheviks, and the main subject is the Jews. The majority greatly praised the Poles; only one person turned out to be a philo-semite, or rather one voice in the dark that belonged to a Russian semiintelligent. At home I found a genuine panic produced by rumors about a state of siege in which it will be forbidden to enter or leave Moscow. It seems to me that such a point is still far off.

The weather continues to be marvelous. The upset is compounded by P. N. Kapterev's nervous state and the possibility of the arrest of I. F. Ognev, who did not return from Moscow yesterday. I brought rumors of his arrest, and they had preceded me in connection with the arrest of V. F. Savodnik, a sixty-five-year-old histology professor; what do they need him for? During conversation in the train, I heard of the following division of communists: (1) the materialists, or scum, and (2) "the holy ones" who "only think of hewing to their idea." It is possible that such a division arose in the midst of the communists themselves. One senses that we are approaching a real crisis.

28 [September]. A very good news summary; Maloarkhangel'sk, Nizhne-devitsk—such are the distinctive points. The war has crossed into Great

Russia in a most decisive way. There is no news from Moscow. Today is the funeral of the bomb victims. It would be interesting, after all, to know who got the idea of throwing it at such an inopportune moment. The whole morning was occupied with exchange: a felt jacket for potatoes, shoes for butter; we sold a lady's cloak for money and with the money bought flour. A pair of shoes is priced at 1,500 rubles! "The descendants of the Orthodox shall know!" . . .[130]

29 [September]. A day of little news. The last morning train did not run because, they say, of damage to the tracks somewhere. This is a routine phenomenon now. The weather remains magnificent. I am trying to use the free day today in order to get some work done.

30 [September]. Last Friday my wife's uncle, D. K. Aleksandrov-Dol'nik, was killed. He was arrested three weeks ago, together with other notary publics suspected, they say, of being the ones who sold the Metropol out from under the bolsheviks. When people interceded on his behalf, they said in the Cheka: "You don't know who you are interceding for—he is a tsarist procurator." On Thursday the 25th the bomb was thrown into Countess Uvarova's house; on Friday at 8 p.m. he was taken from Butyrki to the Cheka on the Lubianka, where he was shot the same night "by a decision of three" as a former procurator. According to one of the notaries who sat with him in Butyrki and was released after his removal, he became very agitated upon learning on Friday of the execution of Alferov and co. and about the explosion: he already saw himself as the next possible and suitable victim, the more so when his comrades were released and he was not. We know nothing of his last moments. They probably dumped his body at Kalitnikovskoe Cemetery, where they usually dump the victims of the terror.[131] Yesterday all this was very simply told to Nadezhda Vasil'evna, who had learned of his transfer to Lubianka and had tried to send him some food. In the evening there was a very simple, but truly touching memorial service. He perished as one of the victims of the new outburst of the red terror. Having suffered at Shcheglovitov's hands twelve years ago,[132] he has now suffered at the hands of the revolutionaries—such is the fate of men of the well-intentioned middle in the terrible brawl that is called the Russian revolution. We were on good terms with him, despite his somewhat heavy, selfish character. He was

[130] "Da vedaiut potomki pravoslavnykh! . . ." A line from the opening soliloquy of Father Pimen, the chronicler, in Pushkin's *Boris Godunov.*

[131] A cemetery in the southeastern part of Moscow, founded in the late eighteenth century.

[132] Shcheglovitov was minister of justice and presumably the deceased's superior at that time.

an honorable man and an honorable professional, with a broad juridical mind. If the old order had surrounded itself with such people and acted through them, Russia would have had another fate. May he enter the Kingdom of God!

The story with professor I. F. Ognev turned out to be essentially a tragicomedy: he fell into an ambush in the footsteps of his servant, who had gone to look for coal in the apartment of their relatives, the Alferovs. Others went to look for Ognev, and thus higgledy-piggledy twelve to fifteen people fell into the ambush, including the employees of the Rumiantsev Museum, Savodnik and Usova, who live in the same house. I am glad for the poor old man, who got off with two weeks of going hungry.

The Commissariat of People's Enlightenment is pursuing some kind of definite policy vis-à-vis the university to make teaching impossible: it seems they are restricting us to the period from 4 to 6 P.M.—the rest of the space is needed for the "workers' faculty"![133]

The news summary continues to show advancement into Sovdepiia from all directions, except the north.

OCTOBER

4 [October]. I have returned to the Posad after only four days, and it seems that an eternity has passed. The cause is the tragic death of D.K. I thought a long time while traveling yesterday about how Nina will take it and whether her present illness will influence her reaction to the sad news. But my note, which she received yesterday, already explained everything to her; she understood and took the news as we all did, with quiet despair. I am trying to determine the essential character of the present moment; it is, of course, more serious than a year ago when the outbreak of "red terror" was the consequence of the attempt on Lenin's life. The pressure from without has grown stronger; they themselves recognize that decisive days are at hand. They say they have decided not to evacuate Moscow, but to defend themselves here. All this may create especially difficult moments—moments of mortal danger, savage arbitrariness, and terrifying cruelty. We are progressively approaching the situation of Paris in May 1871; but then it was Paris alone, while now we are still in the center of a very large territory from which there is no way out to liberty. Those who remain in this territory are faced with experiencing

[133] The "workers' faculties" (rabfaki) were preparatory courses designed to funnel worker-students into the universities. The first rabfak opened at Moscow University in October 1919, but they had been introduced at some other Moscow institutions as early as February 1919.

all possible horrors before the tragedy comes to its logical end and the remains of Russia assume a normal appearance, and the old woman—the Russian intelligentsia—will have to set about repairing her ruined hut. Yesterday I was at comrade Riazanov's with a petition about Liza Rar; he was very polite and even asked for news of her husband. I don't know what causes him to accept such petitions—a natural responsiveness or the desire to build bridges? In the last few days a sensational rumor has been circulated that the bolsheviks want to shut down all studies in the higher schools, with the exception of the medical faculties. This, of course, is a gesture of despair (or stupidity?), but perhaps it would be better to break off the stupid comedy of studies when there are neither students nor places to lecture: the bolsheviks have seized the best auditorium in the university, the building of the historico-philological faculty, for the "workers" faculty—such a stupid name had to be invented—and will probably give their "Karla-marla" there.[134] We have to lecture in the building of the law faculty or at the Poltoratskie courses. Some historians are inclined to favor the latter building; I have decided to remain in the university and not to leave it voluntarily.

Returning to the murders of the last few days, I think that old personal accounts are significant in them: I was convinced of this by an article in *Izvestiia VTsIK* for October 3 entitled "Sashka-katorga." It consists of insinuations against A. A. Volkov originating in a milieu close to the zemstvo of Iaroslavl' province.[135] Most likely its author, or those like him, were not uninvolved in Volkov's death. It is possible that old personal accounts also played a role in the death of D. K. Denunciation reigns as never before.

Butter already costs 500 rubles, and flour 3,300. Yesterday they published in the newspapers Lenin's telegram calling for delivery of bread to the cities. Vain illusions, because everything that is left is being used for the transport of troops, and there is no longer anywhere to transport bread from. Only the Moscow-Nizhnii and Moscow-Arzamas-Kazan' lines remain. All the rest have significance as purely military roads. Hence the concern to get flour at any cost.

6 [October]. All day Sunday was passed in exchanging goods. We stocked up with five sacks of potatoes and nearly two puds of millet, and it now

---

[134] That is, "Marxist mumbo jumbo."

[135] The *Izvestiia* article, signed by one Sergei Zarevoi, seems to confirm Got'e's suspicions about personal scores. Volkov is described as a former right-winger in the Iaroslavl' zemstvo who habitually behaved in an insulting way toward the plain folk. He was known as "hard-labor Alex" among the left-wing zemstvo employees because of his denunciations against zemstvo doctors and statisticians, which led to expulsions from the province and arrests. The article ends, "Iaroslavians will say thanks for his execution!"

remains to stock up on flour, which, it seems, is hardest of all. The ring
is tightening and the time must be foreseen when real hunger will have
to be experienced. Nina is busy with preparations for the winter—the
most elementary and unexpected, such as drying turnips. All these are
matters of life or death arising from the contemporary situation. Fortunately, her strength has increased a little and her condition has improved.
Two evenings I cleaned and cut turnips myself. At 9 o'clock I collapse
into bed and sleep eleven hours; perhaps that is the result of general
weakness, perhaps it is the consequence of the shocking impressions of
last week. Yesterday's news summary was favorable for the whites. The
reds admit the loss of Livni and Dmitriev (Kursk province) and the
movement of Denikin cutting the Gomel'-Briansk line. Thus Denikin,
apparently, is not so much deepening his breakthrough as he is broad-
ening it to the west in order to cut off the bolsheviks remaining in the
Ukraine and in the east, and to cut off the parts of the red army operating
on the border of the Don region to the south of the Griazi-Tsaritsyn line.

A new phase in the question of shutting down classes in the university
is reported: supposedly an auditor of Shaniavskii University, Kandelaki,
supported by the vile Pokrovskii, proposes to close the philological faculty
for being counterrevolutionary. P. N. Kapterev reported that the question will be resolved on Monday in the Central Executive Committee, no
less.

9 [*October*]. In Sergievo again, owing to the fact that in the Rumiantsev
Museum they are exterminating the bugs that are eating the ethnographic dummies. I intend to take advantage of it to get some more work
done. On Tuesday I began teaching in the university. Six auditors came,
for the most part old ones, already familiar. They put me in the smallest
law auditorium, which is designed for four hundred persons, uncomfortable and barnlike. For convenience I moved all classes to one day—Tuesday. Yesterday the comrades admitted they have lost Voronezh. The
whites, moving, as it was said in *Izvestiia,* toward Usman', and according
to rumors already from Griazi to Kozlov, are cutting off the red army
located between Novokhopersk and Kamyshin. For that they need to
take only Griazi and Kozlov, the railway hubs. On the other side, there
is much talk about a movement around Orel to cut off the Briansk-Ka-
luga line. The rumors are very much in agreement among themselves,
regardless of whether they come from ordinary citizens or communists.
Correspondingly, the mood in Moscow, I would say, is not bad, despite
the extraordinary local disquietude. In particular, in the last few days
there were searches in the university and in the Higher Women's
Courses, and the Cheka sniffed at something in the Historical Museum.
This created a state of panic in the Rumiantsev Museum as well. Part of

the cache had to be removed and part put in another place.[136] All morning and part of the afternoon yesterday were spent at this. Another original feature: Count P. S. Sheremetev told me yesterday that in his discussion with comrade Riazanov regarding his two murdered sons-in-law, Gudovich and Saburov (they were killed together with D.K.), Gol'dendakh asked him: "Is Gudovich a count?" On hearing the affirmative answer, he noted, sympathizing with Sheremetev and apparently himself indignant with the order of things: "That is quite sufficient!"—that is, it is enough to have a title in order to perish.

10 [October]. A quiet day. There is no news from Moscow yet. I worked on my *Time of Troubles*, giving it the final touches from the editorial standpoint. Today in the bazaar ten eggs cost 200 rubles, butter, of which there was a great deal, 520 rubles a pound.

12 [October]. P. N. Kapterev brought a lot of good news from Moscow; the only thing is, you don't know whether to believe it all. In any case, the movement on Tula is apparently taking shape, perhaps even bypassing Orel. Next, the bolshevik army on the Don has wavered; that is the news that alarmed the bolsheviks and forced them to postpone the matter of the historico-philological faculty. There are many indications of their confusion. Prices are rising at an even greater rate: here today eggs are 200 rubles, milk 210 rubles, meat 560.

14 [October]. Yesterday and today preparations for moving back to Moscow. We are putting our quarters here on a winter footing, and although there is very little to take with us, quite a lot accumulates all the same. A new big affair has taken shape these last few days: the Rumiantsev Museum is to take under its protection the library of the Theological Academy. This must be done in the name of the future. For me this is the sought-for legal grounds for coming here. Living here, you lose the last half-real notions about reality. On the one hand, vague favorable rumors reach us; on the other, the newspapers are dull and vague. It is as if they want to conceal everything.

18 [October]. I could not write in Moscow, because I was afraid to, not knowing where to hide my notes. A great deal has changed in two weeks. A tremendous assault on Petersburg has come to light, one unlike any

---

[136] Got'e is apparently referring to something that was subject to confiscation—possibly including the diary.

before.[137] Today the bolsheviks are confessing that they have lost Krasnoe Selo, and Trotskii's article in *Izvestiia* points to the possibility of fighting in the streets. In a word, Petersburg could slip out from under the authority of the bolsheviks. In the south the situation is also favorable; an advance past Orel, according to rumors even past Mtsensk, although the latter requires verification. The bolsheviks are retreating very quickly between Voronezh and the Volga. On the other hand, the bolshevik foray toward Kiev must be considered a minus; they boast that they have taken it, although the general impression is that something is not right in their reports, which are very short and unclear. At best it is nothing more than a raid; that is what the majority thinks, at least. This week for the first time they began to talk about what might happen in Moscow if Denikin gets here; there is speculation about whether the bolsheviks will defend themselves in Moscow itself or will clear out of it in good time. For the time being, opinions differ—it seems there is an equal number of supporters of the one and the other. There is also much talk about Denikin's tactics for the immediate future—will he go head-on for Tula or will he bypass Tula and the Oka (the ancient "coast" through Kaluga)?[138] So far, one can only notice the desire of the bolsheviks to restrain him by pressure on his flanks at Grafskaia-Uman' and from Kiev to Briansk.

I have not seen Lenin and I have not been at Sukharevka; it seems I should hurry, but I suppose I will do only the second and see only one of the two great manifestations of the Russian revolution that remain unknown to me. Our E. V. Iur'eva has been released from Butyrki; she left the prison apparently shaken by what she experienced there. I learned from P. N. Kapterev the details of how the condemned are transported. They are summoned for dispatch "in town, with personal effects"; they get to the murderers last. They call ordinarily after 4 p.m. and until late evening; and this time is the most frightful in prison. Among more or less well-known persons, one of the socialistically inclined Russians, Volk-Karachevskii,[139] was killed. I submitted the manuscript of *The Time of Troubles*; I was told that "permission has been received" for its publication. I, however, think that its contents are too contrary to contemporary currents and that it would be better to print it later.[140] One

---

[137] Iudenich's drive on Petrograd was at its height at this time. In mid-October it seemed likely that both Petrograd and Moscow would fall to the Whites. This was the moment of greatest crisis in the Civil War; it was over by the end of the third week of October.

[138] *Bereg*. Got'e refers to the strategy of the Tatar approaches to Muscovy.

[139] V. V. Volk-Karachevskii was a member of the Popular Socialist (PS) party who was implicated by the Cheka in the "National Center" affair.

[140] Got'e's small book (152 pages) finally appeared, through the State Publishing House, in 1921: Iu. V. Got'e, *Smutnoe vremia. Ocherk istorii revoliutsionnykh dvizhenii nachala XVII stoletiia* (Moscow, 1921).

more note: the question of firewood for the Rumiantsev Museum depends on whether the haulers (they have to haul it from Berendeevo station on the Iaroslavl' railroad) are given a certain rather small quantity of tobacco, salt, matches, and cigarettes. That is what the well-being, or rather the possibility of functioning, of the museum and public library depend on. We came to Sergiev Posad again to exchange various things. In addition to the wish to be free from everything superfluous, there is the fear that our house will not remain in one piece if fighting occurs on the terrain of Moscow itself.

20 [October]. The news is dichotomous: on the one hand, the bolsheviks are boasting that they have taken Fastov, have gone over to the offensive against Orel and Voronezh, and have retaken Gatchina. On the other hand, Krasnoe Selo and Gatchina have been lost and the troops are being withdrawn to the Petersburg-Vitebsk railway line, Novosil' has been lost, and a defeat has been suffered near Tsaritsyn. In addition, tickets on the Nikolaevskaia railroad are being sold only as far as Malaia Vishera.[141] Today I received for the guardianship of the Rumiantsev Museum the library of the Moscow Theological Academy—a magnificent library and in perfect order. It will be pleasant to facilitate the rescue of this book treasure.

25 [October]. This entire week, ordinary in terms of everyday life, has been very distressing in terms of general matters. Orel and, it seems, Voronezh have been taken back and a big stalemate has developed near Petrograd, which was not taken, although everything had looked is if it would fall. We don't know the real reason for all this, but the effect of these facts on the feelings of the inhabitants, which had just taken wing with hopes, is oppressive. There can be no doubt that there are lies in "their" reports, as always, but again, to calculate the quantity of lies and separate the lies from the truth is impossible, and that is the second cause of dismal moods. There lies ahead the agonizing question: has it really fallen through this time, too? Will they now really jump out of the hole in which, it seemed to us, they were already sitting? Are the others weakening or will they find the strength again? Those are the agonizing questions that are relentlessly demanding answers. In any case, a new stalemate is under way, a new delay for the optimistic anticipations of last week, or even of the several preceding weeks. One wants terribly to get out of this awful country, which is rapidly approaching a state of complete primitive barbarism, and one senses that all wishes are in vain, that we are sitting in the most horrifying and somber prison. Nina's health

---

[141] That is, about 125 kilometers south of Petrograd.

also disturbs me to the highest degree: winter is approaching and all our hopes for a summer recovery were vain, and winter will come with her organism even weaker. There is no way out of this hellish circle of thoughts.

26 [October]. All morning I kept having dark thoughts about hunger, about Nina's health, and about how everything around us is endless and interminable. In the morning I went to look at the Vifaniia library—a good collection of almost ten thousand volumes based on the libraries of Platon, Filaret, and Makarii.[142] I saw the ruined church of the Vifaniia seminary—a large and dirty hall, and in it a platform that is used or could be used as a stage.

27 [October]. It turns out that there has never before been such a difference between what is reported and what is happening in reality. I came from Sergievo in circumstances that I had never traveled in before. The train was crowded to five times over the norm. I could get into the car for only half the journey. All the passengers carried sacks of potatoes. The fare was 600 rubles in kind (eggs, 230; meat, 650). The mood was good-natured, but there was bitterness and fatigue in the air. The museum was opened today. I am glad, because that allows me to see many people and occupy my time.

NOVEMBER

1 [November]. I have to give up writing at home. It is too dangerous. It has been a long time since I was in such depressed spirits as I am these days. The Petersburg adventure has burst, for a long time, if not forever. In the south the retreat of Denikin from the vicinity of Orel, Elets, and Kromy has begun. It is impossible to understand what is going on; there is no reliable information. But everything is very similar to the first days of Kolchak's retreat: a strike in the center, retreat in the center, and firmness for a while on the flanks. I would be very glad if I were mistaken, but I fear it is just like that. Even now there are many optimists; they continue to hope for something, but I am sick at heart. It is possible, of course, that it is a matter of nerves on my part, too. God will it! In any case, I think that we are stuck with the bolsheviks for a third winter. My already depressed frame of mind is reinforced, in the first place, by the fact that our house is not heated. Up to 350 cars of firewood were desig-

[142] Platon Levshin (metropolitan from 1775 to 1812), Filaret Drozdov (1825–1867), and Makarii Bulgakov (1879–1882) were eighteenth- and nineteenth-century metropolitans of Moscow who were renowned bookmen.

nated for the museum, but this firewood is in Berendeevo on the Northern Railroad, and the railroads are requisitioning all the firewood that arrives in Moscow and (according to rumors) are sending it to the railroads leading south from Moscow, which don't have a log of wood of their own. They haven't taken our wood yet, but there is a great danger that this will happen. In the meantime, it is 7° in the apartment and our brains are beginning to rattle in our skulls from the cold. Another, more precisely the third, cause of my depression is Nina's health. It is not worse, but I am terrified by the prospect for her of such a winter as that which threatens us. Finally, the matter of hunger is becoming so urgent that you think that no matter how many things you sell there still won't be enough money, and when everything has been sold you will have to lay down arms and helplessly surrender. In the realm of curiosities: in Tikhomirov's memoirs, which he finished reading to me shortly before my departure from Sergiev Posad, Prince L'vov[143] is called "a political deaf-mute." A brilliant and accurate description. N. A. Berdiaev has submitted an application for extension of the exemption [from confiscation] of his library. M. N. Pokrovskii resolved: "I have no objections"; but, according to rumors, Berdiaev is in the Ukraine. Such is the state of information about employees of the Commissariat of Enlightenment.

4 [November]. Red army victories all along the line. The situation at home has not changed. Impossible cold. The sale of things is going full speed ahead. I am quitting reading the newspapers and am determined to turn everything over to the will of . . . I don't know who. More than ever, I fear that the small group of civilized Russian people is being thrown to the whim of fate and will be left to expire in a country where civilization's death sentence has been signed. There is only one thing worth striving for—exit abroad. If anybody lives to see that, good luck to him. But, alas, who among us will survive until spring?

5 [November]. Bread has risen to 150 rubles. Everything is being confiscated everywhere. I don't read the newspapers because they are worthless. My wife's health is getting worse. The railroads are at a standstill. The specter of death by famine is looming. A. I. Iakovlev reported just now that certain big-wigs in the commissariat openly admit that all is lost, but add: "But. . . ." We are all perishing because of that "but."

8 [November]. The rest is silence.[144] That is how my view of the world of the last few days can be described. Unrelieved gloom. One can only await what happens, without making any kind of plans or calculations. Yester-

---

[143] That is, Prince G. E. L'vov, head of the first Provisional Government.

[144] This sentence is in English in the original.

day's festivities were much more modest than last year.[145] No kind of handouts to the inhabitants except a half-pound of white bread to the children. The school lunches are much skimpier than last year. Everything that was left has been given to the red army men. I didn't see the demonstrations, but in places they were thin, and in other places people were herded into them by force. The crowds of demonstrators that together with troops made up an adequate number of people in the necessary places were collected by those means. I am beginning to think that we will be left to rot in a blockade for an indeterminate time, in the course of which four-fifths of the civilized Russian people remaining in the bolshevik prison camp will die off. In the end, former Russia will after all fall like a ripe fruit into the embrace of international capital.

10 [November]. The situation remains the same. I have gotten Nina into a sanatorium; we are to go on the 20th. I am beginning to fear that this won't be enough. Her health worries me endlessly. My only thoughts: to subsist, to get my wife treated, and to hold out until spring. Boring, vulgar, disgusting. Life and activity are dying out almost everywhere. Today I took a look at the Archive of Foreign Affairs and our museum—it makes you sick to look at them. A typhus hospital is being transferred to the old building of the university; yet another method for killing Moscow University.

13 [November]. The problem of food supplies overshadows everything else except the problem of heating. The essence of the matter is that the bolsheviks, who have no reserves of any kind, are determined to close all institutions, thinking in this way to save fuel for the railroads, for which they have no firewood. Traffic is coming to a standstill even on the railroads. As a result of that we are sitting here without firewood, in the museum as well as in the university, and, finally, at home. The only time you feel decent is sitting home in the evening in one room, which we heat with the help of a little iron stove. Then the woe and the worries temporarily recede into the background and you seem to forget them, but in the morning they take hold with renewed force.

14 [November]. I received a copy of an interesting document, which I am appending here.[146] The fact is evident that this scum is going somewhere, but it remains quite unclear why? The sum of private information is that no one is fighting in the south. Paraphrasing the reports of their own press, the crazed Muscovites embroider on them as on a canvas and are

[145] That is, the celebration of the anniversary of the October revolution.
[146] No document corresponding clearly to this place in the text can be found in the archive, and therefore the allusion remains unclear.

making up stories about all kinds of negotiations with the Entente and suchlike stupidities. The fact remains: the situation is hopeless; flour costs six or seven thousand, meat 650 rubles, eggs 300 rubles a dozen. We spent 1,000 rubles yesterday buying 10 eggs and 4 pounds of soap. They say that lectures are being canceled in all the humanities faculties; for the time being, only temporarily, until spring, with maintenance of salaries. It will be interesting to see what all this will be like tomorrow.

17 [November]. The heavens themselves are taking up arms against us. Since morning there has been a snowstorm and blizzard like in mid-February. One can imagine how this must affect the condition of the railroads, and consequently our provisions. It would be good if this devastation affected the bolsheviks as well; but in the given situation, their agony is our agony. The temperature in our apartment is zero. We have moved in to my aunt's place; therefore, any semblance of a home has been destroyed. You live on the run, not knowing where to rest your head. In the future we will have to count on the evolutionary path. Who will survive and wait for its results, I don't know. If matters develop by evolution, that smells of years of such a mixture of doctrinairism and Pugachevshchina that no living soul will survive. This mixture is precisely the main essence of the Russian revolution, its *Saft und Kraft*; and it is the guarantee of the destruction of all that is alive in Russia. Existence in Moscow is measured only by those little stoves that have been installed in certain rooms: this is the life style of Eskimos or Samoyeds. A small touch: there is an offer in the Rumiantsev Museum to buy firewood at a speculative price from a person who is both a speculator and a member of the Cheka of the Vindava railroad. Typical for the Russian revolution.

18 [November]. The pseudo-Dutchmen who have ensconced themselves in the house of my aunt, E. A., commenced after her arrest to take part in the looting of the house, and yesterday, we were told, they got drunk on the remains of her wine. A scene worthy of the great Russian revolution, which is nothing other than one vast robbery. I also heard that a house in Kuntsevo and the house of Countess Uvarova in Karacharovo have been plundered: there the peasant communists cut the Persian rugs into pieces and divided them among themselves. The same kind of plundering is beginning in my aunt's house. On her business I went yesterday to see the main official of the so-called political Red Cross, the attorney N. K. Murav'ev, who was also a revolutionary in his youth.[147] Dry and

---

[147] The Political Red Cross or Committee for Aid to Political Prisoners was set up in Moscow, in an office on Kuznetskii Most, some time in 1918 in order to provide information about, and legal and material aid to, political prisoners. Nikolai Konstantinovich Murav'ev (1870–1936) was a well-known lawyer who appeared for the defense in many

imposing, a graying blond of about fifty; polite and self-assured; he received me while warming himself at an iron stove in a well-furnished room, where I saw a lot of beautiful china collected in a big cupboard. He occupies a small but attractive mansion, which they apparently don't touch.

23 [November]. I have returned from four days of wandering. The evening of the 19th, Nina and I left Mertvyi Pereulok on a sleigh that was kindly put at our disposal by the principal head of institutions of higher learning(!).[148] It was a real sleigh ride, and a pleasant one, on a road freshly covered with snow, which would have been reminiscent of old times if only we hadn't gone along completely darkened streets. In the morning we moved on to Shchelkovo. There were no horses there from the sanatorium and we had to ask for them by telephone. Nothing can happen in Russia without a great deal of disorder! In order to get back to Moscow in time, I left for Grebnevo, that is, the sanatorium, on foot without waiting for the horses, but I was given a lift along the road by a kind villager who was returning from having fulfilled his wood-hauling duty for sovdep. In our conversation he vehemently cursed the comrades. The sanatorium is located in the Grebnevo palazzo, which I had once seen on the trip from Pushkino to Berliukovskaia Pustyn'. Such grandeur! Such beauty of a life long past and perished![149] The sanatorium produced a good impression on me. Having had a stroll and a chat with Doctor Grinevskii and with M. M. Bogoslovskii, who is receiving treatment there, I set back off on foot and about one and a half versts from the sanatorium met Nina, who was clearly tired from the rather drawn-out journey. The most interesting spot on the road is the Shchelkovo factory settlement, where all the signs are red; obviously, everything is in the hands of the sovdepists, and the factories (Rabenek, Chetverikov) are standing irreversibly still. The provisions warehouse had been burned the day before in order to hide the traces in water.

I spent the 21st and 22d in Sergiev Posad and, despite the mess there,

---

political cases before and for some time after the Revolution. He had been chairman of the Provisional Government's Extraordinary Investigatory Commission on the fall of the old regime. He was one of four members of the Moscow Committee; its chairman was Ekaterina Pavlovna Peshkova. There were similar organizations in Petrograd and several other cities. Some of them apparently survived into the mid-1930s. See *Pamiat'. Istoricheskii sbornik*, vyp. 1, pp. 313–24; 2, 523–38.

[148] That is, by Pokrovskii.

[149] Shchelkovo is thirty-eight kilometers from Moscow on a branch of the Iaroslavl' line; it is eight kilometers further to Grebnevo, which was one of the grand old estates of the Moscow region. The great manor house described by Got'e, which still stands, was built during the reign of Catherine II by General Gavriil Il'ich Bibikov.

I felt a certain spiritual relief as always. I found the libraries that have been entrusted to me in order. The affair of the monastery has also settled down: it has been reestablished, but with only forty-three monks as caretakers. According to the chairman of the Preservation Commission, Count Iu. A. Olsuf'ev,[150] these are the best monks. If that is so, the monastery has lost nothing. It is very typical that they go to Olsuf'ev for all instructions: I was myself a witness to how they asked him what to do with the church wine, when to open the Trinity Cathedral, etc. He gave me the impression of being the veritable guardian of the monastery. Among other things, he told me that during the discussions with the sovdep, this phrase was dropped by its chairman, a Balt military clerk, Venalainen: "We will kick your uncle out of his grave." I went for the first time to have dinner in a soviet dining room: indescribable filth, and portraits of the god Marx and his disciples everywhere. For twelve rubles I received a plate of bad fish soup and potato loaf. My trips came off quite successfully. I left for the Posad an hour late, but I rode for only three hours; we came back in three hours, too, despite the snowstorm and blizzard. Considering the present condition of the railroads, that is splendid. The impression from the dark cars, into which floods of people looking for places burst on the outskirts of Moscow, is terrifying: it is a kind of cold Gehenna. The *Niflheim*[151] of contemporary Bolshevy—cursing, shrieks, requests to move on somewhere and squeeze together, and all this is drowned out by cries of "Comrades!" Before the stations nearest to Moscow, and progressively as you get farther from Moscow, the conversations become calmer, but they all turn around the sore subject— who is responsible for the horror we are living through? Yesterday I had a good look at the notorious students who occupy the monastery and were going to Moscow, and I heard how one of them assured a certain female resident of the Posad that everything is fine—a typical socialistic youth from among the Russian intelligentsia: a superficial, stupid, ignorant neophyte of the new religion of socialism.

There is nothing to be said about general matters. Everything is going in the worst possible way. I fear, however, more than ever that we will be left to rot endlessly in a blockade. Despite all the assurances of the comrades that there are those who want to enter into agreements, I have a very hard time believing it. It is impossible for the victors of the peace to enter agreements with bandits who have violated the elementary principles of public and civil law! And there is no need at all for it.

[150] Count Iurii Aleksandrovich Olsuf'ev (b. 1879) was an art historian, an employee of the Sergiev Posad "branch" of the Rumiantsev Museum after it acquired the monastery library.

[151] That is, the underworld, the land of the dead.

25 [November]. The situation remains entirely unchanged. But for us there is neither gladness nor heroes in their advance. I have the feeling that all is lost. It is − 3 degrees in the apartment; I am spending the night in refuge at my mother-in-law's. My son is staying in bed to avoid getting a worse cold. My wife's sister, Tania, is getting married to her cousin, Alesha Gvozdev, in the commissariat, in order to get forty arshins[152] of calico, which are generously distributed by the bolsheviks to those who get married through their offices. I am appending a letter of Liza Rar from prison: it is a typical document.[153]

27 [November]. Yesterday I lectured at the archive institute. In front of me sat a proletarian girl in a kerchief. What can she get out of my lectures? I received the *Historical Archive* published in Petersburg, with good articles by the Petersburg historians, including the already deceased Lappo-Danilevskii and D'iakonov. A good book, written by former people.[154] They say the archive dictator, Riazanov, is dissatisfied with its overly old-fashioned contents. Cold reigns as before in the apartment, in the museum, and in the university. An enemy that the bolsheviks can't conquer, either. Today I met the cobbler Skuriatnikov, who used to sew the shoes of all stylish Moscow; today he is fed by a cobbler who probably worked for him—he has lost everything and they shot his only son.

28 [November]. I am almost certain that the victors of the world want to asphyxiate the bolsheviks by the same means with which they asphyxiated Germany. The only unfortunate thing is that we will die along with the bolsheviks. Yesterday I met a finely dressed old man, undoubtedly of good society, who was begging alms.

DECEMBER

1 [December]. A two-day trip to the Grebnevo sanatorium. Nina's health is in the same state so far. My hope is for a long visit for her there, which might restore somewhat her overtaxed strength and allow her to live

---

[152] *Arshin*: the Russian yard of twenty-eight inches.

[153] See Appendix, Letter 8: letter of Liza Rar from Butyrskaia prison, November 14, 1919.

[154] *Istoricheskii arkhiv*, kn. 1 (Petrograd, 1919). This collection of articles, which was not continued until the late 1930s, was published by the Main Archive Administration. It consisted mostly of articles on sources and archaeographic matters by Petrograd historians. Aleksandr Sergeevich Lappo-Danilevskii (1863–1919), a lecturer on Russian history at Petersburg University and an academician, was best known for his source publications and work on historical theory and method. An obituary is included in the 1919 miscellany.

through the winter. I recognize that this is the last, or one of the last, gambles, and I spent many troubled hours under the influence of those thoughts. This is one more example of the victims of war and revolution. Her organism could not withstand the shocks, her nervous system cracked, and a predisposition to sugar paved the way to the ravaging of the organism. Since her temperament is not inclined toward combating illness, this, too, created new, unfavorable conditions. And this is the re-sult—she is an invalid, and our home has been swept away and reduced to nothing. All at once today the news came of the death of two old Rumiantsev Library employees—S. I. Sokolov and V. I. Bezsonov. A dire warning for the winter, and, in general, for all of us. That is the fate that looms for all of us who don't succeed in fleeing this hell. Yesterday I did nine versts on foot from the sanatorium to the railroad and five versts around Moscow with a pud of potatoes on my back—in all, fourteen versts. This is also a feature of our life. General affairs are without change. The bolshevik rumors about negotiations are exaggerated, it seems; gloom surrounds us as before and is preparing to engulf us.

4 [December]. Yesterday was the funeral of V. I. Bezsonov. Out of for-getfulness I accidentally went into the neighboring parish church, at the end of Ostozhenka. Three people were being buried there, but V. I. was not among them; I realized that I had to go into the Church of the Res-urrection next door, and there I found two bodies, including the one I was looking for. And what was in the other neighboring churches? Could it have been the same thing? After a miserable service, poor V. I., in a coffin with cracks, was placed on a simple sledge and dragged to Vagan'kovo.[155] A marvelous genre picture. I continue to live like a gypsy, since Volodia is coughing and can't be brought home. I am on the move days at a time in order to get one thing or another—food, medicine—now for Nina, now for Volodia, or for general use, and in the end every-thing becomes so wearisome that at times you grow discouraged. I've got to find the strength to sit down and write something, if only in order to earn money for bread—but it is quite impossible. And so endlessly, with-out a glimmer of hope, without end. On Tuesday the 2d, two students from the Women's Courses and three university students came over; I worked with them in the bedroom, the only more or less warm room; the lecture and seminar were interrupted by a fuss over the stoking of the little stove. Such are the conditions of teaching in Moscow University in the 170th year of its existence. The bolsheviks are expecting an attack from the west. It is hard for blind moles to say what kind of attack this

---

[155] Vagan'kovo Cemetery, founded in 1771, is located in the northwestern part of the city. Many prominent Muscovites are buried there.

will be. Everything that has happened so far rather demonstrates the lack of seriousness of the campaigns against the RSFSR and the peculiar way the powers-that-be have of howling before they are seized by the throat in order to cry later, when the imagined danger is past: "we are unconquerable." A purely Jewish tactic. There is only one objective indicator: the quasi-delegation of the Red Cross has been kicked out of Poland and now the Poles who were getting ready to go home are not being allowed to leave here. The university has died; the museum is dying; Nina's health is not improving. What else is in store?

5 [December]. I am sitting here without news of Nina. I don't know whether Tania didn't arrive, or did arrive but is not communicating anything. There are rumors of plague in the east; the typhus is apparently spreading. There is talk again that the Poles are being released from Moscow. No other changes. I am very concerned about what they want to do with Turkestan; they are paying special attention to that country. What for? In order to make it a base for a campaign against India, or in order to install a model communism there? In any case, if it were offered to me to go there I would be full of fear and apprehension.

10 [December]. On Friday the 5th I set out on my customary tour. I carried nearly thirty pounds of provisions for my poor Nina. I walked in the evening to the station past Theater Square, which was illuminated by the bloody light of the sign of the Seventh All-Russian Congress of Soviets, which hung in splendor on the columns of the Bolshoi Theater. Access to the theater was being jealously guarded by those who used to be called soldiers, in fine new sheepskin coats and fur coats: the worker-peasant government has set itself off from the people even more sharply than the tsarist government. I was going with a troubled feeling because Tania had not come at the appointed time and had remained at the sanatorium. At the station I learned at Lelia's that Tania had sent a letter saying not to worry, that she was staying until my arrival so that Nina would not be bored. Nevertheless, Tania's letter sowed dark thoughts and forebodings. The Kurdiumovs were upset from the search that had just taken place at their friend and neighbor's, Manteufel, the émigré baron and menshevik and chief of traction for the Northern Railways, who was arrested for malicious sabotage and taken to the Cheka because they found somewhere a not entirely ruined locomotive that was not being used. I had to spend the night on the train, where I was graciously given refuge by the head of one of the distant districts who had arrived in Moscow. It was a simple second-class car that had become his private property—like all the upholstered cars of the second and first classes, according to him. Such is the state of things in the RSFSR. On the 6th, I completed my journey with-

out hindrance, and at 12 o'clock I was in Grebnevo, where I learned from
M. M. Bogoslovskii, whom I met in the courtyard, the shocking news
that my Nina was in a hopeless state. The illness had suddenly worsened
sharply and come to its natural dénouement, a "diabetic coma." Everything had happened all of a sudden the evening before. At 3 o'clock Nina
suddenly began to talk excitedly, and at 5 o'clock she had already fallen
into the sleep from which there is no return. It lasted thirty-one hours,
and she died on the night of the 6th at 11:30 P.M. No one expected such
an outcome. Even the doctors didn't expect it, at least not so soon. On the
morning of the 7th, Tania returned to Moscow to inform the old folks
and prepare Volodia. I remained there to be with her and prepare for the
funeral. My dear friend M. M. Bogoslovskii did not leave me for a minute. Such a sensitive and beautiful soul, such a warm and responsive
heart, and together with that, such restraint. Everything was arranged
quickly and smoothly—both the administration of the sanatorium and
the local clergy were unusually attentive and obliging. The only complication was the building of the coffin (that is a characteristic feature of the
moment); there were no boards to be found anywhere, and to make it
they knocked down the fence in the greenhouse; nevertheless, the coffin
was ready Monday morning. At 1 P.M. she was carried to the church;
funeral vespers were peformed at 5 o'clock, after which the priest summoned M. M. Bogoslovskii and myself to tea. My first thought was to
refuse, but he invited us so cordially that we went, and had an excellent
time: a small room, intensely heated, an affably puffing samovar, fancy
cakes, honey, coffee with milk, and butter—old-fashioned cordiality; my
spirits were momentarily lifted. Among those present were two former
people—Major General V. M. Petrovo-Solovovo of H. I. M.'s Suite, and
the Riazan procurator V. P. Zvonnikov, who assured us with one voice
that it is possible to have some kind of life only outside of Moscow. Tania,
Lelia, my brother Vladimir Vladimirovich, E. K. Wilken, Al. Al. Gvozdev, and N. V. and Lipa Dol'nik arrived in the evening and were received and lodged in the sanatorium with unusual cordiality.

On the 9th, my nameday, the funeral service was held and Nina was
placed in the cold church, lovely, stylish, light white and blue, like the
gates of heaven where my devout one has been transported; then, having
thanked everyone for their generous participation, we set off on the return journey on foot.

Today, the 10th, I made the rounds of various sovdepiias and rather
easily received permission to bury her in Novodevich'ii Monastery. Our
poor Volodia is bravely experiencing his first great grief: he understands
much, but tries to restrain himself and hides his grief in his little child's
soul. Our task will be to support in him the worship of his mother, which
she so deserves. She died by slow torture, the innocent victim of the brutal

appetites of the Germans and the hysterics of Russian revolutionaries. The horrors of the war were the disease's point of departure; the impossibility of extracting Nina from the seething cauldron of Russian outrages brought her to a fatal end. May the Prussian Junkers be cursed, and the Russian scum with them. My poor boy and I are the genuine wreckage of the sea of life. I will not be able and will not want to rebuild the edifice of our material well-being; will I be able to do the one thing that lies ahead of me, to fulfill the one obligation I have before Nina—to bring up Volodia, a fine, richly gifted boy with great and good instincts? That will be the final battle in life. It must be won, but there is no confidence, as I no longer have confidence in anything. So far all my wagers on public affairs have been lost; now my main gamble in life has been lost. I have become a lonely old man who has entered that period in life that can be called cemeterial. Everything dear to me, all the people I loved—all are in the grave, with the exception of a light in the window: Volodia. To wander among the gravestones, that is all that is left to me in my personal lot. *Addio, le sante memorie!* Greetings, lonely old age, which I always feared more than anything, even when I would jokingly tell Nina that I was sure I would die earlier than she and that she would not avoid being a widow.

I have dwelt too long on personal feelings, which I have avoided in these notes. But after all, my personal catastrophe is directly linked to the general catastrophe, and therefore I describe it here. When I arrived in Moscow and asked what the lies are in Moscow, no one could answer anything. No one reads the newspapers. Moscow is in a state of decrepitude and is not even producing rumors. It seems that any negotiations, if in fact there were any (which I doubt), are finished, broken off, and that we have again plunged into some kind of hopeless bolshevik darkness, from which mortal man has no way out; a way out will perhaps come in some years when we will all have long since followed my dear Nina into "the land where there is no sadness or sorrow."[156]

17 [December]. All these days I have continued to live with my personal grief. General affairs have retreated far away. I recall an episode from one of Salias's novels:[157] a rich merchant who had lost everything in the plague dug his own grave, lay down in it with his face to the wall and ceased thinking. I remind myself of that merchant. I simply no longer think anything and expect nothing. Only I still can't understand that

---

[156] Words of a Slavonic funeral prayer.

[157] Count Evgenii Andreevich Salias de Turnemir (1840–1908) was a well-known historical novelist.

everything around me has suddenly become empty and that I am condemned to eternal loneliness. Today I began to occupy myself with matters, and it seemed to me that this was better, but as soon as I remain alone with myself I find myself thinking that as soon as I reach the Posad or the sanatorium, I will tell about something to my dear Nina, who is no more and never will be. The factual situation of the last few days was such: on Thursday morning I picked out a place in Novodevich'ii Monastery and arranged with the gravediggers to have the grave ready by Saturday. In the evening I went to spend the night at Lena's, and on Friday I left for Grebnevo together with M. V. Sergievskii,[158] who volunteered with astonishing courtesy to accompany me. We were at the sanatorium at 11:15 A.M. The Father Superior was already waiting for us; we agreed that we would leave at 4 o'clock. Until then I sat all the time in M. M. Bogoslovskii's room. It goes without saying that both Sergievskii and I received the same cordial reception at the sanatorium as on the previous days. At 4 we left the sanatorium on foot for the church, placed the coffin on the sledge, and tied it down. At 4:45 P.M., sitting on the side, we set off on the road. At 8 P.M. we were in the village of Pekhro, fifteen versts from the city gates, where we stayed until 2:30 A.M. The coffin stood on a cart in the courtyard. We had a nap in the tavern where, of course, we did not get by without all kinds of questions. When we set out, it had grown much colder, the moon was shining, and the whole sky was sown with stars: Orion, Sirius, Jupiter, and, finally, Venus—it all passed before our eyes. She so loved to go for rides, and her last ride was in this magical setting. But the horse was already fatigued and we went more slowly; we actually went on foot more than we rode, as we needed to run in order to warm up. We were at the gates at 5:45, after which began the journey across Moscow, by the longest way that exists—it lasted two and three-quarters hours, which equals approximately twelve versts. We were at the monastery gates at 8:30. The whole way we did not meet a single policeman, and no one asked us about the purpose of our journey. So ended that unique journey, possible only under the bolshevik regime. The rest was nothing remarkable. Nina's second funeral passed as it should—there was everything except the service, just as in Grebnevo there was everything except the lowering into the grave. Despite the bolshevik decrees, I was able to get a place for myself, too, next to my Nina, and thus to acquire landed property at a time when such property is being rejected. I always liked the cemetery of Novodevich'ii Monastery, because the monastery itself is beautiful, and also

[158] Maksim Vladimirovich Sergievskii (1892–1946) was a philologist, a graduate of Moscow University (1916) and a professor there (1925–1946).

because a circuit road runs near the new cemetery: and may young life play at the entrance to the tomb . . . !¹⁵⁹

Yesterday there was a mass in the Rumiantsev Museum arranged by my coworkers, who are in general very sympathetic toward me.¹⁶⁰ Both days I felt a terrible fatigue and an irresistible desire to sleep.

19 [December]. I have completely lost interest in general affairs. I now experience and understand the feeling of the calm of the grave. I see and know that I no longer have a homeland, nor a family, that my life is coming to a standstill, unneeded; there remains only my son, who must be saved—that is the entire purpose of my life and work.

22 [December]. I traveled to the Posad. As always, that journey had a calming effect on me. The proximity to nature, the relative quiet. Only the return by railroad was agonizing.

24 [December]. My spiritual state is turning into a kind of petrification. Day after day passes, and you think, thank God, another day less. The Russian tragedy has entered the phase of gloom. Vas'ka Nikiforov of Zaprud'e visited me and brought some rusks as a present. I sent my regards to all Zaprud'e, but I deliberately asked that regards not be sent to Aleksei. Our house, cattle, and inventory are intact. He asked me if I didn't want to go to the village. I answered that for me the village was dead and that I would go there no more.

25 [December]. Another boring day. The talk continues, and they continue to write about some kind of danger from the west. I think it is a matter of a danger imagined by the Jews; they are shouting, and all the others shout after them.

26 [December]. I. A. Il'in told me of his chat with Kamenev; the latter was surprised that the Russian intelligentsia was not with them. I think the Russian intelligentsia deserves that the bolsheviks think it should be with them. The pestilence is spreading on all sides; in their newspapers

¹⁵⁹ Lines from a poem by Pushkin, "Brozhu li ia vdol' ulits shumnykh . . ." (1828), whose theme is reflection on mortality and the wish to be buried in one's native place:

I pust' u grobovogo vkhoda	And may young life play
Mladaia budet zhizn' igrat',	At the entrance to the tomb,
I ravnodushnaia priroda	And indifferent nature glow
Krasoiu vechnoiu siiat'.	With her eternal beauty.

¹⁶⁰ Got'e's archive contains a touching letter of condolence signed by seventy-six of his co-workers at the Rumiantsev Museum.

today I noticed Clemenceau's declaration that the Western powers will encircle soviet Russia with barbed wire. I think this is what will happen, despite the rumors that are circulating about Polish intervention.

29 [December]. S. D. Bakharev recounted his odyssey to me. He was in Saratov province, went from there to Kashira on a brake platform, on an engine, and on foot, and has now gone to work for the railroad as a clerk. He barely manages to feed his family. He heard the most horrendous stories—two reliable instances of cannibalism; university laboratory assistants are eating dogs and cats. And all this was told quietly, calmly, and without a murmur. Yesterday I sat all day with Volodia, who, thank God, is healthy and well nourished. I have a feeling of moral fatigue such as I have not experienced for a long time. Rumors about some kind of attacks from the west are continuing. Today they were saying that the bolsheviks are hurriedly shifting troops to the Polish border. Where is the truth and where falsehood?

31 [December]. The most terrible year for me is ending. Ahead there is nothing—neither in private life, nor in general prospects. The revolution has devoured everything that was most dear to me and has left me for the time being a fragile burden in the form of a young son, whom it will be *more than* problematical to raise under current conditions. For days on end I experience heavy, indescribable melancholy from which there is no exit, as there is no exit from our life. Cold, hunger, moral and physical death—that is the lot of everyone who does not adapt or speculate. Today I heard that they intend to send the Belgians packing as well. The lucky Wilkens. May God let us live long enough to follow them.

1920

❋

January. I am beginning the notes on January 5th because the state of bewilderment I am in not only doesn't pass, it is still increasing. There is nothing ahead but terrible loneliness and fear of hunger (I am greeting the new year alone with my juvenile son). On Saturday I went to the Vvedenskie Hills to make the only visit planned for the holidays—to the grave of my parents. Everything was covered with snow there, an abomination of desolation that had never occurred there before. The journey through Moscow—dirty, befouled, snowed in, stripped, and full of garbage—produced, as always, a most depressing impression on me. A visit to Liza [Rar] produced a no less heavy impression: after the palace, she is taking shelter, together with her children and husband, in two very small rooms where the servant used to live; everything has been taken away and they are being threatened with eviction.

9 [January]. Three days of so-called rest. I tried to sit at home; a heavy state of mind. The depression grows stronger rather than passing. I am vainly trying to get received by comrade Kamenev on the subject of E. A. Got'e's release.[1] Access to the current generals is much harder than to the former ones. There are new rumors of some kind of movement from the west. They are officially reporting the taking of Dvinsk. By whom? I am trying not to listen to anything, and I myself no longer believe anything.

12 [January]. On Saturday, together with E. V. Got'e, I again set off to seek a meeting with comrade Kamenev. In the place where passes are given out, they informed us that only his secretary, a comrade of the female gender, Krylenko,[2] could receive us—she was not in right now but should be arriving. That was at two o'clock. We waited patiently until a quarter to four in premises that had once sheltered gentry coming to town for the winter months, now befouled beyond imagination. At

[1] Got'e went to see Kamenev, at this time Chairman of the Moscow Soviet, on behalf of his uncle Emil' Vladimirovich's wife.

[2] This may have been Ol'ga Vasil'evna (b. 1896), the youngest sister of N. V. Krylenko. See Max Eastman, *Love and Revolution* (New York, 1964), pp. 338–43.

half-past three the following telephone conversation occurred: a great many comrades are waiting here, they have been waiting for two hours already; can they be admitted? An affirmative answer followed, after some hesitation, and we crossed the square into the former governor general's house. Here we were admitted no farther than the front hall, as comrade Krylenko had announced that she would come out there to receive us. After another forty-five minutes, there appeared a small, sprightly, and, it must be admitted, amiable girl, who played her role very smartly, heard us out, took the documents, and announced that we should call her on Monday at 2 P.M. about the results of our visit. While waiting for her, we scrutinized the faces—either Jews or Russian gorillas. It is no accident that this joke has been circulating the last few days: "On what is soviet power based? On Jewish brains, Lettish riflemen, and Russian fools." Fabulous rumors are again circulating in Moscow, this time about the Poles. But, alas, it is not the Poles who will save Russia! Millet costs 9,500–10,000 rubles a pud.

13 [January]. From comrade Krylenko I received the reply that comrade Kamenev has not yet acquainted himself with the case. I think that we will not be summoned. The case will take its usual course, and it is up to fate to decide whether or not my aunt will survive in the Cheka. Some are persuaded that the year 1920 will see some kind of solution. I think that must not be expected. Old Russian society is being transformed into fertilizer and humus for the future. For me that future appears to be completely dark.

21/22 [January]. I wrote nothing for a whole week, since the time I left Moscow. The cause is still the same: the impossibility of being certain that the journal will not fall into the wrong hands. The main event of this time is the report of the official press about the lifting of the blockade against Russia. Everyone has been carried away again. Once again they fail to notice, or don't want to notice, that the official reports reflect only what the authorities want to report for internal consumption, not the objective truth. Personally, I am not drawing any conclusions from these reports for the time being: they are not distinguished by clarity, and in any case I have no certainty that something contradictory won't be reported tomorrow. Nonetheless, thoughts are glimmering in connection with these rumors about the possibility of legal exit abroad; this possibility appears dimly somewhere in the distant future.

In Moscow there have been some kind of celebrations in memory of Herzen all these days. The rulers of the earth are appearing at ceremonial meetings; also appearing are the inveterate orators—comrade Sakulin and Lemke.[3] A meeting of the "university" is taking place together with the society of destroyers of Russian letters,[4] and at this meeting of the university there is not one professor in attendance, or almost so, despite the fact that "free admission, heated premises" has been temptingly added to the posters hung on the university fence. I will add that on the same poster, above the boastful program of the solemn meeting in memory of Herzen, someone's hand, more contemporary in spirit, had inscribed with a pencil two truly indecent words—p.... and c.... Poor Herzen. How grieved he would have been by all these bolshevik wakes. We in the museum had to set up an exhibit in his memory, too. Such anguish it was to do it; such a feeling of uselessness and needlessness was in my soul when, not wanting to be branded a saboteur, I exhorted dear old V. F. Savodnik to fetch down the exhibits and put them out in the display cases. Today (the 22d) there is an evening at the Malyi Theater, where the Jew Tsederbaum-Martov will say something, and those poor nags on their last legs, Iuzhin[5] and Ermolova, will read something from his works.

I sat home all day today and ran out only to my "purchase," to the monastery, trying to get a cross put above my Ninochka. That, too, is problematical. However, I discovered a secret, which is very simple: here, too, the palm has to be greased. The trip to the Posad has improved my mood a little, in that I have rested. It is so good to sleep in the quiet of the Posad. And I slept for twelve hours out of every twenty-four. Here the relative spiritual calm that I had acquired there has again disappeared: es machen mir meine Gespenster sogar einen Tagesbesuch![6] Despair, the unrelieved despair of loneliness has seized me with a new force, and I feel more than ever before that you can't get away from yourself.

E. A. Got'e, on whose account we went to see the secretary of comrade Kamenev, has been released, but on the eve of her liberation they came for her again to arrest her. She came home on the day of the funeral of her sister, about whose death she knew nothing.

[3] Pavel Nikitich Sakulin (1868–1930) was a *marxisant* literary critic who wrote books on the sociology of literature. He was made an academician in 1929, shortly before his death. Mikhail Konstantinovich Lemke (1872–1923) was an extremely prolific historian and publicist, specializing in the history of the Russian revolutionary movement. He supported the Bolshevik regime and was in these days an indefatigable lecturer and propagandist. He joined the Communist party in 1922.

[4] "Obshchestvo gubitelei rossiiskoi slovesnosti," that is, Obshchestvo liubitelei rossiiskoi slovesnosti, the Society of Lovers of Russian Letters, a literary-scholarly society attached to Moscow University, founded in 1811.

[5] See n. 93 for 1917.

[6] Got'e quotes from one of Heine's *Lyrisches Intermezzo* (1822–1823), no. 37. See n. 35.

24 [January]. Yesterday I participated in the meeting of the State Academic Council of the People's Commissariat of Enlightenment, which was supposed to decide the question of the staffing of university libraries. Pokrovskii chaired. Almost exclusively nonintelligentsia people participated, with the exception of comrade Volgin, who with a stupid and insolent look demanded special measures to protect the interests of outside borrowers at the university library. Special interest was aroused by the situation of the library commission, which these people absolutely wanted to pack with representatives of the communist students and a representative of the commissariat. A certain young man—apparently a representative of the communist students in this council—distinguished himself in this matter: he wanted to stick even representatives of the district soviets in the library commission. His face was typical—a low brow, a malevolent expression of lips and eyes. The comments of Pokrovskii himself were interesting—exuding open hatred of the university and the professors. The participating communists exchanged remarks about politics among themselves, and here one could sense a tone of exultation and confidence that they are the conquerors of everyone and everything. Alas, Russian reality for the moment gives them superficial grounds for saying so. The library commission was buried. Aside from that, I presented Pokrovskii a memorandum on the need to buy books abroad. It was answered that now is just the time to prepare for this buying. God willing!

29 [January]. Ivanovo-Voznesensk. I have again not written for the same reasons. Now at liberty, having left on tour and ensconced in a sanatorium regime in Ivanovo, I am sitting down to write for a whole week.

On January 25 I was at the beloved grave in the morning. I spent the whole day at the nameday party of my belle-soeur, Tat'iana Nikolaevna. In the evening I left for the university, where there was to be comradely conversation and a cup of tea. About 150 people had gathered in the administration hall—the council in its numerical complement of the epoch of the Provisional Government. The rector opened the meeting with a report of some statistical data. The most interesting was the information that the number of students in the university (combined) exceeds 26,000 persons. The report met with general laughter. The general sense of the report data was that the university had done what it could, but *after a gallant fight* had to submit to the bolsheviks[7]. Then the deans talked about the situation of the faculties, with Grushka and Martynov[8]

[7] This sentence is in English in Got'e's text.

[8] Professor Aleksei Vasil'evich Martynov (b. 1868) was a surgeon and member of the medical faculty of Moscow University.

speaking the most academically. Reformatskii[9] spoke very stupidly, with the tone of an archdeacon, reporting that 1919 was a better year in the university than 1918 (!?). Vinaver[10] very aptly said that the faculty of social sciences is the illegitimate son of the university in search of legitimation. If he did not say this in those precise terms, such was the sense of his speech. The meeting was enlivened by tea with sugar, cookies, and black bread with butter. There were still other speakers after the deans, but I heard only Kizevetter, who as usual sparkled like seltzer water: he gave off light but no heat. He said that Russian scholars are like the sentinel of Catherine's time who was posted to guard a rose and was not relieved but forgotten, while the rose withered in the meantime. That would be true, but he then went on to argue that the Russian people is a statist people, and that it will reconstruct the state that it had so long and persistently built. I think he himself didn't believe what he was saying.

From the university I went to a party of actors of the Chamber Theater,[11] where I had been invited by the nameday celebrant, Tat'iana Nikolaevna. I decided to pull myself together, not to spoil their mood, and to have a look. A revival of forms of the past, of that long-gone bachelor life when I now and then, quite rarely, dipped into bohemia—that is what I got from this digression, and also the possibility to drink some alcohol, to the amount of two or three jiggers, which represents no small interest at the present time. These people are self-sufficient; more than that, they are full of themselves. Looking at them, I understood what makes them like bolsheviks: they have just a few doubts about anything as the bolsheviks do. The night was almost sleepless; I went to bed at 6 A.M. On Monday the 26th there was a general meeting in the museum for reelection of the employees' committee. Elected were those who were ordered by someone or other, and as a result Kozlov got onto the committee and Georgievskii did not. I allow for the possibility that Vinogradov wanted this, but it turned out extremely stupidly. One less competent person and one more smart aleck. Such triviality and boredom, these elections; they exude such uselessness.

On Tuesday—departure for Ivanovo-Voznesensk to give an episodic course of lectures. Because of imperfect arrangements, I learned that I was going only three hours before the departure of the train. I set off in a good mood, carrying two bales on my shoulders. The ticket had already been bought, and I settled very well into a relatively decent first-class car

9 Aleksandr Nikolaevich Reformatskii (1864–1937) was a prominent chemist (and brother of the even more prominent chemist Sergei Nikolaevich Reformatskii).

10 Professor Aleksandr Markovich Vinaver (b. 1883), formerly of the law faculty, was the first (elected) dean of the new faculty of social sciences. His specialties were law and economics.

11 Kamernyi teatr, the new dramatic theater founded by A. Ia. Tairov in 1914.

in which by no means everything had been broken, and which was relatively clean. I neither saw nor felt any lice, or "semashkos"[12] as they now call them. It was in general like old times in the car. Only in the morning did two communists crowd into the corridor—both of the "holy" type: one was a fool of a laborer, from the metalworkers, the other was a more intellectual type, who had probably spent time in exile and emigration. They argued between themselves about questions of party tactics, dropping words like "comrade," "I excuse myself,"[13] gubkom, gubkhoz, ispolkom, gubnarobraz, and the like.[14] The main point of their argument consisted of whether *collegia* were needed in the institutions and who should be in them. The metalworker stood for decreasing their numbers and significance; the émigré defended them; both were accustomed to mass meetings. Both were yelling and neither out-argued the other.

I slept very well in the train, but I was awakened by the stops: in Khot'kovo for some reason we stopped for about three hours; in Aleksandrov—from 4 A.M. to 12 noon. It was not the first time I have traveled by rail in the dead of the sovdep era, but I am still outraged by these senseless stops, to which I should have become accustomed long ago. The main thing is the feeling of being in a country where any sense of *punctuality* on the railroads has been lost, the very concept of punctuality has been lost, and every stop can drag on for an indeterminately long time.

The usual ruin is felt at the stations everywhere; the only passengers are lice-covered red army men, gray, resembling lice themselves. And truly, the former gray heroes—inert like lice that have eaten away the Russian land. We arrived in Ivanovo-Voznesensk at 11 P.M., and I crossed the entire town on foot with another professor, a meteorologist from the Petrovskaia Academy, and reached the dormitory at 12 o'clock. I slept superbly. Today I visited the dean, the secretary, and the office, and agreed about the lectures, of which I will give six, beginning on Saturday. In general, I got my bearings properly and came away with the impression that living here is like being in a sanatorium—you get away from your affairs; no one disturbs you; you can get some rest and bring something back.

But the general mood does not change. There is a persistent feeling of a ruined life and a ruined country; I recall the words of Dante that I read the other day: "Vivere senza speranza in disio." And here, away from Moscow affairs, you feel more than ever that only thus is it possible to live in Sovdepiia. Here, of course, they are interested in the news of Mos-

[12] Nikolai Aleksandrovich Semashko (1874–1949) was commissar for health.

[13] *Izviniaius'*. This form is still widely used in Soviet Russian speech, and is still considered to be uncultured. Cf. French, *Je m'excuse*.

[14] Gubkom: provincial party committee; gubkhoz: provincial economic administration; ispolkom: executive committee; gubnarobraz: provincial education administration.

cow, but there is no real news, and nothing to tell. Only one thing emerges from the Moscow rumors of the last few days: something is happening between the rest of the world and the bolsheviks, and this "something" permits a certain hope for the possibility of departing abroad.

31 [January]. Thus far my Ivanovo impressions continue to be fine. You feel relieved of Moscow. It is the same as a stay in a sanatorium. Pleasant conversations with intelligent people in the evenings. So far the most interesting is Pontovich, either a German or a Pole, but russified. There is something of Goncharov's Stolz in him.[15] In the evening conversations the tongue is loosened and the brain limbers up. That doesn't mean that the feeling of grief disappears. On the contrary, it is frequently sharper than ever. For example, yesterday I was looking over Herzen's works and read part of his correspondence with Natasha. How painful and sad it became. In a word, even if "you want to forget, to stop loving—you love all the more, stronger."

Today I stocked up on provisions at the market. I have got to eat well myself, too. Ivanovo-Voznesensk is a very curious town. It was formed entirely of hamlets and villages and factories, grown together, so the result is something extremely incoherent and absurd: a town without a center, filled with shacks, among which palazzos of the former bourgeois tower here and there.

FEBRUARY

1 [February]. I still feel like I am on a sanatorium regimen—I rested the whole day. In the evening there was the first lecture. The audience was mixed; after the lecture some Moscow students from the [Women's] Courses came up and chatted. I was once more convinced how small the world is. This morning I toured the Burylin[16] museum: a local bourgeois and exmagnate spent a lot of money and collected everything imaginable. As always in such cases, there are many good things and a lot of junk. I intend to sit quietly and rest for the remainder of the day. During my walk I saw many local palaces occupied by soviet institutions. Everywhere there is the same picture of plunder and violence. It is sad to look at the frozen, dead factories. Here, too, when you go out of the "sanato-

[15] Pontovich, apparently, was a professor in Ivanovo-Voznesensk. Stolz was the half-German "devotee to work and efficiency" in Goncharov's novel *Oblomov* (1859). Mirsky, *A History of Russian Literature*, p. 183.

[16] Burylin had had one of the largest factories in Ivanovo-Voznesensk; it manufactured cotton goods.

rium," you feel that there is only one solution—to leave this terrible, ruined country.

2 [February]. Today I obtained some sunflower oil, but in order to get it, I had to have a bottle. Luckily, I met on the street one of the professors' wives with whom I had become acquainted here, and she brought me out two bottles from her milk-woman's, who happened to be living across from the place of our meeting. If it weren't for that accidental meeting, I wouldn't have gotten the oil. After that expedition, I sat at home and grieved. I felt the emptiness and futility of my present existence with rare clarity. I am needed only by Volodia! Later, I got myself together and went to the lecture. There were about thirty people. The audience was attentive; the lecture cheered me up a little. In the evening I again sat down with Herzen's works in Lemke's edition.[17] I am looking them over for a small report in the Society for Russian History and Antiquities. That narcotic still works. It should be used. Bolshevization got lost somewhere and didn't oppress me today. There are no rumors or newspapers, and thank God!

3 [February]. A day without external events. A snowstorm. At home all day. A lecture in the evening; despite the weather, the auditors came and were attentive. I spent the whole day looking over Herzen's works. There is much in common with me in his feelings after the death of his wife. Reading his letters for the years 1852–1853, you feel how hard it was for him and how he was tormented by the problem of raising his children. And he had material security and didn't have to worry about the day to come. All morning I thought about the desirability and possibility of departure and, despite all possible woes and failures, I came to the conclusion that I should leave if it becomes possible. I will take Volodia, and come what may. Here, neither I personally nor my work is needed by anyone.

4 [February]. I am making the first preparations for my return to Moscow. I thought a lot about what to do if the possibility of going abroad should arise. Reason persistently dictates staying there for a long time, regardless of all the difficult aspects of such an outcome. When I was having dinner today in the local student dining room, I once again came to the same conclusion: around me sat savages who imagine themselves to be the reformers of mankind. What can be done with such people, with such a nation? In the evening I tried to arrange practical exercises;

[17] A. I. Gertsen, *Polnoe sobranie sochinenii i pisem*, 22 vols., ed. M. K. Lemke (Petrograd, 1919–1925).

five people responded to my invitation, for the most part local autodidacts. I don't think anything will come of it.

5 *[February]*. The newspapers are reporting on the peace with Estonia. It is possible that an air hole between Sovdepiia and the world will be created temporarily. It would be good if one could succeed in arranging for the ordering of foreign books through that air hole. The song about the good lad and melancholy is profoundly true.[18] You can't get away from yourself. Whether at night or during the day, going to a lecture or in the midst of studies at home—I think constantly of the irretrievable, irredeemable loss, of the fact that I had everything and now there is nothing. This thought resounds in me like a funeral knell. *L'angelus* of my life.

7 *[February]*. The time has come to sum up my stay in Ivanovo-Voznesensk. I am going to Moscow today. In general, the impressions are excellent. A fine reception, amiable and courteous attention. Complete quiet in warmth and repletion over the course of ten days. During that time there have been no Moscow rumors, no strain; toward the end, on the last day, an excellent bath. It would be very good to live here with a family; good in the sense of calm and the relative (it seems?) possibility of forgetting about the existence of the bolsheviks. However, to live here would not be a complete solution to the problem; the deterioration of material conditions is occurring steadily here as well, with a lag behind Moscow of several months. If the general conditions don't change, then in time things will be impossible here, too. Moreover, it would be harder to clear out abroad from here than from Moscow. In any case, my stay here was a genuine rest for me.

I think that I was also calm here and tried while at rest to delve into myself and think over my situation. It must be admitted that it is revolting:

> Nel mezzo del camin di nostra vita
> Mi ritrovai per una silva oscura

con un piccolo bambino, one must add to Dante's words; it is almost impossible to raise a son without his mother, especially in the present conditions. *Eine Lebensgefährtin wiederzusuchen*—the thought is sickening. To leave oneself would be simplicity itself; with Volodia—to take him to a foreign country without a mother, without a governess—it would be more than difficult. It is impossible to find a governess. Nina's family can be relied upon, but the grandmother is fragile, Tania is not for hire to

---

[18] The brave youth begs his companions to cast him into the Volga to drown his sorrow from unrequited love for a maiden. A. I. Sobolevskii, *Velikorusskie narodnye pesni*, vol. 5 (St. Petersburg, 1899), nos. 105, 106.

work for me, and Lelia is weighed down with her own family. The general condition of life is impossible. For the future, I see in Russia only dying. All this took shape before my eyes with extraordinary clarity here. Providence or fate will show what is to be done. I only think that if it becomes possible to leave together with Volodia, one should see in this the hand of fate and leave without hesitation. As long as I am in Moscow I will gladly return to Ivanovo-Voznesensk.

11 [February]. The return trip to Moscow was quite all right, but rather long. We arrived in Aleksandrov at 11 A.M., but waited there until 11 P.M., when we were attached to the Iaroslavl' train. The boredom was very great, but it was diminished by sitting in warmth. We walked into town to find dinner, but were told that red army men had arrived today and, besides, there was a gathering of some kind of activists, therefore the visiting professors were asked to visit the following day. We left Aleksandrov at 11, and arrived in Moscow at 6 A.M.; 7 hours, 105 versts, that is, 15 versts an hour. But this was for the better, as we could walk about Moscow in the daylight.

In Moscow all kinds of unpleasant things of the usual type loomed, but I don't care about them. I feel myself in the mood of Pecherin (his verses about the boat). Yesterday it was learned that professors are receiving a ration—it is still not clear what kind. Apparently, the bolsheviks need to be able to say to Europe that scholars are in favor here. I found Volodia in fine fettle and well. That is the only comforting thing.

They have stopped heating the museum again and this time positively until spring. That will bring new and irreparable ruin to the affairs of the library—cold once again, and again your fingers begin to freeze. Try to work in those conditions! The general situation is unclear, and I can understand little of it. I will say only one thing: it is not the Poles who will save Russia.

14 [February]. "Senza sperare vivemo in disio"—that is the correct Dante verse that I cited earlier in distorted form: it describes my mood best of all, in both general and in concrete affairs and relations. Professor V. M. Khvostov has hanged himself, apparently as a result of an acute attack of melancholy. I had not seen him for a long time, and his experiences in the last year of his life were far from clear to me. Formerly this was a man who valued himself more highly than he should have, self-infatuated and self-admiring. In the first year of the revolution, he was constantly predicting what would happen next with the Russian revolution, and was always wide of the mark. Later on he himself saw the futility of his predictions and, perhaps, lost faith in his foresight. However, as late as last year when we were still having discussions about Compréhension

Réciproque, Khvostov still betrayed confidence in himself, his importance, and his future—how he savored, for example, talking about how
he would give lectures in Paris. The idea occurs to me that, having irrevocably decided to die, he must have said, almost like Nero: "What a great
scholar is dying!"

How fed up I am with the museum! Vicious cold again; everyone
around either doesn't come to work or is sick, and I have to do everything
for everybody.

16 [February]. Two more days in which nothing new has happened. It is
still and dead in the soul. Brain and body are freezing, for the frosts of
Candlemas are extremely hard. Somewhere in the far distance the possibility of leaving glimmers. Whither and what for? You sometimes try
not to ponder those questions.

19 [February]. Rumors of a new bolshevik campaign against the humanities faculties and, perhaps, even of their complete destruction. Well, that
would only be logical. They don't need the humanities since they don't
serve practical party purposes. The faculties will be replaced by party
schools, short courses; that is, there will be in our field what already exists
in the field of the technical sciences—poor half-educated technologists
will be created, and scholars will be simply destroyed, as an unneeded
luxury in the worker-peasant republic. If they would take the next logical
step and set free all the humanities professors to go where they please—
how good that would be!

Arrests are continuing in Moscow—today they grabbed Iu. V.
Sergievskii[19]—on a denunciation from Spassk, they say. Despite their
cries about some kind of new era in bolshevism, everything remains the
same. A picture I contemplate every day can serve as the emblem of
everything that exists: on the corner tower of the archive there is represented a figure whose features you can't make out, and under it is the
legend "We reject the old world." All around it everything is strewn with
shit and pissed upon such as it never was under the old order. I positively
return to my thought of long ago that the reformers of Russian life should
have in the first place taught people how to use latrines.

There is the same haze on the general horizon as before. Out of ennui
I continue to occupy myself with putting in order the postal stamps that
have come to the museum. About the museum, incidentally: they have
stopped heating us altogether, and it is now below zero inside the build-

[19] This was probably Georgii Vladimirovich Sergievskii (b. 1886), an art historian and
historian of Western Europe. He was arrested in the roundup of the members of the so-
called "Tactical Center" in February 1920 (see n. 21). "Georgii" and "Iurii" are two forms
of the same name, "George." Spassk is probably the town in Riazan' province.

ing; the ink is freezing, hands grow numb. No one comes to work, and whoever does come runs off to dinner. What kind of productive work is possible? Death, cold and hungry, is everywhere. And reports of deaths are pouring down like rain.

23 [February]. I spent four days at Lelia Kurdiumova's at the "bridge-construction depot" at the intersection of the Ring Road and the Petersburg Highway. Life was good from the external point of view; that is, there were bliny and even a little alcohol, so there was the illusion of something old.[20] I will be silent about the state of the moral atmosphere, since there is no need to write about the intimate side of the family's life. That is better. They live in the summer house of some rich man, Pavlov. The summer house is built on a low place where, of course, it is damp, in a wood, which the comrades have already cut down to the ground and ruined. The summer house had embellishments; many roofs, henhouses, barns, etc. I wouldn't even put a doghouse in this place. Nevertheless, the great embellishment is completely befouled and bears all the marks of horror and ruin. I will add that inside the electrical fixtures have been removed and stolen; and there are plans to ruin all the rooms of the main house for the needs of the depot. Such is the local picture. Next door is the station of the Ring Road, "Bratsevo," which is embellished by a cemetery of thirty-five or forty dead locomotives. I was told in this regard that this is a very small cemetery, that there are even more corpses at the other stations. On the way there, past the Tver' Gate, the roads are covered with snow; there is a cemetery of dead streetcars near the former racetrack, the rails snowed over. Strel'na with its tropical garden has practically all frozen. In Vsekhsviatskoe, dismantled houses and peeling signs, just as in Moscow. In a word, from the Moscow point of departure to the point of arrival—nothing but undisguised death and ruination, like everywhere else in former Russia. I had not been beyond the Tver' Gate for about four years, and I confess that the impression was oppressive, despite all the dulling of nerves.

In Moscow there is a new series of arrests, to which people close to the Union of Public Activists[21] are being subjected; they say that several ac-

[20] It was Shrovetide. Lelia Kurdiumova was Got'e's sister-in-law.

[21] The *Soiuz obshchestvennykh deiatelei* was an organization of nonsocialist political and military figures that dated back to the August 8–10, 1917, conference of public figures (see n. 70 for 1917). This was one of several veins of anti-Soviet organization linked to the Tactical Center that was being mined out in 1919–1920 by the Cheka. The leadership of the Tactical Center was arrested in February 1920; twenty-eight people were tried on this account in August 1920. The characterization of the Tactical Center as a highly organized anti-Bolshevik network for counterrevolutionary action, which was made by the prosecution in the August 1920 trial, was surely an exaggeration. See S. P. Mel'gunov, "Sud istorii nad intelligentsiei," in *Na chuzhoi storone*, 1923, no. 3, pp. 137–63.

tivists of the cooperative movement, supposedly suspected of ties outside official channels with cooperative activists living abroad, have also been arrested. Whatever the case, there is again a wave of unrest and despondency in Moscow. In general affairs the situation remains incomprehensible to us, who are informed of nothing.

News has come that M. M. Khvostov has died in Tomsk from typhus; he was my university comrade, a good scholar, a lively and caring person who was for a long time the main figure in world history at Kazan' University.[22] Of how many more victims will those who are fated to survive the others in the "twilight of Russian life" learn?

24 [February]. The matter of the arrests carried out over the last few days continues to be illuminated by rumors in the same tones as a few days ago; the aspiration to establish ties with the cooperativists living abroad, the aspiration of the Cheka to demonstrate its utility, somebody's betrayal and somebody's stupidity. In the museum committee we debated the necessity of creating some kind of agricultural enterprise, for otherwise they will certainly force us in the summer to participate in productive labor—that is, in other words, to return forcibly to primitive forms of life.

28 February. The diary is progressively acquiring the character of alternating notes. My constant migrating and the continuing absence of security for notes of any kind hinder the work. Today the Poles revealed their appetites, which, by the way, did not surprise me. They demand a plebiscite in the areas that belonged to Poland before 1772. Well? It serves the Russian fools right; a people that has ruined in three years what it took five hundred to create deserves its fate. The bolsheviks on this account are howling about the "Polish imperialists," but the latter will either get everything they want or we will be threatened with a new war, whose burden will fall on Simple Ivan, who was assured in 1917 that he was very tired. I have again put on the agenda a trip abroad to buy books. There was a meeting on that subject yesterday in the Commissariat of People's Enlightenment. The attitude was very cautionary; in that institution they apparently want the foreign books to travel to Moscow. For all practical purposes, I will probably have to take the entire organization of an expedition on myself, but will I be able to go there? Everything will depend on whether they will let Volodia go with me or not. Qui vivra, verra. Perhaps there is not so long to wait. We are waiting for the professor's ration, but when will they give it? Nothing more precise is heard.

---

[22] Mikhail Mikhailovich Khvostov (1872–1920), a specialist in ancient history, had taught at Kazan' University since 1900. He also wrote about the history of modern Europe. According to the *Soviet Encyclopedia*, Khvostov died on February 25.

Everyone seems to have calmed down; meanwhile, they are still not progressing from words to action. They are saying that seven persons—I will name those I haven't forgotten: D. M. Petrushevskii, D. N. Anuchin,[23] A. A. Eikhenval'd,[24] Timiriazev, Gor'kii, Volgin, and someone else— have already received special rations, not only for themselves but for their families as well, with special letters from the Council of People's Commissars. How flattering to feel oneself a scholarly *oprichnik*[25] of soviet power and the soviet state. I return to yesterday's meeting at Pokrovskii's: he is skeptical about an exchange of wares and proposes that the book expedition be given money to the extent of 300–400 million paper rubles. "What of it? That is only one-fourth of daily production," he added. Even bearing in mind the bolsheviks' programmatic aspiration to destroy all forms of money, I don't understand where they are going with their insane financial policies. I wrote quite a lot, despite numerous hindrances arising from the fact that for two hours someone was constantly taking turns talking to me, and from the fact that in the end hands and brain became stiff from the cold. It is colder in the museum than outside.

MARCH

3 March. In the meeting of the State Academic Council on Friday the question was raised of destroying all the faculties except the medical faculty. Thus, after all kinds of rearrangements, the bolsheviks have decided to abolish the university as such. There will not be a long wait to learn what will be put in the place of the abolished faculties: something or nothing. In other words, will this be the finale of a destructive tragedy or a comedy with a change of costume? Today the meeting in the State Publishing House "on sending agents abroad for buying books" was pallid and boring. My plan is simpler and more realistic. I didn't have much trouble getting several of the basic propositions of my memorandum ac-

[23] Dmitrii Nikolaevich Anuchin (1843–1923) was an anthropologist and geographer, one of the founders of Russian academic anthropology, and first chairman of the geography department at Moscow University (from 1885 until his death).

[24] Aleksandr Aleksandrovich Eikhenval'd (1864–1944) was a physics professor at Moscow University and a leading specialist on electromagnetics. He emigrated in 1920.

[25] An oprichnik was a member of the special army of bodyguards and police agents (*oprichnina*) created by Ivan IV in 1565.

The academic or professors' ration seems to have been the result of Gor'kii's efforts to help scholars. On December 23, 1919, Sovnarkom passed a resolution "On the improvement of the life of scientific specialists," and beginning in early 1920, two thousand special rations were made available. They were allocated by the Commission for the Improvement of the Life of Scholars (KUBU). See Fitzpatrick, *The Commissariat of Enlightenment,* p. 82.

cepted. One could sense the general recognition of universal helplessness and, at the same time, of the need to establish relations with the world abroad. In the last few days flour has risen to 13–15,000 rubles, millet to 16–17,000. The food problem is becoming more and more difficult. The desire is growing ever stronger in me that there be peace, and only peace, in which freedom of movement would be restored. I don't need anything more.

6 March. I have decided to take action to find a way out of the impending catastrophe, material and physical. There was a discussion with the Yugoslavs—Bakhrushin and I on our side, Ilić and Jovanović on the other. Jovanović is an interesting fellow, of a clearly pronounced Yugoslav type—big nose and brown hair. He talked with us apparently sincerely and frankly: from his viewpoint and that of the radical party to which he belongs, the appearance of Russian scholars in Serbia is very desirable; but, being here, they can do nothing nor can they say anything for certain. Whichever one of them gets out of here will make an effort in behalf of the matter. Bakhrushin's and my impression is that if the affair goes successfully, something may come of it. Jovanović averred that he still believes in Russia's future, that the bolsheviks distinguish themselves by an extraordinary capacity for lying, that he does not believe them about anything. In his opinion, Russia must overcome the crisis of bolshevism herself, from within. Yesterday as well, two hours before the appointed conversation, I was at a meeting of the "scholarly sector" of the People's Commissariat of Enlightenment in the presence of Pokrovskii and Lunacharskii. Besides them there were Artem'ev and Ter-Oganesov[26]—an Armenian carrot-top with a smart-alecky look who, they say, has won favor with Lenin. I declaimed my memorandum and found complete sympathy. "They" seem to recognize clearly the necessity of establishing cultural ties with other countries, and all the bolsheviks present accepted the basic propositions of my plan; it now remains to get it through the collegium of the commissariat and then through the Commissariat of Foreign Affairs, and to decide the question of the people who will go. I decided to sustain the affair to the end, whether or not I am able to take advantage of it. A base in the Baltic region apparently pleases them. The wish to give the entire undertaking a certain businesslike character was apparent in the conversations. The expedition should be small in size, and the needs of more or less all the interested institutions should be reflected in it. For the first time I saw close up comrade Lunacharskii-

[26] Vartan Tigranovich Ter-Oganesov (b. 1890) was an astronomer with an appointment in the Moscow Mining Institute.

Lunaparkskii-Lupanarskii.[27] A vigorous man of about forty-five, of a very healthy and well-fed appearance. His self-satisfaction is apparent in his every movement, every word. It is unlikely, however, that he has much authority among his comrades. It is apparent that they, too, consider him an empty person. Before the meeting, I had the occasion to talk with Pokrovskii and to raise the question of the transfer of Russian professors to the south. "You raise a very vital question," he said to me. "We should move not just people, but whole institutions. The existence of forty-two institutions of higher learning in Petersburg is abnormal and unthinkable. Petersburg will not be preserved in its former state and will not regain its former significance. I even think the capital will not stay in Moscow." "Where do you conceive of it, in Khar'kov or Kiev?" "Perhaps, but more likely in Odessa. In the future the center of the republic will form there. Life must move to the producing provinces." On the question of transfers to the south, he said: "Perhaps you will present your ideas on this question." Today I talked about this with Bakhrushin, who is raising the question himself. But what views of an important bolshevik on the Russian future! Apparently all of northern Russia appears to them to be one vast wasteland.

The bolsheviks have killed Kolchak.[28] Thus do they destroy all outstanding Russian men. Lice and a gray swamp of gorillas. That is the immediate future of former Russia.

10 March. The general situation is unchanged. There are interesting rumors, from D. I. Ul'ianov[29] through A. I. Iakovlev, that there are no armies in the south, neither red nor white, that a detachment of five hundred men is considered a very big force. The anarchy and disintegration in the south are complete. No offensive of the whites is to be expected—of which I, incidentally, was convinced long ago. A great many continue to expect something from the Poles, but by all indications the Poles have forgotten nothing and have learned nothing. The bolsheviks are convoking a scholarly commission in Moscow, which is collecting data on border delimitations with Poland. That means bargaining will begin, and all the lands the Poles want will be conceded, with the calculation of dismantling all of Poland later by means of propaganda. It seems to me that neither here nor abroad is it understood that Russia, by means of artificial selection, can become the receptacle of all the communists and hooligans from all over the world. It will be the same as it was in Geneva in Calvin's time: all the Jews and communists from the entire world will

[27] Deprecatory plays on the name Lunacharskii, which could be translated as "Moonstruck": "comrade Luna Park," etc.

[28] Kolchak was shot by the Bolsheviks in Irkutsk on February 7.

[29] Lenin's brother, Dmitrii Il'ich, who was in the Crimea.

gather here, and all nonsympathizers will be eliminated from here, will either die off or leave, and then international hooliganism under the name of communism will reign over the stupid, barbaric Russian people. And that will be its grave, dug by the Russian intelligentsia.

For me these days have been days of provisioning—I received three puds of flour through an "organization" that was thought to have been long gone. It is a characteristic feature of Russian meanness that those of our colleagues who did not want to risk depositing money in that "organization" have demanded their share and made a whole scandal, now that it has unexpectedly succeeded in bringing flour to Moscow. Afterward I looked after the notorious professor's ration, which, in general, is rather decent.

12 [March]. A meeting with S. F. Platonov. His appearance is not bad; a great deal of energy, as always—it just flows from him. Iakovlev and Bakhrushin dined at my place together with him and we asked him many questions. His views do not differ much from ours: evolution, with practical types devouring the ideologists in the beginning, and then they themselves being swallowed up by speculators. According to him, life is not so bad in Petersburg, at least for those who receive a ration; but the city is insanely and relentlessly declining. In Platonov's opinion, in the future it will be an enormous Russian harbor—and that's all. He has no doubts at all about this future for Petersburg.

The incident with the flour has been happily resolved. After long debates, a general meeting of the "collective" approved a deduction of two pounds each and satisfied all those who had not received [anything] to the extent of ten to fifteen pounds per person. Yesterday and today I implemented my professor's ration. Thanks to that handout, Volodia and I can feel somewhat secure, at least for a time.

13 [March]. Today is the day designated for cleaning houses and institutions; therefore everything is closed, and there are fewer people in the museum than ever before; and meanwhile, most likely, no one is doing anything at home—thus the usual picture obtains: the measure undertaken leads to unexpected results, moreover directly opposite to those intended. Forty-eight rations have been given to the museum; today they were divided up; a difficult operation—to pick forty-eight people from three hundred, when all are equally hungry. By chance I had in my hands today three issues of *Vie Parisienne* for September 1919—still the same laughter, jokes, sparkle, and wit. The war did not stop life there. *La brave vielle France* remains the same—laughing and in good spirits. Mieux vaut de rire que de larmes écrire, pour ce que rire est le propre de l'homme.[30] Rabelais's philosophy remains the philosophy of his descendants. What a contrast with the land of lackluster climate and lackluster communism.

15 [March]. The customary excursion to the monastery on Sunday. It is beginning to thaw; the old sun warms, "and may young life play at the entrance to the tomb, and indifferent nature glow with her eternal beauty."[31] Yesterday I visited B. I. Ugrimov,[32] whom I hadn't been to see for about fifteen years; I reminisced about bygone days with him and his wife; thirty whole years stretch out behind us. Today I read the letter of Countess E. A. Uvarova written from Poltava in November. It evoked a different world, which, alas, has perished, this time it seems for good. The old countess gives lessons, digs in the garden, and has unearthed a dolmen. The little Countess Ekaterina Alekseevna has left for Salonika.[33]

17 [March]. The news of the counterrevolutionary coup in Germany, which was published yesterday, does not impress me very much.[34] The man in the street has begun to speak again and is making all kinds of suppositions, is hoping for something. Ich aber verhänge das Fenster des Zimmers mit schwarzen Tuch: Es machen mir meine Gespenster sogar einen Tagesbesuch.[35] My sorrows have made me a gloomy philosopher. Even if Western Europe changes its attitude toward Russia as a result of that coup, the results of such a change will not be evident soon. It seems to me that this coup may even temporarily fortify Russian authority: both Germany and the Entente need Russia. And now they will try to get as much good out of her as they can in an effort somehow to eliminate the bolsheviks.

19 [March]. I made the acquaintance of General Brusilov, who is living out his days in bolshevik Moscow, conducting himself with dignity and independently of the bolsheviks. He receives nothing, is needy, and is selling his bookcases, which the Rumiantsev Museum is buying from him. If I had been told five years ago, amid the thunder of the Eighth Army's successes and later in 1916 amid the successes of the southwestern front, that I would some day be doing small favors for Brusilov, I would

---

[30] "It is better to laugh than to write of tears, for it is in man's nature to laugh."

[31] Lines from a verse by Pushkin. See n. 159 for 1919.

[32] Boris Ivanovich Ugrimov (b. 1872) was an engineer, born in Moscow.

[33] E. A. Uvarova was the daughter of Countess Praskov'ia Sergeevna Uvarova ("the old countess"; see n. 155 for 1917).

[34] The reference is to the Kapp Putsch in Berlin (March 13–17, 1920).

[35] "I, however, hang the window of the room with black cloth: so my ghosts pay a visit even in the daytime." Cf. n. 6.

not have believed it. He produces the impression of a cheerful, intelligent, and firm old man.

The prospects for a trip to Iur'ev have changed somewhat today; comrade Pokrovskii is now in favor of a small expedition; it is possible that, if the affair doesn't change several times more, this is better for us. Today I must write another memorandum about this matter.

German events are vague and unclear; it will take some time. Today Volodia and I are fasting, and on account of that occasion we are spending the night at home for the first time since our catastrophe. It is difficult and sad.

21 [March]. A muddle in Germany. My impression is this: the left has raised its head along with the right, but in sum the moderates will probably win again, and they will gradually move rightward. I do not regret the failure of the Junker adventure; it is they who more than anything else wanted to destroy Russia and did the most to that end of all the external enemies. They are talking of some kind of disturbances among the peasants and in the factories. I don't believe in them, or at least I don't count on them. The bolsheviks will crush all the protestants in turn with the help not of the Latvians and the Chinese, but of the burned-out Russian scum, which is capable of anything and stops before nothing. All around there is talk of nothing but the rations. Apparently some number of them are being given to the Rumiantsev Museum; I think that this is the only means of preventing the flight of the employees in all directions. Several hundred rations for academics or pseudo-academics have been distributed in Moscow. They say that in a few days the comrade-people's commissars will give another 1,300 or 1,800 rations for Moscow. And that is a real event, because 2,000 rations will save the entire Moscow community of scholars, or, more exactly, its remains.[36] I think that it costs nothing to give 2,000 rations; despite all the destruction, they are supporting a couple of million red army men loafers and all kinds of communists. At the same time, these figures convince me once more how small is the number of more or less civilized Russians. Such a number cannot preserve the country from complete barbarization.

25 [March]. I am again in Ivanovo-Voznesensk. The journey went quite satisfactorily; four of us rode in a two-place cabin and slept in a stack. It is the first time I have slept on an upper bunk that way. The most unpleasant part of the journey was walking across Moscow with a pud's weight on my shoulders, bearing in mind the Moscow mud as well. Here there is the customary cordiality and affectionate reception; although

---

[36] The total number of "academic rations" distributed was about two thousand.

since Kizevetter came at the same time as I did, my lectures have suffered a little. Today I spent the whole morning arranging matters of provision and clerical affairs and only sat down to work after lunch. The usual feeling of relaxation after Moscow; the weather is magnificent, spring-like; and by association of ideas I have persistent memories of former joyful springtime trips to the Crimea. And, by the law of contrast, my present circumstance as a man condemned to eternal solitude presents itself with even greater horror. It seems to me that recently I have become even more attached to Volodia, but I am more and more fearful for him and feeling sorry for him. How is he going to grow up? To take him abroad—and I think that if the possibility arises this should be done—means to condemn him to the possibility of even greater poverty than we are experiencing here; to leave him here means to condemn him to possible spiritual ruin. Figure that out. But departure from Sovdepiia is after all the only possibility, although a weak one, of achieving a decent life. Here everything is in the past—youth, happiness, my chosen work, and even any kind of bearable human life. In the last few days I have been overwhelmed by spiritual gloom as never before. The image of the happy past won't go away, and I am less than ever inclined to yield to the inevitable. On the outside everyone marvels at my restraint.

26 [March]. The stay in the Ivanovo-Voznesensk Polytechnic Institution is again beginning to have its salutary effect on me. I once again feel that I have landed in a sanatorium for several days. Moscow and all the events have gone far away. I went to listen to Kizevetter's lecture and noticed that he is not free of imitating Kliuchevskii: the pronunciation of certain words with accented "o," and accent patterns that are not characteristic of A.A. in conversation, suddenly appear in the lecture. I had never heard his university lectures, and therefore this visit was especially interesting to me. His customary qualities and shortcomings show up in his presentation—liveliness, imagery, plasticity, on the one hand; a certain pursuit of the [felicitous] phrase, on the other. In the evening, conversation at Pontovich's. Several of the professors were gathered, and Kogan-Bernshtein,[37] a student of Struve, introduced the subject of the mechanics of the Russian revolution in comparison with the French and the English [revolutions]. There were quite a few conjectures about how Russia might emerge from the revolution; of course, we didn't resolve that question, but we had a fine time.

[37] Sergei Vladimirovich Kogan-Bernshtein (or Bernshtein-Kogan) (1886–1951) was an economist (economic geographer) who in the late 1920s taught at the Moscow Institute of Transport Engineering and at Leningrad University.

27 [March]. The sanatorium regimen continues to produce results. I have a feeling of respite from Moscow. The first lecture went successfully, in my opinion, despite the late hour and the competition of A. A. Kizevetter. There is so much free time that we go to listen to each other. Is this not an idyll in the scholarly Athens called Ivanovo-Voznesensk?

29 [March]. The idyll was ruined the morning of the 28th by the arrest of A. A. Kizevetter. It happened between 9 and 10 A.M. I got up at 10 A.M. and went out to the lavatory, where it was whispered to me: "a search at Kizevetter's!" While I was washing, there was a knock and A.A. came in and said to me quite calmly: "They are taking me again." Then he wanted to leave me his lecture notes, but they wouldn't allow him to. It was mentioned in the order that the arrest had been carried out by instructions from Moscow. Rumors are circulating here that many arrests are going on in Moscow; everyone is puzzled about their cause. There was to have been an evening in memory of Herzen that evening in the Pedagogical Institute. It was solemnly canceled because "due to independent circumstances" (how ironic those words sound!) A.A. could not take part in it. I finished here, at last, the book of M. de Vogüé, *Le Roman russe.*[38] An excellent, brilliant book, not only well written, but correctly perceiving much in Russian life and literature. I have the idea more and more often that observant foreigners have seen in us much that really exists but that we have not seen at all for lack of perspective.

30 [March]. They have taken Kizevetter to Moscow. Yesterday evening we—that is, Petrushevskii, Pontovich, Bernshtein, and I—went around to various places to find out if that rumor was true or not, and in what conditions he had to travel. They answered from the Provincial Cheka that there was no need to fear typhus infection, since with him they had sent their own people, "whom they also value." When we learned for certain that he was being sent off, it was already late to send him food; but we imagined that he must have had enough of it. *Izvestiia* printed a most curious announcement inviting, on behalf of the Cheka, the SRS, "right and left," who had escaped from prison to return to it without fear that their confinement would be harder. Isn't there a connection between this escape and the arrest of Kizevetter? There is certainly nothing impossible in it. Despite the sad outcome of Kizevetter's trip, the professorial idyll continues. Yesterday Petrushevskii, Pontovich, and Bernshtein listened to me, and the lecture apparently produced a good impression on them.

[38] The first edition of de Vogüé's book on the Russian novel was published in Paris in 1886; the thirteenth edition was published in 1916.

31 [March]. A day without incident. Marvelous summer weather. I am again experiencing the effects of the sanatorium regimen of Ivanovo-Voznesensk. My lectures continue to enjoy unexpected success.

APRIL

2 [April]. The news brought from Moscow convinces me that Kizevetter was arrested in connection with that same case of the public activists.[39] In this regard, P. told me interesting things about how L.'s[40] wife betrayed him out of jealousy. O, Russian slovenliness and frivolity! Then the conversation turned altogether to the Russian, and specifically Kadet, cliquishness that permeated the zemstvo and town unions: in order to succeed there, one had to belong to the *Russian Gazette* group or to the Kadet party. We then turned to Kadet methods: it turns out that very important affairs were entrusted to the most frivolous people—for example, Iu[reva?]. In regard to the latter, I remembered that she had told me, when I asserted that no struggle was possible and that the only solution was to leave: "Go off to your Kadets! But what of their chattels?"! This was a cry from the heart and a true reflection of how the Kadets treated their own, people devoted to them. And strangers they simply cast off, even worse than the bolsheviks. My good spirits continue. I am trying to get some rest and store up energy. I am very satisfied with the lectures. I bought up everything I could. Now I want only to see Volodia.

3 [April]. The end of my stay in Ivanovo-Voznesensk; we leave this evening. The impressions are just as good as the first time; however, I feel the need to go to Moscow, where I will be closer to the machinery that will help me to keep closer track of my fate. According to the newspaper reports, a schism over the principles of autocracy and collegiality has occurred at the congress of the RCP.[41] Some think that this may have some significance. I don't share that opinion: it is only a lovers' quarrel.[42]

---

[39] See n. 21. Got'e was probably correct in his surmise. See D. L. Golinkov, *Krushenie antisovetsogo podpol'a v SSSR*, vol. 2 (Moscow, 1980), pp. 11–21.

[40] "L." was probably Sergei Mikhailovich Leont'ev, a zemstvo man and Kadet party activist from Rostov district, Iaroslavl' province, who had been a member of the Union of Public Activists from its inception.

[41] RCP = Russian Communist party. The Ninth Party Congress was held from March 29 to April 4, 1920.

[42] Got'e refers to the criticism of overcentralization and unresponsiveness to local party groups leveled at the Central Committee at the congress by the so-called Workers' Opposition and Democratic Centralists. See Schapiro, *The Origin of the Communist Autocracy*, pp. 221–24. Got'e's characterization of these differences within the Party was astute.

9 [April]. Nearly a week in Moscow. I haven't been writing for the usual reasons. The first thing I learned in Moscow was that the matter of a trip abroad for books has been irrevocably postponed until foreign-trade relations are set right. That means a delay of several months, at best. I found no other disappointments here, but it has been a long time since I had such a flood of spiritual gloom as I have these days. And analyzing it, I see that it is a cheerful and calm gloom—the result of a clearly recognized cool and calm horror in regard to what is and what will be. The death of all Russian life is an already accomplished fact, without hope of rapid resurrection. When you see this dirty, ruined city, full of savage, beastlike people, you are overwhelmed with shame and horror. Yesterday and the day before, I happened to pass along some Moscow streets that I had not been on for a very long time, and perhaps this walk through the Moscow streets acted on my psyche even more strongly: you think yourself accustomed, but it is still painful and irritating to belong to a suicide-nation that has defiled everything. A routine visit to the beloved grave has again caused me to discover new acquaintances in the cemetery of Novodevichii Monastery—this is where the old civilized Moscow that has not left but remained behind is moving; like all of Russia, it is dying without heirs or estate, not just dying, but completely dying out. The only comforting thing, perhaps, is that the intelligentsia that prepared the ruin of Russia with its own hands is dying out with all the others.

They say that after Easter we are supposed to recommence classes in the university; only no one knows where we will give lectures, since we have been irrevocably thrown out of our lecture halls.

I am going with Volodia to Holy Week services, but I haven't the former mood—all is wormwood, dust, all the past has died.

12 [April]. Easter with beautiful weather. The general situation remains the same. I am ever more firmly convinced that everything we are seeing will last endlessly. Some news has arrived from places that were in the hands of the whites: in Kiev there were binges and drunkenness, accompanied by unneeded severity. The same in Rostov. A great number of people who are fleeing in all directions has accumulated in Rostov; I heard that V. B. Pokhvisnev has fled to Serbia. According to the rumors, the arrests and arbitrariness in Kiev and Odessa are worse now than in Moscow. According to the stories, it is expected that the bolsheviks will hold on in Kiev for a long time. Provisions are cheaper than in Moscow but are growing dearer every day.

On Easter I was with Volodia and Tania at Novodevichii Monastery; coming and going from there we met at least a dozen acquaintances; crossing the cemetery, I found some more familiar graves. I got the impression that all of Moscow, in the person of her best representatives, is moving in there—those are the paths predestined by fate for civilized Russians: *auswandern* or *aussterben*. Only [their] miserable remnants, together with the best elements that will rise above the present stinking dregs, will perhaps create something on the site of the present ruins.

Gloom in the soul; a solitary and sad Easter somehow especially encourages it. Manch Bild aus vergessenen Zeiten steigt auf aus seinem Grabe. . . .[43] To get out of this unbearable state, one wants to travel as much as possible, if only along the borders of expanding Sovdepiia, until the Lord delivers [one] from it. I have also decided to make two copies of my work of many years—the second volume of the history of regional administration—and deposit them in the Rumiantsev and public libraries so the work won't perish.[44]

16 [April]. Completely summer weather. I took Volodia to Lelia at the summer house; I remain a bachelor. I went there by the Ring Road, having learned to my amazement that trains are traveling on it. The general situation remains the same. Perfidious Albion is playing the role of mediator in the liquidation of Denikin. Today I went to see M. N. Pokrovskii about business of the Rumiantsev Museum. I was given to understand that it would be useful for the Rumiantsev Museum to establish ties with the Commissariat of Foreign Trade. In the office of the faculty of social sciences I was told that the problem of finding a place to lecture is acute. I nevertheless announced that I will begin lecturing on the 20th; however, on that day I will continue to lecture at home.

18 [April]. On the conversation with Pokrovskii: he said that "there is no machinery at all" in the academic section of the Commissariat of Foreign Trade and that we should take advantage of that situation and take things there in our own hands; that is typical for the prevailing muddle of ideas and for the impotence of the rulers.

I have heard of the arrival here of some American who was connected with public health and the Red Cross. He was fed a lot of stories about how they are ridding Russia of "the tsarist lice." According to the rumors, the American, who came to supply someone with some kind of provisions, acted deaf and dumb and produced the impression of a naive person who will believe anything. I received my "labor booklet": it is the same passport, but much worse than the old ones.

[43] "Many an image from times forgotten rose up from its grave. . . ."
[44] Got'e deposited the two typescript copies in the manuscript division of the Rumiantsev Museum and in the Petrograd Public Library. The second volume was finally published in 1941: *Istoriia oblastnogo upravleniia v Rossii ot Petra I do Ekateriny II*, vol. 2 (Moscow, 1941).

Campa[45] has returned from Italy and is saying that all is by no means well as regards socialism and even local bolshevism in Italy. Is everything he says true? We intend to question him in detail, but one must bear in mind here "qu'il a la mentalité d'un commis voyageur." O. M. Veselkina quite correctly made that remark about him. The Moscow optimists will not stop their empty gossip and rumors. The most unrealizable hopes will not die, but it is high time to part with them and understand that ahead lies a long, difficult period that very few will survive. They buried I. A. Pokrovskii yesterday.[46] That is a great loss in the poor world of learned Russian jurists and in the quantitatively no less poor world of tough Russian men. There was one student in uniform at the funeral. He reminded me of the general at the wedding.[47]

21 [April]. I was in the People's Commissariat of Enlightenment at a meeting of the commission on the distribution of books. It was proposed to nationalize all stores of books and to distribute them with the help of an institution called Tsurka.[48] Present were several famous soviet workers, such as Angarskii-Klestov[49] (a red-headed dolt) and comrade Vladimirskii,[50] who spoke more intelligently than the others at this meeting. A certain comrade Pichit, the representative of Tsentropechat',[51] objected the most to Tsurka, but he suffered complete defeat, and when everyone had left, Pokrovskii and the controller of the People's Commissariat of Enlightenment, Markus, guffawed wildly, repeating: "We have killed Tsentropechat'!" The picture of internecine squabbling was clear. They were rejoicing that they had brought harm to their own institution.

[45] Campa was probably an Italian colleague of Malfitano.

[46] Professor of civil law at Moscow University.

[47] The reference is to the practice of inviting senior officers to give "tone" to a wedding. See Vladimir Dal', *Tolkovyi slovar' zhivogo velikorusskogo iazyka*, s. v. "General" ("konditerskie generaly").

[48] Tsurka (Tsentral'noe upravlenie raspredeleniem knig; Central Administration for the Distribution of Books) was established in response to a Sovnarkom decree of April 20 on the nationalization of book stocks and other printed works. *Dekrety Sovetskoi vlasti*, vol. 8, pp. 59–60.

[49] Nikolai Semenovich Klestov (party pseudonym: Angarskii) (1873–1941) was a long-time Bolshevik writer and editor who served as head of the press division of the Moscow Soviet.

[50] Mikhail Fedorovich Vladimirskii (1874–1951) was another longtime Bolshevik, a former zemstvo doctor, prominent in the soviets (Moscow soviet and the Executive Committee of the Congress of Soviets) and in party and government institutions (at this time he was a member of the Bolshevik Central Committee and served as assistant commissar of internal affairs of the RSFSR).

[51] The acronym for the long title of the Soviet agency for the distribution of printed matter, founded by a TsIK decree of November 26, 1918, and the forerunner of Soiuzpechat'. The rivalry described here was between the commissariat and the institutions of the Soviet.

I was exhausted all these days by the burden of meetings.

There is nothing on the general horizon. I heard an interesting story about some German communists, supposedly, who have come here. They are demanding for themselves factories that they themselves will select; they are demanding land to work, with the right to evict the peasants, whom they do not fear because they will be armed to the teeth. In all, as many as 200,000 of them are supposed to appear. The soviet authority will probably let them in. I see in such a turn of events the beginning of the peaceful conquest of Russia by foreigners.

26 [April]. I have just returned from a trip to Troitsa; things are not well there. The commission that has arrived to "liquidate" the monastery is headed by the defrocked priest Galkin, who was a member of the Union of the Russian People under the old regime and very much wanted to be a bishop, but did not receive a bishopric.[52] Together with local bolsheviks he is pursuing a deliberate policy of plundering the monastery, and it will be a miracle if they don't succeed in it. All this is somehow sensed involuntarily when you are there; the heavy feeling is communicated and you get infected by it. Returning from there, I didn't go all the way to Moscow, but set off on foot from six kilometers [outside of town] through Rostokino, Ostankino, and Petrovsko-Razumovskoe to so-called Bratsevo[53] to my Volodia. The environs of Moscow had many charms and were beautiful in their way, but the woods around Ostankino are almost all cut down, and in Razumovskoe they have begun to cut the park beyond the pond. That is the beginning. Destruction and desolation—that is the predominant impression from a stroll about the environs of Moscow. The summer houses are empty; suffice it to say that on Saturday evening, with wonderful April weather, there was only one human figure in the entire main avenue of Petrovsko-Razumovskoe. I got the same impressions on Sunday from a stroll to Pokrovskoe-Glebovo and Ivan'kovo.

I found nothing new in Moscow for the two days that had passed. However, there are reports of new arrests among the Kadet party; on the other hand, other Kadets have been released, for example, A. A. Kizevetter, who was freed to the custody of comrade Riazanov with the obligation to appear for judgment of the tribunal if demanded. He looks well; he says only that he was terribly bored.

A certain disarray reigns in the university milieu; since there is no

[52] Mikhail Vladimirovich Galkin (Gorev), a former priest, was an antireligious publicist who edited the journal *Revolution and the Church* (*Revoliutsiia i tserkov'*), the main antireligious organ of the day.

[53] Bratsevo was a former noble estate with an imposing Alexandrine mansion about eighteen kilometers from Moscow near the Riga railroad line.

room for lecturing on the Mokhovaia, they intend to protest, while at the same time the building at Devich'e Pole stands unused. I think that under the given circumstances a protest is a superfluous and unnecessary thing. Some sort of protest is also being prepared in the University Council. It, too, seems unnecessary, since the university as such has been killed by the successive measures of the bolsheviks, and until the university is called upon to reconstitute itself, all our efforts will be in vain.

A meeting with out-of-work German scholars did not come off; I still don't know why.

On the road from Troitsa, I. F. Ognev told me that L. M. Lopatin[54] left a manuscript with prophecies, written by spiritualist means and concerning what we are now experiencing. Since both L.M. and I.F. are above any suspicion of altering the truth, the manuscript should be of extraordinary interest.

29 *[April]*. Some kind of war is getting under way again in the southwest: the Poles are stealing up on Kiev. The everlasting feud of the Russians and the Poles, in which neither side can understand the other, is beginning again. As the Russians couldn't understand that the Poles must be allowed to go their own way, so now the Poles can't understand that by seizing the West Russian territories they are opening an era of new wars between Poland and Russia in the future. Exactly the same opinion is held by the Serb, Jovanović, at whose place Bakhrushin and I had tea yesterday. There were no practical discussions about a trip to Belgrade, nor could there have been, but all the same perhaps something will come of this friendship. They say (D. N. Egorov's story) that the bolsheviks are preparing, or have prepared, a Polish revolutionary government headed by Dzherzhinskii, but that this was supposedly discovered and produced a big impression.[55] *Se non è vero.* ... In any case, Dzherzhinskii is officially listed as having gone somewhere. I saw a letter written by Lunacharskii to the City Committee of the RCP, which has seized the building of the Literary-Artistic Circle, concerning Serov's portrait of Ermolova, which belonged to the Circle and is still there: insofar as the committee

[54] Lev Mikhailovich Lopatin (1855–1920), professor of philosophy at Moscow University, was a leading proponent of Russian Idealist philosophy. He had died on March 21, 1920.

[55] "Relying on the support of the Red Army, the revolutionary workers and poorest peasants of the liberated regions of Poland created at the end of July [1920] their own government—the Provisional Revolutionary Committee of Poland (Pol'revkom)" (from the official Soviet history of the Civil War, *Istoriia grazhdanskoi voiny v SSSR*, vol. 5 [Moscow, 1960], p. 144). The members of Pol'revkom, formed in Bialystok (Belostok), were Dzherzhinskii (Dzierzynski), Feliks Kon (1864–1941), Iu. Markhlevskii (Julian Baltazar Marchlewski, 1866–1925), E. A. Prukhniak (Pruchniak), and I. Unshlicht (Jozef Unszlicht, 1879–1938). Markhlevskii was chairman of the committee.

is the *de facto owner* (how skillfully is the legal designation given) of the portrait, he, Lunacharskii, finds it desirable that the committee should make a gift of it to Ermolova herself on the occasion of her fiftieth anniversary, or to the Malyi Theater. That is the limit!

There was a meeting with A. A. Brusilov at Iakovlev's; he recounted interesting things about Nicholas II. It turns out that when [Nicholas] arrived in Mogilev after the abdication, he suddenly informed Alekseev that he had reconsidered and wanted to leave the crown to his son. Alekseev vainly tried to make him understand that it was already too late and that it was impossible to change anything. He made [Alekseev] call Rodzianko "by direct line" and inform him of the wish of the ex-emperor. Rodzianko not only couldn't bring the subject up, he had to conceal the proposition altogether. It is curious how Nicholas gave the adjutant generalship to Brusilov when he was in Galicia in 1915. Nicholas II was dining at Brusilov's headquarters, and on arriving to dinner he said to him: "Well, I am dining with you today, so congratulations on being my adjutant general!" That was almost an insult, Brusilov added—to give an adjutant generalship not for merit, but for a dinner.[56]

Yesterday and today there was a meeting of the faculty and of the University Council concerning the expropriatory policy of the so-called workers' faculty. Nothing will come of all this. The great Pan has died![57] Moscow University has died! And God knows when it will be resurrected. I am continuing my line of conduct. I went and participated as long as the faculty and the council had a concrete meaning and purpose. But now there is nothing to do in them.

MAY

2 *[May]*. The Polish offensive is intensifying, but it doesn't make me happy. Polish-Russian relations are only getting more muddled, because as only a very few Russians have clearly understood that the Poles must be given freedom, so in Poland, now intoxicated and, as always, arrogant, there are few who understand that *Poland will secure* her freedom only within her ethnic boundaries. The movement eastward, which has a chance of support from Western Europe and even the support of certain Russian elements so long as the bolsheviks are ruling in Russia, will become in the future a source of constant wars and will repeat the calami-

[56] This scene is described in Brusilov's memoirs, published in 1929: A. A. Brusilov, *Moi vospominaniia* (Moscow, 1929), p. 123.

[57] "The expression 'the great Pan has died' signifies in literary speech the decline of Hellenistic culture, and in general the end of any historical period." N. S. Ashukin and M. G. Ashukina, *Krylatye slova*, 2d ed. (Moscow, 1960), pp. 620–21.

tous relations between the two peoples that have existed for centuries. And for the near future it will only serve to intensify all sorts of oppression and horrors. But why are the Poles moving now, instead of earlier? Perhaps because it is precisely now, when the attempts of Denikin, Kolchak, etc. have finally failed, that the idea of a unified, indivisible Russia has also perished and therefore it is possible to snatch the most from the Russian lands. But such fools were those who, in preparing to restore Russia, thought to do this without any compromises, internal or external: neither to the peasants, nor to the borderlands—nothing. I will repeat the immortal words of Kliuchevskii: they have again failed "to show the muzhik that he is a fool and to get along with the borderlands." Truly, it is impossible to imagine a people more stupid in regard to social issues than the Russians.

The celebration of the First of May was turned into a *subbotnik*.[58] Here in the museum they cleaned the garden and cleared the remains of snow away from the walls of the book repository; they did very little, of course, and talked more, and the young people simply enjoyed themselves. The city was covered with posters of the usual vile appearance, but there was little red cloth; there is probably a general shortage of it. On the 30th I had another chat with Pokrovskii about buying foreign books. I had to cram many basic truths into him; from this strictly and narrowly businesslike chat I came away with the impression that he is so tired that he is not completely normal. Others had told me about that, but I was only then able to observe it myself. It was very characteristic that he seriously called the hysterical Polish proclamation printed in *Izvestiia* on April 30 "a declaration of war with Poland."[59] *Ils se gobent* and are sincerely assuming the tone and language of the old days. Saturday evening and Sunday at Lelia's where I returned Volodia, who was in Moscow for two days. The funeral of poor Shura Grave was very moving; there were

[58] "One of the forms of unremunerated volunteer labor of Soviet workers for the good of society, which characterizes their communist attitude toward work" (*Bol'shaia Sovetskaia Entsiklopediia*). The subbotniki were initiated by some Moscow railway workers in the spring of 1919: in response to an appeal by Lenin to improve the railroads, fifteen Communists of the Moscow-Kazan' depot worked into the night of Saturday, April 12, 1919 (whence the name: the Russian word for Saturday is *subbota*), and repaired three locomotives. This act was publicized and organized mass subbotniki soon followed.

[59] *Izvestiia* for April 30, 1920, contains no "Polish proclamation" as such; it does contain the proclamation of the Soviet government "To all Workers, Peasants, and Honest Citizens of Russia," which described Polish aims as the seizure of all the Ukraine and the enslavement of the Lithuanians, Belorussians, and Russians in their territory. This was the opening of the main phase of the Polish-Soviet war, the Polish offensive that would culminate in the taking of Kiev on May 6. On April 21 the Polish government had concluded a treaty with Petliura's Directory by which Poland recognized the independence of the Ukraine and the Petliura government agreed to the annexation by Poland of Eastern Galicia, Western Volynia, and part of Polesie.

speeches at graveside; speaking were several students and one—quite banal, it is true—professor (D. L. Cherniakhovskii, a fool of a bolshevik or SR).[60]

5 [May]. The Polish offensive continues, and Kiev, if it hasn't been taken, is in any case lost in advance. The event of the day is the formation of a "special convocation" for taking military measures against the Poles. Brusilov heads the convocation; its members include Polivanov, Klembovskii, Gutor, and other general castoffs of the great war.[61] Some want to see in this signals of a certain turn to the right by the bolsheviks. I don't think so; it is more likely a matter of using the generals as puppets; and for the generals it is a golden opportunity to get on rations, since the civil war has supposedly ended and now a war with foreigners has begun.[62] For the bolsheviks, the generals are a screen behind which it is easier for them to conduct their policy: this hiding behind generals and staging of a national war are a standard ploy. It is unlikely that anything useful will come for Russia from the resumption of a state of war: the attempts to establish order in Russia with the help of the whites have perished irretrievably as a result of stupidity, incompetence, and quarrels; Russia has become definitively bolshevik, and for the outside world Russia and bolshevism are probably now almost synonyms. And the way out of this is as follows: the struggle against bolshevism will be a struggle against Russia with the help of the borderlands, which are marching on Russia and will tear off her all they can. And so a new weapon is introduced into the struggle of the world against bolshevism—Russian national feeling. But who will it work for? Not for the good of Russia, which must be defended against the Poles, but for the good and the entrenchment of bolshevism, which, behind the screen of national feeling and the exploitation of the names of Brusilov, Polivanov, and others like puppets, will continue to undermine the world and will attempt by force of arms to introduce communism and anarchy as widely as possible. That

[60] Aleksandr Aleksandrovich Grave was on the medical faculty of Moscow University. This was perhaps the same Cherniakhovskii identified earlier by Got'e as his former upperclassman. See n. 20 for 1919.

[61] A Special Convocation attached to the Commander in Chief of All Armed Forces of the Republic for the reason stated by Got'e was officially convened on May 9. Its chairman was General Brusilov and its other members were Generals P. S. Baluev, Aleksei Evgen'evich Gutor (1868–1938), A. M. Zaionchkovskii, Vladislav Napoleonovich Klembovskii (1860–1921), Dmitrii Pavlovich Parskii (1866–1921), and Aleksei Andreevich Polivanov (1855–1920).

[62] In the polemic with Denikin at the end of the first edition of his memoirs, Brusilov defends his decision to "stay with his people" no matter what, but also notes that at this time the penurious material conditions he had lived in since the revolution began to improve. (Brusilov, Moi vospominaniia, pp. 235–36).

is why I expect nothing good from the new developments of the last few days. As before, there is no ray of hope, and the material and moral situation of us who are war prisoners, vanquished by the international communists, can only get worse in the months to come from the war with Poland.

7 *[May]*. The newspapers are full of comments of general capitulation. The bolsheviks are broadcasting that the generals have recognized the necessity of bolshevik authority, and they are shouting this *urbi et orbi* in the literal sense of that expression. They have printed Brusilov's letter in which he offers to establish the convocation and does not refuse service to the bolsheviks.[63] Today I heard the proposition that Brusilov, perhaps, wrote that letter in response to an offer to assume a more responsible post, but that he took refuge in this way behind the convocation. In any case, the bolsheviks are now exploiting this influential name, as they are exploiting patriotism at the same time, and will exploit whatever is necessary to achieve the goal they have set themselves.

I was at Lelia Kurdiumova's summer place to say goodbye to Volodia before my trip to Petersburg. I returned from there by the northern part of the Ring Road to Kursk Station. The locomotive cemetery stretches from Serebrennyi Bor to Vladykin; there is an endless park of dead cars in the Kazan' marshaling yard. Kursk Station is all dirty and downtrodden; from there I went along Vorontsov Field past the former German mansions, which are now either plundered or occupied by some kind of international troops. Khitrov market is empty. On the Varvarka some girl asked me if I didn't know of any hotel in Moscow, as they were going from station to station, were very tired, and wanted to spend the night. I had to answer her that there used to be hotels in Moscow, but I don't know if there are any now. My path led to the university, to a meeting of the Society of Russian History and Antiquities—a quiet corner redolent of Old Rus' and Old Russia.[64] The habitués of the workers' faculty club,

---

[63] Brusilov's letter offering to establish a special convocation on Poland was published in *Izvestiia* on May 7, 1920: "It would seem that in such circumstances [the Polish intention to 'seize all the lands belonging to the Polish Kingdom before 1772' and perhaps even more] it would be desirable to call a convocation of people of experience in military affairs and in life for detailed discussion of Russia's present situation and of the most efficacious measures for avoiding a foreign invasion. It would seem to me that the first task ought to be the arousal of the people's patriotism, without which there will be no sound fighting capacity."

[64] Obshchestvo istorii i drevnostei rossiiskikh was the first scholarly historical society in Moscow, founded in 1804 under the aegis of Moscow University. It was liquidated in 1929. The society was principally devoted to the study and publication of historical documents.

which has grabbed the entire old building after the seizure of the new one, were stamping their feet above us, but we continued our business.

Apropos, I want to note why I stubbornly do not go to the faculty and the University Council. I was their most meticulous attendee when their work was work, and responsible work at that. Now there is no work at all either at the faculty or in the council, they have no rights and almost no responsibilities. So it is better not to waste precious time.

I heard that some kind of big swindle has been discovered in the dining room of the museum: they were selling salt at Smolensk [market], of which they had large reserves since they were hardly feeding anyone, and this at the expense of their hungry comrades. There you have the Russian scum!

Petersburg, 9 May–20 May, 1920. I had planned this trip long ago, as a means of changing scenery and forgetting myself a little, and in order to finish, at last, my work on the regional administration of the eighteenth century with some information in the Archive of the State Council. I kept putting it off until "things got better." Alas, I did not wait for that "better" and decided that I cannot wait that long. As one does not travel in Sovdepiia except on business, a business trip was arranged from the museum for selection of books from the Public Library and other places. I traveled with my colleagues Kiselev and Petrovskii.[65] We left in the morning in one cab, which was hired for 5,000 rubles, and sat, like cooks used to do, on our suitcases. There was a pleasant surprise at the railway: we were admitted with our reserved-seat tickets to a completely clean second-class car of the latest construction, with wide benches and wide windows; there were eight of us in the compartment, but the public was quite decent, and as we three had the upper bench and half the lower at our disposal, we arranged for sleeping quite satisfactorily. The train traveled twenty-three hours; there was no crowding anywhere, and we traveled as in the good old days. There were no buffets, here and there only soviet swill, called coffee, and suspicious pieces of something called meat. On the other hand, there was milk for sale, and in places butter and eggs. Milk was 150, 180 rubles a glass, and near Petrograd 250 rubles; butter was about 2,500 rubles; eggs—at midway in the journey—100 rubles each, toward Petrograd 150. As we had our own reserves, the diet was adequate and decent. For the return trip we were even more fortunate, for the three of us we were given a first-class compartment (double) in an international car. In the same car there were two other compartments occupied by returning Muscovites, and there were almost no Jews, amaz-

---

[65] Aleksei Sergeevich Petrovskii (b. 1881) was a member of the ranking staff of the Rumiantsev Museum; he later became head librarian of the Lenin Library.

ingly. On entering the car, both going and coming, we forgot altogether about lice and typhus.

Approaching Petrograd, I turned my mind to what I would see on leaving the train, and the first thing that struck me was the sign "Entrance to Kronstadt forbidden" gracing the platform. As if people only come to Petrograd in order to get to that horrible laboratory of the Russian revolution. The self-indulgence and self-glorification of the revolutionary lout is evident in this. Znamenskaia Square remains as it was with its hippopotamus in the form of Alexander III.[66] There were few people on Nevskii Prospect, but the signs were intact and some shops were open. That created a very pleasant first impression, of something less ravaged than Moscow. Near the Public Library I separated myself from my traveling companions (May 10, the day of arrival) and set off for information. The Imperial Public Library, as always, was cold, formal, but amiable. And it is still physically cold, because some especially intelligent commission had forbidden until a few days ago the opening of windows, as that is supposedly bad for the books. I made the acquaintance of E. L. Radlov,[67] who produced a very pleasant impression, and with the "government commissar" Anderson, a red-headed Balt and revolutionary greenhorn, as S. F. Platonov described him. From the Public Library I went to the building of the ministry of popular enlightenment and searched there for one of the new library organs. I roamed about the huge building just as though in the castle of Sleeping Beauty—everything was empty and literally enchanted. From there I went to the Senate building on the English Quay, where the Main Archive Administration is presently located, where I found S. F. Platonov, who right off took me in and thus resolved the worrisome problem of where I was to lay my head.

In Platonov's family I received the kind of friendly reception and warm endearment that you often don't get from genuine relatives and old friends—and that, too, of course, made an imprint on my stay in Petrograd.

On May 11, I began my work in the Archive of the State Council, experiencing the kind of involvement that I frequently got from archival work in the old days. What a joy to sit with the documents, knowing that no one will bother you and that there is no need to hurry anywhere. Five days of work made it possible for me to finish my work of many years and proceed to the final elaboration of those places in the work

---

[66] The site of the Moscow station is now called October Square and the statue of Alexander III by Pavel Trubetskoi stands in the courtyard of the Russian Museum in Leningrad.

[67] Ernest Leopol'dovich Radlov (1854–1928) was a prominent philosopher and a translator and commentator on Aristotle and Hegel. From 1917 to 1924 he was director of the public library—that is, he was Got'e's counterpart in Petrograd.

(*Regional Administration*, volume 2) that until then weren't getting anywhere.

Aside from the archive work, which was my main purpose, I fulfilled
the museum tasks together with my comrades; for that we had to frequent certain Sovdep institutions and talk with the comrades (Sevtsen-
tropechat', the Petrograd branch of the State Publishing House). All this
was very boring and tedious, but as a result we nevertheless provided the
museum with quite a few sources for books, albeit on the condition of
finding the means for getting them to Moscow. Apparently it will be
impossible to find any means other than soliciting a heated boxcar or just
a passenger car and bringing them to Moscow in it.

The rest of my time was devoted to visiting Petersburg acquaintances,
for the most part among the history professors. I will now turn to the
sum of impressions that I brought back from Petrograd.

Those people in whose midst I mostly circulated, that is, our historians,
live more stably and cheerfully than our Muscovites; they don't experience the decrepitude that has overtaken almost all of us. They are not so
bothered by the bolsheviks, because they are further from the central
bolshevik authority, and at the same time, Petrograd remains a large Russian cultural center, even the largest, as before, and therefore the bolsheviks cannot treat the Petrograd bourgeois intelligentsia as they do in the
provinces. In Petrograd there are all the benefits, and none of the minuses, of the government's removal. Moreover, in Petrograd it is possible
to *publish*, which is practically impossible in Moscow. There is a certain
advantage in this for our brethren. The rations, which everywhere generally facilitate a certain calming of the nerves, were introduced earlier
in Petrograd, and they are more accustomed to them than in Moscow.
All of this contributes to a calmer *resignation*. I cannot call their mood
otherwise, because everyone with whom I talked sees things as being
hopeless, and if they are counting on anything, it is only slow evolution.
I saw, however, more oppressive scenes: for example, in the family of
Shmeman,[68] a member of the State Council and Senator of the First Department. He works in the office of some communal operation; the family is scattered, they are selling their things; he himself has declined
greatly and sees salvation only in a *sharp* and prompt sudden change. I
saw the former director of Imperial theaters, Teliakovskii,[69] who has a
small position on the Nikolaevskaia railway and supports himself by
petty speculation.

[68] Nikolai Eduardovich Shmeman (1858–1918) was a former member of the State
Council and of the first department of the Senate.

[69] Vladimir Aleksandrovich Teliakovskii (1860–1924) was director of the imperial theaters from 1901 to May 1917. He has left memoirs: V. A. Teliakovskii, *Vospominaniia,
1898–1917* (Petrograd, 1924).

Externally, Petrograd is better than Moscow, because it is much cleaner. When they cleaned the snow from the streets, they piled the dirt in the middle of the street with the streetcars and removed it with the help of the latter. There are more streetcars than in Moscow, but far fewer horses and automobiles; the latter in particular creates, for the most part, an impression of emptiness—not the absence of people, of whom there are enough, although immeasurably fewer than before. I have retained the impression that two strata for the most part have disappeared from Petrograd: the upper, aristocratic and governing, and the lower—all those countless Novgorod, Pskov, Tver, Vologda, and other muzhiks who used to come here for work in the trades. The Neva is very empty—ever so rarely a tug with a barge of firewood goes by on it. Only past the Nikolaevskii Bridge can one see quite a few ships of the Baltic Fleet standing calmly offshore, while the "ornament and pride of the revolution" in bell-bottom trousers stroll along the embankment with their ladies under arm. They are especially numerous around the Fortress and near the English Quay, where they have seized the entire quarter, evicting its inhabitants. As a counterweight to this, one can say only one thing—in Petrograd there are a lot fewer Jews than in Moscow (L'un vaut l'autre). There is no doubt that Petrograd lacks its former decorum. Suffice it to say that in the warm evenings of this unprecedentedly early summer I saw young boys swimming in the Swan Canal and grown leaders of school and other excursions of the gorilla breed swimming at the Point.[70] Kamennoostrovskii Prospect, where I lived, was very empty: in the marvelous evenings of early May there were only "workers" hauling lilacs in carts from the summer places of Kamennyi Ostrov, where formerly the pavement here would have been groaning from the carriages. The factories are silent, there is no smoke, the air is clean, and therefore on Kamennoostrovskii, beginning almost from the Fortress, the mosquitos swarmed in hordes.

In respect to food, I was placed in very good conditions. I brought quite a lot with me, and I prevailed upon N. I. Platonova to take most of it; the rest, the smaller part, went for my lunches, and thus I didn't have to go to the dining halls and waste time there at all. During the last few days, I bought a few things at the market. Going about the market (on the Petersburg Side), I saw that more or less everything is there and that the prices were almost the same as Moscow's: bread, 350; millet, 400; butter, 3,000.

I was in two places where the public was not allowed earlier: the Stroganov and Kamennoostrovskii palaces. The first is a genuine *palazzo*,

[70] The tip of Vasilievskii Island where the stock exchange building is located, a formal architectural ensemble.

such as are shown for money in Genoa and Venice. The second has been greatly spoiled by a hospital that was set up in it by its owner, Princess Saxe-Altenburg, in the first months of the war; however, the front rooms, which retain the flavor of Alexander I, have been preserved in it: little rooms, probably his personal apartments. The palace is also still interesting because it is probably the only intact work of Bazhenov.[71]

The sum of my Petrograd impressions was rather positive. The causes for that are presented above. I left with the thought that Petrograd is not a dead city, but a sleeping beauty, who some day will wake to a new, although perhaps a different life than before. In any case, it has preserved in these terrible years its significance as the most civilized of Russian cities.

21 May. I didn't go all the way to Moscow, but got off in Khovrino and went directly to Pavlov's summer place near the Ring Road. Crossing Khovrino, I met S. D. Bakharev, who has finally managed to get a job as plant manager of a sanatorium. He invited me to drink coffee and to my indescribable amazement led me to a summer house where we had lived in 1879. Fate plays with us in small matters as well as large. I found Volodia in good shape. The walk to the summer house took fifty minutes.

22 May. All is well in the museum. There are no scandals. All is right at the cemetery, too. I returned to Bratsevo, where I stayed all day Sunday.

24–28 May. Muscovite life has taken its customary vile course. A gloomy disposition, dissipated a little by the trip, has again set in in my soul. Endless discussions and universal [. . .] gossip, mutually contradictory rumors. I am completely unable to work productively in my two rooms. Gloomy thoughts about how to live a solitary existence and how to raise my Volodia. Some kind of hints again from the commissariat about the matter of book acquisitions abroad, which is leading to nothing—that is the atmosphere I circulated in all this week. I have hardly read the newspapers and I catch myself wanting to know all at once how the war with Poland will end. At first the bolsheviks were frightened, then they howled victory, and now they are dejected again. But I don't believe either their shouts or the idle gossip of the bourgeois who languish in captivity. One thing can be said—that it is not a joking matter and that

[71] Vasilii Ivanovich Bazhenov (1737/38–1799) was one of the few great native Russian architects of the eighteenth century. Got'e's remark is a little mysterious, since a number of Bazhenov's projects were still intact, including the magnificent building of the Rumiantsev Museum in Moscow (Pashkov dom, 1784–86).

some kind of result is indeed possible. O, God—any kind of release from this dead end.

29 [May]. I have left with Volodia for a six-day excursion to Pestovo and Sergievo. I had not been in Pestovo for two years. Everything is run-down, but the proprietors are behaving cheerfully. In the gallery there is a theater of a cultural enlightenment circle where Volodia Reiman directs gorillas; the living quarters [?] of the ex-bourgeois are in the outbuilding. We walked there from the station in three hours, with three-quarters of an hour of stops. The central building of the house remains untouched. I am trying to sit there; I haven't the least desire to take walks or move about—not from physical tiredness, which I don't feel, but from moral weariness. My eyes wouldn't see anything. Writing or reading are the only things I am still capable of doing.

31 [May]. A marvelous day. In Pestovo there is a play of the gorillas in the gallery. They are performing *Marriage.*[72] After that there is a ball until 6 A.M. Volodia Reiman is the director. The proprietors' energy in defending their nest is admirable. The fact that they still live here is due to their energy, too. But it is still painful to see everything around that has been defiled by the monkeys in human form. It seems to me that I am not I and am not here. The forms are old, the content is new. More than ever I feel that our existence is not even living, but some kind of posthumous pale reflection of former life. We are no longer people, but "pale souls of cattle."[73]

JUNE

1 June. A perfectly calm day in Pestovo. The frame of mind is the same, but you rest physically when taking in nature, which is radiant with its eternal beauty, even here in the boring north where we are.

2 [June]. Removal to Troitsa. On the railroad we got on a train filled with women going to the bazaar in Troitsa. All morning today was spent on business, for the most part in connection with the transfer of the monastery library to the status of our Rumiantsev "branch." The monastery, closed and desecrated, produces a painful and sad impression. Hooligans with guns stand in front of the cathedrals, which were unsealed only for Trinity, and guard the seals. There was selling of antireligious and anti-

[72] A comic play by Gogol.
[73] "Dushi blednye skotov."

clerical literature during the hours of services on Trinity. Instead of extinguishing faith, they are fanning it. Always the same mistake.

3 [June]. Continued rest in Sergiev Posad and complete absence of any kind of news. We got here well. Little news in Moscow. Everything is the same.

On Whit Monday there was indignation when they wanted to seal up the cathedral again. The women howled. Some attribute significance to this, as a symptom. I don't think these trifles will do any harm to the bolsheviks.

11 June. All these days Moscow has again been living on rumors. The offensive of the Poles brought the defeat of the Russian bolsheviks near Borisov, which they themselves have admitted in their bulletins, albeit with reservations and omissions, as always. The simultaneous attempt to press from the south led in Moscow to the revival of all kinds of rumors, hopes, and even plans. I remain completely filled with skepticism. Nothing has happened so far that could be considered a blow to soviet authority. And the process of rotting from within of this unfortunate corpse called Russia can continue indefinitely; I have always said this and am prepared to repeat it indefinitely.

The latest attack on the university: the workers' faculty, which has taken away all our lecture halls, now wants all university affairs to be decided in the administration, including curricular matters, in order simply to devour everything that remains. When the administration, or rather its professorial part, objected to this, the workers' faculty and the communist students announced that they will take the matter to the commissariat. But the commissariat itself appears to be washing its hands. It would be more logical to simply close up and destroy everything.

12 June. I observed the mores at the bridge-construction depot: arrests; threats of shooting, almost; compulsory labor [. . .]—one perceives with particular clarity the charms of the socialist order, which border on slavery. The general situation is still the same. England continues to conduct "morganatic negotiations with the bolshevik scum."[74] I think that only *brave vielle France* is conducting an honorable and consistent policy. But, alas, I very much fear that in the future her Russian sympathies will go over irretrievably to Poland, until that Slavic soul gets France into a mess, as the Russian God-bearing people and its rotten and unprincipled intelligentsia has already done.

[74] Here Got'e probably quotes a phrase picked up from the British press.

15 [June]. The shameless liars have announced that the Poles have blown up the Vladimir Cathedral in Kiev, and are appealing to Orthodox sympathies. Well, are they lying this time, too? I think that in this affair all their behavior will be like the fable of the wolf and the cat—they will convince no one and will not really succeed in raising anyone against the Poles.[75] But how fatiguing and revolting is this running in place with its retreats and advances! When and where will there be an end to it?

18 [June]. I have written little these days, because I was finishing the second volume of my *Regional Administration*. Yesterday evening, or it would be better to say in the still of the night, I finally dotted the last "i" on my twelve-year labor. "The long-awaited moment arrived, my years-long work is finished. What is the incomprehensible sadness that secretly torments me?" Is it tormenting me because I in fact "stand like an un-needed day-laborer"?[76] I did in fact finish this work in order to bring the job that had been started to an end before the liquidation of my scholarly studies. This unneeded work can be continued only for my own pleasure, as a narcotic substance in order to forget, if only for a time, all the horrors and the desperate boredom that is gradually overcoming me. I want nothing more than peace and oblivion.

Today I happened to be in the Military-Historical Commission where a paper was being read about the "Riga operation" in August of 1917; that is, the flight of the demoralized Russian army from the vicinity of Riga. The paper was being given by General Parskii,[77] a wrinkled lemon of an alcoholic type. Among the distinguished personages present was the notorious Vatsetis,[78] with a shaved clown's mug, apparently an intelligent rogue, but nothing more. The generals talked about how they were beaten, and I did not have the feeling that anyone among them felt particularly sorry for himself, for the army, or for Russia. Formerly mess expenses, now rations—that is all that counted and counts for the Russian

---

[75] *Izvestiia* for June 13 was full of stories about the Bolsheviks' taking of Kiev on the 12th and the Poles' "vandalism" during their withdrawal from that city, including blowing up St. Vladimir Cathedral. But later Soviet histories of the Kiev campaign and of the city of Kiev make no mention of damage to the St. Vladimir Cathedral or other cultural monuments. The reference is to Krylov's fable, whose moral is that of Galatians 6:7: "For whatsoever a man soweth, that shall he also reap."

[76] The quoted phrases are from Pushkin's poem "Trud" ("Work") (1830).

[77] General Parskii, former general and commander of the northern front, was at this time a member of the Military-Historical Commission for Studying and Profiting from the Experience of the War of 1914–1918.

[78] Ioakim Ioakimovich Vatsetis (Vacietis) (1873–1938), of Latvian peasant background, had been a colonel in the old army who went over to the Bolsheviks with his regiment in October 1917. In 1918–1919 he was commander in chief of the Red Army. At this time he was a member of Revvoensovet, the supreme military council of the republic.

leaders. The auditors were for the most part monkeys, genuine simian mugs, summoned to make up the new Russian officer corps to the glory of the world proletariat. It was interesting, but I left with a feeling of pain, shame, and pity.

The general situation is confused. How to reconcile the morganatic negotiations of comrade Krasin with pressure on the soviet republic, and the wild whooping of Lenin in his letter to the English workers with someone's desire to enter any kind of discussions with the comrades.[79] When will they understand in the West that however rotten the seedbed of bolshevism may be, it is still dangerous for Europe? The lice-infested bedlam, as Churchill called the RSFSR the other day,[80] remains a bedlam, full of shameless liars who are prepared to swindle all and sundry, who hold nothing sacred, lie right and left, and set themselves the task of undermining the European states wherever they can. Their rapprochement with the Turks, who are rebeling against the Entente, is typical; they are on friendly terms with the Turkish Pan-Islamists, Nationalists, and Young Turks who raised the Caucasian mountaineers against Denikin and have now come to red Moscow. Representatives of these people have come to us in the museum.

22 [June]. I am spending a week in Pestovo. Of all the summer residences and nooks, this is the last that remains for me and has not been completely lost by its proprietors. In order to get here you have to conquer twelve versts by foot, with a pud-and-a-half burden on your shoulders. The weather was not too hot; however, having done the thing, I felt tired; my legs were especially tired—all the rest held up very well. How many old memories are connected with Pestovo. The joy of early youth, the later span of time in the days of the Reimans' magnificence, quiet friendship in the company of Nina. Now everything is rundown; the remaining proprietors cut and split firewood, carry water, cook, and even wash, in order to live in warmth and in their old corner. We live like everyone else here, and participate in the common work; my responsibilities include carrying water and firewood and watering the garden. Such

[79] Krasin had been in London since late May, negotiating with the Lloyd George government about Soviet-British relations in general and trying to keep the British from helping Poland in particular. Krasin's meeting with Lloyd George on May 31 was the first meeting of a representative of the Soviet government with the head of government of one of the great powers. Richard H. Ullman, *The Anglo-Soviet Accord* (*Anglo-Soviet Relations, 1917–1921*, vol. 3) (Princeton, 1972).

Lenin's letter to the English workers was written on May 30 for transmission by a visiting delegation of English workers. Lenin used the letter to protest against British aid to Poland and to justify the Red Terror, abrogation of freedom of speech, etc. (it was England's fault for supporting the White Terror). *Pravda*, June 17, 1920.

[80] I have been unable to locate the source of this phrase attributed by Got'e to Churchill.

are the pastimes of the contemporary professor. But one gets a lot for it. In the first place, the society of people you love—and there are not so many of them left. Then there is the countryside—our nasty and vile countryside, but after all attractive in summertime. The day before yesterday I went with Volodia Reiman, on the sly, three versts to the mill to buy flour and, also on the sly, brought home a pud and a half (how typical this is for contemporary mores and customs). It was a fine cool, damp evening, and the "gray" night descended little by little. That is just what I like in the summer in our latitude. In the country here there is quiet and temporary oblivion. And both body and soul yearn for rest. It has been four days since I heard anything about politics.

24 [June]. Another two days of complete calm without any news from the bolshevik world. Only the necessity of performing various chores reminds one of what we are living through. I have specialized for the most part in the sawing and chopping of firewood and the carrying of water. Nevertheless, there is quite a lot of time left for study. More than ever, living in this long-familiar place, I am losing the desire to take walks. I am especially willing to replace walks with work. I heard from O.L.U. a story about a letter from Osorgin (*Russian Gazette*)[81] to someone that had been confiscated by the military censors; it described spiritualist seances that took place before the war, in which everything that would befall Russia after the war was foretold. If this is compared to what I heard from I. F. Ognev about similar seances, the impression is big and impressive. In this regard I can't help recalling also a small seance in the town of Simeiz in July 1915, in which Nina, Tania, the Kaluga pair, Kupriianova, and Baidakova participated;[82] some spirit announced to them (1) that in 1917 there would be a revolution in Russia, (2) that Nicholas II and Aleksandra Fedorovna would be killed, (3) that Alexis would not rule, and (4) that neither Russia nor Germany would be victors. The last one seemed to me altogether wild, but it came true all the same.

27 [June]. Return to hateful and filthy Moscow after a week in the country. On the whole, everything that concerns me is more or less all right. The general situation remains the same. Wrangel has probably moved a little in the south. When will there finally be an end to this terrible war? In the train I heard this interesting story: at the conference of school workers in Sergiev Posad it was remarked that so-called political literature (that is, simply agitational, bolshevik) is not being checked out from

---

[81] Mikhail Andreevich Osorgin (Il'in) (1878–1942) was a longtime foreign correspondent for *Russkie vedomosti* who reported from Italy and had covered the Balkan Wars. After the revolution, he became a prominent émigré writer.

[82] The "Kaluga pair" may have been relatives.

the rural libraries at all, and in this regard the communist members of
the conference declared that if they were to start distributing it by design,
they would be beaten up or killed. In a word, bolshevik propaganda in
the village is unthinkable at the present time. That is a very interesting
fact. Without a load I easily walked the distance from Pestovo to the
station in two hours and five minutes, and even made it to the Sergievo
train, which I managed to get on rather easily.

JULY

2 [July]. A week in Moscow. A most destructive mood. Complete confusion. There is running in place everywhere on the fronts. I once again
and for the thousand-and-first time think that all these offensives are
only woe and disaster for us, that the affair should be allowed to follow
its own path and then the results will become apparent in several years. I
bade farewell to the Wilkens today. Lucky people—to live in the civilized world, breathe freely, and arrange one's affairs as reason and inclination dictate. But it will be strange in Moscow without the Wilkens.
Looking at them and getting out of my state of confusion, I think again:
how to get out of here. Now a new scheme is in the offing—an expedition
to Reval[83] to extract bibliographical data from foreign journals there and
to collect information. I am dreaming of leaving to see Volodia this evening.

Yesterday A. S. Nikolaev reminded me of what Rozhdestvenskii[84] and
Platonov had already said in Petersburg: May 5th was Solov'ev's[85] hun-
dredth anniversary and we, the Moscow historians, have not responded
to that event at all. That is how what we are having to live through affects
us!

7 July. Pestovo. Once again I am drinking the cup of oblivion for several
days and am getting away from the direct impressions of Moscow. My
personal situation can be described as a desire to square the circle. I sit
and think how to solve the problem of the remainder of my life, how to
escape from the emptiness and boredom that surround me. In the end, I
think I should try to get out of the situation by leaving Russia. If it doesn't
work out one time, it will work out the next. Here nothing is to be expected either in public or in private life. Today my friend Shambi
brought some news from Moscow. The unchangeably hopeless situation

---

[83] That is, Tallinn, the capital of Estonia.
[84] Sergei Vasil'evich Rozhdestvenskii (1868–1934) was a professor of Russian history at
Petersburg University best known for his work on sixteenth-century landholding.
[85] S. M. Solov'ev. See n. 76 for 1919.

of the violently murdered country and nation shows through his customary pessimism [*sic*]. Russia is dying, delivered into the power of bribes, chauffeurs, the third element, ignorant chatterboxes—people who spent time in the law faculty but did not become lawyers, smart alecks, fools, and robbers who have gone over to this government with the magnanimous help of the socialistic intelligentsia. The rudder of history has accidentally turned Russia in this direction; it could accidentally turn her in another direction. I am more and more convinced that chance, simply chance, is the true motor of history.

Here one passes the time, as before, between intellectual and physical labor; today Shambi and I cut up almost an entire birch.

9 [July]. We continue to work—sawing wood and gathering hay. No news at all, excellent weather. I am glad that at least my Volodia is enjoying the wonderful air and the country. I don't want to think about how the problem of our life will be solved, for there is no more painful thought than that.

11 [July]. There was a search at the former steward's on suspicion of speculation—by denunciation, of course, although that particular type is mixed up in all sorts of things. During the search, he brought out a box of money and put it under a bush on the porch. It was gone in less than a quarter of an hour: someone stole it. Such are the mores in this country. The thieves were apparently the peasants who had moved onto the territory of the estate without authorization. Everything else remains the same. Quiet anguish in the bosom of magnificent weather. I am eating and sleeping well. What else? I am enjoying swimming. Is that so little? I am engaging at leisure in pedagogy with my son. I have begun to do some reading for a projected future work explaining the present Russian situation. I read Khomiakov. God, what drivel, what unrestrained phrase-mongering in his publicistic articles. Angles-Uglichans-Slavonians.[86] It is the limit of foolish and pretentious nonsense. And this is one of the most important Slavophiles!

12 [July]. St. Peter's Day, which I used for a trip to Troitsa so as not to make a regular workday of it. There I prepared for receiving the monastery library, keeping the monk Aleksei and S. P. Mansurov[87] attached

[86] "Anglekane = Uglichane = slaviane." Got'e refers to the Slavophile philosopher Aleksei Stepanovich Khomiakov (1804–1860), who wrote on religious themes. In question here, apparently, was some specious etymological argument about cultural-religious ties between the English and the early Slavs.

[87] Sergei Pavlovich Mansurov (d. 1929) was a philosopher and historian of the church.

to it. The act could not be signed, because the commission for allocating the monastery buildings had not yet finished its work and had not transferred the library to the section on museum affairs, which in its turn is supposed to transfer it to us. What bureaucratic red tape! In connection with the library, I had the pleasure of meeting today with comrade M. T. Smirnov, the chairman of the executive committee of the Sergievo sovdep (God, what a title!). I saw before me a rather decent-looking and amiable person, but definitely the type of limited and stupid person from among the people's teachers who believes in communism and bolshevism and is, moreover, according to the rumors, honest. Undoubtedly, this is one of the most dangerous types holding sway in our time. However, for these days it was easy to come to terms with him.

In the evening, the trip to Moscow in unbearable heat. Here, apparently, there have been no great scandals, judging from everything I learned at the apartment upon arrival. The general news is that Wrangel has not been crushed, but the bolsheviks are pushing back the Poles. It is impossible to get to the heart of the matter and figure out what is going on. On the way home, I was thinking and came to the conclusion that I am most depressed when I am traveling, when you witness external life, and when, against that terrible background of ruin and gorilla debauchery, you see your own isolation and the wreck of everything. The simian mugs in the train, the soviet whores in infinite number on the walls of disfigured and defiled Moscow have had a more depressing effect on me than ever before. Never has the feeling of hopelessness and entrapment stood out so clearly and never has the desire to flee, without looking back, far, far away, in any direction, been awakened so strongly. I will make an attempt in this direction again; who knows, perhaps I will some day get results—I will save myself and will save Volodia for a cultured life.

15 [July]. Not quite the usual ending of seminar work. A walking excursion to Kolomenskoe, D'iakovo, and so-called Chortovo gorodishche[88] was enterprised at the request of my students. S. V. Bakhrushin and the young Vinogradov couple joined the small number of students. Despite the heat, the excursion came off very pleasantly. We talked a lot on historical subjects, and at Chortovo gorodishche I gave a small lecture. The young people expressed a desire to repeat similar excursions. Kolomenskoe has changed little in the four years since my last visit; it must be admitted that the palace administration kept it in rather rundown condition, too.

He was a member of the commission for the preservation of the Trinity-St. Sergius Monastery.

[88] Chortovo gorodishche is a hillock near D'iakovo that is an archaeological site.

18 [July]. I came to Pestovo for one day, after a revolting Moscow week, whereas I had counted on coming for about ten days. The entire week passed in the usual boredom, anguish, and suffering, and it seemed everything was fine, when suddenly yesterday an extraordinary event occurred, fully in keeping with the entirety of contemporary life. A search—or in the terminology of the commissars, an "operation"—was conducted in the museum (and also in the Historical Museum) by order of the Cheka. I was approaching the museum from the Dol'niks in the morning when I ran into two employees coming from the museum, who told me that all the buildings were surrounded by red army men, and that they were letting everyone in but no one out. I of course went there and learned that at 5 A.M. twenty-four commissars with twenty-four red army men came to the chairman of the building committee, Georgievskii, and presented a warrant for closing the museum for seven days and conducting searches throughout the premises of the museum, and for detaining suspicious persons. At 7 A.M. Golitsyn, Vinogradov, Dolgov,[89] Romanov, and I (who was absent) were alerted, and the search in the museum began, for the most part in the basements; their job was to find underground passages to the Kremlin and weapons, and incidentally gold and diamonds. After a search of the entire basement floor, they searched the employees' apartments. The search at my place lasted an hour and a half; the same at the Menzbirs, although I was not present for it. The comrade commissar went about my two rooms and then undertook an examination of my writing desk, where he found nothing, as he nowhere found anything. At first he was polite, but reserved; later he became more familiar and asked if he could smoke; he was not interested in the flour. In general, I cannot complain about any kind of impropriety on his part. At first I found it unpleasant; later I became indifferent, and I spoke with him quite dispassionately. I cannot say that this person made a particularly bad impression on me. Among the searches, only the search at comrade Raiskii's[90] yielded substantial results: 160,000 rubles in banknotes, partly Nicholaevan. They kept the employees locked up in the museum until 4 P.M., whereupon they all left, having confirmed that the museum was closed to the public for seven days, but that the employees must be at their stations. Afterward there followed a meeting at which it was decided to inform the People's Commissariat of Enlightenment about everything and await further developments. They found no underground passages; as for weapons—only four Japanese rifles from 1904, located in the ethnographic division. They sealed two basements. On the

---

[89] Semen Osipovich Dolgov (1857–1925) was the curator of manuscripts and old books at the Rumiantsev Museum.

[90] Comrade Raiskii was apparently a Bolshevik who lived on the premises of the Rumiantsev Museum.

whole, they were polite. They said that we were probably fed up with them, and that such a search made no sense—either everything had to be rummaged through or the affair abandoned. They were apparently embarrassed by the large quantity of boxes. I successfully got out my things that were lying in the library and removed them in their presence. I don't know what awaits us next, but in any case I have been punished by having to sit in Moscow for several extra days.

22 [July]. In Pestovo again, after two days spent fruitlessly in Moscow. For the period from Sunday to Wednesday morning the affair did not progress. The museum was closed; moreover, on Monday they ordered it closed even for work. I went with Vinogradov to Pokrovskii and to Lunacharskii. The former apparently really knew nothing about our entire affair. He advised us to wait the prescribed time and then reopen. Lunacharskii reported that he was indeed informed about everything, but that this "was not directed against us; only a few circumstances had to be checked." My impression was that they don't think our affair is serious, but that if the Cheka should blow it up, they would not intervene for us. The most improbable rumors about this episode are circulating in Moscow. It is claimed that puds of gold were found at Golitsyn's, and boxes of weapons at [. . .] in the division. The rumor started in our dining room that there was a new search in the museum on Monday that 80 commissars came in several cars. Some sort of delegation from Khiva that happened to be in Moscow and toured the museum in the company of a Cheka agent was mistaken for a search party. Such is the life of learned institutions under the dictatorship of the proletariat.

All of Moscow is preparing for the festivities in honor of the congress of communists.[91] On Red Square there are structures somewhat reminiscent of the coronation. In addition to arches, they are putting up a huge tribunal in the form of a mountain, similar to the mountain in the church at Vifaniia.[92] Anguish and gloom in the soul from all this.

23 [July]. Yesterday A. K. Vinogradov reported to me on the telephone that Pokrovskii said that the museum cannot be opened. He is waiting

[91] That is, the Second Congress of the Third International (Comintern), which met in Moscow from July 21 to August 6, 1920.

[92] The church in the monastery at Vifaniia near Troitsa (founded in 1783) "has the form of a mountain inside, on which there is a throne in the name of the Transfiguration of the Lord, and beneath, as if in a cave, there is the church of . . . Lazarus. Here there is preserved the wooden coffin in which St. Sergius was first buried. Worshipers gnaw the coffin, as according to popular belief this cures toothache." *Entsiklopedicheskii slovar'* (Brokgauz-Efron), vol. 6, p. 606. Vifaniia is the Slavonic form for Bethany, the town in which Lazarus lived; it is separated from Jerusalem by a huge mountain.

for the appointment of a commissar. In general, the situation of the museum is completely uncertain. I decided to remain in Pestovo today. I have this feeling: the university has perished, and now the museum has perished. There are no more "cultural trenches" at all. There is nothing more to defend, and nobody to defend it for. The closure of the Public Library for an indefinite period, for a reason unknown to the institution, is highly revealing about the RSFSR.

25 [July]. The next news was better. On the 24th I received a report by telephone that the museum is opening on Monday and that everything is all right, and that a barge of firewood has even arrived. A. K. Vinogradov's tone was more optimistic and gayer. Tomorrow I hope to learn the solution to all this story. Despite the confusion, I was able to spend five days in the country and work at haying, staying with my Volodia, who for me is higher than all other obligations in the world.

30 [July]. On Monday I was in Moscow and found a genuine idyll in the museum: everything open, everything working, as if nothing had happened. A telephone order had come from comrade Lunacharskii and the Cheka—to open, and that's all. There was an assumption that day that they would change their minds again after a few days; but today, the 30th, I inquired by telephone, and everything is going normally, quietly, calmly. If they were really looking for some kind of underground passages, what were they used for? They are just as wild, ignorant, and rude as all that scum that personifies the Russian revolution.

27th—the celebration in honor of the Third International was held in Moscow. The formerly so-called gray heroes marched in measured step with blank mugs, exactly as they marched in tsarist parades, and I wanted in my soul to spit in those gorilla mugs, which, if you know how to beat them, can be made to do anything. The entire center of the city was cordoned off, so that to get to the station, I had to go around by the side streets—as happened at the time of the tsar's arrivals and departures. The employees of genuine soviet institutions were obliged to pass in procession on Red Square that day, and that parade lasted until 6 P.M. I left for Pestovo and here I am again drinking the cup of oblivion.

Today, alas, we were awakened with the news of the death of my cousin, Liza Rar—at the age of thirty, from a strangulated bowel in one day. The Cheka, prison, robbery, eviction, and death—that was her life the entire last year. What is this chain of senseless young deaths—Nina, Shura Grave, and now Liza!? A hecatomb even without an always apparent connection with the ruin of Russia. I know nothing of general politics, and don't want to know. I have become indifferent to everything in that area.

AUGUST

1 [August]. Several quiet days in Pestovo spent at haying work. My specialty is putting the hay on the cart. In addition, I sawed and split firewood with S. K. Shambinago. I intersperse these labors with a little study and with care and concern for Volodia. There was tropical heat all these days.

9 [August]. A week spent in Moscow with all the charms of the bolshevik capital. Tropical, unbearable heat such as Moscow can't recall having had for a long time. With Moscow's heat, her customary stuffiness rose to an unheard of level. One could bathe in sweat without moving. But I had to walk a good deal, as usual, in the first place to make a trip to the Vvedenskie Hills to the grave of poor Liza Rar, who died recently from a strangulated bowel. I can't remember such an uninterrupted series of youthful deaths occasioning unhappiness, grief, orphans, and disconsolate people. Nina, Shura Grave, Liza. These deaths are certainly related to the terrible life to which we have been condemned; all this is closely and directly bound together, the one with the other. I arrived at the Vvedenskie Hills at 7 o'clock, and everything was already locked up. I got through the back gate and was at my graves and at Liza's. Such neglect at this cemetery, once the best in Moscow! I returned by Gorokhovskii Pereulok, past the Geodetic [Institute], where I had not been for a long time; every look at the long-unseen streets of Moscow makes the heart ache in horror from the ruins you see everywhere.

Last Tuesday we quietly and modestly celebrated the tenth anniversary of Prince V. D. Golitsyn's directorship of the museum; Iakovlev, Romanov, Borzov, and I were there. We drank some wine, some vodka, a half-bottle of cognac, and one bottle of champagne. We had a warm and heartfelt talk after expressing our best wishes to the prince. Many of us in the museum still don't understand his true significance: the fact is that this irreproachably decent lord and gentleman is truly the living conscience of the museum—for ten years he has prevented us from quarreling, playing dirty tricks, and intriguing. That sort of thing could have especially flourished in the "revolution," but this was impossible precisely because of his presence. God grant him strength and health for long years, until he carries us to some shore and we can rest from life's storms.

Wednesday—a new excursion: I went to participate in the unloading of a barge of firewood for the museum. We received a barge with 600 *sazhen'*[93] of firewood that arrived in Moscow from the Unzha.[94] It had to

---

[93] One sazhen' = 2.13 meters.

[94] That is, from the Unzha River in Kostroma province.

be unloaded or it would have been taken away, and the guarantee of warmth and life in the museum was in that barge. And so, all the employees are taking part in this work, carrying wood from the barge and depositing it on the ground. I worked two and a half hours, and was even gay, thanks, of course, to very good company. The work went rather smoothly, under the command of D. N. Egorov.

9 August (continuation). I think, however, that this unloading job will last for a long time.

A meeting on Thursday with S. V. Bakhrushin and Rado Jovanović—again, like a month ago, a very lively conversation, for the most part about future relations between Russia and Serbia.

Friday—departure from Moscow with a sidetrip to Pushkino, where I had to arrange for the moving of E. E. Armand's books. Such horror and neglect there, where life once burgeoned! E.E.'s house has been turned into a club; everything has been pilfered, is falling down and leaking; Ad. E.'s house is serving as a nursery, and not a single object has remained in the rooms. The two old women have been stuffed into an old peoples' home and are sadly living out their lives among the ruins of the past. The garden is overgrown, there are tall weeds everywhere, and the gazebos have been wrecked. Horror and abomination.

I continue to avoid the newspapers, because they make me sick. However, the general situation is in fact very interesting and, in addition, it changes every day. Poland has been beaten, and on the 6th and 7th the Russian reds were within twenty-five versts of Warsaw; Kovel', Ternopol', and Buchach[95] have been taken, and they are approaching Siedlce.[96] Europe cannot fail to react to this. In London the discussions with Kamenev-Rozenfel'd and Krasin have been terminated, but that is of little importance, of course. Europe is on the eve of an invasion by Batu[97] or the Huns in the form of Russian "liberators" if it doesn't take care of the bolshevik nest. This constitutes the interest of the moment. The affair can't remain at the former standstill; something must happen.

10 [August]. The end of summer. The air is brisk and there are many yellow leaves, although it remains very dry. The summer is passing, but nothing else changes. And from that—sadness, anguish, and a black mood. I feel as though I am living without my ego, like a kind of hollow person.

[95] Towns in the present-day western Ukraine.

[96] Siedlce is about fifty miles due east of Warsaw.

[97] Batu (d. 1255) was the Mongol Khan who led the invasion of Eastern Europe that began in 1236. He was the founder of the Golden Horde.

13 [August]. I went to Sergievo and prepared for the transfer of the library. I saw a fine scene—the entire square in front of the monastery, with the exception of the hotel (now the sovdep) has been burned out; the corner Piatnitskaia tower and the Holy Gates have also collapsed. The fire started because the Posad comrades set fire to the stalls to cover their tracks after having plundered the wares designated for distribution. This was a continuation of the fire that occurred in Holy Week of 1919. Everything was sad and boring in the monastery, and the grass of neglect is covering it inside. The comrades are again howling that Petersburg is in danger—probably according to the system of Jewish "Gewalt."[98] They are pressing on Warsaw, and on Wrangel, too, it seems. One will have to wait yet for the future conflict with the whole world. With all this, the anguish and black mood are taking over completely; perhaps the weather facilitates this, too—a bit autumnal, grayish, after a good rain in the night. There is no energy for work, and no desire to live and work.

16 [August]. Several days of rest again. The sky is lowering. The hot summer has passed, and because of that, perhaps, the feeling of summer past and impending winter is especially burdensome. I haven't been in such a black mood as these last few days for a long time. I think about myself, my role and significance in the bit of life that remains. It seems to me that all my present existence consists of personal rejection of myself and everything individual. It is a difficult process, especially for me, who loved life and my individual will. Everything for Volodia, nothing for myself—how poorly still I am handling my responsibilities regarding Volodia! For myself I only look inside myself: reading, memories. Externally, nothing interests me, with one exception—to leave Sovdepiia.

23 [August]. Pestovo again after a week in Moscow. There are few personal observations; the days were uneventful. Tuesday and Wednesday (the 17th and 18th) there were few conversations in Moscow; the inclination for rumors and gossip was in a depressed state, which was replaced by a wave of animation on the last day of my stay in Moscow, the 21st. On that day (Saturday) the bolsheviks printed a war communiqué that made it clear that they have suffered a big failure near Warsaw: it was mentioned that the enemy was pressing them in the direction of Pultusk, that they changed to new positions thirty-five versts from Warsaw and have crossed to the right bank of the Western Bug at Brest. This testifies to major changes. The question remains—are these changes accidental and short-lived or is this the beginning of lengthy retreats and

[98] "Hue and cry."

defeats, similar to what it was like with Denikin and Kolchak?[99] One will have to wait for the answer. The bolsheviks have decided to be merciful in the trial of the "tactical center" and, some think, are extending their hand to the intelligentsia. I don't know if that is so, but in any case, it is at least a good thing that there are no death sentences. It appears that the most unenviable role fell to the lot of those who wavered (Kotliarevskii, Sergievskii, Vinogradskii, Ustinov).[100] They have compromised themselves before both sides. Some of them will have to serve time— among them I am not at all sorry for Kishkin, Kotliarevskii, or Mel'gunov,[101] three sorry nonentities who imitated the frog in the fable "The Frog and the Ox,"[102] or for A. L. Tolstaia,[103] who has been at the jam pot like her daddy and Chertkov.

I received an interesting letter from Emma Wilken. I append it here as a document.[104] It seems to me, and to all who have read it, that it has been sent from another world.

The questions of academic life remain altogether unclear. The question arises, shouldn't one try to do something to counter the increasing ruin? Aren't we at fault in this, too? After I get some rest, I will have to think seriously about that. Iakovlev and his family have left for Simbirsk; one less friend and intelligent interlocutor. Will he return?

26 [August]. I went to Sergiev Posad and finished the transfer of the monastery library to the management of the museum. I went to pay a visit to the governor general,[105] but he wasn't there; he had gone to Moscow. In connection with the process of transfer a small episode occurred, which,

[99] See Norman Davies, *White Eagle-Red Star: the Polish-Soviet War, 1919–20* (London, 1972). The Polish offensive that drove the Red Army back to the Bug began on August 16 and reached the Bug by August 19. This was the end of the Warsaw Operation and the decisive turning point in the war, which was finally ended by negotiated settlement in October.

[100] Nikolai Nikolaevich Vinogradskii was working at this time as a functionary in the fuel administration; he had previously worked in provincial government administration. Vladimir Mikhailovich Ustinov (b. 1870) held a doctorate in constitutional law and taught at several Moscow institutions, including the Shaniavskii University and the Higher Women's Courses. "Kotliavervskii" was Got'e's colleague from the law faculty, S. A. Kotliarevskii.

[101] Sergei Petrovich Mel'gunov (1879–1956) was a leader of the Popular Socialist party, a professional historian and journalist. Following his emigration, he published a series of studies and materials on the history of the revolution and civil war, including the history of the Tactical Center. (Mel'gunov's father had been Got'e's high school history teacher.)

[102] Krylov's *Liagushka i vol*. The frog burst while trying to puff himself up to the size of the ox.

[103] Aleksandra L'vovna Tolstaia (1884–1979) was Lev Tolstoi's youngest daughter. She was arrested five times before emigrating in 1929. Alexandra Tolstoi, *I Worked for the Soviet* (New Haven, 1934).

[104] This letter is missing from the Got'e file.

[105] That is, the local commissar.

if looked at from a mystical point of view, may appear to have meaning. In transferring the library, we—that is, the Rumiantsev Museum and I, its representative—began a new affair, and the employees in the library entered a new phase. I asked the librarian, Father Aleksii, to offer a prayer, which he did for the two of us—Mansurov and me. The prayer was, of course, to Saint Sergius. Afterward I went to see Father Diomid, the sacristan, with whom I was supposed to examine the manuscripts located in the sacristy. Father Diomid was in the Trinity Cathedral, which was closed and sealed and can be entered only by special passes. Having asked the guard if Father Diomid was there and having received an affirmative answer, I asked if Mansurov and I could go there. The guard and the guard commanders, young boys, said yes; we went into the entrance chamber and, knocking at the iron doors, which were locked from the inside, we saw the absolutely stunned face of Father Diomid looking out through the small window. He asked us in astonishment: "How did they let you in here? Even I am let in only by special passes!" Then, turning to us, he said: "Do you wish to kiss [the relics of St. Sergius]?" which we did. On August 25, 1920, the relics of St. Sergius were intact and in a good state of preservation. Thus, it turned out that St. Sergius seemed to have answered our prayer and, in making it possible for us to enter the Trinity Cathedral, gave his blessing to the Rumiantsev Museum to watch over his book treasure.

30 [August]. Several days in Pestovo again, with wonderful weather and a bearable mood. The news that reaches us is that the red army has in fact suffered a great blow. But "they" will continue to puff themselves up all the same, for they have no other recourse. I reread the novels of Markevich. This writer, who in his time was censured by the Russian intelligentsia, makes many truthful remarks about Russian society. Especially valuable are the references to its fragility and the absence of strong and stable convictions.[106]

I found several verses of Anatole France. I am writing them down because they harmonize very well with my own profound mood, secret and hidden from everyone:

> *Les mortes, en leurs temps jeunes et désirées,*
> *D'un frisson triste et doux troublent nos sens rêveurs;*
> *Et la fuite des jours, le retour des soirées*
> *Nous font goûter la vie avec d'âpres saveurs*[107]

---

[106] Boleslav Markevich (Boleslaw Markiewicz) (1822–1884) was a popular writer of "antinihilist," or reactionary, novels in the 1870s. His principal work was the trilogy *Chetvert' veka nazad (A Quarter of a Century Ago)* (1878).

[107] Anatole France, "L'Auteur à un ami," in *Oeuvres complètes illustrées de Anatole France.* Tome 1 (Paris, 1925), p. 396.

I am trying not to think of what is happening in Moscow; in any case many unpleasant things are in store there.

31 [August]. Today I began to read the works of Pisarev.[108] Such glib hypocrisy and enormous banality. One sees very well in him the father or grandfather of contemporary supernihilism. All authorities are overthrown, just as now; the first attempts are being made at the "reevaluation of values," with which the Russian intelligentsia vulgarians have been constantly obsessed ever since. In pursuing the new ("We will show the world a new path"), Pisarev and the generations of gorillas that followed him—who falsely imagined themselves to be the renovators of mankind; that is, the most dangerous madmen in the entire human race—have mistaken the permanent acquisitions and invaluable achievements of human civilization for obsolete authorities and have transformed the reevaluation of values into an invasion of the Huns or Batu. And so it is in our days!

SEPTEMBER

1 [September]. Complete isolation. A miserable mood. Those with the strength to endure to the end will have a great deal more to bear.

2 [September]. Thinking of myself, I feel that my life of forty-six years has retreated into the past; there is no link between it and the present except little Volodia. The whole line of continuity was broken with Nina, and now I must build something out of the debris in order to live out the remaining small part of my life. The only advantage in this is that you genuinely understand that all is vanity. Live a life normally and you would regret that it was over; but now—there is no regret.

3 [September]. Poor Russian scholarship—constant blows and losses, but no replenishment by new forces. The winter was terrible enough, and now, in the summer, two such deaths side by side as the deaths of Turaev and Shakhmatov. And in that field there clearly remains nothing but a blank space!

The populists idealized the people *an und für sich*. The populists and Tolstoi with his well-fed lord's nonsense summoned everyone to descend into the lower classes. Various sorts of idiots tried to develop the people with diversions and theater. But not one of these "developing" and pro-

---

[108] Dmitrii Ivanovich Pisarev (1840–1868) was the preeminent nihilist literary critic of the 1860s.

gressive souls found it necessary to inculcate a feeling of duty, honesty, and honor in that people. And now we are reaping the just reward of bad character.

5 September. Nina's birthday. I observed it with Lena Reiman and Volod'ka. Emptiness. Judging from the news received, the general situation is almost as serious as a year ago. How will it end?

8 [September]. Until recently, I always knew what I was doing and what, in my view, I had to do. And now I don't know what to undertake at present, or when something needs to be arranged. What should I strive for—for departure? But Volodia is so small. Reject this idea? That would mean ruining him and what remains of me, although I don't care at all about the latter. Is one to believe that something will come of it, that something will take shape out of the unmitigated pogrom called the Russian revolution? But what is to be done when that belief is not there, when you can't see the germ of anything good. Try to build a new personal life? But invisible bonds bind one fast to the beloved past; responsibility and duty require me to be the tutor of my dear fragment of that past; and, of course, it is late, late. Life has ended at forty-six—further there is only existence, as long as it lasts, relieved by a few, ever rarer, friends and by one's work, which in the existing conditions of life is not needed and whose result can't even be published. The official work in the museum is difficult and boring. God, how I am sick of it! To direct the work of two hundred hungry intelligentsia idlers, and in the name of what? In order to preserve the institution, knowing that you will not preserve it *by that*! Teaching?—it has been reduced to nothing. My notes, in spite of me, are taking on a subjective character, which I earlier tried not to give them. But what is to be done? The tone could be sustained when there was something of one's own, but when there is not, when all has disappeared, the cry of the soul involuntarily extends to diary entries.

The last days in Pestovo. Yesterday, as an exceptional phenomenon this year, it rained. Autumn has drawn near with rapid steps.

11 [September]. The last day in Pestovo, tomorrow to Moscow. I think of this with complete indifference, although it seems painful and difficult to arrange anything at all.

14 [September]. Moscow engulfed me with her stench, physical and moral. Everyone is again full of rumors. Fortune has shifted on the western front. At the same time, it seems that serious attention is being paid to Wrangel. Boring and empty. Volodia and I were at the monastery, where everything is in order.

16 [September]. Comrade Steklov turned up in the museum for a book, and so one more link has been added to my small collection of personal bolshevik impressions. This is a thick-set, tall Jew, who is betrayed not by his looks but by his accent. He was polite, even emphatically amiable. The self-satisfaction of a well-off Semite who feels he is the boss shows through his every word and gesture.

The comrades continue to be beaten as they have never been beaten before.

22 September. I haven't written because there was no time. The impossibility of keeping the notes at home makes it very difficult to keep them regularly. As for the general background, events are developing in the same direction. "They" are getting beaten as they have never been beaten before, but all that has been done so far is little—they must be not only beaten, but finished off. If a way out is found now, even a temporary one, they will again recover and everything will continue as before, for these will only be blows on a pillow, as all blows against tsarist and soviet Russia have been until now. In order to achieve the destruction of the bolsheviks, the pillow must be torn so that the feathers scatter. If the negotiations in Riga lead to anything, the bolsheviks will throw all their forces against Wrangel. If anyone is thinking about the overthrow of the bolsheviks, there must be no peace in Riga.[109]

24 [September]. The general situation remains the same. The rumors are growing and spreading. They tell of enormous losses, for the most part of prisoners and internees in Prussia, and of the evacuation of the big towns of the south. A commission for acquisition of books abroad has been formed under the People's Commissariat of Enlightenment. I don't know what will come of it. For the rest, everything remains unchanged and just as dreary.

26 [September]. The general situation is still the same. Bolshevy reminds me of a pillow being beaten; it yields, but if they should stop beating it, it will take its normal shape again. The question is, will they beat it until the down flies out of it? I am going to saw wood.

30 [September]. Three days of sawing wood in Domodedovo on the Riazan'-Ural railroad. Wonderful weather, very good company consisting of nine representatives, male and female, of the Rumiantsev Museum, good

[109] Peace negotiations between Poland and Soviet Russia had begun on August 17 in Minsk, and were continued in Riga. Preliminary peace conditions were agreed upon on October 12; hostilities ceased on October 18; the final peace treaty, known as the Riga Treaty, was not signed until March 18, 1921.

food, and relatively satisfactory lodging for the night made a pleasant, although not easy, picnic of this expedition. The sawing of wood was done by five professors of Moscow University, three young ladies, and one professional sawyer, divided into three groups of three. I was with M. V. Sergievskii and N. S. Voskresenskaia. Both were excellent workers and good companions. We relatively easily produced three cubic sazhens in three days. I was not greatly fatigued; on the contrary, it seemed to me that working under the marvelous September sun is better than sitting in the museum and talking nonstop with various people for five hours at a time. In the evenings we sat and chattered very animatedly about travels and scholarship, and on the last day Borzov and I even dragged out old museum gossip. We spent the night in the building of an old teahouse on a big piece of felt spread on straw. It was hard, but there were no bedbugs, so it was quite bearable. I returned in a cheerful and lively mood. The situation in Moscow remains the same. The onslaught against the bolsheviks has not yet ended.

OCTOBER

4 [October]. The general situation is the same. There is again talk on all sides about how the bolsheviks are bad off, that they are frightened, etc. Now, in addition, there is persistent talk of a new schism among them and of how the most extreme group, led by Bukharin, has the best chances. Of course, if they get in a very bad way there will probably be a moment when their sting will be especially painful.

We have been discussing the question among colleagues of whether it is necessary, desirable, or possible to honor Solov'ev on the occasion of his centenary. Bakhrushin and I were in favor of a celebration. Bogoslovskii and Liubavskii were against it. As there was no unity, we had to consider the question closed. Bogoslovskii argued that we should be silent since it is impossible to say what needs to be said. We argued that a great deal can be said about Solov'ev that is worth hearing and that can't be considered a patently hostile act even by them. Which of us is right? I myself don't know for sure.

A commission for ordering books from abroad has been set up again in the commissariat. I am trying. What for, I don't know myself. For the first time in my life I feel I have become a genuine fatalist. Come what may; I myself don't know how to arrange the remains of my life.

6 [October]. They have made peace at our expense. Today's news about a truce between the bolsheviks and the Poles has depressed me. I was not very hopeful, but they were beating the pillow, and as long as they beat it, there was a ray of hope. Now it will fill out again; again a respite, again a resurgence, and a new phase of hopelessness for the slaves. Everything else pales before the recognition of this fact.

7 [October]. I learned something about how people travel to Reval. Not everything will be easy and well, even if one succeeds in leaving here to go there. One of the difficult questions is the technical one of how to go farther, in case of success. There is little hope, but one has to try all the same, especially now that it is becoming clear that there is nothing to be expected in the future.

9 [October]. Yesterday I went on business about ordering books from abroad to the collegium of the Commissariat of People's Enlightenment, which was meeting in the Egorov house in the Alexandrine Garden. The director, Markus, went and asked the cleaning women for a standing lamp. One woman would not give a lamp in his absence, fearing that it would be stolen. There was a commotion today occasioned by the collection of clothes; as I had the stupidity to substitute for the chairman of the building committee until tomorrow, I got caught up, as they say, in a dreary story. I read the *Berliner Tageblatt* for August. The attitude toward us is coldly correct. It is clear that all Europe understands that it is impossible to have anything to do with the bolsheviks. But the liquidation of the war is a difficult thing and the Entente has many other problems on its hands. The rout of the bolsheviks in Poland was especially strong at the bewitched place where Samsonov perished in 1914.[110]

11 [October]. Without change. The cause of peace has bogged down. In the university the candidacies of two professors who are to be admitted to the "presidium" of the university are being discussed.[111] We decided to nominate two victims. An anecdote: the junior employees are nominating the doorman Uteshev for assistant rector. That is the limit.

[110] The forest of Tannenberg, where General Samsonov killed himself on August 17, 1914, after the destruction of his army by the Germans in the Russian army's disastrous East Prussian campaign at the beginning of the First World War.

[111] On September 29, 1920, Narkompros announced the creation of a "temporary presidium" of Moscow University, replacing the University Council. It consisted of three representatives of the university staff (two regular professors and one from the rabfak), one representative of nonacademic staff, the "military commissar" attached to the university, and three representatives of Narkompros. Henceforward, the rector was to be elected by this presidium. Professors were to be appointed by the Academic Council of Narkompros. This was the end of faculty autonomy at the university, although it did not mean the complete subservience of the university to the commissariat. See Fitzpatrick, *The Commissariat of Enlightenment*, pp. 84–88.

12 [October]. A talk with Pokrovskii about buying books abroad. It turns out that it is our fault that the matter has not gotten anywhere so far. Everything we prepared turned out to be not what was needed; a new audience has been set for tomorrow.

The peace negotiations have been delayed again. Something there is not right.

15 [October]. It has turned out that comrade Pokrovskii doesn't want me to go to Reval or to Riga and, apparently, my French name has something to do with this. As a practical matter, I could, perhaps, insist, but it is clear that they will not let me out with Volodia; in that case, I'm not interested. However, that and the fact that they have after all concluded some kind of peace raises point-blank the question of principle concerning emigration. If not immediately, then at some other time. Now, apparently, everything depends on Wrangel; what will come of it? In any case, a period of silence will follow the period of rumors. On Thursday, the 13th, I dropped in on the meeting of professors and instructors of the university that elected two dummies to the new "presidium." A sorry and sad scene, but saddest of all is our latest rector, Novikov, a pitiful little coward and nonentity nurtured by the Kadets!

17 [October]. I went to Troitsa and came back the same day; it is dull and boring there; what was dear to me there is no longer; the monastery itself is gone. Everything was all right from the business point of view.

The peace has been signed. Only the territorial terms have been published so far: they are giving up half of Volynia; half of Podolia; Grodno; Vilna; and part of Minsk province.[112] If the Poles have indeed taken this, then in the future a union of Russia and Germany is naturally in order, and it will be directed against Poland.[113] This is also very useful for the Ukrainians of the Petliura type: just don't make friends with the Poles. However, all this may perhaps be reexamined in time. According to reports, the troops of Savinkov and Balakhovich, numbering 50,000 (and some say more) men, stand opposite the red army on the western front.[114] That means the war with the bolsheviks will continue, and every day may bring us new surprises. All the same, I fear that it will be impossible or, at the very least, very difficult to reconstruct the one and indivisible [Russia]. All the Russians have suffered failure: the tsarist regime went down the drain and everyone in it [. . .]; the ruling bureaucracy, because

[112] That is, the western parts of the Ukraine and Belorussia, significantly to the east of the Curzon line.

[113] This, of course, is precisely what happened in 1939.

[114] Savinkov was the main organizer of a Russian force on Polish territory for fighting the Bolsheviks—the so-called "Third Russian Army."

it was unable to organize a palace coup; the Kadetoids and the Kadets in the form of L'vov and Miliukov, because they were unable to organize the revolution and direct it; the SRs, in the form of Kerenskii, because they fraternized with the bolsheviks; the bolsheviks, because they destroyed and besmirched everything that remained at the time of their seizure of power; the entire people, because it was able only to destroy, at the incitement of the firebrands, and then was capable only of silence when it was being fleeced and compelled to fight for the Jews. Who can put that all together and repair it?

19 [October]. I was invited to the "Narkomat Vnesh. Torg."[115] in regard to the matter of distributing the books acquired in England by "comrade Krasin." I was in the company of Kaufman, Levi, Frenkel', and Katsenelenbaum, and also one Rivka. Isn't that Russia!? One must, however, give them credit for having more sense than comrade Pokrovskii. Today I was in Narkompros to see the Jew Grinberg,[116] who positively produced a good impression on me. A sensible and well-intentioned person; the Petersburgers don't have a good opinion of him for nothing. But God, what an accent! Today something like martial law was suddenly proclaimed and many officers were arrested. What were they frightened of?

I received a letter from the Erofeevs—addressed in fact to the Wilkens, and in the event of their absence to me. It is so interesting that I am appending it here.[117]

21 [October]. Arrests are taking place among three groups: the SRs, former dignitaries, and officers. No one yet knows why. They say a new conspiracy has been discovered. I think there is no conspiracy at all, but they need to create one for some reason. There can be no lengthy and durable peace, either. And they themselves don't believe in it. Something is seething all around, but we here continue to be completely blind. More than ever before, I feel that Russia is a second Mexico. It will take a long time to get out of the mess made by Nicholas II, on the one hand, and the Russian intelligentsia criminal-dreamers, on the other. There is enough [mess] for our unhappy century. The tragedy of civilized Russians is very similar to the tragedy of the Titanic. They were going along and unexpectedly ran into an iceberg. Now we are all unseaworthy wreckage, we are floating on the ocean and drowning one after the other, or we are

[115] The Commissariat for Foreign Trade.

[116] Zakharii Grigor'evich Grinberg (1889–1949) had been a member of the Petrograd collegium of Narkompros before holding the same position in Moscow. In 1920 he was head of the organizational division of Narkompros. From 1921 to 1924 he was in the Berlin trade commission, with the job of buying books.

[117] Letter of the Erofeevs to the Wilkens, no date. See Appendix, Letter 9.

already conscious of having drowned. More and more I include myself among the latter. My last thought is to at least save my child.

I am appending the letters of Erofeev, L. N. Krasil'nikova,[118] and Platonova,[119] and an unsent letter to the Wilkens.[120]

24 [October]. The situation is obviously critical. A lot of information from V. I. Picheta about his stay in Riga. The bolsheviks have concluded peace in order to stay in power at any cost. The Poles, in Grabski's[121] words, have recognized that it is better for them to do business with the bolsheviks than with Wrangel. The peace is unacceptable for Belorussia and the Ukraine since it gives half of both regions to the Poles. I rather consider this a useful pedagogical measure for the Russian idiots: they might just be cured of antipatriotism and self-determination of the nationalities. Although, to tell the truth, not only the Belorussians and Ukrainians, but the Saratovites of the Sakulin type and many Muscovites of the SR and PS persuasions ought to be given in apprenticeship to the Poles.

A meeting in the "N. K. Vneshtorg" in the building of the stripped Merchants' Bank (God, what they have turned this favorite Moscow center into!) on the subject of buying books abroad. There were five Jews out of eleven people; two—Kaufman and Lapirov-Skoblo—were intelligent, the rest were pale and colorless.

In *Izvestiia* for Saturday, the 23d, there is an open letter from our museum treasurer, N. V. Kozlov, about his resignation from the SR party and his intention to become a member of the RCP. He explains his action by the fact that he got tired of sitting in prison and that the *Izvestiia* editorial office didn't want to print a declaration only about resignation from the SRs. In fact, however, he doesn't intend to join the RCP. O, the mores of the Russian louts!!

26 [October]. The rumors have subsided. That is a usual phenomenon after especially stormy moments. I have written a draft decree on procedures for buying books abroad. That is the length one has to go to. Today there was an announcement about the twenty-fifth anniversary of the scholarly activity of comrade Pokrovskii. The reptile press is full of reptilian lies.

[118] Letter of L. N. Krasil'nikova, dated June 6 [1920]. See Appendix, Letter 10.

[119] Letter of Nina Sergeevna Platonova, daughter of the historian, dated August 26, 1920. See Appendix, Letter 11.

[120] Letter of Got'e to Emma Wilken, dated August 10, 1920, unsent. See Appendix, Letter 12. Got'e's penciled note at the end of the letter reads: "Letter not sent, because they wouldn't take it."

[121] Wladyslaw Grabski (1874–1938) was a Polish scholar and politician, a deputy to the first three dumas (Polish National Democrat). For a time in 1920 and again from 1923 to 1925, he was Polish prime minister.

29 [October]. "They" are full of bourgeois prejudices. The bolshevik Arakcheev, comrade Pokrovskii, is celebrating his twenty-fifth scholarly jubilee. This alone is a bourgeois prejudice! But the jubilee (twenty-five years ago he gave his first lecture) is even being celebrated, they say, with a banquet. In this regard, the petty scoundrel Storozhev has burst out in the newspaper *Communist Labor*[122] with an article in which he slings mud at Kliuchevskii, talking about his "alcoholic vice." With the conclusion of the breathing-space peace, as should have been expected, the rumors in Moscow have fallen like a stone to the bottom.

NOVEMBER

2 [November]. The concern of the day is the withholding of the academic ration. What is concealed behind this? What surprise? One should think we will find out within a few days. The general situation is once again one of hopeless winter boredom in all respects. Sitting in the winter lair is more bearable since our house is being heated. I had a long discussion yesterday with the engineer Pereverzev; it turns out that this kindly figure is also an old revolutionary, an SR of 1905, and was the chairman of the railroad union![123] Ou la révolution va-t-elle se nicher!

4 [November]. Various rumors are circulating about the situation in the south. Some are spreading the rumor today that they have already been beaten. It will be very interesting to see what will happen in the next few days. A new Marne, meaning by this going over to the attack from full retreat, or are these rumors lies and did they really succeed in wiping out Wrangel? I have just returned from O. M. Veselago's, where I saw the Grushkas and David Ivanovich Ilovaiskii,[124] who has arrived from Rostov. On the way home I was asked for my "documents," but they were polite.

5 [November]. New assaults are looming over the Rumiantsev Museum. They say it has been decided to put it under the administration of "Glav-

---

[122] Vasilii Nikolaevich Storozhev (1866–1924) was a Russian historian educated at Moscow University, a longtime collaborator of Pokrovskii.

[123] Vladimir Nikolaevich Pereverzev (1867–1944) had been the chairman of the first railway union and a leader of the Union of Unions during the revolution of 1905.

[124] David Ivanovich Ilovaiskii (1878–1935) was a paleontologist and professor at the Moscow Mining Academy (later the Moscow Oil Institute).

Polit-Prosvet"(!)—poor Russian language![125] They say this institution is run by hysterical women communists like Mrs. Lenin and especially Meshcheriakova.[126] This has supposedly been done with the object of including the Rumiantsev Museum and the Public Library in the network of library exchange. If that is all true, it means we are the object of their construction, which is worse than any destruction. A. K. Vinogradov brought us the news of this; but today he is already behaving more cheerfully. Knowing his impulsiveness, one might think the affair is not so awful. However, who knows? It is possible that the cause we husbanded for three years will collapse from one stroke of the dictator's pen, which, they say, crossed out the condition about a special administration for the Public Library and the Rumiantsev Museum.

8 [November]. It seems the disaster was in fact exaggerated. A decree on centralization of library affairs has been issued, half of which will probably not be carried out.[127] In any case, I am no longer particularly worried. The bolshevik holiday passed modestly; on the very day of the celebrations, they were able to print only something about "reconnaissance raids" concerning Wrangel. That means the conquest of the Crimea has fallen through. S. F. Platonov arrived on Saturday and is staying with me. Many pleasant conversations, as always. Gatherings at my place, at Bakhrushin's, at Bogoslovskii's. S.F. gave a lecture about family characteristics among the descendants of the Emperor Paul and Mariia Fedorovna. He said not a single trite word about the imperial family and hardly a word about Nicholas II. Those who were expecting piquancies were probably disappointed.

10 [November]. The reds are squeezing Wrangel again. All efforts are obviously being made to crush him before the occurrence of possible new complications. The bolsheviks are always lucky because their opponents are always divided among themselves and can never agree. Today I carried home on my back two puds of potatoes and a pud of cabbage. I carried the cabbage together with M. A. Menzbir. An old man with a

[125] The Glavnyi politiko-prosvetitel'skii komitet (Main Committee for Political Enlightenment) was officially established on November 12, 1920. It was subordinate to the Narkompros but was also an organ of the Party central committee. Its main function was the coordination of political propaganda in the country. Glavpolitprosvet was abolished in 1930.

[126] A. I. Meshcheriakova's connection with Krupskaia went back to the mid-1890s, when they had taught together in Sunday schools for workers in Petersburg. At this time she was working in the library section of Glavpolitprosvet.

[127] A decree on centralization of library affairs, prepared in Narkompros, was passed by Sovnarkom on June 22, 1920. It called for setting up a commission to create a centralized library system, which was to be part of Narkompros.

bad heart dragging fifty pounds of cabbage—that is a spectacle worthy of Sovdepiia. I received a letter from A. I. Iakovlev, which I attach;[128] I think we will not soon see him in Moscow.

14 [November]. The reds are mopping up the Crimea and will probably finish the job. Force will break a straw, especially when the straws are not a sheaf, but a scraggly bunch. One more attempt at struggle is collapsing. That is as it should be when the entire antibolshevik camp, insofar as it consists of intelligentsia and civilized people, is consumed by discord, and when the "God-bearing people" will always submit only to the one who is able to hit it in the mug. The other day I heard the following: Supreme Commander Kamenev received a house to live in. He didn't like the house, so he chose another, but he liked the furniture in the first one and ordered it removed. This is what the Russians in whom are combined the spirit of military requisitions and socialism have come to. I read Staniukovich's *Around the World on the Korshun* to Volodia: God, what a stupifying specter of the spirit of the sixties! How highly the Russian sailors thought of themselves, and such contempt for the peoples conducting colonial wars—for the French in Indochina, for example.[129] If he could see the Russian people and the Russian "intelligentsia" now.

16 [November]. They have finished mopping up. It is likely that what was announced to us today was in fact being anticipated for some time, because Wrangel has apparently left.[130] And various persons of his entourage have left, too. Only the small fry and those stupid bourgeois who thought they had hidden in the Crimea remained behind. The last antibolshevik refuge in Russia has perished with the fall of the Crimea. From now on the struggle can only be from without; all that lies within former Russia is doomed to decay and further ruination. If anyone nurtured any illusions, he now has one illusion less.

I went to Troitsa. The rescue of libraries is, after all, a kind of constructive work, and therefore I get a certain satisfaction from arranging things there. At least I felt that yesterday. Sunday there was a wake for L. M. Lopatin. There was a public resembling the old-Muscovite [public] in the large auditorium of the Psychological Institute. They honored dear L.M., who had personified the old Moscow University, the old civiliza-

---

[128] Letter of A. I. Iakovlev, dated October 23, 1920, Simbirsk. See Appendix, Letter 13.

[129] Konstantin Mikhailovich Staniukovich (1843–1903) was one of the "plebeian novelists" of the 1860s whose convictions were generally radical. According to Mirsky, Staniukovich was the only Russian novelist of the sea in the nineteenth century. Indochina occupied a prominent place in his stories.

[130] Wrangel had left the Crimea on November 14.

tion, the old houses between the Arbat and Prechistenka. This was a genuine requiem for the Moscow that is gone forever.

17 [November]. One thing can be said—the departure of Wrangel was decided on the spot much earlier than we knew about it. This is demonstrated by the bolsheviks' own half-admissions and by the fact of the leaders' departure. Lunacharskii has sent a paper to Narkompros, forwarded to the museum, proposing that a person experienced in library affairs be assigned to organize a library for him, his own, which is in disorder. There you have the level of patrimonialism that obtains among our masters.

21 [November]. I have learned that Karakhan is occupying the entire Kharitonenko mansion.[131] The entire very fine library from the Got'e house in Mashkov has been delivered to him there, incidentally; there were almost four thousand books there. The Archive of the Ministry of Foreign Affairs was almost destroyed—because it so pleased comrade Pokrovskii. In the end the reform came down to a cutting of the staff and the firing of the professorial element, including Kizevetter, who was given a second ration for this. What nonsense! The new presidium has begun to function in the university; D. P. Bogolepov was made the new rector—they say he is a good man, but quite stupid and, moreover, a fanatic; that is, the worst type of bolshevik.[132]

26 [November]. There is more and more talk of internal dissension among them. Only it is impossible to tell whether this is the wishful comment of the depressed bourgeois or whether it actually corresponds to the true state of things. I think it is only a lovers' quarrel. They are always sufficiently in agreement to scoff at the public. These last few days I have been under the influence of an obsession—to leave, to leave at any cost, for any destination. I have now come to the idea of the inevitability of denationalization, for I do not anticipate a resurrection from this people and this country, which have been thoroughly demoralized by deceit and vice. Today I heard a sensational rumor that America is supposedly demanding convocation of a constituent assembly by March 1. Even if

[131] Lev Mikhailovich Karakhan (real name: Karakhanian) (1889–1937) was a prominent Soviet official and diplomat who at this time was assistant commissar for foreign affairs.

[132] Dmitrii Petrovich Bogolepov (1885–1941) was a longtime Bolshevik and former deputy to the duma (Fourth). A Privatdozent on the law faculty before 1917, he worked in the finance commissariat before being appointed rector in November 1920. He lived up to Got'e's apprehensions: he was a vociferous enemy of the "bourgeois university" and proponent of the rabfak—to the point that he ran afoul of Pokrovskii (the creator of the rabfak) and was dismissed in May 1921.

that were the truth and even if the bolsheviks were to agree to it, there wouldn't be anyone to elect besides the bolsheviks themselves. The realm has fallen and will not revive.

28 [November]. All of Russia can be bought up according to the just-published decree on concessions.[133] If that decree is put into effect, the foreigners will swallow up Russia. Here is the question—what is this, the usual desire to dupe, or the realization of that phenomenal intrigue about which there is more and more talk, the swallowing up of Russia by the foreigners? Who will dupe and swallow up whom?

30 [November]. A *politkom*[134] has been appointed for the university. Given the presence of the "presidium," this measure seems superfluous to me. In the newspapers today there is a proclamation declaring all srs, Wrangelite officers, and political prisoners sitting in Butyrki and the camps to be hostages; they will be shot if any terrorist attempts are made on "their" people. In general, a dull and oppresive mood.

DECEMBER

6 [December]. A trip to Tver' from the 1st through the 5th to give lectures in the local institute of popular education—something like a semiuniversity. The balance for the trip: thirty pounds of bread and 22,000 rubles. With them I bought two and a half pounds of butter, twenty eggs, and one grouse, which I brought home. I lectured on archaeology. The audience was very grateful and receptive. A good reception. I was fed well; the accommodations were clean. The town is very similar to all the other Russian provincial capitals of the second rank. The only surviving antiquity is the cathedral, which was quite disfigured, however, in the eighteenth century. The relics of Michael of Tver' have not been touched.[135] There are interesting remnants of the eighteenth century, undoubtedly going back to Sievers:[136] the central Millionaia Street and part

---

[133] A decree "on the general economic and legal terms of concessions" passed Sovnarkom on November 23, 1920, and was published in *Izvestiia* on November 25. *Dekrety Sovetskoi vlasti*, vol. 11, pp. 251–53. Got'e's reaction to this minor step in the direction of establishing normal economic relations with the outside world is a measure of his apprehensions about both the Bolsheviks and the Western "imperialists."

[134] Political commissar.

[135] Mikhail Iaroslavich (1271–1318), prince of Tver' and grand prince of Vladimir, was one of the many "prince-martyrs" to be canonized by the Russian church.

[136] Count Jacob Johann von Sievers (Iakov Efimovich Sivers) (1731–1808) was a prominent statesman during the reign of Catherine II and chief architect of the great statute on the provinces (1775), which set up the provincial administration of Russia that re-

of the embankment consist of houses with the same façade that have been only partly disfigured by later construction. The octagonal square with government offices is very handsome. The town has been stripped, like all contemporary Russian towns; in the course of three days I saw several of the usual bolshevik removal operations; in particular, [I saw] them hauling books from the theological seminary to the library—on a wood sledge, with the books scattering fanlike along the street and the girl accompanying them cursing.

During the time of my absence, a decree was issued on the reorganization of the faculties of social sciences and on the compilation of lists of persons who can teach in them.[137] This is either a complete rout of all of us or a false alarm. I think it is something between the two. They were saying today, incidentally, that the decree has already been dropped. Much is being said about concessions, but without adequate foundation. The essence of the matter, in my opinion, is still not apparent. Today is a year since Nina's death. I have still not come to my senses from that catastrophe. I spent the morning at the monastery.

9 [December]. My nameday, which for me has been permanently canceled because Nina's funeral was held on that day. My servant has left for several days in the village. We are experimenting at life without a servant. For beginners, two and a half hours this evening went to various housekeeping trivialities, and the evening is lost. And it is that way almost every day. The general situation is unclear; there are no new facts or phenomena on my horizon.

14 [December]. I heard an anecdote about Taine. Having seen *The Power of Darkness*[138] in Paris, he said: "Ces cochons mystiques me déplaisent." How characteristic that is of the speaker and of those of whom he spoke. I heard this from O. M. Veselkina, who heard it from Prince A. D. Obolenskii (the former Ober-Procurator of the Synod), he from Iu. N. Miliutin, and Miliutin from Anatole Leroy-Beaulieu.[139] The bolsheviks de-

---

mained until the fall of the old regime. He was for many years Governor General of Novgorod, to which jurisdiction Tver' belonged.

[137] *Sobranie uzakonenii i rasporiazhenii rabochego i krest'ianskogo pravitel'stva*, 1920, no. 93, art. 503. The decree did not contain personnel lists; it directed Narkompros to compile such.

[138] Tolstoi's best-known play (1887), a moralizing work—its main themes being the nature of evil and the atonement for sin—cast as a realistic drama. "Abroad it was received enthusiastically because its ruthless realism was a new and piquant thing to the Western palate." Mirsky, *A History of Russian Literature*, p. 310.

[139] Aleksei Dmitrievich Obolenskii (1855–1933) was a prominent career bureaucrat who had served as Procurator of the Holy Synod briefly in 1905–1906; he was one of Witte's closest collaborators in the preparation of the October Manifesto in 1905. Iurii

stroyed Sukharevka today. We will see what the results will be. Everything is in flux and is constantly changing, without, however, any perceptible benefit to us.

18 [December]. For want of anything to do, they are now gossiping in Moscow about various changes in the composition of the bolshevik government. They are talking about how one leaves and another is appointed in his place exactly like they used to talk about how Nicholas II fired his ministers or Rasputin performed his exploits. The other day I went again to Grinberg to talk about buying books abroad. He says this question will be resolved soon. After that *démarche* I will be still and shut up, since if the most intelligent and well-meaning among them does nothing, the others certainly won't. It has already been ten days since Masha the cook left and we, that is I and my two boys (Volodia and my nephew Iura),[140] are doing everything ourselves except the preparation of food, which takes place in the apartment next door.

24 [December]. A trace of Masha turned up today: they won't let her back into Moscow because the term of leave on the paper issued to her was overstayed. Thus the "local authorities," instead of facilitating a rapid return to service (Masha is reckoned to be in the service of the museum), detain such a person even longer. I am writing this as a minor curiosity in our life full of curiosities.

All these days I have been in a very confused and changeable mood. You positively don't know today what you are going to think and feel tomorrow. You come to the philosophical conclusion that you must wait, for everything around you is in flux, now rapid, now slow, but nothing ever remains for even a minute at rest or even in any kind of steady state; and who knows where or when this mad race will carry us. The news from those who have gone abroad is not always good: they say that Dima Got'e in Zurich is selling some kind of machines. Lipa and Emma Wilken are working, each receiving 300 francs, which is not enough. Only those who have money are happy; or someone who finds a money-maker. So one has to wait, and seize every opportunity to establish ties abroad and set oneself the goal in life to somehow, sometime, get out of

---

Nikolaevich Miliutin (1856–1912), son of the great reformer Nikolai Alekseevich Miliutin (1818–1872), was a journalist and editor, and a leading figure of the Octobrist party. Anatole Leroy-Beaulieu (1842–1912) was a liberal French scholar-publicist who wrote one of the best books about modern Russia, *L'Empire des Tsars et les Russes* (3 vols.; Paris, 1881–1889) (English translation: *Empire of the Tsars*); he also wrote a book about Nikolai Miliutin, based on Miliutin's personal papers, *Un homme d'état russe* (Paris, 1884).

[140] Iurii Kurdiumov, the son of Got'e's sister-in-law. He was to die of tuberculosis in April 1921 (see entry for April 18, 1921).

this horror, and for the time being to be patient and to take from this life all one can.

They say there is discord in their midst; according to gossip and rumors, they are quarreling at the eighth congress, but after all "it is only a lovers' quarrel." The only fact is that "Narkompros" has been smashed. Lunacharskii—a rope-dancer who is an embarrassment even for the soviet government—has been assigned a nursemaid, a Latvian intelligent from among the front-line commissars.[141] They say that our Zmei-Gorynych[142] Pokrovskii is falling, too. But their replacements will be even worse.

28 [December]. I continue to be completely indifferent to what the comrades are doing at their congress. The exterior look of the Bolshoi Theater is just as sinister as before; there is the same guard past which the comrades admit the comrades with equally important mien on both sides. A stupid, arrogant rabble that can be instilled with any kind of rubbish and will believe it. As before, I continue to wash the dishes and do various other agreeable household things while waiting for the return of my cook. I have even learned to fry potatoes. Today I went on foot over six versts from Mytishchi to the children's sanatorium, where my nephew, Dima Kurdiumov, has been placed; I went with his mother. More than twenty versts were covered in the course of the day, and a stroll like that is to be considered an episode that gives variety to our existence. The rumors and gossip have fallen off, like a stone in a well.

30 [December]. Again a kind of phase of black mood for the end of the year; everything seems inconsequential and superfluous. The hordes of Huns are carrying out their task, and their cowering servants are doing even more. Today I was told about some kind of conference on artistic matters, where the actor Meierkhol'd[143] and the poet Briusov especially distinguished themselves in their persecution of individual creativity and

---

[141] Lunacharskii and Narkompros had come under attack from the Party leadership in the autumn of 1920 for supporting the autonomy of the Proletcult. Narkompros was subjected to extensive reorganization at the end of 1920, which was carried out by Evgraf Aleksandrovich Litkens (1888–1922), acting as a kind of organizational tsar imposed from without. Although Litkens's name was Latvian, he was a native of St. Petersburg. Neither Lunacharskii nor Pokrovskii lost his position as a result of these changes, however. See Fitzpatrick, *The Commissariat of Education.*

[142] An evil dragon of the Old Russian *byliny* (heroic folk poems) ("Dobrynia i zmei").

[143] Vsevolod Emil'evich Meierkhol'd (1874–1942), the theater producer and director, had been appointed head of the theatrical department of Narkompros in the summer of 1920 and immediately launched a revolutionary attack on traditional theater (he coined the slogan "theatrical October" on October 11, 1920).

inspiration—in their desire to replace all this with "production" in matters of art. The demented whorehouse is expanding ever wider.

31 [December]. One more year of bolshevism is expiring. The same emptiness and dejection as a year ago. There is nothing ahead; I am appending an excerpt from a letter of Emma Wilken received by E. A. Got'e.[144]

[144] Letter of Emma Wilken to Got'e, dated November 20, 1920. See Appendix, Letter 14.

_1921_

❄

JANUARY

1 January. On the occasion of New Year's Day, Volodia and I slept at home and are now sitting together. The only pleasure is the hope of sitting home for a while and going nowhere. But that hope is a bad thing, too.

4 [January]. I am getting ready to leave for Pestovo for a week. The bolsheviks are threatening that someone is preparing to make war against them. This is occurring because they themselves are Jew-cowards and also because they simply won't get along without a war. Masha has returned and reported that she traveled there for 2,000 rubles and got a return ticket for fifteen pounds of flour and ten pounds of oats.

7 [January]. Christmas in Pestovo. I managed to get away for several days. The nerves and organism are so worn that the main desire is to lie down and sleep. I am lying down eleven hours a day and am sleeping more than nine; I don't know to what extent a week spent here will fortify me for further continuance of the bustle of Moscow life, which is terribly exhausting, but I've got to make the most of it. I am trying to use these free days to get on with some work that had come to a standstill in Moscow; so far I am succeeding. The situation here has worsened since summer. The "M.Ch.K."[1] has taken root and commandeered part of the house. There is talk of possible new seizures; the woods are being chopped down; but still it is good here, mainly because you are among good people and because you have gotten away for a week from cursed Moscow, where bolshevism continues to boil in its stinking cauldron.

I have recently come to the firm conviction that all means are permitted in relation to them, as they permit themselves everything. In particular, the appropriation or use of a thing belonging to the "RSFSR," in whatever form or circumstances, should be considered permissible and is not theft.

---

[1] The Cheka of Moscow oblast'.

9 [January]. Several quiet days of rest. They go by one after the other, leaving an impression of spiritual peace. A comic note: yesterday evening we had guests, among them two former people—a marshal of nobility, G. I. Leont'ev, and a saloonkeeper from Mytishchi, Stepin, an actor *dans ses moments perdus*, who declaimed a scene from *The Robbers*.[2] All this peacefully coexisted around the tea table.

I am trying, while sitting here, to comprehend the meaning of the present moment in the history and evolution of bolshevism. They are in a temporary moment of external lull and are talking a lot about internal construction. They are undertaking reforms that are being interpreted by some as a communist reaction; in fact, everything they are undertaking is nothing other than the fable "The Quartet": No matter how you sit, you will not do as a musician![3] However, now and for the duration of their existence, they do not consider themselves to be guilty and will seek to lay the guilt on others.

12 [January]. The end of my stay in Pestovo. Thaw and springtime with wet snow. The week spent here was a week of rest and sad thoughts, and sometimes the joyful absence of thoughts. The sad thoughts, which accompany the end of the old year, all come down to the same thing—it is impossible to live like this. That which was formerly Russia has ruined itself for a long time. We are already has-beens, but the young must be saved. I have the responsibility of saving Volodia from the barbarity that has enveloped this land and threatens him. But how can this be done? The country, in one form or another, is doomed to enslavement by foreigners. And there is no point in cursing anyone: a people that has ruined itself has no right to demand anyone's help and sympathy. And who is to be helped? The surface scum, even if we were to call it cream? It is only rootless scum, swill.[4] The people?—these are not people, but gorillas, who are only capable of committing excesses and scratching their asses. Let them perish, let them bear the yoke of slavery of the bolsheviks and of the foreigners. The task of those of us who do not perish is to create a new fatherland for ourselves in place of the one that itself refused to be one.

14 [January]. Moscow greeted me with her usual anxieties and agitations. There are again ominous rumors about smashing the university and about various impending and imminent calamities. The contrast between

---

[2] The play by Schiller.

[3] Krylov's fable "The Quartet" ends with the nightingale telling the monkey, the ass, the goat, and the bear: "And you, friends, no matter how you sit / As musicians you will never be fit."

[4] That is, the intelligentsia.

the quiet days in the country and this boiling in a dirty cauldron with sewage is very great indeed.

The last few days I have been thinking about my feelings toward the Russian people. It seems to me that I pity and despise it. I pity it because I cannot get over the thought that I am a part of this people; I despise it because this people, in the person of its leadership, could not understand that to fail to carry the war to its logical end is a sign of weakness and pusillanimity; moreover, when among the outstanding public activists there were those who, like D. N. Shipov in his memoirs,[5] were not ashamed to write that they considered owning land a sin yet owned it all their lives, then this means that they are the worst kind of fools. And fools cannot lead a people and a country. Pusillanimity, weakness, and stupidity—those are the characteristics for which I despise the Russian people and the Russian intelligentsia.

15 [January]. Sasha Gartung has died. Toward the end he was a communist and a prominent party activist in either Tambov or Morshansk.[6] He began by wanting to be a priest; for a long time he was a fanatic Kadet, but in 1917 he went out of his mind and became either a Popular Socialist or an SR, and he ended as a bolshevik. What a typical example of the spiritual instability that is so common in unhappy Russian society. A torn-up neurasthenic and instinctive misanthrope, he was for me the very type of the Russian failure by his own fault, who, in an almost fatalistic fashion, had to become a communist. I had a visit from Serezha Solov'ev, who has become a Catholic priest.[7] When I asked him if this is his last metamorphosis, he answered me that if a man has gone topsyturvy three times, one should hope that he will not go on to do it a sixth time. But I think that he is not through somersaulting yet. Here is an example of a gifted Russian in whom "spiritual strength had long been absent." What is to be done with this cursed people, which gives us types like the persons just mentioned?

The rumors are now devoted to the matter of the expulsion of professors for unreliability. It would be good to be included among them. The attendant Klimentov has reported [to the authorities] that the "superiors"

---

[5] *Vospominaniia i dumy o perezhitom* (Moscow, 1918). Dmitrii Nikolaevich Shipov (1851–1920) was a leading figure in the zemstvo movement and a founder of the Octobrist party in 1905. His worldview, on which he expounds at length in his memoirs, was a kind of conservative populism, combining elements of Slavophilism, Tolstoianism, and noblesse oblige.

[6] According to Gartung's letters to Got'e, it was Morshansk.

[7] Sergei Mikhailovich Solov'ev (1885–1943), the namesake and grandson of the great historian, was a Symbolist poet and mystic, a youthful friend of Belyi, and a disciple of Blok and of his uncle, Vladimir Solov'ev, whose biographer he was. He became a Catholic priest on Christmas Day, 1920.

in the museum were not being made to clear snow. On account of that, everyone was dragged out today, up to and including the prince and myself. The rest in Pestovo is already coming to naught.

19 [January]. There is persistent talk about events that are expected to break in the spring. There is talk at the same time about uprisings and disturbances inside Russia. What conclusions can be drawn from all this? None at all. Isn't all this only the reflection of the desires of all the unfortunates who are languishing in the big prison called Sovdepiia? This witticism has been going around Moscow for several days: what will this all lead to? The answer consists of the words "hammer" and "sickle" spelled backwards.[8] That is how the grief-stricken bourgeois amuses himself. The other day I received a bit more news about those who have gone abroad. It is possible to get along there with modest resources. My God, how I want to shake off the dust of former Russia! But there is really no hope at all.

The question of smashing the university has been put off for a long time, so it seems. They can't even perform the fable of "The Quartet" at all satisfactorily. One of the few comforts is pleasant and intelligent conversation. I have experienced that pleasure several times recently.

23 [January]. Days without particular news or events. But such inveterate liars all have become, and how they love to repeat all sorts of rumors! The notorious presidium of the university has replaced itself with some kind of bureau, by means of excluding unsuitable individuals. This new institution has established a commission for sorting out the little people, that is, the professors, and has sorted them out at its own discretion. The proposals of this commission, unapproved by anyone and apparently even eliciting disapproval "from above," have been the source of all the conversations and gossip passed on from mouth to mouth. It is even shameful. The impression from the information about the university is that here, too, they will be unable to do anything or create anything.

24 [January]. I received an interesting letter from A. K. Vinogradov, which I append here as documentation.[9] I sawed wood for a whole hour for heating my house and for the glory of Sovdepiia.

25 [January]. The saddest St. Tat'iana's Day, probably, in the entire 166 years of the existence of Moscow University. I very much wanted to be

[8] *Prestolom*—"to the throne," i.e., a restoration.
[9] Letter of A. K. Vinogradov to Got'e from Riga, dated January 17, 1921. See Appendix, Letter 15.

at the mass in the Church of St. George on Krasnaia Gorka,[10] but I couldn't do it because of museum business, about which below. Afterward, tea in the Psychological Institute, the last refuge of scholarship in the university buildings. It was pleasant and agreeable there, although it was strange to feel as if one were at an illegal gathering within the walls of the university. In the evening I had supper at Shambinago's; we celebrated both the university and a nameday. We spent the time in warm conversation.

The museum business that prevented me from being at the mass consisted of a sudden inspection of the museum, carried out officially by Narkompros, but unofficially by the Cheka. Apparently there was a denunciation that we have a bourgeois society, that we are conserving some kind of tsarist things, and that we are all of us always away on business trips. The inspectors were two: one was a well-disposed and civilized person from Narkompros, Shchik, and the other was a Latvian of the Cheka type. Deflecting the blows was not so hard, thanks to the former. It seems the affair has turned out all right for the time being.

30 [January]. A trip to Sergievo. Everything went well. I was unexpectedly able to return the same day, since the train made good time even though it left an hour and a half late from Moscow; on the way back it even left on time and arrived on schedule. On the way in the train I heard an argument between some dissatisfied peasants and a bolshevik who was defending the soviet regime. The bolshevik finally had to be silent in the face of the unanimous dissatisfaction of his adversaries.

The inspection turned out all right; it was undertaken as the result of a denunciation originating in the family of the attendant Klimentov, and for some reason was directed especially at Vinogradov. The same opinion and the same conversation is heard everywhere: everything is crumbling. But will this crumbling continue for long? The bolsheviks are sending troops to fight the rebelling muzhiks in Tambov and Voronezh provinces.[11] An antibolshevik jacquerie—this was something unthinkable three years ago!

[10] A hill in the Presnia district.

[11] The Tambov rising, or "Antonovshchina" (after the name of the leader of the partisan movement there), began in the summer of 1920 and reached its height in the winter and early spring of 1921, when the whole of Tambov province and several neighboring provinces were involved in the fighting. This and several similar regional uprisings (particularly in western Siberia) in the winter of 1920–1921 were one of the main factors compelling the Bolsheviks to abandon forced requisitions and turn to the NEP, "The Peasant Brest." But it took a full-scale military campaign in the spring and summer of 1921 to suppress the Tambov uprising.

All these last years there was never talk so early, before spring, about impending events and springtime opportunities. Now, on the contrary, there is a great deal of talk. I, however, remain a skeptic. In my opinion, they are still dickering there: France is afraid to release Germany from its paws, and Germany is trying to jump out of the hole, offering to her Western partners to destroy the bolsheviks in return.

A few days ago, A. I. Iakovlev arrived from Simbirsk and D. N. Egorov arrived from Ekaterinburg. Summarizing their stories, one can see that the provinces are unbelievably gray, that the darkest and wildest elements dominate, that what remains of the cultured population either is in hiding or has been morally crushed. In Ekaterinburg, things are apparently so bad that Egorov warns against going there, whereas earlier he was an importunate advocate of the journey. Incidentally, he says that he was able to find out about the death of the imperial family. They were all executed, or rather shot, by sentence of some tribunal; at least they were killed without any taunts. The bodies were hauled away and burned. Along with them were killed the servants, Doctor Botkin, and Tatishchev.[12] The most energetic member of the family was Tat'iana Nikolaevna,[13] who had made active attempts to free herself and her family. What a beautiful page [in the history] of the great and bloodless [revolution]! How terrible, at the same time, was the crime of Nicholas II and Aleksandra Fedorovna, the real murderers of their whole family, which they crippled morally and then destroyed.

It frequently occurs to me that if the current Russian émigrés succeed in returning some day, those who have suffered bolshevism here and survived it will have to endure an onslaught. The prototype of this was the return of the Kadet professors to Moscow University in 1917[14]—self-infatuated, disdainful of everything and everyone, having forgotten nothing and learned nothing—that is how all these doleful figures of 1917 of doleful memory will arrive, I think.

[12] Doctor Evgenii Vasil'evich Botkin, the imperial family's physician, was killed with the family in Ekaterinburg on July 16, 1918. General Il'ia Leonidovich Tatishchev, the tsar's aide-de-camp, was killed there somewhat later along with other members of the family entourage.

[13] Tat'iana was the second daughter of Nicholas and Alexandra. She, it was generally remarked, was the daughter who followed in her mother's footsteps and displayed a sense of personal authority.

[14] The reference is to the numerous professors who had resigned in 1911 in the "Kasso affair" and then returned to the university after the February revolution in 1917. For a list of their names, see the article by B. I. Syromiatnikov (one such himself) in the "Granat" encyclopedia, s.v. "Moskovskii universitet." In all, more than a third of the faculty resigned in 1911.

In the university, the "dean," comrade Volgin, has crossed off a great number of courses, including my course on historiography. I will continue to give it, paying no attention. We'll see what happens next.

People who had seemed lost do turn up occasionally. I am attaching the letter I received today from V. D. Korsakova.[15]

7 [February]. Vinogradov arrived from Riga. It is his opinion that no intervention should be expected. I think the same. It is curious that all Moscow is talking these days only about the apocryphal speech of Briand supposedly printed in *Matin* on January 18.[16] It is going the rounds even though no one has read it. The eternal desire of the man in the street to find an outlet for his hopes. Egorov's story about Ekaterinburg closely resembles the contents of the memoirs of Gilliard, the children's former tutor.[17] This is very interesting, because it reinforces and strengthens the impression.

10 [February]. A dole has been issued by the soviet authorities to those who received the academic ration according to the list of March 1920. It consists of a jacket, three changes of shirts and underwear, six pairs of socks, and a pair of shoes and galoshs. The galoshs were distributed at the "Bogatyr'" warehouse, where they were handed out to us by an obvious counterrevolutionary and anti-Semite; the rest was [distributed] in the former Shanks store.[18] The jacket they gave was the kind that used to cost 25 or 30 rubles. It was strange to collect all this in a store where I used to shop for the highest-quality goods. And it was all given free of charge! What generosity and solicitude!

I was finally able to learn the contents of Briand's declaration. Its sense is this: that intervention is possible only if the comrades start to climb out of the borders of the RSFSR. How far that is from what the Muscovite

---

[15] Letter of V. D. Korsakova to Got'e, dated January 22, 1921, Krasnoiarsk. See Appendix, Letter 16.

[16] The government of Aristide Briand had been formed on January 16, with Briand holding the portfolio of foreign affairs as well as the prime ministership. His first speech in office, to the National Assembly, was made on January 20 and was printed in *Le Matin* on the 21st (not the 18th). It contained two brief paragraphs on Soviet Russia: one declared that there would be no relations with Russia until the appearance of a "truly representative" government, one that would accept the engagements undertaken by previous Russian governments; the other said that there would be no French intervention in Russian affairs so long as the Bolsheviks remained inside their own frontiers.

[17] Pierre Gilliard, *Treize années à la cour de Russie (Peterhof, Septembre 1905–Ekaterinbourg, Mai 1918). Le tragique destin de Nicolas II et de sa famille* (Paris, 1921).

[18] Bogatyr' was a factory on Bol'shaia Bogorodskaia Street that made rubber products; Shanks & Co. was a haberdashery firm on Kuznetskii Most founded in 1888 by James Shanks.

bourgeois was construing. I received a letter from Ivask, which I am attaching.[19]

11 [February]. The heat is being turned off here. Two months of extreme cold are in store. The task now is to supply enough fuel for the little stove in the bedroom. There you have the main concern of the day! A man who has arrived from the Crimea came to see me today; the journey lasted twenty-two days. Such is the brilliant situation of Sovdepiia!

13 [February]. The question of rations and heating is becoming acute. How vile it is! I have just looked out the window at the funeral of Petr Kropotkin.[20] He was being carried in an open coffin to Novodevichii Monastery. There was a "tail," a crowd was walking with flags and an orchestra. The crowd was rather impressive, but on the radio and in reports it will probably assume even greater proportions. The crowd was walking both in front of and behind the coffin. There were intelligenty and students in it, but in general it was that gray mass which is the typical property of our time. Anarchist groups with black flags occupied a very prominent place. Dull, simian, uncivilized, barbarian faces.[21]

15 [February]. The ration was issued without reduction; an ominous sign; perhaps the bolsheviks are not going to give any more alms at all, and the professors will no longer stand, like beggars on the church porch, waiting to be thrown their daily bread.

Today I presided at the general assembly of the museum; it was stormy and shameful. A band of intriguers, led by G. P. Georgievskii, Nikitiuk, and principally the treasurer Kozlov and the descriptive cataloguer Smirnov, tried to establish some sort of super administration of their own. In general, they failed, but the future is pregnant with complications. What a dirty trick! The key factor, of course, was the employees, whom they mobilized by means of food-supply issues.

20 [February]. Few events. The general mood remains the same. Most of all, further deterioration is anticipated. The museum passions have subsided. The jugheads have gotten their comeuppance in the labor

---

[19] Letter of U. G. Ivask to Got'e from Riga, dated January 10, 1921. See Appendix, Letter 17. Udo Georgievich Ivask (1878–1922) was a prominent bibliographer and bibliophile, and an employee of the Rumiantsev Museum.

[20] Prince Petr Alekseevich Kropotkin (1842–1921), the revolutionary patriarch and theoretician of anarchism, had died in Dmitrov on February 8. He had returned to Russia in June 1917 after thirty-one years of exile in Western Europe.

[21] On Kropotkin's funeral, see Paul Avrich, *The Russian Anarchists* (Princeton, 1967), p. 229.

union. The university affairs remain in the same state of decay. I made the acquaintance of a representative of the Finnish diplomatic mission. This is a young Balt, a theosophist, who made himself understood rather poorly in English. A praiseworthy feature is that he is looking for acquaintances with real Russian people. He asked what Russian scholars are doing; I explained to him that they are dying. He expressed amazement that so many are working for the bolsheviks and that the entire Russian intelligentsia has not left. I asked him in response, incidentally, how all the Western powers could reconcile themselves to the bolsheviks' treatment of their fellow countrymen living in Russia.

I am sorting out the German books that have arrived from Riga. I am reading ecstatically Buat's little book about Ludendorff, translated from French into German,[22] and am waiting for the memoirs of Ludendorff and Hindenburg, which have also been acquired for us. The building is no longer being heated, it appears for good. We will have to freeze for a month and a half.

24 [February]. Disturbances are occurring in Moscow. These are the first workers' disturbances under the soviet regime. They say that there were three killed and that the red army men refused to fire. Many are deluding themselves with the most optimistic hopes; others are skeptical. I think that these movements are interesting as the first swallows of spring and an indicator of accumulated discontent. Further developments depend on circumstances that will become apparent in the future. Either this is the beginning of the end or it is the continuation of a long process of decay. A.S.N. and A. I. Andreev have arrived from Petrograd;[23] they brought the news of M. M. Bogoslovskii's election as a member of the Academy of Sciences. I find that it would have been hard to make a better or more worthy choice.

I have been reveling these days in the book of the French general, Buat, about Ludendorff. It is a very interesting and objectively written book. In it I at last found the technical secret of the Allies' victory in 1918: fresh new American divisions, whose strength was greater than expected, gave the Allies a numerical advantage and allowed them to "suck dry" the German reserves. The mistake of the German command was to wear out the Germans, who were exhausted from the war, and to seek until the last moment a solution to the war on the field of battle.

[22] General [Edmund Alphonse Leon] Buat, *Ludendorff* (Lausanne, 1920) [German edition]; and *Ludendorff, avec un protrait hors texte* (Paris, 1921).

[23] A.S.N. was probably the Petrograd historian and archivist, Aleksandr Sergeevich Nikolaev (see n. 257 for 1918). Aleksandr Ignat'evich Andreev (1887–1959) was a Petrograd historian who worked in the Academy of Sciences. He was a specialist on the history of the eighteenth century, Siberia, and Russian geographical discoveries.

28 [February]. The rumors are all alike. The internal *Zusammenbruch* is coming rapidly to a head. There are small disorders. These are all signs that everything around us is in flux and nothing remains unchanged. Some draw the conclusion from this that everything will soon be finished. I continue to disbelieve that. My Petrograders have left, passing among the travails. Yesterday there was a meeting of the historico-philological faculty devoted to Shakhmatov's memory.[24] I gave a paper, "Shakhmatov as a historian." It seems to have gone over rather decently.

MARCH

2 [March]. The rumors are not subsiding. Communist military cadets are being sent to Petrograd. Nonetheless, the situation remains unclear for us, since they are trying to hide everything. I am beginning to be attracted by archaeological work in the Academy of Material Culture: there is in it a certain illusion of some sort of scholarly work.

6 [March]. A rebellion has broken out in Kronstadt and has not yet been crushed.[25] Moscow is divided into two halves: one is the pessimists, the other the optimists. The former decide all questions in the negative beforehand; the latter expect all kinds of good things. I think that the uninitiated are not in a position now to understand the possibilities of tomorrow. A one-kopeck candle can set fire to a city; on the other hand, even a big bonfire can be put out.

12 [March]. Black days for the Rumiantsev Museum; V. D. Golitsyn was arrested on the 10th. What is going to come of this incident? The events in Kronstadt remain unclear for the uninitiated and uninformed.

17 [March]. According to rumors, Golitsyn's arrest is not connected with the Rumiantsev Museum, but is to be explained by some kind of personal accusations against that fine and harmless person. How will incarceration affect his health? He is already sixty-four after all. In the meantime, the

---

[24] The great philologist A. A. Shakhmatov had died the previous August in Petrograd.

[25] The rebellion in Kronstadt had begun on March 1 with a mass meeting of 15,000 sailors. The nonviolent insurgency was suppressed by direct military attack on March 17, after three unsuccessful attempts on March 8, 10, and 12. Although it was crushed, the Kronstadt rebellion was instrumental in bringing about the government's abandonment of "war communism" and the turn to NEP. Along with their demands for the restoration of true lower-class ("soviet") democracy, the Kronstadt rebels demanded an end to food requisitioning and restoration of free trade. See Paul Avrich, *Kronstadt, 1921* (Princeton, 1970).

direction of the Rumiantsev Museum with the title of director has been
entrusted to Vinogradov. Some are accusing him of all kinds of things
and consider him the culprit in the incident with the prince. I don't share
that opinion, but I think (1) that whatever the case with the prince, it is
precisely Vinogradov, as the only person acceptable to the bolsheviks,
who could receive his inheritance, and (2) that thanks to his ambition, he
is satisfied with his appointment and, perhaps, was unable to hide adequately this satisfaction.

The general situation is apparently not as simple as it seemed the first
few days.

21 [March]. It is amazing how variously the bourgeois are interpreting
the fall, or rather the end, of the Kronstadt revolt. Some are dejected and
see in it the greatest misfortune; others assign absolutely no significance
to that affair. I think that it is only a small episode in the process of the
gradual attrition and downfall of the remains of Russia.

24 [March]. The general atmosphere here continues to be depressed and
boring. My museum job completely depresses me. It is a kind of continuous stifling and marking of time, especially when one has to sort out all
the boxes brought to the museum over the last four years—and all this
as a result of the denunciation made by the attendant A. O. Klimentov,
who was discontented because for a long time he was refused the room
he wanted.

28 [March]. Continuing the same work, I have opened about fifty boxes.
This is amazingly productive and interesting work! The results are astonishing. There is nothing that is not of significance for the museum,
with the exception of one chest of junk and my forgotten basket of dishes.
The most varied reports about V. D. Golitsyn: some are very propitious;
others say that he will be held there longer, because he is being blamed
for something. The general mood is very boring, and it is taking possession of me, too. Perhaps it is the influence of spring, when one always
has the desire to go off somewhere far, far away. And instead one sits in
enslaved demoralization on a leash in disgusting Moscow, which has entirely lost its former appearance. My only distraction is reading Ludendorff's memoirs, which are extremely interesting.[26]

31 [March]. V. D. Golitsyn has been released without being charged, but
he is being threatened with expulsion from his apartment—a new disaster, from which he must be protected. Decrees about so-called free trade,

[26] Erich von Ludendorff, *Kriegserinnerungen* (Berlin, 1919).

in which the stupid bourgeois is rejoicing.[27] In my opinion this is only the latest deceit, which will be cast off at the first convenient opportunity. Yesterday I listened to a very interesting reading by Prince S. M. Volkonskii—reminiscences of his grandfather, the Decembrist, and the story of how he left the position of Director of the Imperial Theaters.[28] Another new detail for the comprehension of the mysteriously empty but at the same time tragic personality of Nicholas II. Such evenings in the company of educated and intelligent people, with interesting stories, remind me of the fable, or rather the setting, of Boccaccio: the plague on all sides and spiritual delights in select company.

APRIL

4 [April]. Rumors about new decrees of an emancipatory character; however, you can't make out whether this is the cry of bourgeois-philistine souls, which are always either frightening or comforting each other without fail, or have the bolsheviks really gotten themselves into a fix—a new page that is turning in our tragedy, or, more precisely, our tragicomedy of a stupid people and a stupid society, which is deprived of genuine healthy egoism, yet still reproaches now the Entente, now Germany. I read the memoirs of Stankevich, the sr type, friend of Kerenskii and commissar attached to the army in the Kerenskiada of unforgettable memory.[29] What dregs are both the author and what he writes! How difficult it is to work in the museum these days! How I would like to be rid of it all!

10 [April]. All the rumors are again about the decrees; I am beginning to think that the iron law of life is vanquishing even bolshevism. One must, however, preserve caution and not count too much on any decrees, which can be taken back tomorrow. Mrs. Trotskii, whom I hadn't seen for three

---

[27] The first of the decrees legalizing private trade was published on March 29. *Sobranie uzakonenii i rasporiazhenii rabochego i krest'ianskogo pravitel'stva* (Moscow), 1920, no. 149; *Izvestiia*, March 29, 1921.

[28] Prince Sergei Mikhailovich Volkonskii (1860–1937) had been director of the imperial theaters from 1899 to 1901. He was the grandson of the Decembrist Prince Sergei Grigor'evich Volkonskii (1788–1865). His reminiscences about his grandfather, written in February 1921, are preserved in the Manuscript Collection of the Lenin Library, f. 56, 15.36. His memoirs were published in Berlin in 1923: *Moi vospominaniia* (3 vols. in 2); an English translation appeared in London: *My Reminiscences* (2 vols.), n.d.

[29] Vladimir Benediktovich Stankevich (1884–1968), a chemist by profession, was an sr military commissar of the Provisional Government. He left memoirs: *Vospominaniia* (Berlin, 1920).

years, visited the museum yesterday. The same moth or flea, a nonentity of a charwoman, neither amiable nor unamiable, sour but not malevolent. I think the new "director" Vinogradov invited her, as an icon is invited, to bless his directorship—a kind of prayer service. I have read the documents published abroad about the murder of the royal family—a typical page of the Russian revolution, which leaves one with very painful feelings.[30] And how many other such pages have there been? The Russian émigré press—that is, journals and books—has begun to be received in the museum. There is much of interest in them from the point of view of verifying rumors and impressions. One of the most painful things is the brochure about the Crimean catastrophe.[31] The Russians are everywhere bunglers, incapable of organizing their affairs.

12 [April]. I have reached the end of my rope. My nerves have acted up so I don't know what to do with them. The occasion was insignificant—an invitation to go to a meeting in the Book Chamber[32] for discussion of a plan for some kind of bibliographical institute. I listened to the fools and wretches Bodnarskii and Shchelkunov[33] playing with others' welfare in order to gain favor with the bolsheviks, and I wasted time contemplating the petty demon Stepka Krivtsov, my communist cousin.[34] It is strange and stupid that just such a petty and insignificant event can drive you out of your wits. Bourgeois rumors about the breaking of the treaty with England, talk of reductions in living space, and suchlike filth and abomination ad nauseam. God, what melancholy and boredom! I can't concentrate on work; I can barely finish my lectures. I have begun checking the second volume of *Regional Administration* with the help of V. M. Ryndina,[35] which is a small pleasure for me in this vast sea of boredom and melancholy.

[30] N. A. Sokolov, *Ubiistvo tsarskoi sem'i* (Berlin, 1921).

[31] S. Smolenskii, *Krymskaia katastrofa (Zapiski stroevogo ofitsera)* (Sofia, 1921).

[32] The Russian Book Chamber (presently the All-Union Book Chamber, Vsesoiuznaia Knizhnaia palata) was founded in Petrograd in 1917 as a national center for bibliographic registration and statistics. It was moved to Moscow in 1920.

[33] Bogdan Stepanovich Bodnarskii (1874–1968), a prominent bibliographer, was president of the Russian Bibliographical Society and director of the Book Chamber. Mikhail Il'ich Shchelkunov (1884–1938) was another prominent bibliographer and an employee of the Rumiantsev Museum.

[34] Stepan Savvich Krivtsov (b. 1885) was a professor in the Institute of Red Professors in the early 1920s. A reference work published in 1930 identified him as a member of the Society of Marxist Historians and a specialist in historical materialism, dialectical materialism, and Leninism, head of the methodological section of the Lenin Institute, and a member of the Communist Academy.

[35] Vera Mikhailovna Ryndina, an employee of the Rumiantsev Museum. She and Got'e would be married on August 4, 1921.

18 April. A trip to Tver' to give lectures. The reception was just as good as before; a small but attentive audience. Four days spent outside of Moscow have a marvelous effect: several days during which you don't think about Moscow, Moscow affairs, or the museum with which I am fed up. Of course, that is the case until you enter into the life of the provincial town, because it is even worse there than in Moscow, even judging by external appearances, by the faces you see. However, there, too, women have a better appearance than men: their external appearance rather converges with the general European, the bourgeois; but the men, with their service jackets, shaved heads, and service caps pulled down on the backs of their heads, produce, as everywhere, a repulsive impression. It was a great pleasure yesterday to go out of town to the bank of the Volga, to a little pine forest on the dunes. Out of the wind under a pine, I read for three and a half hours and finished Ludendorff's memoirs. The return to Moscow was satisfactory; we got on without tickets with the help of the railroad Cheka and rode all the way on our suitcases in the corridor of a second-class car. Wonderful weather; looking out the window, you want to get out of town, to the country. Near Tver' the birches were already taking leaf—this is the 5th of April, old style; what does the summer have in store for us?

I haven't heard about the latest annoyances, but I did learn of the death of my little nephew, Iura Kurdiumov; the poor little boy died of children's consumption in three months. But even without that, Moscow immediately produced her usual oppressive impression. Ludendorff's memoirs are one of the most interesting books I have ever read. He says by no means everything, and in general says only what he wants to; but the psychology of that remarkable representative of the German military milieu is extraordinarily interesting and instructive. Proud self-assurance, preserved even at the moment of collapse; what an antipode of the Russian intelligentsia mire! However antipathetic the German military milieu may be, it is still more worthy of respect than a nation of Poshleikins and Sergeant Prishibeevs.[36] Even after the catastrophe, Ludendorff is proud he is a German and appeals to others to be proud of this; Russians could not say this of themselves, and especially not now.

24 April. The week that has passed since the return from Tver' was stormy and unpleasant. Museum events are developing. The prince is still being threatened with eviction; someone wants to inspect our buildings;

---

[36] Prishibeev sergeants: from Sergeant Prishibeev (*unter Prishibeev*), the hero of Chekhov's story of the same name (1885), the archetypical busybody and abuser of the authority of his rank. The provenance of *Poshleikiny* is unknown to me.

some enemy is circling us somewhere and is sneaking up on us. Another story is too Sovdepish not to record. Certain people in the form of the militia appeared to my acquaintances, Kotel'nikov and Zhukovskii, and announced that all their property was to be confiscated. Taking measures to save their property, they distributed some things among their acquaintances, myself among them, and asked them to come by the following day to take some more things. I went with Iura Reiman, and in front of their gate we received packages. I brought mine home successfully, but Iura was taken to the commissariat with napkins and tablecloths. I extracted these things with difficulty from the commissariat; incidentally, from the conversation with a "comrade," it became perfectly clear to me that a painstaking tail was put on everyone who entered and left that apartment.

The general situation is becoming more and more complicated and confused. Only one thing is clear—an economic collapse is unavoidable.

26 April. A trip to Troitsa. On the way I learned that Khot'kovo also no longer exists as a monastery.[37] Apparently a crusade has been proclaimed against the church with special force. Everything is calm in Troitsa. The ride in the train was disgusting. On the way to Moscow I dropped in to see Lelia. From there, from the sixth verst, I came home on foot—11 versts, 1 hour and 45 minutes. For Easter they are giving out "salt and beans" instead of all the promised handouts. Obviously, the masters have few reserves.

29 [April]. Good Friday; in keeping with tradition, I am going about the churches with Volodia, but this year I have no enthusiasm at all. In addition, I have been beset all these days by a kind of weakness—I want to lie down and sleep, and nothing more. They are talking about some sort of attempts by M. Gor'kii to arrange a dalliance of the professors with Lenin, in order to improve the living conditions and situation of the professoriate and to dump Pokrovskii. The dalliance has not yet come off; I fear that this is only a provocation. They gave five pounds of kerosene in the ration instead of meat and butter. Isn't that laughable?

MAY

7 [May]. Easter has vanquished the First of May; such, at least, was my opinion, derived more from stories than from personal impressions. The

---

[37] Khot'kovo Monastery was located southwest of Troitsa, near Abramtsevo.

mass meetings were not successful; the bells rang in full force; the performances on the streets were simple holiday fetes. Afterward I spent three days in Pestovo, where we are expected for the summer as well. I am glad, because that is a solution for my Volodia. Marvelous weather; the dry spell has given way to a storm and rain; the bird cherries are blossoming, the lilacs are blooming, and the lindens are coming out. When it blossoms all at once, the poor northern countryside manages to leave a strong impression, especially when you enter it after the cursed city.

I was supposed to leave for Petersburg today, but tickets can be had only for tomorrow.

Today I solicited for the return of Tania's ration; its removal practically threatens the poor old people with starvation.

17 [May]. A week spent in Petrograd. I went there in a *wagon-lit*, and returned in a rather dirty first-class compartment. Thus, the journey itself was a regular *Erholungsreise*.[38] Petrograd has not gotten worse over the year of my absence from it. The weather was wonderful, and [Petrograd] was just as charmingly handsome as a year ago. Lodging was prepared for us in the Marble Palace, where the Academy of the History of Material Culture is now housed. The room had a view on the Neva; I couldn't take my eyes off it. The purpose of the trip was rest and relaxation; officially, I was on the council of the Academy of the History of Material Culture[39] and took advantage of this in order to clarify my future activity vis-à-vis the commission for the study of Central European antiquities, which has been established in Moscow. From this point of view it seems I achieved some results. There was a lot of free time. I took advantage of it in order, as a craftsman-historian, to examine the palaces. I was in the Winter, Anichkov, and Marble [palaces].[40] It was sad, and grand, and it was painful to look at this grandeur that had fallen through its own fault. The Winter Palace inside is very majestic, stylish, and beautiful. The apartments of Alexander II, where part of his soul reposes, were characteristic, as were the apartments of Nicholas II, where there

[38] A vacation trip.

[39] The Russian Academy of the History of Material Culture was founded on April 18, 1919, succeeding the Imperial Archaeological Commission, which had existed since 1859. In 1937 it became an institute of the Academy of Sciences. In 1959 it was renamed the Archaeological Institute.

[40] The Anichkov and Marble palaces, built by the Empresses Elizabeth and Catherine II, respectively, for favorites, are two of the most impressive eighteenth-century palaces in the city. The Anichkov Palace, on the corner of Nevskii and the Fontanka, is presently the Pioneer Palace; the Marble Palace on the Neva quay near the Winter Palace, so-called because of its unusual marble façade, is a Lenin museum.

reposes his hollowness and the capriciousness of Aleksandra Fedorovna. The comrades have disfigured much, but enough remains so that the Winter Palace has not lost its *cachet*. The worst is that in the rooms that were reserved for visiting sovereigns, they have built a little stove for the anticipated arrival of Lunacharskii. In the Anichkov, Alexander III's study is of interest. It is big, simple, and dark, but majestic. In the Marble [Palace] the comfortable rooms of K.R.,[41] reveal taste and intellectuality. The rest of the time went to visiting friends and acquaintances; the customary cordiality and welcome.

In general, Petrograd has preserved its Europeanism, which is greater than Moscow's; the mood of the people I saw is more practical and calm. They breathe easier and work more and better than we do. The news that penetrates there from abroad is almost the same as what penetrates to Moscow: contradictory, and provoking the most varied moods—good for some, bad for others, and yet others are dying to return. I walked a lot—I walked to Smol'nyi, which is all surrounded by guards, like the Kremlin.[42] At the State Duma[43] there is a sign: The Comrade Zinoviev Workers' University. On a square on the Admiralty Embankment I saw a pig foraging. The hospital ship *The People's Will* is lying on its side in the Neva. That is symbolic: the People's Will in the water. Children are swimming in the canals near the Summer Garden, like last year.

21 May. A week in Moscow. The same aimless and senseless bustle as before, as always. The same gray swamp without a ray of hope ahead. The Rumiantsev Museum is on center stage again, with the intrigues that have crept into the light after the replacement of Prince V. D. Golitsyn. Yesterday he was asked by a delegation not to leave the museum. Thank God, at least that was achieved.

24 [May].   "Proletarian rejoice!
                        In place of bread, eat cock!"[44]

[41] K.R. was the nom de plume of the poet Grand Duke Konstantin Konstantinovich (1858–1915), a grandson of Nicholas I.

[42] Smol'nyi, the building of the former institute for daughters of the nobility, was the seat of the Petrograd soviet, the Military-Revolutionary Committee, and the Bolshevik party at the time of the October revolution. After the Bolshevik government moved to Moscow in March 1918, it remained the seat of the Petrograd soviet and of Party headquarters for the city and province.

[43] That is, the Tauride Palace (Tavricheskii dvorets), originally built by Catherine II for Prince Potemkin in the 1780s. From 1906 to 1917, it was the seat of the state duma, and for several months in 1917 of the Petrograd soviet and the Provisional Government as well. The palace presently houses the Higher Party School.

[44] "Proletarii torzhestvui / Vmesto khleba kushai khui."

That is the inscription decorating the sign of the Academic Center of Narkompros, No. 18 Volkhonka. It is typical for the present moment, when the bolsheviks, like crazed cats, are rushing madly about a building collapsing from fire. I am reading the *Archive of the Russian Revolution*, published by Gessen in Berlin. In Nabokov's article, "The Provisional Government," the characterization of the members of that improvisional government is interesting.[45] One doesn't need that kind of praise!

25 [May]. Ten years since the death of Kliuchevskii. A memorial service and meeting in the Society of Russian History and Antiquities. We recalled his horror at the prospect of a Russian revolution. A fine survey of Russian historiography for ten years by Bogoslovskii. I am attaching A. I. Iakovlev's letter.[46]

27 [May]. An excellent promenade with students and several young anthropologists with the goal of archaeological reconnaissance. The route: Neskuchnyi [Palace]—Mamonova dacha—along the bottom of the Sparrow Hills—Potylikha—the Country Court.[47] At Mamonova dacha we apparently found a Stone Age site; and behind Country Court—a magnificent ancient settlement, not yet studied by anyone. Where have the Moscow archaeologists been sitting up to now, and what have they been thinking of?

The bread situation is growing acute. One thinks about the months to come with alarm.

31 May. The general situation is unchanged. I sense some kind of impending shift, which can be defined like this: better to hold onto power and give up something than the other way around. However, this shift will be slow, contradictory, and full of deceit, and accompanied by the desire to turn back at every given moment. I continue to read émigré literature, and after the *Archive of the Russian Revolution* I have taken up K. N. Sokolov's *Denikin's Government*.[48] It is a very interesting book. Un-

---

[45] *Arkhiv russkoi revoliutsii*, 22 vols. (Berlin, 1920–1927). Nabokov's memoir on the Provisional Government appeared in the first volume (pp. 9–96). There is an English translation: *V. D. Nabokov and the Russian Provisional Government, 1917*, ed. Virgil D. Medlin and Steven L. Parsons (New Haven, 1976).

[46] A. I. Iakovlev's letter to Got'e, dated May 4, 1921, Simbirsk. See Appendix, Letter 18.

[47] The promenade took place south of the city in the area between the Moskva River and Moscow University. Mamonova dacha is a former estate in the Sparrow Hills (now the Lenin Hills) overlooking the river. At the time of Got'e's visit, it was a city park; it is presently the site of the Institute of Chemical Physics.

[48] K. N. Sokolov, *Pravlenie generala Denikina* (Sofia, 1921).

bearable heat. An urge to get fresh air. I have received a letter from Florovskii in Odessa, which I am attaching here.[49]

JUNE

1 [June]. Tropical July heat; the brain is melting. We were supposed to go to the Sheremetevs' Mikhailovskoe.[50] But nothing can be done simply in Sovdepiia—even getting an automobile for which all the papers are in hand.

5 [June]. The same kind of heat; it is hard to think and even harder to study. I read Struve's book, *Reflections on the Russian Revolution.*[51] There are many good thoughts; I will note two that fully coincide with my own: (1) the Kadets' greatest mistake was to turn leftward after 1905, because after 1905 the danger was precisely from the left, not the right; (2) the Russian revolution was an act of state suicide.

The rumors are all the same. No new changes thus far.

7 [June]. A page has turned in my life today.[52]

15 [June]. A trip to Troitsa, where the next day an excursion of thirty-five people from the Rumiantsev Museum also arrived. It was very warm and nice. On the way home Vovulia[53] and I got off at Bratovshchina and walked to Pestovo in the cool evening. In Pestovo I lay almost all the time in a chaise longue and rested. Nature has a calming effect and makes you forget about the bolsheviks. The house in Pestovo has been declared a state theater! Such rubbish has to be invented! In Moscow there are quiet rumors about something the future will bring. The rumors are inconsistent and unclear, but somehow one senses that something is changing. The crazed cats are racing about the burning house before leaping out the windows. The bolsheviks have reexamined the Dzhunkovskii affair and have decided that he is so proper that he can be released to freedom,

---

[49] Letter of A. V. Florovskii to Got'e, dated May 17, 1921, Odessa. See Appendix, Letter 19. Antonii Vasil'evich Florovskii (1884–1968), the brother of the theologian G. V. Florovskii, specialized in the history of Russia. He had been a student of E. N. Shchepkin at Novorossiiskii (Odessa) University. In 1922 he was expelled from Soviet Russia and became a professor at Charles University in Prague.

[50] An old estate with a manor house in the classical style and a large park that had belonged to the Sheremetevs, about forty-five kilometers southwest of Moscow on the Kaluga Road.

[51] *Razmyshleniia o russkoi revoliutsii* (Sofia, 1921).

[52] This appears to be a reference to Got'e's relations with Vera Mikhailovna Ryndina.

[53] Volodia: Vladimir, Got'e's son.

but ... bearing in mind the complications with Japan (!?), he must continue to sit in Butyrki![54] Such is their logic.[55]

June 24. Little has changed in Moscow in the course of a week. All the same muddle and nonsense. They say that the Jews of all nations who have appeared at the congress of communists[56] are arguing among themselves and are divided into two factions—one, supposedly led by Trotskii, shouts that [they] should go on smashing to the end and is preparing to make war with the West, beginning with a pogrom of Latvia; the other, supposedly led by Lenin, wants to step backward. Some supposedly find that communism in its implementation in Russia is *total kompromittiert*. The rumors of an enormous crop failure in the Volga region and in the south are being confirmed: in Saratov, bread is 10,000 rubles a pound; in Rostov, 5,000 rubles; in Moscow, around 3,000 rubles. Potatoes in Moscow have leaped in a week from 40,000 to 80,000 a pud. Cherepnin [?] has arrived from the Crimea. Of the little he told, I caught (1) that Wrangel made a mistake in completely neglecting the urban population, among whom a terrible agitation of a bolshevik character broke out; (2) that our industrialists abroad are sitting high and dry because they are paid no attention. From this I conclude that the capitalists of Western Europe are waiting for Russia to fall into their hands like ripe fruit, and will then hire our fools as stewards at best, as people who know local conditions. Today I had the visit of an Estonian, who brought me greetings from L. I. L'vov,[57] who finally managed to successfully get out of happy Sovdepiia.

30 [June]. I am attaching a letter from our director that I received upon returning from the country.[58] I have demanded an explanation and have shown him the frivolity of his ideas. But it is characteristic of him. When I showed it to Egorov, he said that in my place he would be very offended. I will bring to his attention once again, by the way, that I am not

[54] General Vladimir Fedorovich Dzhunkovskii, a former governor of Moscow, assistant minister of internal affairs, and division commander in the World War, had been arrested by the Cheka in September 1918. It was assumed that he was the leader of an anti-Soviet organization in Turkestan that was discovered by the Cheka about that time—the so-called Turkestan Military Organization (TVO). It later turned out that the Dzhunkovskii involved in that affair was only his namesake, one General E. Dzhunkovskii, former assistant governor general of Turkestan.

[55] To the entry for 15 June, Got'e added the note "(Letters of Iakovlev, Florovskii, and Riazhskii)." The letter of G. A. [?] Riazhskii could not be found.

[56] The Third Congress of the Comintern met in Moscow from June 22 to July 12, 1921.

[57] Lollii Ivanovich L'vov (b. 1888) was a writer and poet. After emigrating, he was a frequent contributor to Struve's *Russkaia mysl'*.

[58] Letter of A. K. Vinogradov to Got'e from Riga, dated June 28, 1921. See Appendix, Letter 20.

at all against being delivered of the office of associate director. But in essence, all this is of so little concern that I quickly forgot about it.

In the university they intend to admit mainly graduates of the rabfaki and children of "the poorest peasantry," and all others by competition. Fine methods for implanting culture and civilization! I had an unpleasant confrontation with a certain comrade Tovstukha,[59] who wanted to take out publications from the museum in violation of the rules. A genuine type of communist-bolshevik from among the veterans of penal servitude or hungry émigrés—bilious, irritable, morose, nasty, skinny, perhaps consumptive, unquestionably hating and despising all nonbolsheviks. The general situation is unchanged. Cholera and famine are spreading in the south and southwest.

JULY

7 [July]. Famine is approaching at a rapid pace. They apparently recognize that the situation is bad, at least to the extent that Muscovite rumors can be believed. They are talking about wires that have been sent with an appeal for help for the starving, and about the wires that have been received in response, in which it is supposedly stated that they are ready to help, but not a pound of bread will be given to this government. They say that the procuress M. Gor'kii went to the Patriarch with a request from the authorities to appeal for help to the foreign churches.[60] They are talking about articles in foreign newspapers where there is supposedly talk of intervention. In Moscow efforts are being made to form a committee for aid to the starving, composed half-and-half of "public" activists and moderate bolsheviks; but thus far it has not been able to form be-

---

[59] Ivan Pavlovich Tovstukha (1889–1935) was a functionary in the Commissariat of Nationalities who in 1921 became head of Stalin's personal secretariat. Tovstukha had experienced Siberian exile before the war.

[60] As Got'e notes, the worst period of the entire revolutionary epoch in terms of food supply was just beginning in the summer of 1921. Two drought years in a row (1920 and 1921), the ruthless requisitioning policies of the regime under "war communism," and the general devastation of the Civil War converged to produce full-scale famine in the central and eastern agricultural regions, and even in parts of the Ukraine. The worst phase of the famine lasted from early summer 1921 until the 1922 harvest, which was abundant. In the summer of 1921, the Bolshevik government was obliged to resort to extreme measures. On July 11, an appeal for food was issued over the signatures of Patriarch Tikhon and Maksim Gor'kii. Herbert Hoover responded to this appeal, and as a result American Relief Administration famine-relief operations began in Russia in August (ARA help had been offered in 1920, but the Soviet government would not allow the ARA to run its own operation in the country; this time that condition was accepted). At the height of its operations, the ARA was feeding more than ten million people daily. The ARA activity in Russia continued until mid-1923. See H. H. Fisher, *The Famine in Soviet Russia* (New York, 1927).

cause the authorities clearly don't want this and, moreover, the moderate elements are at odds with the extremists—the Kremlin with Lubianka. However that may be, Moscow is again full of stories; everyone has pricked up his ears. In any case, the famine is delivering the bolsheviks a blow stronger than all the Kolchaks and Denikins put together.

15 [July]. I saw off M. M. Bogoslovskii[61] and was very busy. The whole day today was spent on excavations at Kolomenskoe. To get there, moreover, we went by the Ring Road and ran into a new railway rate, increased four hundred times or nearly that. Instead of 20 rubles—7,600 rubles. Rumors circulated in the evening that it has already been revoked because it has brought chaos, confusion, and even unrest in its wake. To what extent the rumors of revocation are true I'll find out tomorrow when I go to Pestovo. This rate, to tell the truth, is of a counterrevolutionary character and was made in order to anger the citizens of the RSFSR.

All the same rumors have been circulating these last few days. They add that in response to the appeal of the prisoner-patriarch the answer has been received that in the present state of affairs they can only pray for the Russian people. Both the rumors and the incredibly stupid decrees make one ever more persuaded that the RSFSR is on the eve of collapse. But will the eve last for a long time?

22 [July]. Moscow is filling up with rumors. They are coming from the bolsheviks as well. Their newspapers write about some kind of intentions from outside. What is this—deceptive hopes again or something more solid? In any case, disintegration progresses apace. What fools are those worn-out public activists who took part in the conference on hunger. And from whom is anything good to be expected? Kishkin-Hieronymus Amalia von Kurz-Galop who should have stuck to his physiotherapy, or the fool Katia Kuskova, or that blank space Golovin?[62] No, let the bolsheviks disentangle what they have done!

AUGUST

4 [August]. For a space of almost two weeks I have not kept notes because I was not in Moscow very often (for that time see the Pestovo notes).[63]

---

[61] Bogoslovskii was apparently moving to Petrograd to take up his new position in the Academy of Sciences.

[62] The Third All-Russian Food Conference opened on June 16, 1921. The non-Bolshevik participants mentioned were N. M. Kishkin, E. D. Kuskova, and Fedor Aleksandrovich Golovin (b. 1868), a prominent Kadet and former president of the Duma (2d).

[63] The Pestovo notes for June–September 1921 have been placed at the end of the main entries for September.

The general situation is changing only very slightly and hardly noticeably, but still in the same direction toward further disintegration. There are now great difficulties in the printing of money, and therefore [my] salary is being withheld. It is apparent that they are convulsively searching everywhere for money, but don't know where to find it; they are threatening to introduce payment for apartments and for electricity. They are raising the railway fare inordinately, and are promising some kind of new taxes. However, all this will have no effect on the process of disintegration, just as the notorious committee of quasi-public activists headed by Prokopovich,[64] Kuskova, and Kishkin—a committee that rumor has pithily christened with the marvelous name of Pro-ku-kish, will not help in the struggle with famine.[65]

Today I went to the Sovdep "to get crowned" with Vera Mikhailovna.[66] The registration of marriages is a regular operetta. There are three tables in a big room for this purpose; opposite is the table for registration of births. The registration procedure lasts ten minutes, then you are led to some Jewish secretary who interrogates you one more time and signs the paper. They say there are sometimes lines. We left in a very gay mood.

25 *[August]*. See the Pestovo notes for the gap.

In Moscow: the most amazing rumors about relinquishing power, about a coalition ministry, about the opening of restaurants (they say that for a license to open the Iar[67] the bolsheviks are asking 30 billion, but are getting 25). Prokukish is failing because the bolsheviks won't let them go abroad. I don't know what will happen next, but I feel that the time of an "administration for the affairs of the former Russian Empire" is approaching.

I have been elected chairman of the Moscow section of the Academy

---

[64] Sergei Nikolaevich Prokopovich (1871–1955) was a prominent economist and statistician. In the history of Russian Marxism, he and his wife, E. D. Kuskova, were known as revisionist "economists" of the turn of the century. Prokopovich had been minister of trade and industry and then minister of supply in the Provisional Government. He and his wife were deported from Soviet Russia in 1922.

[65] This was the Central Commission for Aid to the Hungry attached to the VTsIK, founded by a decree of July 18, 1921. The chairman was M. I. Kalinin. It was called Prokukish after the first syllables in the names Prokopovich, Kuskova, and Kishkin.

[66] Got'e married Vera Mikhailovna Ryndina. The Russian expression for "to get married" is *venchat'sia*; literally, "to be crowned." In this case it was the civil act; the religious ceremony was held on August 12, 1921. See the entry for 16 August in the Pestovo notes.

[67] Originally founded in 1826, Iar became one of the most fashionable restaurants of Moscow in the second half of the nineteenth century. It was located in Petrovskii Park on the Petersburg Highway (now Leningrad Prospect) in what was then the outskirts of town.

of the History of Material Culture; I presided today for the first time.[68] New cares. I yearn to settle down at home and study.

27 [August]. I was sent to a meeting of Kominolit. That is not a mineral, but an institution that is responsible for supplying the RSFSR with foreign books.[69] It is headed by a Kiev bolshevik from among the landlords and bourgeois, Otto Iul'evich Shmidt,[70] a quite handsome young man. He is casting himself in the role of a civilized person. Around him sat rude and mischievous monstrosities—about ten gorillas who understood nothing of what they were supposed to do. The meeting took place in the building of the Azov-Don Bank. I was summoned for purposes of informing them, as they desire to "collect materials."

28 [August]. I have stayed to guard the museum, since everyone has left and Vinogradov decided in a fit of panic that it must be guarded. The general situation remains the same. I am reading Struve's *Russian Thought* (No. 1, published in Sofia).[71] The diary of the fool Gippius is interesting; it turns out that she and her fool Merezhkovskii were in the SRS.[72] The characterization of Fr. Iv. Kreiman in the reminiscences of Evgenii Nikolaevich Trubetskoi is very interesting.[73]

[68] The academy and its successors maintained a special Moscow section until 1945, when its headquarters were moved to Moscow.

[69] The Interdepartmental Commission for the Purchase and Distribution of Foreign Literature (Mezhvedomstvennaia komissiia po zakupke i raspredeleniiu inostrannoi literatury) was created by resolution of Sovnarkom on June 14, 1921.

[70] Otto Iul'evich Shmidt (1891–1956) had taught mathematics at the University of Kiev during the war. At this time, he was working in Narkompros and was head of Gosizdat, the state publishing house. Shmidt later had an extraordinarily varied career, which ranged from editorship of the first Soviet encyclopedia to polar exploration. He was elected to full membership in the Academy of Sciences in 1935.

[71] *Russkaia mysl'* (Sofia), no. 1–2 (January-February 1921).

[72] Zinaida Nikolaevna Gippius (Hippius) (1869–1945), a metaphysical Symbolist poet and writer of fiction and essays, was for many years the literary lioness of Petersburg, in the company of her husband, Dmitrii Sergeevich Merezhkovskii (1865–1941), a poet and philosophical novelist and essayist known outside of Russia for his historical novels, especially his *Leonardo da Vinci* (1902). Gippius and Merezhkovskii had been associated with the SRS since the time of the 1905 revolution. They were vociferously anti-Bolshevik. The diary in question was part of Gippius's "Petersburg Diary," kept while they were living in Petrograd in 1918–1919; they fled Soviet Russia toward the end of 1919 and eventually settled in Paris. "Dnevnik Zinaidy Nikolaevny Gippius," *Russkaia mysl'*, 1921, no. 1–2, pp. 129–90; no. 3–4, pp. 49–99; Zinaida Gippius, *Peterburgskie dnevniki (1914–1919)* (New York, 1982).

[73] Prince E. N. Trubetskoi's memoirs were published serially in *Russkaia mysl'* over the course of 1921 and appeared in book form the same year: *Vospominaniia* (Sofia, 1921). Another collection of reminiscences was published the same year in Vienna: *Iz proshlogo*.

30 August]. A second meeting of Kominolit, which is nothing other than the domination of the Scientific-Technical Section of VSNKh (!!!) over all the other libraries. The venal scoundrel Reformatskii[74] fought for the STS more than anybody else. All of Prokukish has been arrested. This is a flop for the bolsheviks, since it will after all produce some kind of impression in Europe. For the fools from Prokukish this is the best and most honorable way out of a foolish situation.

SEPTEMBER

4 [September]. Vinogradov has left to visit his family and has been gone for two weeks. Therefore I can neither go to Volodia nor bring him home. A stupid situation.

The general situation is muddled. They are putting up some sort of smoke screen again, and in Petrograd they have perpetrated a nasty affair with executions.[75] They are trying to invent some kind of story with Prokukish as well. They say that some have gotten themselves good and well [into prison] there. I do think, however, that the fall of Prokukish will not remain entirely unnoticed abroad. I read the latest work of L. Andreev—*The Diary of Satan*.[76] An overdrawn but powerful depiction of a nihilist-bolshevik preparing to blow up civilization.

7 [September]. The crazed cats seem to have hurled themselves to the left. This is the latest shift: there will be many of them, hither and thither. September is the classic month of cruelties. Now there are again horrors in Petrograd and Moscow; they are trying to lay it on thick around Prokukish. The situation with Vinogradov is unchanged—and I am still unable to leave to get Volodia.

19 September 1921. Moscow. Autumn once again; the usual fuss is beginning; the general mood is confused and little understandable. They are talking about war, but no one thinks there will be one.

[74] Got'e apparently refers to Professor Aleksandr Nikolaevich Reformatskii (1864–1937), a prominent chemist who taught in several Moscow institutions.

[75] Got'e refers to the so-called Petrograd Battle Organization affair, which allegedly involved the discovery of a vast plot to organize an armed uprising. Implicated were survivors of the Kronstadt rebellion, the National Center (Professor V. N. Tagantsev), people with ties to Iudenich and Wrangel, and the intelligence services of Britain and the United States. By order of the Petrograd Cheka, more than two hundred people were arrested and many were shot. D. L. Golinkov, *Krushenie antisovetskogo podpol'ia v SSSR* (Moscow, 1980), 2: 110–16.

[76] *Dnevnik Satany* (Helsingfors, 1921).

21 [September]. Yesterday evening there appeared in our entrance-way a drunk young man, who threatened and cursed for a long time when he was thrown out of there. According to the documents he presented to the armed guard and to the no less armed "director" Vinogradov, he was a member of the RCP, Aleksandr Petrovich Minkin, former commandant of Trotskii's train and a former member of the VTsIK. Tow-headed and shabby, with an unremarkable face, quite unsteady, apparently knocked off all his foundations, if he ever had any, he alternately shouted that he would shoot everybody and begged to be shot. He was apparently equally prepared for the one or the other. A typical representative of the "Russian revolution."

26 [September]. Friction with the Poles. What is behind it? We don't know, as we don't know anything in general. It seems there is an inclination to liberate Prokukish. For the rest, the customary Moscow confusion: meetings, assemblies, completely unnecessary busywork, and fatigue as a result. The museum particularly irritates me and takes up time.

28 [September]. Once again a kind of calm. Once again the bourgeois in Moscow are depressed. Money continues to fall headlong. A sazhen' of firewood is 275,000; shoes, 375,000; one gold 10-ruble piece costs 395,000 rubles. Meanwhile, I saw the matter of introducing a new ruble on the agenda of Sovnarkom that was given to Otto Shmidt. The latest new stupidity! A calm in the museum and the university.

PESTOVO NOTES, JUNE–SEPTEMBER 1921

19 June. Trinity. Yesterday I cheerfully marched sixteen versts; the weather was gloomy, rain. That, however, doesn't affect the psyche. Rest—that's what is needed and is attainable here. The general impressions from Moscow remain that something ought to begin changing. This is suggested by my instinct, which I used to trust unconditionally, then stopped trusting altogether, and now trust with doubts. I just read in the SR Parisian *Contemporary Notes* the reminiscences of Breshko-Breshkovskaia about Kropotkin and Louisa Michel.[77] What a stupid article and how pretentious is the blind, utter fool its author!

A play in the hayloft yesterday. Very decent actors played Spazhinskii's *In Old Times*.[78] Although I remember the ensemble of the Malyi

---

[77] Katerina Breshkovskaia, "Tri anarkhista: P. A. Kropotkin, Most i Luiza Mishel' (Vospominaniia)," in *Sovremennye zapiski* (Paris), 1921, no. 4, pp. 100–27.

[78] A play by Ippolit Vasil'evich Spazhinskii (1844–1917).

Theater (Rybakov, Ermolova, Leshkovskaia, Maksheev, Pravdin),[79] I watched [these actors] with some pleasure. At the end of the play, a soviet *intermezzo*: checking of documents. Incidentally, it turned out that they caught not deserters, but bandits who had supposedly come here. The affair was accompanied by a shot, at which a part of the audience rushed in panic onto the stage. Afterward the holiday continued with a ball in the gallery of the house, which was dirtied as if they had brought litter there on purpose. The actors, and then we, were offered tea; the young people took part in the gorillas' dances until 6 A.M. and afterward played catch. That is how they amuse themselves in Sovrossiia.

21 [June]. After two days of holiday with the inevitable influx of guests, the calm that is usual for Pestovo has returned. I put on trousers with variegated patches on the knees and behind and split wood, weeded the garden, and brought water, and now I am writing reminiscences about the irretrievable past and about my Ninochka. Tomorrow morning it's off to Moscow.

26 [June]. Peace in Pestovo after five days of Moscow life. We came together with Shambi. I am reading Miliukov's *History of the Second Russian Revolution.*[80]

27 [June]. A quiet day; I am studying in the coolness. I think frequently of those who are in Moscow.

28 [June]. The same; rumors don't penetrate here. Miliukov's book—that is, the first part, which is all I have—leaves the impression of being to some extent an apology for himself and the Kadet party; for the rest it is a rather clear and accurate picture of that *course a la mort* that lasted from March to October 1917, and in which the greatest fault lies not with the bolsheviks but with those who tolerated [them], such as that same Miliukov or, especially, L'vov, and particularly with the criminally stupid and base moderate socialists, various srs, pss, etc.

I am also attaching a letter from Malfitano.[81]

[79] All actors of the Malyi Theater: Konstantin Nikolaevich Rybakov (1856–1916); Mariia Nikolaevna Ermolova (1853–1928); Elena Konstantinovna Leshkovskaia (1864–1925); Vladimir Aleksandrovich Maksheev (1843–1901); Osip Andreevich Pravdin (Treuleben) (1847–1921). Pravdin became the first commissar of the Malyi Theater following the February revolution; after the October revolution, he was one of the theater's directors.

[80] P. N. Miliukov, *Istoriia vtoroi russkoi revoliutsii,* vol. 1 (in 3 parts) (Sofia, 1921).

[81] Letter of Malfitano to Got'e, dated July 21, 1921, Paris. See Appendix, Letter 21.

JULY

5 [July]. Nothing but rest and calm during these three days in Pestovo; we planted turnips as a cooperative for feeding the Reiman family in winter.

11 [July]. Bad weather, to which we had grown unaccustomed. I am ruminating on the Moscow rumors, although here you somehow retreat especially far from everything that is happening in Moscow. We chased off the boys who have been taking apples and raspberries from the garden.

18 [July]. The commotion in my soul caused by the new rate was resolved without difficulty. My ticket was good until August 1, and Volodia and Iurochka traveled free, since it turns out that in the RSFSR children under sixteen ride free. Thus we got here successfully. But here I constantly experience some kind of moral and physical depression. Examining myself, I think that this is—(1) a natural reaction after a certain amount of excitement recently, (2) the result of damp and cloudy weather, (3) the result of unusually unpleasant and troublesome days in the museum, and (4) thoughts about the consequences of this new rate. This is undoubtedly a sign of the breakdown of the RSFSR; it is apparent that they are convulsively grabbing at everything in order to fix something and hold on. The increase of the rates by several hundred times affects everyone, and if the bourgeois or the intelligentsia must accept it, the workers and suchlike elements will become even more dissatisfied. But the main thing is that the freight on shipped food products will increase hunger in the big towns, including Moscow, as a result of the terrible costliness of provisions. I think a great deal about Vera Mikhailovna. How will she get back? Still, the instructions supposedly guarantee the possibility of returning under the old terms.

Here there is peace and quiet as always. I am gathering mushrooms and turning the hay. Volodia is still healthy, thank God.

23–26 [July]. Peace and quiet, interrupted by rain that hinders the hay-gathering.

31 July, Sunday. I was in Moscow only one day last week. Afterward I returned to Pestovo, where I will stay until tomorrow. On the 28th we celebrated Volodia's nameday; Vera Mikhailovna and Tania Dol'nik were there. The setting was almost prewar: pies, candies, and the like, and an excellent mood. On Saturday, S. K. Shambinago brought various news, which all points in the same direction, even taking into account the usual exaggerations of the teller.

On Tuesday the 26th, on the way from Pestovo to Moscow, I visited the village of Muranovo, which belonged to Baratynskii and Tiutchev, where I was the guest of N. I. and F. I. Tiutchev and O. M. Veselkina. A very beautiful estate. The house was built by Baratynskii; now it has been completely turned into a museum, where reminiscences about Baratynskii, Tiutchev, and I. S. Aksakov are framed in a wonderful setting of bronze, marble, portraits, and old furniture. After the tour, which depressed me because I hadn't expected anything of the kind, there was a discussion with N. I. Tiutchev and Trapeznikov. Both are completely in agreement that the museum must survive the bolsheviks and remain in this house.[82]

8 August, Monday. Here all is the same: peace, mushrooms, of which I brought back four baskets, and deep sleep. There are busy days ahead in Moscow, since my arrangements with Vera Mikhailovna are coming to a successful conclusion.

A. I. Iakovlev arrived. His stories about the situation in Simbirsk fully confirm everything that is being said about the Volga region. He recounted to me his discussion with Pokrovskii, which I record here:

"Mikhail Nikolaevich, what are you doing? You have brought the Russian people to the point where your names will be inscribed in history with fiery letters of damnation, and the people will tear you to pieces."

"I don't know what letters our names will be inscribed with, fiery or some other kind, but *unfortunately* the people will not tear us apart, as it did not tear apart the government in 1891. We will feed the children, probably with the help of America. They will give us nothing, but will themselves do the giving and feeding."

"Is such an agreement already concluded?"

"Yes, almost concluded. The experiment in socialism is finished and will not be repeated again."

I make the following deduction: even such paranoiacs as Pokrovskii are becoming convinced that it is all over; but they don't leave because they have nowhere to go and "unfortunately" the people itself will not settle with them. But if the Americans will themselves be operating here in the RSFSR, others will climb in after them and this will be the beginning

[82] Evgenii Abramovich Baratynskii (1800–1844) and Fedor Ivanovich Tiutchev (1803–1873) were major Russian poets who lived on this estate (their families were related by marriage). The manor house was constructed by Baratynskii for his family in 1841–1842. Nikolai Ivanovich and Fedor Ivanovich Tiutchev were the grandsons of the poet. The estate remained in the hands of the Tiutchevs until 1920, when it was transformed into a Tiutchev museum.

of peaceful intervention or infiltration by foreigners, and that will be followed by a restructuring of the administration—gradual, of course.

I heard a typical report about the dissatisfaction of the communist military cadets, reproaching Lenin, Trotskii, and co. for having led them into a dead end.

I heard from K. S. Kuz'minskii[83] that no military preparations are being made; that means either that there will be no military intervention, or if there is, that it will not meet any resistance, since all understand that there is nothing to resist with.

About Prokukish—entirely cheerless news: they are powerless and helpless, and they are dead men who sit there; according to competent judgments, either the bolsheviks will try to preserve them at any cost, in order to show their worthlessness to all, or they will themselves try to provoke an explosion and even their own arrest in order to salvage their position.

16 August. I came here with Vera Mikhailovna after the wedding. It is our *voyage de noce.* The weather is marvelous. The wedding was on Friday the 12th, at 11 A.M. in the church of the former Serbian residence. Afterward there was coffee at the Ryndins; later on I was in the museum. At 5 P.M. we had a dinner for the four witnesses. In addition, there were Tania Dol'nik, E. A. Kolychevskaia, who answered for us in the museum, and A. I. Iakovlev, who brought us a bit of vodka. Unexpectedly for ourselves, the dinner was very gay and lively. In the evening we paid a visit to M. M. Ryndin,[84] and the following morning, at 10 A.M., Aleksandr Sergeevich Nikolaev had a working coffee at our place, after which we left for Pestovo.

A few days ago, K. D. Korsakov[85] appeared on the horizon, directly from Siberia into one of the Moscow sanatoriums. This is one more of the revenants of the past, returning to Moscow after long illnesses and wanderings. At our dinner we commented at length on the decrees on the partial return of houses and on permission to sell spirits. All these are concessions, signs of the times. A. I. Iakovlev told about his visit to the Englishmen of Hodgson & Co. who were staying in Moscow; the conclusion was that *there is nothing to be done here,* and *we are here for information.*[86] In addition, it seems they are sincerely amazed that in Russia everyone is dissatisfied with the soviet regime. Talk of military interven-

---

[83] Konstantin Stanislavovich Kuz'minskii (1875–1940) was an art historian and member of the State Academy of Arts.

[84] The bride's father.

[85] K. D. Korsakov and his wife had corresponded with Got'e earlier in 1921 from Krasnoiarsk, where they had been living for two years.

[86] The italicized words are in English in the original text.

tion is subsiding, but the idea of peaceful intervention seems to be growing and developing; however, it may seem to me like that because I share
that idea myself.

I am attaching Emma Wilken's letter, from which I learned, incidentally, that my money is safe.[87]

12 September. I wasn't here for an entire two weeks. It is the fault of
Vinogradov's disappearance, which appears ever more puzzling to me.
The last few days the women in the museum have even been saying that
he has fled abroad. That is not like him; but I wouldn't be surprised even
by that. On Friday the 27th I was at last relieved by Egorov,[88] and I left
for Pestovo in order to spend several last days here and then move Volodia to Moscow. Today I am waiting for Vera Mikhailovna, who is also
supposed to bring news from Egorov.

We are having marvelous days of the September variety already; all
the woods are yellow; it is warm during the day, and the evenings are
cool. The retiring summer is making us a gift of its last rays.

Yesterday, the 11th, we experienced a few difficult minutes here: there
was a Cheka inspection of the small, unlucky theatrical circle directed by
Volodia Reiman. The affair arose from a denunciaton by one of the Moscow actors, who are not being paid adequately. Two persons appeared.
One was a Jew with an astonishing facial expression, typical, however,
among the bolsheviks and Chekists: a mixture of cruelty and some kind
of boundless despondency. Looking at him, the heart bursts from utter
anguish. The other, a Russian, played a secondary role and was silent for
the most part; apparently one of those that are still being taught the business. In the evening they stayed to spend the night, then disappeared
"like smoke" at the sun's first rays. How painful it is to feel oneself in the
power of these suspicious characters!

It is very hard to understand the general situation as I left it in Moscow. It appears there is some kind of hitch in the bolsheviks' backward
march. But is that so, or is it an impression created by the Petrograd
shootings and the incident with Prokukish? Several of the chief figures
in the latter, in particular pro, ku, and kish, apparently face something
serious. But such blind and stupid people they are! Their whole démarche was founded solely on the overriding desire to play some kind of
role at any cost. At any cost—but in order to play a role! How typical
this is for the so-called Russian public activists. Such complete and hopeless fools they are. And yet, apparently, Russian reality can create only

[87] Letter of Emma Wilken to Got'e, undated, Antwerp. See Appendix, Letter 22.

[88] Got'e's colleague on the history faculty, D. N. Egorov, also worked in the Rumiantsev Museum. In 1919 he had been appointed Director of the World History division.

such public fools. There are all kinds of such fools abroad, and if they show up here, there will be so much foolishness that the last remains of Russia will be drowned in it. Looking on all this, there is again awakened in me the desire to leave, together with the desire to cease being a Russian.

17 September. The last day in Pestovo. The summer is over—the fourth summer under the bolsheviks. How many of them are left? The last days were passed at chores. We finished the hay; we dug potatoes—work that I hadn't seen since my childhood in Zagran'e. The situation here is complicated by the arrest of Volodia Reiman, which occurred on Monday evening. We went with him to Pushkino—he on that business and I for Verochka. He remained in Pushkino, and when we were returning, we were met by a policeman with a warrant for [his] arrest. Volodia was obliged to leave Pushkino owing to the search and arrest of his boss in the theater, Mel'nikov, and learned of his own fate on arriving home. He left on Tuesday, apparently for a long stay [in prison], despite the triviality of the whole affair.

Shambi brought rumors about the general situation—it is becoming more confused, both without and within. Such is the impression.

[End of Pestovo notes.]

OCTOBER

1–4 [October]. A trip to Petrograd. I rode there and back with N. D. Protasov[89] very successfully. Both ways on a rapid train that takes fifteen hours, stopping at the big stations. In this ride there was a certain illusion of the past, which was destroyed by the sight of the gorillas sitting in the compartment. An *artel'shchik*[90] with his papa, who had been saved from one of the starving and looted regions, traveled with us on the way there; and on the way back [we had] a group of young communist red army men, proud of their calling, smooth-shaven, even on the backs of their heads, and completely ignorant.

I spent three days in Petrograd. There was a meeting of the council and administration of the Academy of the History of Material Culture; a certain businesslike character in both. I saw quite a few people; I spent an evening at Platonov's. Everyone there is under the influence of the latest pogrom of Petersburg University, analogous to the Moscow po-

[89] Nikolai Dmitrievich Protasov (b. 1886) was a librarian, a specialist on archaeology and art history, and a member of the Academy of the History of Material Culture.

[90] A member of a workers' or peasants' cooperative association, an *artel'*.

grom, but afflicting them later than us. In addition, all the scholarly institutions there are sitting without money and without salaries, so that few people are even showing up for work. Nevskii has been covered with handicraft shops and cafes; there are foreign wares in the city, attained by contraband. They say that the sailors are trawling for mines, but in reality they are trading with the foreign schooners that approach them. Yesterday I saw a Petersburg flood for the first time in my life. It was a very beautiful spectacle, which we contemplated from the first floor of the Marble Palace.

Nothing new in Moscow; autumn slush and ennui. N.P.K., according to his relative arrived from Norway, says that the Russian question is only the fourth in a series of major international questions; in first place there is the German question, then the Japanese-American, then internal questions, and only then the Russian.

9 [October]. The off season for rumors is beginning. All are calming down, for they have ensconced themselves with the bolsheviks for the winter. There is slush in social relations, too, complete boredom; if there wasn't a certain amount of comfort at home, one could hang oneself. Everything has been killed off in the university. It is unknown when and where classes will begin. But I have never been so little interested in the university as now, when it practically doesn't exist. Our museum has arranged a Dante exhibit. The world would have lost nothing without it. There was a big theft in the Historical Museum. As near as can be made out, many professional bandits turned rulers use this [sort of thing] in order to make a profit.

14 [October]. Decrees about the institution of a state bank, about establishment of a budget, about regulations—everything testifies to new concessions by the bolsheviks to the iron law of life. In Moscow, the phase of burglaries continues, both in public institutions and in private houses. If we in the museum are going to be heated, it is only thanks to private means and bribes. My mood is revolting and my *taedium Russiae* is growing apace, together with *Hinausweh*.[91] Yesterday there was an article by Steklov in the newspaper about the collection of articles, *Change of Signposts*, which appeared in Prague:[92] a group of flabby Russian intelligentsia-renegades—Kliuchnikov, a greenhorn admitted to graduate study in civil law at Moscow University; the hysteric lawyer Bobrishchev-Pushkin; Luk'ianov, who escaped from Petersburg in 1918—got the urge to

[91] That is, the urge to leave.
[92] *Smena vekh* appeared in Prague in July 1921.

go to Canossa to the bolsheviks.[93] If what is written about them is true, then in the first place they are late, and in the second place, either these are unprincipled fools or they have simply been bought. Gredeskuls[94] or Prokukishes? The one and the other are equally vulgar and vile. O, despicable Russian intelligentsia!

18 [October]. All the same. An augmentation of prices on the railroads has been designated for three weeks to help the starving, at the rate of 1,000 rubles per verst. They say this will begin on the 20th. The result is being felt already: bread is 3,500 rubles instead of 2,800. The other day I saw V. A. Rozenberg, once the all-powerful editor of *The Russian Gazette*.[95] He is modest and even ingratiating in search of employment. He asked if Volgin is of any significance. I replied to him that we can thank *The Russian Gazette* for that creature to whom we owe the destruction of Moscow University.[96]

[93] Iurii Veniaminovich Kliuchnikov (1886–1938), a specialist in international law, had in fact been a Privatdozent at Moscow University before the Revolution. He was an active opponent of the Bolsheviks during the Revolution, and minister of foreign affairs in the Kolchak government before emigrating to Paris. He returned to Soviet Russia in 1923 and became director of the section on international politics in the Communist Academy. He perished in the Ezhovshchina. Aleksandr Vladimirovich Bobrishchev-Pushkin (1875–1958) was a lawyer. Sergei Sergeevich Luk'ianov was a journalist, the son of a former Procurator of the Holy Synod. He had belonged for a time to the Kadet party. In 1920 he emigrated to Paris, where in the course of the 1920s he joined the French Communist party and became a TASS correspondent. He returned to Russia in 1930, and apparently perished in the camps sometime in the late 1930s. It is interesting that Got'e does not mention the contributor Nikolai Vasil'evich Ustrialov (1890–1938), another former Privatdozent of the Moscow University law faculty, who was the principal ideologist of the movement, *Smenovekhovstvo*, that took its name from the 1921 book *Smena vekh*. Ustrialov remained in Kharbin until 1935, when he, too, returned to Soviet Russia only to perish in the purges three years later.

[94] Nikolai Andreevich Gredeskul (1864–?), a law professor and former Kadet duma deputy, had probably attracted Got'e's attention as one of the group of twenty-four Petrograd professors (the Group of Red Professors, as they were known) who in the spring of 1921 had issued a declaration calling for cooperation between the professoriate and the Soviet regime, identifying the proletariat as the true defender of science, etc. Gredeskul's views were close to those of the Smenovekhovtsy.

[95] Vladimir Aleksandrovich Rozenberg (1860–1932).

[96] V. P. Volgin was appointed rector of Moscow University in December 1921, replacing D. P. Bogolepov, but he had been a member of the "presidium" since its creation, and a member of the State Academic Council (Gosudarstvennyi uchenyi sovet, the body in Narkompros that was charged with approving all school curriculums, teaching materials, and staffs) since 1919. Volgin had been employed as a writer for *The Russian Gazette* from 1911 to 1914; he reported on the current situation in England, the United States, Germany, and Asia, and reviewed books on international history.

25 [October]. Situation inchangée. Lenin's speech about the new economic policy is receiving much comment.[97] In my opinion, these are the words of an absolute liar and insolent fellow whom it costs nothing to play with words, as it costs him nothing to juggle with ideas and people. The bolsheviks are announcing the Emperor Karl's arrival in Hungary by airplane.[98] But here there is no one to fly in, even if they wanted that. My lecture in the university was scheduled for today. I arrived and saw the door was locked. I went and made an official statement about this incident, which may give an idea of what is going on in the former university. I saw M. P. Keller[99] off abroad. How envious one gets of people who are able to leave! The other day I received an offer to take part in the affairs of the Historical Museum. I accepted the offer with pleasure.

27 [October]. An attempt to rob our apartment was made today, according to a method worked out to the smallest details. To begin with, the first one came and asked if X lives here; on the way out, he tried to jam the lock. Then a second one came secretly and ran into M. A. Menzbir, which saved us. Pokrovskii has officially raised the question of selling certain things from the Hermitage in order to sustain the bolshevik treasury. It is proposed to curtail the museums and scholarly institutions and make them find their own means of support.

30 [October]. There is much talk on the subject of the note about willingness to recognize the debts.[100] Some believe it, others do not. I think that this is one of the naturally successive stages in the bolsheviks' downfall. Of course, they are doing it with the secret desire to dupe everyone; but whether life will permit them to dupe their opponents or will oblige them to make new concessions—that is the question. I think the second is more likely.

They celebrated the twenty-fifth anniversary of D. N. Ushakov to-

[97] Lenin's speech about NEP, "2-i Vserossiiskii s'ezd politprosvetov, rech' tov. Lenina," was published in *Izvestiia* in three parts on October 19, 21, and 22.

[98] On October 21, the Emperor Karl made his second unsuccessful attempt to take power from Admiral Horthy in Hungary (the first had been on March 27, 1921). He arrived in Oedenburg and marched on Budapest with an improvised force. He was captured by a government force and exiled to Madeira, where he died on April 1, 1922.

[99] Count Mikhail Pavlovich Keller (b. 1883), of German Baltic noble background, was a well-known bibliophile and member of various bibliographical associations. For a time in 1921 he took employment in the rare book department of the Rumiantsev Museum, but emigrated to Latvia in October 1921; he was able to do this by opting for Latvian citizenship.

[100] The government note on its willingness to recognize the Russian state debts, "Deklaratsiia o priznanii dolgov," was published in *Izvestiia* on October 29, 1921.

day.[101] I am against official jubilees, especially at the present time. The celebration was conventionally warm. Since Ushakov was my classmate, I felt by ricochet that this was something like a first memorial service. Ambivalence could be felt in the speeches: on the one hand, collaboration; on the other, hatred for the bolsheviks.

From there I went directly to the ceremony in honor of V. I. Ger'e's memory. Bogoslovskii, Savin, Egorov, Liubavskii, and Bakhrushin spoke. It was a little long, but very warm and very solid.

A drastic reduction of personnel in the bolshevik institutions. They are destroying all the Muzo, Izo, Lito, Mono, etc.;[102] that is, they are destroying all their own efforts at construction: the economy is strangling them.

31 [October]. I have finished reading Witte's memoirs.[103] One of the most interesting books I have ever read. Witte appears as a very intelligent, statesmanlike-intelligent, and also a talented person. True, the careerist and egoist is visible in him, but he may be excused for that as an intelligent person among that multitude of fools in which he circulated. One gets an extraordinarily valuable impression of Nicholas II. Nicholas completely lacked a sense and understanding of the law and legality. In addition, he was petty, envious, and unforgiving and could not tolerate having anyone higher than himself around; as a weak person, he was also a liar. It is hardly an exaggeration: much that Witte says is confirmed by other sources. Witte talks about his retirement in exactly the way Prince S. M. Volkonskii talks about his retirement from the directorship of the imperial theaters. Witte extols Alexander III, but I don't think it is only out of a wish to contrast him to Nicholas II. Very interesting are the chapters on the preparation of the Japanese war, in which Nicholas played a much more significant role than is generally thought; on the

[101] Dmitrii Nikolaevich Ushakov (1873–1942) was a prominent linguist, a dialectologist, and lexicographer. *Tolkovyi slovar' russkogo iazyka*, 4 vols. (Moscow, 1935–1940).

[102] That is, the music, graphic arts, and literary departments, and the Moscow education department, of Narkompros. Got'e's obituary notice for these institutions was premature. See Fitzpatrick, *The Commissariat of Enlightenment*.

[103] Although the year of publication on the title page was 1922, Got'e appears to have read the first volume of the Berlin edition of Witte's memoirs. Its publication was first announced in the Berlin émigré newspaper *Rul'*, on October 30, 1921. It is possible, however, that he had read Yarmolinsky's one-volume English translation of the entire memoir: it appeared several months before the Berlin edition and thus well before Got'e's mention of it; moreover, his comment does not suggest that he had read only part of Witte's memoirs. Graf S. Iu. Vitte, *Vospominaniia, t. I. Tsarstvovanie Nikolaia II* (Berlin, 1922). *The Memoirs of Count Witte. Translated from the Original Russian Manuscript and Edited by Abraham Yarmolinsky* (London, 1921). See B. V. Anan'ich and R. Sh. Ganelin, "Opyt kritiki memuarov S. Iu Vitte," in *Voprosy istoriografii i istochnikovedeniia istorii SSSR. Sbornik statei* (Moscow, 1963), pp. 298–374.

Portsmouth negotiations, where Witte achieved a fantastic success; and on his meetings with Wilhelm. Playing the fool with Nicholas, Wilhelm entangled Russia in sordid affairs, and the simpleton Nicholas went so far as to conclude an alliance with him in Björke against his ally France.[104] What an excellent minister of foreign affairs Witte would have made if Nicholas II hadn't hated him. The premonitions of the war and revolution are very interesting. You often forget the book was finished in 1912.

NOVEMBER

2 [November]. I read Change of Signposts. The book is better and more interesting than one could have thought from the excerpts from it that the bolsheviks are using in their lectures and speeches. This is the voice of those émigrés who are having a hard time of it or are disenchanted. There is no impression of subornation, but the main polemic is directed against various groups of émigrés and against the ex-leaders of the ex-parties. For the first time in the émigré press I hear respect paid to those who are carrying on cultural work here in spite of everything. And it is not all praise for the bolsheviks: their dark sides are not hushed up. On the other hand, they overestimate the bolsheviks: they don't know the Russia of 1921; they are not aware of the disintegration, robbery, and theft that are destroying the remains of the bolshevik regime. The voice of Russian messianism is also here—they don't want to understand that there is no world-future in Russia and that Russia has demonstrated with her Pugachevshchina that she is the lowest race. In almost every article there is a mixture of truth, ignorance, and falsehood, both conscious and unconscious. There is a lot of hysteria; but there is no noticeable insincerity. Yet it can't be denied that the touching naiveté of the Russian intelligentsia is combined in this book with its incurable feebleness and flaccidity.[105]

---

[104] On July 24, 1905, while cruising on their yachts, the German Emperor Wilhelm and Nicholas II signed a treaty providing for mutual aid in case of attack by another European power. It was opposed by the foreign offices of both countries and ultimately had to be abandoned because the French would not accept it.

[105] The Smenovekhovtsy, or National Bolsheviks as they came to be known, advocated an end to opposition to the Bolshevik regime and the return home of those who had emigrated, essentially on the grounds that the Bolsheviks' victory in the Civil War and their fighting of the war with Poland proved that they had taken on the historic national mission. The introduction of the NEP of course reinforced that conviction. The Bolshevik government immediately authorized republication of the book in Russia. Perhaps the main element in the outlook of the Smenovekhovtsy that set them off from Got'e and

4 [November]. I was supposed to go to Petrograd on business of the Academy of Material Culture. I received a reserved Narkompros seat. It turned out to be a third-class seat, the fourth on the bench, in a car with broken windows in which people were standing in the corridor. I conscientiously sat down in my place, but afterward I was seized by horror of that stuffiness and crowding, and also of the insult that I was supposed to travel in that mess. Five minutes before the departure of the train I rolled out of the car and returned home.

5 [November]. G. A. Riazhskii recounted a lot about Siberia; another new confirmation that there were all the same diseases there as here—chiefly thievery, embezzling, and that terrible Russian dishonesty. The question of inviting the bolsheviks anywhere is not even being raised in Europe: their appeal about the assumption of debts and about being invited to Washington was a blank shot.

7 [November]. The fourth anniversary of the Tatar yoke. Dully boring thoughts—the same weather, the same celebration. More precisely, there is no celebration at all, only here and there, rarely, tattered red flags are dangling.

A chat with I. L. Tomashevskii, former assistant procurator of the court and chamberlain, but of Polish origin.[106] Now the *polska krew*[107] in him has begun to speak and the inveterate and gloating Pole in him is making himself felt. How easily such transformations take place. However, what is there to say when the Russian people is nothing else than "a son-of-a-bitch, a Kamarinskii muzhik"[108] running bare-assed down the street; he runs and runs, farts and tugs at his b. . .s. Isn't that a picture!

There are only acid critical responses in the newspapers to the supposed desire to pay the debts. However, it would be strange if it were otherwise. Bread is 3,500, and meat is an average of 10,000 rubles a pound.

9 [November]. The situation is unchanged. A persistent yearning these days to remove my family and myself and leave forever. I am rapturously reading the interesting memoirs of Czernin.[109]

---

like-minded academics of nationalist and statist orientation was their populist belief in the genius and "statism" of the common people ("the touching naïveté of the Russian intelligentsia").

[106] Ivan Leont'evich Tomashevskii (Tomaszewski) was also a former chief judge of the Third Moscow Criminal Court.

[107] "Polish blood."

[108] A character in a popular song.

[109] The war memoirs of Count Ottokar Czernin (1872–1932), the Austrian minister of

12 [November]. On my book about the Time of Troubles comrade Po-krovskii inscribed, "Who reviewed this filth?"[110] A high distinction. I am reading Count Czernin's memoirs: a very interesting view of Wilhelm and a lively characterization of Franz Ferdinand—a real figure comes to life.

14 [November]. Another crisis of impecuniousness, more precisely absence of "gov-notes,"[111] is beginning. Again no one is getting paid anywhere; I need "millions" and there is nowhere to get them. Bread has risen to 4,000; butter, 40,000; a mug of milk, 5,000. Prices are even higher in Petrograd. There is no doubt that the general economy of "Sovrossiia" is stifling that misshapen edifice. They say of the recognition of debts that it is Jews haggling with Jews.

16 [November]. The general picture is unchanged; I ask myself, has the pile of manure budged or has it not budged? Sometimes it seems yes, sometimes no. "The days rush by like minutes; the weeks are shorter than days."[112] It is four years already that we are twirling like squirrels in a cage, and all to no end. The only comfort is scholarly study in the evenings.

23 [November]. The general situation remains the same. The ruble is soaring catastrophically: a 10-ruble gold piece costs more than 700,000 rubles; butter, 60,000; bread, 4,800. I have 1,500,000 rubles at home and they are equal to 750,000 two months ago. And all this can go on for a long time. In the end, however, the future will take shape in the form of an administration for the affairs of the bankrupt debtor, "the former Russian Empire," and the general assembly of creditors will consist for the most part of foreigners. I don't know if this prognosis of mine is correct.

It is becoming difficult to work with A. K. Vinogradov in the museum: with all his major positive qualities as a worker and defender of the museum's interests, he is an operator, a careerist, and a lout. He is hard on the nerves: an example is the appended letter of the 20th of November, in regard to which he had to voice quite a few bitter truths.[113]

Yesterday I gave a talk in the Historical Society about Witte's mem-

---

foreign affairs from 1916 to 1918, were published in 1919: Ottokar Czernin, *Im Weltkrieg* (Berlin and Vienna, 1919).

[110] That is, "Which censor passed it?"

[111] *Gos-znaki,* the currency printed by the Soviet government.

[112] "Dni begut, kak minuty; nedeli koroche dnei."

[113] Letter of A. K. Vinogradov to Got'e, dated November 20, 1921. See Appendix, Letter 23.

oirs. There was a big audience; representatives of the old world were present. There were animated discussions about the talk. I enjoyed myself. The American professors Coolidge and Golder[114] were at the talk: both have expressionless faces.

25 [November]. The extent to which you don't know now in the morning what will happen in the evening: yesterday at 4 P.M. we got the sudden news that the Cheka is sealing up our branch division in Likhov Pereulok, that is, the former diocesan library. It turns out that the priests serving there got the idea of taking the arm of the prelate who was visiting them, and this happened in the presence of communists; as a result, the communist cell informed the Cheka, and we had to make a formal response, as a result of which the day and the evening were lost in the bustle. But all these days were very busy.

A decree about money. Ten thousand will be called a ruble. I don't think it will yield the desired results. Today I learned from a reliable source that A. N. Savin is lecturing in the Institute of Red Professors, which, by the way, consists entirely of Jews.[115]

27 [November]. A new rise in prices; some explain this as a "denomination" of money, but I think this is simply the customary and normal road the bolsheviks are taking to their death. I went with Bakhrushin to visit the American Harvard history professor, Coolidge. We spent an interesting evening. We heard a few things of interest about life in Europe and about the new books on history and politics that have been published in the last twenty-five years. The acquaintance with him should be maintained.

[114] Archibald Cary Coolidge (1866–1928) was professor of history and director of the university library at Harvard. He had been acting secretary of the American Legation in Petersburg in 1890–91. In 1919 he was attached to the Peace Conference and in 1921 he joined the ARA as Chief of the Liaison Division of the Russian Unit, which was responsible for communications with the Soviet government and the press, as well as for repatriation cases. On Golder, his former student who was there in several capacities, see the Introduction to the diary.

[115] The Institute of Red Professors was founded by decree of Sovnarkom on February 11, 1921, as a graduate school for the training of "red professors" in history and the social sciences. Admission was to be restricted to Party members recommended by the Central Committee or provincial committees, although a few non-Party members were admitted from the beginning (four of ninety-three in the first year). The initial teaching staff included several non-Marxists in addition to Savin. If Jews were numerous in the institute, as Got'e suggests, it must have been among the students; the teaching staff was predominantly non-Jewish. The director and rector of the institute was M. N. Pokrovskii. Studies began in the fall of 1921.

DECEMBER

1 [December]. I have received a summons to give testimony in the Moscow Cheka on the case of the Likhov Pereulok library. I was at the meeting of the Socio-pedagogical Section of the Faculty of Social Sciences, where I had to go in connection with one particular matter. The so-called faculty consisted of Savin; Konovalov,[116] who has been removed from the staff (which is why he is also leaving the post of secretary); N. G. Tarasov[117] with a saccharine smile; several precocious youths, including our V. K. Nikol'skii,[118] who has apparently taken the role of professor in the new formation; and two individuals completely unknown to me. Revolting and boring. Two scoundrels fell out over the university elections of a "presidium": Kostitsyn, a bolshevik mathematician,[119] and Kubitskii,[120] a scoundrel philosopher. The first called the second a papier-mâché man who absorbs all bad odors. The second is appealing to the moderate professoriate and is finding a response in that promiscuous bleating ewe, M. M. Novikov.[121] A small but redoubtable gang. Butter is 70,000.

2 [December]. A visit to the Moscow Cheka. A pass from the commandant. I went into the courtyard of the building of the Moscow Insurance Society. It was clean. The building was clean. In order to get to room no. 37 I had to go along long corridors and came out in a room with windows facing Malaia Lubianka. There was no one; then a young man of intelligentsia appearance came in and asked: "Are you here to see me?" The chamber was a room, or rather part of a room set off by a wooden partition. He gave me a questionnaire sheet to fill out. Then there began a very polite conversation, whose point was to find out where the books in the basement of house no. 6 of Likhov Pereulok had come from. I told him all I could and he asked me to advise him what to do in order to

[116] Dmitrii Grigor'evich Konovalov (b. 1876), a specialist on the history of religion, was a member of the faculty of social sciences; he later was a member of RANION.

[117] Nikolai Grigor'evich Tarasov (b. 1866) was a historian and an art critic. In the early 1920s he participated in several published efforts to provide a Marxist interpretation of art history and social science theory.

[118] Vladimir Kapitonovich Nikol'skii (1894–1953) graduated from Moscow University in 1916; he became a professor there in 1930. His early work was devoted to seventeenth-century Russia, although he later wrote on primitive society and the history of religion.

[119] Vladimir Aleksandrovich Kostitsyn (b. 1883) was an astrophysicist and professor on the mathematics faculty who was a longtime bolshevik activist.

[120] Aleksei Vladislavovich Kubitskii (b. 1880) was a professor of philosophy at Moscow University and later a member of RANION. He was a specialist on Greek philosophy and Idealism.

[121] Novikov had been replaced as rector by D. P. Bogolepov in November 1920.

figure it out. I said that the best thing would be a combined commission of representatives of the Rumiantsev Museum, Narkompros, and the Moscow Cheka, with which he completely agreed. The end of the conversation was like this: "This case must be liquidated as soon as possible." The inquest-conversation lasted about forty minutes and was entirely correct. On leaving I had to present my pass, which remained with the guard. The new state bank has nothing to do, because there is no business in it at all; this report comes from members of the administration. I am not surprised.

8 [December]. A sad event has occurred since the other day. My uncle, Eduard Vladimirovich, professor of the Higher Women's Courses (the Second University), died. He was an original, profound, and charming person, a subtle thinker, and an unusually delicate, private man, as one of his assistants called him in a graveside speech. He did not give all he could have given in his life. He was an excellent doctor with a large practice, but he did not amass a fortune because he was extraordinarily honorable. He was a scientist with original views, but he did not make a big name for himself because he was too modest and lacked the high-handedness that various Ostroumovs, Zakhar'ins,[122] and similar representatives of Russian medical art possessed in abundance. He was an amazingly kind person, but he was not popular among his medical comrades because he was the complete opposite of the type of Russian medical man. The rudeness and amoral lawlessness of the majority of Russian doctors disgusted this man, who was a European in both appearance and internal makeup. For me this is a great loss; he was a person with whom one could always have a heart-to-heart talk; he suffered with our sorrows and rejoiced in our joys. He was alienated from life after his wife's death in 1915; the revolution gave definitive impetus to his *taedium vitae*. He said many times that he looked on everything around him like a man who had already died. Only reading interested him, particularly memoirs of the eighteenth century, predominantly French; he withdrew spiritually among the rationalist philosophers and wise skeptics of that age, who were the closest to him spiritually. The funeral services were very touching; they cost 5,000,000 rubles, the equivalent of 4 gold imperials, that is, 40 old rubles. Since he lived in a soviet house, the unpleasant task of removing his affairs had to be undertaken immediately to avoid robbery.

[122] The names of famous predecessors of Eduard Vladimirovich Got'e in the field of therapeutics, Aleksei Aleksandrovich Ostroumov (1844–1908), and Grigorii Antonovich Zakhar'in (1829–1897). Got'e was considered a representative of Ostroumov's school as Ostroumov was of Zakhar'in's.

All these days have been occupied with liquidation of his affairs and his life.

16 [December]. There are no changes. All is the same. The bolsheviks are like crazed cats in a sack. They are all seeking a way out but can't find it. In the opinion of some, this foreshadows their rapid end; in the opinion of others, it is an indicator of the fact that it will not soon be possible to overthrow them. These are all subjective judgments where the man in the street's point of view collides with the historical. Reason says more than ever before—*wir müssen durch!* But feeling resists. Truly, *qui vivra, verra.* I am very tired. Fuss and bother after the death of Uncle Eduard; now in addition, the grave illness of my wife's father is unsettling, especially if you take into consideration that all my job activity is also a kind of marking time that frays the nerves. You patch one hole and another immediately appears, and so on endlessly. I haven't written anything about the university for a long time, but that is because it no longer exists; its constituent parts remain, but it itself does not exist, and it would be best if we, its old veterans, were to go off to the side, restricting our relation to it to our obligations to the students, so long as there are such and so long as we are given the possibility of teaching. If I am going to continue my activity as an expert on Polish affairs, I will do so because two hatreds struggle within me—for the bolsheviks and for the Poles. [There is] the off chance, moreover, that even a tiny bit can be done to help former Russia!

20 [December]. The celebration of St. Nicholas's Day is much more sumptuous than a year or two or three ago. Meanwhile prices are soaring wildly: bread is 9–10,000, although in Moscow, as before, it is possible to get everything. The Moscow bourgeois are spreading the most amazing rumors about the congress of soviets that is supposed to open—some expect a rightward shift, others a shift to the left; the one and the other are depicted in the sharpest and most decisive forms.

21 [December]. This is how I spent the day today:

   8:30 - Mass, the twentieth day for Uncle Eduard Vladimirovich
  10–11 - Lessons with Volodia, interrupted by four visits
     11 - The museum office
 11:30–1 - Sorted books in the university library
   1–2 - Museum council
     2 - In the Academy of Material Culture
 2:15–3 - Library
     3 - Dinner

3:30–4:30 - Commissariat of Foreign Affairs: Polish affairs
5–6 - Lecture for the library courses
7–8 - Meeting of the Commission on Antiquities of Central Russia
8:30 - Came home
This is a very typical schedule for the present time.

The illness of Vera Mikhailovna's father is dragging on and getting worse.

23 December. I have received a proposal to participate in the commission of experts on the matter of releasing various objects and documents to the Poles on the basis of the Riga treaty.[123] I do not think that I have committed a sin in accepting it, for I am convinced that the Poles have remained and will remain the enemies of Russia, and that in defending ourselves from them we are perhaps working for a future hypothetical Russia. So far I saw yesterday only the assistant chairman of the Russian delegation, comrade Mrachkovskii,[124] a communist lawyer—dry, businesslike, polite, and civilized enough, but with an unpleasant, hard expression on his face.

I have just become an associate of the Historical Museum; I was at the council meeting and at a meeting of the historical section. Work there may be pleasant even in the present conditions. Gold has fallen sharply; they say that the bolsheviks have asked the Jews what they are to do; the latter advised them to dump gold on the market and request an account from the big advance negotiators. Several of the latter will probably crash; the Jews will buy up gold at a cheap price, and in a week or two gold will again head for the sky and the bolshevik treasury will pay for the expenses and losses.

26 [December]. A Christmas present from the Americans, Coolidge and Golder: a *food packet* with a very kind letter, which I append here.[125] One pud of the finest wheat flour, twenty-five pounds of rice, fifteen pounds of sugar, three pounds of tea, a tub of lard, twenty jars of condensed milk. I admit I was touched, and contented, and a little upset. The Congress of Soviets leads one to expect something; so far I see nothing, but changes are impending all the same. Vera Mikhailovna's situation is the same and

---

[123] The Riga Treaty had stipulated that Soviet Russia was to return to Poland all spoils of war and scholarly and cultural treasures removed from Polish territory since 1772.

[124] Sergei Vital'evich Mrachkovskii (1888–1936), himself the child of exiled revolutionaries, was an Old Bolshevik. In the 1920s he was an ardent supporter of Trotskii; he was one of the defendants, along with Zinov'ev and Kamenev, in the 1936 show trial, and was executed in August 1936.

[125] Letter of Coolidge to Got'e, dated December 24, 1921, Moscow. See Appendix, Letter 24. The italicized words are in English in the original text.

drags on. I feel that I cannot intensify my activities any further; I have reached the limit; it is not the total amount of them, but rather the dispersion that these activities engender that won't permit increasing them.

Bread is 9,000; one pound of sausage is 65,000.

28 [December]. Situation inchangée. I listened to a lecture by A. A. Grushka on Dostoevskii. It is interesting when all his antibolshevik speeches come out in the form of [.....]. Despite the terrible situation of the country, I remain cheerful for some reason.

31 [December]. A typical occurrence: the director of the administrative board of Narkompros, the Jewish upstart Nevel'son, wanted to put up his mama, so he seized an apartment of the Moscow section of the Academy of Material Culture. The administration of scholarly institutions, which fears Nevel'son or doesn't want to spoil their relations, won't lift a finger to help the offended institution. I am going and pleading. The optimists are expecting some kind of decrees. The bolsheviks are writing that someone wants to recognize them. One more year of Russian death is over.

1922

✳

1 [January]. What are the auspices for this year? Apparently, a further shift; a difficult period of starvation. Will this year be worse or better than last?

5 [January]. The Christmas preparations are bigger and more widespread this year than in past years. In the first place, there is more money; in the second, everything can be bought, and therefore a Christmas tree is prepared and a goose is purchased. The guarantee of two communists was demanded for the commission of experts on Poland. At first I didn't want to do this at all, and in any case excluded the possibility of turning to the university and Narkompros communists. I finally turned to two of the people who are least unacceptable to me—Otto Shmidt and N. Trotskaia. I think that in doing so I am doing something base, but the cause of defending Russian archives and museums is a good cause, and the hatred for the Poles roused by their insane policy vis-à-vis Russia is just as strong in me as hatred for the communists.

15 [January]. I passed several days in Pestovo. I mostly slept there; the rest of the time I sat and read, infrequently going out for a walk along the road in front of the house. That was the best possible Christmas rest. I feel that my nervous fatigue has passed and that I have much more strength. Upon returning I found everything more or less all right at home. A great deal is unclear on the general horizon. Something is changing, something is being prepared. And money continues to plummet. A mug of milk is 25,000; bread, 11,000.

17 [January]. The ministry of Poincaré constitutes a spoke in the wheel of the RSFSR.[1] For the time being, it is difficult to judge further. I am continuing to read English and German books about the war with great pleasure: for example, Kleinwächter's *Der Untergang der Österreichisch-*

---

[1] The government of Raymond Poincaré, the former president of the French Republic, was formed on January 15, 1922. It pursued a program demanding forced reparations from Germany and Russian recognition of the tsarist debt.

ungarischen Monarchie.[2] I am accumulating a large store of knowledge and impressions. Bread is 13,000.

22 [January]. The 7th was the wedding of Lenochka Shambinago.[3] In the museum church. Tails and bright ladies' dresses. Afterward tea and snacks at home. It was gay and in the old style. Everyone is talking about the Genoa Conference.[4] I think that it might after all bring us something, as a further stage in the shift. Prices are rising like never before: bread is 20,000. I received a letter from M. M. Cherkasskaia in Khar'kov—*Une lettre navrante*; I am appending it here.[5] It is a brilliant illustration of the bolshevik regime. I heard a story from Vl. Gv. that in order to get two railway cars for sending troops to the Finnish border they gave a bribe of three puds of flour. That, it seems, is the limit. A strange situation. I remain in good spirits, but meanwhile the general economic situation is becoming ever more impossible. Today there was a meeting in "komindel"[6] on Polish affairs; comrade Mrachkovskii is a typical provincial lawyer; his assistant, a whorehouse pimp; and the same confusion in the business at hand as everywhere.

25 [January]. St. Tat'iana's Day. Mass at St. George's on Krasnaia Gorka. There was another solemn mass at the former Ascension Monastery, so that the university community was split in two. That is only to be regretted. The day was spent in the usual bustle. Dinner at Tat'iana Al. Shambinago's, where a little was drunk; later—an early evening at Tania Dol'nik's, whence I set off at 11 P.M. for A. A. Grushka's to a professors' party. Liubavskii, Menzbir, Gulevich,[7] Martynov, Bogoiavlenskii, Severtsov,[8] Poznyshev,[9] Bogoslovskii, Il'in, Shambinago, Orlov,[10] and others were there. There were after-dinner speeches until 3 A.M. The general

[2] Friedrich S. C. Kleinwächter, *Der Untergang der Österreichisch-ungarischen Monarchie* (Leipzig, 1920).

[3] Apparently the daughter of S. K. Shambinago.

[4] The Genoa Conference on the Russian problem and general economic problems, in which both Germany and Soviet Russia participated, met from April 10 to May 19, 1922. It broke down over French insistence on Russian recognition of the tsarist debt.

[5] Letter of M. M. Cherkasskaia to Got'e, dated March 24, 1922. See Appendix, Letter 25.

[6] The Commissariat for Foreign Affairs.

[7] Vladimir Sergeevich Gulevich (1867–1933) was a biochemist and professor of medicine at Moscow University. He became an academician in 1929.

[8] Aleksei Nikolaevich Severtsov (1866–1936) was professor of biology at Moscow University and an academician. He was a founder of the field of evolutionary morphology.

[9] Sergei Viktorovich Poznyshev (b. 1870) was a former assistant rector and member of the law faculty of Moscow University. He was a specialist in criminal law. He later headed the social sciences division of the Lenin Library.

[10] Aleksandr Sergeevich Orlov (1871–1947) had been a professor at Moscow University and was a leading specialist on Old Russian literature.

theme was the revival of Russia on monarchist foundations. A general description: one of those present, M. S. Fel'dshtein,[11] remarked that in the prewar period, speeches such as those being given would have been impossible. The mood was cheerful. It was said that St. Tat'iana's Day was on the whole celebrated in a much livelier and more energetic way than in previous years. A lull in the newspapers and rumors. Bread has reached 28,000.

31 [January]. America is dealing with the bolsheviks like a rich lord with an indigent drunkard. She is giving [them] a handout but does not sit [them] at table with her. The bolsheviks are coming closer and closer to a final crash, and yet they are trying to put off the final reckoning by means of lies and the employment of all possible means. Many expect that they will surrender even before the Genoa Conference, but I think that there, too, they will try to prolong their existence by lies. This episode shows how they have become accustomed to lies: in the commission of experts (that is, in the so-called Russo-Ukrainian delegation) the bolsheviks have decided to lead the Poles by the nose until March, occupying their attention by submitting matters that are unneeded by either side, and they are entrusting this vile game to the scholar-experts, or to several of them, at least.

The current financial situation is very interesting: the fixed budget has already cracked, they can't print money fast enough, and therefore they are leaving the timid departments, such as Enlightenment, for example, without money. Soon they will probably forbid paying [wages of] less than a certain sum but will pay out less than that sum, so like it or not they will have to fire half [the employees].

Prices are holding at the previous level.

FEBRUARY

4 February. On Wednesday, the 1st, there was a meeting with the Poles. As many as fifteen head of them had gathered. Importunate demands. It is offensive, from the Old Russian point of view, to hear all that they are saying and demanding. And yet, seeing and hearing this, I couldn't decide which of the two sides is the more antipathetic to me, and it appears, strange as it may seem, that the Poles disgusted me less. On the same day, there was a meeting of the professors in the university, which decided to begin a strike in consequence of the terrible situation both of the university as a whole and of the teachers. I did not participate in that meeting

[11] Mikhail Solomonovich Fel'dshtein (b. 1885) was a specialist in state law and political theory.

and in general I have a passive attitude toward this strange and, to my mind, absurd enterprise. Since the university is unnecessary and practically doesn't exist anymore, the bolsheviks could care less whether we strike or not. I think they will either smash the university and the professors, the way they smashed the Committee for Aid to the Starving, or sternly order us to return to work within three days and then fire us. Well, come what may; I don't support the strike but I will not break it.

All these days a situation of a kind of impasse surrounding us. I am more than ever convinced that "they" are approaching their end, but I am also more than ever convinced that their end will not be the beginning of Russia's rebirth. Russia will not revive for a long time.

6 [*February*]. An example of a stupid affair. On the day after the announcement of the strike, in the morning, an unknown lady came to Shambinago and announced that "things were not well tonight at Grushka's." We are informed; the news goes further; everyone is on the alert. T. A. Shambinago,[12] as usual, made up an explanation that this was because of the conversations on St. Tat'iana's Day. In fact, it turns out that although there was indeed a search, they were looking not for Grushka, but for a certain Ivanova.

The professors' strike has ended successfully, thank God. A delegation went to see comrade Tsiurupa,[13] Lenin's assistant, who cursed Narkompros. The professors were ordered to elect a committee that will review the Narkompros budget. Gulevich, Kostitsyn, Stratonov,[14] D. N. Egorov, and Sergievskii were elected. The issuing of the academic ration, which was cut off on Pokrovskii's order, was commanded restored. Thus, unexpectedly to me, the professors won a victory. The bolsheviks did not undertake a new pogrom of the university, and that must be considered both a novelty and a success. Yet if they had wanted they could have divided, replaced, and even routed the fragile professors' milieu. Classes start tomorrow.

Today I visited the ARA for discussions about feeding the professors from America. The Morozov mansion on the Spiridonovka; many Jews who speak both Russian and English. A long wait because my companions, Severtsov and Iasinskii,[15] had decided to be offended. It turns out that the Jews had not even announced us. When the appropriate per-

[12] Tat'iana Shambinago.

[13] Aleksandr Dmitrievich Tsiurupa (1870–1928), a longtime bolshevik and associate of Lenin, was vice-president of Sovnarkom.

[14] Vsevolod Viktorovich Stratonov (1869–1938) was a mathematician and astronomer. He had been elected dean of the physical-mathematics faculty in 1919.

[15] Anton Nikitich Iasinskii (1864–1933) was a medievalist and specialist on Czech history. He had been a professor at Moscow University until 1919, at which time he was named a professor at the Moscow Archaeological Institute.

son—an American German (perhaps a Jew, but not necessarily), Mr. Burland[16]—came out and learned who we were, he immediately received us politely. It turns out that the American universities want to feed Russian scholars; a campaign has been launched by Russian scholars who have gone to America. I think something will come of this.[17]

The general situation is unchanged. They continue to expect something, and I think that changes should follow.

Iakovlev writes from Simbirsk that they are eating corpses and rats there.

11 [February]. The Cheka and its branches have been abolished as of the other day.[18] I am not exaggerating the significance of this event, but I am not underestimating it, either. The same people will stay there, at least for the immediate future, but when they are replaced they will no longer be superdepartmental dictators, but only bureaucrats of the department of internal affairs. The very range of the department is narrowed; in general, its resources have been somewhat reduced. They were provoked to take this step not by a wish to do something good, but by the same iron law of life that has already forced concessions and will turn them to dust. For the time being no other events are visible on the horizon.

As is becoming clear from the activities of the commission elected by the professors, there is nothing for support of the institutions of higher learning, but they are still busy with promotions in Narkompros: they intend to establish a central library on popular enlightenment. The irrepressible scoundrel and fool Charnolusskii is submitting a project, and the fools from Narkompros are supporting it. Paper will tolerate anything!

13 [February]. I visited Coolidge for the last time: he is leaving for America. That is too bad. He is an interesting, sympathetic, highly cultured, and sincere American. He will leave a pleasant memory. Perhaps life will

[16] Elmer G. Burland was head of the ARA Food Remittance Division in Russia, which handled the distribution of individual food packets.

[17] The Food Remittance Division had a "group" or "bulk" program that permitted groups or organizations in America or elsewhere outside of Russia to target classes of individuals in Russia for receipt of the food packets, rather than specifically named individuals, which was the general rule of the system. See E. G. Burland, "The Intelligentsia: Some Aspects of General Relief in Russia," *A.R.A. Bulletin*, Series 2, 61, pp. 4–12.

[18] The Cheka was replaced by the GPU (Gosudarstvennoe politicheskoe upravlenie, or State Political Administration), whose formation was announced at the Eleventh Party Congress, which met at the end of March 1922. As Got'e surmises, the change was meant to signify the routinization of political-police work and the reduction of its scope. Unlike the Cheka, however, the GPU was empowered to arrest Party members.

bring us together once again; perhaps—"the grasshopper hops, but doesn't see where."

21 [February]. The general tendency remains the same. The sum of rumors and conversations for the last few days is as follows: the bolsheviks are really intending to go to Genoa with unimaginable plans. Chicherin has summoned Vorms and ordered him to draw up a project on how to transfer all the gold from America to Zurich and to issue a unified world currency on it. You can't make out whether this is unbounded impudence or the same old stupidity. There is complete chaos and disorder in Narkomfin.[19] Now the Jewish bolsheviks there are saying to the "bourgeois economists" that the latter were right when they foretold their complete bankruptcy. A Canossa to foreign capital is unavoidable. What we don't yet know are only the dates and the means. The news from the places of famine is so horrible that I try consciously, closing my eyes, not to think and not to talk about this unheard of disaster. Perhaps that is very bad, but I declare it openly.

24 [February]. Cases of banditry in Moscow are increasing greatly; in all other respects—*situation inchangée*.

28 [February]. Rumors about Lenin's illness; idle folk are saying that he is supposedly raving that the Mother of God is pursuing him. It is apparently true that he is not entirely well.[20] There is confirmation from all sides of the note of the 21st about a complete economic collapse[21] and, in particular, of the fact that this is recognized by the important bolsheviks themselves. But delay they will, for they have nothing to lose. Thefts and burglaries are becoming more and more frequent. In Moscow they say that the cutback in the Cheka staff has yielded a large number of robbers. I saw S. I. Lebedkin,[22] who has arrived from Sevastopol': they are dying from hunger there, too. I am attaching a sad letter of I. F. Rybakov[23] from Poltava, where things are obviously not pleasant either. Yesterday my roof began to leak and flooded the whole room in the course of the night; such is the state of Sovdep roofs.

[19] The Commissariat of Finance.

[20] "[Lenin] fell seriously ill towards the end of 1921 and was forced to rest for several weeks. During the first half of the following year, his capacity for work was reduced and was constantly deteriorating." Moshe Lewin, *Lenin's Last Struggle* (New York, 1970), p. 33.

[21] *Izvestiia* of February 21 carried several stories about the crisis in Moscow's fuel supply and the related collapse of the transport system.

[22] Sergei Ivanovich Lebedkin (b. 1884) was an anatomy professor; in the later 1920s he taught at the Belorussian University in Minsk.

[23] Letter of I. F. Rybakov to Got'e, dated June 4, 1921. See Appendix, Letter 26.

MARCH

4 [March]. Appeals to war are being heard. This is either saber-rattling or a cry of despair. I don't think they could win a war. Relations are growing tense in the commission with the Poles. The Poles are yelling that they are being offended, and are themselves robbing Russia. The bolsheviks are appealing to the patriotism of Russian scholars. It makes a funny picture. But I am beginning to feel a distinct hatred for the Poles.

7 [or 8] [March]. The funeral of M. M. Ryndin lasted six days, since we got permission to bury him in Novodevichii Monastery only two days after his death. The burial order was gotten [in exchange for] a pair of galoshs from Glavrezina. The bearing-out was only on Sunday the 5th (he died on Thursday the 2nd), the burial service was on the 6th, and his burial was only today, since the grave was not ready. Ninochka's funeral in November 1919 cost 30,000; Uncle Eduard's funeral in December 1921 was 5,000,000; M. M.'s funeral in March 1922 was 33,000,000. Bread costs 60,000 a pound.

The general situation and my attitude toward it remain unchanged.

11 [March]. A ticket to Petrograd costs two and a half million, and this figure is not shocking. In all the history of Sovdepiia there has not been such a devaluation of money as these days. Yesterday I was at the annual meeting of the Archaeological Society; the old days were remembered. There is news from the countess: she lives in the Banat, in the town of Belaia Tserkov'.[24] Today I was at a meeting of Kubu[25] and we talked about a classification of five categories; it seems they decided that this is all nonsense, which in fact it is.

15 [March]. The last two days there has been a certain animation in the newspapers and there have been rumors. It is my impression that "they" greatly fear the Genoa Conference and at the same time are trying to frighten all the inhabitants of the RSFSR and all of Western Europe with saber-rattling. I think the former have become stupefied and the latter are laughing.

17 [March]. I have never been so convinced of the phenomenal sociopolitical stupidity of the Russian people. They are talented fools.

The prognosis for today: the Genoa Conference may not succeed—

[24] That is, the Banat of Temesvar, the area divided between Rumania and Yugoslavia by the Peace Conference in 1919. Bela Crkva is now in the Vojvodina.

[25] That is, the Commission for Improving the Living Conditions of Scholars. See n. 26 for 1920.

both sides will dig in their heels and pour forth their mutual unacceptability. Then a moment could occur that the most persistent communists apparently foresee: a war, since it is better for their idea to fall in battle than for them to surrender their positions without a fight. If the war is conducted on that side not by bands and not by Wrangel alone, the issue should be decided quickly, because they have no one they can rely on except 20–30,000 bandits, fanaticized fools, and communist cadets. It would be enough for the opposing side to occupy the line Petrograd-Moscow-Khar'kov-Rostov in order to put an end to it all, for they cannot hold on in the Volga region: they simply risk being eaten there.

23 [March]. A week of intense study. There just isn't time to do my own work. There is a lot of work everywhere, even in the Polish commission. Mrachkovskii is a strange figure—a bolshevik, a communist, and at the same time undoubtedly a kind and sympathetic man, although one with the pyschology of a provincial barrister.

Another hitch on the general horizon. The bolsheviks don't want to yield any more, and the Genoa Conference is apparently coming unstuck. They are taking advantage of that and rattling their sabers.

Bread is 100,000 rubles; everything else goes accordingly. They say that the financial organs are no longer in a state to sustain parity with the rate of the gold ruble and that this rate will be abandoned beginning in April.

27 [March]. The question of church treasures is growing acute. There are arrests of clergy in Moscow. Demonstrations in Petersburg. In *Izvestiia* there is an *interview*, or what is supposed to be an *interview*, with the patriarch, whose words are intelligent, logical, and even bold. "The tsars took, but also gave, but the present government is looting."[26] Today is a day of joys and disenchantments. Naze shelved my money but left it in Russian bank notes! On the other hand, I received an ARA packet. I am not grieving about the money. Perhaps we can scrape some up. A cordial letter from Uncle Emil'. They are leaving for the Genoa Conference but are saying that not one decent person has gone with them among the experts. General Zaionchkovskii visited us today. A very interesting man.

28 [March]. A sudden change in the trip to Petrograd: I will have to go tomorrow instead of the day after tomorrow. It is always like that with the bolsheviks—there is no stability, even in petty matters.

A stupid speech by Lenin at the congress of communists. I don't understand how it is that many people still consider that vulgar smart aleck

[26] "Golodaiushchie u Tikhona," *Izvestiia*, March 26, 1922.

to be an intelligent man. They are going to Genoa, as they put it, to a contest, to haggle.[27]

I. A. Il'in is asking me to be his arbitrator: I am appending his letter,[28] as well as the letters of Emma and Uncle Emil'.[29]

APRIL

30 March–4 April. A trip to Petrograd on business of the Polish delegation and of the Academy of Material Culture. The trip was very successful; thanks to the fact that the trip was on business of the Commissariat of Foreign Affairs, I traveled in a diplomatic car on the way there and in a wagon-lit on the way back. There, as always, a marvelous reception; I saw many people, and rushed about the Imperial Public Library, the Archives, and the Hermitage. Because of the illness of A. A. Vasil'ev, I even had to chair at the council of the Academy of the History of Material Culture. As always, a cordial welcome at the Platonovs and from other Petrograders, who receive me with traditional Muscovite hospitality. It is interesting to note once again that they live there without the rumors on which we feed. The last day I dined at Pivato, which has newly reopened.[30]

The Germans have entered into an agreement with the bolsheviks. From the Germans' side these are logical steps for the destruction of Russia; for the bolsheviks it is an attempt to jump out of a hole. It would be useful for our Germanophiles to know all this.

I took the journey with Mrachkovskii. Il gagne beaucoup à le connaitre. A kind and gentle person. Qu'est-il allé faire dans cette galère?

9 [April]. Moscow is experiencing the plundering of churches. The soviet government, as always, is cruel and stupid. In sum, some further accumulation of hatred is occurring; the church will be elevated higher from the persecution, and the government will rob the last public treasure reserve. From my point of view, all this is for the better.

All has grown still before the conference. Everyone is conjecturing about what will happen. The bolsheviks seem to have stopped making any further concessions for the time being. It is possible that the cause is

[27] The Eleventh Party Congress met from March 27 to April 2. Got'e refers to Lenin's long "Political Report of the Central Committee," which was made on the morning of the first day of the congress. Lenin, *Sochineniia*, 3d ed., vol. 27, pp. 225–59.

[28] Letter of I. A. Il'in to Got'e, dated March 27, 1922. See Appendix, Letter 27.

[29] Letter from Got'e's Aunt Emma and Uncle Emil', dated February 20, 1922, Zurich. See Appendix, Letter 28.

[30] The 1914 *Baedeker* lists the restaurant of Pivato Frères, Morskaia 36.

the expectation of what will happen in Genoa, where they have gone with a pile of absurd counterproposals. Among the rumors that are nevertheless circulating, it is interesting to note the persistent reports of an uprising in Turkestan, where the bolsheviks are reaping the fruit of their policies. It is too bad that as a result all the Russians there may be slaughtered.[31]

Moscow has never been so dirty as it is now, thanks to the slow and tedious spring.

Bread is 120,000; everything else in accordance; gold [.....] are 12,000 [sic]. Today I finished with all my job responsibilities and tomorrow we are all going to Pestovo for ten days.

10–20 April spent in Pestovo. We arrived almost in wintertime. Damp weather, a lot of snow, fog; freezing at night. We are leaving in full summer. Sun, 25 degrees in the daytime; 7–8 degrees above at night. We have dinner on the balcony, and we take walks not only without an overcoat, but today even in nothing but a shirt. The last snows are thawing before our eyes, the sleepy frogs are crawling out, the larks are singing, the butterflies are fluttering. While the streams were big, Volod'ka and I busied ourselves with various hydraulic installations; now "I sit in the sun all day" and warm myself like a good old tomcat. I sleep well, and my heart is calm, since as long as I am here I don't give a hang. I am gathering energy for the spring season.

The principal delight is that ten days are being spent in complete isolation from "general conditions." It is as if there were no bolsheviks at all, as if there were no Genoa Conference, either. Everything has temporarily faded away somewhere. There is only one desire: to go away somewhere as far as possible from it all; to go far, far away to the seashore, to the south where there is sun and warmth—not the transient pleasure that one gets in this stupid country with its stupid climate, but nature's constant blessing. To the devil with all the politics and all the nervous strain that again await [us] in Moscow. Everything we have received here gives us strength for further struggle and activity, and many may justifiably envy us.

24 [April]. Immersion in conversations about the Genoa Conference upon arrival in Moscow. The conclusion of the Russo-German agreement has

---

[31] Got'e refers to the recent activities of the Basmachi, the Islamic nationalist bands that had been fighting against the Bolsheviks in Central Asia since 1917. United under Enver Pasha, who had come to the region in 1921, they took over a considerable part of Turkestan in the spring of 1922. Fighting against the bolsheviks continued through most of the year, and the movement was not entirely liquidated until after the turn of the decade.

horrified some and made others joyful.[32] No one knows what is really happening in Genoa, because it is impossible to believe what they write in their newspapers. All the same they are lying, repeating, and explaining endlessly. Personally I *senza sperare vivo in disio*—I am waiting to see what will happen and how this will affect our fate.

MAY

1 [May]. I have again not written for a whole week. This has happened because there were scholarly meetings four evenings in a row. Two of them were devoted to analysis of Vipper's book about Ivan the Terrible.[33] The book is interesting, although it has defects. But even more interesting is its author—an undoubtedly gifted man, but a hysterical old woman in religious, or antireligious, matters, which are the same thing in this case. After thirty years of preoccupation with the implanting of socialism in Russia, he has become a patriot of the most conservative type and is trying, apparently, to make up for what has been ruined—for, as he himself said, he regrets the old Russia, in whose downfall he took a hand.

Two evenings were devoted to construction meetings, as there are no more shelves for books in the Rumiantsev Museum, and we had intended to build a new book depository.[34] This is insanity, of course, but the affair must be carried through to conclusion in order to relieve ourselves of any responsibility. It is characteristic that 75 billion have been allotted for the work, but it turns out that 250 are needed. Will Narkompros allot them? Not likely. But in my opinion it was right to pursue the matter to the end. In addition, I was busy with an arbitration suit between N. I. Polianskii[35] and Il'in—an affair that could only have occurred on our shaky soil.

The general situation is such: they have been given an ultimatum in Genoa. The answer has not yet been made public. If the affair blows up they will get out of it with the agreement with Germany. I don't expect large results from it, but even small ones will not soon be felt. If they

[32] Got'e refers to the Treaty of Rapallo between Soviet Russia and Germany, which was signed on April 16, 1922. The treaty provided for resumption of normal diplomatic relations between the two countries, most-favored-nation treatment, and mutual renunciation of all claims.

[33] *Ivan Groznyi* (Moscow, 1922). Robert Iur'evich Vipper (1859–1954) was professor of world history at Moscow University from 1899 to 1922. He lived in Latvia during most of the interwar years, returning to Moscow in 1941. Vipper was a prolific and wide-ranging scholar who wrote books on the history of classical civilization, the history of Christianity, and historical epistomology, among other things.

[34] See Figure 9.

[35] This may have been Nikolai Nikolaevich Polianskii (b. 1878), a law professor.

agree, they will deceive their opponents further, and the affair will require new attempts at resolution that cannot be foreseen now. Today they held a big demonstration on the occasion of the first of May, with a Red Oath of Allegiance for the army.[36] Beautiful weather. I am sitting at home the whole day and see some frenzied youths with blank faces and red flags, wiping the sweat from the heat, who pass from time to time in small detachments. However, there was, and perhaps still is, a definite animation in the city. They are trying to impart a grand sweep to the demonstration in order to influence Genoa and Europe generally. We will be informed about the results of the conflict only on Wednesday, when the first newspaper appears—regardless of whether they have broken off or agreed.

I came across several issues of *Temps*[37] for March; I was amazed how well they are informed there about our affairs. How pleasant to read a newspaper for all men. Reading it, how one wishes to shake off the dust and fly off far, far away. Will that ever come to pass? Now I have only one clearly expressed desire in life—not to die without having been abroad.

The rise in prices seems to have declined for the time being: bread is 120–130,000; *ryzhiki*, as they now call gold coins, are 24 "lemons."[38]

From the first of May the streetcar is 100,000 per station. The railroads have been raised to unheard of proportions.

7 [May]. Genoa has not fallen through yet, but nothing will come of it. There will be a rupture, a general one, but, as the bolsheviks say themselves, they will try to make a deal with each separately, with England and Italy in particular. They say the English capitalists are investing money in German industry. That would explain the policy *de ce maquignon de Lloyd George.*[39] Russia will be milked and exploited by English money and German resources. The only question is, what will come of it. France's position may not be shaken by this, since she has the United States and Japan standing behind her, not counting the Little Entente.[40] But things are no better for Russia from all that, and our situation does not improve. On the contrary, from all this muddle the idea of a great-

[36] The first Soviet oath of allegiance for the armed forces had been adopted in March 1918.

[37] The liberal Paris newspaper.

[38] A ryzhik is a kind of small, reddish mushroom. A "lemon" (*limon*) was a popular ironic corruption of "million" (*million*).

[39] Lloyd George's policy toward Germany concerning reparations and other postwar arrangements was generally conciliatory.

[40] The treaty alliance between Czechoslovakia, Yugoslavia, and Rumania, consummated in 1920–1921 to forestall restoration of the Austro-Hungarian Empire.

power Russia will fade more and more, the more so that it is in no one's interest to restore her from without, but all are ready to milk her last juices. The bolsheviks are trying the patriarch.[41] This is a moment of enormous importance for the Russian church. They will either leave him in peace or execute him. If they don't execute him, it will only be out of fear of Europe, and they don't fear everyone, but only those with whom they have to do business and those who are needed by them. Germany, our main enemy, will not intercede for the patriarch. Will both Anglo-Saxon powers, or either one of them, do this? That is the whole question, to which I would not dare to give an affirmative answer. His own people will not stand up for the patriarch, either, for the Russian muzhik, who alone in Russia has yet to be destroyed, doesn't give a damn about the patriarch, as he didn't give a damn about the tsar. Find a way out of that situation! There is no way out; Russia will remain a corpse, and there is only one logical solution—to break away from the once dear but now stinking corpse and try to find a new fatherland, for it is impossible to live without a fatherland.

8 [May]. Eleven death sentences have been delivered in the first church trial.[42] No one expected that. It produces a painful and onerous impression. It means that everything remains as before and nothing has changed. They remain the same and have once again bared their teeth. There is probably a definite aim here—persecution of the church. I think the next question is the destruction of the patriarch[ate] and the entire hierarchy of the Russian church. How is all this to be reconciled with the desire to establish relations with Europe?

16 [May]. I haven't written because this whole week was somehow especially full of agitation, and in the evenings I was hurrying to finish my

---

[41] On May 5, the Moscow Revolutionary Tribunal ordered the trial of Patriarch Ti-khon (Belavin) on a series of charges of anti-Soviet behavior, conspiracy to overthrow Soviet power, etc. The principal indictment resulted from the patriarch's appeal to the faithful on February 28 to oppose removal of major church treasures by the government, ostensibly for use in famine relief. The investigation of the case continued until June 1923, when it was turned over to the Supreme Court of the RSFSR. On June 16, 1923, the patriarch wrote to the court, admitting his guilt, vowing loyalty to the Soviet regime in the future, and asking for his release. The court postponed the case and released Tikhon, and in the spring of 1924 the case was dismissed altogether. See John Shelton Curtiss, *The Russian Church and the Soviet State, 1917–1950* (Boston, 1953).

[42] In April and May, the Moscow Revolutionary Tribunal tried seventeen churchmen on the issue of withholding church treasure. Eleven of them were sentenced to death on May 7; six were pardoned, but five, including Anatolii Petrovich Orlov (1879–1922), rector of the Theological Academy, were actually executed. The indictment of the patriarch, who appeared as a witness at this trial, ensued from it.

course on archaeology and frequently sat up until late at night. The priests have so far not been executed, and there is hope that they will not be killed. But on the other hand, a great general danger is looming over the church, and the bolsheviks have apparently succeeded in provoking a schism in it. A group of churchmen, for the most part not of clerical origin—hysterics, charlatans, and scoundrels, such as S. Kalinovskii, my one-time student at the Polivanov Gymnasium, or the popular preacher from Petrograd Vvedenskii, who is all but a lecher, or madmen such as "Father Ivan" from the Church of St. Tikhon at the Arbat Gates (apparently honored by the cook Masha), and led by Bishop Antonin, who is all but a syphilitic—have taken it upon themselves to found a new church, leaning on the bolsheviks.[43] And the bolsheviks, with their help, will create a new red church and depose the patriarch. This can be expected in the near future.

The bolsheviks are simply making a mockery of Genoa, and the whole thing is hanging onto existence only from the efforts *de ce maquignon de Lloyd George*.

23 [May]. Calme plat. The conference has collapsed. They are now busy with the trial of the srs[44] and, it seems, of the church as well. But the intrigue of Vvedenskii and Kalinovskii and co. also seems to be collaps-

[43] Got'e refers to the Renewal (*Obnovlenie*) or Living Church movement, which preached the compatibility of socialism and Christianity and the need for reform of the church. The Obnovlentsy had supported surrender of church treasures for famine aid and had testified against the opposing churchmen in the 1922 trials; in 1923 they called a church council that dismissed Tikhon from office and elected a Supreme Church Administration to replace the patriarch. As Tikhon and his followers did not submit to the ruling of this council, the result was a second schism in the Russian Orthodox Church. The Soviet government gave some support to the Renewal movement but never completely surpressed the patriarchal church. Eventually, the patriarchal church regained predominance and a degree of cooperation from the state under Tikhon's successor, the Locum Tenens Metropolitan Sergii, who was finally elected patriarch by a church council in 1943 with Stalin's blessing.

Sergei Vasil'evich Kalinovskii (1886–193?) was a Moscow priest with a history of political activism, first on the right and then on the left. In 1919 he had tried to form a Workers' and Peasants' Christian-Socialist party. He was a founder and editor of the liberal movement's journal, *The Living Church* (*Zhivaia tserkov'*). Before the end of 1922, he had left the church and become a professional antireligious propagandist. Aleksandr Ivanovich Vvedenskii (1889–1946) was the central intellectual figure in the Renewal movement. He had graduated from Petersburg University before becoming a priest there. Bishop Antonin (Aleksandr Andreevich Granovskii [b. 1860]) was a learned monastic clergyman. He became Bishop of Narva in the Petersburg eparchy in 1903.

[44] On February 27, 1922, the gpu announced a forthcoming trial of those srs who had been members of the Central Committee, plus other individuals in the sr party, on charges of crimes allegedly committed against the Soviet state during the Civil War. The trial of thirty-four srs was held from June 8 to August 7, 1922.

ing. At yesterday's meeting in the conservatory, Vvedenskii, they say, was almost not allowed to speak. *Supposedly* Antonin himself has disavowed them. I remember Kalinovskii as a student of the Polivanov Gymnasium. I gave him a "D." He was a stupid, slippery urchin with a repulsive mug, who could be seen in the Cathedral of Christ the Savior in a surplice putting hassocks under the bishops' feet. Later he became a priest of a pronounced black-hundreds-intriguing type. By the natural course of evo- and revo-lution, he is now a revolutionary-bolshevik priest. And such people are coming to be in charge of the church! However, everything must perish in this country, including the church.

27 [May]. The calme plat continues. The basic feature of the present moment is a complete lack of money. No one anywhere is receiving a salary. According to rumors, the bolsheviks have decided to improve their affairs by this means. But the ability to buy is being lost from the lack of currency, and all business is at a standstill; prices have even gotten a little cheaper, but they have gotten cheaper from lack of demand. A. N. Bernshtein has died.[45] I could never understand what came over him and the so-called Aktsentr, where he was for a long time Glivenko's assistant.[46] Was it really only to study in practice how madmen pretend to be sane?

31 [May]. The calme plat continues. There are no rumors, or very few, or they are such that they are not even worth remembering. The lack of money also continues. I got out of a very difficult situation only by selling the first part of the archaeology course I have written for twelve million a printer's sheet. That will allow me to exist for three months. The extent to which the bolsheviks failed in Genoa is now becoming clear. It is perfectly clear that they are sitting in their dead end and cannot get out of it; but the affair is once again going nowhere, and it again seems to us that all this is immutable and endless, and again there is anguish and a feeling of hopelessness, and again, as never before, the wish to get out of here. Shchepkin, Leont'ev, Filat'ev, and Mel'gunov—that is, the main figures of the Tactical Center—have been arrested. The same old story.[47]

[45] A. N. Bernshtein was a neurologist and psychiatrist.

[46] The Academic Center (Akademicheskii tsentr) was attached to Narkompros. Ivan Ivanovich Glivenko (1868–1931) was a historian of European literature, an Italian specialist, who was a professor at Moscow University and a member of the Academy of Arts (and later of RANION).

[47] Shchepkin, Leont'ev, and Mel'gunov had received ten-year prison terms in the Tactical Center trial in August 1920, but they had been amnestied and released in 1921. G. V. Filat'ev was a Menshevik member of the Union for the Resurrection of Russia, one of the constituent elements of the Tactical Center.

JUNE

1–4 [June] in Pestovo. Again several days in the fresh air and the country. The contrast between the outrageousness of human life and the serenity of nature invariably astonishes me every time; it astonished me this time as well. I left under the confused impression of the new arrests carried out in Moscow, whose victims were again Shchepkin, Leont'ev, and several others. Now (I received this news here already through G. M. Leont'ev)[48] they are saying that they were arrested in order to deport them abroad. If that is true, it is a new orientation that should be exploited as soon as it reveals itself more clearly. You have to leave, otherwise you will be an accomplice in the crime and won't speak your piece, however weak and insignificant it may be, in regard to the mockery to which Russia has been subjected. And the mockery continues, persistently and incorrigibly. They have, after all, killed five priests, including the kind and respected A. P. Orlov, simply because he was the rector of the theological academy. The remark on this account by the scoundrel and renegade Galkin was a good one: he declared that the death of the five priests was a good warning to the counterrevolution in cassocks. They plundered the church and, having plundered it, betrayed it—to those Galkins, Kalinovskiis, and co. There is persistent and insistent talk that Lenin has a very advanced stage of progressive paralysis. A fine finale for the leader of the Russian revolution—the best and most appropriate possible. He is dying of syphilis after having infected and ruined all Russia with syphilis.

15–20 June. Petrograd. I traveled third class. I was disenchanted at first; then it turned out that a whole bench was at my disposal; there were few people and a lot of fresh air. I spent the five days in Petrograd with the customary pleasantness and cordial welcome. Among the business matters: a discussion about cutting back the staff of the Academy of the History of Material Culture; delivery of a package of books for the Rumiantsev Museum; and arrangement for publication of my *Archaeology* by Brokgauz and Efron.[49] I did all the business; I received 100 million, but couldn't change it upon arriving home. The white nights in Petersburg with a view on the violet Peter and Paul Fortress from my window was charming. I sat and strolled until 3–4 A.M. with Farmakovskii and Shileiko.[50] Once there was even a small orchestra in one of the first-floor

[48] This was probably S. M. Leont'ev's brother.

[49] The book was finally published in 1925: Iu. V. Got'e, *Ocherki po istorii material'noi kul'tury Vostochnoi Evropy do osnovaniia pervogo russkogo gosudarstva. I. Kamennyi vek. Bronzovyi vek. Zheleznyi vek na iuge Rossii* (Leningrad: Brokgauz-Efron, 1925).

[50] Boris Vladimirovich Farmakovskii (1870–1928) was a prominent archaeologist, a specialist on ancient cultures of the Black Sea littoral. Vol'demar Kazimirovich Shileiko

drawing rooms: Farmakovskii turned out to be an excellent musician. I returned in second class with hard benches, but I slept well and again had a whole bench.

20[?] [June]. I slipped through Moscow; Verochka came for me; she went for purchases and tickets, and I sat home in order to avoid the Rumiantsev Museum.

20 June–3 July. Pestovo. Rest, complete oblivion, then gradual penetration of Moscow rumors. There are few apparent changes. As for events, only the murder of Rathenau, it seems from the communist side.[51] I think it is not a minus for us if there is one less talented German Jew. The trial of the SRs is dragging on further and will likely drag on for a long time yet. Here you somehow forget all this, and only one thought keeps repeating itself—how to go abroad. If it would only turn out to be possible next year. Here there is enough anguish, anarchy, and confusion for many years. The needle is moving, but slowly and unevenly. If only one could rest and come to one's self. But here there are mushrooms, swimming, and good air; it is, of course, a surrogate, but not a bad one.

2 July. My birthday—forty-nine years old, and I have to construct my life all over again. The news brought from Moscow doesn't change the general picture. In The Hague the bolsheviks are being boorish as usual, and just as little will probably come from these meetings as from Genoa. There is panic in the museum over the staff cutback, and they even summoned me from here. But I couldn't find the strength to go.

9 July. A week spent in Moscow. I have not experienced anything so nightmarish for a long time. The staff cutback, in the first place: we had to throw out eighty-nine people. I have never performed a baser or more vile act in my life. The awareness of the injustice [of it all] and the awareness of the intentional and unintentional injustices that you commit in the process; and, most importantly, the awareness that this action is the beginning of the destruction of the library, which will now proceed uninterruptedly; yet with it the demands that will be made on it and the responsibility that will lie on me will grow steadily. Whence the conclusion—it is necessary to save oneself. It is all the more necessary to save oneself since the situation in which we find ourselves is dragging on endlessly and, therefore, the hope that I nurtured for five whole years—to

---

(1891–1930) was an Assyriologist and a poet, and a professor at Petrograd University from 1922 until his death.

[51] Walther Rathenau, the German foreign minister, was assassinated on June 24, 1922, by right-wing nationalists.

bring the library to some kind of logical end point, where I might say "Lord, now lettest thou thy servant depart in peace. ... For mine eyes have seen thy salvation"[52]—that possibility, I am now convinced, is fading completely. It is hard to work; there is no hope at all ahead for improvement of this work, and at the same time it threatens to fill up everything and leave no room for anything else. The risk of responsibility is growing; one can lose one's health at this as well. This means I must leave, but leave intelligently and carefully. The next few months must be devoted to this. At the same time, I must begin to think practically about how to get out of Russia, and it is easier to leave from an unresponsible post than from a responsible one.

There is nothing new in regard to general matters; all the same boredom, unless one counts the new hecatomb that the bolsheviks want to make of the Petrograd church trial, where eleven men, headed by the metropolitan, have again been sentenced to death.[53]

The week spent in Moscow was also difficult because there was a terrible, suffocating heat. Never has that cloaca seemed so unbearable to me.

Pestovo, 16 July. Again a week in Moscow and two days in Pestovo. The same worries again in Moscow, although perhaps to a lesser degree than in the preceding week. I recognize that my activity in the Rumiantsev Museum as one of its administrators will no longer be useful. So long as I thought that I was protecting the library for a better time, I was patient. Now I see that this patience will have to be prolonged to the day of my death, which will come even sooner than it ought to owing precisely to the constant nervous strain, the tension, and the unending minor nervous irritation. And all this to no end, *car tout cela durera bien autant que nous*, and we can only look into the past "with the bitter gibe of the deceived son at his profligate father."[54] Everything is changing around us, but when the Russian social organism finishes the digestion of the undigestible substances of the revolution, it will already be too late for us. Whence the conclusion that it is necessary to leave before we are thrown out with shame.

We visited Golder. He is no less interesting than Coolidge, even livelier than he is. A proposal to ship off my materials; I think I will accept

---

[52] Got'e quotes the opening of the canticle known as the Song of Simeon (or *Nunc dimittis*), Luke 2:29–32.

[53] The verdict handed down on July 5 in the Petrograd church trial, which was similar to the one of April–May in Moscow, actually condemned ten men to death, of whom four, including Metropolitan Veniamin, were in fact executed; some eighty others received lighter punishments.

[54] "Nasmeshkoi gor'koiu obmanutogo syna / Nad promotavshimsia otsom": the last two lines of Lermontov's poem "Duma" (1838).

it. This may yield a turning point in my plans for the future; in any case, it will save the materials.[55] We will have to leave Pestovo on Sunday, since tomorrow the potatoes in the garden have to be weeded. However, that task is better than activity in the Rumiantsev Museum. The general situation is without change. They are wrecking The Hague Conference just as certainly as they wrecked the Genoa [Conference].[56] Complications in Germany are accumulating.

23 July. Pestovo. Life in Moscow is so agitated that it is impossible to write anything. Moreover, it is so stuffy in the rooms that the brain is numbed and refuses to work. In general affairs, rumors, and mood there is the former lull and ennui. They are negotiating lazily in The Hague, are doggedly trying the SRs, and have stopped talking about Lenin's health. My mood is foul, almost exclusively because of the Rumiantsev Museum, toward which I am again experiencing the feeling I already experienced in 1908–10—the internal atmosphere has grown so dense that one wants to flee, no matter where. I don't remember if I wrote in my notes about how I was arbitrarily excluded from the categories of qualified scholars that were established back in December 1921. The Moscow Kubu (Commission for Improving the Living Conditions of Scholars) included me, on an equal footing with my colleagues (Liubavskii, Kizevetter, Bogoslovskii, Iakovlev), in the fourth category, which is defined as "outstanding." But later, all the qualifications underwent a new scrutiny in the Central Kubu, where Pokrovskii is in command, and the members are Volgin, Glivenko, and others unknown to me, and the defenders of our interests are Pavlov for the natural [sciences][57] and Bogoslovskii for the humanities. And there, at Pokrovskii's insistence, supported by Volgin and Glivenko, Egorov, Iakovlev, and I among the historians were demoted to the third [category], and Bogoslovskii and Liubavskii were promoted to the fifth. I have nothing against their promotion, nor that of many others, it seems—for example, the clever Ukrainian[58] Petrushevskii—and I resolved firmly not to react to that in any way, both because it would be useless and because I consider it unworthy of me. But it is interesting for the general picture that is taking shape from fragmentary

[55] See the Introduction. Got'e refers here to the diary and the letters he had appended to it.

[56] The Hague Conference (June 15–July 19, 1922), agreed upon at Genoa, included all the participants in the Genoa Conference except Germany. It continued discussion of the Russian agenda—debts and claims—without result.

[57] Aleksei Petrovich Pavlov (1854–1929), a geologist, had been professor of natural sciences at Moscow University since 1886. In 1916, he was elected to the Academy of Sciences.

[58] *Khitrogo khokhla.* Petrushevskii was born and educated in Kiev.

accounts about what is happening in Tsekubu.[59] It turns out that places had to be cleared for their own, for bolsheviks, and so it turns out that I am worse than Veselovskii, and Egorov is worse than Petrushevskii. (They are saying, but I don't know it for sure yet, that even Kizevetter has been demoted to the third category.) In regard to myself personally, however, I strongly suspect that I was demoted for my *Time of Troubles*, which earned me the active disfavor of Pokrovskii. I heard just such an opinion from another party. If it is so, that only does me honor. I have written this down here because I consider the whole affair typical for our time.

[59] The Central Commission for Improving the Living Conditions of Scholars.

Appendix

*

Letter 1

Paper submitted 1 September 1918
Append to sheet 11 of the notes.

To the Moscow Extraordinary Commission for Combatting Counterrevolution, Crimes of Office, and Speculation

From Citizen Iurii Vladimirovich Got'e, residing in the First Tver' Commissariat at Bol'shoi Znamenskii Pereulok, No. 4.

Petition.

Upon arriving in Moscow from the leave granted me for the summer vacation period of 1918, which I spent within the boundaries of Tver' province, I was apprised by the building committee of the fact that the Moscow Extraordinary Commission for Combatting Counterrevolution, Crimes of Office, and Speculation (Speculation Department) has assessed me a fine of ten thousand rubles for the acquisition in April of this year of one pud and five pounds of sugar outside the rules established for receiving sugar; moreover, it was indicated in the paper sent to the building committee that the mentioned fine is being assessed against those who obtained the sugar as representatives of the bourgeois class.

I consider it my present duty to explain that I live exclusively by my personal labor, having supported my own existence and that of my family for twenty-five years only by a salary received for personal labor and service. I have never exploited the labor of others and have never engaged in any kind of speculative enterprises; at the present time I am working in soviet institutions. I have never had and do not at present have any kind of outside nonlabor sources of income nor any savings, such as a current account or the like.

These circumstances make it entirely impossible for me to pay the fine leveled against me and in addition give me grounds—as a person not belonging to the nonlaboring bourgeoisie and, as the attached attestations show, in the service of the RSFSR—to request the Extraordinary Commission to review the decision taken in my regard and to annul the fine assessed against me.

If the commission does not find it possible to annul the fine against me completely, I request its reduction and payment of it through monthly deductions from the salary I receive for service in Moscow State University and the Moscow Rumiantsev Museum, which constitutes my only means of existence.

I attach herewith attestion no. 2174 of Moscow University, and no. 436 of the Moscow Rumiantsev Museum.

Letter 2

[Letter of Nina Nikolaevna Got'e to Got'e, dated August 26 (September 8) 1918, Zagran'e.]

To 15 September

Dear Iurochka,

More than ever, we should be together in order to resolve all the questions with which life is confronting us. It is hard to communicate by letters. I will try to be logical. Upon receiving your letter, I thought for a long time about what to do: of course, if it were not for Volodiushka, there would be no question—I would rush to you immediately, but seeing how he eats an egg with pleasure in the morning and drinks a minimum of a pot of milk a day, I am determined to stay a little longer—perhaps until the 21st or 22d. I don't know if I can hold out any longer.

As for sending packages to Moscow, the situation has gotten significantly more difficult. A.S. returned the package I sent yesterday with a polite note that as of yesterday acceptance of any edible packages is forbidden by the Supply Division, and permission of the township Committee of the Poor is required to send any (at least until the 1st). After talking with Lena, I am determined to go there and present a petition, although I have no faith in success. What I should do with Lial'ka is a problem. I am writing a letter to A. Gr. today.

Thus there will be no food coming from Zagran'e, the more so that Volkov reported yesterday as well that one of the soviet bosses told him that bread (of any kind—rye, oat, wheat, barley) will be confiscated by armed force, except for twelve puds per person per year; food products as a whole will be left, of course, only for those who will be present, so that Zagran'e will do us no good in the near future. The only way out is for me to sit here until the census so that they would leave us thirty-six puds, but considering the uncertainty of its time I will not likely wait it out.

In regard to the sugar story, I hope that it has been liquidated in a way that is beneficial for us.

Now about the apartment: I am infinitely sorry for Tania and I sincerely envy their leaving. We will not be touched as long as you occupy your positions. And if we move anywhere, it should not be in order to wander about Russia, but to go to Siberia or best of all to blessed France—I have reached the end of my rope, too, and sincerely sympathize with you. I would not give it a second thought (you can always find a crust of bread in France with the help of your friends) if it weren't for my parents, whom I cannot leave in this nightmare—my soul would never rest. But it would certainly be best for Volodia to remove him somewhere far away—the endless talk of hunger and possible disorders produce a very negative effect. When I told him yesterday that we are staying for the time being in Zagran'e, he answered me: "It is good here, but isn't Papa alone?" The endless disorder and upset affect him, too.

I think that if the Frenchmen haven't left Russia yet, it would be good to put up two of them in our rooms (I don't want Germans *no matter what*). Perhaps they could also help us out with food—they manage to get something. We will have to rent, of course, without meals and preferably to men.

Another thought has occurred to me that you, perhaps, share. If the Kurdiumovs are not in line for a state apartment, shouldn't we join up with them? We have a certain amount of flour, and they, it is true, will have a state ration of food products. The cost of food should be divided, insofar as possible, proportionately to the number of mouths. We would provide the apartment, sharing it like this: they would get the bedroom and the children's room. We would set up in the study—a bedroom for me and Volodia with a corner for him; and in the living room—a study with a couch for you. The dining room would be a common room. The children will probably enroll in Gymnasium and will study their lessons in the evening. If possible, we should hire a French girl in common for two or three hours when you are home, so it will be a little quieter. This, of course, is only a proposal that should be very thoroughly discussed. Think about it yourself, and talk with Mama privately. There is the problem, of course, of the servant (Masha could be made only a cook without being involved in the rooms). This scheme will not work, either, if the Kurdiumovs want to hire someone for the children; it would be literally impossible to stick him anywhere. The advantages of such a merger, it seems to me, are: (1) having one's own people in the house, (2) taking meals together, (3) sharing a French girl and a servant, (4) helping Mama, who is wearing herself out, I think, without a corner of her own. The minuses are: (1) living with Mitia (although he is not likely to be home often), (2) eating up our reserves faster with such a big family, (3) a house full of people, (4) more trouble for me, thanks to Lelia's helplessness with the children, although if Iura and T. are in Gymnasium, the problem will be significantly simpler, (5) Mitia's solvency. Think about it. Of course, our life will be complicated by such a scheme, but perhaps we should join forces in order to feed ourselves more easily and to double up with our own people. There will be no unpleasantness, I hope, with Lelia. Of course, you may utterly destroy my arguments, but since I won't be able to talk with you for a long time, I am writing you what I would say in person. The best for us, of course, would be to rent the rooms to the Frenchmen. The second scheme is also a solution.

I feel all right. I am not eating any potatoes at all. I am on a diet of mushrooms, beans, and kasha, which I have found on the estate. There is nowhere to buy meat; there are almost no eggs—only enough for Volodia, and occasionally I make fried eggs; the cows give little—they have stopped milking three of them. My spirits are low, like everyone else's—my thoughts are almost always in Moscow.

I end for the time being, my dear. I embrace you and ours warmly. Write something about Papa. Did you ask at the university shop about potatoes?

Your Nina

26 August 1918

Letter 3

[Letter of V. Bok to Got'e, dated September 12, 1918, Novgorod.]

To 16 September

Deeply Respected Iurii Vladimirovich:

I was not in Novgorod when your telegram arrived, and that is why I am able to write you only today.

Vladimir Vladimirovich, thank God, is alive and well, but remains under guard. A day or two before the Moscow assassination attempt and the Petrograd murder, the case of your brother, and also that of the assistant procurator Troitskii and others, were sent from the Extraordinary Commission for Combatting Counterrevolution to the tribunal, which intended to free all the prisoners. But then the events in Moscow and Petersburg struck,[1] and all the cases were hastily recalled to the Extraordinary Commission. And on the following morning six persons were shot, including my professional associate, poor V. A. Troitskii. One competent person, whom you also visited here in connection with your brother's case, told me that by some happy accident Vladimir Vladimirovich's case was not returned then to the Extraordinary Commission and it is

[1] The assassination attempt on Lenin in Moscow and the assassination of M. S. Uritskii, the head of the Petrograd Cheka, in Petrograd, both occurred on August 30, 1918.

possibly only thanks to that that Vladimir Vladimirovich, by God's will, was not the seventh victim.

The same person advised me (I went to him about the possibility of freeing the hostages, numbering sixty persons, including our former procurator) to wait a little until the excitement in high places over the Moscow (and Petrograd) events subsides, and then it will be possible to take measures in the Extraordinary Commission toward freeing the prisoners on bail. At present two merchants and one officer have already been freed on bail of 3,000–5,000 rubles. In the Extraordinary Commission everything depends on its chairman; at present that post is occupied by a local man, one Alekseev, a student. They told me that he is a man with a head on his shoulders and good sense, and far from cruel. Therefore, in my opinion, you ought to leave again for Novgorod and take all measures here for freeing your brother. Unfortunately, all efforts of outsiders, nonrelatives, are looked on here as interference in the affairs of others and are therefore completely useless.

I have just learned that the local barrister Bogoliubov, one of the hostages, has been freed on bail. Your brother is not on the list of hostages, but it is clear that he was not released in good time only because of the events that occurred in the capitals. I think your presence in Novgorod and your efforts are extremely necessary, and the sooner the better. I of course consider it my duty to help you in any way I can.

Please accept my assurance of most sincere devotion and respect.

V. Bok

Novgorod, 12 September 1918.

Letter 4

[Letter of Nina Nikolaevna Got'e to Got'e, dated August 28 (September 10) 1918, Zagran'e.]

To 20 September

28 August

Dear Iurochka,

Although there is nothing special to write about, I want to talk with you, if only on paper. The weather today is revolting! It is cold, five degrees, and rain all day. My mood matches the weather.

Lena and Mania paid a visit to the Committee [of Village Poor], which, contrary to their somber expectations, came off very successfully. Both the commandants of Krasnyi Kholm were being hounded by the township: they had wanted to take the best horses and remove the furniture from the estates for messieurs commissars—it was all rejected. They say they have driven the Kaliteevskiis from their estate and looted their property. Perhaps Zagran'e is threatened with the same fate?! Sometimes I am overwhelmed by gloomy thoughts. Heeding them, I am going to send off tomorrow eight sheets, your white suit, and some other things as well. Something unpleasant is in the air, and at times I am terrified over the future of this place. I bought twenty-six pounds of butter at 13.50 a pound per wheel, and Lesha Blagoveshchenskii wants to send them off by fair means or foul. If it doesn't work out now, then maybe after a while.

At times I seriously have the idea of joining up with Mama for dinner for economy's sake. Perhaps it would be easier for them in a material sense, too. We could feed ourselves in the morning and evening. Perhaps I had better talk about this [with her] myself.

Iu. L. is writing desparate letters—but frequently a note is struck that makes it seem she is worse off than anyone else. Lena intends to pull some strings and take some food with her to Moscow for her on the 16th. I want to go with her, but I am forcing myself not to think about that, to hold on for another week for Volodia's sake. I don't know if your brother has been completely released? In that case he will certainly come to Zagran'e, and I will leave with the same horses.

If the affair with the sugar isn't liquidated, shouldn't you call Lena Reiman and settle with them for a while? It seems there is nowhere else to go.

Oh, what I would give to be with you right now. I often get the idea of leaving for somewhere very far away, but where?!!

I am going to sleep—it is 11 o'clock. My itch isn't bothering me *at all*, and I have been sleeping better for several nights.

I embrace you warmly, my dear. Kiss our dear ones. Bus'ka thinks of you often.

Your Nina

The poor Wilkens. Iu. L. wrote that the store is being inventoried. What will they live on?

Letter 5

[Letter of Nina Nikolaevna Got'e to Got'e, dated August 31 (September 12) 1918, Zagran'e.]

To 21 September 1918

12 September

Dear Iurochek!

It is ten years today that we are together, and you are dearer to me now than you were then. Today I am thinking especially often of you and of the environment we were in then, especially that pure, moonlit night when we went along the white road to Sebastopol. No, it can't be that we will never again experience southern nights! I have just returned with Volodia from the play given by the Zagranians—it was a kind of marionette theater; the children liked it very much. The play is being given over four evenings. We had supper with them beforehand. In general, we eat together frequently and are living harmoniously. We have decided to depart together with Lena on the 8th, probably for Rybinsk, so if you intend to go to the Reimans on the 8th and 9th, don't let our arrival hold you back. Go, it is better there than in Moscow. You write that you know I won't stay an extra day—I am doing this only for Volodia, who very much wants to stay a little longer in Zagran'e, and for whom every extra day is beneficial.

This morning we went with Lesha Blagoveshchenskii to send the butter; we sent off thirty-two pounds (including seven pounds belonging to Lial'ka). Tante Marie should not be surprised to receive such a pleasant package from A. P. Blagoveshchenskii. I picked her because she has a name that is unknown to Aleksandr Sergeevich. Warn her about this. As you know from my previous letter, all packages are prohibited without permission of the Committee of Poor, so the butter went as contraband. I am going to the committee in several days about these matters. The weather is not cheering. As if on purpose, good, dark nights with falling stars and rainy days. They milled the rye (seventy-six bushels) and the barley (twenty-four bushels), and put the quite wet wheat in the barn to save it from theft. Last night they stole fifteen sheaves of wheat from us. Today they began to harvest the oats, which will apparently not completely mature. The other day the Krasnyi Kholm commandant and commissar were at the meeting of the township committee; they announced that they need broken horses and the furniture from the estates. The township committee turned them down, but they informed the committee that they will do what they please. In addition, a hospital is being set up in Iur'ev. Thinking they will not hesitate to seize good linen, I took part to the mother-in-law and part to Aleks. Pavl. Perhaps we are after all fated to pass some more time in Zagran'e. Two beds, the dresser and the table, and part of the china have been given to the Obrastsovs.

Where are you right now (11 o'clock in the evening)? I kiss you firmly, my dear, in my thoughts and now I will soon do it in reality. I am writing for the last time. Why yes, you are celebrating today at the wedding. Drink, and forget everything!

I am very disturbed about Mama. Kiss them all for me. How happy I will be to see them.

Masha is after me to go as soon as possible, and is ready to leave for the village immediately.

Letter 6

[Letter of Princess M. M. Cherkasskaia to Got'e, dated September 19, 1918, Khar'kov.]

19 September 1918

Dear Iura,

We received your letter of July 22 a few days ago and were boundlessly joyful, since we have been thinking of our Moscow friends all the time and had had no news from anyone for God knows how long, so all kinds of notions had entered our heads. I was deeply touched that you remembered me on the 22d and I thank you for the [nameday] greetings. If only you knew how we both yearn for Moscow, how we would like to see and talk with those we have known and loved for so many years and who have become even closer to us in our days of bitterness and oppression.

I will not even speak of the degradation and destruction of our motherland: that is such a deep and painful wound that, it seems to me, it will never heal. How lucky is Natasha not to see nor feel the horror we are experiencing; what would have become of her now, she who always took everything so close to heart.

We are all alive, physically hale and healthy (although Belochka is growing very thin) to the extent that is possible at our very advanced age. L.N. is working, and I have had to take up the same old thing again: I give French lessons, but private ones and at my place, and I am glad that there are pupils, otherwise with the present high prices we would be badly off, insofar as we receive no pension since the 1st of March. What a misfortune to have served so many years and to have been left in old age without a crust of bread, since we have nothing at all except the pension. P.P. is also alive, but he is growing weak, which is not surprising since he is eighty-five.

We live very monotonously and modestly, we go almost nowhere, since our legs are bad and horses' legs are dear; that is, the coachmen are inaccessible. At least it is a good thing that we all live in the same house and while away the evenings together, otherwise we would have gone quite wild. We try to speak as little as possible about all the horrors that are occurring everywhere, since all our nerves are on edge, although things have gotten much calmer here since the *b.[olsheviks]* disappeared, at least you no longer fear going out on the street and being stripped as was the case earlier. How good that Zagran'e has survived, at least you have a refuge where you can rest. How I would like to get to you there; remember how we made arrangements about that with you and Nina at our last meeting? You wrote nothing about Lialia: where is he? How is he getting along? What is he doing? Hasn't he married?

Give Nina our greetings and a big kiss. We also permit ourselves as old ladies to warmly embrace you and give you a big, big kiss. May God protect you. Love,

M. Cherkasskaia

Send us a bit of news about yourself now and then. Are the Ramus[?] alive?

Letter 7

[Letter of Aleksandr Gartung to Got'e, undated but ca. May 6, 1919, Morshansk.]

Iurii,

I am taking advantage of the good offices of N. G. Tarasov to report that I have been living in Morshansk since January 6, after having lived until December 19 near the Sampur station in Tambov district at the medical-aid post in the village of L'vov. My wife has remained there, and our daughter is in the former Tambov Aleksandrovskii Institute; it is uncertain whether we will reunite or not. According to my information, my mother has successfully overcome the typhus. I worked as chairman of the Morshansk Commission on Juvenile Delinquents of the medical-sanitary division from January 16, but I was fired as of April 11 because I learned during a business trip to Tambov that there is no such official position. Not bad? At present I am the people's judge for major cases (which are tried by six jurymen).

My life is boring, boring, although I do have a little bit of a social life with a few people. I represent the defense in the revolutionary tribunal with success—imagine—so that the last time even the young ladies made eyes at me. In general, I live like a monk. Soviet power, in my opinion, has become firmly established for a long time—we will not outlive it. Things are bad with my priestly career, too: on the day of my confession to the rector of the former seminary in the Kazan' Monastery during the first week of Lent, Bishop Zinovii was naive enough to offer me a vacancy as a sexton.

How are you getting along, starving and freezing, how do you see the immediate prospects? My quasi-legal situation has turned out to be a complete myth. Send news of Moscow, using the same opportunity as I, that is, by means of N. G. Tarasov. Who is alive, who has died—I don't know anything. Let me know. My respects to Nina Nikolaevna. How is your heir (such irony)?

Yours,
A. Gartung

P.S. Come here to the teachers' courses or the people's university. This latter arranges lectures with debates, in which I usually participate, on Sundays in the summer theater. Last Sunday I had to chair a debate about the intelligentsia and the revolution. Next Sunday, May 11, I should be chairing at a lecture of the washedout half-Jew, G. O. Gordon,[2] on the origins of Christianity. The latter is the head of our division of popular education, very intelligent and interesting and, according to him, he knows you. If he doesn't know you, at least he assesses you correctly.

P.S.S. [sic] You are going to read this, be amazed, and, I think, say: only the grave will mend the hunchback—Sashka is still the same: a mixture of I. A. Khlestakov and F. P. Karamazov. *Do widzenia.*[3]

P.S.S.S. [sic] Rail travel is very fine now—you get lousy in an instant.

Once again, A. Gartung

My address: Morshansk, Pochtovaia St., house no. 55, apt. of K. I. Garshkis.

Letter 8

[Letter of Elizaveta L. Rar to Got'e, dated November 14, 1919, Moscow.]

To the Curator of the Rumiantsev Museum Library
Dear Iurii Vladimirovich,

Can't you find it possible to give me some new translation work, in view of the fact that I have worked for the museum earlier and at present have the time and am very much in need of earnings.

I can turn in the earlier work as soon as I get out of prison, as it is finished in draft.

If some information is needed or for discussions in general, please see my mother at my address in town.

With respect and thanks,

E. L. Rar

14 November 1919
Butyrskaia Prison
Women's Solitary no. 9

---

[2] G. O. Gordon was a philosopher, a disciple of Hermann Cohen. He apparently ended his days in the Solovki concentration camp.

[3] Polish: "Until we meet again."

Letter 9

[Letter of the Erofeevs to the Wilkens, no date, Kislovodsk.]

Dear, faraway friends, all the Wilkens,

Do you know where we are—in Kislovodsk! The cost was great (that is, not a kopeck of money, but in efforts, upsets, and nerves), but the goal has after all been achieved—we are in the south! We traveled for two months, less five days, from Saratov at first to Tsaritsyn in a wonderful cabin on a steamer, and then with a special train in a freight car, at sixteen persons per car; we lived for seven weeks on the bunks in the car. Sema is the assistant head of the 220nd military-construction detachment of the Caucasian front; I am the timekeeper of the same detachment (I am Gena Semenovna). Our detachment was sent here to repair all the local sanatoriums. We were first sent from Tikhoretskaia to Rostov/Don, from there again to Tikhoretskaia, then to Piatigorsk, and finally Sema was sent at the head of half the detachment to Kislovodsk. On the road we suffered especially from the water. We stopped for a week in Nal'chik and sometimes had to drink God knows what kind of water, half sand and silt; for example, we drank water from the Kuban' that was quite brown, like coffee. We stood for ten days in Rostov/Don on the freight tracks; human waste lay everywhere, and at that time there was cholera. We often found lice on ourselves, and it is not easy to wash oneself in a common car. Well yes, that is all past and we all reached Kislovodsk healthy, even grandmother, who never left the freight car.

What can be said of the towns we went through? Tsaritsyn, for example, is a completely dead town; there is only one carpenter for the whole of Tsaritsyn there, and not a single architect. Sema earned 8,000 in three days there. Rostov is a gay, noisy town, everyone is dressed up, there are flowers, music, free trade open to everyone, even in flour. All the medicine in the world. When we went through Armavir the first time, there was everything; the finest wheat flour cost 1,000 rubles a pud, and 800 at the bazaar. When we found ourselves in Armavir again two weeks later, free trade had been forbidden. In Kavkazskaia, Tikhoretskaia, in Armavir, everywhere, Sema was offered a job as architect for 14–15,000 with a free apartment and firewood, but we unreasonable ones were drawn to Kislovodsk, and quite in vain—there is a surplus of intelligentsia here, and prices are very dear: French bread costs 100 rubles a pound, the finest wheat flour 5,000, corn flour 2,000, manna 100 rubles, one pound of buckwheat groats is 100 rubles, rice is 200, barley groats and corn meal are 15 rubles; farmer's cheese is 60 rubles, butter is 400, mutton lard is 200, beef [lard] 280, milk is 50 rubles a bottle, beef is 100 rubles, mutton is 120, potatoes are 600 rubles a pud, apples are 50 rubles for ten, one pound of cabbage is 20 rubles, watermelons are 100 rubles, cherries 60 rubles, currants 50 rubles, eggplants are 10 rubles apiece for big ones, cucumbers are 50 to 100 rubles, honey is 300 rubles, sugar is 1,200 rubles, Swiss cheese is 300 rubles, and sausage is 200 rubles. Of course, we cannot make ends meet here, although Sema gets 7,000 and I get 6,000; moreover we both receive a half-pound of bread a day and the infirmary dinner: soup and kasha; supper is kasha only; one pound of sugar a month each; one pound of vegetable oil, occasionally meat. Mama and Mania also receive one pound of bread per day each, and the others a half-pound each. So we have enough bread and don't bake it; we cook on a kerosene stove or on a stove that the children built themselves in the garden. There is not much occasion to cook, because we always get plenty of soup and kasha, we buy the milk already boiled, and we always take fermented boiled milk, or sour milk, or farmer's cheese. There is running water and plumbing, and a fine toilet. The linen is washed for us by the infirmary steam laundry. All this makes life very easy and agreeable. They put us up, for free of course, in a fine dacha; they gave us two rooms with a balcony, a divine view of Elbrus, a garden full of roses, and a gate that opens directly into a park. Our detachment is repairing all the infirmaries and sanatoriums of Kislovodsk; here Sema is the head of the detachment, but unfortunately in a week they are making him head of the entire 220nd, not only of Kislovodsk, but also of Essentuk and Piatigorsk, and he will have to travel, but the salary will be only 500 rubles more. Life is agreeable in Kislovodsk: the streets are washed every day; a symphony orchestra plays every day for free from 6 to 9 o'clock; there are cafes and restaurants on every corner; on every streetcorner they sell *baranki*,[4] rolls, sweet rolls, kefir, sour milk; in the evening everything is bathed in electric light, it smells of Houbigant and Coty; every day there is a bazaar where you can get anything, there is no need for any reserves, there is even dry cleaning and dyeing. You ask yourself, why are we dissatisfied with this heaven?—because the only reasonable thing to do at present is to *settle on the land*, and we have firmly resolved to do that. The children want it very much, their powers are developing, they have grown much stronger recently—they are always barefoot, half-naked, they have become hardier than they were before. But it is not profitable to settle in Kislovodsk, because wheat doesn't grow here. We consider the best places to be the Kuban' region and Stavropol' province; we are going to aim for there again, but we may have to spend the winter here— that is not bad, because it never gets below minus two degrees.

We met here Ekaterina Evgen'evna Konstan and the Riabovs; Nadia

---

[4] A ring-shaped roll, smaller version of the *bublik*.

Riabova is a music teacher in the people's conservatory, Ekaterina Evge-n'evna is the chairwoman of the union of unemployed. Doctor Aleksinskii, Otto, Savel'-Mogilevich, Speranskii, Polonskii, and many other promi-nent Muscovites are here. We ask ourselves very often, where are you all; perhaps you have already left for Belgium. Our Mania has been waiting for an answer from Ira, but many letters most likely were sent to Saratov after we had left. Write if you receive this letter, we very much want to hear from you. Write, don't forget us. Write as well about all our com-mon acquaintances, and about Mother Moscow. It is often unbearably painful and sad, it is not easy to cut oneself off from everything at our age, but it is still good that we are here, and not in Moscow.

Our address: Kislovodsk. Rebrovskaia Balka
                  Raevskaia Street 37, Lapovits dacha
                  Head of the 22ond Military-Construction
                  Detachment
                  S. M. Erofeev

Mama and Sema kiss you all. Mama feels well, she has even put on some weight, but in her sleep she always sees Moscow; the children, how-ever, say "at home in Saratov" as often as "at home in Moscow." Recently our technician invited Mania and Iura to see *Uncle Vania* (the Art Thea-ter was here), and their conversations the next day caused my heart to burst from memories. I kiss you all. Give my greetings to the Reimans, Iurii Vladimirovich, the Rars, and Elizaveta Andreevna.

Letter 10

[Letter of L. N. Krasil'nikova to Got'e, dated June 6 (1920), Khar'kov.]

6 June
Dear Iura,
    We heard the sad news about the misfortune that has overtaken you from S. V. Giatsintova (the actress of the Art Studio Theater).[5] Words cannot express how shocked we were and how deeply and warmly we sympathize with you; we greatly regret that we cannot personally share with you our sincere sympathy, but you feel it, of course. We did not write to you immediately because S.V. did not know if you were in Mos-cow, and we don't know your address. May the Lord help you to raise and educate Volodia!

[5] Sof'ia Vladimirovna Giatsintova (b. 1895) was a well-known Moscow Art Theater dramatic actress whose career on the stage lasted from 1911 to 1975. See her memoirs (to the mid-1930s): Sof'ia Giatsintova, *S pamiat'iu naedine* (Moscow, 1985).

How sad that P. Mingalev is in such a terrible state; how strange that Anna Sergeevna's wealth was of no good to anyone.

We cannot say much about ourselves: we are aging and growing weak from years, but mainly from the frightful living conditions. We work a great deal and earn our bread by the sweat of our brows, but it is so expensive that we have to sell not only luxuries but even necessities. Like everyone now, we live a very restricted life in all respects, but so far, we are not depressed, we still hope for a better future. You wanted to know about the Lisharev family: Ol'ga Mikhailovna has been bedridden for several months now; she is weak, although she has no disease of any kind. Serezha left long ago, and his whereabouts are unknown. Lelia is here; her daughters are working, and her son is in school. She herself gives English lessons, for her means of support are quite small; she is also selling everything she can. Vava and her husband left long ago for somewhere abroad; we have no news of them.

Where is Lialia? We know nothing about him. If he is in Moscow, give him our warm regards. We both send big kisses to you and Volodia. Good health and spirits to you. May the Lord protect you. Don't forget your old, old friends who sincerely love you.

Give our warm regards to Ol'ga Mikhailovna.

Unfortunately, we did not see your acquaintance. We weren't home when he came by with your letter, and he did not repeat his visit later.

Letter 11

[Letter of Nina Sergeevna Platonova to Got'e, dated August 26, 1920, Petrograd.]

26 August
Dear Iurii Vladimirovich,

I have a big favor to ask of you: it concerns books that are impossible to get in Petersburg and must be sought in Moscow. Under present circumstances this is a risky business, I know, and I am prepared to beg your forgiveness in advance for the boldness of my request, but Papa thinks I can ask you, and, emboldened by his encouragement, I have decided to bother you. The publisher Grzhebin has ordered a biography of Mme. Roland from me; for my work I would have to have at hand a copy of her memoirs, which came out in Paris at the turn of our century; they were published by the Parisian Société de l'histoire de la Révolution Française in two volumes in octavo with commentaries. This book is not here, neither in the public library, nor in the libraries of the academy, the university, or the Higher Women's Courses. Those people who might have it are not in Petersburg at present, and the only thing left for me to do is try my luck in Moscow. If it wouldn't be too much trouble for you to find a copy of this book that you wouldn't mind subjecting to the fortunes of the journey from Moscow to Petersburg, I beg of you to send it here at the first reliable opportunity, which should be forthcoming from us in the near future. On my part, I promise to treat the book well and to return it in early winter not by mail, but with someone we can rely on. Foreseeing in advance that this publication may be lacking in Moscow as it is in Petersburg, I turn to you with my request counting only on a lucky chance and your kindness. Forgive me the trouble I may be causing you with my request, Iurii Vladimirovich; I will be very grateful to you for carrying it out.

The summer has flown by quickly, and a great deal of time has already passed since your visit here, but it seems that you left only week before last, and that impression perhaps makes it easier for me to turn to you with such a bold request as mine. I hope that your boy is well and that the summer has passed smoothly and as calmly as is presently possible for you. Natasha didn't find you in Moscow when she was there at the beginning of July, and my own trip to Moscow didn't work out, which I very much regret now: how I wanted suddenly to get out of here and have a look at the world and other people when the opportunity to make the trip arose. The Maikovs spent some time in Moscow and brought many stories from there, but they didn't see you, so we know nothing of you. We all send greetings and heartfelt best wishes.

With sincere respect,
Nina Platonova

Letter 12

[Letter of Iurii Vladimirovich Got'e to Emma Wilken, dated October 10, 1920, Moscow, unsent; original in French.]

10 October 1920

Dear Emma,

I am taking advantage of an unexpected opportunity to send you these lines by private means. I have written three letters. Have they arrived? I doubt it. Not a word from you, neither for me nor for anyone else. I saw "the lady general" yesterday, and the day before yesterday I saw Sasha. No one has any news of you. We are all getting by as in the past. All the same sorrows and spiritual torpor. They speak of peace, but make war; it is exactly the same with us who are in a permanent state of anxiety. The Pestovians are well; Iura is with me—I have a kind of students' apartment. I think that suits Lena and Iurochka. It suits me, too, because it makes my lair less sad. The weather has been continually good so far, but I think the cold season is drawing near and that Lena is going to escape. Aunt Liza has just returned with the little ones. I haven't seen her yet; I hope to do that tomorrow, which is Lialia's birthday. The poor little boy! A very sad holiday. Poor children, the Rars and mine. What a sad fate to lose mothers like Nina and Liza. We have had news of Emile through Buchbeim. It turns out he is in Switzerland; I haven't got the details to be able to tell you anything about his situation. I think that is all I can tell you about us. It is still the same state of death as during your days in the "cooperative of rations" where we live. Some say that in a few days we will be in paradise: there is a "collection" of warm clothing for the army going on, so they say that when it is completed we will re-don the paradisiacal apparel, while continuing to eat apples (there is an altogether extraordinary quantity of them; everyone is eating them).

If this letter arrives, that still does not resolve the problem of a response. I hope all the same to one day receive several lines from you, in order to learn what is becoming of you. As for coming to see you, I have no hopes for the near future.

I kiss you all.

Iura

I know, by the way, that Vera Mikhailovna Ryndina has written you twice; many persons have done so, I am sure of it. At least we are going to have heat—that is already something.

Goodbye once more; I would very much like to say see you soon, but. . . .

JG

Letter not sent, because they wouldn't take it.

Letter 13

[Letter of A. I. Iakovlev to Got'e, dated October 23, 1920, Simbirsk.]

Simbirsk
23 October 1920

Dear and kind Iurii Vladimirovich,

I received your letter of 8/8 just the other day, but I still feel guilty for my two-month silence. At first I was counting on returning to Moscow myself around mid-September, but then such complicated and urgent worries about living arrangements here descended on me that I had to postpone departure from week to week. I don't know to this day when I will be able to leave here. I have had to take charge of a complicated, half-destroyed school system and come face to face with the fuel crisis. In the course of affairs I am even compelled to engage in the physically very pleasant but very time-consuming job of cutting trees with my own hands. Events (in nature!) have developed quickly: genuine winter has been here for four days already, there was no time to waste, and I threw myself into the battle for existence on the front not of five Moscow rooms, but of an entire institution dependent on me, in and around which three hundred people exist. You can imagine how complicated and confused the bundle of relations and problems is. . . . Physically we have incomparably better conditions here than in Moscow. You know how hard things were for us there, but things are not without terrible dangers here either: our wood still hasn't arrived, and that is very frightening with central heating, since we aren't able to heat our single apartment—the entire big three-story house has to be heated.

I won't say much about how hard it was to interrupt friendly ties and relations in Moscow; how often I have turned in my thoughts to you and our dear colleagues in the business, or idleness, of the museum. The hope does not die in my soul that in the near future, when the main difficulties will have been resolved, I will once again be in Moscow, if only temporarily, *pour prendre une tasse d'air*. It is possible to live here, and I entertain the bold hope, if I succeed in getting a railway car for Simbirsk University, to bring you here for a guest-lecture course. For the time being, however, "Simbirsk University" is only a bluff.

My family are alive and healthy. Ol'ga sends greetings to you and Volodia.

I warmly and sincerely embrace you. Your

Al. Iakovlev

My profound respects to B.I.L., A.B., O. I. Sh., M.M.B., E. V. Ch., N. Ia. Ch., M. S. Shch., and dear Prince V. D. Embrace Sergei Vladimirovich[6] for me.

Letter 14

[Letter of Emma Wilken to Got'e, dated November 20, 1920, Brussels.]

Bruxelles. 8, Avenue Galillée
20 November 1920

Dear Iura,

I am writing, it seems, without any hope that you will receive anything. Several of my letters have returned to me after long wanderings. I have received two letters from Moscow: one from Julietta, without news,

---

[6] Bakhrushin.

and one from Lena. I had no idea that Ninochka had died, and I will also have to endure the death of my Lizusha. It is even harder to endure here, because I yearn to be with the children and E.A. The poor things, how will they handle their grief. I can't imagine how they will arrange their lives without Lizusha. I conclude from Lena's letter that you were healthy at that time, and I hope that everything continues to go well in that respect. We are all healthy. We arrived in fine shape on August 7, but we still haven't settled down. It all seems as if we are still living in anticipation of the resolution of various questions. Lina and I are both working in offices as bookkeepers' assistants. I had never in my life had anything to do with it, but fast figuring helps and I am handling the work. I am glad that there is a lot of it; the less time there is to think, the better. I am busy from 8 to 12 and from 2 to 6. We live all scattered about. Mama and Lina are in a small, cozy two-room apartment with a gas kitchen; I had to sleep on the floor because there was nowhere to put a third bed. The Slosses won't let me go, so I am living for the time being with them. There are lots of reasons to keep me; the main one is that they live a distance of twenty minutes' walk from my work and it is easier for them to spoil me that way. People here have been reborn in the course of the war, they have become more responsive; we get so much kindness and pampering from everyone, they are all ready to help. But so far, thank God, we are getting by, since we have gotten something from the government. Georges and Nina took a trip to Paris; Leva and Liza are there. Georges was able to get an insurance payment. Right now they are living with our Belgian friends, the Michels. They have put the children in a full pension with a governess, where there are sixteen of them; they go to school from there. They have managed with French; they spent two months with the Slosses at the dacha and became skillful at it. The little one does very well in school; they are behind for their age, but will catch up. At the beginning of our stay I did some traveling, I was at Gustave's in Liège; they are having a very hard time of it. Afterward I was the guest of my young friends, the Slosses' sons, both of whom have managed to marry successfully. One has a factory in Pepinster, the other lives in Spa. I enjoyed the walks and the nature. I went to work on the 1st of October, quite rested. Nina and I both earn 300, but yesterday I was already promised a raise. Life here is expensive: full board and lodging costs a minimum of 13 francs; it is cheaper to rent a furnished apartment and cook at home, which is not at all complicated since gas stoves are almost everywhere. At home, food comes to 5 francs, and everything can be had simply and conveniently. We hope to find an apartment for between 200 and 250. Your uncle and aunt are in Switzerland, in Zurich, where they wound up after long ordeals; relatively recently they were wandering about Rumania, where they had a very hard time. Both work as [commercial] representatives, she works more than he, it seems to me. I get letters from Anna Aleksandrovna; she lives in Germany. Life there is very difficult. Natasha lives apart from her husband; he has a job in Berlin, where he can't keep his family, so she has to live with his parents in Dresden.

The weather has been marvelous, and is still holding; it is up to fifteen degrees in the daytime, and zero at night. I go everywhere on foot, although there are all kinds of streetcars going in all directions. Write about how our museum folk are getting along; I remember everyone and send warm regards to them all. I pine for my work every day. How are the parents getting along? The sisters? Write about everyone, I so want to know about everyone. Our people all send their regards.

I give you and your son a big kiss.

Your Emma

Letter 15

[Letter of A. K. Vinogradov to Got'e, dated January 17, 1921, Riga.]

Riga. The Peace Delegation
17 January. Monday. 1921.

Dear Iurii Vladimirovich,

At last I can write to you: a diplomatic courier is going to Moscow today, and I am taking advantage of that to fill you in. My departure was a complete surprise for me: I had to get ready in two days. I barely had time to get a little money for buying books. Before departure, M. N. Pokrovskii informed me of his decision to send A. I. Kalishevskii either to Revel or to Riga, and therefore I cannot develop any large-scale plans for book-buying in Riga. But I have already taken preliminary steps. I bought everything I could from available reserves in Riga—the most important and significant works in all fields published in 1920 and 1921— having received 300,000 Latvian rubles, which amounts in our money to three and a half million rubles. Tsarist money has the same value as Latvian, but a Duma note of 1,000 rubles is worth 230 Latvian rubles. The exchange rate of the Latvian ruble is falling very fast. The German mark is presently equal to four Latvian rubles. It is impossible to get French currency, just as it is impossible to order English books, because the exchange rate is impossibly low and freight is so expensive that, as Kymmel and Rap put it, it is cheaper to publish a book in Riga than to order it from England. The average price of a large edition comes to 100–130 Latvian rubles. There are some amazingly good things, and others of modest worth. I do not buy bad books, with which Riga is crammed, even as an example, but I have been able to put together a small collection of Russian books published in Berlin and Stockholm. The work of the delegation is proceeding normally. I. E. Grabar' and I will finish our reports on the 24th of January, and on Tuesday (the morning of January 25th) we will leave for Moscow with the books. I very much wish that you would meet with Kalishevskii and convince him not to hurry with his business trip and in any case to wait for my arrival. I remain convinced it will be very hard for A. I. Kalishevskii, whether alone or at the head of an expedition. Study of the situation and especially establishment of sound relations with the delegation have shown me that A. I. Kalishevskii won't be able to handle the job. It is hard to get money, even with Moscow's agreement (I will tell you in detail about this when I arrive, since I don't have time to write about it now); it is hard to send books to Russia because of the unresolved international trade relationship (I am not an example, since my situation is completely exceptional at the moment); and the current situation with ordering non-German books is even more difficult—it is impossible to get hold of foreign currency, there are no journals, and therefore everything depends not so much on the customary skill as on familiarity with the tactical peculiarities of our time. It would be best of all, of course, to go to Leipzig or Berlin with the vast millions of reparations, but A.I.K. surely won't manage to do that, I can vouch for it. Everything is taking shape so that you will have to go, that has already been said here. What is going on now in the museum? The reelection of the committee will have to be put off for a week or even ten to twelve days. *Thus far* I am very, very satisfied with the results of the work here. I clasp your hand firmly. Greetings to my esteemed fellow workers and my profound respects to Vasilii Dmitrievich.

Your devoted servant,
A. Vinogradov

Letter 16

[Letter of V. D. Korsakova to Got'e, dated January 22, 1921, Krasnoiarsk.]

Dear Iurii Vladimirovich:

I have not written to you and Nina Nikolaevna for a very long time. In order to find out about your life and activities, I decided to plan my letter to coincide with the time when I formerly congratulated Nina Nikolaevna on her nameday. I greet you and wish you health and all the best.

I think that Volodia must already be a very big boy. Where does he go to school? Are you able to spend the summers outside of Moscow?

Since the 1st of December 1918 I have been working in the Central Library, and from 2 to 8 o'clock I work in the library storehouse, where we sort the books and manuscripts that wound up there in the autumn of 1918 when Kazan' was evacuated.

There had been no news from K.D. since May 1920. Imagine that he has been in the hospital since the end of January 1920: he had recurring typhus (three attacks), then spotted fever, acute pleurisy in the left lung, and now acute pleurisy in the right lung. He should live for a time in a warm climate and take a cure of koumiss in the summer. In one of his letters he asked me if I had any news of you.

When he had almost recovered after acute pleurisy, he intended to move either to Moscow or to Irkutsk. Now there can be no talk of that, since he must be very careful after the second attack of pleurisy.

Varvara Al. is in Saratov province, Khvalinskii district, with the children. Her husband got a job as assistant forester, and they live in the forest. In regard to provisions that is of course better than living in town, but the mail is slow and sometimes, perhaps, it gets lost. Iurii is eight and a half, and Igor' is closer to seven than to six. I saw them at the end of May 1915, so that I practically don't know them.

Is it true that Petrovskii Park and the better part of the park in Petrovsko-Razumovskoe have been cut down?

My regards to you, Nina Nikolaevna, and Volodia. Good health to you.

Sincerely yours,
V.K.

Vozdvizhenskaia 13, apt. 2.

Letter 17

[Letter of U. G. Ivask to Got'e, dated January 10, 1921, Riga.]

Dear Iurii Vladimirovich,

I received your letter at the end of December and was very pleased that you have not forgotten me. I sent the attached letter to Emma Karlovna to Brussels the following day, and as soon as a reply comes from her I will send it on to you at the first opportunity.

Compared to Moscow, life here is wonderful; although many things are rather expensive, it is nevertheless quite possible to live on one's salary. At present there is no one in the chair of the history of Eastern Europe here; if a person of your reputation were to occupy that vacancy, it would be fully provided for materially.

At present the work of restoring to their former locations 500,000 books reevacuated from Russia is coming to an end. This work of grandiose proportions required great efforts and, in addition, a considerable expenditure of money, since labor is very expensive here.

Heartfelt greetings to you and to all my former coworkers who have not forgotten me. I will be extraordinarily pleased to receive from you occasionally even the briefest news about what is going on there.

I firmly shake your hand,

U. G. Ivask

10 January 1921

Letter 18

[Letter of A. I. Iakovlev to Got'e, dated May 4, 1921, Simbirsk.]

Simbirsk, The Chuvash Institute
5/4/21

Christ has risen!

Dear Iurii Vladimirovich,

Holiday greetings to you and Volodia. Our people send heartfelt greetings. We are having the customary holiday adventure—Ivka has gotten pneumonia and Ochagov's grippe [?]. That is probably the result of the scarlatina he had. There is nothing to tell about life in Simbirsk: living conditions have gotten much worse than in 1920. I am still hoping to see you here in May, but the university has been inactive all this time, and things are so slack there that I am afraid we will not be able to arrange anything decent. In any case, I am notifying you in good time. In our institute there is complete nonsense. Only the faintest news about life in Moscow reaches here, usually exaggeratedly optimistic. I am busy with my "dynamic tasks," especially on days off when it isn't necessary to run about in pursuit of a crust of bread. Spring is in full motion here. The leaves have come out, the apple and pear trees are blooming. Just in case, write down a program of your proposed lectures in Simbirsk, so that it can be printed or lithographed in advance in case the lectures are held.

I embrace you.

Yours,
A. Iakovlev

How is V[asilii] D[mitrievich] G[olitsyn]? I have heard nothing about him since my departure.

Letter 19

[Letter of A. V. Florovskii to Got'e, dated May 17, 1921, Odessa.]

Dear Iurii Vladimirovich,

Please accept my sincere greeting after a long interruption. It will be conveyed to you by either Leonid Petrovich Grossman[7] or Il'ia Semenovich Vugman. These two persons have been sent to the capitals by the Odessa Public Library, whose head I now am, to obtain northern publications and to arrange for uninterrupted supply to the library of all the books of the federation. If you find it possible, please show them whatever help you can in fulfilling this task and acquaint our delegates with the new conditions of library work and its new plans and prospects. The Odessa library aspires to be included soon among the state libraries, and that is why it needs to become familiar with the activities of the state libraries of St. Petersburg and Moscow.

Odessa is so poor in new literature that it is only the rare publication that finds its way into the public library. We lack a great number of scholarly publications in Odessa and we know about them only from the *Literary Bulletin* (there is no full set of it in Odessa!!) and suchlike publications.

Our work in Odessa as far as printing goes is just getting established. I personally have had nothing printed since 1919, although I have written a few things. Right now I am busy with archival work on the history of the peasant reform—there is a possibility of publishing some individual essays in the near future.

The scholarly works of Moscow reach us haphazardly. We have not seen the collection in honor of M. K. Liubavskii in Odessa, nor a great many other books from 1917–21. Grossman or Vugman can give you the details about everything.

Please give my regards to M. M. Bogoslovskii, A. I. Iakovlev, and V. I. Picheta.

Yours with sincere respect,
Antonii Florovskii

5/17/1921
Odessa, Ul. Petra V., 24, apt. 3
or Odessa Public Library, Khersonskaia 13.

[7] Leonid Petrovich Grossman (1888–1965), a native of Odessa, was a prominent literary scholar, later known for his work on Dostoevskii.

Letter 20

[Letter of A. K. Vinogradov to Got'e, dated June 28, 1921, Riga.]

6.28.21

Dear Iurii Vladimirovich,

I have been placed in the difficult position of being unable to come to an understanding with you regarding your participation in the general work of the museum. Talking more, and more often, would only aggravate the issues and put them on an unhealthy plane. That would harm us both, and therefore I have decided to write you and ask you to consider this letter of mine my final word on the subject under discussion, after which I will draw conclusions only in regard to changing my own position.

I agreed with great distress to become director of the museum, and I was genuinely counting on your help.[8] I am so far from having had it, that the main material for my judgment is the defects of the Academic Council, its lack of contact with matters that are of the greatest urgency to the museum, rather than any positive actions by you as chairman. There is not a group that has not pointed out the necessity of your presence in the library. The theft of books in the library departments is growing. You are not taking appropriate measures: (1) reregistration of readers with a new record based on documents, (2) demanding signatures on the checkout slips, etc., etc., etc. For some reason, others are obliged to think about all this for you. You have not examined on the spot a single one of the libraries that have been turned over to us, you have not been to see a single institution involved in ordering books from abroad (for example, the Scientific-Technical Division of VSNKh,[9] which has received hundreds of boxes).

It is hard for me to enumerate everything concerning which *we have the right to expect initiative and a number of persistent actions on your part.* The area closest to you is the one you have paid least attention to—what can be demanded and expected of the rank-and-file intelligent or non-intelligentsia person who looks at the museum exclusively from the point of view of his own interest? The authority of the institution and its dignity, and the rights that go along with it, have been reduced to a threatening minimum.

In addition, I must tell you that for all practical purposes you are absent half the workweek, which amounts to a good half of the spring and

[8] Vinogradov was appointed director of the Rumiantsev Museum following Prince V. D. Golitsyn's arrest in March 1921.

[9] Supreme Council of National Economy. At this time VSNKh was in effect the Commissariat of Industry.

autumn months, and that does not even take account of your immediately forthcoming long leave. All this transforms our work and the work
of improving the material situation into some kind of stupid farce. I am
expending a great deal of moral and nervous energy. You have been using the interest on those expenditures, but now you are destroying the
base capital. Your work and mine would be less nerve-racking if you
were to give just a little more to D. I. Egorov, N. F. Garelin, and me. If
this does not happen, don't raise the matter of this letter with me but
think of finding a more complaisant director than I.

Yours, A. Vinogradov.

Letter 21

[Letter of J. Malfitano to Got'e, date July 21, 1921, Paris.]

Institut Pasteur   Paris, 21. VII. 1921
25 rue Dutot
(XVe Arrondt)
Tel. Saxe 08–27
        18–14

Dear Mr. Gautier,

Your letter has caused me the torment of knowing one is not in agreement with those one loves and esteems. No doubt nothing is genuinely
true if one is entirely in agreement with one's friends in believing it. But
believe me, I am convinced that at present it is extremely difficult to have
clear vision. You know that the only principle I consider beneficial is
sincerity. You are sincere, certainly; our friendship was born of our reciprocal sincerity. My present opinion is dictated by the hope that conditions
can be developed in which it will be less easy to lie. These conditions are
summed up in Equality. I am writing to you in haste because otherwise
I would think a lot about my letter, to the point that I would never write
it. I am ashamed before all my friends in Russia, you in the first place.
Not for having changed my opinion, but because of the illusions I entertained when I was in Moscow. I cannot prove that these are still not
illusions, but I tell you very sincerely that my great love for Russia is the
motive.

I have passed your letter on to Avenard through the intermediary of
his father-in-law, since he lives in the country and we don't see each other
often. Write to me again. You can be sure of [. . . . .] and of my esteem.
Kiss your child for me.

Yours,
J. Malfitano

Letter 22

[Letter of Emma Wilken to Got'e, undated but mid-1921, Antwerp.]

My Dear Iura,

I have just received your letter and hasten to reply, as I sense that you will be waiting impatiently for my answer. I send you and Verochka (I permit myself not to use her patronymic, Mikhailovna) my parental blessing, I heartily congratulate you and wish you all the best. The others here join me and also send you their best wishes; only Mama said that she is sorry that it happened, because it makes her lose hope of ever seeing you.

You don't know me well if you fear a reproachful look from me; just imagine that I am trying to look at you as tenderly as possible, and looking now at your Ninochka, whose portrait I brought with me to Antwerp, I feel that she would not condemn you either. It seems to me that now, as has been the case for some time now, she and I understand each other without words. I thought a lot about you this winter; it is hard to live alone in your circumstances, and Volodia is still at an age where he needs a woman's care. You could not have made a better choice. I am confident of Verochka, I appraised her good heart during our work together; you yourself know very well my feelings toward her. I am content for you and for Volodia. You were both so spoiled by the constant concern of Nina, whose thoughts were entirely concentrated on your well-being.

Sasha Rar has distressed me by considering that all this is not as it should be; the evidence is that, although he was ostensibly on good terms with me, he couldn't bring himself to write me a single word, despite the fact that he got my letters. You write nothing about V.M.'s father; he produced a very good impression on me, but I hardly know him, I saw him only a couple of times. Thank you for the letters; if my letters give you pleasure, yours are even more important for me. All my yearnings and wishes are concentrated on seeing my old friends again.

It has already been two weeks since I started my new, this time independent, work; I am having no luck in one thing—I cannot find a place for the office, although adequate funds have been allotted; they avoid my charges and don't want to let them in the house. Personally, I have settled in well, I found a very attractive room with a window on the garden; the landlords look after me and think that I am an agreeable tenant.

I have got myself an annual ticket commencing August 1st, and I will go to Brussels during the week as well as on Saturday; the express trains take forty minutes, without stops; the entire trip takes one and a half hours, faster than we used to get to Listviny.

My work is not easy, the main snag is that I can't develop in myself, as the main committee demands of me, indifference to all that I have to confront. Sitting in London, all our bosses sort out the technical side of things from our reports—from whence and whither the wave of émigrés is going, what kind of delays there are, why someone or other has not got to America. On the basis of all this information, they work out various rules to help and lighten the fate of the émigrés in general. There is another conference in Geneva right now, where they are all discussing various questions. The literature on these questions is already large and interesting, and I assimilate it easily, I have gotten used to English. All this is fine, but they all don't have to deal with individual cases; we who work on the spot have to see much grief, and I stick to my own particular opinion that in certain cases if you don't deal gently with people, there will be no trust and you will never get to the truth. It is possible to be of great help, sometimes just by giving directions about what is required to board a steamer. In addition, we have the possibility of communicating with the committee in America, which makes inquires about relatives there on the spot. I got angry when they printed the notice about my appointment here, because it was written that I speak all the Slavic languages perfectly; how do you like that? The American doctor with whom I work while arranging steamer embarkations is convinced that it is the truth, since thus far I can communicate with everyone. All those coming from Yugoslavia, Poland, and Galicia understand me very well. I can't communicate with the Rumanians, but they mostly go through France. All our folks are well. Georges took the family to the seashore today, to a little village near Ostend, where he will spend a week himself. My Mama groans and is never satisfied; it seems her life, too, is going all right. I turn over half of my salary; Lina gets more, so we don't have to be as concerned whether she will want something or other. It is hard to sit in town in the heat, but what can be done? Perhaps we will go to see Nina and the children when Georges returns, but that is little. I am sorry for her, I can't bear to look at those who live worse [than I], and I always want to keep up with those who live better. I give a big kiss to you, Verochka, and Volodia, and I beg of you not to forget your old friend.

Emma

What you gave to Naze he has kept in the same form; therefore we were unable to use it.[10]

[10] The reference is to rubles that were being held for Got'e abroad.

Letter 23

[Letter of A. K. Vinogradov to Got'e, November 20, 1921, Moscow.]

20 November 1921

Dear Iurii Vladimirovich,

In my absence you received a certain Stefan Rygiel in the museum, and in the process he was allowed to examine the museum and the library, if not in an exceptional manner, then at least not in the same manner as other visitors. I wish to inform you that such receptions of foreign nationals must not be allowed at the present time or in the future. I request you to report this order to the Academic Council and to make it known without fail in all departments of the museum. The presence in Moscow of Polish citizens who are legally registered in the People's Commissariat of Foreign Affairs is a matter of either diplomatic or commercial interests; therefore, there is no basis for supposing that the Pole you received had a purely scholarly interest in the museum. The reception of Stefan Rygiel was a major error on your part, one that could entail grave consequences for you and for the museum. Apprising you of this with great regret, I request you to take pains to spare me the necessity of having to give you self-evident instructions, insofar as you, being a member of the museum administration, are thereby obliged to burden your memory somewhat with the rules and regulations in all areas concerning the life of the museum.

A. Vinogradov

Letter 24

[Letter of Archibald Cary Coolidge to Got'e, December 24, 1921, Moscow.]

Moscow, Dec. 24–'21

Dear Professor Gautier:

I hope you will not object to my advertising the work of the American Relief Administration. We have just instituted a new system by which it is possible for Russians who have friends or relatives in America to receive from them what we call "food packets." We are looking forward to great results from this, including much satisfaction to ourselves. Now this is Christmas time, a time when we like to send a few presents, and I am going to ask you and your family to give me the pleasure of accepting this sample of ARA work, of letting me feel that if you have not friends in

America you have American friends who can add to your Christmas cheer.

With best Christmas messages, believe me,

Very sincerely yours,
Archibald Cary Coolidge

Letter 25

[Letter of M. M. Cherkasskaia to Got'e, dated March 24, 1922, Khar'kov.]

24 March 1922

Kind and Dear Iurochka,

I have been meaning for a long time to write you a few words to thank you for your heartfelt condolences and for sharing in my grief, but I have still not been able to get hold of myself, and there is also the high cost of [mailing] letters, which deprives me literally of any communication with dear ones. How sad and painful it is! Having experienced solitude, you understand what I am going through, and at my age and in such a difficult time. They have taken everything away from Lelia and me, we live very meagerly, without a servant, and now, with our high prices (black bread is 95–100,000 a pound, potatoes are 40,000 a pound, ten eggs is 400,000, etc.), you might say we are going hungry. We are both working like machines: she gives English lessons, and I French; both of her daughters also work, but all that is not enough—we are having to sell the last of what is left, that is, dresses, linen, etc., and now they have even separated us, evicted us from our former apartment and put us on different streets, so that it is hard for me with my old legs to go to her and we see each other only twice a week, although we love each other as before. I am glad for you, that your life has again been resurrected. I would very much like to meet your wife, but, alas, that will never be! I have neither the energy, the money, nor the decent clothing to show myself anywhere. Now I go nowhere even in Khar'kov, except to Lelia's, and there isn't any time to. I think about the approaching holiday with horror and sadness; it will be very painful and sad without my unforgettable L.N. How sorry I am for Eduard Vladimirovich, and in general all those deaths you informed me about. And how are your pretty cousins—are they alive and how are they faring? Do you know where and how Ekaterina Pavlovna Samarzhi is living, and also ask Kolia Tiutchev if he knows anything about Krapotkina and Kavalinskaia. Give him my greetings and tell him that I don't write to him because I am unable to pay 7,500 for a letter. I am taking advantage of [a letter] to L.N.'s niece to write to you. Imagine that it has been two years since we heard anything about Serezha. Lelia and I grieve heavily about that. In case there is no opportunity before the holiday, my felicitations to you and Kolia Tiutchev beforehand, may you celebrate it joyously.

You ask for my exact address. The address is as before, to my name, Chebotarskaia 45, apt. 1. My cousin lives there; she receives all the letters and brings me mine, but all letters come quite irregularly, because the postman refuses to deliver often. I also live on Chebotarskaia, no. 49, but mostly Jews live here and they don't know me well. I am addressing this letter to Mokhovaia, because I don't remember your address. My greetings to your wife, I kiss you and your son. Where is your brother? May God protect you. Loving you as ever,

M. Cherkasskaia

Lelia sends kisses to you and Ol'ga Ves.
Write sometime, only in bigger characters, brighten up my life and gladden me with some news.

Letter 26

[Letter of I. F. Rybakov to Got'e, dated June 4, 1921, Poltava.]

Poltava, 6/4/1921

Christ has Risen, Dear Respected Iurii Vladimirovich!

I am very glad to have found in Ol'ga Nikolaevna a living bridge between the past and the present, between you and us. I wanted to add "provincials" to the last word, but I couldn't because I am really not sure where the "province" is now. It would be hard for me to say where people are moping more and are further removed from cultural blessings—there or here!

I am very grateful to you for the kind autumn letter and the greeting you sent me through Baliasnaia. I have not only preserved a grateful memory of you, I can say quite sincerely that I love you. I did not write for a long time only because your letter greatly depressed me and there was a great deal of grief around me then. ... Now, whatever may be there, spring has come and people have become more joyful by force of cosmic laws. And I can really rejoice, even though I pine a great deal for my family (my wife and little daughter have been living for about a year already with the grandfather near Odessa) and grieve that my health seems to be giving out. And why not rejoice: I have been freed from all administrative responsibilities, collegia, commissions, leaving me only lectures to give and work in the archive. In the morning I climb down into the cellar and work on the materials of the equity court and the inventories of the Little Russian regiments; the lectures are in the evening. I am also busy with church-community affairs and have even become a member of the reformed Eparchial Council representing the laymen, together with two respected archpriests, two young priests of the "new wave," a former teacher of the theological seminary, and a respected elder eparchial figure. I frequently meet with the ranking hierarch, the archbishop Parfenii, who was a suffragan in Moscow from 1894 to 1904. He is a very kind, educated man, with published works on the history of the Poltavshchina and archaeology; he remembers Kliuchevskii very well. Don't be distressed and don't laugh, dear Iurii Vladimirovich—our hierarch is also a Ukrainian, who was once head of the official commission for the translation of the Gospels, and the new "consistory" is also Ukrainian, the mass is already being conducted in the Ukrainian language in six churches of Poltava, and there are a great many such churches in the eparchy. Baliasnaia and I always speak Ukrainian, by the way. One more fact: the local pastor, a lecturer in our institute, who has been conducting mass in the Russian language for a long time, is now preparing to conduct it in Ukrainian because he considers it "a powerful weapon of propaganda."

I greatly regret that I can send you now only the poorest compiled brochure from among my books; I don't know if I will please or disappoint dear Aleksandr Nikolaevich Savin with it. I am also sending volume one of the transactions of the learned society, which you probably lack. I beg of you to write, dear Iurii Vladimirovich. Please give my heartfelt greeting to Mikhail Mikhailovich,[11] Matvei Kuz'mich,[12] Bogoiavlenskii, Savin, Egorov, and all the good people, and kiss your son for me. All the best!

With love and devotion,
I. Rybakov
Poltava, Shevchenkovskaia, 20

P.S. I have asked kind Ol'ga Nikolaevna to take along a little sugar for your son. I.R.

[11] Bogoslovskii.
[12] Liubavskii.

Letter 27

[Letter of I. A. Il'in to Got'e, dated March 27, 1922, Moscow.]

27 March

Dear Iurii Mikhailovich,

I am sitting out a mild flu at home and therefore I am addressing you in writing.

At that meeting of the Juridical Society where I gave a speech on behalf of the council, there occurred a certain conversation between N. N. Polianskii and me that entrained a great number of other conversations and organizational consequences and is now being settled through an honor court of arbitration. Being conscious of the rightness, restraint, and deliberateness of my actions, I ask you not to refuse the role of arbitrator on *my* behalf. Polianskii has invited M. N. Gernet.[13] In order for you to be able to weigh the entire episode and understand the state of affairs, I call your attention to Mikhail Solomonovich Fel'dshtein, who is fully and impartially informed about everything. His telephone is 2–70–22; between 11 and 12 A.M. he is usually taking breakfast.

As referee I would very much like to see A. A. Grushka, who responded with more than simple readiness in a preliminary conversation. The proceedings are being delayed while he is ill, as I am in his footsteps, as is the election of the chairman of the Juridical Society.

If you would like to read my speech for the full picture, it is always at your disposal in a large, clear, pencil-written manuscript (*liber lectu plane iucundus et elegans*).

If you would like to give me your answer orally after being filled in by M. S. Fel'dshtein, I will be glad to see you at my home daily from 12 to 2 or from 5 to 11 in the evening (Znamenka, Krestovozdvizhenskii Pereulok, 2, in the courtyard, apt. 36, sixth floor, the telephone is out of order).

I am purposely not expounding *anything* to you on behalf of my "prejudiced" person; I would only like to bring this affair to its end "honorably and scrupulously."

Your "theoeides,"[14] it would seem,
I. A. Il'in

[13] Mikhail Nikolaevich Gernet (1874–1953) was a professor of criminal law at Moscow University and a prolific publicist. He is best known for his *History of Tsarist Prisons*, 5 vols. (Moscow, 1941–1956), which he wrote late in life after having lost his sight.

[14] "Godlike."

Letter 28

[Letter of Aunt Emma and Uncle Emil' Got'e to Got'e, dated February 20, 1922, Zurich.]

Dear Iura,

Both your letters have reached us, and many thanks for them; that was the first substantial news from you since the day of our departure. We were informed of the death of Uncle Eduard; that did not greatly shock me, because I knew of his heart disease and was prepared for that sad news. I am infinitely sorry for him; how much more good he could have done if fate had decided otherwise. I am the last of the old men. After a year and a half's journey by way of Bessarabia and Rumania, we have been able, thanks to the help of friends, to settle here in Zurich, Gloria-strasse 70, where we have also taken up a trade to support ourselves—a commission and agent business. Emma started the former, she goes by recommendations to various people and families and takes orders for all kinds of edibles and household items from samples she has with her, and then delivers them. As for the latter, I wrote to Weiss and other friends upon arriving here and got through them a beverage dealership, and then through a local native I got the same for German beverages. It is still a matter of the future, although it began to yield a noticeable profit last year already. That will be a big help. The clientele developed by recommendations of friends, and since the houses have turned out to be very good ones, business is growing. I can't say that we are getting rich, no, but we are supporting ourselves with our own labor and are a burden to no one, and that is an enormous moral satisfaction. Our health is all right and our strength is holding up, even though we have to be on the job twelve hours a day. That is what I can say about us.

Many thanks for the information about the Archaeological Society; I will inform the chairman, with whom I am in correspondence. It will please him. Take the chairmanship, don't refuse. I am glad the building has been preserved. Give my regards to all who remember me, both in the society and in the museum. I can inform you of an interesting detail. The La Barthe engravings were engraved by the father and son Lorin in Herisau in Switzerland by order of Walser, who published them.[15] I learned that here, and on the 13th drawing there is without a doubt a signature in the right-hand corner; isn't it an original? If you see Oreshnikov, give him my heartfelt greeting. Where is his family? I am very

---

[15] Gérard de la Barthe was a late eighteenth-century French landscape painter who lived from 1787 to 1810 in Petersburg and Moscow, where he painted a series of views with figures that were engraved by various engravers.

glad that you have married; that is extremely good for your son, and I am very pleased that such a sympathetic new niece has appeared. May fate give much happiness and good health to all three of you. Give our best wishes, good health, and greetings to all our people from the smallest to the greatest. Where do the Reimans live? Give our felicitations to Champignon. Is his wife still living? Where are Lialia, Josephine, Sasha Rar and his relatives? I heard that Snegov has replaced Sobinov. When did he begin singing? In a word, anything you can relay about our friends and relations, write it all, and thanks in advance. If any of our people join you in writing to us, many thanks, and I who send you this epistle am writing to all our people. We kiss you all warmly and remain your

Aunt and Uncle Emil'

2/20/22

Index of Personal Names

❄

Biographical notes on individuals are provided at first mention in the text only. Italics indicate the location of biographical material.

Adler, Friedrich, 245, *245 n.46*
Afanas'ev, General, 197
Afanas'ev, Aleksandr Nikolaevich, 111, *111 n.41*
Aksakov, I.S., 425
Aksin'ia, 207
Alad'in, Aleksei Fedorovich, 56, *56 n.101*
Aleksandr Sergeevich, 469
Aleksandra Fedorovna, Empress, 29, *29 n.9*, 36, 101 n.17, 269, 368, 402, 413
Aleksandra Ivanovna, 185
Aleksandra Pavlovna, *40 n.45*, 46, 162, 469
Aleksandrov, Fedor, 38, 206, 207, 212
Aleksandrov-Dol'nik, D.K., 307, 308, 309, 311
Alekseev, General Mikhail Vasil'evich, 59, *59 n.112*, 105, 178 n.179, 355
Aleksei, Father, 301, 370, 379
Aleksei Ivanovich, 202, 207, 210, 326
Aleksinskii, Doctor, 475
Alexander I, 128 n.77, 188 n.196, 363
Alexander II, 121, 238 n.31, 412
Alexander III, 40, 109, 139, 360, 413, 432
Alexandra. *See* Aleksandra Fedorovna, Empress
Alexis, Tsarevich, 368
Alferov, Aleksandr Danilovich, 293, *294 n.111*, 305, 307, 308
Alferova, Aleksandra Samsonovna, *305 n.129*
Alice, Princess, 29 n.9
Anacharsis, 128, *128 n.77*
Anan'ich, B.V., 432 n.103
Anderson, 360
Andreev, 170 n.171
Andreev, Aleksandr Ignat'evich, 405, *405 n.23*
Andreev, Leonid, 44, *44 n.59*, 421

Andreeva, Mariia Fedorovna, 219, *219 n.251*
Anet, Claude. *See* Schopfer, Jean
Angarskii, Nikolai Semenovich, 352, *352 n.49*
Anna Ioannovna, Empress, 27 n.2, 116 n.48, 243 n.42
Antip'ev, Nikolai, 43, 46, 161, 165, 167
Antipin, P.S., 238
Antonelli, 120
Antonin, Bishop, 455, *455 n.43*, 456
Anuchin, Dmitrii Nikolaevich, 341, *341 n.23*
Apostol, P.N., 96 n.3
Apraksin, 128
Arakcheev, Aleksei Andreevich, *188 n.196*, 388
Armand, 217, 300
Armand, Ad.E., 376
Armand, Arkadii Evgen'evich, 214, 217
Armand, E.E., 376
Armand, F.A., 72, 207
Armand, Inessa (née Stéphane), 5, 72-73 *n.168*, 207, 208 n.230, 282
Arndt, Walter, 30 n.13
Arsen'ev, Nikolai Sergeevich, 60, *60 n.117*
Artem'ev, D.N. 235, *235 n.23*, 250
Artsybashev, Mikhail Petrovich, 271, *271 n.82*
Asafova, N.M., 12 n.24, 303 n.125
Ashukina, M.G., 355 n.57
Astaf'ev, 134
Astrov, Aleksandr Ivanovich, 305, *305 n.129*
Astrov, N.I., 276
Avenard, Henri, 116, 126, 129, 145, 160, 202, 213, 221, 222, 250, 487

LIBRARY OF CONGRESS CATALOGING-IN-PUBLICATION DATA

Got'e, ĨŪ. V. (ĨŪriĭ Vladimirovich), 1873-1943.
Time of troubles, the diary of Iurii Vladimirovich Got'e.

Translation from Russian.
Includes indexes.
1. Got'e, ĨŪ. V. (ĨŪriĭ Vladimirovich), 1873-1943—
Diaries. 2. Soviet Union—History—Revolution,
1917-1921—Personal narratives. 3. College teachers—
Soviet Union—Diaries. 4. Librarians—Soviet Union—
Diaries. I. Emmons, Terence. II. Title.
DK265.7.G66A3 1988   947.084′1′0924   87-33017
ISBN 0-691-05520-3